Celebrating Children

Equipping People Working with Children and Young People Living in Difficult Circumstances Around the World

This book, with its accompanying resources were produced by a partnership facilitated by Viva Network. Rather than starting more children's charities, Viva Network creates networks and partnerships amongst people already helping children, so that more children receive better help. www.viva.org

Celebrating Children

Equipping People Working with Children
and Young People Living in Difficult
Circumstances Around the World

Editors
Glenn Miles
and
Josephine-Joy Wright

First published 2003 by Paternoster
Reprinted June 2006

Paternoster is an imprint of Authentic Media,
P.O. Box 300, Carlisle, Cumbria, CA3 0QS, U.K.
and
P.O. Box 1047, Waynesboro, GA 30830-2047, U.S.A.

09 08 07 06 05 04   1 2 3 4 5 6 7

ISBN -13: 978-1-84227-060-8

ISBN -10: 1-84227-060-5

Cover Illustration

Detail taken from an original by sculptress
Michèle Greene, entitled 'Waiting'.
Used by permission, copyright © Michèle Greene 2002.

Typeset by Profile, Culmdale, Rewe, Exeter,
and printed and bound in Great Britain by
Bell & Bain Ltd., Glasgow.

– Contents –

Part One: Understanding the Child in Context

Part Two: Key Issues in Listening to Children

A time for preparation and training – Protecting the child and the worker –
Questions to consider

Part Six: Development, Evaluation and Monitoring of Programmes

Part Seven: Development of Self and Staff

Part Eight: Case Studies from around the World: Children and Projects

– Illustrations and Tables –

– Editors –

Glenn Miles is 'Children at Risk' facilitator for Tearfund UK in Cambodia, which involves capacity building, networking, research and training. With a background in child health nursing, for the past fifteen years he has been involved in community child health and child welfare focused in Southeast Asia. He has done evaluations and research with child health and welfare projects in India, Pakistan, Sri Lanka, Thailand, Cambodia and the Philippines. He holds a masters degree in maternal child health from the Centre for International Child Health (University of London) and a diploma from All Nations Christian College. He is currently doing doctoral studies at the University of Wales, Swansea, in their Department for International Childhood Studies where he is exploring children's perceptions of child abuse and their influence on policy and planning in the Cambodian context. He has co-authored, with Paul Stephenson, the Tearfund 'Child Development Study Pack' and a series of six Tear-

fund 'Children at Risk Guidelines'. He is married to Siobhan, a nurse practitioner, and they have three beautiful girls aged two, five and seven years.

Josephine-Joy Wright worked in a day nursery at the age of sixteen and since then God has given her a passion for 'children at risk' and a vision for enabling workers. Dr Wright is trained as a clinical psychologist. She studied at universities in Bristol and in the Midlands before working in Wales and England, principally with the National Health Service. She specializes in the fields of trauma and abuse and national and international disaster-related work. Her work has taken her to many countries including China, Columbia, Bosnia and Croatia, Liberia and Kenya. She currently works within the Viva Network, facilitating the international development of courses to train workers with 'children at risk', and within the NHS as a consultant clinical psychologist with children and adolescents.

– Contributors –

Alastair Ager is director of the Centre for International Health Studies and Professor of Applied Psychology at Queen Margaret University College, Edinburgh. Professor Ager has extensive experience working with refugees and humanitarian assistance workers and has published over 50 academic works. He has field experience across southern Africa, southern Asia, the Caribbean and Eastern Europe.

Rushika Amarasekera has worked as a psychologist in advocacy, training and rehabilitation of children who are sexually abused and exploited for over ten years. She has been involved in training government staff, health, legal and social welfare professionals, and schoolchildren with the Lanka Evangelical Alliance Development Services ESCAPE programme.

Ela Balog established the Institute of Christian Pedagogy for the Evangelical Theological Seminary in Osijek, Croatia in 1994. During the war, she organized a rehabilitation programme in Italy for Croatian children affected by the war. She is the editor of

the children's Christian magazine *Latica* and is actively involved in various boards in the field of Christian education.

Cheryl Barnes has led church-based children's ministries, counselled children and families and been involved in school outreaches in Zambia, Zimbabwe, Zululand and Singapore. She has lectured on 'Children at Risk' in various institutions and is involved in piloting distance learning for children's workers.

Steve Bartel has been a primary school teacher and spent time aboard the relief ship 'Anastasis'. He and his wife now work in Columbia with YWAM. Their programme includes street evangelism, a drop-in centre for street children, a crisis shelter, a halfway house, a transition school and long-term 're-parenting' homes.

Colin Bennett is lecturer and tutor at Moorlands Bible College, UK.

Ros Besford is a member of Tearfund's 'Children at Risk' team and has spent time working in Eastern Europe, Latin America and Asia.

Sue Birchmore has worked with World Vision in various capacities and is now involved with programmes helping refugee families return and rebuild their homes, trauma healing programmes for children and educational and psychosocial programmes for children in refugee camps.

Dan Brewster is the associate director of the Program for Asia for Compassion International. He has been involved in relief work and child and family development ministries in Africa, South America and Asia for 24 years. Dr Brewster has studied and written extensively in the areas of child and community development, missions and mission strategy.

Tri Budiardjo has worked in Cambodia with World Vision and is now director of the Christian Children's Fund, Indonesia. His educational background is in theology and economics and he has just published a book called *The Bible's Views on Children*.

Sally Clarke is resource directory co-ordinator at Viva Network, Oxford, UK.

Kathryn Copsey has spent time exploring the most effective ways of supporting church-based children's workers in communicating the Christian faith to non-churched children. She has worked as a children's resource editor with Scripture Union and set up CURBS (Children in URBan Situations), an innovative project that provides resources and support for urban children's workers.

Gustavo Crocker has served as the international director of Nazarene Compassionate Ministries and has been involved in programmes in 62 different countries. Dr Crocker also served as field management director for Compassion International and currently works with World Relief. He has written several books and articles.

Ojoma Edeh is a professor at Millersville University, Pennsylvania and is the founder and executive director of MOM (Ministry of Mercy), a ministry to children with disabilities, orphans, street kids and abandoned teenagers and women in Nigeria.

Steve Gourley has worked with children in especially difficult circumstances in Cambodia since 1996 with organizations such as World Vision, the International Labour Organization and the Cambodian League for the Protection and Promotion of Human Rights. He has specialized in developing community-based responses to child labour and broader child protection issues.

Laurence Gray manages World Vision Cambodia's 'Children in Especially Difficult Circumstances' programme, which includes projects for prevention, protection and advocacy with street children, child labourers, urban poor communities and children who have experienced sexual exploitation.

Gill Grant has worked with children affected by HIV/AIDS in London and is now director of the Bethany Project in Zimbabwe.

Patricia Green began Rahab Ministries in Bangkok, offering support to women working in prostitution, in 1998. In 1971 she set up Landmark Homes for Girls, offering care to troubled teenagers in Hamilton, NZ. She is a social worker and accredited minister.

Susan Hayes Greener is director of program development at Mission of Mercy in Colorado Springs. She has taught child development and education courses and has done research in the areas of emotional intelligence, social psychology and public health. She has served as executive director of an Early Head Start Program, working with poverty-stricken mothers and children and has also worked with Compassion International.

George Hosking, a psychologist and clinical criminologist, works with offenders and victims of violence. He is the research co-ordinator of WAVE, an international charity dedicated to reducing child abuse and violence through tackling root causes, and also serves on the Parenting Education and Support Forum and the Children and Violence Forum.

Coleen Houlihan is a teenager who lives in Hertfordshire, UK. She uses her poetry to find a voice in a world of fear, where life has often failed to make sense and she has felt alone and negated. Her poems echo her determination not to be defined by her past and to find a rebirth of hope for herself and others walking on the same road.

Belinda Johnson has travelled and worked in many countries around the world and currently lives and works in Kazakhstan with Teen Challenge Kazakhstan.

Amanda Jones is a systemic psychotherapist working in the Traumatic Stress Service at the Maudsley Hospital, as well as in the psychotherapy unit at Charing Cross Hospital.

Pam MacKenzie has worked as a teacher in the UK and Yemen and as a trainer in language, literacy and education. Dr MacKenzie runs 'International Network for Development', which focuses on providing education for marginalized groups, and works with the tribal church in India.

Heather MacLeod currently works for World Vision's Partnership Office as the international child protection co-ordinator. She has also worked addressing and protecting the holistic health needs of children in Romania, Rwanda and eastern Zaire/DRC.

Emily McDonald first worked with children in Bolivia in 1991 and now runs Viva Network's training activities. She has co-taught courses on 'children at risk' in several countries.

Patrick McDonald is the director and founder of Viva Network and the senior associate for 'children at risk' of the Lausanne Movement. He has worked with children in Bolivia and has travelled widely in Latin America, Africa, Asia and Europe in an effort to bring unity and common purpose to Christian ministries helping hurting children. Patrick has written a book called *Reaching Children in Need* as well as numerous articles.

Heather Mkandawire is project co-ordinator for the Bethany Project in Zimbabwe. She has worked with the project since it started in 1995, training local communities in community-based orphan care and managing a growing team of community volunteers.

Bryant L. Myers is vice-president for international program strategy for World Vision International, where he has worked for 25 years. Dr Myers has written several books and serves on the boards of Iwa, Evangelicals for Social Action, Arab World Ministries and Viva Network.

Kelly O'Donnell is a psychologist with YWAM and Member Care Associates, based in Europe. Dr O'Donnell writes and consults in the area of missionary care, focusing on personnel development, crisis management, team building and family life.

Wanda Parker has worked with at-risk kids for over 30 years in inner cities, rural areas and *barrios*. She is presently the executive director of Kid Hope, which empowers Christian ministries to mentor at-risk kids towards a Christ-centred, hope-filled future.

David and Pauline Pearson are the founders of the Churches' Child Protection Advisory Service (the working name for PCCA Christian Child Care). David, PCCA's director, has been involved in child protection for more than 30 years. Pauline, a social worker, has extensive experience with children and adults who have been abused.

Valeria Peres works as a missionary to children in crisis in Cambodia. She is a WEC missionary seconded to the YWAM Hagar Foster Care Home project.

Sharon Prior is a lecturer at Moorlands Bible College.

Cressida Pryor works as dramatherapist and psychologist in an NHS adult mental health setting in the UK.

Tom Riley has worked in the Balkans and Croatia. He joined the Novi Most team as deputy director in 1997 and selects and trains overseas personnel.

Carmen Rivera is the director of Mosoj Yan ('New Way') in Cochabamba, Bolivia, which serves street girls through a programme of education and spiritual transformation.

Trudie Rossouw is a consultant child and adolescent psychiatrist. Dr Rossouw presently works in an NHS setting in the North East London Mental Health Trust in the child and adolescent service.

Wasan and Chariya Saenwian have worked with children in various ministries and have been the managers of Christian Care for Children with Disabilities in Bangkok since 1996.

Raymond Samuel is the founding director of SISU, a childcare agency which reaches about 2,000 children in need. He has worked with less privileged children in the tribal groups of Maharastra and Gujarat states of India. He is working on the prevention of female infanticide practice in a community in Tamil Nadu state.

Peter Sidebotham is a consultant paediatrician working in Bristol, UK. Dr Sidebotham has been involved with health projects in Asia, Africa and Eastern Europe and has direct ongoing links with health and community development programmes in Asia through Servants to Asia's Urban Poor.

Paul Stephenson brings a background in education, community development, qualitative research and programme evaluation to his current post as manager of Tearfund's 'Children at Risk' programme. He has worked on child-centred research, policy and resource development and in development and relief in Latin America, Africa, Asia and Eastern Europe.

Don Strongman works for Habitat for Humanity International Asia Pacific based in Bangkok, Thailand. He has 20 years of experience as an educator in public schools.

Eileen Taylor was a missionary with OMF and is a Christian counsellor.

Subhadra Tidball has been the director of Save Lanka Kids, a project under Community Concern Society, Sri Lanka, since its inception in 1997. Save Lanka Kids aims to empower Sri Lankans to prevent child sexual abuse. Subhadra has also illustrated and written children's literature.

Andrew Tomkins is director of the Centre for International Child Health (CICH) at the Institute of Child Health, University of London, which promotes the health and welfare of children and their families in poor countries through excellence in research, teaching, consultancy and advocacy. Professor Tomkins has worked in Nigeria and the Gambia, developing new research projects on child health, nutrition and development. He has worked with Tearfund for 20 years and is now vice-chairman.

Gundelina Velazco has taught in universities in the Philippines, written extensively and conducted assessment and therapy of street children and trained workers. Dr Velazco is currently the psychologist of Scripture Gift Mission International, working to conceptualize, develop and research Bible-based materials for 'children at risk'.

Keith White and his wife lead a Christian residential community for children in need in East London. Dr White is an associate lecturer in sociology at Spurgeon's College, London. He is president of FICE (UK) and founder trustee of Christian Child Care Forum (UK). He has written and edited several books, chairs the editorial board of *Children.UK* (an Internet magazine) and edits the annual journal of NCVCCO.

Nigel Williams is chief executive of Childnet International, a charity he founded in 1995 to ensure that children benefit from, rather than being hurt by, using the Internet. A Cambridge graduate, Nigel has worked in the civil service, computer industry and as a lobbyist for CARE.

Andreas A. Yewangoe is a minister in the Christian church of Sumba, Indonesia. He teaches at the theological faculty of Artha Wacana Christian University in Kupang, West Timor, Indonesia and is chairperson of the communion of churches in Indonesia.

– Foreword –

Children are a priority for the King and his kingdom: they are many, they suffer and God's unambiguous mandate in their favour shouts for urgent action. They are both key to the great commission and an essential expression of the great commandment. The Christian response to children today stands at a crossroads. Most children at the turn of the century are 'children at risk', or children that need more than mere words to demonstrate the love of God. They are hungry, homeless and hurting. Faced with the urgent need to nurture and protect these children, many Christians respond compassionately and even sacrificially, but most struggle to engage effectively and consistently. The increasing need for professional standards in care poses a defining challenge for the church.

I have been involved in Christian child development for several years and I have been fascinated and exhilarated to see this textbook come into existence. It has been created by an amazing group of people with huge compassion for and commitment to the children they write about. It is a very diverse group, ranging from 'front-line' practitioners to academics of world renown, united by their love for Jesus and their commitment to see children reach their full potential.

Anchored in events taking place some two thousand years ago, compassionate Christian care provides a formidable legacy of transformation. Institutions of care, welfare and education have often been inspired and supported by the Christian movement. Today 25,000 service-providing projects reach some 20 million children worldwide. This outreach employs more than 100,000 Christian workers and costs the church billions each year. This vast effort is now finding a sense of connectedness and belonging through Viva Network. The movement is gaining momentum as churches worldwide call for holism and governmental agencies outsource substantial chunks of the caring industry.

The training and equipping of workers is pivotal to the success of the church. This book is more than simply a collection of articles: it is part of a systematic process aimed at creating a new generation of highly trained Christian child development workers. It is the most comprehensive collection of current Christian knowledge concerning care for children and I trust you will find it informative and illuminating. Above all, I pray that God will speak to you as you read through these pages about ways in which you can make a difference in the lives of children around you, children in your neighbourhood, in your city, in your country and on your continent. May you be exceedingly effective on their behalf as we together serve our master, the King – Jesus Christ.

Patrick McDonald, Founder and Director of Viva Network

– Preface –

Celebrate. What does the word mean? We usually associate it with a joyous occasion or a special event. How does this word apply to children living in danger-fraught, exploitative situations – to children who may have been forced into becoming child soldiers, to seven-year-olds who have been given drugs during the day to make them brave to fight and alcohol at night to numb the pain? Or to young girls thrown into the proverbial lions' den to face terror-filled nights from a pimp's order to service ten men and so lose their innocence and self-esteem? Only holistic healing that restores damaged spirits and provides God-inspired hope will ignite celebration from at-risk and exploited children. Healing and hope is what this book is all about: preparing and equipping childcare workers for ministry that results in celebration for both the workers and the children.

Children are precious and valuable because they have been created in the image of God.

This truth is foundational to our celebration of children. God declares that children are his best gifts. Throughout Jesus' ministry, he continually set the example as he celebrated children. His arms were ever open and ready to receive each and every child. He loved them, touched them, healed them and blessed them. He often used children to illustrate the truths of the kingdom: 'I tell you the truth, unless you change and become like little children, you will never enter the kingdom of heaven. Therefore, whoever humbles himself like this child is the greatest in the kingdom of heaven. And whoever welcomes a little child like this in my name welcomes me' (Matt. 18:3–5).

We also celebrate the potential God has placed within each child: gifts and abilities both for their personal development and for blessing others in their families, churches and communities. As these gifts are developed and celebrated, children are led to trust God's unique plans for their lives (Jer. 29:11). Childcare workers have the awesome responsibility of enabling children to become all God has intended for them to be.

Our ultimate goal is to have children carry on their celebrations as they worship at God's throne. The psalmist reminds us, 'From the lips of children and infants you have ordained praise' (Ps. 8:2). The loud hosannas of children welcomed Christ at his triumphal entry into Jerusalem. At his return, their praise again will welcome Christ's presence.

As you use this book to prepare for effective ministry to at-risk children, may you be inspired to renew your efforts to restore hope-filled celebrations to children who are dearly treasured by their heavenly Father.

Phyllis Kilbourn, Author and Founder and Director, 'Rainbows of Hope'

– Acknowledgements –

When we undertook to edit this book we had no idea what a mammoth task we were attempting. It has involved many groups and individuals in its conception, design and production. The book springs from a series of Viva Network facilitated workshops on training for people working with children. In particular, workshops at Bawtry Hall, Doncaster and Cherwell, Oxford helped to develop the curriculum outline, which was initially conceived by Gundelina Velazco, a psychologist from the Philippines who was then working as a consultant to Viva Network in collaboration with Emily McDonald, Viva Network's training manager at the time.

The following people were involved in the curriculum development process. They are listed according to the organizations with which they were working at the time of their involvement, and they represent some of the key Christian NGOs, universities and seminaries working in this evolving area: Ela Balog, Evangelical Theological Seminary, Croatia; Steve Bartel and Katrina McClean, YWAM Columbia; Richard Birkebak, YWAM University of the Nations; Stuart Christine, BMS, Brazil; Kathryn Copsey, CURBS; Gill Dallow, London Bible College; Wynand de Kock, Cornerstone Christian College; Patricia Green, Rahab Ministries, Thailand; Dario Lopez, CEMMA; Johann Lukasse, YWAM Brazil; Doug and Janna McConnell, Pioneers; Joe and Wanda Parker, Say Yes! Children's Club, USA; Raymond Samuel, Society for Integrated Social Upliftment (SISU), India; Teresa Santos, AMAI, Brazil; Vicki Shaver, Scripture Union, Scotland; Mikel and Karen Neuman and Jennifer Sah y Loeung, Western Seminary, Portland, Oregon, USA; Glenn Miles, Tearfund, UK; Josephine-Joy Wright, NHS, UK and Viva Network; Avril Fanner and Laura Sandidge, Pathfinders; Susan Greener and Laurent Mbanda, Compassion International; Margaret Apudo, Daystar University, Kenya; and Raquel Ovalles, Asian Theological Seminary, Philippines. The following Viva Network staff also played a key part in the process: Gundelina Velazco, Dave and Charity Scott, Emily and Patrick McDonald, Pauline MacKinnon, Deborah De Kock, Sonia Wilson, Karen Lamprecht and Jennifer Weiss. The course, which was compiled from these workshops, was drafted by Josephine-Joy

Wright, working firstly with Emily McDonald and secondly with Vicki Shaver and Glenn Miles.

Without the help of our friends and family this project would not have been possible. Glenn is especially grateful to his beloved and supportive wife Siobhan and children Zoë, Hannah and Sarah who allowed him to work on this during time which really belonged to them. He is also grateful to his assistant Romanear Thong for his support and encouragement and to Paul Stephenson and Ros Besford at Tearfund UK. He is thankful to his parents for their wonderful example of good parenting and encouragement in everything he does. Also thanks to all the 4M2C! prayer partners.

Josephine-Joy is most grateful to her family and friends and the children with whom she works for loaning her to a project which so often took her to another world. She is especially grateful to her dear friends Eileen and Roy Taylor, for loving her and even at crazy hours being constant and there in so many ways emotionally, spiritually and practically. Thanks go to the Taylors, to Tom Riley, Dorothy and Michael Hoy, her home group, Claire and Terry Trimnell, Sarah and Richard Ewers and to many others who steadfastly stood in the pathway of Satan in Jesus' name when Satan tried repeatedly to sabotage God's purpose in bringing this course and book to fruition. She is grateful to her brother Dave and to Jamie from Viva Network for their IT expertise and care; to Dave Scott and the Viva Network staff; to her brothers Quentin and Dave and sister Fiona and their families for sharing her joys and concerns at various points on the journey; to her nieces Vanessa and Chloe for sharing her excitement as the book became a reality; and to her friend, Tom Riley, for showing God's light and direction in the confusion at the eleventh hour with his love and wisdom, and for believing in her.

A huge thank you needs to go to our commissioning editor, Jeremy Mudditt, for walking two naïve editors through their first book with such compassion and patience. Without one other person, this book would never have been produced – Tara Smith, our copy editor, has been a real star, a light in the darkness with her forbearance, wisdom, kindness and laughter. She is really our third editor. Thank you, Tara.

Above all, we are grateful to God for giving us a task that enabled us to grow, to be challenged, to work together, to share such joy and to learn so much from being there when wires got crossed and emotions became tangled in tiredness. We also thank the children for sharing themselves with us and for allowing us into their worlds.

We are grateful that, between us, the book can now be born and released for God to use to do his miracles in children's lives.

Amen.

Glenn Miles and Josephine-Joy Wright

– Introduction –

Every book has a 'story', and this one is no exception. This book grew out of an international working group of Christian organizations and agencies caring for children. This group had been convened, with the help of Viva Network, to design a training course to equip people to work more effectively with children living in especially difficult circumstances of loss, trauma and abuse across the world.

The group recognized that we needed a source textbook both for students and teachers of our course (*Celebrating Children*) which would also be a practical and academic resource for other courses and for workers in the field. The resultant textbook has taken the course syllabus as its framework, covering key issues facing both the children and the workers. Its basis is healthy child development, biblical and research-based practice and a dialogue between micro and macro perspectives.

We chose the title out of a desire that our work with children should not focus on them as problems, or put them in neatly labelled boxes. Rather, our work should be a celebration of who children are and what God wants for them. Our hope is that the children with whom we work will be transformed and released to celebrate who they are and to worship God for themselves. The words 'celebrating children' can therefore be understood in three ways:

1. Our celebration of children for who they are: precious and valuable because they are made in the image of God.

2. Children celebrating because they are everything God intended them to be.

3. Children coming to a place where they can celebrate and worship at God's throne.

The 47 chapters, including the numerous case studies in this volume, were written by more than 50 different experts concerned with the needs of children. Contributors include professors in prestigious universities, practitioners in the field and people working with large sophisticated government-funded programmes and with small, sustainable community-based initiatives.

The chapters cover topics such as biblical and missiological studies, various applied social sciences such as sociology, psychology and development studies, practical health, management, organizational issues and policy studies. The book examines global causes for children being vulnerable, or 'at risk', as well as issues facing individual children and those working for them.

There are many people already working with children who are looking for an introductory text that will enable them to learn about the important issues. There are others who have had training in one area but need input in other areas. For example, many Christians have secular childcare training but want to know what God thinks about childcare ministry. Conversely, there are those who have had biblical training and would like to work with children but who do not know where to start looking for information.

Sunday school teachers and youth leaders should understand that the children in their care are not only spiritual beings but may well also be 'children at risk'. Leaders need to understand the physical and emotional needs of these children. People working in childcare projects need to have as a priority the right of the children in their care to hear and experience the gospel. We hope that this book will challenge everyone working with children to

improve their practice. After reading this text, the reader will be equipped to meet the *Celebrating Children* course objectives:

1. Describe the process of holistic child development within the child's own context (familial, cultural, etc.) according to a variety of theoretical frameworks and explore how these frameworks apply in practice, within a range of cultures.

2. Describe the biblical perspective on children in the contexts of their families and communities, in the church and in God's kingdom. Apply this perspective in principle and practice, following Jesus' example of listening to, honouring and involving children and his mandate for us to do the same in our work with them.

3. Identify factors that impact child development – on the global level and for each individual child and his family. Understand how these factors work either positively to enhance the child's resilience, or negatively to place the child at risk.

4. Identify principles of social transformation through a study of the history of Christian work with children and its impact on current practice and church awareness and involvement.

5. Demonstrate an understanding of effective ways of working with children and their families and how you will implement them.

6. Analyse the methods of assessment and evaluation and the models of prevention and intervention that are essential for effective work with children.

7. Explore the knowledge and practical skills required to be an effective 'children at risk' worker in context. Describe the strengths and vulnerabilities of the Christian working with 'children at risk'.

A central principle running through this book is that we, as well as the children, are on a journey of learning and transformation. The text favours the participatory approach, in which children and workers grow together to effect change – rather than the adults operating from a position of power over the children. So often it is the children and young people who are the lights in the darkness and signposts on the way. They dare to challenge, dare to ask, dare to love, dare to be out of their depth with each other and with Christ while we as adults stand on the river bank (Ezek. 47:1–6).

Adults can enable children whose lives are ruled by fear to dare to get close, dare to hope, dare to be, dare to own and to enjoy who God made them to be. We need to work together, underpinned by mutual honouring and compassionate love. Secure adult-child and adult-adult relationships should act as channels of God's healing power and as mirrors of his gift of himself to us. In this way we can become lights and signposts for children and for one another, pointing to Christ. This book seeks to help us to be witnesses to one another of his new life through biblically-rooted, evidence-based best practice.

This book gathers together current expertise, in a constantly growing body of knowledge, as a tool to enhance the development of those who work with children. Our prayer is that this book will assist readers in their practice, empower them to use their current knowledge and skills more effectively, help them to identify their areas of developmental need and stimulate their courage to trust God and to reach out to change, learn and be renewed. As a result, children will feel heard, will know they are valued, loved and honoured and will be released to enjoy Christ's freedom and grow up in the wisdom and stature of God and become 'oaks of righteousness' (Isa. 61:3b). Then God will be glorified and our work will be done.

– Abbreviations –

AERDO	Association of Evangelical Relief and Development Organizations
AMAI	Agape Missionary Association International
ARC	Action for the Rights of Children
CCPAS	Churches' Child Protection Advisory Service (PCCA)
CEMAA	Centro Evangélico de Misiología Andino Amazónica
CICH	Centre for International Child Health
CRC	*UN Convention on the Rights of the Child* (1989)
CURBS	Children in URBan Situations
EMQ	*Evangelical Missions Quarterly*
FICE	Fédération Internationale des Communautés Educatives
GCOWE	Global Commission on World Evangelism
IDS	Institute of Development Studies
IMF	International Monetary Fund
MOM	Ministry of Mercy
NCVCCO	National Council of Voluntary Child Care Organisations
NHS	National Health Service (UK)
ODA	Overseas Development Assistance
SCF	Save the Children Fund
SGM	Scripture Gift Mission International
SISU	Society for Integrated Social Upliftment
TCI	Teen Challenge International
WAVE	Worldwide Alternatives to ViolencE
WDA	Women's Development Association
WEC	World Evangelism Crusade
WTO	World Trade Organization
WVI	World Vision International
YFC	Youth for Christ International
YWAM	Youth With A Mission

– PART ONE –

Understanding the Child in Context

Introduction THE *early stages of child development research focused on ethological and anthropological investigations: assessing the way in which children worked with their environment, and particularly with their social and cultural worlds. Over the past 50 years, as researchers have tried to analyse children's development in more depth, the focus has shifted from contextual to individual investigations. However, both a theological and a sociological framework would emphasize that, while we do need to understand the development of the individual child, that development can only really be understood in context. That is, we need to look at how the child impacts upon his world, how his world impacts upon him and, in the manner of true integration, how the two are transformed by one another.*

This first part begins with Kathryn Copsey's comprehensive reflection on 'what is a child?'. Glenn Miles writes in Chapter 2 about how children see themselves, using a case study with militarized children in Southeast Asia. Chapter 3, then, offers a comprehensive look at what the Bible says about children that is foundational for all of the material in this volume. In Chapter 4, Glenn Miles explores how culture in particular impacts the development of children. Susan Greener then provides an assessment of the key contextual factors, followed by Keith White's overview of the theoretical frameworks that may assist our analysis. Paul Stephenson critically appraises the key issue of children's rights in the concluding chapter in this section. The authors provide different windows on the world of the child in context which, in sum, provide a sound framework for the rest of the book's discussion. **Josephine-Joy Wright**

– CHAPTER 1 –

What Is a Child?

Kathryn Copsey

USHA is ten. She has been ill and has left school after just two years. Her auntie is teaching her to become a tailor. She cares for her two younger sisters and helps the family with their work. Her mother washes clothes and Usha fetches the water. After they have been ironed and washed, she delivers them and collects the money.

Yasuko is four. She attends the local kindergarten where she wears a little yellow hat, a uniform and carries a school bag like all the other children. She practices her violin for an hour each day, enthusiastically supported by her mother. Building character is important in the Kobayashi household, and Yasuko is brought up to respect discipline, tradition and the value of hard work.

David is eight. His family was caught in anti-government guerrilla warfare. He saw his father, mother and baby sister brutally killed as he hid in the bush. He ran away and was found by an aunt and uncle who had managed to escape. Together they fled across the border to a refugee camp, which already housed some 3,000 people.

Debbie is eleven. She has long blond hair, a mountain bike, wears designer clothes and has her own pony, which she rides most days. She lives in a large, four-bedroom house in a rural location. Her mother is a teacher and her father runs a business. Debbie will soon get treatment by an orthodontist so her front teeth will look perfectly level. It will cost her parents in the region of £4,000.

Raoul is thirteen. He has been living on the streets since he was eight. He never knew his mother and, when his father died suddenly of a heart attack, he was left with no family and nowhere to live. He took a bus to the big city, where he slept in a doorway. He met up with other street children and quickly became wise in the art of street survival, mingling with petty criminals, drug pushers and pimps. He has recently found his way to a refuge for street children, which is the only caring community he has ever known.

Here are five images of children from five different continents. Which, if any, of these is closest to your own picture of what a child is? Which best represents your own childhood? Is there a difference?

Think of the word 'child'. Write down the first three words or images that come to your mind when you think of this word. Where do your images come from? Your own childhood, children you know, children you have seen today, children you have seen in pictures, children you have seen on television? Are your images mostly negative or positive, or are they neutral?

Now do the same for the word 'childhood'. Did you think in terms of a period of time? If so, when did it start and finish? Did you think in terms of activities or significant people? If so, what or who were these?

Now talk to someone from a different cultural background, perhaps from another country. What are their images of children and childhood? In what ways are they the same as or different to yours?

As you have thought through these issues, you may have been aware that your images of children and childhood come from many different sources. You will have been influenced by the way you were brought up, by your memories of your own childhood, by the views of your parents, relatives and friends, as well as by neighbours, teachers and others in your community. You will have been influenced by what you have seen or read. In other words, you have been influenced by your own *experiences*. You have also been influenced by the *culture* in which you have grown up, and this includes your ethnic background, social class and gender.

Ariès (1962) suggests that 'childhood' is a comparatively recent invention that is specific to certain cultures at certain times in their history. Thinking of childhood as a time for play is a Western notion. In many cultures, particularly in agricultural communities, children are expected to take their place as part of the family work force, caring for younger siblings and learning adult responsibilities. In Western societies where parents usually work outside the home, children are largely cut off from the world of work. Education is about formal learning in a school setting, whereas play and learning in rural communities, where work is inextricably bound up with survival, tend to be about preparation for taking on adult roles.

The important point to note from all of this is that views of children and of childhood are not uniform. Social, political and economic issues all shape our views. These, in turn, shape how we relate to and work with children.

A further issue to note in our exploration of 'what is a child?' relates to what age range we are using to describe a child. This book and the associated syllabus (see Appendix) use the definition adopted by the CRC, which defines a child as a person below the age of eighteen, unless the laws of a particular country set the legal age for adulthood as younger than eighteen.

The child in context

When trying to describe a child, we first of all need to remember that a child does not exist in isolation. A child exists in context and, in order to understand that child, we must also understand his or her context. Thus a child is born of a mother into some form of family, which is part of a neighbourhood, part of a community, part of a village, town, city, country, and so on. Directly or indirectly, the child is affected by all of these systems as he or she grows up. Urie Bronfenbrenner (1979), an American psychologist, has emphasized the importance of studying 'development-in-context' by proposing an 'ecological' model of development where 'ecology' refers to the various environmental settings which the child experiences (see also Chapter 5, 'Factors That Optimize Development', below). Bronfenbrenner suggests a model in which there are four nested circles (see Figure 1). The basic level is the microsystem. For a child, one microsystem might be the home, another might be the extended family, another might be the school, and a fourth might be the peer group. At the next level, the mesosystem links the various microsystems. For example, the home situation may affect whether the child works or goes to school. The third level is the exosystem – settings that affect the individual indirectly. For example, the child may not directly experience a parent's work environment, but he may experience the effect that long working hours have on the family. The final level is the macrosystem, which refers to the ideological patterns of a given society and the way in which social and political institutions are structured. Thus a war might affect the working patterns of a family, which in turn affect the patterns of home life and family caring.

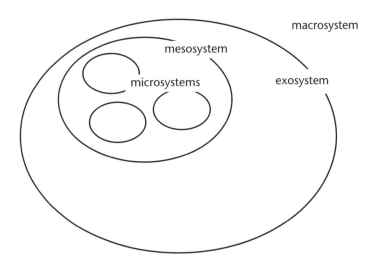

Figure 1: Bronfenbrenner's ecological model of human development

If we are to take seriously the context within which a child is growing up and the various systems which affect her, then it is essential to start *in* the child's world where she is now – not where we would *like* the child to be. This means that we must put aside our own preconceptions and be aware of our own cultural bias in order to do three things:

- come alongside the child and see the world through her eyes;
- build up a relationship based on trust and the offer of long-term commitment;
- earn the right to be heard.

If this is our starting point, then we will be better able to hear and understand the children's own stories and to stand beside them in their pain. Henri Nouwen (1993, p. 123) said:

> I now realize that only when I can enter with the children into their joy will I be able also to enter with them into their poverty and pain. God obviously wants me to walk into the world of suffering with a little child on each hand.

The child as a whole person

God created human beings with bodies, minds and souls. Adults have a tendency to compartmentalize these aspects, particularly in the Western world: this is 'secular', that is 'spiritual'; now I am 'thinking', then I will be 'doing'. But children do not naturally make such distinctions. For them, life is a whole. And, in order to understand a child fully, we need to look at all of the elements that make up this 'wholeness': the physical, social, mental or cognitive, emotional, moral and spiritual elements. We need to look at each child 'holistically', just as Jesus did in his encounters with individuals in the Gospels.

The physical aspect

Growth is one of the most obvious signs of physical development. This process begins even before birth, as the fertilized egg grows into a foetus in the womb according to a fixed schedule. This growth continues after birth for nearly twenty years. Children all over the world mature in the same sequence. A baby will first hold its head up, then learn to sit alone, roll over, stand and eventually walk. This sequence is fixed: a baby will not be able to stand before she can roll over. However, the age at which each stage is attained can vary greatly. Developmentalists have researched the average age-span at which children reach each stage, and children who progress before or after this span are classed as early or late developers. In some cases slow development may be due to the effects of a premature birth, early illness, a difficult pregnancy, or poor health or malnutrition on the part of the mother. In other cases, it may simply be that the biological time clock of the baby is slow or that the baby has no real desire to walk if he can progress just as easily by scooting along on his bottom.

From conception, many of the new baby's characteristics are fixed – such as gender, eye colour, hair colour, and so on. But other characteristics – such as height and weight – are influenced by diet and physical environment. There is a continuing debate among developmentalists concerning how much the environment (nurture) can influence a child's development, and how much development is controlled by genetic inheritance (nature). Some theorists see development as a continuous process that occurs gradually, over a long period of time. Others see development as a discontinuous process, in which children develop ways of thinking, feeling and behaving which are qualitatively different as they grow older. All developmentalists would acknowledge the importance of the social context within which the child is growing up and would see the need to recognize both the similarities and differences between children of different cultures in order to obtain a theory of development which is truly cross-cultural.

The social aspect

Unlike some animal species, which come into the world able to survive on their own, the human baby is virtually helpless at birth. She is dependent on her parents or other caregivers for food, warmth and protection. Although a baby exhibits certain behaviours that elicit interaction from adults (such as crying, smiling, responses to visual and auditory stimuli), it is primarily down to the adult to maintain the level of social interaction. Gradually, through this interaction, the baby develops her own 'social repertoire' of responses, learning to distinguish familiar from unfamiliar faces and to take turns so that true interaction can take place.

Research has indicated that what is important for the child at this early stage of development is to have one or two consistent caregivers with whom she can build up a bond of security and trust. The caregiver does not necessarily have to be the mother. The key is that the primary caregiver must be available and responsive to the child and provide a secure, consistent environment. It is also important at this early stage to be aware of the child's emotional needs and of the long-term impact of bonding in early years.

Some research has suggested that children build up internal representations of early attachment relationships in their minds, called *internal working models.* These are cognitive structures based on the day-to-day interactions with the mother (or other caregiver) and on the expectations and emotional experiences associated with these interactions. As the child grows older, this working model changes to account for new relationships and experiences. Where a child experiences a secure attachment and relationship, her internal working model of caregivers will be that they model behaviours that are available and responsive. Where her experience has been of an insecure attachment with inconsistent and unresponsive behaviours, this has implications for the child's later social and emotional development. While this theory cannot be applied uncritically to attachment patterns in adult life, it can provide a useful framework for thinking about the long-term effects of early attachment experiences (Cassidy and Shaver, 1999).

So it is the *early* experiences of social deprivation, in particular those types of situations that surround 'children at risk' (for example armed conflict, dysfunctional families, life on the streets), which have the most deleterious long-term effects on children. By the age of seven a child has internally formed her responses to the outside world, which will remain with her for life. If she has found that the world is basically an unsafe place, that adults are not to be trusted, that carers desert you, then such experiences will largely determine her adult patterns in life. This is not to say that there cannot be a significant intervention in her life to change her responses, such as a major reparative experience. For example, she might experience God's love through the intervention of the Holy Spirit – either on his own or by his working through a caring adult.

As the child grows older, her circle of adult carers expands beyond the primary caregivers. In some countries the primary caregivers may include older siblings or members of the extended family such as aunts, uncles or grandparents. In the West, the primary caregiver is often the mother and perhaps also the father. The circle then expands to include siblings, grandparents, aunts and uncles and eventually childminders, day-care staff and teachers. Each of these individuals extends the horizons of the infant, fulfilling different roles for her. Relationships with siblings are particularly important to the developing child. Research into sibling relationships has shown how important brothers and sisters are as social partners and has revealed the rich and complex relationships they have with each other, which show great depth of emotion and understanding and often a love/hate relationship.

The cognitive aspect

The study of children's cognitive development has been profoundly influenced by the work of Jean Piaget (1896–1980). Piaget brought a scientific approach to the study of knowledge. While many aspects of his theories are now challenged, few would deny the invaluable contribution he has made to our understanding of the way in which children think. In particular, he has had a major impact in the field of education. His research encouraged the development of a child-centred approach to education, for he argued that children think differently from adults and view the world from a different perspective. He also encouraged the idea of 'active' learning – learning by discovery – where the focus is on the learning process rather than on the end product.

Piaget suggested that children go through four stages in the development of their thinking, and that they do so in the same invariable order. Within these stages, changes in the structure of the children's intelligence take place. Piaget called these structures schema, or mental operations. They can be applied to any idea or activity in the child's world. As the child's thinking develops, the structures evolve from one stage to the next.

In the first stage (*sensori-motor*, ages 0–2), the infant begins to act on her environment physically. She begins to learn about her world through her actions and her senses. In the second and third stages (*pre-operational*, ages 2–7, and *concrete-operational*, ages 8–11), she learns to form internal representations of these actions. The actions become symbols in the mind, but because they are still closely tied to the physical, to concrete objects, this is called the 'concrete' operational stage. In the fourth stage (*formal operational*, ages 11+), the child learns to work with these representations as abstract or hypothetical problems, divorced from the original concrete situations. The child thus develops the ability to reason logically.

Piaget's theories have been challenged in a number of areas. Margaret Donaldson (1978) in particular suggests that children are able to take on board the perspective of another at a much earlier age than Piaget would imply. She also observes that they are not so limited in their ability to reason deductively as Piaget would suggest. Other research indicates that Piaget underestimates the importance of social interaction through shared meanings and the role of language.

Margaret Donaldson also raises a number of other issues that have an important bearing on how we understand and work with children.

1. She stresses the need to consider the whole child when seeking to explore what a child understands or is able to do. Assessing a child in a laboratory setting may not present the full picture. More can be learned by observing how the child responds in a natural setting with which she is comfortable and familiar.

2. Donaldson also states that it is important to consider a situation from the child's point of view. In an experimental setting, the child is actively trying to make sense of what the adult is asking her to do. She may well be responding to what she thinks the adult must mean rather than what is actually said or asked.

3. Finally, while affirming the importance of formal education – the need for a child to learn to work with abstract modes of thought – she suggests that we need to understand that, for children, thinking is 'embedded' in its context. It needs to make 'human sense' to them; it needs to take account of what they are bringing with them into the situation.

Another major challenge to Piaget's theories has come from the Russian psychologist Lev Vygotsky (1896–1934). He stresses the role of social interaction as key to the child's developing understanding – the intervention of the adult (or peer) who challenges the child to move on to new knowledge by means of the relationship. The relationship and interaction that take place with the adult are crucial (Donaldson, 1988).

The moral and emotional aspects

Research has indicated that these two aspects of a child's development are inextricably bound together. If a child does not understand that an action has caused distress, then he is unlikely to conceive of that action as being wrong. In fact, the development of moral understanding in a child closely parallels that of emotional understanding, and research has indicated that this is the case across cultures.

It is important to make the distinction here that we are speaking about the development of moral reasoning, or how we *think* about morality, rather than whether or not we *act* upon it. Kohlberg, who followed on Piaget's initial work in this area, proposed three principle stages in the development of moral thinking: *preconventional* (up to nine years), in which the individual reasons in relation to the possible effect upon himself of breaking the rule; *conventional* (adolescents and most adults), in which 'being good' is important – upholding rules set by society; and *post-conventional* (minority of adults over twenty), in which the person is guided by more general moral principles underlying rules.

It is interesting that these stages parallel different stages in emotional development. Around the age of six, children think of emotion in terms of an emotionally charged situation that produces a visible, physical result. By the age of ten, children tend to label mental processes that affect their behavioural or emotional responses to situations – for example, 'forget it' or 'think positively' about it. Older children develop this further by making a greater distinction between what emotion they display in response to what other people say and what they are actually feeling.

It would appear from this that all children, regardless of their family backgrounds, begin life with the sense that certain actions are wrong. Yet children vary a great deal in terms of their willingness to abide by or disregard these principles. Their home backgrounds and the contexts in which they live significantly affect this variation in how they act upon their moral reasoning. This moral reasoning is paralleled by the understanding, which develops between the ages of four and ten, that the emotional state of one person can affect the emotional state of another – for example, 'if I am angry and I hit you, I will make you cry'.

The spiritual aspect

Genesis 1:26 says, 'Let us make man in our image, in our likeness'. What does it mean to say that we have been made in God's image? Clearly it does not refer to a physical similarity, as God is spirit. It must, therefore, refer to inner, more intangible qualities.

If we believe we are made in the image of God, then we must take seriously the idea that all of us, including children, have an inborn spirituality. Otherwise we find that we are in danger of saying that it is only when we become Christian that we have a spiritual side. So we can be deeply spiritual without having a faith as such: faith is the framework that we put around our spirituality. Thus we might put an Islamic, Buddhist, Hindu, Orthodox, Jewish or any of a number of different faith frameworks around our spirituality. Sometimes we are in danger of neglecting or negating the fact that children, made as they are in the image of God, already have spirituality. What we need to understand is that their spirituality can be a springboard to faith (Hay and Nye, 1998).

What, then, are the qualities that naturally tumble out of children, those qualities that Jesus encourages us to learn from when he urges us to 'become like a child'? In other words, what characterizes a child's spirituality? What qualities does a child carry within by virtue of having been made in God's image?

Here is one summary. Children are:

- Open:

  To nature – children exhibit a sense of awe and wonder

  To feelings – children tend to be direct, in touch with their feelings

  To others – children naturally tend to have an open, welcoming nature

- Able to be present:

  Children tend to live in the 'here and now' and think in concrete terms

  Children have a gift for perception – what we really mean, how we feel

  Children tend to accept things at face value, taking as much as is needed for a given time

- Uncomplicated:

  Children can find belief easy and uncomplicated, they do not need to analyse

  Children can find trust easy if they are brought up within a trustworthy environment

  Children have simple, basic emotional and physical needs

It is clear, however, that the majority of the children with whom we work do not exhibit these qualities, because their spirituality has been severely damaged. There are many ways in which this happens. We may simply be unaware of it, we may fail to recognize it and therefore fail to nurture it. We may rubbish it, crush it, clutter it; we may allow it to be lost under the weight of a materialistic, consumerist culture. We do this, for example,

- If we give children the message that feelings are wrong
- If we offer children environments that have no beauty, that are soulless and fail to help them discover a sense of awe and wonder in what lies around them
- If we destroy their sense of trust and openness through various forms of abuse and insincerity
- If we fail to meet their basic emotional and physical needs
- If we make belief too cognitive, too complicated, failing to recognize the value of affective learning
- If we kill their imagination and their sense of fantasy.

David Hay (Hay and Nye, 1998), from the Children's Spirituality Project, speaks of children's spiritual awareness being artificially blocked out by a secularized society. He identifies the ways in which we damage a child's spirituality as:

- A squashing of the sense of awareness
- The crushing of mystery
- The rise of individualism and the breakdown of the family
- A pushing out of consciousness of the fundamental questions of meaning such as 'Who am I?'

Thus, by the time a child is ten or eleven in Western society, and even earlier in some other areas of the world, spiritual awareness is edged out. In effect, the image of God in the child has been scratched or spoiled. She inherits a false self, a damaged self. We want to be able to use a child's spirituality as a springboard to faith, but the degree to which this spirituality has been damaged (the image scratched) will affect the child's ability to move to faith. It is very difficult for a child to understand what it is to trust Jesus if she has lost the ability to trust. It is very difficult to marvel at the God of creation if there has been nothing in the environment to nurture that sense of awe and wonder. We first need to *repair* a child's spirituality – to reawaken it – before we are able to put the framework of faith around it.

– Questions to Consider –

1 Describe what is meant by a 'holistic' view of child development and how this relates to our work with children.

2 Compare three different theoretical frameworks for understanding children's cognitive development and discuss the pros and cons of each theory in practice.

3 What have we learned from the research of Hay and Nye and others about the spiritual life of children? How do these findings affect our work with children?

– Chapter 2 –

How Do Children Describe Themselves?[1]

Glenn Miles

CHILDREN are described, in many ways and by many people, in terms of how they relate to the person describing them. There are many dangers when labelling children, and we must be careful that we do not 'put them in a box'. Giving children opportunities to describe/picture themselves may reveal much about them that surprises even the experienced carers. This chapter describes how militarized children were given the opportunity to describe their past, present and future through the medium of drawing and how this was used to benefit them.

The act of drawing is an integral part of play and is generally enjoyed by children of all ages. When provided with materials, most children will draw. Art has also been used as a diagnostic tool to gauge intellectual or emotional development, as a therapeutic tool and as a communication tool to understand children's world-views and explore their beliefs and opinions.

Some psychologists have attempted to use art to determine the intellectual or emotional status of children. Machover (1949) developed the classic personality test based on children's drawings of a person. Art has been used extensively to diagnose psychological disturbance in children, but Cox (1992) suggests that evidence indicates that while drawings may be a reliable global assessment of a child's emotional adjustment, they cannot give any indication of specific strengths or weaknesses. The age and ability of children will affect what they draw and, while children themselves may understand why they have drawn something and what it is, adult interpretation is highly subjective – leading many psychologists to question the value of projective drawing measures with children. Pridmore and Bendelow (1995) point out that the emphasis of psychologists in using art has tended to be on diagnosing abnormality and non-conformity.

Nevertheless, a number of professionals have begun to recognize the use of drawing in dialogue with children, specifically when trying to find out children's opinions and understandings of situations. This use of drawing focuses on building on strengths and empowerment. Art therapy is generally associated with the Freudian psychoanalytic theory that confrontation and expression of blocked and suppressed feelings is therapeutic (Freud, 1976). It is felt that children might gain some relief from drawing and be able to deal with the underlying tensions generated by being in situations of conflict. Erikson (1968) took Piaget's theory of assimilation (bringing order and control to poorly understood feelings) through play, to propose the possibility of deliberately recreating different situations with children – using, for example, drawings and drama.

Goodwin (1982) suggests that art enables children, especially those severely traumatized through sexual abuse, for example, to communicate in ways that they might be unable or unwilling to do verbally. Gross and Hayne (1998) suggest that 'drawing can be used to facilitate children's ability to talk about events, particularly those events they might otherwise find difficult to describe or understand'. Thomas and Silk (1990) have commented that no controlled evaluations have been conducted with children to demonstrate that expression of emotion in art is, in fact, therapeutic. They did say, however, that interest in art as a therapy has increased as the process of drawing has been recognized as a powerful means of overcoming barriers of communication.

Rae (1991) has conducted research with children that suggested that drawings facilitated discussion about children's emotional reaction to hospitalization. Butler, Gross and Hayne (1995) found that of the children aged between three and five years old experiencing the same event (a visit to a fire station), the half who did drawings reported significantly more information than the half who did not. Drucker, Greco-Vigorito, Moore-Russell, Avaltroni and Ryan (1997) used drawings to interview five- to nine-year-old children of substance abusers, asking them to describe a recent incident. Children who were asked to draw reported more than three times as much information than did those who were only asked to tell.

Pridmore and Bendelow (1995) suggest that, 'using children's drawings in conjunction with writing or dialogue can be a powerful method of exploring the beliefs of young children, which inform . . . behaviour'. They go on to emphasize the ethical advantage of using these child-centred approaches, which incorporate the children's own ideas, beliefs and metaphors. In Woodhead's multi-culture research project (1998) with working children from a wide range of jobs, 'young people were encouraged to represent their feelings and beliefs in whatever way most meaningful to them, including drawings, mapping, role play as well as group discussion'. The significant point here is that the children had control over the methodology.

According to the CRC, it is every child's right to be able to communicate, and art is seen as one means of communication. Article 13 says that children have the right to freedom of expression, to be able to impart information and ideas of all kinds by all means, including in the form of art. As importantly, Article 12 says that children have a right to be heard and that their opinions should be taken into account when making decisions that affect them.

Even apart from potential psychological benefits, using drawings with children is an effective way of finding out a wide range of information. The aim of the research in this case study was to understand children's perceptions of hope for their own futures, for the project and for their state/country so that the programme could be developed accordingly. To hope is to believe that something positive, which is not presently visible, could still materialize. Hope is one of three key Christian principles (the others being faith and love). Kilbourn (1995) suggests that restoring hope is key to the recovery of war-traumatized children. It has been suggested that a traumatic event or series of events can develop in such a way so as to block out the past and the future and focus only on the present. Lazarus (1999) suggests that hope is in fact an in-built coping resource against despair. In circumstances where we feel that we want to try to improve a situation, we need to recognize that most children have the ability to assist in this process themselves. Could encouraging children to draw their expectations for the future actually foster hope as they consider future possibilities?

Case study of how children were able to 'picture themselves'

Research was conducted with sixty militarized refugee children without accompanying parents, in two centres in Southeast Asia. All of the 52 boys and eight girls (aged 9–16) living in the two centres participated. Some children had been militarized (living and working with the resistance army) for up to six years.

In preliminary semi-structured interviews with centre leaders, it was suggested that children had often been 'picked up' by the 'resistance' military army as refugees separated from their families in the looting and burning of their villages. Some children had seen family members and friends tortured and killed. Many parents would have been killed and, due to the insecure nature of the region, it was not always possible for the remaining parents to be located.

These children were therefore used by the 'resistance' army to work for them – gathering food from the forest, cooking, being porters, carrying weapons and later being trained in weapon use. Some children had been trained as snipers. The ongoing destabilization of the state from which they came meant that most children had had limited access to education and health care. Children were being forcibly conscripted into the government army (which the resistance were fighting against). Furthermore, the neighbouring country to which they would need to go to in order to escape was not welcoming and refused to give refugee status. Indeed, Human Rights Watch sees forcible deportation as being in direct

proportion to increased economic co-operation between governments. In one sense, the care of the 'resistance' for the children was an act of mercy – since the alternative might have been to leave them to die in the jungle.

The international community does not favour the 'resistance' military group, and therefore it receives little support. With a reputation for opium smuggling, the resistance were keen to promote an improved image at an international political level. They are aware that the CRC strongly suggests that children, especially those under sixteen years of age, should not be militarized (there is an increasing lobby to increase this age to 18 years). They had therefore invited a development agency to help provide accommodation and education for the 60 children, which was how the two centres came into being. The intention is that more children will be 'made available' in the future as the programme develops and resources become available.

Although the project was not submitted to an ethical committee, ethical concerns were considered. It was recognized that, in doing ethical research, children need to have the freedom not to be involved. This is not easy in a situation where to withdraw in front of the group might lead to 'loss of face' – a particular concern in Southeast Asia. However, it was felt that the method of drawing and the openness of what was required gave children the opportunity to draw as much or as little as they liked. While project organizers recognized that bringing up the past might be painful for some children, there is insufficient evidence that the drawing of traumatic events causes further trauma and much psychological theory (though little evidence – see above) to indicate that the opposite is in fact true.

The research was conducted in the children's familiar 'breeze block' classroom. Although children were not forbidden to look at their colleagues' work, this was not encouraged. The children were asked to draw three sets of pictures as follows:

Page 1. On a large sheet of paper, divided into three parts, in the first section they drew a picture of themselves in the country from which they had fled. In the second section, they drew themselves now. In the third section, they drew themselves in the future, picturing what they would be doing.

Page 2. How they saw the centre in which they were living in the future.

Page 3. The country from which they had fled: a) now and b) in the future.

After the exercise, children were asked individually to explain what they had drawn. Then the children discussed the drawings with key staff members. The following is a breakdown of the results.

Page 1. Most children had ideas about what they wanted to do in the future. Out of 52 unaccompanied refugee boys, 24 boys indicated in their drawings (usually through holding guns, but sometimes in uniform) that they had been 'soldiers' in the past. Twenty-two boys drew themselves as soldiers in the future but, interestingly, 13 of the boys who had been soldiers drew themselves as 'something else' in the future. Thirteen of the boys who had been 'something else' drew themselves as soldiers in the future, leaving only 11 boys who drew themselves as soldiers in the past and also drew themselves as soldiers in the future (usually in a higher rank, denoted by epaulettes). Other children drew themselves as farmers/buffalo herders in the past, rather than students, even though they had been pupils for varying time spans (perhaps because of the disruption to school). Significantly, none of the children chose to be farmers in the future. Some of the children drew themselves in the future as teachers (9 children), preachers/evangelists (7 children) and in other jobs (doctor, politician). Most children drew themselves in the present picture as pupils, but several drew themselves with

their hands up in worship, which could indicate the importance of their new-found faith.

One child drew a picture of a brother in the past picture who was absent in pictures of the present and future, which suggested that he had been killed. When the child was asked about this, he replied that the brother was in fact in the other centre for unaccompanied children. This may indicate that art was being used as a form of communication to adults that was not so easily done verbally. In this case it led to a reunion between siblings, but it illustrates the importance of a non-intimidating open dialogue between adults and children. Children, and particularly former child soldiers, might consider that directly asking adults for something would lead to discipline, even though the intention of the adults might be the opposite. This indicates yet again that clarification is vital.

Page 2. Most of the children drew pictures of a bigger and better centre – with, for example, a school for 'accompanied' refugee children from the locality, increased sports facilities and a guest house. This perhaps indicated the value they placed on guests from outside developing relationships with the children. The drawings were generally positive and hopeful.

Page 3. Children drew some disturbing pictures of their country, as they perceived it now, clearly in a war situation. Some of the pictures illustrated traumas the children had been exposed to, such as being driven out of a burning village and being witness to torture and killings. One child drew a picture of a tiger caught in a thorn bush, wounded but fighting to get free. The tiger is a mascot, or symbol, of his people and graphically illustrated their situation.

As is often the case in qualitative research, mistakes can prove to be fruitful. One teacher misunderstood the instructions, and she originally asked the boys to write a narrative of the situation in their country now and in the future. When some of these were translated it was fascinating to see that, although the children's written descriptions of the situation reflected the melancholic nature of the 'resistance' armies' songs and poems, their drawings gave a more hopeful picture of the future – with multiple colourful high-rise buildings, roads and cars, contrasting with the thick green jungle of the current conflict location. Significantly, no child's picture of the future was the same as the past. More research is needed to explore this.

Methodology

Asking children to *vocalize* their responses has limited value because children's vocabulary is restricted according to their ages and abilities. A child's ability to articulate his opinions and feelings is not the same as an adult's, and he is therefore open to misinterpretation. Adults may intimidate children, and therefore access to information that children have may be restricted. Children may prefer not to disclose information in a face-to-face interview that they might disclose in an anonymous self-written questionnaire or other non-directive exercise. Children may also have insufficient time to give a considered response.

Drawing responses can be positive because drawing is fun for both children and researchers. Drawing may enable children to relax and concentrate their thoughts. It 'breaks down barriers' of communication and allows the artist to express emotions. Possible flaws in the method include the following: children could fabricate events in the process of drawing, as they are often encouraged to in artistic expression of ideas; interpretation of more abstract ideas by adults is subjective (and in this case it may be better for children to interpret the drawings themselves); children may feel their drawing ability is limited and be embarrassed to show it to adults, thereby drawing what they find easiest rather than what they want to communicate. There will also be cross-cultural variations in what children draw in research being conducted cross-culturally (and even within the cross-sub-cultural differences between adults and children).

Pridmore and Bendelow (1995) and Pridmore (1996) suggest that the draw-and-write technique generates more information because drawing enables all children, including young children and children with special needs, to participate. It enables researchers to treat children as subjects rather than objects. It enables children to have time to reflect and gain control over their own ideas. Children can express ideas through drawing for which they did not have words and then seek help to write about these ideas. It allows for the study of difference and range rather than seeing children as a homogenous group. Gross and Hayne (1997) suggest that the draw-and-tell technique generates more information because drawing helps children feel more comfortable and relaxed in an unfamiliar situation. Drawing may also facilitate memory retrieval. Drawing helps children to arrange and organize their narratives, giving them the opportunity to tell a better story. Collins, McWhirter and Wetton (1998) suggest other advantages of the draw-and-tell technique used in their study of pre-school children and sun protection. Even though a child may have drawn a scribble, to the child this scribble has meaning that can be discussed. All children are able to describe their pictures and give answers in response to questions asked by the researcher. Research provides quantifiable data that can be used in programme development. The research takes a short time to administer and is relatively easy to analyse.

Backett-Milburn and McKie (1999) describe some of the disadvantages of this technique. Drawing requires knowledge (of the appearance and structure of subjects or objects to be drawn) and skill (children become more skilful in drawing as they get older). Children's drawings cannot be regarded as direct translations of mental states and images on paper. Children (and adults) will reproduce pictures of dominant discourses in the culture. The fact that children can produce drawings and statements about topics can mask critical reflection on what these data actually mean and how this has been affected by the research process. Analysis is often done quantitatively when it is really a qualitative methodology.

Conclusion

The general impression gained from what children had drawn in this study was that they were hopeful about the future, even though there are currently no political or social indications that things are likely to improve. Essentially, the children are currently illegal refugees, not accepted by their 'host' country and unable to return to their own country.

This exercise gives us some insight into children's sense of hope for the future. It provided specific information on some aspects of how the programme could be developed in the future, such as ideas for physically developing the centre and its facilities. It also provided a launch pad to discuss and develop vocational training opportunities, and it gave staff working with the children further insights into how the children themselves were thinking. The staff and teachers recognized that these insights added to their understanding of specific children and of the group as a whole. It also encouraged the staff to think about the importance of communication. The children seemed to enjoy the activity of drawing and appreciated that somebody was interested in their opinions and their personal futures as well as the future of their people. It may be useful to repeat the exercise in a year's time to compare whether their hopes have changed or developed.

Using drawings in this way seemed to be a useful and fairly quick way to gain a great deal of information in a short period of time. This is important where research time is at a premium. However, much more information could have been acquired with more time. And, apart from the controversial psychological benefits, using art was a useful tool to open up communication between children and adults.

Children should be given the opportunity to express themselves and describe themselves. This will give invaluable insights to the carers as well as benefiting the children.

Figure 1: 'This is me before when I was a soldier'

Figure 2: 'This is me now'

Figure 3: 'This is me in the future as a teacher'

– Exercise –

1 Brainstorm a list of descriptions for children and 'children at risk'. What do you come up with? You will probably have many adverbs that can be divided into resiliencies and vulnerabilities, but how do children describe themselves?

2 Give children a large piece of paper divided into three sections. Ask them to draw:

a) me in the past

b) me now

c) me in the future.

Then ask the child to describe 'their story' to you, or to a trusted worker.

I have tried this with former child soldiers, children who had been sexually exploited and children who had been in orphanages. The results were exciting and gave new insights to staff that had worked with the children for years. It once again demonstrated to me the importance of listening to children.

3 An alternative exercise is to ask children, as well as the adults with whom they work, to write about their perceptions of growing up and then consider how different the responses are. The following lists illustrate the need for care when designing such exercises, since children have to think into their perceived futures to write about their perceptions of growing up. For adults, on the other hand, the task is a reflective as well as a projective one. These two lists also highlight the differences in perception between adults and children. Whereas children often choose concrete, visible, self-focused examples, the adult responses are primarily more emotionally complex and abstract.

Children	*Adults*
• To be at peace with myself, my family and friends	• To be resilient and competent
• To get a good job	• To grow well and develop immunity against infection
• To be loved	• To show initiative and motivation
• To get out as soon as possible	• To be as intelligent as possible
• To be big	• To be useful citizens
• To love someone special	• To be peaceful
• To be smart	• To develop their talents to their potential
• To play football better	• To be smart, personable and employable
• To live in a safe place	• To grow spiritually and bear fruit
• To change the way that people think	• To develop pro-social temperaments
• To have enough to eat	• To study well at school and achieve good grades
• To be beautiful	
• To stop adults spoiling our world	

- To find out what God wants me to do
- To understand myself
- To discover what I am good at
- To fight against wrong things
- To avoid being hurt by bad people

- To be able to sort out problems
- To be healthy and without disability

Note

1. Modified and reprinted by permission of the Association of British Paediatric Nurses and Sage Publications Ltd from G. Miles, 'Drawing Together Hope: "Listening" to Militarised Children', *Journal of Child Health Care* 4.4, 137–42. © Association of British Paediatric Nurses and Sage Publications, 2000.

– Questions to Consider –

1 How can children's drawings help us to gain a picture of children and their worlds?

2 Give an example of your use of drawing as a technique to assist children's self-expression, detailing your assessment and theoretical perspective. How do you think the child perceived the exercise? Assess how effective you feel that the technique is in helping us to hear children's voices.

– CHAPTER 3 –

What the Bible Says about Children

Josephine-Joy Wright, Tri Budiardjo and Andreas A. Yewangoe and friends[1]

Sons are a heritage from the LORD, children a reward from him. (Ps. 127:3)

Unless you change and become like little children, you will never enter the kingdom of heaven. (Matt. 18:3)

Train a child in the way he should go, and when he is old he will not turn from it. (Prov. 22:6)

When I was a child, I talked like a child, I thought like a child, I reasoned like a child. When I became a man, I put childish ways behind me. Now we see but a poor reflection; then we shall see face to face. Now I know in part; then I shall know fully, even as I am fully known. (1 Cor. 13:11–12)

A focus on relationships

CHILDREN are on a journey of growth, of being and of becoming. Nowhere is that more powerfully seen than in the Bible. The Bible charts a journey of our relationship with God as his children. This book also reflects that journey for, rather than being simply another childcare reference, it is designed to be a powerful resource for effecting God's 'transformational development' (Myers, 1999) in his world. The Bible demonstrates powerfully that children are an essential part of that transformational development, being 'in amongst us' and showing us how we can enter the kingdom of God (Matt.18:2). But they require the nurture and training of adults to effect this transformation in their lives.

A key theme in the Bible is our relationship to children, mirrored in God's relationship to us as his children. Much of God's pain in the Old Testament, caused by his children Israel, finds a parallel in the love and pain that we experience in relationship with our children. As children move towards maturity they wrestle to be weaned, to express their ideas and authority. Our goal in the midst of this process is to pass on the faith to our children (our biological children and the children in our communities) so they can defeat the world through faith (1 John 5:4, CEV). But this journey is not just about the world's framework of wrong behaviour bringing consequences and punishment or good behaviour bringing no consequences and no boundaries or meaning. God's relationship with Israel shows us powerfully that there is a different way. While children do need unconditional love, safe places to learn and clear consequences for their actions, they also need a way back – through forgiveness and repentance. Through these acts of grace we enable them to be bold in Christ. Just as an eagle teaches her chicks to fly by allowing them to fall through the air and then catching them and taking them back to the nest (Deut. 32:10–13), God allows us to fall. Yet his arms are always there to catch us and he shows us that our mistakes are opportunities for learning – that they are beginnings, not ends. God longs to shelter and comfort us (Matt. 23:37).

God's provision of a Counsellor (defender, helper) in John 14:16–18 demonstrates the depth and everlasting provision of his love for us, his children. This Counsellor, the Holy Spirit, the Spirit of truth, will be with us for ever. The Greek words for 'with' that are used in this passage (*'para'* and *'meta'*) emphasize that the Spirit will watch over and be alongside us. The Spirit will also be living deep 'within' us (*'en'*). Jesus will not leave us as 'orphans' (v. 18). The Father will never abandon his children – this is a powerful picture for us to learn from. Many children are vulnerable because they are deprived of this type of relationship with God and with others that is a foundation for healthy development. God's primary focus is for us to be in relationship with him as our Father and to be in healthy relationships with one another. His focus is not on resolving poverty or even socio-economic problems, but rather on relationships. This fact challenges our current view of what the key issues are facing missions and agencies working with children. Certainly good food and shelter are needed for healthy development, but our work needs to mirror God's own primary focus on relationships.

Key biblical themes and points of good practice

Health and maturity

The Old Testament illustrates the theme of journeying into maturity in the stories of Joseph and Moses. In the New Testament, Ephesians 4:21–24 speaks to us of Christ's command for us to put off our old selves. James 1:2–5 and Hebrews 6:1–3 also speak of God's desire for us to grow into maturity and wisdom so that we can have unity in the body of Christ and use our gifts fully for God's purposes. Even though Isaiah speaks of God's frustration with Israel's repeated unfaithfulness and rebellion against his laws, God does not give up on his children even when they do not listen or return to him (Amos 4) because he loves them (Isa. 14:1; Hos. 11:1–11; 14:4). God keeps on encouraging her to mature and obey – appropriate obedience being one of the signs of his people.

The World Health Organization refers to health as,

> not merely being the absence of disease but also the physical, psychological, intellectual, spiritual and social well-being of a person.

The CRC codified a holistic view of the well-being of children, referring in Article 17 to '. . . promotion of his or her social, spiritual, and moral well being and physical and mental health', and in Article 27 to '. . . the right of every child to a standard of living adequate for the child's physical, mental, spiritual, moral and social development'.

All dimensions of children's development must be nurtured in age-appropriate ways, including their moral and spiritual development.

Protection and nurture

Children, if they are protected, nurtured and allowed to hope, will be 'a new generation whose identity is clarified and who may become agents of change and vision bearers for a new and better future' (World Vision, 2001). Isaiah 61 speaks powerfully of God's ability to transform his people to become agents of change and instruments of healing in his world as 'oaks of righteousness' (v. 3b).

There are four issues that we need to consider as we look holistically at what the Bible says about children. First of all, we need to understand what the Bible says about children in order to understand God's mandate to us in relationship to children and young people. Secondly, we need to be able to make sense of their worlds. Then, thirdly, we need to know how to be as Christ with them to enable them to grow up 'in wisdom and stature, and in favour with God and men' (Luke 2:52). Finally, we need to know how to help orphans and those who are hurting and living in difficult circumstances. We need to be able to reach out to them with God's love (Jas. 1:27; Isa. 58:10; Ps. 68:5).

There is a strong movement in the non-Christian Western world towards child-centred practice. Although this is an admirable and necessary socio-political shift from seeing children simply as appendages of their parents or as 'non-person' objects within their communities to be trained and disciplined into submission and obedience, it is essential that we do not swing too far the opposite way in our enthusiasm and elevate children above adults or see them as mini-adults. Doing so destroys the gift of childhood and burdens them with decisions and expectations beyond their years. In Christian childcare books of 20 to 50 years ago, children were seen as substandard – as less than whole, valuable, thinking, creative, loving human beings.

Children are called to honour and obey their parents. By the same token, parents need to protect, care for, discipline, guide and teach their children. Adults must have authority over, and be stewards of, children and creation. Children belong to their parents in the sense of being bonded to and linked with them by the fact of their births. Parental authority is necessary for healthy child development as it provides security and boundaries.

Christ's example of respect

Our practice needs to follow the example Christ set in his treatment of both adults and children, as well as the example of God's relationship to his children, Israel. We will see how God uses people of all ages to do his work, employing individual gifts and qualities that belong uniquely to different people at different ages. For example, there are times when God requires someone with a child's directness, passion and truth to speak out and unlock a situation, such as David did when he stepped out with an offer to confront Goliath – even though in human terms it seemed to be a crazy thing for him to do. David trusted in God, believing in the impossible and in the simplicity of his world when adults were bound by fear and by what they could see (1 Sam. 17:26). At other times God requires a mature, diplomatic approach with a person who is strategically aware of the issues, such as when his own Son tackled the questions from the Pharisees (e.g., Mark 7:1–23). As a young boy, Jesus illustrates how children ask deep theological questions and inadvertently challenge current thinking in a way that sheds light on the whole picture (Luke 2:46–50). Children in the Bible reflect such potential at all ages. Jeremiah was called to be a prophet when he was only a child (Jer. 1); Esther became queen as a young orphan; Josiah became king at eight years of age and was renowned for being a very good king (2 Kgs. 22:1–2); Mary, the mother of Jesus, was chosen as a young girl to bear God's Son (Luke 1:29–38).

Christ set children 'among' them – that is, within families and communities. To be 'in the midst' does not always mean to be in the centre. Sometimes children will need to be in the centre, at other times they will need to lead or be taught or be under the shelter of our protection at the side of things. At all times they will need to be considered as valuable in their own right and loved, honoured and empowered to grow up in Christ's image within the body of Christ (Gal. 4:19). We need to be aware of and honour children in our work while keeping Christ as our example and centre.

We are called to take care of his children. All people are made in God's image. The issue of when we become children of God is a theological minefield, beyond the scope of this chapter. Non-Christian children are certainly cut off from the fullness of the Father's love. This love is restored at our adoption when we commit our lives to Christ. But all children, both Christian and non-Christian, need love – and we need to be instruments of that love in God's world. The Bible shows us how to relate to God, to one another and to ourselves in right relationships and deeds. We will now turn to explore more fully what this means to us as biblically based practitioners.

Three cords

Our relationships with God and with children are mirrored in the symbol that he uses for working together effectively – the three cords that are better than one. We need one another. We are intrinsically relational beings in community with one another, formed in God's image and in relationship to him. We need to help one another to grow in Christ, guided by our Father's footsteps. Using this framework to look at what the Bible says about children, and pulling together diverse theological perspectives, three key interrelating themes emerge: who children are – their identities in their relationship with God; what children need from the world – their primary relationship with their parents and their relationships with others; what children give to the world – their relational influence on others around them.

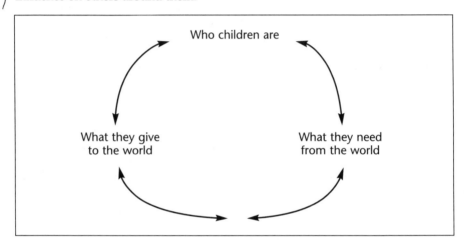

Figure 1: Key themes from the Bible

The key issues for each of these themes are demonstrated in the following figures. Unfortunately, they are constrained by the two-dimensional printed page. They need to be considered as an interweaving story, a three-dimensional narrative reflecting the way children live within their worlds. We cannot understand them by analysing them from the two-dimensional Greek didactic chains that often bind our adult thinking. Rather, we need to try to think with the free-flowing thought processes of the Hebraic culture within which Jesus lived.

Figure 2 is a working model illustrating the ever-changing boundaries between the four developing worlds of the child. It would be ideally represented as a sculpture of four moving orbs representing these different worlds with God represented as a light from behind, penetrating and transforming both the orbs and their dynamic interplay.

This figure needs to be seen as a poetic picture. The boundaries of the circles represent the boundaries of influence on the four worlds. The ways and extent to which the worlds overlap and interrelate will vary as the child develops. The permeability of the boundaries will also vary with the child's development and life experiences.

For example, in a very young child, the child's and parent's worlds will overlap

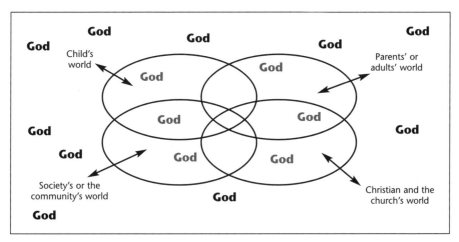

Figure 2: A dynamic representation of the inter-world relationships affecting and
being affected by children within their context[2]
(The exact form of this interaction will vary over time, depending on developmental
factors and the child's life experiences in his particular situation.)

quite a bit. As a healthy child develops, these two worlds will move apart and the
influence of society's world will grow. In adolescence, young people are very
open to the influence of both society's values and Christian values and beliefs as
they search for meaning and purpose in their worlds. If the parent's and child's
worlds stay very close together, the child's development is stunted and the child
cannot develop his own identity. If parenting is detached and abandoning, the
child may isolate herself in fear or may be vulnerable to the non-age-appropriate
influences of society's and even the church's worlds. The Bible advocates
gradual, appropriate interplay between these worlds as the child develops.

Both adolescents and young children are often very spiritually aware and open
to God, since the boundary between them and God is very diffuse. We need to
make use of this potential and openness and sensitively nurture our children's
spirituality within a holistic context.

Many of us, in our own journeys, have not allowed ourselves to be who we are
in Christ. Some of us have spent our lives shut away in pasts that have become
our prisons, shutting out God's healing and revelation. We may have never been
able to let go of our pasts (Phil. 3:13; Isa. 43:18–19) or trust God to redeem and
restore our futures (Joel 2:25). We may have never been able to receive from the
world what we need – we may have never been able to share with the world who
we are and our joy at becoming ourselves in Christ. As we come to realize more
fully who we are in Christ, we can enable his children to be free and to grow in
faith and maturity, to be witnesses throughout the world (see Fig. 3).

Who children are

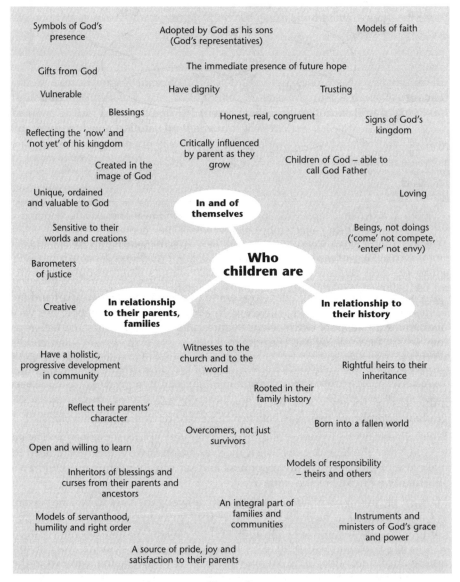

Figure 3:
What the Bible says about who children are: Their identity in relationship to God

A blessing

From the very first mention of children in the Bible, God makes clear that children are a blessing. After God created the first man and woman, God trusted the 'task' of raising children to men and women. Eve considered her first-born son as a blessing (Gen. 4:1). She was the first of many to be blessed by the gift of children (e.g., Gen. 21:6; 1 Sam. 2:1–10). At Jesus' baptism, God declares his delight in his Son: 'You are my Son, whom I love; with you I am well pleased' (Luke 3:22b). Children have intrinsic dignity and are able to praise God and to be used by God to fulfil his purpose and overcome evil (Ps. 8:2; 1 Sam. 3:10; 17:32). Children are a source of pride, joy and satisfaction to their parents and families. The biblical examples of children born to barren women illustrate the profound importance of children in fulfilling and carrying on the promises of God. Children are vessels through which God's blessings continue from one generation to the next. Each child has inherent value, and each one is unique. Even identical twins do not share fingerprints. 'Before I formed you in the womb I knew you, before you were born I set you apart' (Jer. 1:5). Here, as well as in Psalm 139:13–16, God relates to the unborn as a unique individual. When we lose sight of this truth we risk overlooking children, as Jesse overlooked David, or exasperating them (Eph. 6:4).

Children belong to God and should be recognized for their inestimable worth and dignity – not for what they produce and accomplish, but for who they are as God's own handiwork. Children had status and dignity in the Old Testament – they were an essential part of the Jewish family unit. Children were valued not so much as persons in their own right but 'for their potential, as future adult members of the covenant community (boys), or as guardians of the family and bearers of the next generation (girls)' ('Children in the Way', National Society for Promoting Religious Education, 1988). Rather than being symbols of innocence or sentimentality, adult members of the community viewed children as needing protection, education, guidance and discipline, as lacking in wisdom and understanding, as vulnerable as adults to the consequences of sin (General Synod Board of Education, 1988). Like trees, as people mature and grow God uses them for different purposes and gives them different gifts. Strange's (1996) exposition on children in the early church shows how this was the prevailing view of children until recently, resulting in very constricting childcare and faith teaching practices.

Adopted by God

Adoption as the legal process as we understand it had no place within Jewish culture and Hebraic custom (Cranfield, 1975, pp. 394–403; Hendriksen, 1980, pp. 258–64). A man would take the children of his dead relatives into his family out of social family duty, not as 'adoption'. There was, however, within Hebraic custom a ceremony of adoption. This ceremony took place when the father judged that the son had reached a stage of maturity and appointed him to be *his representative*. Whatever the son said or agreed to hereafter, it was as if he was speaking with his father's voice, with his father's authority. The same words were used at Christ's baptism as at the ceremony of adoption (Luke 3:22b). This understanding of adoption powerfully illustrates how we, as adopted children of God, are his representatives here on earth. Paul spoke of children's relationships to God in terms of their inheritance (Rom. 8:17). Paul was speaking here as a Roman, a Jew and a Christian writing in Greek. As a Roman Christian, Paul was powerfully aware of the parallels between what Christ has done for us in our adoption and what happens when a slave is adopted (Stibbe, 1999). Paul would also have been using the term 'adoption' within his understanding and experience of Roman law in which adoption was considered a very serious business (Barclay, 1962, pp. 105–107). In Roman law, a son never became of age – he was always under the absolute power and control of his father. This fact helps us to understand why the idea that God the Father gave his children free will to choose life or death (sin) was so threatening to the Romans.

In the Roman ceremony of adoption the son was symbolically sold ('*mancipatio*') three times. On two of these occasions he was bought back by his birth father ('*patria potestas*'). On the third occasion a ceremony called '*vindicato*' followed, in which the son legally became the adopting father's possession. The consequences of this adoption process include the following:

- The adopted person lost all rights in his old family and gained all the rights of a legitimate son in his new family. In the most binding legal way, he received a new father.

- The adopted son became heir to his new father's estate. Even if other sons were born at a later time, his rights were not affected. He was inalienably co-heir with them.

- In the eyes of the law, the old life of the adopted person was completely wiped out. All debts, for example, were cancelled. He was regarded as a new person entering into a new life, disconnected from the past.

Seven people bore witness to the ceremony. For Christians, the Spirit is our witness – as he was as Jesus' baptism.

As children of God, we are representatives of the Father. Although we are to put away childish things (1 Cor. 13:11), we can call God '*abba*' (Aramaic), or 'daddy', as a reflection of our childlikeness and intimacy with him. But, as we grow, Paul says that we can call God 'father' (Greek), symbolizing a matured relationship including respect, responsibility and honour.

We are completely part of his family as Christians – 'the old has gone, the new has come' (2 Cor. 5:17).

> If our sense of significance derives from sonship not slavery, then we will be able to achieve God's purpose in our lives. The reason for this is that we will be ministering for the Lord out of a sense of gratitude rather than a need for God's approval. (Stibbe, 1999)

As children of God we do not have to earn our right to be adopted – that is a free gift from God. In the same way, we do not have to earn our right to be loved. But as we mature in Christ we come into a deeper experience of the essence of our adoption.

> The work of the Holy Spirit is to create in believers the spirit of adoption . . . We are regenerated by the Holy Spirit, and so receive the nature of children; and that nature, which is given by him, he continually prompts and excites and develops and matures; so that we receive day by day more and more of the child-like spirit. (Spurgeon, 1958, p. 27)

Children are an example

Jesus did not consider children to be simply an essential and valuable part of the family that had not yet achieved adult status. In fact, he said, adults often need to learn from children and their patterns of discipleship (Matt. 18:1–4; 19:14). Children need love, encouragement, care and guidance, and they are also valuable in their own right. Parents have a spiritual and moral duty to take care of their children (Matt. 18:5–6). They are God's stewards, caring for children whom God has adopted into his family (see Fig. 4).

[handwritten margin note: Shouldn't we always have the intimacy + closeness to be able to call him "Daddy" over "Father"?]

What children need from the world, from us

Used by God even if not perfect

Appropriate discipline

Allowed to have and take appropriate responsibilities

Discipleship

Education

Holistic teaching about
• Scriptures and God's commandments
• Their history and what God has done for them
• About family – roles, value, essence

Affirmed as wise and knowledgeable

Love in action

Guidance – secure boundaries

Introduction to the mystery of the cross and Christ

Mentoring

Roots

Honesty

Protection

Reality

Unconditional, responsive love modelled on God the Father

Safe places to grow

Affirmation

Let go

Security

Good food

Significance

Practical care

To be delighted in

Community

Role models

To be in relationships

What children need from the world

Truth

Consistency

To be allowed to be children

Continuity

To be believed in

Space and means, nurture and instruction to explore and develop their faith, prayer and worship

Respect

To be welcomed and enabled to feel welcomed

Hesed (belonging love)

Openness to them

Honour

Forgiveness and a way back within and outside the church family

To be seen and noticed and loved as they are – as children not just those in need

Allowed to make mistakes

Mercy

A learning environment where mistakes are opportunities, not ends

Grace

Clear responses to their fears and questions

Not to be burdened by parents or others

Allowed to ask questions

Their normal everyday place in family, group, church (not special exceptions)

To feel invited and included

Attitudes and opportunities which invite participation

Encouragement

Provided with an environment and atmosphere where they feel they belong

Enabled to grow

Their place within the family is honoured

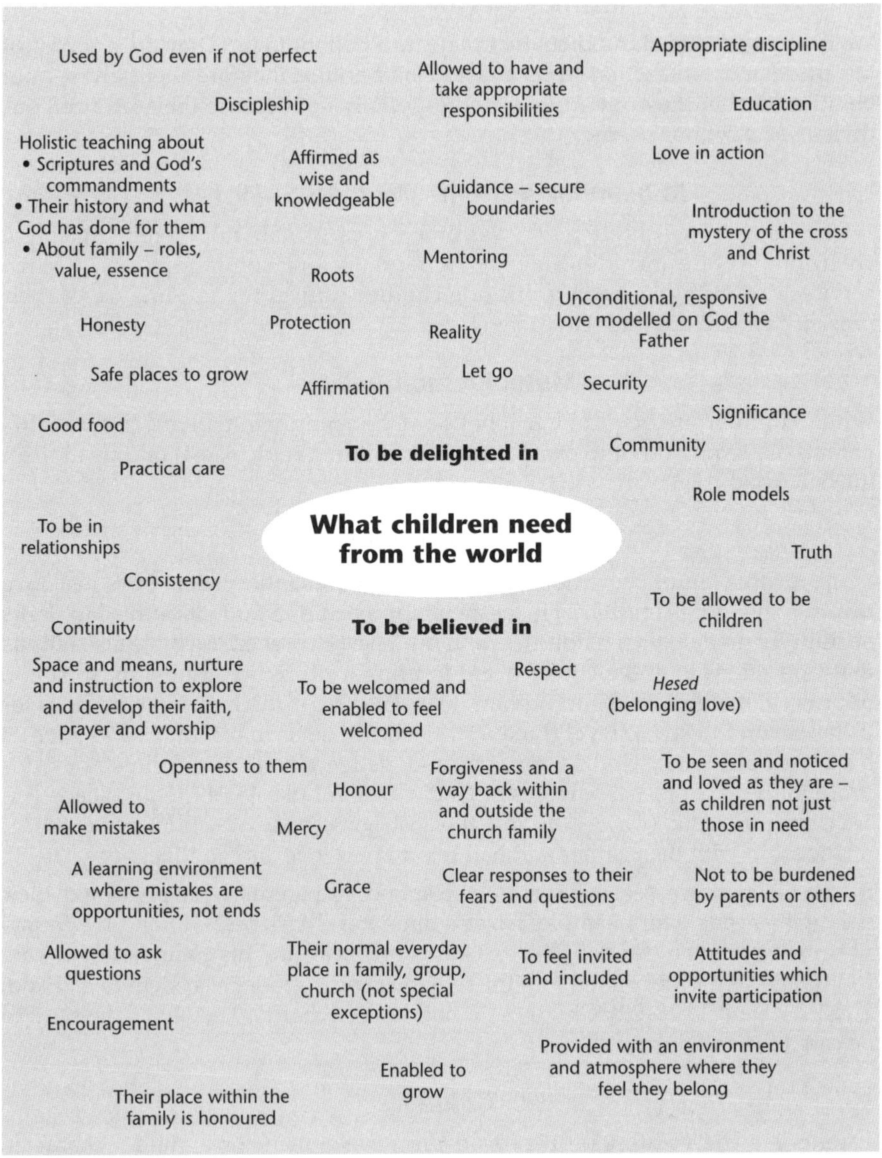

Figure 4: What the Bible says about what children need from the world, from us: Their relationships to parents and adults

Love (Hos. 11:1–11)

It was God's love for Israel that meant that he could not give up on them even when they were disobedient and rebellious. It is a powerful illustration of the love that we need to give our children – unconditional, clear and unending.

handwritten margin notes: Yes – but people in his name in general regardless of age / welcome all

Honest affirmations and encouragement
as they are, for who they are

We need to tell and show them that they are a delight to us. They are a source of joy, pride and satisfaction to us and to God because they are themselves – not because of what they can achieve, and especially not because they can fulfil our dreams or meet our needs.

To be made welcome (Matt.18:5; 19:14)

When we welcome children, we welcome Christ. We are not merely greeting a child, but we are including her in the fabric of our community life. Church services, for example, need to include children, affirm the importance of their presence and accept their childlike ways.

Mutual responsibilities

While children are required to obey and honour their parents (Deut. 5:16), parents are required not to exasperate their children (Eph. 6:1–4) or to lead them into sin (Matt. 18:6).

Practical care

Many people think that the Bible portrays a romantic vision of Jesus' love towards the 'little children'. He let them approach him and sit on his lap. Jesus beautifully models such tenderness and intimacy. However, the Bible also tells us that God reigns to execute justice and to bring forth righteousness for the poor, oppressed, marginalized and orphans (e.g., Pss. 68:5–6; 82:1–4). God provides for us far beyond the basic level (Luke 11:13) – he made us in his image and gave us his own Son, Jesus. God's provision and patience with Israel illustrates this profoundly, as do Jesus' parables of God's love in Luke 15 of the lost sheep (vv. 1–7), the lost coin (vv. 8–10); and the lost sons, both of whom were out of relationship with their father and had rejected his love and goodness (vv. 11–32).

In the Gospels we see Jesus readily respond to parents who presented their children's needs – for example, Jairus's daughter (Mark 5:22–43) and the Syrian Phoenician woman (Mark 7:24–30). God is practical, and his compassionate care for his children is translated into the religious and socio-legal system (e.g., Exod. 22:22–23; Deut 14:28–29). Children do not deserve charity. They have the right to be cared for and nurtured.

Guidance

Parents are the greatest influence on the development of a child's character, through their relationship with them through birth (or adoption), their intimacy and the extent of their shared experiences. Parents need to model how God guides us. 'I will instruct you and teach you in the way you should go; I will counsel you and watch over you' (Ps. 32:8). 'If you go the wrong way – to the right or to the left – you will hear a voice behind you saying "This is the right way. . ."' (Isa. 30:21).

To be enabled to grow in their faith

John Westerhoff's description of four stages of the faith journey are helpful here

(Westerhoff, 1980). We begin as young children with an 'experienced faith', feeling inevitably part of what is around us, dependent on experience and interaction. 'The child explores and tests, imagines and creates, observes and copies, experiences and reacts.' So faith comes first not through theological words, but through experiences of trust, love and acceptance. The question, Westerhoff says, is not, 'What do I tell my child?', but 'What is it like to be Christian with my child?'.

Then comes 'affiliative faith'. Westerhoff talks about how we need to belong to, and participate in, an identity-conscious community of faith with opportunities to deepen religious feelings through creative activities, to share in the community's stories and to experience awe, wonder and mystery. Beliefs and attitudes are more consciously taken over from a significant other person or valued group; there is a need at this time for acceptance and belonging.

The third stage is a 'searching faith' that strives to work out a consistent personal faith with reference to an authority within, rather than to the authority of other people. Typically, there will be elements of doubt and critical judgement and a need for experimentation as alternative understandings and traditions are explored. Those at this stage need to commit their lives to people and to causes.

Finally there is an 'owned faith', which holds the tension of truth viewed from different perspectives and finds new meaning in myth, symbol and ritual.

> Now people most want to put their faith into personal and social action, and they are willing and able to stand up for what they believe, even against the community of their nurture.

This movement from experienced faith through to owned faith is what Westerhoff sees as conversion – a major change in a person's total behaviour, which may be sudden or gradual. He says that:

> to reach owned faith (our full potential) is a long pilgrimage in which we need to be provided with an environment and experiences that encourage us to act in ways that assist our expansion of faith.

We need to create opportunities to enable this to happen. As Hadden Willmer argued at the 2002 Cutting Edge Conference at De Bron, Holland, we need not ask children to make adult decisions – rather, we need to give them the opportunity to enjoy being children. But, as Keith White countered and complemented at the same conference, we need not see children as simply adults in waiting. They are fully formed representatives of Christ, able to be instruments of his power and grace. Organizations from this conference put forward proposals to the Lausanne Convention 2004 concerning the place of children and how their needs were considered by those working with them.

Discipline

Just as a book with no margins cannot communicate the power and beauty of its message, so children need secure boundaries to develop and reach their potential. In an informal study a few years ago, one of my colleagues asked the young people with whom she was working what they most wanted in life. She was stunned by their response: 'Someone who loves us enough to tell us clearly what to do, what is okay and not okay'. Not the latest books, not the latest music, but *love* – demonstrated through caring enough to give secure boundaries even when it is painful to follow them through (as it was, and is, for God). Parents have the most profound influence on their children's character development and on the way that they relate to their internal and external worlds. This is a great privilege and responsibility.

Over the years, theories of socially and politically acceptable discipline have varied greatly. But the CRC is clear that we do not have a right as parents and adults to abuse our children – physically, spiritually or emotionally. The biblical mandate for us is, in fact, the opposite. When we read that 'he who spared the rod hates his son' (Prov. 13:24), the rod referred to is the shepherd's rod. This verse has often been taken out of context and used on its own to justify corporal punishment. It is difficult if we live in a culture in which hitting children is accepted as the norm and even good practice. But the shepherd did not use his rod to hit his sheep. If he did, they would not have come to him when they were in danger but would have avoided him out of fear, and he would have lost them. The shepherd used his rod to cajole, prompt and guide his sheep along the way that was safe to go. In the same way, we need to guide children so that they can learn the wise and safe route through life (Prov. 29:15). The shepherd also used his staff to lift his sheep out of places of danger. We need to be willing to go into difficult places to help our children. We do not help them by condemning them from the wings when they get in danger through drug taking, sexual activity, and so on. When we use the rod and staff in this way, they are a comfort to us and to our children (Ps. 23:4). We need to use our authority as parents and adults appropriately – not to abuse but to protect, guide and help children to learn the true, non-manipulative consequences of their actions. In doing so we model God's relationship with us, his children.

To be believed in

Jesus is very clear that our pasts do not need to define us, that we can change and that he believes in us. Parents and adults need to give children a hope for the future, to encourage them to have dreams. Children need to know that we will support them as they step out and take risks and follow their dreams (even if these dreams are not ours for them). God's model is to provide consistent love and be there as they fly.

To be taught

Children need education and also to learn about their historical and scriptural roots and God's laws for wise living (Ps. 78:2–8; Deut. 4:5–9), such as observance of the Sabbath. Children need to be taught how to function within their families and fulfil their socio-legal requirements without compromising their faith. They need safe people who can teach them the skills for living such as how to have healthy relationships, good boundaries, how to manage conflict effectively and how to enjoy and work with their feelings and those of others. They need to be taught these things in the context of faith and God's everlasting love.

To be children

Children need childhoods. They are not responsible for their parents' ultimate physical and emotional well-being. Although children are to honour and respect their parents (Eph. 6:2), and that involves caring for them, for children with psycho-spiritually healthy parents such a mutually honouring, biblical relationship will usually yield healthy development for the child. But God never spoke of the distress that Israel caused him in a way that implied that Israel had to behave in order to make God happy. Too often, parents or adults say, 'You made me. . .'. This is a lie. We cannot, as adults, be made to do or be anything. We have choices. We make decisions. We need to challenge this lie in ourselves and in others so that children are free to be themselves as children, not their parents' parents.

A healthy childhood is a secure foundation for a healthy adulthood. Children need opportunities to play, to be safely irresponsible in an age-appropriate way while slowly learning to take responsibility. Children are often more aware and in touch with creation than adults. They are often passionate about its care and experience this more fully than adults. We need to learn from and delight in this so that we can regain our childlikeness and our openness to God in his world. The worlds of children and of parents and adults need to complement each other if both are to grow up and fulfil God's purpose in their lives.

What children give the world

Figure 5 presents us with a wealth of potential and possibilities. The blessing of children is not so much in what they are, but in who and how they are – unique, creative, challenging, wondering at the happenings of the world, living and being within their worlds, saying the unsayable, praying the 'dangerous prayer', thinking the socially unthinkable, being honest and real. They are superb witnesses to one another and to adults. The witness of my three- to five-year-old Sunday school class doubled the size of the class in three years and brought four sets of their parents to faith. Children are significant to God, and to us.

Often we struggle to put these three relational cords of biblically-rooted good practice into action in our communities in which children live and grow. Rainbows of Hope, run by Phyllis Kilbourn (the author of many significant publications in this field), developed a statement of belief that does just that:

> Every child is created in the image of God and, therefore, is a person of immense worth and significance, no matter what his or her racial, social or cultural context. Children were, and are, important to Jesus' ministry and should be equally important to ours. Ministry to children must include evangelism and discipleship. Every child is endowed with God-given gifts and potential that need to be developed and celebrated in the church community. Ministry to children is not just a means to an end, but is rooted in our conviction that children are worthy of ministry. A parallel ministry to families is vital to prevent child abuse and provide healthy homes capable of spiritual nurture.

Each one of us, child or adult, is a child of God on a unique, preordained, purposeful and creative journey. As we travel, we grow in our faith and experience the fullness of our Father's love for us, having accepted him into our lives and having been forgiven and adopted by him. That is our biblical mandate. If we can learn how to walk with children – sometimes being led by them, often guiding, protecting and teaching them, but always honouring them – then we will all come into the fullness of God's kingdom and grow more like Christ.

> Blessed are those whose strength is in you, who have set their hearts on pilgrimage. As they pass through the Valley of Baca, they make it a place of

springs; the autumn rains also cover it with pools. They go from strength to strength till each appears before God in Zion. (Ps. 84:5–7)

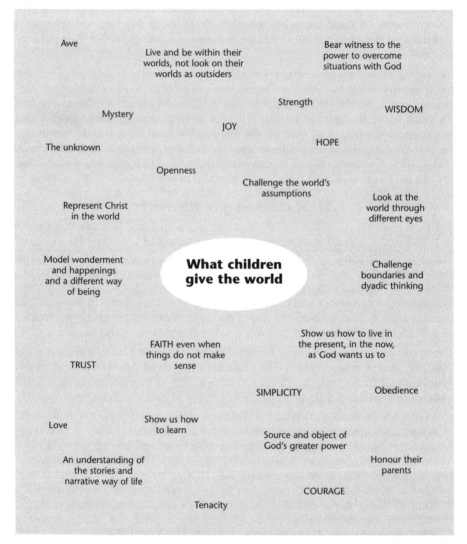

Figure 5: What the Bible says children give the world: Their relational influence on others around them

Notes

1. This chapter is the result of a creative process of consultation with and encouragement from God and friends. Josephine-Joy would like to express her heartfelt thanks to: Tom Riley, for his inspiration, insightful wisdom and steadfast care; Dave Scott, for his perceptive comments on the wider perspective and theological interpretations; Chris Scupham for advice on spiritual adoption and Greek translation; Eileen and Roy Taylor, Helen Powell and Claire Trimnell for their reference-hunting and constant support.

2. Developed by Adrian Datta, Tom Riley and Josephine-Joy Wright, 2002.

– Questions to Consider –

1 Describe the Bible's view of children. How does this view affect our practice?

2 How would you answer someone who expressed the view that God does not really care about children and families? Use references from the Bible to argue your response.

3 Write a summary statement that encapsulates your theology of ministry with children, incorporating biblical truths about who children are, what they need and what they give the world.

– CHAPTER 4 –

The Development of Children in Their Families and Communities

Glenn Miles

Biblical child development

JESUS himself 'grew and became strong; he was filled with wisdom, and the grace of God was upon him' (Luke 2:40). The account of his childhood ends with the statement that 'Jesus grew in wisdom and stature, and in favour with God and men' (Luke 2:52). So Jesus developed mentally (wisdom), physically (stature), in favour with God (spiritually) and in favour with men (socially). If this is how a perfect human being developed, then every human being should follow the same pattern. If any one of these areas of human growth and development is neglected, then the individual involved will be damaged.

Family cultures and communities

The extended interdependent family structure in the Bible has far more in common with stable rural families in developing countries than with fragmenting nuclear families in more developed countries. Hebrew families were located within a larger 'house'. These houses were united by marriage and kinship (and adoption) to form clans; several clans constituted a tribe; the confederation of tribes made up Israel. An interdependent Hebrew household consisted of between 50 and 100 people. In contrast, the average nuclear family in more developed countries today is made up of three or four people. Relatives may be many miles away, with tenuous or non-existent economic ties. The family tends to be a unit of consumption rather than a unit of production. These trends in more developed countries are also apparent in bigger cities in developing countries. Families are separated from their extended families as they migrate to the cities and, in many cases, husbands look for work in the city apart from their families, which leads to even further fragmentation of the family.

In a world witnessing the increasing disintegration of family life, Christians have sometimes attempted to preserve the family structure found in Scripture without necessarily separating what is cultural from what is biblical. This can lead to a false idealism about what families are really like. Scripture does not present a particularly 'rosy' picture of the family. There is fratricide, rape, incest, adultery and murder as well as love and loyalty – both within households and beyond them.

In the Old Testament, as in many communities today, houses, clans or tribes were economic, social and political units. Whole households, including children, worked together on the land. Marriages were arranged, as they are in many parts of the developing world today, and marriage was a covenant between two families – not just between two individuals. A 'bride price' was paid to seal the covenant (Gen. 34:12; 1 Sam. 18:25). Arranged marriages were one way of successfully uniting dynasties, provided that the parents were loving and concerned primarily with the welfare of their children. Both then and now, however, arranged marriages can be dominated by the extended family. Parents sometimes make all the decisions without involving their children, and the choice of partner may be made primarily on financial grounds. In some cultures, when dowries are not paid it is considered the right of the family to abuse the spouse. In extreme cases, for example in India, this has led to severe 'dowry' burnings, in which paraffin is thrown on women and they are set alight to punish them and their families for not coming up with sufficient money.

Another model found in developing countries is the patriarchal marriage, characterized by dominion and control over women and children. Neither women nor children are consulted in decisions that affect them. Although historically and geographically the church has not distanced itself from this as it might have done, this model stands in contrast to the traditions of Judaeo-Christian understandings of marriage (that is, as an institution created by God for the union of man and woman, to be characterized by *mutual* submission, respect and service). Marriage is a covenantal relationship. Marriage and family life are important to God. Christian parents are called to listen to and respect their children, just as children are called to listen to and respect their parents.

What, then, are some of the reasons for this apparent disintegration of family life?

Marxists blamed worsening economic conditions and decreased welfare support, but changes in cultural values – the new individualism and its expressions in divorce, out-of-wedlock births, single parenting and careerism – must also be considered. The emphasis is on the needs of the individual rather than the group in postmodern society. As a result, even the marriage commitment is seen as tenuous. If one of the partners feels that his or her needs are not being fulfilled, they feel free to end the partnership. Marriage no longer offers security for the couple or for the children.

In more developed countries, many of the economic, political and social functions of the family have been taken over by the state, banks and schools. Public and private worlds have become more separate.

While some conservatives have felt that the phenomenon of women working outside of the home has in itself led to a breakdown in the family (thereby holding women responsible), others believe the family crisis follows from the fact that men's commitment to housework and childcare has not kept pace with this (putting the responsibility onto men).

The 'globalization' of many nations means that they are also inheriting many of the problems of more developed countries. The shift to the city means that many families cannot move as clans, but only in nuclear families. Competition rather than interdependence can then become the familial and cultural norm.

Conflict/war situations can have a devastating effect on family life. Families can be separated for extended and indefinite periods. There can also be loss of life and injury that contribute to the stresses.

Political ideologies can have profound effects on the family. In Cambodia during the Pol Pot era, the family rice pot was broken as a symbol that the new regime would do away with the need for the family. The Angkor (the new regime) would provide everything.

In many cultures in developing countries it is considered an obligation for a son or daughter to earn an income for their ageing parents. This may mean moving to the city and sending part of the money home. While in many cases this employment is honourable, sometimes it may still be acceptable for children to go into prostitution – as their obligation to their parents is judged to be more important than the 'morality' or safety of the employment.

There are many explanations for the breakdown of the family, and it probably results from a combination of different factors. However, as Christians we also recognize the role of personal choice and personal sin as well as corporate sin.

What is God's concern for families in each society? What would God have us promote, discourage, protect, challenge?

What does Scripture say about families?

The 'family' can be an institution in which God's grace is experienced and where people find nurture and healing, thereby growing as persons in their individuality, in their social relations and in their relations with God (Barton, 1993). However, 'the family' can become perverted by sin as people are disloyal, compete for power and neglect responsibilities.

Even in the context of a society that was made up of extended interdependent family units, Jesus emphasized his relationship with his heavenly Father (Luke 2:41–52) over that with his parents, and he described the disciples as his 'mother and brothers' over his own family (Mark 3:34–35). Later on, Jesus says that those who love father or mother more than Jesus are not worthy of him (Matt. 10:37). When one potential disciple was ready to follow Jesus, but first asked to bury his father, Jesus' response was blunt and harsh (Luke 9:57–60). At the foot of the cross (John 19:25–27), Jesus says to Mary 'Dear woman, here is your son,' and to the disciple he loved he says, 'Here is your mother.' These passages could point to the idea that the new family of God takes precedence over the biological family.

In a world where many children have a father who is absent because of divorce, war or simply excessive work demands, the discovery of God as a heavenly Father, perfect and reliable unlike any human parent, can be healing and liberating (see McClung, 1985). Men still, however, need to be encouraged to take their responsibility for their children seriously. It has been suggested that God sent angels to ensure that Joseph took his responsibility in fathering Jesus seriously and did not abandon Mary as he might have done. Tom Beardshaw of Care for the Family has suggested that God himself 'went to some trouble to make sure there was no risk of the breakdown of the marriage of Joseph and Mary, thus ensuring that there were two parents'.

Thomas Aquinas (Pope, 1994) described how children are made in part in the image of their parents and therefore naturally belong to and are valued by them. But they are also made in the image of God and belong to and are valued by him. He uses the Ephesians 5 analogy between fathers and the sacrificial love of Christ. This love is steadfast and unbreakable, reinforcing the long-term commitment of fathers and husbands to their children and wives.

Paul describes the church as a family. The New Testament church met in households. Christian hospitality was like welcoming near and distant relatives. Those baptized, according to Paul, have been adopted by God (Rom. 8:15–17; Gal. 3:26–4:7). Their siblings are other Christians. Their inheritance is the community of believers (Mark 10:28–31). In a culture where the family took precedence over all other relationships, the New Testament church was to reach out to the Gentiles, to the unlovely and even to enemies. Clapp (1993) suggests that 'Paradoxically, a family is enriched when it is decentered, relativized, recognized as less than an absolute'. The Christian family is therefore not a safe haven apart from the world, but a powerful witness into the world. Even vulnerable families need to learn the responsibility (but also the joy) of reaching out in hospitality rather than focusing on the fears associated with a 'bunker' self-preservation mentality.

Nevertheless, it may be important, theologically, not to reduce religion to matters of family life. A danger exists in theological terms, that the worship of God might be supplanted by devotion to the 'family,' that God might become a 'household God' and no more.

What is the importance of parenting?

The Population Council's *Families in Focus* (Bruce, Lloyd and Leonard, 1995) recorded that the number of female-headed households has risen significantly in almost every country in the world since the mid-1970s. Marital dissolution occurs for 40–60 per cent of women in their forties in several countries including the Dominican Republic, Ghana, Indonesia and Senegal. The divorce rate was 55 per cent in the United States in 1990, and divorce rates have doubled since 1970 in the UK, Canada, France and Germany. One per cent of births are out of wedlock in Japan, compared to 33 per cent in northern Europe, 70 per cent in Botswana and 27 per cent in Kenya.

The secular views of the 1960s and 1970s in more developed countries considered that more divorce, out-of-wedlock births, stepfamilies and single parents did not mean that families were declining. In the 1980s and 1990s, however, research has indicated that divorce and single parenthood do have negative consequences for both children and women, and that the family structure is important for the development of children.

A study in the US (McLanahan and Sandefur, 1994) concluded that children growing up outside of biological, two-parent families were twice as likely to do poorly in school, twice as likely to be single parents themselves, and one-and-a-half times more likely to experience long-term unemployment. The results did not depend on race, education or age.

Furthermore, this study also showed that stepfamilies had no advantage over single parents. Both were less successful in raising children than intact, biologically-related families – even though the average income of stepfathers is higher than that of intact families. This fact challenges the idea that family income is more important to the well-being of the child than family structure.

Parenting, and by implication lack of it, is the 'single largest variable implicated in childhood illness and accidents, teenage pregnancy and substance misuse; truancy, school disruption and under-achievement; child abuse; unemployability; juvenile crime and mental illness' (Hoghughi, 1997). It has therefore been described as 'the most important public issue facing . . . society'. *huh!*

However, although a reasonable consensus exists about 'bad parenting', secular experts cannot agree about the opposite, 'particularly in a diverse and rapidly changing society'. Christians, on the other hand, do have some scriptural guidance on the role of parents and the role of the church in supporting the family.

Fathers make a vital contribution to the cognitive and emotional well-being of their children (Snarey, 1993). However, studies suggest that the single most important family trend in the US is the growing absence of fathers from their children (Blankenhorn, 1995). Nearly 30 per cent of children under the age of eighteen do not live with their fathers, and nearly 50 per cent of children under eighteen will spend several years without their fathers present in the home. Fathers that leave the family are also generally unwilling to contribute to the child's financial costs. A study in Chile found that 42 per cent of fathers were not contributing financially after the child's sixth birthday (Sachs, 1994).

Scripture presents parenting in the context of marriage. This does not mean that in ministry we ignore those who are parenting out of the context of a marriage relationship, but it does mean that we value the relationship between parenting and marriage – especially within the church. The church also needs to address individualism and find ways to stop men from drifting away from families and parenthood.

The church's role in underpinning and supporting parents is vital. The church must support parents and families so that they in turn are better able to support children. 'God himself trusted His own Son to humankind as a vulnerable child, requiring that Son to be nurtured by a frail but able family and community, symbolically provid(ing) a model of trust and responsibility . . .' (Viva Network, 1997).

In the Old Testament, while children were entirely subject to the authority of the head of the household and counted legally as his property, 'there was much greater concern with the *responsibility* of the father for his children than with his *rights* over them' (Deut. 21:18–21; 24:16; 2 Kgs. 14:5–6) (Wright, 1997). Parental responsibility to teach children the truth about God and godly living was vital. Proverbs 6:20 encourages children to keep their father's commands and not to forsake their mother's teaching. Proverbs 22:6 talks about the responsibility of parents to create a desire for spiritual things in children from a young age. The 'Shema', the Hebrew confession of faith, was to be impressed on children 'when you sit at home and when you walk along the road, when you lie down and when you get up' (Deut. 6:4–9).

In the early church, parents were encouraged to 'bring [children] up in the training and instruction of the Lord' (Eph. 6:1–4), and fathers were encouraged not to 'embitter your children, or they will become discouraged' (Col. 3:21). These instructions follow instructions to the children to obey their parents. Since Paul's letters were written to be read aloud to the whole church to which they were sent, the fact that he addressed parents and children is very significant. Firstly, he assumes that children belonged to the community of the church and that they would be present at the church gathering when his letters were read. Secondly, he encourages mutual responsibilities for parents and children. This was a challenge to the common assumption at that time that the parental role carried with it unlimited authority over the children of the family.

Although parenting does require sacrifices, 'loving your neighbour as yourself' is key (Browning, 1999). 'Love as equal regard' provides a balance between modern individualism and the older ethics of extreme duty and self-sacrifice. This understanding of love is especially important for mothers and wives who have disproportionately carried the burden of enacting self-sacrificial models of Christian love'.

Who are the widows and orphans?

Different cultures and societies have different family structures. While children can most benefit from being in a two-parent family, this is not always possible. Both the Old and New Testaments mention the responsibility to orphans/the fatherless. Being an orphan in ancient times meant deprivation of support, loss of legal standing and becoming vulnerable to those who would exploit the weak. God is the defender of the fatherless (Deut. 10:18), and the covenant community is encouraged to be similarly compassionate (Exod. 22:25–27). The early church maintained a concern for orphans. James 1:27 describes a 'pure and faultless' religion as characterized by those who 'look after orphans and widows'.

The difficulty for the church today is that there are so many children who do not fit neatly into the two-parent family structure. Children may be separated from one or both parents through war, disaster, accident or the ill health of a parent. Some countries will have culturally appropriate ways of absorbing orphans – for example, into the extended family or into a monastery. In other situations, the loss of life may be so great (due to war, disaster and HIV/AIDS) that the community has limited capacity to absorb children who do not have both parents. In the case of children in situations of war/conflict, tracing parents of children and vice versa is vital.

Sometimes children are brought up by only one parent because of divorce, desertion, domestic violence or unwed motherhood. Although we are not to be patronizing or prejudicial towards the one-parent family, we need to find out their needs by asking them and then take responsibility as a church to support them. Similarly, orphans living as 'child-headed households' will need the love and support of adults, but they may not need adults to take over all responsibilities. They, too, should be asked what they feel that they need, and the assumption should not be that they are incapable and incompetent.

Where a marriage is fragile, if the church is able to support and strengthen the marriage it may enable relationships to be restored and prevent divorce and family breakdown. Similarly, where parent-child relationships are strained, supporting parents in a loving community may prevent child abuse and inter-generational violence.

It is essential that the church ministering to lone parents and their children understand how they got into the situation, because the issues that they face will be so different in differing circumstances. There may be violence and abuse to deal with, or widowhood, desertion or promiscuity. Appropriate responses require understanding, and there are no simple solutions. It is also important not to overlook lone fathers. Mostly widowers, these men are usually excluded from women's informal networks (a vital coping strategy for most single mothers).

Conclusion

We began with exploring the context of the child by looking at Jesus, and here we will end as well. He was born a vulnerable child into a vulnerable family, part of a vulnerable community, and yet he grew to become everything God wanted him to be, assured of God's love for him. The church has a responsibility to provide a supportive and caring 'family' for all children, whether or not they have a biological family, and as those with a special burden for children we need to encourage this support and care.

– Questions to Consider –

Read the story of Jesus' birth, considering how God trusted Mary and Joseph with his own Son (Luke 1:26–38; 46–49; 2:1–7). 'God himself trusted His own Son to [Mary and Joseph] as a vulnerable child, requiring that Son to be nurtured by a frail but able family and community, symbolically provid[ing] a model of trust and responsibility . . .' (Viva Network, 1997).

1 What can we learn about the importance of parental responsibilities?

2 What can we learn about Mary and Joseph's devotion to God?

3 What can we learn about how we should respect parents and involve them in child-care practice?

CHAPTER 5

Factors That Optimize Development

Susan Greener

THE story is an old and familiar one. Two children are born into similar circumstances. Their surroundings are filled with stress, illness, loss, violence and trauma. Yet one child becomes a productive citizen, able to hold a job, marry and raise a family. The other one seems irreparably damaged by childhood experience, unable to function in society. Why is one child a survivor and the other a victim?

Human development is not that simple. Child development researchers recognize that there are consistent paths of human development, but that there is also significant individual variation within those paths. Development is not something that just 'happens' to children. They are not passive recipients of life events, but active players who bring individual characteristics and past personal experiences to every situation, making every child's personal experience a unique one within a general child development framework. The question then is, 'what qualities within the child and in the child's environment promote healthy outcomes despite unfavourable life events?'

Theoretical foundations of child development in context

In order to explore factors that optimize children's development, one must first explicitly state the assumptions concerning the relation between the child and the familial, social and cultural context. In the early twentieth century, developmental theorists tended to see children as passive beings, driven either by barely controlled internal impulses or pre-programmed responses to environmental stimuli. The study of children was focused on the individual child, often in a laboratory setting. Thus, the child was looked at in isolation from the family, community and culture. This early research did, however, provide a great deal of knowledge about the course of children's development in the areas of cognitive, emotional and physical change.

Over time, theories have become more complex, recognizing that no one develops in isolation and that research must look at children in their contexts to truly understand child development. Several such theories have been influential, such as Urie Bronfenbrenner's ecological systems theory (1993), which sees the child developing in a complex system of relationships affected by multiple environmental levels. Although Bronfenbrenner acknowledges the importance of context, the theory does not specify how children develop. Socio-cultural theory (Vygotsky, 1934/1987) focuses on how culture (values, beliefs, customs) is transmitted from one generation to the next. According to Vygotsky, children must interact socially to learn how to function within their social group.

A new direction in developmental theory builds upon the past – incorporating context, yet also describing the course of child development. According to dynamic systems theory (Fischer and Bidell, 1998; Thelen and Smith, 1998), children function as complex beings in a physical and social world. The child's mind and body are integrated into the greater environment in a dynamic way, with the child actively reorganizing his or her own behaviour in response to any change in the system. The system is composed of a group of interacting, interrelated and interdependent components (child, environment) that form an organism that is constantly in motion. The image most frequently used to describe a system is that of a mobile (like a toy that is hung over an infant's crib). There are objects dangling from strings hung from interlocking crosspieces, and any slight movement of one object causes all the other parts of the mobile to move. The pieces are completely interdependent and cannot move without affecting all other parts of the system.

Changes in the system include changes in the child, such as brain maturation or other developmental progress, as well as alterations in the environment. These alterations include common, everyday experiences of learning and interaction with others, as well as more stressful experiences such as exposure to infection, abuse, death in the family, separation, war or other types of trauma. It is assumed that children are active participants in their own development and that influences within the child's system are bi-directional and reciprocal.

In other words, the child not only is impacted by the environment, he or she also has an impact on the surrounding world and the people in it. Likewise, both nature (or biological influences) and nurture are important in forming the developing child. And because the system is in constant flux, human beings are capable of change throughout life – therefore both early and later experiences are important in development.

System components

The child comes into the world well equipped to interact and to learn. Each child has a genetic blueprint that determines sex, temperament, appearance, maturation schedule and health status. Children can be classified into several temperament categories based upon such qualities as activity level, regularity of bodily functions, distractibility, adaptability, attention span and persistence, intensity of reactions and positive mood (Thomas and Chess, 1977). Children may be easy, difficult, slow-to-warm-up or a blend of the three categories.

Obviously, a healthy, attractive child with an easy temperament will elicit different responses in social interactions than an ill, unattractive child who is difficult to soothe.[1] Shortly after birth, the child begins to experience patterns in social responses that influence his perception of the world. However, what is most important is how the child's characteristics and the caregiver's response fit together. Each child is unique and has unique child-rearing needs.

Positive outcomes depend on child-rearing conditions. Is that child's temperamental style valued in the culture? Is the caregiver sensitive and responsive to the child's individual needs? Is the caregiver willing to invest the effort to help the child achieve optimal adaptive functioning? What kinds of supports are available to the caregiver to assist him or her in caring for the child?

It is obvious that it is the interaction between systems that creates the context for child development, and that environmental factors play an important role. In fact, the environment has an impact on child development before the child is even born. The pregnant mother makes decisions that may have a positive or negative impact on the developing child. Her health habits – such as smoking status, nutrition, exercise, exposure to infectious agents and toxins and general health status – can improve or diminish the child's development. The availability of health care and childbirth practices impact the developing foetus as well.

The child is born into an environment that includes various components: immediate family members, parenting style and beliefs, a physical home environment and institutions that directly interact with the child (schools, churches, health clinics, etc.). There are other environmental influences that do not interact directly with the child, but that impact her nevertheless. For example, community characteristics – such as working conditions, crime rate, unemployment levels, educational opportunities and health services – may impact the child either negatively or positively. Finally, the child lives in a culture that places a certain value on children, that has laws supporting or undermining children's rights, and that has customs that enhance or discourage child development.

Impact of stressors on children's development

Resilience and vulnerability factors can occur at any of the aforementioned levels. The child, the immediate environment, the broader environment and the culture all contribute to the dynamic system that can optimize or diminish child development – or that may have very little impact at all. Although it may seem obvious, stressors (experiences or influences that disrupt a child's ability to function) do have additive effects in children's lives. Some stressors are more disruptive than others and require major readjustments on the part of the child in order to adequately cope with the distress. A child can typically handle a major stressor, even if it is chronic. However, when negative conditions are added, the maladjustment is multiplied (Capaldi and Patterson, 1991; Sameroff et al., 1993). Unfortunately, stressors do tend to occur together. For example, marital stress, illness, domestic violence, substance abuse and crime are more common in impoverished communities.

The timing of stressors is particularly important in determining their impact on children's development. Children are more vulnerable to certain types of stressors at certain points of development. For example, the developing foetus, because of developing organ systems, is extremely vulnerable to maternal illness, drug use, malnutrition and environmental toxins.

Also, during the first three years of life, while the brain is attaining 90 per cent of its adult size, the child is greatly impacted by trauma, abuse and neglect. Young children rely on the caregiver to regulate their experiences so that they are manageable and appropriate. The child needs a safe, secure foundation from which to explore new experiences and assimilate them into their brain structures. When the environment is chaotic, unpredictable, devoid of stimulation, abusive or traumatic, the child's actual brain structure is altered, thereby negatively impacting all future development (Perry and Pollard, 1998). Finally, children are more vulnerable during developmental transitions, such as adjusting to school or puberty (Rutter, 'Continuities', 1987).

Consequently, the impact of a stressful event will depend on the age of the child and his position along the life course. Death, loss, divorce, war, disease and other stressors will affect children of different ages in different ways.

Divorce as an example of a stressful event

Divorce is a stress that many children around the world experience. The reader may be thinking that it is not nearly as stressful as the events in the lives of street children or those impacted by war. This is certainly true; however, divorce has been well researched and it does affect all of the systems that have been discussed. Divorce involves loss, separation and significant change for the affected child.

Divorce is not a single, stressful event in the life of the child, but rather a series of events or transitions involving changes in living arrangements, income and family roles (Berk, 1999). The child's own characteristics, parental adjustment and social supports within the family and the community all impact the ease of the child's adjustment. Prior to a divorce, marital conflict will have already increased the stress level in the life of the child. The poor quality of the marriage relationship increases tension in the home and may expose the child to domestic violence.

The divorce itself often necessitates not only a change in the family members living together and child custody arrangements, but also a change in the actual home address due to altered economic circumstances. The child then loses a familiar environment, as well as the support of neighbours and friends. Moreover, stressed parents are not as attentive and are often disorganized in their parenting strategies. The child frequently has to adjust to different parenting rules when passed from one custodial parent to the other. The child may also have to adjust to remarriage and possibly the addition of step-siblings or the birth of half-siblings. Thus, divorce not only removes one parent from the immediate environment. It also severely disrupts the relationships, routines, structure and social supports in the child's life.

A child's age at the time of divorce has a significant effect on his reaction. Younger children have difficulty understanding the reasons for divorce and often engage in self-blame, increasing their fears that the parents will abandon them. They may display intense separation anxiety and are also likely to fantasize that their parents will reunite one day (Wallerstein, 1983). Older children are better able to understand the reasons for divorce, but they may still react strongly and negatively and engage in rebellious and delinquent behaviour (Doherty and Needle, 1991). However, some older children respond by becoming more mature, taking on responsibilities for household tasks and sibling care (P. Hetherington, 1995).

The temperament and sex of the child also affect response to divorce. As would be expected, temperamentally difficult children have a much more difficult time coping with divorce. In contrast, temperamentally easy children are less often targets of parental anger and often emerge from the stress of divorce with enhanced coping skills (P. Hetherington, 1995). Boys with difficult temperaments have an especially hard time adjusting to divorce, and they often react with increased non-compliance and defiance. Because they tend towards disobedience, boys are less likely to receive social support from parents, teachers and friends. In contrast, girls are more likely to internalize stress and experience depression and anxiety.

The most important factor in predicting healthy adjustment to divorce is effective parenting (E.M. Hetherington, 1991). The effective parent works to minimize disruption and stress, while providing clear rules and warm, sensitive interaction with children. Divorce research points to the importance of a caring adult who is willing to nurture a distressed child and provide a secure environment.

Resilience

Every human being experiences stress, and manageable stress is recognized as being important in developing new coping strategies and adaptation skills. Elimination of all stressors would be neither desirable nor possible. In fact, the further one moves from the child's immediate environment, the more difficult it becomes to eliminate the stressor. For example, it is easier to teach parenting skills to the mother of an abused child than it is to change a cultural belief system that condones domestic violence. The goal of the caregiver and child-care worker then becomes twofold: 1. to eliminate unmanageable stress when possible, and 2. to promote resilience in individual children so that they are better able to cope. Because exposure to trauma cannot be completely controlled, it is important to support qualities that encourage coping in all children, regardless of risk status. Resilience has been defined as 'the capacity to spring back, rebound, successfully adapt in the face of adversity, and develop social competence despite exposure to severe stress' (Konrad and Bronson, 1997).

Much longitudinal research has been conducted in various cultures to determine those qualities that best describe resilient children, and the findings have been quite consistent. The qualities fall into three general categories: individual qualities; qualities of the child's environment; and social/interpersonal skills. Grotberg (1995) has developed a simple classification system to label these three areas: 'I am', 'I have', and 'I can'. The qualities listed in each category below are a compilation of various sources in the resilience research literature (Benard, 1995; Berg and Van Brockern, 1995; Berk, 1999; Werner and Smith, 1992).

It is not expected that any one child would possess all of these qualities, resources and capacities. These skills are, obviously, also age-dependent and develop according to the developmental time frame mentioned above. The greater the number of assets, however, the more options the child has to choose from in meeting negative experiences and the greater her flexibility in developing effective coping strategies.

Individual qualities: 'I am'

Resilient children are:

- More likely to have an easy temperament. In other words, they quickly establish regular routines in infancy, they are generally cheerful and calm, and they adapt easily to new experiences. The child is aware that others like him or her and does things to elicit positive responses from others.

- High in self-esteem. Self-esteem is the judgement one makes about one's own worth and the feelings associated with this judgement. Self-esteem gives children confidence to approach new situations, and it protects the child against failure and criticism. Resilient children refuse to accept negative messages about themselves.

- Optimistic and have a good sense of humour. Finding the positive or funny aspects of a negative situation helps the child cope with the stress.

- Loving, empathic and altruistic. They care about others and express that concern in word and action.
- Autonomous and responsible. They have an appropriate locus-of-control. In other words, they are able to determine which events are within their sphere of influence and which events are the responsibilities of others.
- Resilient children work to solve problems for which they feel responsible and adequate to the task.
- Future-oriented and purposeful. They believe that they have a future and plan for it accordingly.
- Strong in moral thinking and spiritual connectedness. They have a clear sense of right and wrong and feel that right will be victorious. That moral sense is often rooted in belief in God and connection to a body of faith.

Qualities of the child's environment: 'I have'

Resilient children have:

- Affectionate ties. They need unconditional love from adults who play a significant role in their lives. These adults may be parents, other family members, teachers or others who interact frequently with the child. Love from significant others can sometimes compensate for poor family relationships.
- An environment characterized by warmth, closeness, clear guidance and high expectations. Caregivers provide clearly defined rules and routines, expect the child to follow them, and have clearly outlined consequences for disobedience. Children are praised for following rules and routines and are not harmed by caregivers. In addition, care giving characterized by warmth and nurturing may also improve the disposition of temperamentally difficult children.
- Role models. Children need adults, older siblings and peers who model acceptable behaviour. Role models clearly demonstrate adaptive behaviours, as well as ethical behaviour, within the family and to outsiders.
- Encouragement to be autonomous. Adults, especially caregivers, encourage the child to perform tasks independently and to ask for help when needed. Caregivers are sensitive to the child's developmental timetable and adjust expectations accordingly.
- Opportunities for meaningful participation and giving back to others. Children are given the opportunity to make developmentally appropriate decisions regarding their lives and experiences. They are able to take active leadership roles and are able to assist others in a significant way.
- Support systems. Resilient children have access to educational, health and social services to meet needs that the caregiver is unable to fulfil.

Social and interpersonal skills: 'I can'

Resilient children can:

- Approach new tasks with the attitude that the task is manageable and can be accomplished successfully. Because resilient children have higher self-esteem, they are able to see themselves as capable and competent in meeting new challenges.

- Exhibit social competence. They are responsive, able to elicit positive responses from others and flexible in their ability to move between social situations.

- Communicate effectively. These children are able to communicate their needs and feelings and are able to interpret the communications of others accurately.

- Solve problems. They are able to think critically and creatively and to plan, and they are resourceful in seeking help from others when unable to solve a problem on their own. They are also self-reflective and strategic in their approach to problem solving.

- Manage feelings and impulses. Resilient children recognize that in order to elicit positive responses from others and gain support to solve problems, they must be able to regulate their strong negative emotions and impulses.

Conclusion

All children will encounter stressful circumstances during their lifetimes. For some, the stress will come from common, everyday experiences and will be manageable – especially if the child is grounded in a warm, supportive and stable family environment. For many other children, trial will come upon trial, and the child will not have the benefit of a solid foundation to provide a 'secure base' (Bowlby, 1979) during troubled times. Yet it is important to recognize that one of the most important roles of caregivers is to build every child's capacity to cope with adversity. This can be accomplished at several levels.

Some children will have natural reserves based upon their attractive appearance and temperament, and some children will begin at a deficit due to negative personal qualities. However, temperament, although fairly stable, is not set in stone and effective care giving can diminish the severity of negative qualities (Berk, 1999). It is the fit between child and caregiver that is paramount.

All children need role models and teaching to build multiple coping strategies, whether this means altering one's response to environmental circumstances, changing the environment or seeking help from others to deal with problems. The more assets a child brings to a stressful situation, the more likely he or she is to effectively meet life's challenges, learn from them and actually emerge stronger and more capable than before. With adequate support from caring others, children who live in constant stress can be survivors and not victims of their circumstances.

Note

1. Although this type of statement tends to make people uncomfortable, because we like to believe that appearance and difficult temperament do not affect our responses, especially if we are Christians, we are all prone to giving the benefit of the doubt to attractive, easy people. There is much research evidence to support this notion – not only in parenting, but also in the justice system, employment practices, salary scales, etc. This chapter lists universal resilience-building tactics.

| |

– Questions to Consider –

1 Imagine a particular child that you have worked with or one that you know well. Think of that child in terms of a dynamic systems perspective. What qualities does the child bring to his or her physical and social worlds? What is the quality of interaction between the child and caregiver systems? What environmental conditions influence the child's development? What resources are available to the child? How do cultural beliefs influence the child and his or her treatment by others?

2 Choose a problem that is familiar to you (such as homelessness, abuse, war, etc.) and analyse how the problem impacts children in terms of contextual levels (caregiver, immediate environment, broader environment, culture). What types of interventions to decrease stress could be used at various levels?

3 Think about a project working with children with which you are familiar. How could strategies for promoting children's resilience be integrated into this existing programme? What type of interventions and training would be appropriate for parents, caregivers and workers with children at risk?

– CHAPTER 6 –

Key Theoretical Frameworks and Their Application

Keith White

EVERY child is an individual. Each family, community, tribe and culture has its unique or distinctive characteristics. Very different historical forces have affected children and their social settings. The study of child development reflects the complexity of an enterprise aimed at finding coherent frameworks for understanding children worldwide, while at the same time acknowledging the many and varied characteristics and factors that make up each child's life experiences, life story, life-chances and personality.

The search for frameworks has taken into account the importance of some or all of the following:

- Biological and genetic factors;
- Learning, and the child's immediate social and personal environment;

- Unconscious experiences and reactions and the part they play in development;
- The impact of wealth and poverty on the child, his family and community;
- Historical factors such as war, famine, population movements, disease;
- Global and sociological processes like globalization and modernization.

A general map of child development

One of the most useful conceptual tools for checking that nothing is overlooked in assessing child development is that developed by Bronfenbrenner (1979) (see also Figure 1 in Chapter 1, 'What Is a Child?'). Placing the child at the centre of a number of interlocking systems, Bronfenbrenner suggests four basic elements or sub-systems:

1. *Microsystems.* These include all of the settings in which a child has direct personal contact, experience and interaction. The most important are likely to be the parents and family (or family substitute) and the school.

2. *Mesosystems.* These are the connections and links between the microsystems. Although home and school are distinct places and worlds (for most children), the quality of each environment will affect the other.

3. *Exosystems.* These are defined as systems the child does not necessarily experience directly, but which have an effect on him or her because they influence the microsystems of family, school, and so on. The parents' work, faith, community and friends are all examples of such systems.

4. *Macrosystems.* These include poverty, wealth, neighbours, ethnic identity, the wider culture in which family and community are set, global trends and processes.

It is impossible to label these systems in ways that are universally sensible or accurate. Cultural factors will stretch rigid classifications. The neighbourhood or village may be much more important as a microsystem in some societies than others, and some exosystems may be microsystems in other settings. What Bronfenbrenner helps us to do is to remember the different systems and levels that affect every child. Frameworks and studies very often focus on one or two of these, to the exclusion of others. With this general framework in mind, let's explore the nature/nurture debate and then move on to some of the more well-known theories of child development.

The nature/nurture debate

There has always been a lively tension and debate between those who stress what the child inherits and those who stress what the child learns. The central issue is how determined the personality, behaviour and life-chances of a child are, irrespective of other factors and choices at work as the child grows up. Among the important elements mentioned in the case for the 'nature' side of the argument are:

- *Genetics.* Recent research has shown the effect of genetics on a broad range of behaviour. Temperament, cognitive abilities, pathological behaviour, height, weight and appearance all owe much to heredity.

- *Inborn ideas.* This is a very controversial subject in every way. Philosophy itself is divided at this point! But it does seem that certain responses are programmed, or conditioned, by principles that a child 'inherits' rather than by what he or she learns or chooses.

- *Maturation and growth.* There is a universal sequence of physical changes from conception to maturity including growth in size, shape, hormones, muscles and bones. This happens without thought or intention.

By 'nurture', we mean the totality of influences on the growing child. If everything were determined before the child was born (by 'nature'), then parents, teachers and carers could have no significant impact on the child. It is clear that, although the child is not a *tabula rasa* (clean slate), the contributions of other systems are significant. Different inputs will have different effects.

There are some skills that may emerge without the support or encouragement of parents, while others are totally dependent on the external intervention. An example of the former would be physical strength; an example of the latter would be a child's ability to speak a second language.

Another factor is the timing of the environmental influence. At certain stages in a child's development, she is particularly sensitive to external influences. If stimulation of body or brain is missing at a key period of a child's life, the result may be retarded or stunted development. It follows that a consistent and rich immediate context is important for the realization of a child's potential. Generally speaking, the early years and months are of the greatest significance, and therefore the microsystems of home and school are key. It is here that support and attention should be concentrated to facilitate the child's development.

An international textbook, however, has to be particularly sensitive to the cultural systems of which family, community and friends are a part. The study of child development has itself tended to be Eurocentric in origin and assumptions, and this distorts both analysis and conclusions of child development studies in other cultures. For example the 'Western' ideal of the child growing into independence takes for granted the fact that individual choice and responsibility are inherently desirable. Two-thirds of the world would tend towards a more communal, or collectivist, understanding of development. Here membership in coherent and lifelong groups is valued highly, and the goal of development is one of interdependence.

This is not just a matter of academic or theoretical interest. It can affect the minutest and most intimate interactions with children – for example, in the areas of breastfeeding, toilet-training, notions of privacy and assumptions about what constitutes maturity. Our very concepts of what we might mean by 'good-enough-parenting' (a phrase coined by D.W. Winnicott, 1960) will vary considerably from culture to culture. So, too, will our understanding of what we deem to be legitimate rights and responsibilities vary.

In the 1990s, much attention was paid to the different outcomes of children who had experienced setbacks (whether by nature or nurture). The issues of vulnerability and resilience have been alluded to by Susan Greener in Chapter 5 and will be discussed more fully in the next section. Most would agree, in the light of much cross-cultural research, that the interplay between nature and nurture is complex. To understand the interplay, it is vital to give due weight to cultural factors – especially given the Eurocentric bias of the very terms and concepts used to describe what is going on.

The main theories of child development

There are four main theoretical frameworks for studying or understanding child development and the institutions and services that have grown up in different parts of the world. In practice, the philosophies of most of those who work with children exhibit some degree of 'pick-and-mix', but it is important to have some grasp of the nature and roots of the various possible perspectives.

Biological and evolutionary theories

These theories are sometimes referred to as 'socio-biology', and they stress the commonalities between humans and other species on earth. They assume that humans have developed from other species and that many of the same principles of behaviour and development apply. Among the famous and popular writers in this field are Konrad Lorenz and Desmond Morris. A key concept is that of the 'gene', and there is a lively debate about how altruistic or selfish the individual gene, or person, is.

One of the problems of applying such biological analyses to human behaviour is the question of consciousness and awareness in humans. ('Creationists' would, of course, emphasize the distinctives between species rather than the commonalities.) On the other hand, it is becoming clear from much recent research that genes do have a very significant part to play in the formation of individual character and identity. Although some stress the contribution of the biological make-up of a person, no one argues that it is the only influence.

Learning theories

Learning theories stress the 'plastic' nature of human development. There are biological limits, but within these there is enormous scope for individual variation and learned behaviour. Pavlov is famous for his experiments with dogs and food. In essence, he saw that particular stimuli resulted in certain reflex responses. Learning is a process that introduces new stimuli. The association of a particular stimulus with, say, a person, can linger throughout life and provoke conditioned emotional responses affecting emotional and psychological development.

B. F. Skinner developed the theory and practice to show that conscious praise and reward can reinforce desirable behaviour (responses), while undesirable behaviour can also be reinforced (negatively) if a child finds it attracts sympathy or attention.

The common thread tying these theories together is the underlying belief that children have the ability to learn behaviour and the power to shape their environment.

Psychoanalytic theories

Famous psychoanalytic theorists include Freud, Jung, Bowlby and Erikson. In contrast to Skinner and Pavlov, these theorists underline the critical part that the unconscious plays in child development. In order to survive, we develop unconscious strategies or mechanisms (sometimes called 'defence mechanisms'). Alongside the obvious natural stages of physical development of children, there are also emotional stages to be negotiated and overcome. The ability of a child to develop depends to a large degree on the nature and quality of attachments to significant adults in their early lives. Such attachments comprise both conscious and unconscious elements. Early experiences can have lasting effects, both positive and negative, later in life.

Behaviour can be modified to an extent by reward and reinforcement, but the power of the unconscious is such that it can override or stifle conscious intent and patterns. For creative child development to take place, unconscious blocks and regressions need to be identified and overcome.

Cognitive-developmental theories

One of the most famous figures in this field is Jean Piaget. He and others stress the child's own exploration of the world in which she finds herself. The child is an active participant in his or her own development. Through the process of exploration, a child adapts to an environment and in this way makes discoveries that lead to new and more developed concepts and understandings. Once again there are stages of development, but these are not so much about emotional as cognitive development.

Conclusion

If we accept Bronfenbrenner's analysis and assume the respective contributions of 'nature' and 'nurture' to the development of children, it is possible to conceive of an integrated understanding of child development. Biology and genes, learned behaviour, the unconscious effects of significant relationships and events, as well as the active exploration of the child, all play a part. It would be foolish to ignore or underestimate any one of these perspectives. In practice, different interventions may be appropriate at various stages in a child's life, and they will probably derive from more than one of the theories outlined.

These different theories raise our consciousness of the number of factors likely to be in play at any given time in our own care for 'children at risk'. We may also be able to listen more carefully to what the children are communicating when we reject monocausal explanations. We will appreciate the significant and complementary roles of parents, family, teachers, peer groups and others in the process of development. We should likewise be sensitive to cultural differences and the unconscious values we may bring to any assessment of a child's situation. Any intervention or programme will need to operate at various levels.

These theories also have implications for the training and development of those involved in responding to the needs of 'children at risk'. Not only will there need to be a range of expertise, but there must also be genuine understanding of the local culture and systems. Intervention is likely to be a collaborative exercise.

- Questions to Consider -

1 Describe and critically analyse two of the main theoretical frameworks relating to child development. What are their strengths and weaknesses?

2 If you were beginning to map the child development issues in a project, how would you undertake the task from a theoretical and practical perspective?

3 Take a few minutes to write down some of your assumptions about child development, focusing particularly on issues of nurture. Now reflect on how these might be perceived by someone from another culture. How will being aware of some of your own biases affect your practice?

- CHAPTER 7 -

The 'Rights' of the Child and the Christian Response

Paul Stephenson

RIGHTS-BASED programming now dominates the agendas of child-centred governmental and non-governmental institutions. Rights cannot be ignored, although some institutions still choose to side-step engagement with the CRC for philosophical or ideological reasons. This chapter sets out some historical background and contemporary developments in the area of children's rights and outlines three perspectives that inform these institutions. The final section on religious groups focuses predominantly on Christian viewpoints. Further work needs to be done to explore more deeply the perspectives of different faith groups.

The history of the CRC

From good intentions to soft law

Witnesses to the suffering of children during the First World War laid down the foundations for child rights. Eglantine Jebb played a key role in drafting the 1924 Declaration of the Rights of the Child (Yates, 1998). Informed by her Christian beliefs and outraged at the plight of children caught up in the conflict, she developed a series of rights distinct from those afforded to adults. Her primary aim was to protect and nurture children, guaranteeing certain moral entitlements such as love and understanding (Boyden, 1997). The Declaration, and the subsequent manifestation of it adopted by the UN in 1959, was the first global treaty that focused on a particular section of the community – namely children. However, the Declaration was a statement of good intent without any real force. Subsequent international instruments, such as the United Nations International Year of the Child and the CRC were seen as important advances on the Declaration. They both give greater scope for children to advocate and speak for themselves, bestowing not just protective but also enabling rights on children. Ultimately, the CRC, by its advocacy, was the agent for changing the widely-held view that children are objects of international human rights law, so that they are now regarded as subjects of rights (Ennew, 1999).

As 'soft law', the CRC gains force as nations draw upon its principles to draft and amend legislation. Although the CRC is not international law, pressure will be put on ratifying nations to bring their legislation into line with it. An example of this can be seen in UNICEF's *New Global Agenda for Children*. Target 19 states that: 'In each country, all legislation should be in conformity with the CRC by 2005' (UNICEF, *New Global*, 2000a).

At its adoption by the General Assembly of the UN in 1989, nation states rushed to sign and subsequently ratify the CRC. Within the first five years, 191 of the 193 member states had signed and ratified the CRC. Only the USA and Somalia stood aside for differing political reasons (the USA because it felt that current federal law upheld the rights of children sufficiently, and Somalia because of a lack of representative government in a time of civil conflict). A desire to protect and help children provoked the universal enthusiasm for this international treaty and its unprecedented uptake. Despite this momentum, the implications and implementation mechanisms of the CRC were less than clear.

UNICEF: The reluctant champion

A decade later, the debate is over and the impact of child rights now dominates the child welfare community: academics, policy makers and practitioners alike. After a sluggish start, the CRC now frames the programming approaches of major international agencies and NGOs. Article 45 identified UNICEF as the lead UN agency 'to foster effective implementation and to encourage international cooperation in the field covered by the convention'. However, the agency showed an initial reluctance to participate in the drafting process, finding it difficult to transform itself from a service provider to advocate. It stumbled hesitantly into the first World Summit for Children in 1990, which played a lead role in galvanizing the international community to sign up to the CRC. Despite this early hesitancy, UNICEF now plays a leading role in championing children's rights.

The 1990 summit endorsed a plan of action based around 12 broad goals to be achieved by the year 2000. Although noble intentions guided the summit, subsequent national plans of action failed to meet their targets. Budget restrictions, regional armed conflict, corruption, crippling debt and structural adjustment programmes were all blamed as these targets failed to be reached. In some cases, situations actually deteriorated for children (Chen, 2001). However, part of the problem lies in a poor understanding of what a rights-based approach should look like.

The second World Summit for Children in 2001 sought to promote a rights-based approach to meet targets and goals in line with key provisions of the CRC. The UNICEF executive board states in its report setting the stage for the 2001 summit that: 'In the light of the near universal ratification of the CRC, a rights-based approach should underpin all future action for children' (UNICEF, *Emerging Issues*, 2000).

Rights of passage: Achievements and challenges

The debate over how to implement a rights-based approach continues. Ennew argues that this debate, in parallel with the history of children's rights, is controlled and mediated by adults. She claims that while the CRC makes children the subjects of rights, they have yet to take their 'meaningful and rightful place' at the tables where policies are decided and evaluated. The exclusion of children in the rights debate is not the only contentious issue. Anthropologists, social scientists and religious groups also accuse the child-rights movement of insidious cultural imperialism and interference in the affairs of sovereign states and families.

While these debates play a vital role in mediating the implementation process of the CRC, one can point to some significant achievements over the past decade that demonstrate the validity of the rights-based approach. For example:

- Issues relating to children's rights have been put on the political 'agenda'.
- There has been an increased focus on especially disadvantaged groups. Children with disabilities, HIV/AIDS affected children, militarized children, access to education, sexual exploitation, street and working children are now widely debated at both international and national levels.
- There has been an increase in state responsibility for children following ratification, and a setting of global standards.
- Non-governmental organizations have become increasingly involved in the children's rights field, and several played a lead role in drafting the treaty.
- Coalitions, networks and organizations that focus on children's rights grew in the 1990s, and there was also a movement by established NGOs away from 'needs-based' to 'rights-based' approaches to child welfare.
- There has been a greater demand for more and better information relating to all aspects of children's lives.
- There has been a growing realization that children are not simply passive objects or victims, but rather active participants and subjects of their own development who make important contributions to society.
- The CRC has provided a powerful tool for grass-roots activists to campaign on social and political issues affecting children.
- Children's rights have opened doors for a human rights discourse in countries such as China.
- The CRC has given rise to a wide range of new, supplementary international human rights agreements concerning children. These include optional protocols to the CRC and related conventions (e.g., the optional protocols on sexual exploitation and recruitment of under 18s into conflict; the ILO Convention 182 on intolerable forms of child labour, and the Ottawa Treaty on Land Mines).

- Finally, ratification of the CRC has led to changes in national legislation in favour of children. Although this does not always mean improved services or provision for children, it does provide the necessary legal framework for advocacy and, ultimately, implementation.

Who's right?

While undoubtedly fostering some significant advances in children's welfare over the last few years, the CRC provokes strong and contentious debate. Three key groups can be identified as contributing to these debates: the children's rights movement, the child studies group and religious groups. While these may not be all encompassing, they provide a useful illustration of the issues that need to be addressed to achieve the successful implementation and impact of the CRC. The following section summarizes the key aspects of each group's position on the CRC.

Child rights movement

Michael Freeman describes the children's rights movement as a 'motley assemblage of lawyers, philosophers, educationalists, etc., whose primary goal is to disseminate and propagate children's rights' (Freeman, 1998). Those within the movement seek to make rights reality. They view the CRC as the moral and ethical foundation for 'propagating the personhood, integrity and autonomy of children (protecting their rights)'. Universal rights, therefore, provide a global standard against which the welfare of children can be measured. Most importantly, they establish a direct relationship between the child and the state, granting children individual human rights. Children need special rights, argues leading international child rights consultant Judith Ennew, because they are children: they have no voting rights or status, and therefore are much more vulnerable to exploitation and violence. The 1948 *UN Universal Declaration of Human Rights*, she argues, while it includes children, is not specific enough in this regard.

The primary concerns of the children's rights movement, according to Freeman (1998), can be identified as follows: to challenge discrimination; to make a problem of the relationship between age and status; to present the moral case for treating children's rights seriously; to document information about wrongs done to children – at home, school, work or in the street; to explore the limitations of laws and conventions designed to improve the lives of children, granted that 'rights without services are meaningless and that services without resources are impossible'; and to advocate for the recognition of children's rights as part of a cultural revolution, recognizing the role that rights can play in the reconstruction of a society.

Leading thinkers from the child rights movement recognize that the CRC creates tensions around issues of universal norms versus cultural relativism. Their argument is pragmatic. Without the universal conceptualization of child welfare within the CRC, there would be no foundations for progressive global action and activism in favour of children. They argue that the language of the CRC does give 'due account' of the dimensions of class, gender, culture, belief and disability. The future success of the rights movement, they say, depends upon constructive interpretation of the CRC in parallel with its full implementation.

The child studies group

Over the past decade, the growth of childhood studies coincided with the development of the children's rights movement. Those contributing to the sociology of childhood discourse encompass a variety of views and differing emphases. They set out to demonstrate that childhood is not a natural phenomena, but rather a social construct; that childhood is largely an adult invention that serves to 'propound versions of social cohesion' (Freeman, 1998). They set out to analyse how childhood is seen as a period of immaturity, inadequacy and inexperience measured against the desirable state of adulthood, and they attempt to explain why childhood is described in terms of 'difference', requiring that it be referred to in terms similar to those reserved for other forms of deviance.

Within the broad areas of study in this field, the step of understanding children's rights is a historical event that changed our view of children and childhood. The CRC, argues Boyden, an anthropologist and leading child rights critic, embodies a particular view of childhood favoured by the industrial North. The rise of the CRC coincides with the globalization of culture, especially that of youth and the more romantic notions of childhood integral to Europe and North America. These norms include the cult of the individual, the 'differentness' of childhood with the attendant overemphasis on passivity, vulnerability and helplessness, and increasing levels of state intervention in the lives of family and community.

However, this group recognizes that the CRC is here to stay and that they therefore need to engage constructively in the debate. The group also realizes that pursuing an argument whose ultimate answer blows in the winds of cultural relativism offers little hope of affecting real change in the lives of children. But trying to bring the universal into conjunction with the particular is 'a process inherently fraught with ambiguity' (Jenks, et al., 1999). The tone and language of the CRC lends moral authority and political force, but how can this be made relevant across cultures, gender and class? Jo Boyden sees a way ahead for the CRC that would mitigate against the worst excesses brought about by its unchecked enforcement:

> . . . a more liberal vision in which the convention provides a flexible framework that brings cultures together around children's rights and children's welfare rather than an instrument of censure endorsing a single model of childhood . . . cultures are allowed some latitude to proceed towards the global goal in their own way and in their own time, situations are negotiated and not imposed and children assume an active role in these negotiations. (Boyden, 1997)

Finally, there is a sense that the rights discourse places too little emphasis on social relationships and human needs and duties. In this aspect, the child study group shares similar concerns with the religious groups.

Religious groups

Commentators on the CRC claim that its roots lie in Judaeo-Christian thinking (Boyden, 1997). However, for Christians the language of rights in a secular society plays to the increasing individualization of society as claiming rights becomes a blunt tool to vindicate individual rights at the expense of others. The interpretation of human rights is key here. Christian thinking sees that 'human rights are not something to be demanded, but something given and conferred on others by active obedience to God' (Miles and Stephenson, 2000).

Christianity and human rights

Christians claim that God is the independent standard of right and righteousness, and that he holds human beings responsible and accountable to him; 'It is our *responsibility to God for others* that is primary' (Wright, 1980). This is a responsibility marked not by guilt – 'It's not my fault' – but by obligation. In other words, it is to be under responsibility to God for the person or people in a particular situation. This may result in individual rights being deferred in the interests of others, as modelled by both Jesus and Paul. Thus rights are not simply to be claimed or enforced, but they are the result of active responsibility to God for others. In his letter to the Ephesians, Paul sums this up in verse 21 of chapter 5: 'Submit to one another out of reverence for Christ.' By acting out God's intentions for humanity, human rights – harmonious, loving and just relationships between people – can be achieved.

The Bible does not view children as lesser beings, but as complete humans made in the image of God (Ps. 139). A Christian view of rights takes this into account. Biblically, children are subject to God-given rights, but this is held in balance with their responsibility to God and obedience to their parents as the primary caregivers. Parents, at the same time, should not 'exasperate' (Eph. 6:4) their children, but 'surrender any right they feel they have to act unreasonably' (Study Notes, NIV Study Bible, 1990) towards them. Neither parents nor state can claim ownership of children. All human beings are 'children of God'. Within Christian teaching, both children and adults should be treated with the love and respect accorded to 'children of God', thus upholding their rights.

This interpretation of human rights and child rights differentiates the Christian approach to rights-based development from the secular approach. The omission of the divine dimension presents a particular perspective on rights, one that Babu Gogineni, Director of the International Humanitarian Society, says should be guided by 'personal ethics, nationality and conscience' (de Berry and Stephenson, 1999). Secular NGOs are careful to avoid religious input or bias into their programme and training. They take a more litigious approach, empowering children through making them aware of their rights and how to claim them.

At the Nazareth Conference on 'Children's Rights and Religion' in 1999, speakers representing the three major monotheistic religions of the Middle East sought to justify and lay claim to the religious values and traditions that underpin the CRC. Imans, rabbis and priests alike referred to how the CRC was 'in line' with Scripture, saying that the CRC emerged out of a 'universal morality of which all religions are an expression' (Fr. George Khouri).

Legal and ethical conflicts

However, on closer scrutiny, subsequent speakers identified conflicts of implementation in terms of some religious laws and values and the CRC. While the CRC sets itself over and above other institutions, the question was raised as to how then to implement the CRC in family and religious settings that have other priorities? Such conflicts existed in Sharia law on, for example, the lack of provision for female inheritance and Islamic paternalism that undermine the practical entitlement of children to rights (Safir Sayed). Further conflict was noted with regard to Jewish laws on marriage, adoption and conversion (Anat Horowitz). Christian fundamentalists argued that the CRC undermines the God-given right of parents to raise children (Kimbrough-Melton).

Difficulties also lie in the interpretation of Article 14, which states that the child can exercise the right to freedom of religion. This creates tension with the Declaration of the Elimination of all Forms of Discrimination Based on Religion or Belief. This stresses 'the liberty of parents to ensure the religious and moral education of their children with their own convictions'. The outworking of Article 14 of the CRC has in practice pitted children against parents in terms of choice. The CRC attempts to balance the 'best interests of the child' with their evolving capacities to express their interests or wishes. Test cases thus far have shown that the best interests argument holds sway over the rights of the children (Veerman and Sand, 1999). In these particular cases, these interests included those of the state, the child and the parents – in that order. Getting this balance right is critical to the religious groups who perceive that the CRC creates the legal precedent to allow children to exercise their right to freedom of religion over the parental right to 'ensure the religious and moral education of their children with their own convictions'.

Fundamentalism

Although the conference attracted a diversity of faiths and religious perspectives, it did not truly represent the wider spectrum of opinion that can be found within each faith. An interfaith dialogue tends to attract the more liberal wings of different faiths. Despite this, issues raised mirror the wider debates and dissensions that can be found among the more fundamentalist groups.

Such groups agree on key issues that emerge from a particular interpretation of the articles of the CRC. Those most vehemently opposed to the CRC base their arguments on the assumption that the CRC is one of a raft of international treaties emanating from the UN that seek to increase its hegemony over the thoughts, policies and socio-cultural values of the international community. Dallas K. Miller QC is a Christian lawyer in Canada. His views represent those of a substantial group of fundamentalist Christians, Mormons and Muslims opposed to what they see as the subversive agenda of the UN.

> Although several of the provisions offer generally positive, non-offensive platitudes, a substantial portion of the Convention undermines parental rights. Thus threats to the family generally fall into three categories: 1) the transfer of God-given parental rights and responsibilities to the State *(Article 3)*; 2) the institutionalization of rebellion by vesting children with various fundamental rights which advance notions of the child's autonomy and freedom from parental guidance *(Articles 12, 13, and 14)*; and 3) the establishment of bureaucracies and institutions of a national and international nature designed to promote "the ideas of the United Nations" and to investigate and prosecute those who violate their children's rights *(Article 16 and 17)*. (Miller, 2000, italicized references to the CRC added by the author)

Richard G. Wilkins, a professor of law at Brigham Young University, believes that the *Declaration on Human Rights* sufficiently provides for the protection of and provision for children. The CRC, in his view, is unnecessary. Wilkins argues that, along with the international criminal courts and the vast UN conference system, the CRC is just another step in empowering the UN to intervene in the sovereignty of other nations (Wilkins, 1999).

Miller and Wilkins approach these issues from the perspective of citizens of nations with good law and welfare provision for children. The fears they articulate are the fears of like-minded groups who detect a gnawing sense of moral decay within their societies fuelled by the perception that the libertarian agenda is predominant in national and international politics. They also sense that their very way of life and their freedom of religion are under threat. They feel that by taking opposing views and waging semantic wars over UN treaties in the back rooms of UN conferences they can hold back the pervasive liberal tide.

What they do acknowledge, however, is that this argument weakens in the light of the potential impact of the CRC in developing countries. In many ways, their arguments resonate with those expressed by the children's studies group. Although these make strange bedfellows, the children's studies group recognizes the threat to sovereignty and enforced cultural imperialism, paralleling the concerns of religious groups. However, the issues that face children in Canada, for example, cannot be compared to those faced by their peers in the Sudan or Colombia. The strength of the CRC lies in its near-universal ratification. This creates a global unity of purpose and standards that can provide a safer and better world for children. Legislation and policy that seek to outlaw the use of child soldiers, or exploitative forms of child labour, have been made possible by the existence of the CRC.

Christian evangelicalism

Some high-profile evangelical Christian non-government organizations and churches view the CRC in a pragmatic way. World Vision, for example, now professes to follow a child rights-based approach to development. Tearfund, an international NGO with partners in over a hundred countries, prefers to view the CRC as a useful tool that forms part of an advocacy strategy. It sees that the CRC arguably provides the 'best opportunity to move forward the process of meeting the needs of the world's poorest children' (de Berry and Stephenson, 1999), but that its implementation provides a great challenge and potential dangers. It also believes that the championing of rights is implicit to a Christian approach to development. Tearfund believes that God holds Christians responsible for acting towards people, including children, with respect while upholding the rights that God has given to them.

The debate is growing among evangelicals in South America about the pros and cons of the CRC. Some of the more conservative churches view the CRC with suspicion, citing an upsurge in disrespectful behaviour among youth as a direct result of new legislation related to the CRC (Castro, 2000). However, others argue that in countries dominated by conflict and poverty the CRC acts as a wake-up call to the church and governments. Not only does it provide a basis for action, but it also challenges the assistential approach taken by the church in its children's ministries by overcoming the concept of the child as 'an object of compassion' to seeing children as 'full subjects of their rights' (Herrera, et al., 2000).

Faith-based and rights-based approaches

It could be argued that the CRC gives secular organizations a new ethical vision that provides the moral guidance for their programming. In a way, the CRC has become the 'doctrine' for these agencies to define their moral and compassionate humanitarian mission. A rights-based approach may be the twenty-first century's reinvention of the first wave of child welfare organizations that were driven by a faith-based approach.

However, faith-based and rights-based approaches are not mutually exclusive. Human rights uphold religious freedom and religious values uphold human rights. The key difference lies in why and how rights should be upheld. For people of faith, rights are the outworking of a relationship between people, and between people and God.

Conclusion

Having outlined the different perspectives of three groups on the CRC – the child rights movement, the children's studies group and religious groups – it is clear that a variety of opinions are held even within each of the groups. However, despite the differences, the overriding consensus holds that the CRC has put children at the heart of the international aid agenda. As Ennew states, 'At the start of the twenty-first century it is no longer possible for policies concerning children to be developed without at least nominally taking children into account as subjects of rights, however mistaken or hostile some notions of child rights may be' (de Berry and Stephenson, 1999).

What do emerge from this brief analysis are the differing perceptions of and approaches to rights-based work. The child rights movement seeks universal ratification and resources for effective implementation and efficient monitoring. The child studies group warns that there are 'no short cuts' in achieving children's rights (Boyden, 1997), and that simply enforcing the implementation of rights could be damaging to complex cultural situations. Finally, the religious groups see much in the CRC that complements faith-based work. However, some perceive a hidden child rights agenda that seeks to undermine parental rights and religious laws.

Leading proponents of the CRC claim that it is flexible and open to interpretation in different cultures and contexts. How it is implemented depends on the outworking of state legislation at the national level and resourcing that enables services to be provided. Not only that, but holistic approaches should be developed which take into account all aspects of the CRC to ensure that the approach that is adopted in the field and in practice also enables the best allocation of resources possible. All rights need to be considered simultaneously. For example, not considering Article 12 (considering the views of children) at all times may lead to ineffective service provision.

Much needs to be done by all institutions interested in children's welfare to enable implementation in the spirit of the CRC. The differing perspectives described here could contribute constructively to ensure that the CRC fulfils a positive role in enhancing children's well-being.

– Questions to Consider –

1 'Jesus gives us the right to be called children of God.' Discuss how this biblical promise relates to the rights/promises detailed in the CRC.

2 Describe how the CRC developed from a historical perspective. How do you think the CRC principles for good practice affect our global understanding of children's needs?

3 What are the key aspects of the CRC for Christian practice? How can we use it to inspire rather than restrict our practice?

✳ PART TWO ✳

Key Issues in Listening to Children

Introduction LISTENING to children is important because they are made in the image of God and have inherent worth. This means that they are as important as anybody else is and that what they say needs to be given due weight according to their age and ability. Even in the process of listening we must get down to the child's level and try to see things from his perspective – because we can listen and still not really hear at that deeper level where we truly connect with the person's intended meaning.

Children should be included in decisions that affect them. They will have insights about some of the reasons why they are at risk, and possible solutions, simply because they are closest to the problem. Children should be heard not because they are never wrong, but because adults are not always right and sometimes adults can make decisions that are more to do with maintaining their power over children than considering their best interest.

Even when we are committed to including children in the consultation process, it is not easy. We must therefore consider more creative methods of listening – rather than not doing it because it appears too difficult.

Josephine-Joy Wright describes how to listen to children supportively as well as how to enable their involvement. Gundelina Velazco follows this by describing how to involve children in assessment, evaluation and practice. Laurence Gray describes the 'right' of the child to speak and be heard as recommended in Article 12 of the CRC and gives a Christian response to the critics. Steve Gourley draws on his experience of participation to describe how to listen to children and involve them in programme and policy planning that affects them. Finally, Glenn Miles describes the use of advocacy for and with children and explores the ethical issues of listening and not listening to children. **Glenn Miles**

– CHAPTER 8 –

Listening to Children and Enabling Their Involvement

Josephine-Joy Wright

THE young girl sat in the rocking chair, curls tumbling as a shield around her face, her body taut in jeans and oversized jumpers designed to hide her 'shame'. She trembled, eyes darting at me as I sat, still, still and gentle, waiting. Usually any self-respecting teenager thought twice about seeking help. It was not cool or trendy. But then, she did not appear to have much self-respect. To have allowed herself enough care to come was a miracle.

Into the heartbeat of my room she came, into a room filled, unknown to her, with prayer and love. She sat and breathed. For ten long minutes she sat – and I sat too, Christ's wisdom stilling my humanity which would have filled the minutes with adult nonsense. Slowly the words came – words of emptiness, of pain, of abandonment, of longing, words of betrayal and rejection. Slowly words found the media – in clay, in colours, in the Russian dolls' fragmented completeness. As the weeks went by she grew bolder, sharing the reality of the rape, the humiliation, the bullying, the favouritism. One day she asked: 'Why do you stay here with me, why do you care? It's as if you really love me.' Our eyes met. We did not need words. She knew the truth. She was loved.

A few weeks later came the plea. 'Jo, I cut my arms, I try to kill myself, I starve myself to the point of fainting. I'm depressed, I ditched out of school, I'm morose, isolated and wretched, high on drugs, or lower than low with self-hatred. What more do I have to do to make them hear, to make mum and dad see me, to make them listen?'

That cry led to a series of materials and posters which I designed with her and other children and colleagues to teach and help others to understand children's worlds and needs. Some of these ideas I will share with you, for the lessons that we learn about what children and young people need are as much from the young people themselves as from the textbooks of our models and frameworks. We need both, working together to really enable children to grow.

In this chapter we will explore what we mean by supportive listening and therepeutic listening, what the needs of children are in this respect and how good listening can be effected both by the worker and by the child or young person.

Listening is part of the dynamic process of communication, which involves understanding and appropriately responding to the signals that we use to indicate our emotional, intellectual, spiritual and physical well-being to one another. If we fail to listen, we fail to communicate. Too often in my day-to-day work with children, most of whom would be defined as being significantly 'at risk', I witness the breakdown of communication as we fail to listen and to hear one another, both as adults and as children. The following wonderful story underscores this truth. (We acknowledge whoever was inspired to write it and apologize for not being able to give them credit by name.)

> Once there was a very small boy who had feelings. He had many feelings and got them every day. His family liked him when he showed his feelings. So . . . he started wearing them on his sleeve. One day one of the parents said she did not like to see his FEAR feeling anymore, so he tried to pull it off. The parent said she would give him some TOUGH to cover his fear. It was very hard to cover the FEAR with TOUGH, so the other parent and grandparents helped. It took many days. "Now you look wonderful," the parents said when it was done. "We've covered some of your feelings with TOUGH. You will grow into a good strong person."
>
> When the boy was a little older he found a friend. The friend also wore her feelings on her sleeve. One day the friend said, "My parents want me to cover up my LONELY feelings and I will be different from now on." And she was! The boy decided to cover his LONELY feelings too, and he got ANGER from another adult. The boy put the big patches of ANGER on top of his

LONELY. It was hard work trying to cover the LONELY feelings.

One day when the boy went to school, some of his LONELY feelings started to show. So . . . the teacher kept him late and gave him some GUILT to cover the LONELY feelings. Sometimes at night when he was alone the boy would look at his feelings. He would pull off the TOUGH and ANGER to look at his LONELY and FEAR. Then he would have to take a long time putting the TOUGH, ANGER and GUILT on again.

One night he noticed his LONELY and FEAR were growing and beginning to stick out around the patches. He had to go out to find some more ANGER to cover the LONELY and got all the TOUGH that his parents could spare to cover his FEAR.

This boy grew bigger and was very popular. Everyone said that he could hide his feelings well. One day his parents said they had a PROUD feeling because the boy had so much TOUGH. But the boy could not find anywhere to put the PROUD feeling because the TOUGH was getting so big. The boy had trouble finding any room on his sleeve for any other feelings. The TOUGH and the ANGER were all that showed.

Then one day he met another person and became friends. He thought that they were a lot alike because they both had only TOUGH and ANGRY feelings showing. But one day the friend told the boy a secret. "I'm not really like you . . . my TOUGH and ANGRY are really only patches to hide my FEAR and LONELY." The friend then pulled back the edge of his TOUGH and showed the boy FEAR. Just for a second.

The boy sat quiet and did not speak. Then, carefully, he pulled back a little edge of his TOUGH and showed his FEAR. The friend saw the LONELY underneath. Then the friend gently reached out and touched the boy's FEAR and then the LONELY. . . . The friend's touch was like magic. A feeling of ACCEPTANCE appeared on the boy's sleeves, and the TOUGH and ANGER were smaller. Then the boy knew that whenever someone gave him ACCEPTANCE he would need less TOUGH and then there would be more room to show their REAL feelings, whatever they were . . . HAPPY . . . LONELY . . . PROUD . . . SAD . . . LOVING . . . STRONG . . . GOOD . . . WARM . . . HURT . . . FEAR . . .

There are so many worlds, so many people speaking different languages and failing to communicate, for example:

1. Male-female
2. Cross-cultures
3. Cross-family norms
4. Parent-child
5. Inter-siblings
6. Across developmental ages
7. Where chronological and developmental ages do not match.

The list is endless, yet most of us would bear witness to the healing power of really being listened to.

In a recent local survey of workers and children who had undergone difficult experiences, I asked them what being listened to and giving the gift of listening to another meant. Following is a synopsis of the results. It means:

- They care.
- You have enough value for the person to want to give you a whole hour, just for you. 'Wow!' 'That's amazing!'
- You could be loved.
- People only listen if they are real, genuine.
- I matter, I'm significant, I'm special.
- Because they want to know me.
- Because they care I have what I need; they understand.
- They won't go away 'and leave me like the others did'.

Mooli Lahad (1997), in his development of storytelling as a vessel of healing for children with traumatic backgrounds, talks about children's need for a 'witness'. He carried out a survey of 400 children who had been traumatized by the events of war and similar circumstances and found that the quality which children most needed in those who cared for them was that of being a 'witness'. A witness by definition is someone who is there, who sees your world, your pain, your joy within you, who believes in you, who is ready to stand for you, hear and defend you. Whether we are called to be therapists or carers in different ways, we are called fundamentally to be witnesses.

Lahad's techniques and his fundamental passion, love for and honour of children, as well as his belief in the healing power of listening and being a witness, brought to mind a new dimension of Christ's command to us to go and be his witnesses throughout the world (Acts 1:8). Yes, we are fundamentally called to bear witness to what Christ has done on the cross, but we are also called to bear his love and to be as Christ in our daily lives to one another, to welcome children, to honour and respect and listen to them, to be witnesses to and with them. Christ is our greatest witness. He has been a witness of our growth and development, our struggles and our triumphs before we were ever knitted together in our mother's wombs (Ps. 139:13). We, too, need to be willing to bear such witness to children's lives. Christ's witness is not that of an onlooker, standing afar, watching with interest as we fight, fear and fail. Rather, he is a supportive, loving witness who is there by the roadside as we stumble, risking getting hurt with us, even taking the hurt for us, and bearing it with us every step of the way. That is real listening. In a way, the title for this chapter is slightly misleading. Often we think of child participation as an extra, a useful and politically correct thing to do. But, in reality, true listening involves total child and adult participation each step of the way.

Why is listening such a key issue?

As we have already stated, listening is the basis for good communication, which validates and honours the participants and enables them to grow and develop effectively (Richman, 2000) and to experience a sense of relief and being accepted as they are (Lahad, 1994). Listening also gives children and adults a sense of 'continuity' and enables them to regain this sense when it has been destroyed by traumatic losses (as Lahad has shown from his studies of war-traumatized young people and their families). A sense of continuity is crucial if a child is to develop a sense of being in the here and now and a sense of the future and a purpose for her life.

Listening through the ages

Although we will shortly explore the fundamental qualities of a good listener, it is useful to reflect first on what listening involves and provides for people of all ages.

White (1999), at the Cutting Edge Conference in Brighton, UK, presented a paper detailing the results of a review of publications on good child development practice and also reviewed how children and childcare are seen in the Bible. He deduced that children of all ages have five basic needs, which need to be satisfied in order for them to develop as healthy effective members of their social, cultural and spiritual context. White hypothesized that these five needs worked together to meet people's core need – to be loved and able to give and accept love. These needs are as follows:

1. *Security.* This includes a safe place, a safe base from which the child can explore (Ainsworth, 1963); reliable, secure and stable attachments (Bowlby, 1979; 1982); and the secure spiritual attachment of a heavenly Father who assures the frightened child: 'Never will I leave you; never will I forsake you' (Heb. 13:5).

2. *Significance.* To be valued, to be given meaning, to be an effective agent of change in our worlds (Rogers, 1980). Garcia (1982) talks about the concept of reactivity, which enables one to develop awareness, avoid passivity and develop effectively. Christ gives us the ultimate significance, as he valued us enough to die for each one of us.

3. *Boundaries.* At the spiritual, emotional and cognitive levels, we need boundaries to grow, to enable us to make sense of our world and to develop reliable concepts of right and wrong and of who we are.

4. *Community.* Christ calls us to live in unity with one another – a task that calls us to practise trustworthy, reliable, loving listening with one another. In listening we hear not just the heart of the person, but we also often hear the heart of the community which they carry within themselves.

5. *Creativity.* We need creativity to be able to use all of our senses to express our internal worlds, not constrained by adult concepts and words alone but enjoying the wealth of vessels of communication and listening mirrored in the world around us.

By looking through these key needs, we can see how good listening enables a child's needs to be met (see Diagrams 1 and 2). As Pam Levin (1980) and other child-development specialists describe, following the example of Erikson's 'Eight Stages of Man' (1956), as children move through their developmental life cycle they have to accomplish certain key developmental tasks in order to develop effectively and holistically. These stages are detailed more specifically in Chapter 27, where we will explore assessing the practical skills of workers in this field.

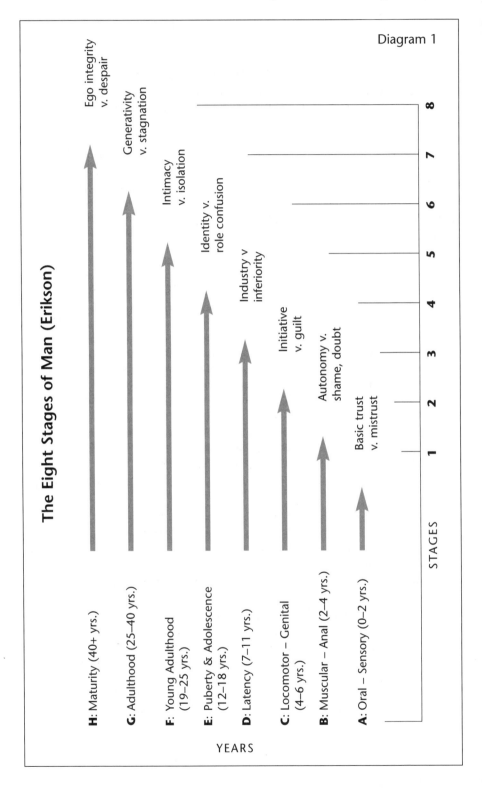

Diagram 1

The Eight Stages of Man (Erikson)

H: Maturity (40+ yrs.) — Ego integrity v. despair

G: Adulthood (25–40 yrs.) — Generativity v. stagnation

F: Young Adulthood (19–25 yrs.) — Intimacy v. isolation

E: Puberty & Adolescence (12–18 yrs.) — Identity v. role confusion

D: Latency (7–11 yrs.) — Industry v inferiority

C: Locomotor – Genital (4–6 yrs.) — Initiative v. guilt

B: Muscular – Anal (2–4 yrs.) — Autonomy v. shame, doubt

A: Oral – Sensory (0–2 yrs.) — Basic trust v. mistrust

STAGES 1 2 3 4 5 6 7 8

YEARS

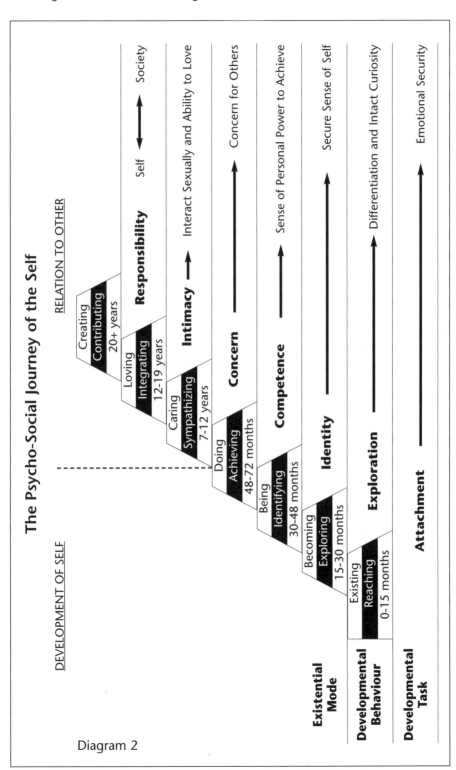

The Psycho-Social Journey of the Self

DEVELOPMENT OF SELF

RELATION TO OTHER

Self ⟷ Society

Responsibility — Interact Sexually and Ability to Love

Creating
Contributing
20+ years

Loving
Integrating
12-19 years

Intimacy →

Caring
Sympathizing
7-12 years

Concern → Concern for Others

Doing
Achieving
48-72 months

Competence → Sense of Personal Power to Achieve

Being
Identifying
30-48 months

Identity → Secure Sense of Self

Becoming
Exploring
15-30 months

Exploration → Differentiation and Intact Curiosity

Existing
Reaching
0-15 months

Attachment → Emotional Security

Existential Mode

Developmental Behaviour

Developmental Task

Diagram 2

The qualities of a good listener

I recently undertook a survey with local school-aged children. I asked them what made a good listener and, conversely, what enabled a child or young person to talk. The results revealed that for them a good listener was one who:

- was genuinely interested in you, and especially in children.
- wanted to hear what you had to say.
- looked at you but did not stare.
- was real and true (what Rogers, 1980, would term 'congruent').
- did not judge you but accepted you ('unconditional positive regard').
- waited to give you time to think before expecting you to reply.
- provided tissues so you knew it was okay to cry.
- did not need you to change or get better to make them feel good, but accepted you just as you were and accepted you even if you did not change ('non-possessive warmth', not co-dependent).
- believed in you that you could make it.
- tried to see the world from your point of view and how you felt in it ('empathy').
- stayed with you long enough for you to feel (crucial for children who are used to hiding feelings).
- waited to be asked to 'come in' to your thoughts and feelings but indicated that they were interested in being let in.
- was aware of the assumptions that they automatically make and tried not to act on them before hearing you out.
- let you stay in your castle if you're not yet ready to come out.

It was fascinating to note how the children had deduced qualities of a good listener that were similar to those postulated by such well-known theorists as Carl Rogers (1980) and Egan (1998). As is well acknowledged in the field of Christian counselling, 75 to 95 per cent of communication (depending on the culture) is non-verbal. Children are very perceptive and often react more to tone and gesture than to words. It is an interesting dilemma that we ask children to shut their eyes when they pray (as we ourselves do). As Robin (age 5) stated, 'I say my prayers with my eyes open so I can hear what I am saying' (Newman, 1972). Children often hear with their eyes and, if we are going to be good listeners to and with them, we need to learn from them a new way of being and seeing as adults. We need to reclaim and give voice to our own child within, to ask ourselves what we and our friends needed as children and then to see and honour the similarities and differences in children today. We need to learn from our pasts but not be constrained by them.

Many of the children with whom we work are used to listening with their eyes, scanning the world for threats, hyper-vigilant to incongruities between our words and our body language that may indicate danger and falsehood. If we are to enable such children to feel that we are genuinely listening to them, we have to be transparent with ourselves and true to the children we serve. Frank Lake, in his book *Clinical Theology*, develops a model of being and well-being that beautifully reflects the purpose and process of effective listening relationships (see Figure 1, below). Through acceptance and sustenance, the child develops the motivation and self-worth to achieve and move towards productivity – which in turn reinforces his sense of acceptance. As Buchannan and Katz (1999) describe in their article on factors associated with high and low self-esteem in children, the experience of being listened to and of learning to listen to oneself is a major factor in enhancing self-esteem. Children with low self-esteem are much more at risk of being involved in offending behaviour, of achieving less well academically and of having mental health and relationship problems as adults (Rutter, et al., 1998).

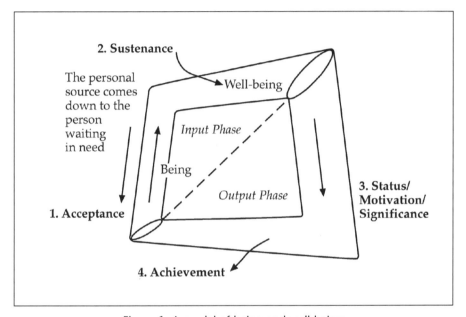

Figure 1: A model of being and well-being

Geldard and Geldard (1997; 1999), Sharp and Cowie (1998) and Milner and Carolin (1999) have produced three very clear, detailed books on communicating with and listening to and with children. A related book from Save the Children (Richman, 2000) also explores this area, as does the work of figures in the Christian counselling world such as Gary Collins (1985), Roger Hurding (1989) and Larry Crabb (1997). The following summarizes the key skills and qualities of an effective listener:

- *Tone of voice.* This needs to be modulated and not harsh, ensuring that the tone is culturally appropriate.

- *Facial expression.* Children respond best to mobile, congruent faces.

- *Eye contact.* Needs to be moderated and culturally and individually appropriate, checking with the children what is non-threatening for them. For example, in China to look consistently at people is to 'invade their soul', whereas in the UK looking at someone means 'I like you and will stay with you and listen to you'. In the Philippines, it is acceptable to break eye contact without communicating anything negative. We need to pace our eye contact, since even in cultures where eye contact is positive, too much can be interpreted as threatening. We need to be aware of the rhythm and timing of children's conversations, which are usually different from those of adults.

- *Seating arrangements.* These need to be explored with the children according to cultural practices regarding eye contact (above), since lack of personal space and the direction of one's gaze can be threatening in some cultures. For example, the Chinese prefer to sit next to the person or at a table so that they can look at the other obliquely. In western Europe, counsellors sit at a 60-degree angle to clients to enable their line of vision not to be directly towards the counsellor, since it is considered rude or defensive to look away. In the Philippines, a counsellor would sit directly opposite the child.

- *Reflective listening techniques.* These help children to feel heard, but they should not be overused or the worker may be construed as patronizing, especially with adolescents.

- *Ask open questions.* Use these unless specific factual answers are required (i.e., How? What happened next? Tell me about. . .? Can you take me into your world?), rather than closed questions, which tend to elicit simple yes/no answers, thus closing the child and the dialogue down.

- *Clarify.* Be sure that you and the child are sharing the meaning, and not just the content, of what is said.

- *Use simple language.* But remember to match your level of language to the child's intelligence so that they do not feel patronized. 'Simple' means enhancing effective communication, not creating a power imbalance between the adult and the child.

- *Space.* Give the child space to think and reply, as well as the right not to reply.

- *Language.* Whenever possible, use the child's mother tongue.

- *Be patient.* Trust takes time to grow. Trust is a *gift*, not a right.

- *Be reliable.* If children are to learn to trust you, they need to know that you mean what you say and will not let them down. If you have to change a time to meet, for example, do not assume that it is all right. Ask them, just as you would ask an adult.

- *Confidentiality is a key issue.* Both the listener and the child need to be clear when confidentiality will need to be broken (i.e., if the children are at risk to themselves or others and action needs to be taken in line with child protection or mental health or criminal risk policies), and when it will be kept. We need to explain how we will document what we hear and where our support comes from *before* we start to listen. It is better to leave children behind their protective 'castle walls' (emotional defences), even if these walls inhibit their spiritual and emotional growth, than to leave them 'naked' because we cannot 'hold' what they have shared and run away – physically, spiritually or emotionally – from them.

- *Appropriate session length.* Collins and others recommend that sessions be kept to 30–40 minutes, but if we are rigid about this we run the risk of cutting children off when they are slowly gaining our trust, relaxing and 'warming up'. Children rarely just start talking about deep emotional aspects of their lives, but they also often find it hard to concentrate for long periods and can experience long conversations as threatening. A child who has been abused, bereaved or traumatized may initially be only able to let you into their world for between five to ten minutes, as any intimacy is dangerous. The time will increase as you demonstrate your reliability and trustworthiness and allow the child to be in control of the relationship while you model safe boundaries.

* *Explore other media and voices for listening, in addition to the spoken word.* These include clay, colours, music, spoken poems, everyday objects in the world around them.

Exploring different 'voices'

Children often listen to themselves and to others through their play. As we learn the qualities of a good listener and what children need, we aim to work with children to find, with them, the voice through which they can communicate and open the gateway into their worlds. Children speak through many different media. They are not constrained by calling creativity 'The Arts' or 'Play', but they use play in its fullest sense as a reflective listener to the drama of life (Jennings, 1993; Cattanach, 1997). This enables them to work through and explore their reactions to their worlds, to develop a sense of mastery and wish fulfilment, to explore ideas about God and humankind, about suffering, beauty, love, hate. If we are quiet, interested and honouring enough, we will be invited into these worlds. We have no right to enter uninvited but Cattanach, Lahad and others bear witness to the power of quiet, reliable, honouring listening as the vessel of trust that enables such children to allow us and, more fundamentally, allows Christ, in to hear, heal and transform. Voices include clay to mould the faces and figures of their lives that they are and can become; stones to sculpt their worlds; sticks in the sand to draw their pain; footballs and scissors to cathect (release) their anger in a safe way; water to pummel and cleanse; paint to explore the colours and forms of feelings; stories to tell and change to work through different endings and beginnings.

We need to take time to watch children, and they in turn will teach us how to really listen, how to really be still, how to talk and listen with many voices. As we learn, we will see how to make pathways between their worlds and ours, working together each step of the way, learning from one another in safety and delight, nurturing one another's resilience and growth. Too often we run before we can walk. We rush in, in our love, our need, our passion and care. But just as the first step for a child and mother as they learn to securely attach is to be together, so must ours be too as we create an environment and a relationship where listening is possible and mirrors Christ's relationship with us.

Such an environment and relationship take time to grow. It is tempting when we are pressured by so many practical needs to let listening time be eroded by logistics. My experience as a therapist, as a worker, as a friend and fundamentally as a child of God, has shown me that to lose such time is not worth the cost. But we can only really learn to listen to children when we have learned to listen to ourselves and, crucially, to God. As we will see in Part 7 of this book, that is the key – otherwise, our knowledge and skills are clanging symbols (1 Cor. 13:1). When we can be still, seek his face and learn from him in silence, then we will really learn to be, to live, to love and to listen.

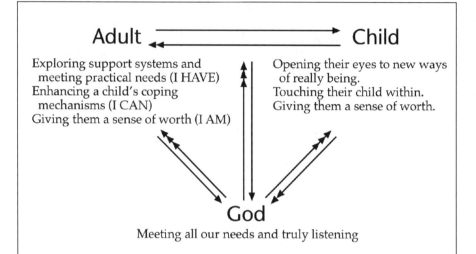

Figure 2: A three-way relationship between adult, child and God

(Figures 1 and 2 reprinted with permission from Frank Lake, *Clinical Theology* [London: Darton, Longman & Todd, 1986])

– Questions to Consider –

1 We often speak of the value of being listened to – what are the benefits for a child or an adult of being listened to and heard? How have such experiences affected you and your development as a person?

2 List the key issues involved in effective listening and discuss how you would apply them to enhance your practice.

3 Describe what happens developmentally when a child is *not* listened to. How can we mitigate this in practice?

CHAPTER 9

Involving Children in the Process of Assessment and Therapy

Gundelina A. Velazco

I⊤ is an exhilarating experience to witness the transformation of a child who is unwilling, inhibited, reluctant, resentful or even defiant towards a helping relationship involving assessment, therapy or evaluation, to being a willing and active participant in this relationship. The objective of this chapter is to provide some insights on how children can be happily involved in their assessment, therapy and evaluation of therapy, based on my experiences in helping children from different levels of society and from different parts of the world. We will look at adult worker behaviours that I found helpful in general, as well as at examples of situations in assessment, therapy or evaluation in which such behaviours were useful and effective.

It has been said that, in many ways, listening is foundational to helping. This is one of the first lessons taught in counselling or therapy classes. This is one of the first skills that we acquire in the helping professions.

Listening can be a very powerful tool. Cameron (2000) prefaced her book on a 12-year study of child sexual abuse survivors by saying that she was not her respondents' therapist, yet that she probably contributed to their healing by listening respectfully to their struggles through interviews in which she sought their viewpoint.

The first distinction to draw here is between listening in such a way that you communicate to children that you are interested in what they are saying and therefore encourage them to express themselves, and listening in such a way that you are able to understand children in-depth and help them to understand themselves better. The former is a subset of the latter. I would call the former 'listening to children's verbal and non-verbal expressions' (as discussed in Chapter 8), and I would call the latter '"listening" to children's thinking'. There is still much work to be done in this area, which will benefit from the experiences of researchers and practitioners and from other branches of knowledge such as cognitive psychology and education. Both modes of listening are indispensable in enabling children's involvement in assessment, therapy and evaluation.

Listen to children's verbal and non-verbal expressions

Much has already been said about the observable manifestations of listening such as eye contact, attentive body language and how to follow what the child says and reflect back to them what they have said to ensure that they know you have heard them. Much has also been said about active listening, attentive silence, reflecting, paraphrasing and summarizing as some other indicators of good listening skills. In addition, I would like to suggest the following.

Actively 'listen' to paralinguistic cues

There are times when children do not or cannot verbalize their thoughts but instead give paralinguistic cues in the form of facial expressions, body language, tone of voice, pace of speech, amount of personal space, gestures and physical appearance.

In actively listening to such cues, the helper is always observant and involved in trying to understand what the child is trying to communicate through such cues and what the cues mean for the child. Listening to these clues involves being sensitive to the cues and exploring them. Statements such as the following can demonstrate active listening:

'You just smiled when I asked you if your mother has come to visit you. Can you share with me the meaning of that smile?'

'I notice that every time the housemother talks to you, you just bow your head. Can you tell me how you feel when you do that?'

'You usually stand farther away from older children than from younger ones when you talk to them. Can you share something about this with me?'

'You appear very well-groomed today. May I know the significance of this day for you?'

Be comfortable and promote comfort with silence

This is more than attentive silence. It is more than keeping silent and looking at the child without hurrying the child and thinking what the child might be saying through his/her silence. Rather, it is being comfortable in a situation when the child has momentarily stopped talking and there is no intermediation of words and sounds between the two of you anymore. The stimuli to focus on have been greatly diminished, and so adult and child stand more 'exposed' before each other.

This is usually an uncomfortable situation, and people tend either to break the silence sooner or later, or to wittingly or unwittingly emit subtle behaviours to prompt the other to say something. Breaking the silence is more natural and easier than preserving the silence.

Corey (2001) talks of 'understanding silence', acknowledging the silence and one's feelings about it, and then pursuing its meanings (pp. 31–32).

Being comfortable with silence is still different from understanding the silence. While understanding the silence is actually doing something about the silence, being comfortable is just being. It requires discipline and adopting a frame of mind that views this moment as part of time itself and not as part of a one-hour session. Of course it is part of a finite session, and obviously you can't stay there as long as time exists, but if one allows this consciousness of finiteness to pervade one's thinking it might somehow be communicated as impatience or translate itself into an observable behaviour of trying to break the silence.

Being comfortable with silence can be cultivated and communicated by being relaxed (deep, slow breathing can facilitate relaxation) and hardly making any movement while maintaining focus on the child. The attentive posture of leaning forward can be just a little more relaxed to signify that at this point you are not waiting for a response and the child is not expected to make any. To further promote the feeling of comfort, you can contemplate the beauty of the opportunity for silence between you and the child – two human beings who can just be, not needing to say or do anything at this moment, but just being.

As you become comfortable with silence, the child does not feel guilty or inadequate with her silence. She learns that you will still be there to listen when she is ready. Being comfortable with silence greatly relaxes the child because the pressure to fill up every moment with interaction is relieved.

Listen to children's thinking

Ginsburg's (1997) book *Entering the Child's Mind* focuses on determining the child's competence through the clinical interview (most of his examples use mathematics and an assessment of children's cognitive competencies). I have found that some of these techniques can be applied in the field of therapy.

Ginsburg writes of 'children's conceptual systems': what is of greater importance than 'objective reality' is the 'child's construction of that reality' (p. 18). He also states that 'an answer cannot be fully understood if it is considered apart from the child's comprehension of the question, from what the child has done to previous questions, from the child's motivation . . . Context is all' (p. 46).

If the child is asked 'How do you feel in this institution?' and the child answers 'Happy', usually the irresistible next question is 'Why are you happy?', or 'What makes you happy?'. The child may then start enumerating the things in the institution that make him happy. There is a difference between these questions and the questions, 'What makes you tell me that you are happy? Would you also say you're happy if your best friend (or mother) or somebody who could take you somewhere else were to ask you?'. The first questions explore the answer. The second set of questions explores the context and motivation of the answer. '. . . What is more important than the . . . answer is the thinking that underlies it' (Ginsburg, 1997, p. 40).

Listening to children's thinking requires an exploration not so much of their answers, but rather of the process that produced their answer . . . or question. Piaget (1976) talks about determining the child's natural mental inclination by observing the questions that the child spontaneously poses.

We must go beyond observation and actually explore these questions in order to determine the concerns of the child that trigger these spontaneous questions. In therapy, for example, if the child asks, 'Are you coming back?', then we know that the child is concerned with our coming back. Whether he likes it or not is something that can be explored. We can ask, 'What made you ask if I am coming back?', or 'How do you feel about my coming back?' instead of jumping to the conclusion that the child wants us to come back and giving a dead-end answer such as, 'Of course I am coming back.'

Involve and empower the child in your work together

Honour the child

In conducting assessment, therapy or evaluation, it is important to communicate to the child that the helping adult honours her as a human being. The helper and the child are in the situation together, with complementary roles to play – the helper and the one being helped – and, from the life drama perspective, both roles are of equal import. A more important consideration is that the child is in therapy because some trauma has happened in his life. But the child is in front of me, there, now, alive, because he has managed to survive. And because he is created in the image of God, the child should be honoured.

It is good to symbolize the thought of honouring. At the beginning of every session with children, regardless of the therapeutic approaches I am going to use, I shake their hands. Usually this is the child's first experience of being given this much importance, which heralds the fact that the therapy is offering an entirely new environment – one which is far removed from the environment of trauma which brought the child to therapy in the first place. This establishes at the outset that the child is important. This also presents to the child a psychological platform, wherein what the child is going to say is important and will be listened to. This symbolically proposes to the child an interaction of mutual respect in which what both people say would be respected.

The shaking of hands should, of course, be friendly (accompanied by a smile) and appropriately tight (neither too limp nor crushing the child's hand), and not cold and businesslike. But neither should it be lingering and so familiar as to be open to misinterpretation, especially by children who have been touched in a sexual context.

It is also important to honour the child in deed. The symbol of shaking hands as a sign of honour will not ring true if the adult monopolizes and controls the conversation, interrupts the child, or rebukes the child for some of the things she says – in sum, if the adult behaves in an authoritative, superior and patronizing manner.

We have looked at some tips on verbalizations that help adults to follow the child, rather than leading and controlling the child in conversation. Besides saying the right kinds of things and avoiding those that are not beneficial, I have also found some non-verbal behaviours helpful. As much as possible, for example, I refrain from standing up during a session with a child so as not to tower over the child at any time. This requires pre-planning so that all of the materials that might possibly be needed are within reach and I do not have to stand up and therefore look down at the child.

We are often told to maintain eye contact. But there are times when a steady eye contact can be perceived as conveying a sense of superiority and an unnecessary show of self-confidence on the part of the adult. Imagine a very distraught child, crying with face contorted in emotional agony. Imagine the adult in front of the child steadily looking at the child's face and saying, 'I am sorry that you had to go through this.' The eye contact and the verbalization would be considered a proper response by current standards. Let us reconsider this:

Now imagine that same adult saying exactly the same thing: 'I am sorry that you had to go through this.' But, while saying this, the adult bows his or her head a little and looks down for a moment, briefly interrupting the eye contact.

The second set of responses, consisting of the bowing of the head and 'being sorry', is more attuned to the emotional state of the child. It is in deference to the emotional agony of the child. The bowing of the head and 'being sorry' are also behaviours that are more congruent with one another. Compared to the response of bowing of the head and 'being sorry', the response of 'being sorry' and maintaining eye contact seems to reflect less regard for the child, not to mention less empathy and less sensitivity.

I am not declaring here that eye contact is obsolete. I am proposing that eye contact be modified or adjusted at appropriate times to show regard for the emotional state of the child and to communicate empathy.

Communicate freedom

At the beginning of every session I tell the child, 'I am going to sit on this chair. That is another chair like this one. You can take that chair or any other chair in this room and put it anywhere you want to sit while we are talking.' This gesture communicates to the child that she has a considerable amount of freedom on this occasion. The realization of this freedom usually sets the child's expression and verbalization free as well. The gesture reflects that the rules of adult-child interaction have changed here: the adult no longer dictates what should be done.

Asking the child to sit where he wants to sit has its diagnostic and therapeutic value, too. One child placed himself at the farthest end of the room across from me at the beginning of a therapy session. I reminded him a few times during the session that he was free to reposition himself whenever he wanted to. Gradually throughout the session he came closer and closer to where I was, as he became more and more able to express himself and resolve his feelings. Eventually he was only an arm's length away from me as he whispered, 'I am not so sad anymore.'

Another way to communicate freedom is to tell the child that they can express themselves through drawing, painting, doll play, clay moulding, dancing, role play, singing, writing, and so on. Sometimes, the mode just evolves in the process of interaction and I no longer have to tell the child what she can do. I was once face-to-face with an elective mute girl, who by that time only spoke with her mother. Not surprisingly, she was failing in school and losing her friends. When I tried to talk to her the first time she was brought to my clinic, she of course did not respond. So I took a piece of paper and some crayons and started to draw. This must have communicated to her that she could draw as well, because she also took a piece of paper and crayons and started to draw. I talked about my drawing to myself, and she also talked to herself about her drawing. At first we were independently talking about our drawings to ourselves. Later, she did not realize that I was already asking her about her drawing and she was responding. We communicated through drawings for some time.

Let them know what they are in for and why

Instead of acting like a laboratory scientist in absolute command, studying some specimen under a microscope, the adult helper is actually better off involving the child by explaining to him what he is in for and why.

This can be done in a way that does not raise the child's defences, but rather provides psychological safety. This involves informing the child what the session is all about in terms that would be acceptable and understandable to her. For example, I might say, 'For this session, I would like you to help me know how I can help you with your nightmares. I will have to ask you to do certain tasks that will let both of us know how you react to certain situations or how some situations might be affecting you. Is that all right with you?'. Or I might say, 'Let's find out today what the effects of our past sessions on your problem with solvent have been. Then let's find out how we can proceed from here.'

Psychological safety also involves creating some psychological structure, such as general, reasonable rules that serve to protect the safety of the child and adult (e.g., 'You can be as active as you want as long as you do not hurt yourself or others.'). Children should also be informed about the length of sessions (e.g., 'Isn't it lovely that we have one hour to talk? How do you feel about this?'), available materials (e.g., 'These are the materials that we can use for our session today – stuffed toys, crayons, paper, some dolls there, etc.'), and the structure of the sessions, if any (e.g., 'Let's talk for some time now, and then later I am going to call in your mother. Is that all right?'). This information provides the child with some regularity that she can count on so that she is not left to guess or be anxious about expectations (Velazco, 1999).

Show that you are comfortable with the child's language

Demonstrating comfort with the child's language involves more than simply using the language yourself. You need to show the child that you are not repelled by their language and that you accept it matter-of-factly. Doing otherwise would inhibit the child's further expression.

As part of one of the on-site training workshops on therapy that I was conducting for psychiatric social workers in the Philippines, there was a time for trainees to bring actual child clients for therapy. They were observed through a one-way mirror and later critiqued. One four-year-old client had experienced sexual abuse and the court needed the child's actual verbalization of the abuse, so the session was videotaped. More than an hour passed and nothing remarkable happened. The trainee was finding it extremely difficult to extract any substantial verbalization from the child about the abuse. One of the reasons for the child's seeming hesitation to talk about the abuse was lack of proper cues from the trainee.

During the break, the trainee was told that she would have to be comfortable with the language surrounding abuse, some of which she might find difficult to use herself (vernacular terminologies for the sexual act are usually taboo and difficult for many people to use in conversation, but very young children are not yet aware of such taboos and can use them without embarrassment). The trainee was coached that, once the child uttered a term, she should use exactly the same term matter-of-factly, without any emotion or judgement, to show the child that it was all right to go on.

When the one-way observation resumed, this was exactly what the trainee did – and only then did the child pour out the whole experience of abuse, using vernacular terms and demonstrating what she meant with the terms through dolls. All this happened within less than ten minutes.

Play to the child's subculture

Assessment has been a very controversial topic in psychology and education. The issue of culture bears heavily on what constitutes proper assessment. 'Each culture and subculture encourages and fosters certain abilities and ways of behaving; and it discourages or suppresses others' (Anastasi, 1988, p. 358).

'Children at risk' (street children, refugees, orphans, survivors of armed conflict, etc.) belong to particular subcultures within their cultures, and we need to consider the complex issues of cultures and subcultures when trying to assess them. Certain methods of testing children are said to be 'culture-common', 'culture-fair' or 'cross-cultural', as assessment is confined only to those experiences that are common to different cultures. Ginsburg (1999) considers this sort of assessment 'culturally deprived' (p. 23), because it removes what is important to individual cultures.

When assessing children, elements that are important to their particular cultural milieu should be included in order to interest and motivate them. This also introduces the idea of fairness, since they are evaluated according to their own cultural standards. The assessment items can, in fact, come from the conceptualizations of people within that culture/subculture. One item in the assessment form for assessing the competencies of children in a rural upland community, for example, is 'Is the child able to weed the fields? If so, how often does he/she pull out the weeds with their roots? (always, often, sometimes, rarely, never)'. The conceptualization in that farming-dependent community is that the more ecologically competent child would usually pull out the weeds with their roots (Velazco, 1985; Church, Katigbak and Velazco, 1989).

In trying to assess the particular groups of children that we work with, we need to have a grasp of concepts that are meaningful in the culture in which they live and start our assessment of both cognitive and affective functioning from there. If a street child's world revolves around drugs, running away from the police, prostitution and begging, then we have to speak this language and dwell in this phenomenology in our assessment.

In some of these children's worlds, a sign of competence is managing not to get hurt or hungry for one day. Social competence can mean good standing in one's gang and not being bullied by other gangs. Hence, if one were to assess the levels of self-esteem or adjustment or the sense of satisfaction among these children, one would have to consider their own construction of what promotes these things. It may not make sense, for example, to focus assessment on their self-perception with regard to grooming, grades or schooling. They can be out of school and very dirty but have high self-esteem.

Arrange for the child's success

In assessing intellectual functioning, we usually start with easy tasks to make the child feel competent, to raise her self-esteem and to encourage her to go on with the assessment. In therapy, we can also arrange for the child to achieve some concrete and mutually agreed-upon goals and thereby feel good about himself. The sense of achievement can be incorporated in different therapeutic approaches.

In 'JC, a Bully No More: A Case of Behaviour Modification Plus' (Velazco, 2000), I discuss the case of 10-year-old JC, once the most problematic child in an institution, who was diagnosed for conduct disorder. He was physically violent towards people and things, stole and did the opposite of what he was told. After ascertaining that he was aware of the problem and wanted to improve, JC, the house parent and I entered into an agreement. Every time he disobeyed the house parents or hurt someone or destroyed something, a stone would be placed in a bottle with his name; the stones symbolized token punishment. Every time he obeyed the house parents or did something good for someone (behaviours that were incompatible with the problematic ones), a ribbon would be placed in another bottle, also with his name; the ribbons served as token rewards. He was told that he could 'buy' stones with ribbons, one for one – that is, one stone for one ribbon. In that way he could get rid of some stones, but he would also lose the same number of ribbons. Therefore, he would have to have many more ribbons than stones in order to have some ribbons left. The idea that he could get rid of the stones meant that, even if he failed, there was still provision for success. JC was in fact very enthusiastic and did very well. By the end of two weeks, he did not have a single stone and ceased to be a problem child at the centre.

'Personification therapy' (Velazco, 1999) is a technique for use by the very skilled psychotherapist. The therapist acts as, or personifies, the problem behaviour to allow the child to confront her problem behaviour in a sort of a verbal reasoning duel. This also allows the child to talk to her problem. The therapist, as the problem behaviour, is at first very strong and provoking. (Therapist: I am your violence. I am glad that you maintain me in your life and you allow me to rule you and affect your life. I know that because of me, you will eventually lose everybody and then there will just be you and me. I like that. Do you like that?) But as the child gains strength and determination to get rid of his problem, the therapist personifying the problem behaviour acts weaker and weaker and allows the child to become more and more powerful over the problem. (Therapist: I am scared when you say that you want to get rid of me. Do you really not want me in your life anymore?) This approach can be quite effective when implemented in an appropriate and supportive environment by a trained therapist.

There are many more therapeutic approaches in which the child's success can be arranged for, thereby ensuring the child's continuing involvement. The basic idea is to structure activities in which the child will most likely prove her competence or, if there is a possibility of failure, to include other activities that will provide ways out of such failures.

It is crucial that children feel a part of their assessment and therapy, but this can only happen when the approach is sensitive and caring. The process of involving children in this way requires the worker to practice many different skills and be in tune with the child on many different levels. When those who work with children create an environment in which children can share freely, and when they truly hear what the children are saying and thinking, they empower children to be transformed and free to become all that God created them to be.

– Questions to Consider –

1 How can we empower children to listen, to feel listened to and to listen to themselves?

2 What are some of the cultural issues that are relevant to the issue of listening? Describe some of these issues and their outworking in your own culture.

CHAPTER 10

The 'Right' of the Child to Speak and Be Heard

Laurence Gray

Your children are not your children
They are the sons and daughters of life's longing itself
They come through you but are not from you
And though they are with you, yet they belong not to you.
You may give them your love but not your thoughts for they have their own thoughts
You may house their bodies but not their souls
For their souls dwell in the house of tomorrow
Which you cannot visit, not even in your dreams.

Kahil Gibran, The Prophet

How well do concepts such as freedom of expression, interdependence and respect for emerging identity describe the relationships between children and their families/communities in a Christian context? Is it important for the cohesiveness of the family/community that the young delay expressing their views and will? If so, does this contribute to the child's development of identity or does it rob the community of the richness of interaction and debate? This chapter will consider such questions in commenting on Article 12 of the CRC and drawing on Christian experience and the Cambodian context, where the expression of tradition, respect and place are changing.

For centuries, Judaeo/Christian tradition has grappled with the concept of children as gifts, rather than possessions. Mosaic law, a reform at its time, restricted the power of the father – who up until this time had been able to sell or give his children away. After the introduction of the law, the father was required to put his case to a judge. God has acted in history through children, who have been linked to blessings and the promise of change. Abraham was blessed with many sons (Gen. 12:1–4). The prevailing Christian view of children places them within the context of the family. Connection to the land is linked to family history and inheritance. Identity, recognition and legitimacy are linked to belonging, and great importance has been placed on maintaining the solidarity of the family. Against this background, are the concepts of children having rights and sharing their views threatening?

The CRC

For Christians, the CRC can be a useful tool that defines specific areas of provision and protection for a society providing the best chance for its children. The CRC also includes a call for the ' . . . *recognition that there are children in especially difficult conditions which need special consideration.'*

The preamble (fifth paragraph) of the CRC recognizes:

> That the family, as the fundamental group of society and the natural environment for the growth and well-being of all its members and particularly

children, should be afforded the necessary protection and assistance so that it can fully assume its responsibilities within the community.

This statement resonates with the historical Judaeo-Christian view, upholding as it does the vital role of the family as a base for the maturing child. Significant sections of the CRC include:

Article 3.2: *'State parties undertake to ensure the child such protection and care necessary for his or her well being, taking into account the rights and duties of parents . . .'* This view is also consistent with the community expectations of the family in preparing children to be productive members of society and assist in common interests such as mutual defence (cf. Neh. 4:14).

Article 5: *'State parties shall respect the rights and duties of parents . . .'* In addition to recognizing the fundamental role the family plays and the role of the state in monitoring children in a family context, a range of commitments to children were also made in the following areas:

• Freedom and civil society (Articles 7, 8, 12, 13, 14, 15, 16, 37)

• Family environment (Articles 5, 9, 10, 11, 18, 19, 20, 21, 25)

• Health and welfare (Articles 6, 18, 23, 27)

• Education, leisure and cultural activities (Articles 28, 29, 30, 31)

• Special measures of protection (Articles 22, 30, 32, 33, 34, 35, 37, 38, 39, 40)

Serious compromise in these recognized standards produces children whose futures are dangerously limited. In such circumstances, the voices of children sound an alarm.

Children's voices: Article 12

The CRC places value on children voicing their own views and participating in decisions that affect them.

Article 12: *'State parties shall assure to the child who is capable of forming his or her own views the right to express those views freely in all matters affecting the child, the views of the child being given due weight in accordance with the age and maturity of the child.'*

This is linked to the concept of freedom as expressed in the *UN Universal Declaration of Human Rights* and is particularly important when the child is subject to judicial or administrative process.

Article 12 acknowledges factors such as age, maturity and context. The participation of children in all matters that affect them has sometimes been seen as undermining the role of the family and the authority of parents. The questions concerning age-appropriate participation are changing and contextual. The French government's comment on this article captures some of this controversy.

> The fears raised by this article have served to justify the attention of parents and educators to language and practices that are contrary to the child's interest . . . Respecting the child's opinion means listening to them but not necessarily endorsing them. The adult decision-maker's task is to add the child's viewpoint to other elements, which might contribute to an enlightened decision.

France is a developed country with a social safety net, and still the idea of children participating in all matters that affect them has been viewed with fear.

In less developed countries that have no effective safety net, fundamental issues of basic need and protection need to be addressed. In Brazil (1990), and more recently in Costa Rica, for example, the state used hit squads of police to solve the problem of street children by killing them. In such extreme circumstances, the right to express a view about the methods that the state uses in response to social problems and provision for children is clear.

In emerging democracies, gaining participation from children and creating space for them at the decision-making table have been noted as priorities. In May 2000, the Committee on the Rights of the Child encouraged Cambodia to continue to ensure that the views of the child were included in all relevant legislation, judicial decisions and administration affecting children. They needed to raise awareness of the importance of this principle in order to change traditional perceptions regarding children as objects who are not subject to rights.

To say that some traditional views are repressive is a strong statement. The Bible gives examples in the New Testament of practices that have lost their meaning or are repressive (Jesus healing on the Sabbath in Luke 14 is one example). Jesus used stories and examples to encourage a change of attitude. Similarly, actions that value children and put the least important first, and which believe in the capacity of children, are transformational. They are not at odds with the Christian faith or the value of the family but they can, in fact, enhance it. Parents and elders find that there are things that they can learn and gain from their children.

Children can make adults aware of new perspectives, unnoticed changes and dreams for the future, both in spiritual and worldly terms. A person becomes spiritually aware well before the age of maturity (maturity being 18, according to the CRC). In America in 1964, the right to participation was being denied children on the basis of race. A six-year-old black girl, Ruby Bridges, taught a nation about the spiritual principle of acceptance. She was the only black child to attend a New Orleans school, and white families had removed their children in protest. There were demonstrations outside the school through which she had to pass daily. Her constant cheerfulness, determination and compassion to those who insulted her surprised every one. She said that she 'prayed for those who condemned her because Jesus told us to feel sorry for people who talk like that'. She was asked, 'When did Jesus say that?'. She replied, 'When he was dying, he asked God to forgive those who were killing him.' For Ruby there was no distinction between religion, spirituality and everyday life (Crompton, 1998).

In Cambodia, children can teach us much about love and acceptance. Children who are stricken with HIV express love and faith in ways that are humbling. Sim watched her parents die and, although she was sick herself, she wanted to pray with others every day and attend church each week. She was five years old when she died, yet she had touched many people with her love and faith. Children teach us so much and have the same spiritual rights as adults – and in many cases they exercise them more.

Barriers to fulfilling dreams

Children represent the future of all countries, and they are the future's human and social capital. Children are able to take part in arriving at decisions that affect their destiny and that of their wider community. In Cambodia, 49.8 per cent of the country's population are under eighteen years of age (National Institute of

Statistics estimate, 1994). Current social issues reduce the potential of Cambodia's future generation. The country is one of the poorest in the region, based on the average per capita income. It has one of the worst records in the region in terms of infant mortality (115 per thousand), under-five mortality (181 per thousand), percentage of income spent on food and limited access to education (especially for girls).

Family separation, high levels of domestic violence and general lack of compliance with the law all contribute to the dislocation of children from their communities. Rural urban drift – in search of security, employment and increased options – is one outcome of these factors. Other consequences include homeless and abandoned children and increased vulnerability to crime or sexual exploitation. Against this background, the children of today will be the leaders of tomorrow and will continue to shape society. The CRC calls for children to be given the best chance possible. The Christian faith also calls for high standards from those who influence or care for children. Jesus' teaching about the kingdom of God belonging to children is but one example (Luke18:15–17).

Table 1 shows some contemporary barriers identified by UNICEF which prevent children from having the best chances in society.

• Poverty	• Poor parenting skills
• Family breakdown	• Domestic violence
• Lack of legal status	• Lack of material and moral support from the community
• Limited laws of child protection	• Extensive presence of land mines
• Weak social service system workers	• Low capacity of social service

Table 1: Social barriers for children

The cost of silence

Children have views on many of these problems – on being hungry, exposed to beatings, used to secure a debt and on being valued as labour or a commodity. These views need to be shared and heard. Any groups who receive low recognition in society are open to exploitation. The fact that abuse can go unchallenged, even if it is publicly witnessed or known, is tantamount to tacit approval.

Unfortunately, the legacy of 30 years of conflict has been detrimental in terms of accepted behaviour towards Cambodia's children. In 1997, a World Vision/IOM study identified the following factors in post-conflict areas that contributed to young women being sold or tricked into prostitution.

• The family is dependent on unpredictable casual work for their income; the family is in debt or lives in extreme poverty.

• The parents of the girl have separated or are divorced or remarried.

• One or both of the parents are dead and the girl is living with relatives or friends.

- One or more of the parents are drug dependent, alcoholics or gamblers.
- The girl is of suitable age for the sex industry.
- The girl is psychologically weak.
- An older sister or relative is already involved in prostitution.

It could be argued that, in addition to being a legal struggle for basic rights, this is also a spiritual battle to set captives free and bring hope to the dispossessed.

Answering a call

God calls us to love our neighbour as ourselves. Whenever we refuse to help one of the least important people, Jesus says we are refusing him (Matt. 25:31–46). Children in the Cambodian context are often the least important members of society, being powerless and too often preyed upon. One way this has been changing at a local level has been as children are given increased opportunities to participate in the life of the community. Increasing the profile of children, their voice and issues is essential. A powerful catalyst for behavioural change is increased awareness.

Profiling children in positive ways, as well as conducting local research on barriers that they face, draw the attention of community members and leaders to improving future options for children. Community leaders have been involved in planning awareness-raising activities for issues such as child rights, domestic violence and gender issues.

Children's clubs have been established in villages in partnership with local authorities and schools. Quarterly events on child rights themes are organized with up to 800 children involved. The clubs are run twice a week and involve a high level of child participation in planning the programme and identifying youth leaders. Partners in this process can be found in churches, community and government. One initiative has involved training on child protection and child rights for ministry of education and district social affairs staff.

These initiatives have involved children's views on local issues of child protection. Activities and partnerships with government at the district level lay the groundwork for establishing local child protection committees in the future. These are some of the formal outcomes, but they all start with challenging the heart of communities and society about the value of children and their views.

Conclusion

Article 12 is challenging because the meaning of participation needs to be applied. This can be a struggle when trying to accommodate different cultural norms and the interests of family/society as well as the individual. Historically, rites of passage mark coming of age and the transition from childhood to adulthood. In the West this is marked by freedom to leave school or to drive a car, and in some countries to own a firearm.

Some of these 'rites of passage' traditions, such as female circumcision, are not in the interests of children and need to be challenged as society changes. Certainly the right to be heard individually and collectively is a significant freedom and, as we have seen above, it can promote greater protection of children's basic needs and add richness to a changing community. Children need to have the right to say 'no' to such harmful cultural traditions. Christians need to embrace rights

linked to expression, participation and freedom. Setting captives free has long
been a call to all Christians. With rights come responsibilities, and children who
organize themselves also find that they need to walk the talk – as the story of
Makara, below, shows.

Sopheap's story speaks of hope, energy and emerging maturity, which come
from recognition and participation. 'Bamboo shoots become bamboo' is a
Cambodian saying meaning that the young of today are the strong resource of
tomorrow. We need to be the sower in the parable and prepare the soil so that the
bamboo shoots grow straight to become leaders of tomorrow like Makara and
Sopheap.

Profiles

Makara

Chan Makara, sixteen, was involved in the
Global March against Child Labor in 1998. He
was one of 20,000 people who walked the
route of the global march in Cambodia and
later spoke to children in 14 different countries en route to Geneva. Four years before he
had worked as a railway station porter,
unloading goods trains at 4 a.m. When he was
twelve, he found out about World Vision's
Street Children project and left the streets. He
was later placed with a foster family and went
to school. He became involved in promoting
children's issues as a peer educator. Today
Makara is finishing high school and works
part-time for a human rights group. He travels
to different parts of the country visiting communities, sharing his experiences and talking
about children's rights. Since the Global
March he has spoken in four countries and
attended several international forums. Makara
is promoting change for children through
advocacy.

Sopheap

I am Cheun Sopheap. I am seventeen years of
age; I am at grade 9 of Siem Reap Secondary
school. I am the fourth of five siblings. My
father, who has got a chronic stomach ulcer,
is a motor taxi driver. Money he has earned is
not enough for affording medicines to cure
his illness. My mum is a road sweeper in
Phnom Penh City. Because of poverty, my
family has moved to live and work in Phnom
Penh City but I am in the 'homeland'. Once,
I decided to leave school in my 'homeland' to
go to Phnom Penh to help my mother sweep
roads. But with counselling and help from the
staff of CEDC Prevention Project of World
Vision Cambodia, I have made up my mind
not to do so.

Everyday I live alone. My school is about 4 km.
away from my village (Svay Prey). I have got
to school by my old bike. In the past (before
having children/youth clubs in my village), I
sometimes could not go to school because the
bike kept breaking down. It is better now
because the club has helped me to repair my
bike.

This year, I have to take a great and difficult
exam for passing to grade 10. My study costs
a lot of money. However, with help from the
members of the clubs, I have less trouble.
Everyday, I have many things to do, homework, housework, club's works. I always
devote most of my leisure time to club activities.

The CEDC Prevention Project of World Vision
Cambodia has set up four clubs in my village.
In the club, there are many activities such as
studying, sporting, sewing, playing, animal
raising, and vegetable planting . . . I actively
participate in almost all clubs' activities. It is
only around six months I have participated in
clubs' activities but to me it seemed that I
have learnt and progressed a lot in decision-
making, co-operation, leadership and group
working.

I recalled that before having the clubs all children and youth did not have much communication, co-operation and study, but now it is
far different. Now, we all are actively in the
process of decision-making, teamwork, collaborating.

I feel I have learnt and got many experiences
from participating in club's activities. I wish all
other clubs' member been same as me and I
envisage that the clubs could last long or forever so that I would have chance to work for
the clubs and get more working experiences.
In the future, I wish I would become a NGOs
staff with my experiences and knowledge.

– Questions to Consider –

1 The Bible speaks of God's gift to us of really hearing us. How does this model affect how we work with children?

2 The CRC speaks of children having a 'right' to be heard – how can we as Christians use this to stimulate our work with children? When, and how, are Christians required to go further than the basic practice of 'rights'?

– CHAPTER 11 –

Involving Children in Programme and Policy Planning

Steve Gourley

Little people, big ideas: Involving children in project design

THE importance of responding strategically to 'children in especially difficult circumstances' (CEDC) cannot be understated. The multitude of factors that contribute to issues such as child labour and child trafficking, for example, suggest that a simplistic, one-dimensional approach will not be effective in either prevention or intervention in the long-term. For this reason, learning to recognize social as well as economic dynamics, and in particular understanding *how children themselves perceive their situation* is a crucial first step in project design. This chapter will present some of the benefits and pitfalls of involving children in project design, and while the examples given focus on child labourers, the observations made will have relevance to responding to 'children at risk' in general.

A matter of perception

A central reason for involving children in project design – as well as at other stages of the project cycle – concerns the difference in perception which can occur between children and adults. This 'conceptual gap' between the way children and adults perceive a situation is magnified not only by the difference in age, but also by the fact that adults, especially cross-cultural Christian workers new to a particular community, are looking in from the outside while children view their lives from the inside.

The misunderstanding that can result from difference in perception can be illustrated by the way humanitarian workers typically react to the situation of child scrap collectors working at the city dump in Phnom Penh, Cambodia. Most assume that illiteracy, a lack of 'marketable' skills and a lack of alternatives force the children and their families to work at the dump ('Why else would anyone work in such horrible circumstances?' is a typical reaction). After spending time with the children at the dump and in their homes, however, World Vision Cambodia's Child Labour Project found that they and their parents often have very clear rationale for becoming involved in the recycling business, as well as for remaining in it even when other options are available.

For instance, the work requires little or no capital, offers flexible hours, is available year-round and is accessible by people of a wide range of ages and educational levels. These are just a few of the advantages which the community sees but which the outsider rarely notices. It is crucial to understand their perspective in order to develop effective interventions. If this is not done, it is unrealistic to expect that the children will stop scrap collecting in favour of another activity which does not provide comparable social and economic benefits.

Benefits of participation

Involving children from the beginning of project planning affords many benefits – for the adults who are designing interventions and ultimately for the children who participate:

Ensures understanding: Only by taking the time to listen to the voices of children can adult outsiders hope to fully understand the experiences and behaviours of children in difficult circumstances. For example, gaining a 'child's eye view' helped World Vision Cambodia staff to understand that child scrap collectors consider the health risks they encounter to be an acceptable part of their work, which is a 'normal' part of their lives. They were not interested in wearing protective clothing such as rubber boots, which they explained caused blisters, or leather shoes, which quickly fell apart. This explained why they rarely used protective shoes donated to them by other groups in the past, and indicated that such a programme would not be successful in the future.

Ensures ownership: Involving children in planning can also help to make sure that both children and parents have a long-term commitment to supporting activities, since they will identify those which are most relevant to their 'felt' needs. The child scrap collectors mentioned above prioritized income generation assistance over health care and even education, which the project was able to provide through a variety of skill training and small business development opportunities. Responding to their requests, as well as allowing the children and their parents to share in responsibility and decision-making after the project began, helped to promote greater ownership of these activities (see Gourley, *Look*, 2000).

Ensures quality: Incorporating the ideas and opinions of children can improve the overall quality and impact of a project due to the increased ownership and focus on felt needs, as noted above. However, this participation is also truly developmental in the sense that it allows them the opportunity to learn to intentionally evaluate and act to improve their lives. For instance, children working in Cambodia's salt production industry who were involved in Participatory Learning and Action activities (PLA) used objects and drawings to analyze their basic needs and problems at work and at home. They also identified and evaluated their ideas and dreams for the future and expressed these to labour inspectors and NGO workers (see Gourley, *Child Labour*, 2000). Finally, allowing children to participate fully in all phases of a project increases their profile in their homes and communities, allowing parents, government and non-government workers alike to see their value and potential. This in turn may lead to a greater respect of their rights in general, and particularly their right to participation as entitled to them by the CRC.

Pitfalls of participation

Despite the potential rewards of involving children in project planning, it is not a 'quick fix' or easy solution to designing successful projects. There are several pitfalls that must be avoided if children's participation is to be effective in producing the benefits described above. The first, and often the most important, barrier to hurdle is *ourselves*: if we do not posses a genuine attitude of faith in the capacity of children to make a positive and meaningful contribution to their own development, their involvement will be reduced to mere tokenism at best, and manipulation at worst. Christian workers should especially be aware of their beliefs and motivations regarding child participation, to ensure that children are valued and treated in a way which honours the Lord and those who have been created in his image. (In this regard, a biblical understanding of humankind as created in God's image and the implications of this in influencing our attitudes and actions towards children is useful, if not essential. Readers are encouraged to seek out and study relevant Scriptures and commentaries on this subject.) Two other pitfalls to avoid when involving children in project design are:

Inaccurate or insufficient information: It is often difficult to collect information that accurately reflects children's situations and views – particularly when addressing sensitive issues involving abuse, sexuality, and so on. It is important that the methodologies used for collecting information are chosen carefully, and that their implementation is monitored. The PLA activities described above are particularly useful in providing children with an interesting and relatively non-threatening way to identify and discuss their concerns with each other and with adults. In addition to such techniques, however, the ability of project staff to cultivate trusting relationships with the children is equally if not more important and should be developed along with practical data collection skills.

Conflicting needs: We have already discussed the gaps in perspective that can occur between children/adults and communities/outsiders. Another gap that is often overlooked is the conflict between the differing *needs* of these groups. This means that the 'needs' of children's workers to achieve specific objectives (whether personal or organizational) may not be in line with the stated needs of the children, their families and/or their communities. The struggle over whose needs will be prioritized and met can result in the further marginalization of children and communities, who because of their vulnerable position have less power in the decision-making process.

An example of this occurred during an assessment of the needs of migrant child salt workers, who clearly stated their prioritized needs for improved employer-provided water and housing and non-formal education. However, due to their objective of enforcing the labour code, government labour inspectors prioritized the instalment of toilets in the salt fields – which were lacking but not preferred by the children (who like most rural Cambodians relieved themselves in nearby outdoor locations) and which were opposed by the employers, who worried about sanitation tanks leaking into the salt being produced. Taking this course of action would divert much-needed financial and other resources away from the more pressing, felt needs of the children.

Conflicts such as these test the commitment of governments, child-focused organizations and individuals to respect the views of the child on issues affecting them and to always act in the best interests of children as required by the CRC. They also test the commitment of Christians to act as servants willing to place the needs of others before their own. Fortunately, an awareness of the potential of such conflicts in specific areas can help to identify and address them before they arise. One way to do this is to complete a Needs Comparison Chart (adapted from a training exercise by Janne Ritskes of Tabitha-Cambodia):

Needs	Children	Parents	Organization	Yourself
1.				
2.				
3.				
4.				
5.				

Identify the top five perceived needs, priorities or objectives of children, their parents or community, your organization and yourself. (Brutal honesty is essential here! Consider your motivations for your involvement.)

Compare the top needs listed for each group. Are there any similarities? Are there any conflicts?

Ask how these similarities and conflicts might impact your work with children. Plan strategies to capitalize on similarities and minimize or resolve conflicts, in discussion with the children and other stakeholders.

Conclusion: Worth the effort

Despite the pitfalls above, allowing children to participate in project planning is a worthwhile and eye-opening experience – both for the children and for the adults involved. Once they are given the opportunity to share their views, experiences and ideas, they will readily prove that big ideas can indeed come from little people.

– Questions to Consider –

1 Child participation is often described as a political expedient in the same way as integrating children with special needs into the mainstream. How can you make participation an integral part of your practice, rather than a token gesture?

2 Describe how you have applied the principles of participation in practice, both at a policy and programme level. What are some of the benefits and pitfalls?

3 How may you have to change your perceptions and practice to make participation an overarching principle of your organization, rather than an option?

– CHAPTER 12 –

The Purpose of Advocacy for and with Children

Glenn Miles

The biblical basis for advocacy

ADVOCACY is sometimes seen as too political for Christians to be involved in, but it is important to see that the Bible is an advocate for advocacy!

Advocacy means standing up for others – often at our own expense. It is based on the fact that people have inherent worth in God and that God is just and righteous. Children, like all human beings, are created in God's image (Gen. 1:27; Ps. 139:13–14) and have a unique relationship with God. This relationship is defined in terms of responsibility. Each person is not only unique with a sense of responsibility towards God (vertical), but each person also has a responsibility towards others (horizontal), who are equally unique. Chris Wright (1995) concludes that, 'A Christian understanding of 'human rights' is therefore different from the secular because [the secular] omits this divine dimension.'

There is no term in the Bible that corresponds exactly to the English 'advocate'. The word *paracletos*, which John uses to describe Jesus (once) and the Holy Spirit (four times), comes very close. When referring to the Holy Spirit, it is translated 'counsellor' in the New International Version. Other possible translations of *paracletos* are 'helper', 'advocate', 'comforter' and even 'paraclete'. In the first letter of John, the word refers to Jesus and is translated as 'one who speaks . . . in our defence' (1 John 2:1).

The picture here is of Jesus' disciples making every effort not to sin but, when they do fall, Jesus is there to plead on their behalf. He is able to do this because, through his sacrificial death, Jesus has turned the righteous wrath of God away from us (1 John 2:2). He was prepared to stand between us and disaster, even though it cost him his life. Having risen from the dead, he continues to plead our cause constantly and consistently (cf. Heb. 7:25; Rom. 8:34).

As our advocate, the Holy Spirit encourages and helps us from within. He is an empowerer (John 14:16) who also leads us into truth (John 14:26). He is particularly present when Jesus' followers face persecution, which often results from speaking the truth in the power of the Spirit (John 15:26).

The Holy Spirit also convicts the world of sin, righteousness and judgement (John 16:7–11). In this context, the Spirit is an advocate in the sense of substantiating (proving) charges against the guilty. In other words, Jesus is saying that when the Spirit comes, what his followers say about sin, righteousness and judgement will have an impact on those who hear their words. This truth may incense them and lead to persecution, or it may cause them to accept the truth and change their ways.

Divine advocacy flows in two directions: from people towards God and from God towards people. The flow from people towards God takes place through intercessory prayer; the flow the other way is prophetic. As advocacy is shown to be a characteristic of God, it must also be a characteristic of God's children. Jesus stands up for the weak and the Holy Spirit empowers the weak. Jesus' followers are called to proclaim justice to the nations, in the prophetic tradition. They must take their stand with the Almighty in defence of the fatherless, widows and strangers (Deut. 10:17–18; 24:17–21; Pss. 10:18; 68:5; 146:7; Prov. 23:10–11; Isa. 1:17; 10:1–2; Jer. 5:28).

Rights

Children have an inherent sense of whether something is 'right' and 'fair'. C.S. Lewis suggests that behind the use of the word 'right' is a tacit acknowledgement of some external standard or norm. As Christians, we believe that this standard is God's righteousness and justice (Isa. 5:16).

'Rights' are not about one person's obligation to act towards another in a certain way because they deserve it or are owed it. Rather, 'rights' are about acting towards one another as God demands. Responsibility for orphans is, therefore, primarily a responsibility to God (Exod. 22:22; Jas. 1:27). In the Old Testament, such acts of charity were enshrined in law. In the New Testament, Jesus underlines the Old Testament principle that the positive face of obligation is love. The greatest commandments are that we should love God with all our being and that we should love our neighbour as ourselves.

Human rights are not something to be demanded, but something to be given and conferred on others – by active obedience to God, as modelled by Jesus.

Involving parents

It is an inappropriate use of power to withhold information from parents that would help them make decisions. Where possible, parents must be given the freedom to choose a course of action that they believe to be in the best interest of the child and family. If everyone has equal 'rights' to life, this does not mean that parents' 'rights' are superior to children's rights. Once again, responsibility and accountability to God for our actions are key.

Involving children

It is also an inappropriate use of power to withhold information from children that would help them make good decisions. Children need to be able to make decisions that are appropriate to their age and ability.

Scripture encourages youth to have an impact on their communities by maintaining personal purity and by obeying God's word (Ps. 119:9). They are also to be exemplary in their speech, life, love, faith and purity (1 Tim. 4:12), to pursue godly virtues (2 Tim. 2:22) and to be self-controlled (Titus 2:6).

The story of Samuel gives a picture of God speaking directly to a child and, through the child, to his people (1 Sam. 3). God gave Daniel, Shadrach, Meshach and Abednego (young men in their teenage years) 'knowledge and understanding of all kinds of literature and learning. And Daniel could understand visions and dreams of all kinds' (Dan. 1:3–17). As a result, they were able to speak out as adults against King Nebuchadnezzar – even under extreme persecution.

Case study: Eradicate Sexual Child Abuse and Prostitution Everywhere (ESCAPE) Sri Lanka

ESCAPE was set up by the Lanka Evangelical Alliance Development Service (LEADS), in response to concern among Christians about sexual exploitation of boys on the beaches. ESCAPE now has a broad-reaching programme involved in rehabilitation, prevention (through education of children and families) and advocacy towards legal reform. ESCAPE believes that knowledge can help to empower children, families and communities. Education is in itself a form of advocacy when it means that children and parents can begin to believe that change is possible and that sexual exploitation of children (prostitution) is neither inevitable nor the only option.

ESCAPE originally used the media to advocate on this issue. For example, short advertisements and documentaries on television have been used to inform children and parents of the problem and to educate them how to prevent it. Newspapers have also been used, in a non-sensational way, to encourage practical public support.

It was considered important to get the church involved in the issues so that they could volunteer to help, pray and be aware of the dangers even within the church community. Training was therefore arranged for pastors, volunteers and youth leaders.

The team has assisted the government in setting up a police vice squad to investigate cases of abuse, and workers have also assisted in training the wider police force. Education becomes advocacy when the police change their attitudes – no longer seeing children as criminals, but seeing them as victims instead. Taking a very low profile, ESCAPE has been involved in a number of prosecutions of perpetrators and pimps. Although this action could compromise the safety of people within the organization, it is seen as a calculated risk.

The attitudes of children and their teachers have also changed as a programme of training teachers in child protection and sex education has been introduced to schools in high-risk areas. A video was produced to show in schools, encouraging children to advocate for themselves in times of danger rather than being passive victims.

Through networking over a few years, the organization has gained credibility at the highest level of government and was asked by the prime minister to make recommendations to improve government policy and practice. As a result, the National Child Protection Agency has been set up and the director of ESCAPE has been invited to be the assistant to the director of the agency.

Practical ways of doing advocacy

The following practical steps for advocacy are based on Tearfund's 'Advocacy Study Pack' by Andy Atkins, public policy advisor, and Graham Gordon, public policy officer, for Tearfund UK.

Step 1: Proposal. Propose advocacy on an issue of concern to you.

Step 2: Information gathering. Gather the necessary information to assess the situation and consider whether you have a potential role in any advocacy activity.

Step 3: Information assessment. Once the information has been gathered, assess the issue or situation to decide whether you should engage in advocacy or not.

Step 4: Planning. Once you have decided to engage in advocacy, formulate a strategy. This will include clear ideas of the issues, objectives, targets, methods and activities, advocates, responsibilities, timescale, success indicators and evaluation points.

Step 5: Action. Take action according to the strategy agreed in Step 4, using the range of methods available. The key to Steps 4 and 5 is co-ordination of all the people involved in advocacy and all the methods being used – lobbying, campaigning, media work and prayer.

Step 6: Evaluation. Monitor actions, evaluate their results and decide what further action is appropriate or how advocacy could be done differently in the future.

(For a full copy of the Tearfund 'Advocacy Study Pack' or the 'Child Development Study Pack' write to Tearfund, 100 Church Rd, Teddington, Middlesex, TW11 8QE, UK. E-mail: enquiries@tearfund.org.)

– Questions to Consider –

1 Read the story of three young men: Shadrach, Meshach and Abednego (Dan. 1:3–17 and 3:8–30). What does this passage teach us about 'speaking out' (advocacy) in terms of: a) preparation, and b) risks?

2 Go through the six steps for doing advocacy above, carefully considering a particular issue or need of which you are aware.

3 Assess how ESCAPE has followed the strategies and suggestions for advocacy set out in this chapter.

CHAPTER 13

The Ethical Issues of Listening to Children

Glenn Miles

THERE is a story of a programme involving street children, for which the programme managers had built a brand new day centre. It had a kitchen, dining hall, day-cots, game rooms, showers and staff all ready to get started with a huge range of activities – but, on the first night, no children came. The previous week, staff had gone out on to the street to invite children and their friends to come and use the facilities, and the kids had seemed to want to come, but when the day came the place was empty. The staff could not understand it. What had gone wrong?

Steve, the co-ordinator, went out for a long walk and bumped into Pablo, one of the natural leaders of the boys on the street, whom he had known for a long time. They sat down together and talked about things. Then, in a rare moment of vulnerability, Steve admitted, 'I just can't understand why none of the street kids are using our new centre.' Pablo looked at Steve and asked him if he had thought about where the centre was situated. Even though it was around the corner, it was only 500 metres from the nearest police station. 'Most of the kids would be afraid of going that close to the police station even if they hadn't done anything wrong,' Pablo said. Steve had a horrible feeling in the pit of his stomach as he realized what he had done. 'But why didn't you tell me?' he asked Pablo. But even as he asked the question he knew the answer. Slowly and quietly Pablo responded, 'But you never asked!'

Is 'But you never asked!' something that children in our programmes might say if we asked them? Or do we value and include their opinions in policy, planning and programme development? Why listen to children? This story illustrates the importance of listening because of the importance of understanding the context. Unless we listen to the recipients of the programmes we are developing, we are likely to miss vital components of what makes it appropriate in the context.

As Christians, listening to children is also about giving them value because they are made in the image of God and therefore have inherent worth. Instead of doing things *for* children, we do things *with* children. Doing things for people without involving them may be necessary in emergencies, but we must quickly move into a situation where we can involve them. We should enable all children – even, where possible, young children or those with learning difficulties – to 'have a say in things that affect them' (Article 12 of the CRC). Otherwise we can be exerting our power as adults in an unhealthy way, feeling that 'we know best' when we actually only have half the picture. Is not 'exerting our power as adults' another form of abuse, the very problem our programmes are trying to address?

More formal listening is known as research with children. Until recently, children were rarely involved in social research. Morrow and Richards (1996) suggest that educational researchers often use teachers as informants, while research on 'the sociology of the family' often uses parents as informants. In both cases, children have not usually been directly involved – even though they were the central concern. In development research that I conducted in refugee camps in Thailand (unpublished), and then in a slum district of Phnom Penh (Miles, Sidebotham and Young, 1994), community leaders were the key informants, followed by the mothers (rarely the fathers, who were less accessible). Only recently have children become more involved in this kind of research. However, it is probably the development of participatory rural appraisal methods in developing countries that has resulted in some of the most creative and participatory methods of research with children (cf. Johnson et al., 1998).

The ethical relationship

The relationship of the child-care worker

If child development workers are doing their job effectively, they will need to allow children to participate in things that affect them by finding out from and/or with children a wide variety of information.

An ethical relationship could be described as 'preventing harm, promoting good, and being respectful and fair' (Sieber, 1993). The child-care researcher, then, first has to acknowledge that the child is worth doing research with, and thus 'establishing a relationship' with, at all. Then, the way in which the relationship develops will decide how much the child is seen as an object, subject or participant.

Object: Something to find out information about

Subject: The focus of the research

Participant: An active player in finding out about something

This will affect the research methods and the research topic. How the child's role is seen may be partly a conscious or a subconscious decision. For example, if the child is seen as a participant or even as a subject, his ideas are more likely to be considered fairly. However, in order for this to happen 'fairly', the researcher needs to acknowledge her own part in the process and be aware of the external (e.g., academic, funding and ethical committee expectations) and the internal (e.g., personal prejudices and attitudes to children's competence) aspects that influence the relationship.

Children have their own separate subcultures with its traditions, values and rules but, because they live within the mainstream of society, there is a tendency to believe that their culture is similar to adult culture. This way of looking at the world, however, is problematic – and even more problematic is the tendency not to realize that it is a problem (Fine and Sandstrom, 1988, p. 34)!

Once children are seen to be able to participate, the next question that needs to be asked is what is the intended and possible impact of the research on children? For the 'rights' lobby, the emphasis is on non-interference: is the research too intrusive or restrictive? And, if so, does it need to be done at all? Is it being done in the 'best interest of the child' as recommended in the CRC?

In a small research project I conducted with militarized children on the Thai-Burmese border (Miles, 2000; see Chapter 2), the concern was that getting children to consider their past (as well as their present and future) might have been traumatic in itself, even though Piaget suggests that play, including art, may be a therapeutic method of dealing with past events. After careful consideration it was felt that a balance could be achieved by looking also to the present and future, taking the emphasis away from the past.

Can it be assumed, however, that the researcher is the best person to decide what is in the children's 'best interest'? Ethical committees may provide an additional safeguard, but researchers should be careful not to pass on ethical responsibility without carefully considering their own responsibilities (Alderson, 1995, p. 38).

The relationship between the researcher and the child is affected not only by intention, but also by how skilled the researcher is in developing the relationship and then in listening to and involving children, as appropriate. It also depends on how aware they are of their limitations and how able they are to adapt to other methodologies. In my research in Thailand (Miles, 1998) and Sri Lanka (Miles, 1999), we chose to work with adolescents – partly because I felt that I had an insufficient understanding of more creative methodologies appropriate for young children. Although self-administered anonymous questionnaires were successfully used in this literate population, they could not be used in most developing countries due to the high level of illiteracy, nor could they be used with younger age groups.

Developing creative methodologies depends on the duration of the relationship between the researcher and the child and the time available to do the research. In a research project, the research relationship can be broken or stop at any point between the choice of the research topic and the presentation of the findings. But if there is time for a good research relationship to develop, it is more likely to have the potential to be ethically fair (that is, for the child to be included in designing and participating in the research).

Concern about the ethical relationship may lead some researchers to avoid doing research with children at all, for fear of exploiting, offending, distressing or misrepresenting them, but a better understanding of the relationship should help them work more effectively (Alderson, 1995, p. 10).

The relationship from the child's perspective

Of course, research is not all about the researcher! The participant and the researcher play equal roles. The child's part in the relationship will depend on his age, gender, ability/disability, ethnicity and social status. The child's exposure to and experience of the issue to be studied is also important.

Neither children nor researchers exist in isolation; they are affected by their respective relationships to others – including peers, parents and teachers – whose expectations and influence could also affect the ethical relationship. Mercer (1995) suggests that a child whose ideas are challenged by other children with opposing ideas progresses intellectually – implying that learning is collaborative. Would it therefore be more appropriate to do research with children in groups rather than with individuals, which is how much research is currently conducted with children?

In my limited research with children in Thailand and Sri Lanka, questionnaire surveys were conducted in examination-like conditions so that respondents would not influence one another. However, Woodhead and Faulkner (1999) suggest that developmental psychologists are finding that interpersonal relationships influence the social construction of knowledge. This has enormous implications for the influence of others on children – during the research itself as well as outside it.

Would children respond better if they could discuss their ideas with friends? Researchers might be concerned that children would 'copy' from each other, thus 'contaminating' the results, but social interaction approaches emphasize that changes in behaviour or attitudes or beliefs are achieved through interaction with significant other people. Is the research environment a learning environment too, or should the two be kept separate?

The ethical relationship is also strongly influenced by democratic traditions of respect for the individual's rights. It must be remembered, however, that in many societies, especially in developing countries, the 'rights' of the community take precedence over the rights of the individual. The researcher needs to consider the vulnerabilities and strengths of the child's community as well as of the child herself.

Trust and respect

A relationship depends largely on trust and respect. In the past, however, when children have been asked for their opinions in questionnaires, for example, these opinions have often not been considered to be useful or worthwhile. Some of the concerns that critics of research with children have are that:

1. Children can't tell truth from fiction.
2. Children make things up to please the interviewer.
3. Children do not have enough experience or knowledge to comment or report on it usefully.
4. Children's accounts are influenced by what they have been told by adults.

Mayall (1994, p. 11), however, has pointed out that all of these drawbacks can apply to adults as well.

Now, more and more, children's opinions are being sought. The danger is that this is being done because it is considered 'important to do so', but the reasons for the involvement and participation of children are often unclear. The question then needs to be asked whether ethical standards are being sought out of fear of criticism from influential sources rather than to truly develop an ethical relationship.

Unless the power differential between adults and children is understood, the ethical relationship will not be fully appreciated either. Woodhead and Faulkner (1999) describe how psychological experiments previously conducted with children were what would now be described as harmful, and therefore unethical.

Issues of consent

Children must be informed about the research, its objectives, how it will be used and its possible consequences. They need to be informed about what is happening before it happens, and they must be invited to participate and have the freedom not to participate without being coerced or bribed. Children and researchers need to agree on confidentiality at the beginning of the project. It may be better for children to be apart from adults who have influence on them when research is being conducted. Anonymity should be adhered to by changing details that might otherwise be recognized. Much research has been done involving children who were not aware of what was happening and who did not have an opportunity to consent. If children are considered to have at least some competence, this practice must be seen as unethical. Ethics in research is about 'preventing harm, promoting good, and being respectful and fair' (Sieber, 1993).

Parental consent is often seen as a key criterion for research with children to be seen as ethical, especially in the medical field. Tymchuk (1992) makes a distinction between the terms 'consent' and 'assent'. Informed consent is where 'someone voluntarily agrees to participate in a research project, based on a full disclosure of pertinent information'. Assent, on the other hand, is 'a parallel process whereby the parent or guardian agrees to allow a child to participate in a research project, and the child assents or agrees to be subject in the research'.

The age of eighteen years is acknowledged in many societies (and by the CRC) to be the age at which children become adults and are competent to make decisions for themselves. But this age varies from culture to culture, and one must ask on what empirical evidence it is based. We should also remember that older children in many parts of the world are not considered to be 'children' at all. They might work hard, fight in armed conflicts and get married well before they are eighteen years old. Although eighteen is often used as a cut-off point after which children do not need parental consent, children at different ages are capable of making decisions, and their competence to consent may depend more on the context and what they are consenting to than their age. If some children are considered to be competent, then the question becomes, 'who decides?'.

The consent of parents or guardians will nevertheless usually be sought. But, to preserve the relationship between the researcher and the child, children should know whether or not information will be passed on to parents, guardians or teachers. They should receive the same level of confidentiality and privacy as adult subjects. Where researchers feel that they must report what a child has said, Alderson (1995, p. 3) suggests that they should discuss it with the child first.

Conclusion

Following are some of the factors involving the child, the child's community, the researcher and the researcher's community that can affect the ethical relationship between the child and the researcher:

a) *The child:*

- Child's age, gender and ability/disability
- Child's experience and exposure to the issue
- Child's own hopes
- Child's socio-cultural background/ethnicity and socio-legal status in society

b) *The child's community:*

- Family's (guardian's) expectations and effect on the relationship
- Peer expectations and influence
- Significant other adults' expectations and influence
- Socio-cultural expectations and influence
- Current environment of the child (how urgent/dangerous is the problem?)

c) The researcher:

- Researcher's experience and exposure to working with children, to the particular issue being looked at and to the context
- Reflexivity of prejudices: seriousness/trivialization of the child's views
- Chosen research topic, level and content
- Hope for outcomes
- Awareness of limitations
- Research methods used and the adaptability of research methods to the specific context

d) The researcher's community:

- Family expectations and influence on the relationship
- Significant other adults present, especially teachers and/or parents and their influence
- Socio-cultural and political expectations and influence
- Academic peers' and/or ethics' committee expectations and influence
- Research donors' needs/priorities, expectations and influence
- 'Rights' lobby's expectations and influence

e) Relationship between the child and researcher:

- Researcher's relationship to the child, including length of time
- Respect and trust for each other
- Perceived competence of the child to the researcher and vice versa
- Information and preparation
- Consent and anonymity assured and achieved
- Under- or over-participation of the child in collecting, interpreting and using the results

It is useful to ask whose interest the research serves: the children's, the adults' they serve, the researchers' or the relevant institutions' and professions'?

Inevitably, the social researcher does have an obligation to develop an ethical relationship, but the process of doing this involves a wide range of factors – some of which are in his control and some of which are not. There is a continuum of 'less ethical' towards 'more ethical' in the ethical relationship. In practice, relationships are not 'ethical' or 'not ethical' but somewhere on the continuum (see Table 1, below). In order for the researcher to be 'more ethical', she needs to be continually aware of the relationship (see Figure 1, below) and of whether the child's best interest is foremost.

– Question to Consider –

Consider a research project with children with which you are familiar.
Look at the way in which it was done and how it involved the children.
Now consider, in the light of this chapter, how it could have been done
more ethically (see Table 1, below).

Less ethical
1. No children are involved at any level.
2. Different groups of children are excluded or, if included, no provision is
   made for particular needs (e.g., children with disabilities are invited to participate, but the research takes place upstairs and no lift is provided).
3. Children are coerced and/or unable to opt out at any point. Children are not
   given explanations or asked to consent. Children's refusal is ignored.
   Children and parents are not given an opportunity to complain.
4. Children are not given any, or adequate, information concerning the purpose
   and consequences of the research.
5. Parents are not asked to consent or, if they are asked, then the child is not
   asked.
6. Confidentiality is ignored or abused. Parents or other adults are informed of
   results without consent from the child. The records are open.
7. Research is not piloted.
8. Research does not benefit children and/or puts children at further risk.
9. Researcher ignores his own prejudices.
10. Researcher has no accountability. Research benefits researcher's career more
    than children's needs.
11. Research information is 'lost' in academic journal.

More ethical
1. Children are involved at varying levels.
2. Different groups of children are included, taking account of their ages and
   abilities, and provision is made for particular needs.
3. Children are able to opt out at any point. Children are given careful
   explanations and asked for consent. A child's refusal is accepted without a
   reason having to be given. Children and parents are given the opportunity to
   complain if necessary.
4. Children are given full explanation of the purpose and consequences of the
   research.
5. Parents are asked to consent where necessary, and the child is informed
   about what parents will be told.
6. Confidentiality is ensured where possible. Parents or other adults are
   informed of results with the full knowledge of child. Records are locked away
   or destroyed.
7. Research is adequately piloted.
8. Research benefits the children and does not put them at further risk.
9. Researcher reflects on his own prejudices.
10. Researcher is accountable to external person/ethical committee. Research
    benefits the children's needs.
11. Research information is widely disseminated.

Table 1: The ethical relationship between the researcher and the child

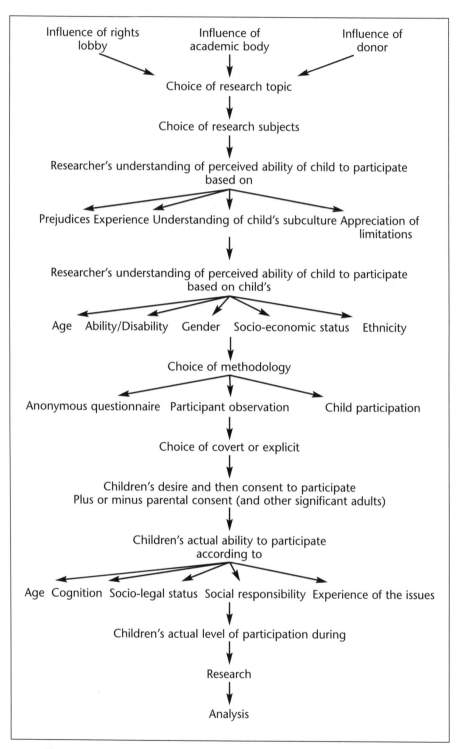

Figure 1: Process in the relationship between researcher and participant

– PART THREE –

Risk and Resilience

Introduction DURING *the past 20 years, there has been a key change in the way in which professionals and researchers view children. They have moved from looking at them in terms of problems in a crisis intervention framework to looking at them through a preventative and health promotion perspective, seeing their potential and not just their problems. Key researchers such as Michael Rutter have been major leaders in this shift. He sought to try to appraise why two children with similar developmental and early years experiences had such different outcomes in terms of their childhood and adulthood progress and potential. He argued that we need to understand not just risk reduction, but also how to enhance a child's resilience.*

Here in Part Three, Bryant Myers and Glenn Miles provide overviews of the key trends and issues in this area of risk and resilience, while Keith White and Josephine-Joy Wright analyse how an individual child becomes 'at risk' and how we can assess his needs and enable transformation. In Chapter 17, Keith White then offers an integrated biblical and theoretical typology of children's needs. Susan Greener examines the particular risk and resilience issues pertaining to children whose needs have not been met as a result of trauma, bereavement or abuse in Chapter 18. Finally, in this section, Josephine-Joy Wright looks into the worlds of such children, exploring how we can enable the children themselves to discover and enhance their potential and work with their own vulnerabilities effectively.

Josephine-Joy Wright

– CHAPTER 14 –

Strategic Trends Affecting Children

Bryant L. Myers

Introduction

THIS summary of global trends is derived from a scan of the fast-changing world of the first decade of the twenty-first century.[1] This assessment describes our world as it sees itself. We need to understand this perspective, because this is the world in which we pursue our respective missions.

Organizations working at the national or local level must use this assessment with care, for any global description is necessarily so general and broad-brushed that it increasingly loses value and relevance as it is applied more closely to specific national contexts. The world of Bangladesh is very different from that of Zambia or Brazil or Germany. Yet, at the same time, much is happening globally that cannot be ignored locally. The future is not determined solely by our immediate context. I would encourage national and local organizations to study the descriptive sections that follow, noting those elements that are also at work locally. To those global forces and trends acting locally, add descriptions of local driving forces and local trends relevant to your organization and its mission. In this way, you will be able to develop a local context for action. Two strategic questions then follow: What does this local context mean to you? And what should you do in response to it?

Strategic thinking is just that – thinking. It is about analysis and synthesis, about distilling your experience in search of basic models that describe how your business works. Strategic thinking is about wondering how different factors in the world and its changing environment will influence and change each other. Strategic thinking is about preparing your organization so that it can carry out its mission in tomorrow's world. The real purpose of effective planning is not to make plans, but to change the models that decision makers carry in their heads.

The work of developing a review of the global context is not the same as predicting the future. In a world that is changing so rapidly, predictions carry little weight. Furthermore, in considering the mix and interplay of driving forces, global trends and likely continuities, we must accept that strategic thinking is hard work, full of ambiguity and always tentative. You and your organization will need to hold conclusions lightly, ever ready to let them go as your context changes. The only thing we can be sure of is that the changes in our world will be too great for mere tinkering. We will have to take big steps.

Our world today: An overview

The first decade of the new century is still experiencing the chaotic aftermath of the breakdown of a world order that had been in place since the end of World War II. Early expectations that the post-cold war period would see reduced levels of conflict and broader economic prosperity have been disappointed. The hope for a better human future seems threatened by a combination of economic, political, cultural and environmental factors over which people feel they have little control. While warlords exploit ethnicity and religion for power and personal economic well-being in private little wars, the international community struggles to find a framework for global leadership and peace building.

There is good news. Child mortality is down more than 100 per cent since 1960. Fertility rates have declined in all regions since 1945, except in Africa. Life expectancy is on the rise everywhere except in parts of Africa, where AIDS is reversing these increases. There has been an increase in human development, measured by income, education and life expectancy, in all the world's regions since 1960. There have been sharp increases in primary school attendance and in adult literacy, especially among women. While only 36 per cent of the world's children had access to safe water in 1965, this has increased to 77 per cent today.

And yet, the poverty in which so many of the world's children live is growing and remains intractable. While the percentage of people living in extreme poverty – defined as less than one US dollar a day – fell somewhat from 1987 to 1998, the actual number of people living on less than one US dollar a day has increased from 1.2 billion in 1987 to 1.5 billion today (World Bank, 2000). Children under the age of five still die from preventable diseases at the rate of

30,500 a day (UNICEF, *State*, 2000). Incomes of rich and poor countries continue to diverge at an alarming rate. Too many countries pay more to debt service than for public service.

There are deep ironies and fundamental changes in direction in our world today. The fastest-growing group of malnourished people comprises those 1.2 billion who are eating too much, or too much of the wrong kind of food. This number almost matches the number of underfed and malnourished people in the world (Brown, et al., 2000). The three richest people in the world have assets exceeding the combined gross domestic product of the 48 least-developed countries. In the midst of all of this suffering and injustice, everyone agrees that children are the future. And yet adults continue to speak for children and, since children are not a political constituency, they too often remain invisible to governments and many others.

Global trends

The Holy Spirit of God

Christians cannot list the trends in human history without affirming with gratitude that, while human action matters, history does not belong to us. History is going somewhere and has a purpose. The sole and most fundamental driving force in history is God. No other driving force or trend can ultimately divert God from what God has chosen to do. The Lord of history cares for the world's children and surely weeps at their pain and suffering. When history reaches its culmination, one of the tests of judgement will be how we cared for the least of these.

We must also note that there is another who is at work in human history. Satan is working tirelessly to bend those parts of the global context that have potential to work for life, and life abundant, and make them life-destroying or life-denying. Rebellion is still the rule in the world, and evidence of this rebellion in the form of the exploitation, abuse and neglect of children is sadly present in every culture.

People have changed

One of the most profound changes of the last century has been the degree to which ordinary people have changed in terms of their self-understanding (Rosenau, 1990). After two hundred years of modernity and its commitments to personal liberty and universal education, ordinary people have become more analytical and less passive in the face of their socio-political-economic environment. Ordinary people are more involved, less ignorant concerning how their world works, more demanding of their social institutions and less easily controlled by those in power. This change in people's self-understanding combines with the technology and communications revolution in a way that sharply increases the power of ordinary people.

This profound shift has a series of impacts on the lives of children and youth. One consequence is the human rights movement and the CRC. The CRC has established 'the best interests of children' as a test for policy, and it is becoming a tool by which children can hold adults accountable for domestic violence, abuse and neglect. A second consequence is the re-imaging of children – they are increasingly seen not as incomplete adults whom society does things to, but as subjects of their own development, as potential agents of transformation. There is a growing call for the participation of youth – and there are one billion of them between the ages of ten and nineteen (UNICEF, *State*, 2000, p. 42) – in decisions affecting children (Edwards, 1996).

Global economy, technology and communications

Global communications, the technology revolution and the unchallenged success of free markets across the globe have created a driving force that some call globalization (Carnoy, et al., 1993). The world is open for business 24 hours a day, and information is available anywhere at any time. While globalization has resulted in the creation of enormous wealth that in turn has created broad general improvement in children's lives, globalization also has a dark side.

Transnational corporations promote, and often create, economic integration as they make investment decisions, move fluidly among multiple currencies and make money by taking advantage of the gaps and inconsistencies between national markets. As firms seek to cut costs, they exploit 250 million children for their labour (UNICEF, *State*, 2000, p. 74).

Global communication is a reality. News and information of all sorts – financial, economic, journalistic, religious, cultural and pornographic – are available all the time, anywhere in the world. News and information are merging with entertainment and affecting the way people across the world are thinking. A global youth culture – listening to the same music, using the same images and wearing the same shoes – is developing, mediated by MTV and the Internet. Children with access to the Internet have access to the best and the worst the world has to offer. Socially unthinkable only 25 years ago, advertising is increasingly targeting children with the sole objective of turning them into life-long consumers. More disturbing still, the Internet and inexpensive travel have created a whole new world for paedophiles and for the sexual exploitation of children.

There is a cultural impact that accompanies globalization. Western cultural norms have permeated and invaded local cultures across the world, covering these local cultures with a sort of false veneer. The 'MacWorld' assumption that having and doing are better than being is broadcast everywhere. Children in rural Indian villages get their images of a better human future by watching 'Who Wants To Be a Millionaire?', beamed by satellite to the only television in the village. The Internet brings development information, crop prices, weather forecasts and calls for ethnic hatred.

Using technology to manipulate information and innovate is the new way to create value, and this is the engine of the new global economy. Those who have the skill, education and intelligence to create value with information will be the core workers of tomorrow. If poor children are not empowered to participate in the global information economy, they face a permanent place outside the world's economic system. UNICEF estimates that 130 million children are not in school, nearly 60 per cent of them girls (UNICEF, *State*, 2000, p. 72). A far greater number of children are in schools that rely on colonial educational systems and rote memory – neither of which prepare children for participation in the global information economy.

The power of identity and the need for meaning

Global communications, technology and economic integration are centripetal forces, drawing things toward a centre, integrating things into a global matrix. Yet everyone needs a sense of identity that is rooted locally (Castells, 1997). Identity in the form of ethnicity or religion is a counteracting centrifugal force, working to disperse power and to make things more personal and local.

As poor children find themselves with no place in the global economy, the attractiveness of their ethnic and religious identity increases. This adds to the attractiveness of fundamentalisms, and the violence that too often results from the manipulation of ethnic and religious identity. Youth are particularly vulnerable to calls to extremism.

Throughout the world, there is a resurgence of interest in spiritual things (Anderson, 1990). The hunger for meaning in the human heart remains unmet by economics or technology. Cyberspace is not human space, and virtual reality does not provide a substitute for the purpose and identity that people need. People are searching for something spiritual that works. Children and youth still generally make life-shaping faith decisions before they are in their twenties.

What better future?

One's vision of a better human future is a driver that shapes what people and institutions work for and how they choose to get there. For the international community, the better human future is peaceful, materially prosperous and democratic. This engenders support for peacekeeping and eradication of material poverty through neo-liberal economics. This is the dominant agenda of most governments, the UN system, the World Bank, the IMF and the WTO.

The global media describe a better human future that has lots of good things, few worries and little responsibility. This message is shamelessly promoted to children and youth. The market system engenders a belief that a better human future is a product of self-interest and limited greed. Sadly, both media and the market have a high tolerance for poverty. Poverty is acceptable as long as it does not affect us.

No one seems to be able to articulate a compelling vision of a better human future that points to the idea of loving God and neighbour, or that promotes the idea that being is better than having. One wonders why the Christian community seems unable to articulate a compelling vision of the best human future – the kingdom of God and a world that is safe for children.

The growing gap between the rich and poor

One of the flaws in the free-market system is that it is very uneven in terms of who enjoys its benefits. Those who cannot participate in the market for whatever reason – structural hindrances, cultural values, physical handicaps, or lack of education or skill – risk becoming an underclass falling further and further behind (Cetron, 1991).

Rich countries have been growing faster than poor countries since the Industrial Revolution, with a recent estimate that the ratio of per capita income between the richest and the poorest countries has increased six-fold between 1870 and 1985 (Pritchett, 1997). Between 1980 and today, approximately 15 countries have enjoyed remarkable economic growth, and their 1.5 billion citizens have seen their situations improve. During the same period, more than a hundred countries experienced economic decline, and their 1.6 billion people, over half of whom are children and youth, have suffered through recessions, currency devaluations, abuse by their own governments and structural adjustment (Bindé, 1998).

The poor and their children often live in the unofficial shadow economy that is estimated at US$9 trillion, in comparison to the 1998 global GDP tabulated by the IMF at US$39 trillion. The shadow economy is the rawest expression of capitalism, existing on barter, bribes and illegal activities, devoid of the protections of regulation and law ('Black Hole', 1999). Illicit drugs, street children, child labour and sexual exploitation of children all find their haven in this shadow economy.

The invisible poor and the lost

The poor and the lost are often invisible to the Christian church –and especially the children. Within a band reaching across North Africa (including most of the Sahel), through the Middle East and into the central Asian provinces of the former USSR, the Indian subcontinent, Southeast Asia and western China, live 1.3 billion people who have little chance to hear the good news of Jesus Christ unless someone goes to tell them (Barrett and Johnson, 1990). Eighty-five per cent of the world's poorest countries are located in this same part of the world, and over 40 per cent of their population are children and youth. Yet only 1.2 per cent of Christian mission giving is being invested there (Barrett and Johnson, 1991), and the efforts that are in place there consist largely of adults planning to reach other adults.

Increasing internal violence and conflict

With the end of the cold war, some hoped that world peace was at hand. Certainly the threat of global nuclear destruction did recede. However, it is painfully obvious that conflict and war are still a significant part of the context in which child-focused agencies work. In 1997, there were 52 civil conflicts and wars going on around the world (according to the International Peace Research Institute, Uppsala University, Oslo, Norway). It is estimated that more than 540 million children live in unstable or violent contexts (UNICEF, *State*, 2000, p. 25). When warlords cannot find adults to serve as soldiers they turn to young people, deliberately brutalizing them into cold killers. There are some 300,000 child soldiers in the world today. More than two million children died as a result of armed conflict in the 1990s, and more than six million were seriously injured or permanently disabled (UNICEF, *State*, 2000, p. 28).

Reactions against the results of global market integration, an unbridled free-market system and technological change take several forms. In some cases, grassroots movements react violently across borders in the form of terrorism and assassination. In other cases, authoritarian states promise greater economic and social security in exchange for relinquishing political freedoms. This leads to violent grassroots reactions that often are organized along religious or ethnic lines.

Civil wars driven not by grievance or ideology but by greed are a more recent phenomenon (Collier and Hoeffler, 2000). Local warlords, unable to extract money from superpowers or governments, turn to exporting local natural resources to pay for their armies and use children as their soldiers. The long-term effects on young men and women traumatized for the social good of these nations are a tragic future reality. These local upheavals are a major contributing factor to increasing numbers of internally displaced people and refugees, the majority of whom are women and children.

Movement of people

When one looks at the world in terms of where its people are located, it is clear that the South dominates. When one looks at the world in terms of where wealth is created and concentrated, the North dominates (Smith, 1999). Just as people have moved to the city from the country in search of jobs and opportunity, the migration of people to the North for economic reasons will continue to be a significant feature of this century.

These new immigrant populations have higher birth rates than many of the receiving populations, creating pressures on school and social welfare systems. Those who migrate bring their ethnic links and religions with them, and this can create social strain in their new culture. For example, Islam's potent anti-Westernism and its fundamentalist movement has its roots among Muslims who migrated to the West and were appalled by the world in which they found themselves living.

Conflict, disasters and environmental collapse have dramatically increased the number of refugees from 2.5 million in 1975 to 22 million in 1998, although it is encouraging to note that this is down from a high of 27 million in 1995 (Brown, et al., 1999). To this one must add the 21 million internally displaced people who have migrated to another part of their own country (US Committee on Refugees, 2000). The great majority of refugees are women and children (UN High Commissioner for Refugees, 1993). These refugee movements raise a range of human rights issues, including the right of protection for women and children. Semi-permanent refugee settlements can promote chronic political instability – as they have in Congo, Pakistan and the Middle East ('Refugees', 1999).

Changing demographics

The world's population growth rate is decreasing, yet its total population is growing – mostly in the South (Brown, et al., 1999). The North is experiencing close to zero population growth and is struggling to find social policies that make sense in the face of ageing populations (Kennedy, 1993). For the first time, Japan has more elderly people than people under the age of fifteen (Landers, 1998). This creates a politics of the elderly, and one wonders what impact a shortage of young adults will have on the social and psychological development of children.

While the West, China and Japan are greying, much of the rest of the world is incredibly young. One-third of the world's population is under the age of fifteen, and eighty per cent of these young people live in the Third World. In a world often inhospitable to them, large numbers of these young people live on the streets, are used to fight wars or are exploited for their labour, sex or body parts. These children need an education, a place in society, a way to become productive. Without these, children and youth represent a latent threat for future violence and social unrest.

The generation of youth now in their teens and early twenties (called Millennial Kids, Generation X, Busters and other uncharitable names) may be a new cohort group with as much world-changing impact as the post-World War II generation, 'the Boomers'. While there are fewer of these young people in each country than in the Boomer generation that preceded them, there are an awful lot of twenty-somethings in the world and, with MTV and the Internet, they are getting connected. There were two billion of these teenagers in the world in 2001. Several scenario-planning groups are wondering if the global teenager is not a new driving force in the making (Scwartz, 1991).

yeah man!

The changing world of children's health

Infectious diseases kill more people every year than natural disasters. It is estimated that 150 million people have died from AIDS-related illnesses, tuberculosis and malaria since 1945, in contrast to the 23 million who died in wars over the same period ('Red Cross', 2000). Children are especially vulnerable.

HIV/AIDS threatens millions of lives and the social well-being of entire nations, especially in Africa and Southeast Asia. Unless a radical new medical option emerges, Africa will lose one-fifth of its adult population or more during this decade (Brown, et al., 2000, p. 4). The social impact is already catastrophic, as teachers, doctors and civil servants are dying. More than 15 million children under the age of fifteen have lost one or both parents to HIV/AIDS, and this figure is expected to double by 2010 (Hunter and Williamson, 2000). Too many African and Thai teenagers are heads of families. The girl child is especially vulnerable to exploitation and abuse (UK NGO AIDS Consortium, 2000). Because of the influence of culture and tradition, stigma and discrimination and land rights issues, she is often not able to develop as she wants.

Malaria, once on its way to containment, is once again a growing risk. Malaria kills 3,000 people, mostly children, every day. Debt burdens, environmental concerns and a country's poor economy result in malaria eradication efforts being underfunded. The gene sequence for the malaria virus is known, but no work is being done to create a vaccine because the market for the vaccine is only in the Third World ('WHO', 1999). Global warming means more mosquitoes and malaria in more places, including areas of the world where malaria has not previously been a threat (Epstein, 2000).

For a time, tuberculosis was in full decline. Now the incidence of tuberculosis is increasing again – partly as a result of the weakening that results from HIV/AIDS infection, and partly due to increasing poverty worldwide, especially in urban areas. It is estimated that 50 million people have developed strains of tuberculosis that are resistant to treatment by existing drugs (Smith, 1999).

At the same time, global efforts at immunization have resulted in polio being on the brink of extinction. A great deal of progress has been made in the promotion of breastfeeding. Broader use of iodized salt has resulted in reducing iodine disorders, the world's single greatest cause of preventable mental retardation (Lederer, 2001).

The emerging power and place of women

Those who study human development now know that women – their education, involvement and leadership – are unarguably linked to much of the good that results from transformational development. Female literacy correlates highly with reduced child mortality, lower fertility rates, improved nutrition (WHO, 1999), better children's education and successful microenterprise development. Particularly among the poor, women do much of the work, produce most of the food and raise the children. No agency can escape the demand that women are to be taken seriously and their needs addressed – particularly if change is to be sustainable. What is new is that more and more women are coming to this new self-understanding and are beginning to find their voice. No longer are women in developing countries satisfied with a paternalistic handout because they need to be 'empowered'.

All of this creates an interesting irony when it comes to the issue of the girl child. Girls still receive less food, less healthcare and less education than boys do. Girls are still subject to harmful traditional practices. If women are the key to transformation, a greater emphasis on the care, nurture and development of girl children must become a priority.

Environmental limits

The world is experiencing limits in terms of what our environment will allow. According to Worldwatch, the world's future will be shaped by the facts of population growth, rising temperatures, falling water tables, shrinking cropland per person, collapsing fisheries, shrinking forests and loss of plant and animal species. The three parallel trends of falling water tables, shrinking cropland per person and levelling off of fish production from oceans combine as a serious threat to meeting the world's demand for food, especially if the population continues to climb as currently forecast (Brown, et al., 2000). Sub-Saharan Africa and South Asia are forecast to have 70 per cent of the world's food-insecure people in 2010 (Pinstrup-Andersen, et al., 1997).

Population growth is high in regions least able to provide for more people. Poverty is leading to environmental degradation (deforestation, soil erosion and misuse of chemical additives), which creates more poverty. Environmental refugees, estimated by some to be as high as 25 million, are going to the cities and across borders (Myers, 1995).[2] The European Union is including an exodus of environmental refugees from Africa in their long-term planning.

Fifty-five countries with almost one billion people do not have access to the water requirement necessary to meet basic human needs (Gleick, 1998). Furthermore, unless new and better ways of water management are developed, fresh water may emerge as the key limitation to global food production. The food supply of 500 million people today is being produced by an unsustainable use of water. The largest water deficits are in India and China, the two largest nations on earth. Some predict that future major wars will be over access to water (Serageldin, 1995). Yet the UN notes that we are currently only able to exploit one-sixth of the renewable water resources that are available (Johnson, 1998).

Consumption patterns in the North make a far higher per capita impact on the environment than that of the rest of the world. A child born in the industrialized world adds more to consumption and pollution over his or her lifetime than 30–50 children born in the developing world (UNDP, 1998). The remnant waste of nuclear arms reminds us that we are better at building things than disposing of them safely.

Fast growing economies in newly developing parts of the world are ignoring the environmental cost accompanying this growth. Some see the environmental system as a zero sum game, while others believe that science and human ingenuity will create answers and solutions. Some believe that environmental concern is something done after development, while others argue that drawing on the current state of environmental knowledge will speed development (Litvin, 1998). These different views combine to create a confused and contradictory context for public policy on the environment.

Conclusion

Children and youth are moving onto the global stage. Over the past several years, there have been two major international meetings focusing on issues affecting children. The Second World Congress on Sexual Exploitation took place in 2001, and the UN General Assembly Special Session on Children took place in May 2002. UNICEF is heavily engaged with NGOs in attempts to create a global movement for children as a way to try and move the world beyond meetings and position papers toward simple, measurable targets to create a world that is safer for children.

That children can be agents of change and participants in their own development is an emerging avenue of new thinking in the development community (Theis, 1996; Jayakumar, 2001. Children's movements for peace in Colombia and for better governance in the Philippines demonstrate the growing power of children and youth as a political constituency. The many dimensions of children's rights are heavily supported by NGOs concerned for 'children at risk'. All of this is well and good, and Christians need to make their contribution.

But do Christians have anything unique to say? What is our vision for a better world for children? Does the kingdom of God include the idea of a world that is a safe place for children to play, grow, develop and contribute? Could we take a lead in modelling Christ's admonition to welcome the children by creating a place and a voice for children and youth to speak for themselves? Is there a way to think about the spirituality of children in a way that affirms that children have a spirituality of their own and that God is already at work in their lives (Cavolletti, 1992), in contrast to the 'empty heads and hearts' metaphor of children's spirituality that gives adults permission to pour in the gospel message? Does our vision for child rights stand on the foundation of the Western enlightenment or on a kingdom foundation of children created in the image of the triune God who welcomes children and threatens those who mislead them with a millstone and a deep ocean? Are we willing to risk our lives to fight the evil in the world that works to diminish and destroy the lives of children?

Notes

1. I am indebted to the following people who provided suggestions for this paper: Paul Stephenson, Tearfund UK and Andrew Tomkins, Institute of Child Health, London; along with my World Vision colleagues, Lars Gustavsson, Director of Relief; Don Brandt, Senior Researcher; and Alan Whaites, Director of Policy and Advocacy.

2. Environmental refugees are defined by the UNEP as 'those people forced to leave their traditional habitat, temporarily or permanently, because of a marked environmental disruption (natural or triggered by people) that jeopardized their existence and/or seriously affected their quality of life.'

– CHAPTER 15 –

A Tool for Analysing Why Children Are 'At Risk'

Glenn Miles

The 'But why?' flow chart

A useful tool when looking at the causes for children being at risk is the 'But why?' flow chart. This chart helps people to think about the root causes of problems that they encounter – looking beyond the superficial answers that scrape the surface to more fundamental issues.

A. Draw or write the issue in a box at the top of a page.

B. Ask 'But why has this happened?' and draw a connecting line between the problem and its cause.

C. You may find more than one cause so that you can make a 'spidergram' going back to the root causes.

The following are some simple examples:

1. A child is at risk of sexual exploitation. . . . *But why?*. . . She is very pretty, and her family needs money. . . . *But why?*. . . There is a demand from tourists. . . . *But why?* . . . **Sin**

2. A child is at risk of sexual abuse. . . . *But why?* . . . She and her parents do not

understand about the risks. . . . *But why?* . . . No-one explained them to her/them. . . . *But why?* . . . Lack of education. . . . *But why?* . . . **Unfair distribution of resources**

3   A child is at risk of sexual exploitation. . . . *But why?* . . . There are few laws and no enforcement of the law. . . . *But why?* . . . The police and government are not committed to the process. . . . *But why?* . . . They want to promote the tourist industry. . . . *But why?* . . . **Personal greed and/or few other national sources of income**

4. A child is at risk of sexual abuse. . . . *But why?* . . . She is left out on the streets late at night. . . . *But why?* . . . Her parents both need to work late. . . . *But why?* . . . **Poverty**

Notice where intervention can/should occur in the 'But why?' flow chart. Personal sin needs to be addressed, but so also does corporate sin. This is why advocacy tools need to be used with governments and corporations. Rehabilitation is needed, but the education of the child and her family are also part of the process.

How can I respond?

Following is a list of questions to help you think through possible responses to these issues:

- What about educating/re-educating parents, teachers, police, government officials, pastors, youth leaders?
- What about lobbying travel organizations to be more responsible in advising clients or lobbying governments to enforce laws?
- Who would be most effective in achieving this?
- How would networking with other groups help to share responsibilities?
- Where does prayer come into the equation? Where should it come into the equation?

Using the completed flow chart, you could ask questions like:

- Which of the causes you've listed do you think needs to be addressed first?
- Which of the causes you've listed do you think the local community could work together to change?
- Which of the causes you've listed do you think you or your organization can change?
- Which of the causes you've listed do you think the local church should be involved in changing?
- Which of the causes you've listed do you think could/should be tackled by the larger church at a political level?

CHAPTER 16

Theoretical Frameworks Defining Risk and Resilience

Keith White and Josephine-Joy Wright

The challenge of transformation

'Walk with me and I will show you who I am;
Walk with me and you can show me who I was;
Walk with me with Christ and He will show us who we can become.'

Too often, those of us who spend our lives walking with children in different worlds are confronted by labels and boxes – boxes into which we put symptoms, analyses and assessments, and labels which we confidently attached to the 'child in context' and hoped a change would result. Sometimes this does work. Sadly, the right labels do bring in funding – and sometimes even a pseudo-awareness of the issues. Unfortunately, even in the world of Christian childcare we find more labels and categories.

Although we need labels to order and make sense of the ways in which we work, we also need to take care that we do not lose our children in the process. How? One of the greatest challenges in the field of transforming lives (our own as well as the children's) is to hold on to the person beyond and within the process and the procedure. Labels and categories too often hide another 'p' – problem. So many of the children with whom we have worked were initially labelled as a 'problem', 'trouble' or 'nuisance'. We need to be still enough to find the child within the pulsating pressures of our times. We need to stop long enough to listen, to stay still enough to hear. Only then can we truly hear the silent voices in the eyes of the children whom we serve. It is hard. We are wooed by the safe world of overactivity; we are pressured by the demands and real necessities of life-threatening situations. Here, then, we will explore another way of being, another way of doing. Before we can do that, however, we need to understand the nature of the risks that these children may be facing.

'High risk': Definitions and contributing factors

Children at high risk are those whose well-being and development are imperilled to the extent that their life-chances, emotional progress and sense of self-worth and identity are all under threat. The high level of risk is likely to be the result of a combination of factors including the stresses and pressures on their communities and families, as well as direct pressure on the children themselves. Unless there is some positive form of intervention or support, such children are liable to move into some form of institutional care, be forced to fend for themselves (often by living on the streets) or withdraw into themselves at the expense of their own well-being. In all of these scenarios, normal emotional, physical and psychological development is likely to be impaired, and the preparation for adult roles and tasks interrupted. The child is at risk of struggling to survive without the necessary means of nurture and support.

The factors contributing to risk range from elements of the microsystems to elements of the macrosystems defined by Bronfenbrenner (see Chapter 6). It is possible for families and individual children under considerable stress from, say, epidemics, poverty and war, to survive. These children and families are termed 'resilient' (see below). But problems in the macrosystems tend to put the more personal mesosystems themselves at risk. War or famine will affect schools, families and communities, putting them under such stress that they may reach breaking point. When these mesosystems are crumbling, the child is likely to suffer. If a family is under stress, a poor macrosystem will further increase the risk to the child. The following list of risk factors is adapted from the work of Philip Barker (1995) in *Basic Child Psychiatry* (Ch. 22).

1. *Genetic factors.* More and more research is being done in the area of genetics. Much physical and cognitive development can be traced to genetic factors. A child labelled 'abnormal' or 'disabled' may encounter the risk of further prejudice and disruption to development. A physical disability may lessen the prospects of mainstream education, for example. Physical or mental disabilities may weaken the family's own ability to provide for the child in the long term.

2. *Pregnancy risk factors.* These include AIDS and a range of infections that can be passed from the mother to the child. Once again, such risks are likely to affect all the systems. In certain parts of Africa the effect of AIDS is such that many children have little likelihood of any consistent adult nurture and support through childhood.

3. *Birth trauma and neonatal problems.* These risk factors can lead to problems associated with genetic factors (see 1., above).

4. *Accidents and disasters.* These can occur both inside and outside the home and can interrupt and stunt normal development. They range from fire in the home to landmines, guns and floods.

5. *Poisons.* These factors include toxic chemical substances, second-hand smoke from cigarettes and radioactive material.

6. *Physical illness.* Illness can affect the child's emotional development, and prolonged illness may also affect education and the family's own systems.

7. *Deprivation, abuse and neglect.* This includes lack of food, shelter and medical care. It can also mean passing on patterns of neglect from one generation to the next. There are significant cultural and geographical variations here. In some areas all other risk factors pale into insignificance compared to these. Some families feel their effects more than others, and these factors are more significant in some cultures depending on what a given culture considers to be important and essential.

8. *Family disruption, including absence of father.* Death, separation, divorce and the need to move from the family home can all contribute to an increased risk to children's safety and well-being. Once again, we need to be aware of the interwoven nature of the different systems.

9. *Parental illness.* Without resilient and healthy parents, children are inevitably vulnerable.

10. *Early school failure.* A failure in the mesosystem at an early age can often undermine confidence and lead to rejection in the mainstream systems.

11. *Institutional care.* Periods of care away from family and community are associated with a combination of the factors listed above. The original reasons for such substitute care are compounded by problems associated with such care systems themselves.

A child is particularly vulnerable when any of the major systems collapses, for at that point the factors listed above will pose even greater threats than they would to a child who lives with intact systems. Many children live in worlds in which all the major systems have ceased to function. These children are at the highest possible risk.

Core needs for transformation

Many researchers have attempted to categorize the core needs of children from many different theoretical perspectives.[1]

A witness

Mooli Lahad (1992), who developed the Traumatic Community Stress Prevention Centre in Israel, carried out a large-scale study of children, asking them what they needed to assist their recovery from difficult happenings in their lives. From their responses, he developed his BASIC – Ph model of areas of assessment (behaviour, affect/emotions, social, intuition/imagination, cognition/thinking – physical).

Crucially, he also developed his storytelling techniques (see also Chapter 8), in which the worker creates a story with the child. The worker's job as storyteller is to enable the child to shape the story with her and thus for her to tell the child the story that he needs to hear. Lahad found that, often, the stories the children told echoed their own lives and enabled them to work through feelings of anger, sadness, pain, disappointment and joy in a safe world. Throughout this process, the children knew that the workers were there with them, *hearing* them, *believing* them, *honouring* them, being Christ to them.

Lahad waits with the children as they explore sad and happy feelings – both of which can be equally scary to a child who is not used to experiencing feelings. Lahad found that the greatest thing that children needed was a *witness –* someone who walked with them in their worlds, believing them, being with them, quietly, noisily, reliably, honouring them with their time, their love, their all. That is what Christ requires of us. Christ's challenge to us is to go and to be his witnesses throughout the world (Acts 1:8). Although we are fundamentally called to be witnesses of what he has done and will do in us, Lahad's work suggests a deeper interpretation of this verse. We are called, too, to be Christ to one another – just as Christ is a superb witness of our own lives, always there, listening, believing, gently but firmly challenging us to become what we can be and what he has called us to be. But change is often frightening. The temptation is often to go back into the safety of the life that we know – even if it condemns and chains us. How can we create an environment in which children and adults are able to adapt effectively to the ongoing and varying stressors in their lives and build resilience?

Our basic needs met

The overriding and core human need, which encapsulates all the others, is that of *being loved and being able to love*. This is not a static or mono-cultural concept but a dynamic one that provides the potential for growth. Based on both theology and good childcare practice, White has proposed that children have five basic needs which need to be met in order for them to fulfil this core need (White, 2001).

1. *Security.* A safe base (place/person) and reliable, secure and stable attachments.

2. *Significance.* To make a difference in their worlds, knowing that they matter and are given importance, meaning and a voice to affect their present and their futures.

3. *Boundaries.* Clear guidelines on care, safety and discipline.

4. *Community.* Children do not live in a vacuum. Christ calls us to be one body, one family, in community. Whether we are running a children's home, a street project or a refugee camp, we need to make sure that in our planning we do not create micro-climates of strange environments so at variance with the surrounding culture that our children are de-culturized. We are called to be in, but not of, the world. We need to reclaim the good parts of a child's culture for Christ, to develop a shared language for children with their world while Christ is transforming them from their world. We should not try to abolish children's cultural identity but rather transform it – otherwise, children have no roots in their world. Christ uses every part of our pasts. Nothing is wasted, nothing is a mistake. Some things do have to be cut off, but so often Christ uses our transformed and transforming selves as a witness to himself. We need to enable children to be vessels of Christ's transforming power too, from a secure base rooted in Christ's love and in the passion and assurance of renewal.

5. *Creativity.* Too often adults expect children to talk in their language (words) and in their ways (on command, in boxes). Adults need, instead, to release children to express their 'voices' in all the ways in which God expresses his love and his voice – music, colour, light, activity, forms, shapes – without constraining it into a box called 'the arts', but rather as a normal part of our creating. Go for a walk and see, smell, hear, feel the beauty and the pain of God's creativity. Adults need to make the space to enable children and young people to rediscover and release their own creativity.

All children and adults need each one of these. If these needs are not adequately met, a child is potentially significantly at risk.

Both Lahad and White see children not as problems but as potentials – not as objects of risk that simply need to be protected, or prevented from coming to further harm, but as people involved in shaping their destinies with Christ.

Nurturing resilience

One of the characteristics of many children who are at risk (as defined above) is their ability to survive despite the seemingly overwhelming odds against them. Even when mesosystems and macrosystems collapse, it is not correct to assume that all children in a given situation will be equally affected.

Over the past few years, a field of childcare practice has developed around the concept of 'resilience'. This study was spearheaded by child development professionals such as Michael Rutter (1981; 'Psychosocial', 1987), who was fascinated by how some children seemed to be able to weather horrendous experiences and not just survive but flourish, while others were severely damaged. Resilience is defined as:

The universal capacity which allows a person, group or community to prevent, minimise, or overcome the damaging effects of adversity' (UNESCO, 1995) – that is, the factors which enable a person to cope with their experiences in an adaptive way and not be damaged by them in the long-term. (Rutter, 'Psychosocial', 1987)

Significantly, Rutter saw a child's resilience as being primarily affected by their social learning – how a child is taught and nurtured to make sense of the world and herself in that world. Studies by Werner and Smith (1992) and Luthar (1993), though inconclusive, tend to confirm that if one or more of the core needs is met in early childhood, resilience may develop. Barker concluded, for example (1995, p. 313), that in resilient children 'a strong emotional bond was typically forged between infant and primary caretaker in the first year of life'. This can be seen as meeting the needs for security and significance. Programmes of intervention should be able to identify and nurture such resilience.

Factors affecting resilience include:

• pre-existing support structures,

• the person's history, particularly if she has experienced a great many significant life events, traumas or losses, and also the person's support structures and her ability to make use of them,

• socio-economic factors,

• the carer's and the culture's history of response and recovery from past traumas.

One of the most practical models of resilience was developed by Grotberg (in Barnard, et al., 1999), who outlined three main factors to consider when assessing children's resilience:

• *I am factors.* These include a child's personality and self-esteem – especially the latter, since low self-esteem in childhood has been shown by Rutter and others to be linked to the incidence of mental health problems in adults, offending behaviour, low academic performance and relationship problems.

• *I have factors.* These include a child's community and family support networks and practical care

• *I can factors.* These include a child's coping mechanisms, such as ways of expressing their anger effectively or working with their feelings and stress.

Grotberg sees 'I am' factors as the fundamental key, saying that they are difficult, if not impossible, to change. (Although as Christians we know that God's transforming power is above and beyond such pre-determinations!) Grotberg says that the 'I have' factors could be enhanced and that 'I can' factors need to be learned.

Grotberg's model, when taken in conjunction with White and Lahad's ideas, gives a clear framework both for assessing and working with the strengths and vulnerabilities of the children whom we walk with and for assessing and working with our own strengths and vulnerabilities. Often, as we walk with children with Christ, he touches, pokes, nurtures and heals us both.

Any child can be 'at risk', as can any child-care worker. We do not help children change if we paralyse our own change by not being aware of, and making provision for, our own needs. Both children and workers will always be 'at risk', potentially or actually, while we live in a fallen world. We can be grateful that we will all be out of a job in heaven. Until then, if we want to make the possibility of transformation a reality, we need to work with change, both positive and adverse change, in an adaptive way by:

- Being a witness to children's worlds and finding witness/es for ourselves.
- Being aware of our fundamental needs from a theological and child-care perspective.
- Addressing the factors that enhance our resilience.

Conclusion

Children can be at risk due to a number of different factors operating at various levels. The greater the number and intensity of these factors, the higher the risk. This analysis may help focus attempts to identify children most at risk. It also provides a checklist of those elements that need to be present in any scheme of intervention. The resilience of some children should not disguise their basic need to love and be loved.

This is our challenge – the challenge to be Christ to one another, the challenge to really love one another as we love ourselves (Rom. 13:9), to honour one another with the 'hesed' love with which Christ honours us. So, while recognizing the usefulness of labels, categories and boxes, let us not constrain Christ, ourselves or the children. As Richard Cole, who is enjoying powerful transforming work with child soldiers in Sierra Leone, says, 'First we love and accept them, we hear and bear witness to them, *then* we assess them. We are just doing what Christ does for us. Only then will their lives (and ours) be changed.'

Note
1. Chapter 17 summarizes a typology of need developed over a period of 20 years in a cross-cultural context. It draws from the major theories and is consistent with a biblical perspective on childhood.

– Questions to Consider –

1 Describe the theoretical frameworks of Rutter, Lahad and Grotberg and how their models of understanding risk and resilience can be useful in practice.

2 Look at your project/organization, or a given example, and identify the key risk and resilience factors operating in practice.

3 Look through Barker's list of 11 risk factors and identify possible points of intervention and prevention.

CHAPTER 17

An Integrated Biblical and Theoretical Typology of Children's Needs[1]

Keith White

IF a child has lost, or is at risk of losing, consistent daily links, contact and bonds with his or her own birth family and kin, the following universal needs must be paramount in assessing the most appropriate potential setting to satisfy as many, if not all, of these needs.

The overriding need of every child is to be loved by, and to love, one or more significant adults. The five needs listed below can best be seen as elements or aspects of this process and relationship. If one or more of these is not met, the capacity of any child to experience and express love will be impaired. If none of these are met over a substantial period of a child's early years, the likelihood is that the child will be emotionally scarred and impaired.

Five needs that must be addressed if love is to grow

Security

Security is the primal need. Without security there is no safe base for exploration, relationships, play and development. Without security dysfunctional defence mechanisms will develop that prevent the child from experiencing love. In psychotherapeutic terms, this is Bowlby's 'secure base' (Bowlby, 1979). In biblical terms, we note that a safe place (from Eden to the ark, the promised land and the new Jerusalem) is the most fundamental image of salvation. Jesus comforts his disciples by promising that 'I am going there to prepare a place for you' (John 14:2).

No intervention, however well intentioned or resourced, will have any effect unless children know that they are safe. This need for safety can be met in many different ways. At Mill Grove, a Christian residential community in the United Kingdom caring for 'children at risk', safety is represented by an actual place that has remained constant for a hundred years, and by people who protect the children as their own.

All alternatives to, and substitutes for, a family must provide such security. It is possible in all settings – adoptive, foster and residential. However, the security of children in these microsystems will be jeopardized if there are poor mesosystems, exosystems and macrosystems. It is also possible for these microsystems to be dysfunctional because of internal conflict or inadequacies. No one type of setting guarantees security.

Significance

Children are people. They are individuals and cannot be treated or dealt with as if they were a group, numbers or statistics. Vital to their development and well-being is the assurance that they are infinitely precious as people – not because of something they have done or achieved, but because of who they are. Each child needs to know that at least one adult is committed to him unconditionally. This means that this adult is prepared to be his for life, and possibly even to lay down his or her life for him.

In biblical terms, this is a wonderful dimension of the whole experience of God and his grace described throughout the Scriptures. God is personally interested in us – not because of our merits or potential, but because of his heart and covenant love. The 'I/Thou' relationship is of eternal significance. It is at the heart of the gospel. It is the ultimate expression of unconditional commitment, in that Jesus Christ sealed the covenant by and through his death.

In theoretical terms, this is the essence of child development. The existence of a committed significant other is the sine qua non of 'good enough parenting', and the emotional health of the child depends in large measure on the quality of this relationship. In the field of childcare, this means that institutions, systems, rotas and training count for nothing unless there is a person with whom the child can have this relationship. The whole dynamic and structure of Mill Grove revolves around this axis. Consequently it is quite different from nearly all other residential establishments for children in the UK.

The challenge of identifying one or more adults unconditionally committed to a child is the primary task of any intervention. The difficulties of finding adults who will commit in this way and of defining and maintaining the relationships cannot be stressed enough. The vast majority of children have parents and kin who are committed in this way – the very existence of a life-long family name is a recognition of this bond. Separation from natural family is very threatening to a child's well-being.

An obvious response is adoption, but this is problematical in certain ways. Although there have been many successful cross-cultural adoptions around the world, they can lead to difficulties of identity, and in many parts of the world potential adoptive families are scarce. Assessment is crucial and time-consuming. Adoptive families need supportive mesosystems and exosystems and should not be assessed in isolation.

Foster care is increasingly popular worldwide, but there can be breakdowns and serial placements. Only rarely does fostering build in an unconditional commitment. (Foster care is therefore most appropriate when there is the prospect of a child being reunited with his or her own family.) Unless there is a permanent fostering arrangement (which is unusual and difficult), fostering is best seen as temporary, or as a complement to other interventions and systems.

Residential settings are many and varied. Large establishments such as refugee camps, asylums and boarding schools will be unable to provide unconditionally committed carers who can function in the place of parents and family. Smaller places, however, may be able to do so. They draw strength from the support of systems and networks of which they are a part. Mill Grove, for example, is a family community residence with a large natural extended family from different generations. It therefore provides children with the vital experience of grandparents, aunts, uncles, and so on – not just two foster parents or a retinue of care workers, as is the experience of many children in care.

The role of the local worshipping faith community is a vital element in the personal support system for all offering unconditional commitment.

Boundaries

Every child and human being needs boundaries if she is to feel safe and able to relate to others and develop appropriately. The term 'boundaries' encompasses rules, discipline and values.

In the Bible, we see the way in which God provides physical, moral, practical, sexual and spiritual boundaries for his people so that they can thrive. The purpose of these boundaries is to enable us to live as we were created to live and be at home in God's world. They provide a healthy setting for the development not only of individuals, but also of communities.

In childcare, the importance of firm and consistent boundaries is universally recognized. Boundaries can be represented in different ways. At Mill Grove we find that the best boundaries are 'lived' ones, and that they are appreciated and respected by children of all ages, backgrounds and faiths. The adults and peers in the child's life will communicate consistent moral and emotional boundaries by the way that they live – for example, by the way they relate to one another (including keeping marriage covenants), by their language and behaviour and by the way they honour promises.

It is important to realize that external boundaries, like rules and regulations, are no substitute for 'lived' boundaries. It is also important to be alert to the many ways in which boundaries can be transgressed consciously and unconsciously. Peer group bullying is one common example of the transgression of boundaries, and it is ever present in large group care settings. Changes of carer are likely to confuse boundaries in a child's mind. Continuity of boundaries between the birth family, culture, tradition, and the new setting is important. A change of culture, language and norms is likely to be detrimental to a child's development. Sometimes, however, appropriate boundaries may be new to children who are entering a care setting. These are not detrimental in themselves, and such an unavoidable change is offset by a caring relationship with a committed and consistent adult.

Community

The Bible recognizes that we are made for community and for relationships. Families are our starting point, but the norm is to find and make bonds beyond kith and kin. The biblical story is one of a community, or people, of God.

The importance of peer groups, play and neighbourhoods is often underestimated. In Britain, for example, the individual child tends to be seen in abstraction or simply as part of a family. Children need to be and to feel part of accepting communities, especially faith communities. Childcare cannot be divorced from the wider world of social relationships. Schools are a very significant aspect of 'community' for children.

The critical element here is the quality of the links between the child's microsystem and the exosystems and mesosystems. It is possible for the substitute caring system to be separated from the wider community. The danger is probably greatest in large residential establishments, which can tend to become cut off from the outside world. Once again, faith communities are a vital resource because they link and support the different systems.

The quality of the political, military and economic conditions of the macrosystem is one of the factors that determines the nature of the community, associations and relationships that are available to a child. Street children worldwide show how the desire for community can lead to the development of dysfunctional or dangerous relationships.

Creativity

Children are essentially creative; they are made in the image of God. If they are to fulfil their potential they must be given opportunities and encouragement to create, to make, to shape, to dance. The Scriptures testify to this aspect of humanity. We are to express ourselves with joy and variety in movement, music, work and play.

The ability and propensity to create are helpful indications of a child's emotional and mental state, as well as measures of the quality of the care they are receiving. Institutionalization is one of the big stumbling blocks in the way of creativity, as are poverty and deprivation. It is important that routine care and organization do not stifle play and self-expression. Education should not be conceived without reference to play and spontaneity. Creativity finds its ultimate expression in loving and being loved.

Conclusion

Although these needs are universal, the ways in which they are expressed and addressed will vary from culture to culture and from place to place. There is no panacea or single model of intervention guaranteed to meet them.

These needs can be used as a standard against which to assess the effectiveness of any proposed or existing form of childcare. It is possible to link them specifically with theoretical and professional frameworks, and also to the ideas of lay people from different faith perspectives. Although this chapter (and this book) has been written from the perspective of the Christian faith, the human needs and experiences highlighted above are universal.

Note
1. This typology has been developed over 20 years in the context of Mill Grove. It draws from the cross-cultural experiences of this community and from the major insights of psychoanalysis and psychotherapy. It uses the framework of Bronfenbrenner (see Chapter 5). In 1999, it was adopted by the Cutting Edge Conference Child Development Group as a standard for assessing the quality of models of intervention.

– Questions to Consider –

1 Provide an overview of the key factors which are important in assessing children's needs. Describe what the Bible helps us to understand about children's core needs.

2 Look at your own childhood development in the light of White's typology. How were your childhood needs met/not met, and how did this impact your development?

CHAPTER 18

The Effects of Failure to Meet Children's Needs

Susan Greener

As a father has compassion for his children, so the LORD has compassion for those who fear him. For he knows how we were made; he remembers that we are dust. (Ps. 103:13–14, NRSV)

BECAUSE of their small size and dependence, children are the most vulnerable members of the human race. The Bible encourages caregivers to care for little ones with the kind of compassion that God bestows on all of humanity. Yet many small ones are exposed to accidents, abuse, violence, disaster and danger, often experiencing significant loss and trauma. Despite adults' best efforts it is next to impossible to protect children from all stress, and many will encounter violence, illness, divorce, death or a natural disaster. For some children, trauma may involve a single, frightening incident, such as being in a severe accident. For others, stress is chronic, severe and often debilitating due to neglect, abuse, poverty and war. Childhood trauma occurs along a continuum, ranging from single events impacting children who come from stable, nurturing environments to the extreme situations where children have been severely harmed and live in constant chaos. Likewise, child neglect and abuse are a subset of childhood trauma, also occurring along a continuum in terms of severity, that specifically undermine the child's sense of security and trust.

Identifying traumatized children

An experience is defined as traumatic if it overwhelms the child, dramatically and negatively disrupting the stability of the child's inner world. In a very real sense, trauma throws the child 'off balance' and creates persistent coping responses that produce a new, but less functional, state of balance. This new, trauma-induced state of balance consumes much of the child's energy and is not particularly adaptive. In a sense trauma robs the child, channelling energies that are needed for normal development toward intensive coping behaviours (Perry and Pollard, 1998). Traumatic events include experiences such as sexual abuse, maltreatment, witnessing violence, disasters, medical problems and death (Perry, 1994). Trauma may directly involve the child, such as experiencing major surgery, or it may occur in the child's immediate environment, such as the death of a parent. Or it may be an event in the child's larger environment, such as witnessing the violence of war. In other words, trauma can occur at different levels, which may impact the child in different ways. Trauma is defined as an unexpected out-of-the-ordinary experience which causes distress and a sense of being out of control. The following characteristics all need to be present if a child (or adult) is to be diagnosed with post-traumatic stress disorder:

1. The child exhibits extreme traumatic stress accompanied by intense fear, horror or disorganized behaviour.

2. The child persistently re-experiences the traumatic event through repetitive play or recurring intrusive thoughts or dreams. The child may re-enact the event during playtime, talk about the event frequently or experience recurring dreams about the event.

3. The child avoids cues associated with the trauma. For example, if the child has witnessed a shooting, she may be upset not only by the sight of a gun, but also by any loud noise that resembles a gunshot. The fear becomes generalized and is triggered by a wider variety of stimuli.

4. The child experiences persistent physiological oversensitivity or over-arousal. A trauma reaction is designed to increase one's chance of survival. As a result of experiencing trauma, a child may become extra-vigilant and over-aroused, hunting for cues that signal imminent danger.

5. The signs and symptoms are present for more than one month following the traumatic event.

6. The child experiences clinically significant disturbances in functioning (Perry and Azad, 1999). The child may engage in soothing behaviours such as rocking, headbanging, or self-mutilation, which can produce an opioid-like (pain-killing or numbing) reaction in the brain (Perry and Pollard, 1998). The child may also experience depression, weight loss, an inability to concentrate, hyperactivity, sleeping problems, irritability or failure to thrive (Evans, 2000).

Children's vulnerability to trauma

Children's vulnerability to trauma is dependent on their personal characteristics, the nature of the event and the characteristics of the child's family and social support systems. Each individual child will have his own subjective perception of the event. Each child must assess how threatened he feels in the circumstances. His perception may be impacted by his previous experiences with traumatic events. Every child has a unique coping style and general level of anxiety. The impact of a traumatic event also depends on the child's sex and age. For example, going without parental touch for several weeks is not likely to bother an adolescent, but it would be very traumatic for an infant. Children under the age of six are more likely to respond to trauma by exhibiting regressive behaviour, fear, anxiety, restlessness, irritability and dependent or demanding behaviour due to their lack of coping skills. Children between the ages of six and twelve are generally better able to cope, but they may also show a lack of concentration, memory problems, learning difficulties, lack of spontaneity, passiveness, depression, aggression and demanding behaviour (Evans, 2000).

Each traumatic event has certain characteristics that will alter its impact. Although trauma occurs along a continuum, there are certain events that by consensus are considered to be traumatic. For example, we would expect a child who had witnessed the Rwandan genocide to be traumatized by the experience. The severity of an event can be assessed by asking the following questions: Was the child physically harmed or exposed to a situation in which he could have been harmed? Was the child in close proximity to threat? Was the child repeatedly exposed to the event? Was the event of long duration or did it occur many times over a long period of time?

It is important to consider the child's family and community context in evaluating the impact of trauma. Certain characteristics of the family and social system can lessen trauma's impact. For example, a calm, supportive and nurturing family, well supported in their community, will provide a stable, secure environment for the child struggling to cope with trauma. On the other hand, if the child's environment is chaotic and anxious with distant or absent emotional supports, the child is far more vulnerable to negative impact from trauma (Perry and Azad, 1999).

When the child receives no assistance from family or other persons, she may exhibit dissociation from the trauma. She will not react or talk about it, acting as if nothing has happened. Essentially this is a 'learned helplessness' reaction, in which the child gives up trying to elicit support from others. To the outsider, it may appear that the child was not bothered by the trauma and that everything is fine. The concept of learned helplessness explains the puzzlement of observers concerning the emotional non-reactivity, passivity and compliance of many abused children (Perry and Pollard, 1998). This passivity is not resilience. Dissociation is more common in females, whereas more aggressive, acting-out behaviours are more common in males, who may exhibit symptoms such as hyperactivity, delinquency, defiance, aggression or cruelty (Barkley, 1995; Perry and Pollard, 1998).

Dissociation protects the child from the pain of re-experiencing the trauma but, because it is successful in this respect, it has an addictive quality. It can become a primary coping mechanism whenever the child is under normal stress and can therefore inhibit, in the long term, the child engaging in relationships and activities of everyday living. Dissociation is linked to the development of long-term mental heath problems including DID (dissociate identity disorder) and PTSD (post-traumatic stress disorder)

How does trauma impact development?

Imagine a setting with a toddler and her mother sitting in a room full of strangers, waiting to be seen by a doctor. The toddler sees a box of toys in the corner and would like to go and play with them, but she has to pass by many strange adults to reach the box. The toddler steps away from her mother but keeps a hand on her mother's knee. She turns to look at her mother's face and the mother responds by smiling and gently encouraging the child to go ahead. The child looks at the toys again and at the room full of people. She takes a few steps forward, but then she runs back to her mother for comfort. After several false starts she goes to the toys, but she remains in eye contact with her mother every few moments to obtain a reassuring smile.

Experiencing new or stressful events is inevitable in the life of the child. As seen in the above example, optimal development allows the child to encounter new experiences while grounded in a safe, secure base. While the encounter takes place, the child needs to feel safe and nurtured. The caregiver needs to supervise the situation in a sensitive way so that the child is able to manage the new experience according to his individual needs and developmental stage. When a new experience is chaotic, extreme or mismatched to the developmental stage, development is disrupted. A key to healthy development and the appropriate development of coping skills is the match between the nature of the experience and the child's developmental capacities (Perry and Pollard, 1998). The sensitive caregiver knows her child well and is able to monitor experiences to create manageable encounters. What may be stressful for one child may not be for another, depending on that child's temperament, experience, sex and age.

These developmental challenges are partially due to actual changes in brain organization and development. By the age of three years the brain has reached about 90 per cent of its adult size, while the body is only about 15–18 per cent of its adult size. The child's brain is most plastic in the early years (Perry and Marcellus, 1997) to allow for maximum adaptability to experience. At eight months, the brain has more synaptic connections (links between brain cells) than at any other time of life as the child prepares to meet any and all new situations with maximum cognitive flexibility. The brain then begins to prune (or eliminate) these synaptic connections based on the child's experiences (Berk, 1999; Perry and Pollard, 1998). Children who have repeatedly suffered from traumas or neglect have less well developed synaptic junctions joining the two sides of the cortex of the brain. They therefore have greater problems thinking through complex ideas and integrating the different areas of their brain's function. Recent studies have shown that psychotherapy and good childcare can help the brain to regain some of these functions.

In other words, experience dictates brain structure and, by the age of three, almost all of a child's brain structures have been organized (Perry, 1999, 'Memories'). If a child lives in a neglectful environment, lacking stimulation, many synaptic connections will be lost. If a child lives in an abusive environment, the brain organization will be altered to cope with trauma. The goal is to maximize stimulation in order to preserve synaptic connections and to lay pathways for adaptive coping and problem-solving skills. Thus, brain development is guided by experience – the brain develops and modifies itself in response to life events and, when a stressful event is of sufficient duration, intensity or frequency, brain changes are not reversible.

To some degree, all organ systems in the body have a type of memory (Perry, 1999, 'Memories'). This memory allows the body to learn from threatening experiences and prepare for future encounters of similar danger. A traumatic experience activates many bodily systems and all parts of the brain. Thus the traumatic image is stored in memories throughout the body, but primarily in the limbic system of the brain (pre-verbal memory). This information is used to activate a fear response in similar circumstances to protect the child from future harm. However, this overgeneralization makes the child fearful of situations that are not truly threatening. For example, children who have experienced chronic abuse in their early years do not have true cognitive understanding as to why they may feel anxious or distressed when a caring adult touches them in a gentle manner (Perry, 1999, 'Memories'). Their bodily reaction to touch has stimulated memory that is not necessarily cognitive in nature and cannot be accessed through words/cognitions, but only through non-verbal feelings and creative/play experiences.

Abuse and neglect as trauma

Perhaps the most damaging type of childhood trauma involves parental neglect and abuse. The negative impact is so severe because healthy child development requires the existence of a nurturing, sensitive parent who will not only provide for the child's physical needs, but also create a safe, secure foundation for encountering the world. The family is the child's primary socializer, providing a context for learning coping and problem-solving skills that are necessary for life success. For the neglected and abused child that safe haven is tenuous, unpredictable or absent, and opportunities for learning adaptive life skills are negligible.

Although a variety of definitions of child abuse are used around the world, there are common dominant themes – these are well articulated in the legal definition used in the Philippines. Child abuse refers to the maltreatment, whether habitual or not, of the child, which includes any of the following:

- Psychological and physical abuse, neglect, cruelty, sexual abuse and emotional maltreatment

- Any act by deeds or words which debases, degrades or demeans the intrinsic worth and dignity of a child as a human being

- Unreasonable deprivation of his basic needs for survival such as food and shelter

- Failure to immediately give medical treatment to an injured child resulting in serious impairment of his growth and development or in his permanent incapacity or death (Lepiten, 1997).

Each of these types of abuse should be defined in turn. Physical abuse includes assaults on children that produce cuts, welts, bruises, burns, broken bones and other injuries as a result of punching, beating, kicking, biting, burning, shaking or otherwise harming a child. Sexual abuse includes inappropriate sexual comments, fondling of a child's genitals, intercourse, rape, sodomy, exhibitionism and other forms of exploitation such as forced involvement in prostitution or the production of pornographic material (Berk, 1999; *Child Abuse Prevention and Treatment Act* [CAPTA], 1996).

Physical neglect occurs when children live in conditions in which they are not given enough food, clothing or medical attention (taking into account the impoverished caregiver's capacity). Physical neglect also includes lack of supervision, refusal of or delay in seeking health care, abandonment, expulsion from the home or refusal to allow a runaway to return home. Emotional neglect involves marked inattention to children's needs for affection and emotional support, refusal of or failure to provide needed psychological care, spouse abuse in the child's presence and giving permission for the child to use drugs or alcohol (Berk, 1999; CAPTA, 1996).

Psychological abuse includes acts or omissions by caregivers that have caused or could cause serious behavioural, cognitive, emotional or mental disorders. This may involve extreme forms of punishment, ridicule, humiliation, blaming the child for the family's problems or terrorizing that damages the child's emotional, social or cognitive functioning. Because the damage caused by psychological abuse is internal, its existence is much more difficult to detect and prove (Berk, 1999; CAPTA, 1996).

Each of these definitions must be placed in cultural context. The values and standards of childcare vary greatly around the world, and these must be taken into consideration when evaluating a child's welfare. It must also be recognized that what may seem like neglect (failure to provide for a child's basic needs) may actually be related to extreme poverty that is outside the control of the caregiver. However, abuse or neglect that arises from poverty or ignorance is still damaging to a child's development.

The context of abuse and neglect

The child's individual qualities, as well as those of the parent, family, community and culture, all contribute to the child's vulnerability to neglect and abuse. Although abuse and neglect occur at all socio-economic levels, additive effects are often seen for children who live in poverty. Domestic violence, abuse, parental mental disorder and lack of access to resources are all more common for children living in poverty (Trawick-Smith, 1997).

The affected child is more likely to have been born prematurely, to be ill, difficult in temperament, inattentive and hyperactive or to have other developmental problems (Berk, 1999). In other words, these children are generally more difficult to parent and require more emotional resources than a highly stressed parent may be able to provide. If there are multiple children in a family, often the most vulnerable one is targeted for abuse while the others are relatively untouched by it.

Abusive parents are more likely to suffer from a psychological disturbance, to abuse alcohol or drugs or to have been a childhood victim of abuse. They are more likely to believe in the effectiveness of harsh discipline or to desire to meet their own unmet emotional needs through their children. They are often ignorant of child development and thus have unreasonable behavioural expectations for the child's age (e.g., an infant should be able to control crying). Abusive parents are likely to be very young with little education. They tend to reside in unstable, stressful family situations, which minimize the quality of parental care (Berk, 1999). Neglectful parents are more likely to be depressed with many life stresses, such as high marital conflict and low social support. The depressed parent lacks the energy and motivation to meet the child's needs. Children of depressed parents are likely to exhibit symptoms of depression as well (Berk, 1999).

Abused children tend to live in family situations characterized by low income, poverty, homelessness, marital instability, social isolation and domestic violence. The families are more likely to be large with closely spaced children and overcrowded living conditions. The family's instability is often characterized by frequent moves, which lessens the likelihood of connections to social supports. The family schedule is likely to be highly disorganized, lacking structure and clearly understood rules for the children (Berk, 1999). These types of family situations not only set the stage for abuse and neglect, but also disrupt all areas of development.

Abused and neglected children tend to live in communities that are socially isolated with few safe places to play and lacking supports, such as childcare, educational opportunities, recreation or churches. Parents in these communities are more dissatisfied with their community situation, describing it as a lonely place to live, where people do not care for one another (Berk, 1999). The cultural context is likely to be one that approves of physical force and violence for problem solving, which may be modelled through community violence, brutality by those in authority or war.

In spite of these general predictors, however, it is vitally important to remember that abuse also occurs in apparently stable family situations, with educated parents, community connections and supports. The above descriptions may be typical, but they are by no means the only possible scenarios for abuse. Conversely, it is also essential to bear in mind that parents who have to deal with all of the above stressors are not necessarily abusive.

The impact of abusive childhood experiences on development

As is the case with any potential trauma, the timing of the experience is critical. A developmental matrix showed that severe trauma occurring before age four resulted in a much higher probability of pre-psychotic and psychotic outcomes for affected children. Children who experienced stability during their first three years of life but who were traumatized later in childhood tended to have emotional and anxiety symptoms that were more similar to those seen in adults (Perry, 1994). These differences in impact based on the age of the child reflect the importance of 'critical periods' in development (Perry and Pollard, 1998).

A critical period is one in which optimal learning or achievement of a development task takes place. For example, infants learn bonding and attachment behaviours over the first 36 months of life. If that process is severely disrupted, it is difficult for these children to establish meaningful relationships later on. Thus, early intervention in abusive or neglectful situations is most effective before the brain is completely developed (Perry and Marcellus, 1997) and negative coping patterns are established. A child living in a situation of chronic abuse and neglect needs to make significant mental readjustments (Berk, 1999) and, after these patterns are established, they are difficult to change.

Abused and neglected children are very likely to experience developmental delays in all domains of functioning: cognitive, physical, social and emotional. These delays are a direct consequence of the poor relationship between the child and the caregiver. The bond between child and caregiver is the major mode of developing children in all domains – to learn language, social behaviours, emotional competence and for intellectual stimulation (Perry, 1999, 'Bonding'). When this relationship is poor, as in the case of abuse or neglect, the child is deprived of the major avenue for socialization and stimulation.

Abused and neglected children are likely to have poorer cognitive and social/emotional skills, including a low tolerance for frustration, poor emotional control and poor school performance. Ironically, some abused children become hypersensitive at reading the non-verbal cues of others. These children have spent so much of their early years in a low state of fear that they are focused on non-verbal cues that may indicate imminent abuse (Perry, 1999, 'Memories'). The child is literally functioning in 'fight or flight' mode to increase the likelihood of survival.

Maltreated children are essentially rejected by those who should care the most for them. This rejection severely disrupts trust in adults, making it difficult for abused or neglected children to form intimate relations with others. Children with disrupted attachment and bonding experiences are more likely to experience developmental delays. If chronic maltreatment took place during infancy, they may also exhibit odd eating behaviours, because the feeding relationship is a fundamental part of the bonding experience. They may also show soothing behaviours (e.g., rocking, headbanging) that are an attempt to release pain-killing chemicals in the brain.

Ironically, they may also display indiscriminate attachment, seeking affection from any and all adults. An uninformed observer may perceive these children as being especially affectionate, but in reality the children are seeking security wherever they can find it without regard to appropriate boundaries. Children with attachment problems may also show inappropriate modelling of abusive behaviour and aggression (Perry, 1999, 'Bonding'; Trawick-Smith, 1997).

Traumatized children in context

Children need to be recognized as holistic beings who live in a specific context. Although a traumatized child may have obvious physical needs, equal attention needs to be given to their psychological, emotional, social and developmental needs (Evans, 2000). All of these areas of function are important, especially as they interact to determine a child's overall well-being. It is especially important to look at the child in the context of her family, community and culture. Every child needs some type of social interaction to learn, thrive and heal, because relationship with others is the foundation of socialization and cultural continuity. If the traumatized child can be placed in a secure, nurturing environment that is consistent with her social and cultural values, she is going to heal more quickly. And the healing of traumatized children is critical for the community. When a community allows children to be traumatized it is essentially compromising its future, because traumatized children are less able to contribute to social survival.

However, trauma affects not only the children, but also the systems designed to support and socialize the young. Healing is more difficult in situations where these support systems are completely disrupted. For example, in contexts of organized violence, such as the ethnic conflicts in Eastern Europe and sub-Saharan Africa, many if not all social supports are interrupted. The violence has physical impact on children in terms of mortality, disease, injury, disability, malnutrition, lack of health systems, deteriorated living conditions and lack of clean water and waste disposal. Moreover, many children are unaccompanied and, as witnesses to extreme violence, they are likely to suffer from severe psychological trauma. In this situation, there is a complete lack of socialization taking place and children do not have the opportunity to develop practical skills and academic proficiency (Evans, 2000). Entire families and villages may be displaced, living as refugees, most often in less than optimal circumstances. Thus, traumatic experiences and their implications need to be conceptualized in terms of the interaction between the victim and the environment (Nader, Dubrow and Hudnall Stamm, 1999).

Even in the midst of turmoil, extended family and community can provide stability, continuity and tradition. When the child remains in the family and community context, coping strategies and socialization techniques that are used within the child's culture can be maintained. Trauma is lessened when the immediate family and community are still together, maintaining familiar structures and practices (Evans, 2000). It is important to use culturally appropriate personal support consistent with the child's culture and customs, preferably within their community. The continuance of traditional rituals, celebrations and practices helps to maintain or re-establish a sense of identity – not just for the child, but potentially for a disrupted community as well (Blackburn, 2000).

The key is providing as much stability and security as possible for the traumatized child. This may necessitate a change in the child's immediate environment, as well as intensive therapeutic intervention and compassionate care. However, the wise interventionist creates this healing atmosphere by capitalizing on the strengths and supports that are available to the child within their familiar context. It is critical to re-establish a sense of safety and trust in the world to provide a foundation for faith in a compassionate God who cares for all (Beacham, 1994) and is 'a father to the fatherless' and who 'gives families to the lonely' (Ps. 68:5, 6; Living Bible).

– Questions to Consider –

1 Explain how traumatic experiences impact the child's physical, spiritual, cognitive, social and emotional development.

2 Develop a fictional case study of a traumatized child. Describe the child's behaviour and explain why it concerns you. Describe the child's interactions with environmental factors and how they have either contributed to the trauma or protected the child from further harm.

3 Evaluate each type of neglect and abuse in the cultural context in which you work. What types of caregiver behaviours would indicate each type of abuse? How do cultural values and expectations impact the definitions of each type of abuse?

4 One of the foundations of spiritual development states that a trusting relationship with a caring adult during early childhood provides the foundation for a future faith relationship with a loving God. Describe the potential impact of child neglect and abuse on future faith development. How would one design an intervention for abused/neglected children to re-establish trust as the foundation for Christian faith?

– CHAPTER 19 –

Exploring and Releasing Children's Strengths, Gifts and Potential

Josephine-Joy Wright

Lord,
When they scribble on the walls, please help me to see a rainbow.
And when I've said something a hundred times
Please give me the patience to say it a hundred times more!
And on those particularly annoying days when I tell them to act their age

Please help me to remember that they are!
And while we're on the subject of age, Lord, when I begin to lose my temper
Help me to remember to act mine!
And through it all, Lord – the fingerprints and runny noses, messy rooms and
    unrolled toilet paper
Destroyed videotapes and broken knick-knacks – please help me to remember
    this:
Some day, these will be the days I will long to have back again.

(by a mother of three, in Morgan and Kuykendall, 1997)

THIS prose poem echoes the thoughts and feelings prevalent both in parents and
in workers with children in so many capacities. When leaders of organizations in
the field of childcare meet together, their conversations often seem to turn to
financial budgets, statistics, resource issues and training requirements. Yet if you
take these same leaders aside and ask them why they do what they do, they light
up with eagerness and childlike enthusiasm to speak of their calling or of the
child who changed their life. They speak of children's potential, their courage,
their joys and the changes that they have made.

This chapter sets aside the statistics and organizational and theoretical issues of
many of the previous chapters in order to help us think afresh about how we can
explore children's strengths and vulnerabilities with them, thus identifying their
needs and releasing their potential to grow.

Several contributors to this book have presented various models of the basic
needs which children are known to have – from empirical childcare research,
field observations and biblical truths and directives. All of these are summed up
in the need to give and receive love effectively, to come into relationship with
others and to come into a relationship with Christ. Crabb (1997) sees such
relating, or 'connectedness', as being the key factor in enabling people to be
healed and transformed:

> There is a power in the life of every Christian waiting to be released – a power
> that can lead to further and deeper change, a power that can help someone else
> to join more intimately to the heart of Christ, the power to heal soul-wounds.
> That power is released by connecting with the hearts and souls of other people
> and allowing God's grace to flow freely through us to them.

Zurheide and Zurheide (2000), in their book on accepting children for who they
are, talk about the importance of grace in our attitudes towards children and its
crucial role in enabling children's potential to be revealed and fulfilled. Crabb
(1997) speaks of how when we operate in grace towards one another and connect
together, God's grace can also flow freely and transform our lives. As Crabb says,
God's grace working within us 'does not fix us or pressure us. He does whatever
it takes to reveal himself to us, which may include probing deeply into our messy
hearts or insisting that we do something that we really do not want to do. But the
core purpose is always the same; not to repair or exhort us but to bring us into a
fuller appreciation of his beauty'.

This picture provides us with a model of how to explore children's gifts and
potential, how to see them with Christ's eyes and with his grace – not as
problems or, conversely, as accolades of successful ministry – as God's children.
This sense of wonder, of mystery and of the grace of God expressed in the lives
of children is illustrated so beautifully in Kimball's (2000) *These Things I Wish for*

You. Kimball muses on his children's potential for pain and possibilities as he urges them to become the people God envisioned them to be. As he ponders the curious eccentric characters of their community with his children, he cajoles them to:

> Heed the old stories and become a character yourself. Throw your hat in the air and let out a whoop when you're feeling good. Jump on horseback just because you've never done it before. Follow a swarm of bees all day just to see where they hole up. Live life for the pure joy of it and let others stand by the side of the road, watching you gallop by, holding on for dear life.

Kimball expresses concern that his children will have their potential defined for them in academic and social 'boxes' and thus lose the essence of their gifts as children. In the business of our work with children there is a danger that we could do the same, rather than discovering and delighting in our children's gifts.

What do children need to be able to discover and release their potential?

Morgan and Kuykendall (1997) speak of parents/carers needing to provide children with nine characteristics/types of love:

- security
- affirmation
- belonging
- discipline
- guidance
- respect
- play
- independence
- hope.

Looking through this list, one can also see it as a list of the holistically healthy child's strengths and gifts. Children's gifts, vulnerabilities and potential span all the primary areas of development: physical, behavioural, intellectual, emotional, spiritual, moral, social, and so on. When we work with children it is vital that we look with them for their areas of strengths and potential as well as enabling them to become comfortable and honest with their vulnerabilities. It is vital to encourage children to discover a delight in themselves as they are, created by God, as well as in what they can become.

Acknowledging children's gifts and potential

One of the most powerful areas in which we are able to bear witness to children's gifts and their willingness to make themselves vulnerable is in their prayers. Their approach to and resultant strengths in prayer often reflect their approach to other areas of their life. Their vulnerability is their strength, and adults need to treasure and nurture it as such. Looking at some of these approaches in more detail, Fuller (1998) explored with children and adults what makes children's prayers so effective. She noticed how children fundamentally need to feel listened to, respected and honoured for their alternative, non-adult view of the world. As Erdich (1995) stated, 'A child is fortunate who feels witnessed as a person outside relationships with parents, by another adult.'

If children are given such witnesses, hopefully by those around them as well as, fundamentally, by God, then they can become our teachers and our instruments of healing as well as recipients of care. Fuller found that children's prayers were characterized by the following:

1. Having a child-like faith, which sees the impossible as possible (Heb. 11:6), and which enables us to enter the kingdom of heaven (Matt. 18:3). Such faith is exemplified by Jabez who, despite his name which means 'pain' (in biblical times the meaning of a person's name was in effect a prophecy about their future), prayed to God, 'Oh that you would bless me indeed and enlarge my territory' (1 Chr. 4:9–10). He refused to be constrained and defined by his past. Children so often bear witness to this attitude in their prayers. We need to affirm rather than rationalize such faith, in order to allow children to dream and hope – it is their strength and gift to other children as well as to adults themselves.

2. Having hearts of incredible grace and forgiveness and compassion (Matt. 9:36), they often exhibit tremendous love, loyalty and care, which can be a blessing but which can also open them up to abuse.

3. Trusting in God's provision.

4. Having forgiving hearts that keep short accounts, and believing that God will cleanse and heal.

5. Praying simply, in a straightforward and honest manner (Matt. 6:7–8).

6. Wanting to be active participants in effecting positive changes, wanting to help.

7. Hearing God speak and being able to own and enjoy this gift, uncluttered by adult rationalization or social nuances or spiritual jargon and concepts.

Such characteristic strengths and potential vulnerabilities are often seen in children despite horrendous abuse and trauma. Somewhere in the darkness there is a fragment of hope. For many children, however, that fragment is so battered they feel death wooing them into further disconnection – not just from themselves and others, but from God and life itself. Our challenge is to help them to reclaim that hope and thus to reclaim their strengths and potentials, which give them impossible visions, startling love and integrity. As one of the children who I share my life with says, 'I used to mainline drugs, now I mainline God. He speaks, I do it, and wow! Much more amazing things happen than ever happened when I took drugs. I wish adults would come inside and believe. Maybe it's too simple for them.' I often think that this young person speaks a sad truth into the adult world. We try to make life so complex and, in doing so, we miss the essence of connectedness and, fundamentally, the essence of life itself.

How can we recognize, restore and renew children's strength and potential with them? How can we hear their voice?

It is essential to recognize that children have voices to which we must listen. We should acknowledge all the facets of a child's personality and build on their strengths as we build relationships with them. We must be willing to be relationship-focused, rather than just task-focused. We must ask children for their responses and ideas – and expect replies. We ought to be aware of and work with children's varying experiences with emotions. C. Goleman, in Stroop (1998), speaks of how many parents have ignored children's feelings, not taken them seriously or have been disrespectful of them. We need to model Christ to children so that they can in turn model him to each other and to the world. Children's strengths and potential can be recognized, given a voice and helped to grow better if children are:

1. Helped to understand and name their emotions, and those of others.
2. Helped to understand the basis of decision-making.
3. Taught by example how to manage and effectively release their feelings (Stroop, 1998).
4. Taught to express ideas clearly and appropriately.
5. Helped to recognize their pattern of working with their worlds and how to change their unhelpful ways of being.
6. Mentored and coached by people who enjoy the child's personality and culture and are aware of their own issues (Collins, in press).

Although Stroop applies the adult Myers-Briggs personality test rather globally and generalizes perhaps inappropriately across ages and cultures, he does present some interesting ideas on key principles for working with children as individuals with different personality traits. He urges adults to try to understand the way the child works with his world because of his particular personality type and to develop ways of working with these traits, rather than in conflict with them. This would help the child to see and believe in herself as God does, rather than condemning herself for her vulnerabilities.

In general, personality tests have a great many problems and are questionable in terms of their validity and reliability in cross-cultural and multicultural settings. Their use is particularly problematic with children who have not had most of their basic needs met or appropriate learning opportunities. The value of Stroop's work comes in his challenge to us to look again at children and to see them for their potential as Christ does – not as problems or profiles, but as blessings. The challenge for those who train workers with children and young people is, 'for us to be vessels, so that such workers can encounter God's heart for children and young people, so that they too catch the vision for God's calling on their lives' (G. Cannings, 2001, personal communication). Doing this will mitigate against worker burnout and enable both workers and children to explore and realize their vulnerabilities and gifts, their calling and potential, thus releasing both to be a blessing to one another and to God through prayer and other ministries.

A prayer of blessing

Lord, you took children into your arms,
Loving and blessing them.
Help me to love and bless children as you did –
My own and those in my church, school and neighbourhood.
Help me to be more like them, in trust, compassion and openness.
Restore in me a child-like faith and a clean heart.
Give me your eyes to see them,
To see the potential You've put within them,
And the unique qualities each is gifted with.
In Jesus' Name, Amen. (Fuller, 1998)

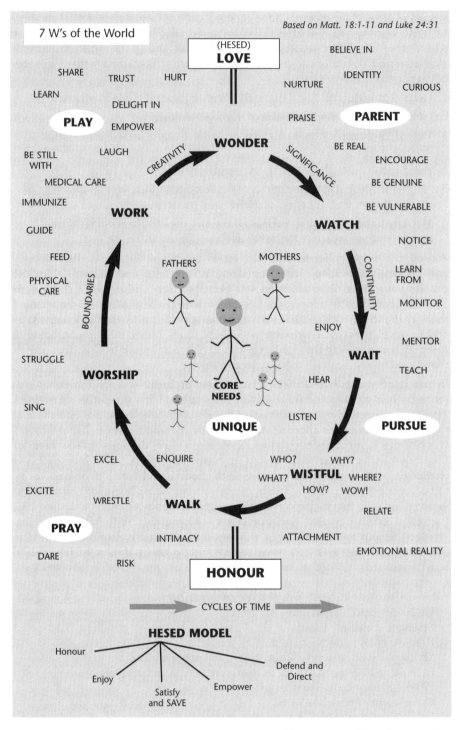

Figure 1: Seven W's of the world: How to enter and be with a child in their world, thus providing their needs and releasing their potential

– Questions to Consider –

1 How does the Bible challenge us to see children's gifts and potential? How do you translate this challenge into your own practice?

2 Give examples from your own practice, or from other projects with which you are familiar, of how children's strengths, gifts and potential can be recognized and released.

3 How does God recognize and release your own 'child within'? How does this affect your work with children?

Putting What You Have Learned Into Practice: Risk and Resilience

Profiles of Children and Projects

THE child and project profiles, found in Part Eight, describe a cross-section of 'at risk' children around the world and the various types of assistance that can be offered to them. Reading through these profiles will enable you to put into practice the various topics covered in Part Three, 'Risk and Resilience'. These case studies allow us to look inside the worlds of the children whom we are discussing and seeking to empower more effectively. Workers and children from around the world provide these superb case studies of children in different situations.

When reading the case studies or visiting projects it will also be useful to consider the programme(s) with which you are familiar and consider:

- What are the similarities and differences between the situations and needs of the children and the risk factors involved?
- What is the project doing to address the root causes of why the child is 'at risk'?
- How are children being listened to and involved in decisions that affect them?
- What can you learn from this for your own context?

– PART FOUR –

Holistic Mission to Children

Introduction THIS *textbook is intended to be holistic. Generally, the Christian approach is implicit – a synthesis of Christian principles and practice and secular research and practice. Sometimes, however, our faith needs to be explicit. This section looks at holistic mission at both the global level and at the level of the individual child.*

Paul Stephenson and Ros Besford critically evaluate the historical and current perspectives on the churches' ministry to children and their families in community – globally, nationally and locally. Patrick McDonald analyses the practical and spiritual implications, lessons and responsibilities for the current practice of the church (including Christian organizations/missions). Chapter 22, by Andrew Tomkins, reviews the scriptural, social, cultural and biomedical basis for the design of child development programmes in Christian organizations from a socio-medical angle. Dan Brewster gives a global overview of 'children at risk' because they have not heard the good news, in what he has coined the '4/14 window'. Then, in Chapter 24, Wanda Parker asks what place the child has in the church. Keith White rediscovers children at the heart of mission in Chapter 25 and, finally, Glenn Miles looks at what the Bible says about why children suffer. Poems by Coleen Houlihan and other young people encapsulate the pain and suffering of searching for the love and affirmation which every young person needs in order to grow into herself and find freedom.

Glenn Miles

– CHAPTER 20 –

The Churches' Ministry to Children and Their Families

Ros Besford and Paul Stephenson

OVER the past 2,000 years, approaches to childcare have changed dramatically. The evolution of childcare, both within the church and beyond, can be linked closely to emerging social constructions of childhood and theological perspectives on charity. Throughout this period, the church and Christian activists have played a role in developing childcare ministries. Arguably, the world-views and doctrines of different denominations and sects of the Christian church, together with post-Enlightenment thinking, have played a hugely significant role in determining the history of childcare. Particular perspectives on sin, morality, salvation, dispensationalism and eschatology provide the motivation and assumptions that influence church work with children both historically and in the present day.

This chapter provides an overview of how Christians have led the way in caring for children and, crucially, in changing social policies for the good of those living in poverty. This historical survey helps us then to identify the way in which the changing definitions of 'children' and childhood have influenced childcare methods around the world.

Our focus here is primarily on the work of Western social reformers. This is not to suggest that these activists had the monopoly on defining childhood and approaches to childcare. It is true to say, however, that many of them were driven by their desire to serve God – and this in turn led to changes in national (and international) policy and practice. These developments became embedded in approaches to childcare, many of which were transported to other cultures by missionaries who were equally driven by their own theology and by that same desire to serve God – in *all* nations.

Theological perspectives and approaches to childcare

It is clear that children had a significant place in Jesus' ministry. It was a child who enabled Jesus to perform the miracle of the feeding of the five thousand (John 6:9), and another child who exemplified humility – a quality essential for entering the kingdom of heaven (Matt. 18:1–3). The New Testament instructs Christians to care for children. Ephesians 6:4 tells parents not to exasperate their children, but to bring them up in the training and instruction of the Lord. Verses 1–3 of the same chapter remind children of their own responsibility to obey their parents in the Lord. In his first letter to Timothy, Paul makes it clear that those who hold office in the church must have good relationships with their children and families (1 Tim. 3:4–5, 12). After all, if the deacons and leaders do not work for mutual respect and trust in their own families, how can they expect to develop this in the church? James provides us with another reminder of the value of children:

> Religion that God our Father accepts as pure and faultless is this: to look after orphans and widows in their distress . . . (Jas. 1:27)

James' instruction is nothing new – the same message is found woven throughout the Scriptures – in Exodus, Deuteronomy, the Psalms and Isaiah.

In Roman times, caring for the children of the poor was an integral part of the life of the Christian community. McDonald and Garrow (2000, p. 58) cite the example of one Roman church that fed over 3,000 hungry people and another that cared for 1,500 widows. This tradition of self-sacrifice and serving the vulnerable carried on through the Middle Ages in much of Western Europe. Those living in monasteries and convents saw it as their duty to care and provide for those who received little or no care and support in their own communities.

Subtle differences in theological perspectives gave rise to different motivations and approaches to childcare. Around the time of the Reformation, it was believed in Catholic societies across Western Europe that certain sacraments – for example baptism – were a guarantee of salvation. This meant that those of a philanthropic nature were duty-bound to look after those abandoned or orphaned children – if for no other reason than to save their young charges from eternal damnation. These children were often cared for in foundling hospitals, where few questions were asked and the process of admittance was altogether anonymous.

At the same time, the growth of Protestantism in England fuelled a desire to care for poor children. This movement was born not so much out of pity for their souls, but out of a desire to 'impose a semblance of virtuous conduct upon the world' (Pullan, 1988). At that time the foundling hospitals so common in France and Italy would have seemed like too much of an open invitation to give up the fight against sin – they provided a 'get-out' clause for those who were unable to face up to the consequences of their actions. People could dump children in these hospitals and not have to care for them themselves.

This split between Protestant and Catholic approaches to children who, through no fault of their own found themselves in difficult circumstances, begins to clarify the origins of the different approaches to childcare adopted by Christian and secular groups. To gain a greater understanding of this wider picture, we need to consider the dichotomy of the eighteenth-century social construction of childhood. The 'child' was defined in two very different ways. On the one hand were those who saw children as inheritors of original sin, and on the other was the optimism of those who believed that the child epitomized all that was pure and innocent.

John Wesley was one who held the former view. He argued that in the best interests of the child, parents should:

> Break their wills betimes. Begin this work before they can run alone, before they can speak plain, perhaps before they can speak at all. Whatever pain it costs, break the will if you would not damn the child. . . . Break his will now, and his soul shall live, and he will probably bless you for all eternity. (James et al., 1998)

Another fervent evangelical of the day, Hannah More, warned that, in the future, society would be subject to 'grave descents on the rights of youth, the rights of children'. She believed that in order to achieve a settled, ordered society, children needed to be taught that they were 'sinful, polluted creatures' (Hendrick, 1994, p. 23). This message gained popularity not only among evangelicals, but also among the upper classes, who were distinctly unsettled by the political and social unrest evident in France and parts of Britain at the time. This view of children as those who harboured potentially dark forces progressed through to Victorian times, where notions of strict obedience and the idea that 'children should be seen and not heard' were propagated, in part through stories and songs that advocated an image of 'gentle Jesus, meek and mild'.

Throughout the eighteenth and nineteenth centuries, it was often evangelical Christians who took the lead in working with poor children. Thomas Coram, for example, created the Foundling Hospital to care for abandoned and orphaned children in the poorest parts of London. Thomas Barnardo was another philanthropist who initially began his work in order to convert the street children he found in Britain's capital city. According to one biographer:

> He had entered the work for missionary purposes to fight a wage with "London sin and vice", to pluck souls from the flames. (Rose, p. 35)

After being faced with the reality of poverty in the city, Barnardo's emphasis shifted to helping the poor preserve some degree of self-respect. Significantly, such Christian work with poor children recognized their intrinsic worth and dignity. It placed a value on these children that society failed to measure. By the time Barnardo died in 1905, he had helped over 60,000 children – thanks in part to his policy of never turning a child away.

Another colossus who played an invaluable part in improving the welfare of many poor children and their families across Britain was Lord Shaftesbury. Like Barnardo, he began his 'ragged schools' in an attempt to 'convert [potential] criminals to Christianity' (Walvin, 1982, p. 116). However, Shaftesbury's work went beyond simply tackling the outward signs of poverty. Through his work both in lobbying government and working practically in poor communities, British welfare policy was changed. This meant that thousands of families would be better off and better able to support their younger members. Shaftesbury devoted his life to working with the poorest of the poor – from chimney sweeps to flower girls – and he was responsible for creating a number of acts and legislation to protect vulnerable children.

Of course, the list is endless. We could include Edward Rudolf, founder of the Children's Society, who began his mission as a Sunday school teacher but was shocked by the numbers of children living and working in the streets of London. Or we could include Elizabeth Fry, the Quaker who set up a school inside one of London's worst prisons for the children of some of the most notorious inmates. Like the work of Shaftesbury, Fry's actions had a far-reaching impact in that they led to the review of the English prison service.

Compulsory education

An alternative view of children and childhood to that proposed by the evangelicals emerged concurrently during the seventeenth century. John Locke published *Some Thoughts Concerning Education* in 1693. This influential document presented childhood as a time of innocence, before the corrupting influences of the world had sullied the inherent purity that was incarnate in the young child.

In Britain, romantics such as the poet William Blake (*Songs of Innocence*, 1789) advocated education for all children, as a process yielding useful and fulfilled adults. The Sunday School Movement, spearheaded by the likes of Robert Raikes, in addition to teaching stories and lessons from the Bible, encouraged children from poor communities to learn how to read and write. Many clergy caught this vision, and churches began to educate young people in Sunday schools aimed at working children who were unable to go to school during the week. In 1870, the Elementary Education Act made education free and compulsory – perhaps satisfying the demands of both parties: those who felt that children needed to be tamed and controlled, and those who wanted to see children reach their full potential as 'useful' members of society.

Compulsory education was to have a significant effect on the construct of the child. Childhood came to be identified as a time that was entirely distinct from adulthood. It was assumed that removing children from the adult world of work somehow made them 'innocent', and thus absolved them of many significant responsibilities. The structures and examinations within the compulsory, formal education system also made it possible to quantify the development of a child. This meant that what was 'normal' could be distinguished from what was not. This idea is still prevalent today in the works of developmental psychologists such as Piaget, Freud and Bruner, who set out definite stages of development which must be passed through in order to become a well-rounded, fully developed person.

Contemporary Western childhood

In contemporary Western culture, the carefree, safe, secure and happy model of childhood is in the ascendancy. The media make much out of the adult nostalgia for childhood. The glorification of adolescent behaviour and Peter Pan complexes merge in television programmes such as the British hit show 'Men Behaving Badly'. Peers celebrate 'childlike' behaviour. Adulthood becomes an extension of childhood as the demand for revivals of recent history sates a need to relive an unburdened past. Freudian journeys of self-discovery, where childhood becomes the map to our present context, influence current psychoanalysis. Childhood has become a Holy Grail – a time not to be touched and tampered with. Children now inhabit a world in which they have freedom to express themselves, but they live in a highly regulated space. Reified as both innocent and potentially evil should they 'fall amongst thieves', images of children have become 'emblematic' of a sentimentalized vision of childhood. Children's functions within the family no longer include responsibility, decision-making and productivity. Children have become a luxury, and perhaps also a right. Parents view children as an expression of future hope and fulfilment. Society sees them as the 'carrier of futurity' (James, et al., 1998, p. 128).

Cross-cultural missions and children

The shifting views of childhood and children are not, of course, bound to a specific part of the world (in this case Western Europe and North America). Cross-cultural mission activity brought many of these concepts of childhood to remote parts of the world. The Apostle Paul set the pattern for mission work in attempting to focus on gospel truths and values as a prime motivator rather than on sociological ideals and cultural challenges.

The theological struggles and cultural biases that defined early Christianity were not short-lived. Even now, mission work continues to fall into the same traps. Throughout the centuries since Paul's time, missionaries have brought Christ and their own culture into every country on earth. Along with the gospel message came the more practical expressions of faith. From the fifteenth century on, missions were often set up along with hospitals, schools and orphanages. The numbers of children that have passed through these institutions cannot be counted. However, we can safely say that many of these children found themselves living dual lives that required them to step out of the roles they played as workers, carers and informal learners in their communities as they stepped into formal education, or the ordered institutional settings of orphanages or boarding schools – perhaps learning a new language, dress code and values system along the way.

Such schooling and care brought with them a package of culturally defined assumptions about childhood. These were shaped and changed over the centuries by an intricate interplay between theological interpretations of how to raise children (Proverbs, Ephesians, Wesley, More), the perceptions of childhood defined by the Enlightenment thinkers (Locke, Blake, Rousseau [*Émile*, 1762], et al.) and a growing body of scientific thinking about children and their development (Piaget, Bruner, Freud, Rogers).

These institutions left a new generation with an identity crisis, as many had made a 'mechanical confession' (Ellsberg, 1991) of Christianity. They either rejected the 'uncivilized' values of their families and communities – or were rejected by them.

Mahatma Ghandi proved to be a strong critic of Western missionaries in India. He was pained by their lack of humility and their intolerance. But what grieved him most was that the missionaries missed the essence of Christ's teaching. 'Confuse not,' said Ghandi, 'Jesus' teaching with what passes as modern civilisation and pray do not do unconscious violence to the people with whom you cast your lot. It is no part of that call, I assure you, to tear up the life of the people of the East by its roots' (Ellsberg, 1991).

Contemporary cross-cultural missions

Several generations on, 60 per cent of Christians live in the 'two-thirds world': 'the centre of Christianity has shifted southward' (*Newsweek*, 16 April 2001, p. 62). Countries that were once considered Christian homelands have become the mission territories of the new millennium. Christianity has become increasingly 'Africanized' or synchretized or culturally adapted to the local context. In sub-Saharan Africa, 1,200 new churches are launched each month (*Newsweek*, 16 April 2001, p. 66). Mission work is now two-way. Missionaries visiting the North focus on rekindling the spiritual fervour that could ignite a revival. Missionaries travelling to the South receive training that calls for partnership, participation, cultural sensitivity and an ability to listen and learn.

Viva Network estimates that the Christian movement worldwide helps more than 20 million children through 25,000 workers. This mix of local church, parachurch and international organizations provides concrete evidence that Christians continue to build on the legacy of the past. Those expressions of care are now increasingly localized. The contemporary Shaftesburys and Barnardos are more likely to be found working in the slums of Mexico City or on the streets of Mumbai. Their ministries may be more rooted and culturally sensitive than those that Ghandi railed against.

Following in the footsteps of their predecessors, cross-cultural missions continue to work with children. One of the most popular callings for Western missionaries is to children on the street. These missionaries no longer see these children as having the potential for evil as did their historical evangelical counterparts. Rather, they see them as innocent victims of a fallen world. Many seek to rescue them and restore their childhood. But this activity itself carries a lingering assumption that a childhood can be re-offered to these children like a package – a place to stay, education and basic healthcare. Is this transferable package all that is needed for a happy childhood?

The Western sentimentalization of childhood influences the way that current Christian ministries work with children. Promotional materials depict 'normal' children as those laughing and being schooled. Conversely, we know that pictures of those on the street or working depict a 'deviant' or 'abnormal' child. Is this how Jesus saw children? Can Christians working with children find any key principles that provide a Christ-centred concept of childhood and children to inform their programmes and practice?

Conclusion

When telling the history of how childhood became defined as a separate stage of human existence, the unheard voice is that of the children. The construction of childhood has largely been an adult affair. The voices of the children of the poor are rarely heard. Now in India and other places where the voice of the working child is gaining strength, a different perspective is emerging about what the children of the poor want. Do they want what adults want of them? What do they have to say about the nature of schooling and their role as actors within society?

A growing body of anthropological and sociological study on children and childhood now challenges the orthodoxy of the developmental psychologists. The perception of the child as helpless and passive is being reconstructed. Those at the forefront of this thinking emphasize the positive contributions children make to families and communities, as well as their opinions, their rights and their resilience (Stephenson, 2001).

Some theologians have begun to search Scripture for a clearer picture of children and their place in biblical society and in theology (White, 2001; Strange, 1996). What is emerging out of these reflections is an image of children as key actors in times of crisis and change. Is this a case of a contemporary theological interpretation mirroring current secular thinking?

Whatever the answer, it is clear that through the centuries the church has been both a leader and a follower when it comes to childcare. At its best, Christian leadership has changed the way that society views and treats children of the poor. Great figures such as Shaftesbury, Barnardo and Eglantine Jebb (founder of Save the Children) showed both compassion and bloody-minded determination to challenge policy and law for the benefit of children. Many unheralded missionaries gave their lives for the welfare of children. Nelson Mandela often praises those at the mission school he attended for giving him the opportunity to be educated.

Jesus Christ subverted cultural notions of what and who children were. He alluded to their perceptiveness and openness when they sang at his triumphal entry:

> But when the chief priests and the teachers of the law saw the wonderful things he did and the children shouting in the temple area, "Hosanna to the Son of David," they were indignant. "Do you hear what these children are saying?" they asked him. "Yes," replied Jesus, "have you never read, 'From the lips of children and infants you have ordained praise'?" (Matt. 21:15–16)

The disciples stopped children from approaching Jesus. Jesus told them to come. At a time when children had no status, Jesus exhorted adults to learn from their qualities and protect them from evil.

Evolving definitions of children and childhood, both sacred and secular, influenced the practical outworking of ministries over the centuries. The debate continues even now, especially as global youth culture and a universal concept of an extended and protected childhood are being exported through media, professional education and policy making. W.A. Strange describes the task of concern for children as an 'integral part of authentic Christian discipleship' (1996, p. 113), offering the caveat that it is an unending task. The challenge to the church is how to work with children in a way that uses the best of what has been learned, while remaining rooted in Christ's teachings and values.

– Questions to Consider –

1 Describe the role and influence of some of the key figures in church history whose work has affected the lives of 'children at risk'. What are the implications of their work on policy development and practice today?

2 Select one of these key figures and discuss how his or her life mirrors Christ's in his or her approach to children.

3 Whom do you see working for children today (a child or an adult) whom you think future generations might regard as an influential figure? What factors shaped your choice?

– CHAPTER 21 –

Practical and Spiritual Lessons for the Church

Patrick McDonald

Introduction

EVERY time has its opportunity and every opportunity its time (Handy, 1995). If ignored, opportunities disappear. 'Children at risk' provide the church with perhaps *the* challenge, *the* opportunity of our time. If embraced, this challenge might well mobilize millions of Christians to reach a generation of needy children. This challenge could become a hallmark of Christianity. We have an opportunity to make Christ and his precepts known – not only to the children touched, but also to the wider world watching.

This is a timely challenge to a church calling for holism, unity and relevance; to a church faced with the immediate task of practising what we preach. In a world weary of rules and ideologies, action is the only evidence of genuine belief. Truth, to be credible, has to be lived, not merely talked. Is the church a gathering of saints, a community of transformation or merely another social club for self-improvement and entertainment?

If the church can't respond compassionately, credibly, consistently and concertedly to the needs of hurting children, then what can it do? Yet if we – as a movement – are to take that challenge seriously, we have to radically restructure current efforts. We have to improve them and expand the overall size of the enterprise. The place of the amateur is increasingly on the decline in a world seeking better performance, higher efficiency and lower risk. If the church doesn't respond, others will.

This chapter explores current Christian endeavours to help children and outlines some of the main trends and challenges facing Christian work now and in the future.

The legacy of transformation

Christ asked all people to follow him, and those that did were later given the name 'Christians', which in Greek means literally 'those who follow Christ'. Christ Jesus cares passionately about children (Matt. 18), and so should those who know and seek to follow him.

The followers of Jesus can enter the twenty-first century celebrating a historic and formative participation in the 'caring' industries of welfare, education and health. From the earliest days of Christian witness, needy children have been a cause for concern and compassion. Down through the ages and right across the world the philosophical revolution emanating from the cross of Jesus has found practical expressions in outreach to children.

The Roman Emperor Julian commented:

> Atheism [at this time Christians were known as atheists, as they rejected the Roman pantheon] has been specially advanced through the loving service rendered to strangers, and through their care for the burial of the dead. It is a scandal that there is not a single Jew who is a beggar, and that the Godless Galileans care not only for their own poor but for ours as well; while those who belong to us look in vain for the help that we should render them. (Neill, 1964)

Contrary to what many believe, Christian care for needy children did not start with the Korean orphans in the 1950s. Christ was born into a world in which care was largely a foreign concept, in which education was the privilege of a small elite, in which the value of life or the rule of law was largely dependent on your deftness with a sword. To my mind, the terror above all was the absence of a philosophical framework providing justice and hope and encouraging goodness and righteousness. The casual acceptance of evil, the unquestioning embrace of depravity and human destruction, both temporal and eternal, speak of a darkness that is hard to fathom.

Being a Dane living in England, I am conscious of the deep scars my countrymen made as they, in the form of Viking raiders, arrived on the coast to rape and pillage. Yet today my country is so utterly different, so transformed, that we are known more for Lego toys, comfortable Ecco shoes and cosy coffee tables with low-hanging lights and plenty of cake than for our strange taste in Viking hats or our fighting spirit. Even the casual observer is forced to ask: What happened? What changed this land so completely and turned a bunch of raiding hooligans into what they are today? The answer – the indisputable, unequivocal answer – is simply: the cross of Christ!

W.A. Strange, in his book *Children in the Early Church*, outlines the philosophical revolution emanating from the cross of Christ. This revolution screamed to the world: 'GOD IS ALIVE', and 'GOD CARES FOR HUMAN LIFE'. He cares enough to die the most ghastly, painful, prolonged death known to humankind. He died that we might live, because life is meant to be lived; life is beautiful, wonderful and full of good things created by a good God; life is eternal and sacred.

Our Lord Jesus stated in the same breath that the greatest in the kingdom of heaven must humble himself like a little child, that indeed entry to heaven requires childlike qualities and that anyone welcoming children in his name would be welcoming him (Matt. 18:1–9). James, Jesus' brother, stated in his typical straightforward way: 'Religion that God our Father accepts as pure and faultless is this: to look after orphans and widows in their distress and to keep oneself from being polluted by the world' (Jas. 1:27).

Children – of whatever blood, social status, ability or appearance – have worth because 'God so loved the world that he gave his one and only Son, that whoever believes in him shall not perish but have eternal life' (John 3:16). In one swift blow, Christ revealed their dignity, worth and significance to every man, woman and child anywhere, at any time.

And this philosophical revolution, explained by Tertullian, Origen and Augustine, began immediately to manifest itself organizationally or, if you will, programmatically. Whether it was Paul and Agabus's disaster relief programme during the Judean famine in the early 50s AD described in Acts 11:27–30, or the work of the churches of Philadelphia, Thyatira and Ephesus, acknowledged for 'service and hard work' in the book of Revelation, we know that the Christian movement from its earliest days has had an impressive track record for helping the needy – including, of course, children.

The early monastic movements developed hospitals, orphan care and education. I come from a Christian community in Denmark, and the land that we live on used to belong to another Christian community, a group of Cistercian monks, who lived there in 1162. This group of brothers was renowned for their compassionate and advanced care for children, and they later formed one of the principal health and education centres of the Jutland peninsula. Throughout the Middle Ages, the Christian movement continued to develop institutions of care and education including virtually all of the medieval universities such as Oxford, Cambridge, Heidelberg, Halle, Sorbonne, Seville and later universities such as Yale, Harvard and Princeton. Out of the first 119 American universities, 104 were started by Christians to acquaint students with the knowledge of God. Out of a graduating class of 40,000 in 1855 (the total number graduating from all American universities that year), 10,000 went on to become ministers (Varghese, 1984). Throughout the Middle Ages, the Christian church remained a dominant force, if not the only force, fighting the corner for 'children at risk'. This fight only gained momentum after the Reformation as famed men like William Wilberforce and Ashley Cooper (better known as Lord Shaftesbury) successfully introduced and defended child rights and people like Pandita Ramabai Mukti, George Muller, William Booth, Mr Fegan, Dr Barnado and many others provided shelter, education and care for multitudes of destitute children. Later on, at the turn of the century, people like Amy Carmichael of the Dohnavur Fellowship in India established front-line care for children and the expanding missionary endeavour established an elaborate infrastructure of schools, health care centres and hospitals and contributed significantly towards the development of leadership for budding democracies the world over.

Later on in the century we meet giants like Everett Swanson (founder of Compassion International), Robert Pierce (founder of World Vision), J. Calvitt Clark and Dr J. Stewart Nagle (co-founders of Christian Children's Fund) and Loren Cunningham (founder of Youth With A Mission), whose faith and work shook their time and created new paradigms of innovative care, compassion and service. Today we look upon people like Primilla Pavamani, Enrique Pinedo, Doug Nichols, Wes Stafford, Robert Glover, Michael Shiferaw, Vera Zhuravleva, Lorenzo Davids, Josefina Gutierrez, Bo Wallenberg, Tetsunao Yamamori, Maggie Gorbran, Karen Hinder, Lucy Palma, Katharine Miles, Francisco Pena and many others who boldly, unashamedly carry the banner of Christ's love for 'children at risk' in our day.

Like no other movement on earth, the Christian church has a heritage of caring for needy children and it is worth remembering and quietly appreciating that even secular care largely stems from the philosophical revolution caused by the rise of Christianity. The energy released by sinners meeting their saviour has indeed had great result. The conviction of sin that leads to conversion involves nothing less than the spiritual birth of the unbeliever who moves from darkness into light, from death into life. The new believer gains status as a citizen of a new community with a new commitment that creates more than an outlet for good intentions – this commitment transforms and empowers those it touches to in turn transform others. The road to maturity in Christ must involve service which, through the power of God, transforms the world.

It is upon the shoulders of unsung heroes that we stand today, at the beginning of a new millennium. We celebrate their victory over temporal struggles, their witness of love and compassion to a cynical, apathetic and disbelieving world, their passion for Christ and their faithfulness to pursue his mandate, his challenge, his command to change the world – one child at a time.

Current efforts

After four years of research, Viva Network is still trying to establish the actual size of what we have termed the 'Christian community of outreach to "children at risk"'. Although no one knows the exact extent or nature of Christian outreach to 'children at risk', everyone agrees that it is, although amorphous, massive.

In the state of Tamil Nadu, India, conservative estimates suggest the presence of more than 1,500 evangelical projects among 'children at risk'. In Nairobi, Kenya, city officials approached Christian leaders to plead with them to form a network of the more than 200 evangelical groups known to work among 'children at risk' in that city. In Lima, more than 100 churches are involved in helping 'children at risk'. When a network of Christian ministry to 'children at risk' formed in Miami, it was thought that there were about 20 groups working in this field in the city. Organizers soon realized that the figure was closer to 40, and the latest figure I had was over 150 groups. In Cape Town a network of 103 groups exists, and the list goes on and on and on.

A 'guestimate' suggests the existence of at least 25,000 projects reaching some two million children in full-time care and tens of millions of children in partial care. Operated by no fewer than 100,000 full-time Christian workers, this global operation is supported by more than a thousand mission and parachurch groups working in more than 192 countries. From Lima to London, from Manila to

Manitoba, from Colombia to Cameroon, Christians in general and evangelicals in particular are reaching out compassionately, and often at great personal sacrifice, to meet the needs of 'children at risk'. The combined expense of this operation costs billions each year.

As vast and compassionate as this response is, co-ordination and collaboration could achieve a huge difference. We must urgently connect people together in a community of peers, in a network that can:

- Co-ordinate existing efforts
- Avoid unnecessary duplication
- Connect people to relevant initiatives
- Create opportunities for collaboration
- Facilitate strategic thinking on common issues
- Develop the capacity to deal with larger common issues such as staff care and training, policy formulation, child welfare, quality control and sharing best practice.

Let us look briefly now at some of the issues facing the Christian response to childcare, especially with 'children at risk'. Keep in mind that any global generalizations serve primarily to point us in the right direction, after which we can contextualize and appropriate what might be useful to our own contexts.

Prayer

The greatest single need facing every member of the Christian childcare community is prayer. I have been astonished at the number of childcare workers who have cited this as their most urgent need. It seems that virtually everyone agrees: prayer precedes power! And power is precisely what is required to tackle the problems faced by 'children at risk': godly power to be as the Lord desires us to be in order for us to do the things he calls us to do.

Isolation

Isolation is perhaps one of the biggest and most crucial problems among Christian childcare workers. The overwhelming sense that 'we are the only ones doing it' is prevalent throughout the Christian childcare community and, coupled with the enormous needs, the sense that all I can do is a 'drop in the bucket' often makes for a very discouraging outlook. Dietrich Bonhoeffer stated a few days prior to his death that 'hope is passionate pursuit of things yet to come'. It is often very hard to feel passionate about a battle that seems to be lost, but fellowship between like-minded Christians working towards the same end can be transforming.

Many Christian ministries lack knowledge of what is available and happening in the world just outside their own front door. I remember vividly when a local network was formed in Argentina. Everyone present at the launch conference stood up to introduce themselves. One man described himself, with a note of pride in his voice, as a representative of 'the only children's prison ministry in Cordoba and probably all of Argentina'. Then he sat down. The man next to him took his turn with a somewhat bemused smile on his face and proceeded to describe himself as representing 'the second only children's prison ministry in Cordoba and probably all of Argentina'.

Things are not always that funny. A good friend of mine – Raymond Samuel, the director of an indigenous Indian child-care project – once recounted to me the tragic result of isolation. He had been working in Maharashtra, distributing food to extremely poor children in some 40 villages that had suffered from an earthquake and severe rains. Children were starving and more supplies were needed urgently. Raymond contacted several agencies but found no response. Six months later the situation was even more serious, but he managed to find a potential supplier in Bombay. Having watched 450 children die in a matter of weeks, Raymond was desperate. He was elated when the supplier said that all the supplies Raymond needed were already on the field and only ten minutes from Raymond's office. Raymond left Bombay and returned to make use of these new-found supplies. But great was his dismay when he found out that the supplies were now three months past their expiry date. Had Raymond known of their existence during the height of the famine, those 450 children might have lived. Instead, the food, the product of toilsome fund-raising, had gone rotten.

I do not think it would be much of an overstatement to say that everyone involved in reaching 'children at risk' has too much to do and too little with which to do it. It must therefore be our first priority to maximize the use of our resources and minimize the extent to which we duplicate efforts or re-invent wheels which have long since been proven unable to perform.

Pursuing excellence

Lack of effective planning, sufficient resources and trained staff means that most child-care projects could be accused of operating unprofessionally. Most projects start in heartfelt response to immediate need and are often not preconceived. They simply happen.

Once they are up and running, however, it is essential that projects are operated professionally. As Christians, we need to do more than simply reach 'children at risk'. We need to raise them as we would our own children. One of the great challenges facing the Christian community of outreach to 'children at risk' is to find ways of combining the enthusiasm, the get-up-and-go of the Christian movement, with the experience and professionalism acquired through two thousand years of caring for children. The children we serve need more than our enthusiasm. They need the longevity of effective holistic care.

Ministry performance standards

Christian organizations need to consider and identify good practice. What does good Christian childcare look like? What does it involve? How is it achieved? Who is doing it? These are all helpful questions to ask, and the answers can be summarized in a code of best practice. It is, however, important to keep in mind that each context and culture creates a unique and often very different environment, and any code of conduct or practice should reflect that context. The best ministry performance standards are often created through local need analysis and participatory reflection at the grass roots. Once standards have been established and agreed upon, these standards can be used by ministries to keep each other mutually accountable and together to pursue yet higher excellence. This type of examination of self and peers can, if carefully managed, be a very helpful, if sometimes humbling, exercise. The formation of networks is again essential for this to happen. It is hard to build a peer group if you do not know where your peers are, or if you do not trust them enough to be vulnerable.

Training

Professionalism, or capacity building as some would call it, must naturally involve training. The Christian church stands at the top of the line of candidates willing and able to handle the global privatization of care, education and welfare. However, if the church is to become a major service provider in these and related areas, we need to make sure that we do so with the highest possible level of integrity and professionalism. This must involve both on-site training and distance learning packages for those unable to leave their projects, to enhance potential workers' awareness of key children's issues. Both types of training need to be properly accredited and certified to enhance effective practice and to provide public credibility.

Caring for the caregivers

A very serious but often unrecognized problem for people in front-line ministry to 'children at risk', is lack of practical, emotional and spiritual support. The inability to find time for fellowship with other Christians, or for personal renewal, together with lack of prayer support, lead to discouragement and early burn-out. Good care for existing workers must be a prerequisite for growth. How can we ask God for more if we do not look after those we already have? It is the breakdown of relationships that often puts children at risk. We desperately need to find a way of restoring those relationships which, by their very nature, will predominately be long-term. Ultimately 'children at risk' need more than social workers; they need mums and dads who will love and respect them as they are, despite all their hang-ups. A child-care worker is in many ways more than simply a service provider – she is a pseudo-parent, who establishes close relationships with the children under her care. All of our pence, pounds, policies and programmes are rather pointless without the child-care workers. They are the noblest part of what we do, which is why it is so shocking to see the level of neglect that they endure as they struggle bravely to meet the overwhelming needs that face them each day (see Part 7 in this volume).

Money

Money is high on the list of needs. We have too much to do and too little to do it with – too many children to reach and not enough money with which to reach them. This is the reality for Christian child-care projects all over the world as the vast majority just scrape by from week to week, making do with 'never enough'. Has God gone bust? Is it just that scrabbling around for resources is a fact of life? Maybe the Lord has exhausted his ministry expenses account, or perhaps he is trying to teach us something by the fact that we only just get by. I believe that the Christian movement has the potential for mass expansion of its efforts to reach 'children at risk'. I am a convinced optimist. I truly believe that we will see a radical change in Christian efforts to reach needy children worldwide and that millions of children will find help and comfort as a result.

However, I am also aware that something fundamental needs to change in the way we underpin these efforts financially. Most ministry to 'children at risk' does not reflect the sufficiency, indeed the victory, of our Lord. Rather, it is affected by the compassion fatigue felt by exhausted donors weary with good causes clamouring at their doorsteps for attention and support. Even where people give generously, funds raised from donations alone never quite meet the need, let alone offer enough support to engender an explosion of ministry in this field. Furthermore, the actual cost of raising funds through smaller donors is high, labour intensive and often fosters a sense of competition between like-minded groups. Radical change is required.

We tend to find money for our work from three sources:

1. The private sector: from our churches, support groups, charities and organizations

2. The public sector: from governments, intergovernmental bodies and local councils

3. The business sector: through business ventures, endowments and income generation projects.

We are reasonably good at developing funding from the private sector but – as a rule – not from the public or business sector. Business tends to distract people from doing ministry. If, for example, you try to run an orphanage and a business at the same time, you will soon struggle to do both – and the demands of paying customers often win the day. Governments, on the other hand, often stipulate terms that disallow evangelism or prayer. Agencies that compromise in this way often end up becoming increasingly 'secular'. Programmes that grow beyond a certain size require highly competent staff, and hiring people for their professional proficiency who do not share the same spiritual commitment can result in the agency sacrificing their sense of calling. These are both real dangers, but it is possible to overcome them both.

Governments and intergovernmental agencies are recognizing the importance and validity of non-governmental organizations (NGOs) as primary service providers in the areas of health and social welfare. Whether it is the Norwegian, Danish or Canadian governments that acknowledge the value of Christian work in their overseas development budgets, or the city councils of Cordoba in Argentina, Nairobi in Kenya or Miami in the USA, the message is the same: let's outsource where possible!

The logic of this hangs together, as voluntary organizations often give governments and local councils more value for their money. These organizations are more likely to be free from corruption, and using them saves councils the cost of their own overheads. What is more, NGOs are largely self-motivated and employ staff whose commitment stems from their convictions rather than their desire for financial reward. Government agencies are realizing like never before that you cannot purchase compassion, but can only encourage and support it where it is found. Compassion is a state of mind and heart and, while opinions vary on what motivates such activism, everyone agrees that it is conducive to effective care.

God gives us a mandate to reach 'children at risk', which it is possible to obey. The way funding is raised now, however, does not allow us to fulfil that mandate. There is a dichotomy, in my mind, between what God seeks to do and the way in which we have gone about it thus far. As the Western world becomes less generous, more and more ways of working with 'children at risk' are developing. A crisis is therefore evolving as good works are on the increase while the funding available for them is declining.

We must push income generation through business ventures, we must facilitate the development of viable and appropriate fund-raising in the less developed world, and we must engage meaningfully and honestly with governmental bodies and partner with them, without losing our Christian witness.

The world has not gone bust. God has not gone bust. There is as much money now as there always has been, if not more, and we can tap into that resource. Many people have a lot of money to give and must be encouraged to give it. God encourages generosity, and we must turn the tide of donor despondency and bring victory in the area of finance.

Networking

I once did two weeks of research in San Salvador, the capital of El Salvador in Central America. I came across six different groups who all told me that 'they were the only ones doing it [reaching children]'. They all wanted to work with street children, and yet none had managed the art. One project worked the city parks and had no halfway house, one group had an orphanage but no outreach team, and one group had a drop-in centre and a halfway house but no capacity to work the streets nor anywhere to send the children to once they wanted to move on.

I bought them all a cup of coffee at a local ice-cream parlour and asked them to share their stories. The result was incredible! In about 15 minutes a connection developed between these groups which enabled all of them to optimize their work at no extra cost. The street team used the halfway house, which sent kids on to the orphanage. None of them had the capacity or skill to run all three, but in a network none of them needed to. No one had yet addressed the issues of family integration or foster care, nor had they thought about connecting to other ministries, the local city council or governmental groups. They had yet to discover the benefits of addressing common needs such as staff training, setting standards, bulk purchasing and strategic thinking and planning. That would be for sometime in the future. But as we drained our cups and set off for the city, everyone felt happy and everyone understood the value of networking.

I am a committed networker. My experience in San Salvador was only one of many such contacts, and the nature of the Christian movement necessitates effective networks if we are to use our God-entrusted resources well. Most of our energy lies in the local church and is focused around charismatic and driven individuals who want to make something happen. That is great – however, if we are to learn from what everybody else has done before us, if we are to discover what resources are available to us, if we are to co-ordinate our efforts with people of like mind and if we are to collaborate on issues of common concern, then we need to network. That involves being able to find and connect to a network relevant to our needs.

Viva Network has sought to develop multiple networks for issues of a local, continental or global nature by bringing together people whose work and values match. My friend Martin is one of the few people I know who become intensely passionate when talking about information dissemination. He compares unwanted information with unwanted goods. You may receive a fantastic pair of pink boots, but if you do not need any boots and you do not like pink, they are no good to you. The same is true of information, which only becomes relevant once it reaches people for whom it is relevant.

It is only through an active network that information can be passed on to where it is needed. I dream of the day when each locality and each field or topic of Christian childcare has a clearly identified, visible 'one-stop shop'. This will be a hub of information, a place where both those who have information, contacts or resources and those who need information, contacts or resources can go.

Once such a central point within the Christian child-care community has been established, the task of information sharing becomes much easier. To be effective, such a hub would need to be staffed by 'networkers' – a new breed of Christian child-care worker able to serve as diplomats, facilitators and convenors. A networker would respond quickly and appropriately, but only in the context of 'network ownership'. The network is only ever as strong as its component parts, and it is therefore the responsibility of all involved.

The need for strategic thinking

Whether geographically (locally, regionally or globally), topically (street children, children at war) or in terms of performance-related issues (training, accountability, recruitment), a crying need exists for the strategic planning of Christian childcare. What's the plan?

We are a community of people who work to help children because of what Christ has done for us and because of what we believe Christ wants to do for children. We may have different organizational tags, flags and mottoes but we are, nonetheless, like-minded. If someone contracts a builder on a big project, the first task he undertakes is to draw up a plan. In the same way, it could be argued that the Lord has contracted us – but who has the blueprints? As I look at current Christian efforts among 'children at risk' it troubles me that so much is being done in certain areas or among certain types of children, and so little elsewhere. The focus of Christian childcare more often than not tends towards areas where there is a history of Christian engagement with a need rather than to where need actually exists. There is a balance to redress.

Another problem caused by the lack of a common strategy is the partial provision of services. Children may be sponsored by one organization to attend school, but the hygiene in their area may be so bad that they suffer from ill health and are rarely able to commit to their studies. Or, a shelter for street children may exist in one area but there may not be a residential home in place to which they can progress. Specialist organizations benefit children in one way but leave other important areas neglected.

The one-stop shop provides an antidote to this problem. Through its forum, the individual strengths of numerous specialist agencies can be harnessed and an overview of who does what, where, can be presented to all concerned – ensuring that the Christian child-care community can reach parts not yet reached.

Research and analysis

Despite significant efforts to help 'children at risk' at a grass-roots level, the evangelical movement has had a fairly marginal input in the areas of research and analysis. Academically and technically, we live largely off the experience of others in our thinking about how to shape good child-care practice and policy. This is not for lack of able thinkers, as many outstanding academics, field practitioners and policy makers belong heart and soul to the evangelical movement but are mostly employed in secular organizations. There they make a vital contribution, but their environment makes it difficult for them to construct and express a Christian response.

A 'Christian working in childcare' is ultimately different from 'Christian childcare'. The evangelical community currently offers little opportunity for service for workers of this calibre. Largely grass roots driven, the evangelical movement certainly has the get up and go to do things others may only talk about, but it does not always stop to reflect on and evaluate its efforts. Many development and child-care organizations look upon the evangelical movement as energetic and compassionate but fail to take it into account as a serious entity. This has much to do with a low level of awareness of the actual nature and scope of our efforts, but I believe that it is also partly our own fault and a result of our failure to conduct serious research into practice, policy and performance.

Empowering the local church

Piedad, a Pentecostal organization in Latin America, discovered that the poor success of their church plant was turned around once they opened a school. Through it they won the trust and friendship of local people and their church grew. The same happened for British Baptist missionaries to Brazil, Stuart and Georgina Christine, who as seasoned church planters turned their attention to children as a way of planting a church. Stuart says that for every child he reaches he wins the respect of 30 adults, and his tale would seem to be true as churches have sprung up right, left and centre throughout the Sao Paulo *favela* where he works.

The Christian movement is one of the largest civic movements on earth today, and its congregations worldwide have three things in common:

1. A heritage of working among 'children at risk' that dates back to Christ

2. A faith that inspires commitment to the needs of 'children at risk'

3. A biblical mandate to care for the needs of others.

These are three good reasons why the local church should be involved in responding to the needs of these children. In reality it has been the parachurch movement, often flabbergasted at the unresponsiveness of the local church, that has done the majority of Christian childcare. As 'children at risk' are reaching the radar screens of church leaders, however, this is beginning to change. In approaching this issue it is important for us to keep in mind the concept of 'sodality and modality'.

Dr Ralph Winter is possibly best known for expounding this issue. The 'sodality' is the classic parachurch agency – focused and committed to a limited range of issues, often comprising a small but committed community of highly mobile people. The 'modality' is classically compared to the local church and is more stationary, broader in scope and with greater permanence. The identification of these two structures is helpful in understanding the different dynamics of operation, but it should not cause us to abandon the hope of mobilizing the local church. The truth is that when local churches seriously commit to single issues it is because clusters of members become, in effect, a sodality. This can be highly successful, both in what is achieved and in the energy it creates for other members by the example of focused commitment.

There is tremendous hope in the prospect of mobilizing and enabling the world's three million local congregations. Local churches have 90 per cent of what it takes to do professional Christian care for 'children at risk'. They own buildings, have pulpits from which to mobilize and inspire, and they are comprised of local people who live throughout the community and who share a commitment to manifest the gospel through their lives.

Essentially the challenges are to 'improve the quality' and 'increase the quantity' of Christian work with 'children at risk'. We must pursue rapid acceleration and improvement of current efforts. So much is at stake – not just the lives and eternal destinies of multitudes, but also the very integrity of our witness.

The integrity of our witness

In Kenya, nearly 80 per cent of the population are reported to be Christians (Johnstone, 2001). Yet, according to Transparency International (Index 1996), Kenya is the third most corrupt country on the planet. What does this say about our integrity as Christians? Surely if the gospel is the truth for the way we live our lives, then it must also be the truth for the context in which we live them and for the way in which our communities are organized. A holistic response to local needs is the loudest way of saying, 'we care'. Discipleship only becomes meaningful when it leads to service. God gave every man and woman the inherent ability to care for children, and childcare provides an obvious entry point to holistic ministry for a local church. What is more pertinent than hungry, hurting children dying on our doorsteps? How can we talk about a loving God if we leave these children without a family? As an African proverb states, 'A hungry stomach has no ears'.

I meet every now and again with the general secretary of the Danish Missionary Council. His name is Birger, and I find him in many ways to be a kindred spirit and an impatient sort of man. In talking of Christian work he keeps saying, as though to himself, '*Det skal vaere noget Godt handvaerk*', which is Danish and in paraphrase means, 'it must be done well, it must be of good tradesman's quality'. '*Handvaerk*' means literally 'the work of your hands', and in Denmark your '*handvaerk*' is a traditional source of great pride and something over which you take great care. It speaks louder of you than words. Christian work with 'children at risk' must always be good '*handvaerk*', because what we do speaks louder than words – not only about us, but also about our master, Jesus Christ.

Future challenge

I believe that Christian outreach to 'children at risk' stands at a crossroads. A response to the needs of 'children at risk' from the Christian community is inevitable as people seek to follow Christ. However, if we continue as we are at present then our efforts may become increasingly peripheral to the overall efforts made in education and childcare. Through networking we can realize and harness our inheritance, our resources and our potential and thus bring about a massive improvement in Christian care for children.

It seems to me that Christ provides each generation with specific challenges and opportunities with which to extend his kingdom. These opportunities represent potential turning points for the church and her witness to the world, and I am convinced that the challenge of reaching the multitude of 'children at risk' is just such an opportunity – an opportunity that I believe is ours to grasp by the power of Christ and his Holy Spirit.

The evangelical movement stands ideally poised for massive expansion of its outreach to 'children at risk'. If we can organize ourselves in functional networks we can make visible the largest body of care currently in existence and expand it greatly. Out of that, a movement of prayer could mobilize every Christian on earth to intercede for 'children at risk'. If we work together, network better and are trained to a higher standard, then we could double or triple the number of children reached effectively. Out of that, more than ten per cent of the three million congregations could be mobilized to reach 'children at risk'. Out of that could come a concerted effort to raise up a body of approximately one million new workers. Out of that, these workers could be provided with decent care and training. And, out of that, evangelical care for children could be seen and known everywhere as a respected and appreciated force.

The challenge of 'children at risk' is as much an opportunity as it is a problem. If tackled well it could provide a multitude of opportunities for service throughout the body. It could – like no other activity – provide credibility for our local and global witness and it could provide a multitude of boys and girls with a sensitive and appropriate introduction to the Father of the fatherless, the high King of heaven, the Ruler of all, the great God who cares for you and who cares for me and who cares for every single child.

To do so, the church would have to move from being a club at the fringe of many societies to being a caring community at the very centre of society. It would therefore have a greater potential to effectively meet the needs of children and their families. To do so, the church would have to practice what it preaches and would have to connect and work in practical unity rather than continue in its bizarre and profoundly unbiblical individualism. The church would have to move out of its cosy trenches and engage meaningfully and effectively in issues of social politics, economics and philosophy. The little children shall lead them.

In doing God's will we shall always find huge blessings. God is no one's debtor. To reach children is certainly God's will, and if the church engages in that it will not only touch the lives of numerous children and gain a solid and credible reputation, but it will also incur the great and powerful blessing of God. Let's get on with it!

– Questions to Consider –

1 It is often said that history repeats itself. What are the good things that we can learn from past practice by the church and Christian missions?

2 How can we avoid making the same mistakes again?

3 If you were introducing a new Christian to the area of the church's responsibility for children and 'children at risk', how would you describe it? How does the local church's involvement with children affect your own work with children? How might you work more effectively with the local church to help children?

– CHAPTER 22 –

The Basis for the Design of Child Development Programmes[1]

Andrew Tomkins

He grew up . . . like a tender shoot. (Isa. 53:2)

Introduction

THIS chapter provides a summary of biomedical and social principles for programme management for the promotion of child development in less developed countries within a framework of Christian values. Child development is here viewed from the following perspectives: spiritual, intellectual, nutritional, physical, social and emotional/behavioural. The chapter reviews the changing social, economic and physical environments and their impact on child health and nutrition and also introduces the concepts of child-centred approaches and community-centred approaches to child development. The challenge for Christian organizations is to reflect on the 'tender shoot' image from Scripture and design programmes that promote the full growth and development of children so that they can be enabled to reach their God-given potential.

Why is child development so important?

Child development is clearly important from a Christian perspective. In Mark 10:13–16, Jesus commanded his disciples to let the children come to him. In the description of Jesus' own development (Isa. 53 and subsequently in the Gospels), it is clear that the 'tender shoot' received nurture from parents, close family and a variety of social, intellectual and physical stimuli from the environment in which he grew up. There is much teaching in the Old and New Testaments (Ps. 145:1–6; Isa. 7:15–16; Acts 2:39), and directly from Jesus himself, on the importance of key values in relationships within the family and society in which children grow up. The Bible also teaches that each individual human being has enormous potential. Jesus himself grew and became strong; he was filled with wisdom and God's goodness was in him (Luke 2:40).

From a societal perspective, the failure to promote child development will result in increasing numbers of adults who are maladjusted, lacking appropriate education and basic life skills, emotionally and behaviourally immature, socially delinquent and physically weak. This has obvious implications in terms of employment and productivity at the family and national levels.

What is being achieved by current child development programmes?

Most child-centred programmes focus on what can be achieved through the 'windows of opportunity' provided within primary education, recognizing that in many communities the completion rates for attendance at primary school are seriously deficient.

Many agencies run child sponsorship programmes aimed at supporting children who might otherwise drop out of school early or not attend at all. They have supported many thousands of children in a range of countries with differing political and socio-economic characteristics. The need becomes more pressing as more and more children grow up in the desperate declining quality of environment of the rapidly expanding cities or decimated rural areas of many less developed countries (King and Elliott, 1996).

Changing social environment

International agencies such as UNICEF and Viva Network have publicized the plight of 'Children in Especially Difficult Circumstances', although they are the first to admit that it is not easy to develop or implement appropriate policies and programmes when there are competing claims for funds to deal with problems that are seen to be more urgent such as HIV/AIDS, control of infectious diseases such as malaria, or relief for the millions of refugees displaced by conflict.

There are widespread changes in the social construction of childhood which go far beyond the more physical problems. In many communities children are increasingly unsure of their worth and place within society. At times children are pressurized to be adults prematurely. Witness, for example, the enormous amount of money spent on advertising for the clothes and possessions of adolescent/adult culture in richer countries. This means that there will soon be more children than ever before who will 'grow up' to their genetic potential physically, but who are very unlikely to achieve their 'developmental goals' as regards their social, intellectual, emotional and spiritual potential. Not only does this have profound implications for human development and economic growth but, from a Christian perspective, these children are not living a life which is 'full' (John 10:10; Dixon, 1995; Watt, 1996).

Priorities for action

Much of the damage to children's lives is the result of rejecting God's plan for humankind. There are many clear guidelines in the Bible which will direct us in establishing what we may call 'kingdom values' (those that we would see if people obeyed God and were empowered by the Holy Spirit). Because these kingdom values indicate that children have a God-given worth, they are important values for all child development programmes – whether those responsible are in agreement with the biblical view of salvation and transformation or not.

Research into the impairment of child development mostly concentrates on evaluating specific interventions, but it is essential to recognize co-existing variables that have a major effect. For instance, it is well known that stunted (physically short in comparison with genetic potential) children tend to perform less well in school, but such children often come from a poor community. Thus not only do they have an inadequate diet but, not surprisingly, they also have fewer books, live in more crowded accommodation, and are therefore socially disadvantaged in many ways. Interventions that seem sensible and biologically plausible, and that intuitively make sense, have not been properly investigated to see if they are just hunches or actually true and can be corroborated by research.

New conceptual linkages can be used to enable a multiplier effect, establishing several interventions concurrently. Choosing the most effective mix will require knowledge of the efficacy of individual interventions, together with a willingness to try and monitor/evaluate new mixes that seem relevant to the local situation.

Perhaps most important here is the demonstration that actions for improving child development may directly target the individual child and the more fundamental causes of problems in society. The arguments outlined below give strong support for the view that 'for child development to be promoted maximally there must be a multi-pronged approach'. Thus we need to include a far wider range of activities than are present within current, conventional child development programmes. There is no 'blueprint' for child development which is suitable for every situation; rather, we must consider a menu of approaches (Silverman, 1994).

The key components of child development

Spiritual life

There are many examples in Scripture of spiritual growth and development among children. Luke describes how Jesus grew up and became strong in the Spirit (Luke 1:78ff.). Paul emphasizes the importance of being spiritually 'rooted and built up' (Col. 2:7). Samuel was only a child when he was aware enough to hear God calling him to work full-time for him (1 Sam. 3). The young servant girl of Naaman's wife had such spiritual insight that she knew that Elisha could heal Naaman of his leprosy (2 Kgs. 5). The boy king Josiah introduced measures to encourage the entire nation to turn back to God (2 Kgs. 22ff.).

Nutrition

Recent comparative international studies emphasize that a good diet and the relative absence of disease are more important than genetics in explaining why many children in economically improving societies are now taller than their parents. Like the 'tender shoot in dry ground' in Isaiah 53, children need nutrients of many kinds if they are to grow to their genetic potential. Stunted children in less developed countries have low IQ scores, even when allowance is made for the coexisting effects of the low socio-economic and poor learning environment in which they often live. Chronic hunger and lack of breakfast have detrimental effects on child development independent of other factors.

Even more important in many communities is the damaging effect on health and development caused by mineral and micronutrient deficiencies such as iron, iodine, zinc and vitamin A. Iron deficiency impairs learning ability and leads to impairment of certain co-ordination skills which are necessary for fine movements such as writing and may even contribute to poor attention span and behavioural disorders. Iodine deficiency, causing goitre, is particularly serious in mothers. Lack of thyroid hormone damages the brains of infants before birth, thereby limiting their intellectual potential as children and adults. In addition, iodine deficiency among schoolchildren reduces their thyroid hormone levels, thereby making them less mentally active. Vitamin A deficiency impairs the immune response to infection and contributes to anaemia, which itself is detrimental to learning. A combination of dietary deficiency of protein, energy, calcium and zinc, along with other deficiencies, accounts for stunting and the impaired cognition and learning that accompany stunting (Kramer, et al., 1995).

There are many references in the Old Testament to the negative impact that injustice by nations or individuals had on the nutritional status of children. Famine during conflict affected children in the Bible (2 Kgs. 6:24–29; 25:3). By contrast, God showed faithfulness by providing food and thereby preventing nutritional oedema (e.g., Exod. 16:4ff.). The striking intelligence and physical health of Shadrach, Meshach and Abednego may be attributed to their plain but sufficient diet (Dan. 1:12).

Health

Several illnesses affect child development. Malaria and intestinal helminths affect a child's ability to function well in school. Many millions of children have visual, auditory or learning handicaps as a result of illnesses that they themselves, or their mothers, experienced. The priority for health-related activities, which Jesus included in his own ministry, has been a motivating factor for many Christian health professionals working in difficult situations with disadvantaged communities. Unfortunately, the professionalism with which many doctors and nurses conduct their work has often been somewhat daunting for those working in child development, and many non-medical workers feel that 'health' is the domain of the professionals. There are obviously special situations where the assistance of health professionals is necessary, but it is increasingly recognized that disease prevention at the community level can start with the involvement of children themselves, such as in the Child to Child programmes (helping children to teach other children, who learn better from their peers and with examples that are relevant to their worlds; Hawes and Scotchmer, 1993).

Intellect

Intellectual inquiry and intelligence are shaped by many factors including genetics, nutrition, exposure to psychomotor stimulation in the pre-school period and an educational culture which stimulates exploration in the home and at school. Malnutrition and infections impair cognitive function and learning.

Jesus' early intellectual jousting with the sages at the temple in Jerusalem was recorded in some detail. While his parents must have panicked when they could not find him, they must have been proud of his early intellectual achievements as he questioned the elders, who were amazed at his understanding (Luke 2:46–47).

Emotion / behaviour

A range of factors, from genetics to culture, conditions behavioural responses to emotional feelings and stimuli. There is no precise and widely accepted method of measuring these. Interestingly, aggression and heightened response to stressful incidents are more marked in stunted children who have higher cortisol levels than better nourished children.

Social awareness

Many young children who are almost entirely self-centred with respect to ownership or handling of belongings grow up to be remarkably more globally aware, caring individuals. The degree of self-centredness is an indicator of social immaturity. Conversely, children often develop strong feelings about what is right or wrong in the world. The strength of passion with which children hold their social values can be striking.

Can child development be measured?

Several systems for evaluating child development already exist, others are becoming established and others require some imaginative and creative thinking and testing in real-life situations before their validity can be established.

Nutrition is the easiest factor to assess, by measuring weight and height. Using 'Road to Health' cards, parents can plot children's nutritional gains under the guidance of health workers. Nutrition in older children can be measured by comparing weight and height against standard charts. The body mass index gives an easy index of thinness that all teachers can calculate. Thus one school or class can be compared with another for the presence of thinness. This is important because of the associated decrease in resistance to infection as well as decreased learning capacity. Haemoglobin is measured by blood tests and interviews regarding the consumption of breakfast before coming to school. Assessment of anaemia in individuals and groups of children is now simple with the availability of battery-operated accurate haemoglobin meters. Anaemia surveys and assessment of anaemia control programmes can now be done using finger-prick samples in the classroom.

Health is also relatively easy to assess. Inspection of the fingernails for length and dirt, and of the skin for the presence of infections such as scabies is easily taught. Children can be questioned regarding the presence of symptoms such as fever, cough, respiratory problems, intestinal worms and skin infections. Nurses can perform simple examinations for childhood infections and can arrange tests for parasitic infection of the blood, urine or intestine. Dental check-ups for the assessment of caries and inflammation of the gums can be performed by mobile dental clinics.

Early child development activities can be measured by the number of stimuli that a child receives, how many toys have been made and used, and whether play activities are well designed and safe. Do children learn songs and rhymes? Do children show more sensitivity to each other's feelings, particularly to younger children? Do health workers include issues of child development in their under-five's clinics?

Intellect can be measured by formal tests of cognitive function, but in practice more countries are now establishing tests of school performance which will enable comparisons of how individuals or groups of children are progressing. It cannot be overemphasized that school performance is the result of a series of inputs, and all the variables – including school facilities, teacher presence and attributes, crowding and socio-economic status at home, together with the home learning environment – need to be considered before concluding that one school is 'better' than another. Standardized school achievement tests in subjects such as arithmetic, spelling, reading, writing and science are increasingly available in many cultures.

Scoring systems also exist to measure the social behaviour of children, such as the Rutter score for anti-social behaviour. These are relatively easy for teachers to use and they have been widely used in cross-cultural studies of aggressive and anti-social behaviour both in industrialized and less developed countries. Programme managers can easily be trained in their use.

If the child is not 'developing', it is important to be sure what the problem is. A child may be very slow to develop intellectually, finding it hard to concentrate on books or any academic activity. Before assuming that the problem is intrinsic laziness, it is essential to consider whether the problem could be compounded by deafness, visual handicap, anaemia, intestinal parasites, absence of breakfast, repeated abuse by a relative or trauma after seeing a close friend killed in a war situation. Child development assessment falls all too frequently between the cracks of various professional disciplines. Teachers assume that the health workers will sort things out. Health workers are rarely aware of what goes on in the school. Social workers are nearly always overburdened by a heavy caseload of severe 'problem' cases, and parents may be so stressed that they are reduced to shouting or hitting the child, their spouses, or both.

Child-centred interventions

Christian ministry

Mark 9:37 emphasizes the special importance of working for the welfare of children. Acts 2:39 clearly states that the Holy Spirit is given for children as well as adults. A child who grows up with ideas of God that are theoretical and abstract is hardly likely to grow spiritually (Tuckey, 1996). Conversely, children are often capable of handling complex issues and may have a remarkably mature understanding of spiritual matters (Matt. 11:25). They may have questions about God and heaven that just do not seem to bother adults (Frangoulis, et al., 1995).

A group of children interviewed in Great Ormond Street Hospital for Children in London were clear that they were going to heaven, but they were seriously worried about how they were going to get there! Was it by bus or aircraft?

Early child development

Love, care, play and stimulation during the first years of life are crucial; they play a profoundly important programming role in how babies will function as older children and adults. An infant's five senses – sight, smell, hearing, taste and touch – are all working from the moment of birth and hearing and touch, including pain, are present well before birth. Early child development activities should be incorporated into mothers' groups, under-five's clinics, crèches, schools and other groups such as scouts, youth groups and church groups.

Nutrition

Nutritional education involves promoting improved diet and the consumption of fortified foods such as iodized salt and supplements such as iron or vitamin A where dietary approaches alone may be insufficient (Tomkins, 2000). Tragically, many children in less developed countries come from homes where children live on the edge nutritionally. School-based feeding programmes may be a very cost-effective way of improving educability, but the correct model in each locality needs to be carefully defined (studies in Guatemala, Haiti and Mexico – Brown and Politt, 1996). Those programmes that involve the children in learning about nutrition and hygiene and preparing school meals are likely to have the greatest impact.

There is increasing evidence that the haemoglobin of children can increase as a result of weekly iron tablets. If deworming is given at the beginning of the school term with a cheap safe drug such as albendazole, haemoglobin and school learning achievement can be improved. Controlling disease, for instance by avoiding intestinal infection with improved personal hygiene and sanitation, and controlling malaria through the use of insecticide treated bed nets are also critical factors in improving health and nutrition (Tomkins and Watson, 1989). Integrated approaches within the curricula include studying diet in science classes, food production and household food security in agriculture and the particular needs of women, especially in pregnancy, in social studies. The best way of improving nutrition is through a combination of learning and doing (Clarke, et al., 1990).

Health services

Health services need to provide preventive, promotive and treatment approaches. Services for school children used to be provided free of charge, but in many countries undergoing structural adjustment programmes such services are now only available on a fee-for-service basis. Thus parents and guardians, and even children themselves, have to make important and painful decisions about what healthcare system they can afford to use.

Unfortunately, many nurses and doctors advising on school health programmes adhere slavishly to their traditional pattern of examine, investigate, diagnose and treat – and they oppose the dissemination of health information among children. New protocols for treatment of school children by teachers are now established (Werner and Bower, 1988). New patterns of disease constantly emerge, such as asthma, which is now present in such epidemic proportions that many student teachers now learn about its management in their college curriculum.

The worldwide epidemic of HIV/AIDS has already had a devastating effect on children (Evans, 1996). Some children suffer directly from the disease itself. More significant, however, is the impact of the disease among the parents on the development of children. Death or disease among parents, one in five of whom may be HIV-positive in some countries, means that parents are often ill, frequently suffering to such an extent that they cannot parent their children or earn enough money for school fees. Ensuring that basic care is available for parents with AIDS is an essential part of limiting the damage that chronic parental illness can have on children.

The importance of providing appropriate levels of screening for handicap and disability must not be underestimated, especially in programmes where, in order to save money, governments have stopped screening services. Children with deafness, partial sight or mental retardation need recognition and help. All too often, behavioural problems arise in children as a result of frustration from handicap. This anti-social behaviour is too often attributed to self-will rather than being recognized as an indicator of an underlying problem. Proper attention to the health of all children in a child development programme is essential if they are to benefit from the learning components of the programme.

School facilities

Desks, chairs and books can no longer be taken for granted, and yet they are essential for the efforts of the teacher to achieve a satisfactory impact. Even more important is the learning environment. Schools can sometimes obstruct learning if the climate is one of fear and excessive discipline and physical punishment. It is all too easy to explain away such behaviour by teachers and excuse such excesses on cultural grounds, but recent research shows that emotional and physical abuse in schools often leads to arrested academic development and to serious emotional dwarfism. Many children are excluded from attending school because of disability. With increasing competition for limited resources within a family, such children may not be sent to school. Even when they are, insufficient resources may be available to meet their special needs. The investment in provision of extra facilities for a disabled child can enhance her learning capacity and also reduce the burden on the family and community when she becomes an adult (O'Toole and MacConkey, 1995). While we can argue that the care of a child with disability should involve some diversion of resources away from non-disabled children, there will be those under intense economic pressure who have to make hard decisions. In making these decisions, it is useful to reflect that Jesus had particular compassion on those with disability. Despite all the difficulties of substandard facilities and educational approaches, it is clear that sustained school attendance can ameliorate the damaging effects of a bad developmental start to life (Myers, 1992).

Life skills

The term 'life skills' has been borrowed from the health education fraternity, who have largely come to realize that making children frightened of something, such as lung cancer, heart attacks or AIDS, is not an effective way of inducing behavioural change. Health educators and promoters have moved towards approaches that increase the level of self-worth (Mailbach and Murphy, 1995). Thus they encourage the avoidance of cigarettes, drugs and premature sex through developing better self-esteem and better confidence and techniques in saying 'no' (Parker and Gagnon, 1995). Not all teachers have the skills to support the development of these skills, and further training for teachers and recruiting health promoters will often be necessary (Lindstrom and Spencer, 1995; Roberts and Dachdev, 1996).

Parenting

Parenting should occur, ideally and according to the biblical model ordained by God, within the responsible, committed relationship of marriage. This does not mean that parents who are single or not married cannot parent well. However, single parents do have a much more difficult task (Hartnup, 1996). Deuteronomy 6:7–9 encourages parents to continually teach their children essential truths and to guide them as they grow up. Psalm 1:3 refers to the fruit that comes from a parental tree. So many children now grow up with bad models of parenting that parenting will have to be taught in child development programmes and schools in the future (Weiss, 1996).

Special situations

Violence

Violence is now a serious problem among children in many communities, and there is an increasing need to include 'conflict resolution' within school and community programmes. There are new challenges for those working with children in difficult circumstances (Zwi and Rifkin, 1995), including war, civil unrest or generally high levels of physical aggression in the community. Schools and children's groups will need additional, appropriately trained staff with skills in helping children through emotional trauma (Goodall, 1979). The appointment of a school 'violence tutor' is necessary in many situations. Again, imagination and skill in working in this area will need to be enhanced by the preparation of teaching materials that will help all children develop their potential as people who care and understand how violence damages themselves and their peers. There are several good examples of these programmes that have arisen out of the work of UNICEF and Child to Child working in refugee camps (Hanbury, 1994).

Children as change agents

The Bible speaks of the lead that children can take in society. Isaiah 11:6 describes how a young child will take on a leadership role. In many societies it is widely believed that children should be seen and not heard. They are expected to be loyal, hard working and obedient in performing household tasks and diligent in school. In other words, they are expected to be the recipients of wisdom from adults and the more that they obey and absorb, the 'better' they will become. Indeed, these societies often actively suppress alternative, innovative exploratory models of child development and initiative. This is not to suggest that good principles of discipline should be discarded, but too many communities regard children merely as a silent, obedient labour force that is to be indoctrinated in 'good values and behaviour'.

Children are, however, enormously resourceful. In a recent Child to Child project in India, the parents complained that their children were asking for soap to wash their hands before eating! Imaginative projects can integrate areas of study such as health and arithmetic, whether the project is held among children who are unable to attend school or not (Hawes and Scotchmer, 1993). Children can have a profound effect on their parents. For example, parents have experienced their children hassling them to stop smoking after school health curricula addressed health-damaging behaviour.

Prayer

Prayer support is very important for the successful outcome of a child ministry which is based on Christian principles. The success of programmes, particularly those in which new activities are being introduced, will require informed, consistent, believing prayer by the child sponsors and other interested parties alike.

Vulnerable children

Orphans, refugees, street children, children affected by HIV and all of those damaged physically and emotionally by violence within their families and society require specific strategies for child development in local situations. In many traditional societies, orphaned children or children of very poor parents may be 'adopted' into another part of the family, especially one that is better off. Similarly, despite the great numbers of orphans from wars or AIDS, many thousands of children are taken into adoptive families (Bayley, 1996). There are scriptural commands to look after the needs of the fatherless (Isa. 1:23). Although it has been tacitly assumed that these adopted children receive the same care and nurture as full blood-related children, recent studies in several less developed countries cast doubt on this assumption. Adoptive children may be used as cheap household labour, may receive considerably fewer opportunities for going to school and are more likely to be abused physically and sexually. Thus children within the same physical household unit may be variously excluded from child development and protection activities. Such adoptive children are more likely to become involved in child labour and much more likely to drop out of school. For many parents, life is extremely hard. They find it difficult enough to afford food, clothes and school fees for their own children. The burden of caring for additional children from recently deceased relatives may be back-breaking, and something tends to give unless there is support from outside the family.

There are important roles for NGOs in family support but effective, sustainable, culturally appropriate strategies need defining. How can organizations support the provision of schooling, nurture, food and housing? Increasingly, HIV/AIDS orphans are becoming household heads at an early age. Organizations have never before had to consider how to support a twelve-year-old boy who has responsibility for clothing, schooling, nurturing and growing enough food for his three younger siblings and himself.

Street children

Millions of children grow up with very little interaction with their parents. The term 'street children' needs to be defined within each local social context. For some, 'working the streets' to get money is a normal daytime activity at the end of which children return to a parental home. For others the contact with parents is more intermittent, partly dependent in many cases upon the degree of abuse and aggression experienced, or lack of food. Rather fewer, but even more important from the point of view of social development or lack of it, are those children who are completely separated from families and who tend to organize their lives in peer groups with similar circumstances. These children are particularly vulnerable and are nearly always untouched by those child-centred activities which focus on schools ('Children at Risk', 1996). The two recurring themes of poverty and exclusion are critical negative influences on child development.

Innovative, risk-taking approaches aimed at improving the welfare and development of street children are urgently needed. It is at this point that it becomes clearer than ever that child-centred approaches alone are not enough. Programmes also need to address the broader issues of income and environment. One of the difficulties facing workers who focus on street children is the lack of documentation of different methods used in the care of street children. Few programme managers write up their experiences so that others can learn. Fortunately there is an increasing number of networks that make their experiences available through newsletters and electronic means (Scanlon, Lynch and Tomkins, 1998).

'Community-centred' interventions

Christian ministry

Christian ministry can provide a theological basis for problem analysis and action if it includes reference to justice, equity and transformation as well as personal salvation. These issues are addressed in many reviews, but implementation all too often lags behind exegesis. Even in Christian ministry for children, adults often establish worship forms and social development activities without consultation with the children themselves, whose opinions they often consider irrelevant.

Physical environment

Improvement of water supplies and sewerage can lead to a reduction of the burden of disease. Improvement in the quality and safety of recreational facilities will improve children's lives and developmental possibilities, even in the midst of poverty. For example, swings and a toy library will help lift the oppressive spirit of despair from families forced by economic, social and political reasons to live in slums, refugee camps and other disadvantaged situations. Improvement in housing decreases the risk of accidents and disease and enables better concentration during homework. The provision of simple buildings with electricity or offering the use of church premises for 'homework clubs' in the evening are effective ways of promoting child development in slums.

Family support

The concept of 'the family unit' varies considerably. In a decreasing proportion of cases this means a husband, wife and children; a single-parent family is often the norm. Families come under many pressures, and support mechanisms to ensure that the family remains intact, so that child development can continue, are increasingly necessary. This may include marriage counselling or encouragement and practical support through groups for both single-parent and father/mother families. Churches need to recognize their enormous potential for providing support for children without 'dads' or 'mums'. Organizations need to consider a wider brief than education alone. If they are really concerned with child development they will begin to work within families, especially during difficult times (Tomkins, 1996).

Access to family planning services is also very important. Child survival, nutritional status and development are compromised if there are too many children who are too closely spaced. Every farmer knows the importance of ensuring that the soil is left to rest to enable it to regenerate, and spacing plants at wide intervals. It is damaging when men make women pregnant very frequently. Safe and ethical technologies are available for child spacing, but men nearly always want more children than their wives. In many societies, the production of a large number of children is equated with virility and a 'macho image'. This compromises the needs and rights of children in less developed countries to grow up in smaller families in order to obtain the necessary resources for their own development. And yet church leaders infrequently address this conflict. It is thoroughly established that child development improves if the mother is better educated, if she is older when she has her first child, and if she has fewer children. Programmes that support a healthy family size and structure need practical support from child development organizations. If we are to have a primary focus on children living with difficult circumstances, especially the very poor, this is likely to require a major shift in emphasis for many current child development programmes (UNICEF, 1996). This chapter has sought to explore what that shift would mean in practice and how such a focus would affect our design and implementation of child-care programmes.

Note

1. I have appreciated the many ways in which I have been able to interact with dedicated staff from Compassion International, Tearfund, Viva Network and other organizations over the years. Their imagination and commitment have been inspirational to the children they serve, and it has also been a major encouragement to other workers in Christian and secular organizations in less developed countries. This chapter, however, does not necessarily reflect their policies. I have also benefited from the input of a very exciting group of researchers at the CICH with whom I am privileged to work. This chapter is an abbreviated version of a paper presented to the Cutting Edge Conference at Ashburnham, UK, 1999.

– Questions to Consider –

1 Over the years, child development programmes have grown up based on passion, policy and political expedients. As Christians designing such programmes, what are the key factors that we need to be aware of?

2 How can we prevent ourselves from being swayed by non-biblical or non-effective influences in child development programmes?

3 Use the framework given by Tomkins to design your own child development programme to address a given difficulty. How did you determine the design and how would you evaluate its effectiveness?

– CHAPTER 23 –

Children 'at Risk' Because They Have Not Heard the Good News: The 4/14 Window[1]

Dan Brewster

"Let the little children come to me, and do not hinder them, for the kingdom of God belongs to such as these." (Mark 10:14)

Introduction

CUTTING-EDGE mission groups today are making some of the most significant advances in the history of Christianity by looking closely at the '10/40 Window', where most of the remaining people groups are who have never had an opportunity to hear the gospel. The concepts of the 10/40 Window and 'people groups' are among the most significant innovations in missions thinking in generations. The 10/40 Window stretches from the 10th to the 40th latitudes – roughly from West Africa across through the Middle East, South Asia and Southeast Asia, and including Indonesia. There are at least four reasons why the 10/40 Window is significant:

1. Most of the world's unevangelized people live in the 10/40 Window. In fact, while it comprises only one-third of the total land area of the world, almost two-thirds of the world's people live there. Ninety-seven per cent of the three billion people who live in the 55 most unevangelized countries live in the 10/40 Window.

2. The 10/40 Window is at the heart of the world's non-Christian religions.

There are 28 Muslim countries in this area, including a population of nearly one billion people. There is one Hindu country, with a population of almost a billion people, and there are eight Buddhist countries with a combined population of over 230 million people.

3. The poorest of the poor live in the 10/40 Window. More than eight out of ten of the poorest of the poor, who on the average have a gross national product of under $500 per person per year, live there. There is a remarkable overlap between the 50 poorest countries of the world and the least evangelized countries of the world. Only six per cent of the missionary force is now working among this 44 per cent of the world's population.

4. The quality of life is lowest in these countries in the 10/40 Window. One way of measuring the quality of life has been to combine three variables: life expectancy, infant mortality and literacy. More than eight out of ten of the people living in the 50 countries of the world with the lowest quality of life also live in the 10/40 Window.

There is another 'window within the window' however, which may be just as significant, and which may enable many frontier mission efforts to be even more effective. That window is what I call the '4/14 Window'.

The '4/14 Window'

Some years ago, Dr Bryant Myers, director of World Vision's MARC Ministries, made an excellent presentation to the EFMA Executive Retreat entitled 'The State of the World's Children: A Cultural Challenge to the Christian Mission in the 1990s'. Myers painted a sobering picture of the numbers and conditions of children and youth throughout the world today, and he noted some of the challenges that this huge and often suffering people group present to mission strategists. The most significant part of his presentation is shown here in Figure 1: in the USA, nearly 85 per cent of people who make a decision for Christ do so between the ages of four and fourteen!

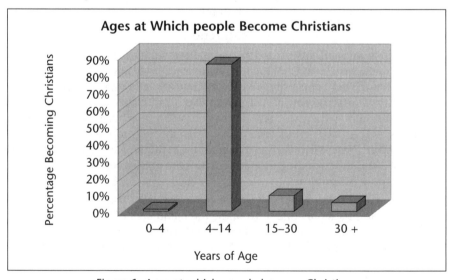

Figure 1: Ages at which people become Christians

The extent to which these data would hold true for populations outside the United States is unclear, although there is much evidence to suggest that they do. At the very least, they confirm evidence that children and young people are indeed 'the world's most fruitful field' (Benke and Bryan, 1977).

Each time I have spoken on the subject I have conducted my own survey, and these surveys have largely confirmed this important missiological fact. My own informal results have yielded a somewhat lower figure than Myers presented. Generally about 60 per cent of the people I ask say that they became Christians between the ages of four and fourteen. Obviously it depends somewhat on how 'becoming a Christian' is defined, and many Christians point to more than one experience – the second often being as an adult. But what, then, shall we say? Perhaps Myers and his sources were wrong – maybe only 60 per cent of Christians made their decision for Christ during these pliable years. But even so, what should this say to mission leaders today?

Children as a 'people group'

The category 'children' is, of course, much too broad to fit the usual definitions of a people group. People groups are typically defined in terms of ethnicity, geography, habitat or social affinity. But such delineations have a distinct adult bias. There are many distinct groups of children and young people who warrant not only ministry to address their physical needs, but also the attention of missiologists in their development of effective mission strategies. Unfortunately, such attention has largely yet to materialize.

We should be concerned about the state of children in the world because there are so many of them. Over one-third of the world's population, 1.8 billion people, are under the age of fifteen. A staggering 85 per cent of these children, 1.5 billion of them, live in the two-thirds world.

Children: A receptive people group

Missiologists are also documenting the reasons for apparent changes in receptivity to the gospel. The shelves of the School of World Mission at Fuller Seminary are brimming with theses and dissertations exploring the reasons for resistance and receptivity. One clear and consistent factor that emerges out of all of this is that people tend to be receptive when their lives are disrupted. The poor and exploited tend to be much more receptive to the gospel. There is no people group today whose lives are more disrupted than those of children and youth.

Bryant Myers reminded us that children are often suffering, unwanted and victimized. Some 40,000 children die around the world every day, many of them as a result of malnutrition and preventable diseases. Children in many countries face enormous risks. Those in the '4/14 Window' remain the most affected and vulnerable group for every kind of disease and suffering.

One evidence of the fact that many children are unwanted is the high rate of abortion, especially in the so-called developed nations. An equally shocking and growing problem is that of street children around the world. I saw first-hand the horror of the street children problem in Sao Paulo, Brazil. I recorded the following impressions in my diary:

> Family abuse is extremely common here in Sao Paulo. There were 42,000 cases of abuse reported in Sao Paulo in a three-year period. Since only 10 per cent or

less of abuse cases are reported, there must have been nearly half a million of such abuse cases. Many children in Brazil die of malnutrition, but many more die because they're on drugs and therefore do not eat. They die of malnutrition, but the real cause is drug addiction.

Actually visiting where the children live was like a descent into hell . . .

We followed the leader over the railing of the bridge, hanging out over the street and then slithered down a steep slope in order to get close so he could peek in a couple of cracks and see who was there. He told us to wait because apparently they were having sex. The counselor (pastor) had a talk with the kids who were under the bridge, and they invited us in. Under the bridge, the kids helped us crawl in through this little hole and drop down into their cave-like area underneath the bridge.

The place was unimaginably foul. The smell of urine and faeces was powerful. Under the structure of the bridge they have some blankets laid out and a few possessions. The amazing and beautiful thing was the relationship Suzanne Holanda, the director of a ministry in San Paulo, has with the kids. She hugged the children and talked with them, and we gathered around and prayed together.

We listened to the young people talk about harassment by the police and about their friends who are being beaten by the police . . . We visited with these kids for half an hour or so, and then climbed back out of the hole and onto the street below.

We all know that these are not the only problems that children face. I had a far too 'up close and personal' exposure to the suffering of children during the Rwanda war last year. In three trips to Rwanda during and right after the war, I personally saw countless children who had limbs cut off, wounds and scars too ghastly to describe and, invariably, horror stories of mistreatment, torture and abuse.

The nature of warfare is changing. UNICEF notes that:

. . . at one time, wars were fought between armies; but in the wars of the last decade far more children than soldiers have been killed and disabled. Over that period, approximately 2 million children have died in wars, between 4 and 5 million have been physically disabled, more than 5 million have been forced into refugee camps, and more than 12 million have been left homeless. (UNICEF, 1995)

The needs and injustices behind such shocking statistics cry out for attention. But the net result globally is a suffering, disrupted people group that is often hungry for the touch of the gospel in their lives. Any mission agency serious about reaching truly receptive peoples in any other 'window' of the world, then, must pay attention to this '4/14 Window'.

Children: A forgotten people group?

In light of all these factors, the relative lack of attention that mission agencies give to children's ministries is curious. What do we have to say, from a missiological standpoint, to the poorest, most numerous, disrupted, hurting – and quite possibly the most receptive – of the world's population groups? Sadly, apparently not much.

Children are often overlooked in mission strategy planning. At the GCOWE 1995 Consultation held in Seoul, Korea, in the 'How do we get there?' section of the planning workbooks, there were suggestions to consider the needs of children and youth. Several of the workshops could be said to have peripherally related to children and youth since obviously there are many millions of Chinese children, Muslim children, urban children and the like. But none of the tracks, nor any of the main plenary or workshop sessions, were specifically devoted to children (GCOWE, 1995).

The picture changed somewhat at GCOWE 1997 in South Africa. There, several of us interested in child ministries and mission strategy were able to include a track focusing on the strategic importance of mission to and through children. An acknowledgement of the importance of the '4/14 Window' was one of the encouraging outcomes of that conference.

Similarly, there is a paucity of articles in the professional missions journals (*IMR, EMQ* and *Missiology*) relating to reaching this most receptive group. The number of articles specifically on the subject of children and missions can probably be counted on the fingers of two hands.

There are a couple of notable exceptions. One is Reapsome (1985), and another is Hansen (1966), in which he suggests that 'the time has come to make the younger generation our prime objective in evangelism. To neglect it', Hansen says, 'would be a strategic blunder. Winning young people must be made a definite goal, and be given priority in our plans.' That observation is still true, but it has not been pursued.

Unfortunately, there is also almost certainly a stereotyping of child and youth ministries. Reapsome (1985), asks 'Are [children] being slighted by more majestic issues, by more serious concerns? Do we, subconsciously perhaps, look down our noses at agencies that work with children?'

A historical emphasis on children through Christian schools

Have children always been a forgotten people group? I have recently enjoyed re-reading portions of the massive *History of Christianity* by the respected historian Kenneth Scott Latourette. Latourette documents the history of the spread of Christianity in a comprehensive and sweeping way, but one must look very hard to see discussions of credible missions efforts directed towards children and youth.

Interestingly, though, his work frequently refers to the impact of Christian schools. For example, Latourette observes the importance of Christian schools in India:

> Protestantism's approach to India was varied. Much of it was through mass conversions, although at the outset these came almost unexpectedly. Some of it was through schools . . . They ranged from village schools which to members of the depressed classes were doors of hope to a world of larger opportunity, through secondary schools, to colleges of university grade. (Latourette, 1975, p. 1353)

We know, too, that an astonishing number of African political leaders came out of the Christian school systems set up in almost all of the African nations during the first part of this century. Presidents Kenyatta, Moi, Kaunda, Nyerere, Boigne and scores of others, not to mention virtually all of the leaders of the African church, are among those whose lives were impacted by this early mission strategy in Africa.

The same was true in Asia. Latourette notes that the leader 'who did most to shape the ideals of revolutionary China between 1911 and the late 1940's was Sun Yat-sen, an avowed Christian who owed most of his formal education to Christian schools' (Latourette, 1975, pp. 1317–18).

It is clear that some revolutionary leaders recognized the powerful effect of Christian schools, and they therefore imposed severe restrictions on their activities. Referring to the takeover by the Communists in China, Latourette writes:

> Religious instruction of youths under eighteen years of age in groups of more than four was forbidden . . . Special theological courses were still allowed, but only by express permission of the state. No believer was permitted to teach in a state school. (Latourette, 1975, pp. 1397–98)

It is possible that the relief and development focus of evangelicals may have absorbed some of the energies formerly devoted to ministry through schools. These relief and development efforts, however, were not normally targeted towards children and youth. But my questions for mission executives are these: With what have we replaced the mission emphasis on children and youth in schools? How are we growing the next generation of church and political leadership?

Child ministries and church growth

Another emphasis that may have absorbed some of the energies formerly devoted to Christian schools is the church growth movement. This crucial ministry has gone hand in hand with the peoples group focus, and it has resulted in the establishment of new bodies of believers in many areas of the world formerly untouched by the gospel. Compassion International's experience is that one of the most significant interventions for church growth is to assist the church develop a child health, education and spiritual nurture programme. If the programme is implemented properly, those churches will grow. In the process, many of those families – both the children and the adults – will come to Christ. We know that children are the church of the future. But we must understand that children and their parents are also the church of today.

Implications of the '4/14 Window'

The '4/14 Window' and social action

The greatest commandment is just as valid as the Great Commission. Yet the adult bias that tends to overlook children in furthering the Great Commission is common among relief and development agencies as well. This is in spite of the 'child survival' programmes that many agencies use and that attract so much government funding. Such a bias is a mistake in terms of effectiveness. UNICEF research indicates that the most significant interventions for *national* development are child health and education (UNICEF, 1988).

Compassion's experience also bears this out. We do not overtly state that we do community development, nor do our funds assist in broad community development activities, but our child development programmes, if well designed, often result in excellent community development. We have found that communities can often unite around the needs of their children even though other issues are divisive. Thus, even if an agency's goal is to do national or community development, many would do well to look more closely at ministry to children.

The '4/14 Window' and leadership development

Frontier mission agencies did us a great service in focusing our attention on AD 2000 and beyond. While we enthusiastically supported all efforts to evangelize the world by AD 2000, I am afraid some Christians assumed that we did not have time to wait for young Christians to mature into their place of leadership. Clearly, however, we must affirm that we can still afford to grow the church. Today's children are still tomorrow's leaders. We should be asking ourselves the following question: What are our strategies for growing the leadership that will be needed to lead the churches in 2025?

Child development is a long-term process. Just as parents know that it takes at least 18 years to 'develop' our own children, so we must realize that child development is a long-time proposition. The result, as was discovered in India and elsewhere, is that many children receive enough Christian training input to equip them to be serious Christian leaders.

The '4/14 Window' and unreached peoples

There is even much potential for reaching into areas of unreached peoples through a strategy of focusing on meeting the needs of this most vulnerable part of virtually every people group. Dr Danny Martin, of Missions to the Unreached, now based in Phuket, Thailand, told me that he would like nothing better than to have child assistance programmes in each of the new churches among the people groups of Asia. Such ministries, he says, would help to consolidate and solidify the new young churches and provide a strong foundation for further church growth and outreach. A missionary working in Mongolia also recently told me the same thing.

Conclusion

The plight of children around the world is well known to most of us, although we perhaps do not take the time to reflect on their needs. Clearly missions, churches and development agencies must deliberately include children in any efforts to relieve human suffering and become more aggressive advocates for alleviating the suffering and exploitation of children. From a kingdom perspective, though, it is just as important for mission agencies to consider carefully the spiritual needs of children and young people, and the potential of such ministries for fulfilling the Great Commission.

At the very least, let's agree that we must not:

1. Ignore the '4/14 Window'. If we do that, we'll only have to deal with them later.

2. Assume that taking children and youth seriously is only someone else's mission.

3. Stereotype those who minister to them.

Note

1. This first appeared as a chapter called 'The 4/14 Window: "Child Ministries and Mission Strategy"', in *Children in Crisis: A New Commitment* (ed. Phyllis Kilbourn; Monrovia, CA: MARC, 1996).

– Questions to Consider –

1 What are the implications of the '4/14 Window' for mission strategizing? What are the implications for your mission?

2 How would you describe to a non-Christian what is meant by the '4/14 Window'? What are the implications for it in practice?

3 From your knowledge of children and 'children at risk', what other 'windows' do you see at a global or community level, and how could we look through them and address the challenges which they present to us?

– CHAPTER 24 –

Discipleship: Helping Children to Find Their Place in the Church

Wanda Parker

Key biblical principles for discipling 'children at risk'

'In your life' discipling

DISCIPLING 'children at risk' demands involvement with every adult who is significantly involved with the child – including primary nurturer, teachers and social service professionals. Due to the iniquities of the fathers onto the children (Exod. 34:7) generation after generation, it takes prayer and fasting to break the 'curse' (Matt. 17:21, NASV). The fasting is not from food. Rather, the discipler gives up things she wants to do for herself in order to 'be there' for the child.

Joshua walked into court and the judge acknowledged him, 'Joshua, it's been a while since I've seen you. How have you been?' Joshua is a discipler who has made a point of getting to know the social service professionals who work with his disciples. The parents of 'his boys' rarely stay in one living space for longer than a month. Each Friday, Joshua and the other disciplers from his church go out on the streets to find the parents and interact with them.

Caleb had been arrested because he had not been attending school. He was living on the streets, going to his one-room 'home' only when he had to. Caleb was terrified of school. Joshua had spent a month going to school with Caleb, sitting in the back of the classroom each day. Caleb continued for a while after Joshua no longer attended with him, but then he stopped going. He had no parent to insist that he keep going. Dad was gone and Mom was either out hustling or wasted. Caleb had grown up fending for himself until he got involved at the church. Joshua had not been able to keep going to school with Caleb because he could not get more time off from his job.

Joshua has been called in the middle of the night to rescue a child; he has given up vacations alone to include kids who have never been out of the city; he has been up before dawn to get to the living spaces of his kids to make sure they are up and ready for school; he has chosen to live in the slums so he is always available for 'his kids'; he weekly tracks down parents. Joshua has been an advocate for 'his kids' with teachers, principals, truant officers, judges, lawyers and yes, even with parents.

Caleb has accepted Christ and recently rededicated his life to the Lord. As this is being written, Caleb is going through a time of teenage rebellion. But whenever a crisis arises he calls on Joshua – his security is with his discipler and the church where he has been nurtured.

A discipler can only work with a few at-risk children

Each discipler must decide how many children he can pour his life into (1 Thess. 2:8). Pastors, seeing the great needs in their communities, will sometimes ask disciplers to work with more children than they have time for. While bigger church programmes can work with up to 20 children, it is impossible for the discipler to devote his life to 20 different children. Jesus poured his life into 12 men. Disciplers may have full-time jobs, their own families and other responsibilities. Each discipler must determine how much time he has available.

Timothy was excited to have a group of kids with whom he could work. He started out with five kids. Those five kids were often in his home, interacting with his own children and his wife. Timothy poured himself into each young man. Often they would be over at his apartment until late at night for tutoring. Gradually, Timothy realized that he did not have adequate time to spend with each of the five. He had to turn four of the five over to another discipler. Breaking these bonds was difficult for Timothy and the boys, and Timothy wished that he had begun with more realistic expectations of himself and his time.

Moses is at Timothy's home every day for tutoring. He goes on vacations with Timothy's family. Timothy's boys consider Moses to be like an older brother. Timothy and his wife are in frequent contact with Moses' mother and other family members. At times it is difficult because what Moses learns at home is contrary to what Timothy teaches him from the Bible. For example, stealing is a way of life for Moses' family.

Timothy's wife has reflected, 'Thinking of the time we are pouring into Moses and the struggle it is, how can these kids ever grow into godly men and women with less concentration of time? How does anyone think it can be done in a large group?'

Things won't always go as planned

Each disciple will make her own choices. Even Jesus' own disciples disappointed him. Peter denied Christ three times in the moment of Christ's greatest need (Matt. 26:69ff.). James and John's mother had expectations of Jesus for her sons (Matt. 20:20ff.). James and John argued over who would be closest to Jesus, enraging the other disciples (Mark 10:41). Peter thought he knew more than Jesus, causing Jesus to rebuke him with, 'Get behind me, Satan!' (Matt. 16:23).

Sarah was a withdrawn, shy eleven-year-old when she first came to the church's after-school programme. She would rarely share about what was happening at home. But Sarah was faithful. If the doors of the church were open, she was there.

Sarah was given some responsibilities, and gradually she began to come out of her shell. She began to bond with the staff. Two years after she first came to the church, she brought along the funeral programme from her dad's funeral. He had been shot and killed just after she had first come to the church. The staff did not even know.

When she entered high school, she began to date. She told her mentor how the guys would pressure her to have sex. When this would happen she would break off the relationship. Then she began to date a guy she believed she truly loved. She held him off for a year.

The staff, who were her support system, had gone home for Christmas when Sarah made the choice to give in to the desires of her boyfriend. She struggled with her choice but was unwilling to stop. Then Sarah found herself pregnant.

Although she has had to relinquish her leadership role, Sarah continues to faithfully come to the church. She is experiencing a lot of denial and shame. The staff continue to work with her, love her and support her, while at the same time allowing her to suffer the consequences of her choices.

It is hard on the staff, who have poured six years of love into Sarah. It has caused them to do a lot of soul-searching, questioning if they could have done more. In the end, however, each child is going to make her own choices.

Disciple young children (Prov. 22:6)

The younger the child is when discipling begins, the better. Ruth was only five when she began coming to church. It was her favourite place to be. She built a close relationship with each of the staff members. She received the love of Jesus and his salvation with open arms. Her face glowed with his love.

At age seven, she would begin her morning with Jesus. She would share with the staff what Jesus was teaching her. Her horrible living conditions gave her ample opportunity to apply the biblical principles she was taught. Again and again, the staff were amazed by how Ruth called on Jesus to get her through yet another difficult situation.

Then, when Ruth was eleven, her family moved. Would Ruth continue to walk with Jesus? Although she was hundreds of miles away, Ruth called every couple of months. She was continuing to live out her faith. Recently Ruth called Naomi, her mentor, to tell her that she had torn up her tarot cards after Naomi had explained what they were. At age fifteen, Ruth is actively walking with Jesus – even though her mentors are hundreds of miles away.

Know the child and be known by the child

Deborah had worked with her girls for a couple of years. They had a trusting relationship. Deborah believed it was time to tell the girls how she had failed, so she shared with them how she had fallen into sexual sin several years earlier. Deborah shared how she had been convicted of her sin and talked about her struggle to forgive herself. The girls sat riveted as Deborah shared.

Deborah did not hide her sinfulness from her girls. They knew who she was, and therefore they were open to sharing who they were. They saw the pain in Deborah because of the mistakes she had made. When Deborah taught them from 1 John 1:9, they were not just words on a page written a thousand years ago – they saw the passage lived out in Deborah's life. The discipling relationship involves a trust that goes both ways. The discipler models a broken spirit, healed by Christ, before the child.

Teach who the enemy is and how to stand firm (Eph. 6)

One of the greatest truths we can teach children is that the battle they are waging is not their own but Jesus' (2 Chr. 20:15–24). Many of the following ideas are adapted from *The Battle is the Lord's* by Tony Evans.

The steps that follow are not foolproof or magical. Each time you work with a child, consider using these steps as a resource for the Lord to direct you. The suggestion is that this be taught one on one when a child or teen indicates a desire to be rid of a 'stronghold' in his life.

1. The child or teen must want the Lord to fight the battle for him. Until he is willing to surrender to Jesus, he will be in control. There cannot be two generals directing the same battle.

2. He must know his position in Christ (Eph. 2:6).

3. 'Since, then, you have been raised with Christ, set your heart on things above, where Christ is seated at the right hand of God. Set your minds on things above, not earthly things' (Col. 3:1–2). *If one seeks earthly solutions, he won't see heavenly responses.* God does not work in the same way that human beings do. Make this concrete so the child can understand. A knick-knack is accidentally broken. The human response is to lie and say you do not know what happened. God's way is to tell the owner the truth, 'I accidentally tripped and the knick-knack fell off the table and shattered.'

4. Jesus has already defeated the enemy (Col. 2:15). Does the child or teen *know* this truth? We can get so caught up in our spiritual emphasis that we fail to see that the child is still hurting. He doesn't know or probably care if Satan has been defeated – he just knows that he hurts (e.g., he has lost his mother). Share a concrete example from your own life to make this truth more real and a source of hope for the child.

5. Satan has no right or authority over the Christian. Jesus Christ has legally set the believer free. But Satan is still bigger and stronger if the believer tries to fight him on his own. Encourage the child to continually ask for the Holy Spirit to empower her for strength and wisdom to overcome.

6. 'Work out your salvation with fear and trembling; for it is God who works in you to will and to act according to his good purpose' (Phil. 2:12–13). There are things the individual should do but, through the whole process, she must

be aware that it is Jesus' provision that brings the change, the freedom. For example, the individual makes the choice to stop lying. She prays and asks Jesus to give her strength to always speak the truth. She asks Jesus to change her heart so she won't feel the need to lie. One day she realizes that she no longer lies. She began the healing by recognizing her sin, confessing and asking Jesus to change her heart. Jesus heard her request and removed her desire to lie.

7. Make a statement from the heart, 'Lord, I can't do this in my power. I'm too weak. I cannot live up to Your standards in my own strength' (Evans, 1998). It is not the words but the heart cry that Jesus responds to. Does the child truly want to change?

Action for the child to take

Once the child understands the above, continue with the following:

1. Prayer is how you stay connected to your general, Jesus.

2. Do not try to stand firm in the midst of the battle alone. Enlist others. Have the child or teen ask seven people to pray for him for the following 31 days. (You should speak to the people first and make sure that they are willing to do so.)

3. James 5:16 indicates that, if we confess our sin to one another and if we pray for others, we will be healed. The child should also ask each person how he might in turn pray for the prayer warrior.

4. Weekly, the child updates the prayer warriors.

5. You, the discipler, walk with them through each step.

6. Teach the child how to pray the word of God back to God.

   One of the great things about prayer, especially if you know the Word of God is that in prayer you can hold God to His Word. I do not mean you can coerce Him, but you can pray like Daniel, "O Lord, hear! O Lord, forgive! O Lord, listen and take action! For Thine own sake, O my God, do not delay, because Thy city and Thy people are called by Thy name" (Daniel 9:19).

   Daniel was reminding God of what He had said about Jerusalem and its people. He was holding God to His Word. Moses did the same thing when God announced He wanted to destroy Israel and start over with Moses (Exodus 32:10).

   Moses went before the Lord and reminded Him of three things (vv. 11–13). He reminded God that these were the people He had rescued from Egypt. Moses reminded God that if He destroyed the nation, the Egyptians would accuse God of doing evil.

   And finally Moses reminded God of His great promises to Abraham and his descendants. Then verse 14 says, "The Lord changed His mind." God was still sovereign in this situation, but from our human standpoint, the intercession of Moses caused God to change His plans.

   Moses knew how to pray. He basically said, "God, if You do this, Your name is going to look bad, and You will be embarrassed among the gods. God, it lies in Your best interest to preserve Your people. You need to forgive Your people."

   I call this putting God on the spot. Moses was able to do this in his prayer because he understood God's nature. Moses appealed to God's grace, knowing that His grace could overrule His wrath.

But Moses had to pray before God would relent. In His sovereignty, God decided that He would allow Moses' prayer to "change His mind."

We have the same privilege as Moses to hold God to His Word in prayer It's not a matter of His reluctance to fulfill His Word, but a test of our faith to believe and act on His Word. That fact has some tremendous implications for our spiritual warfare.

For example, if the devil has been holding you in bondage to a habit you do not believe you can break, you need to hit him with the truth of Philippians 4:13: "I can do all things through Him who strengthens me." When you act in Christ, you have power. (Evans, 1998, pp. 316–17)

7. Help the child to find the verses that pertain to the struggle he is going through. Model the use of the word in prayer as you pray for him.

8. Teach the child what it means to pray continuously (1 Thess. 5:17). Would a soldier in battle drop his weapon while the battle is raging – even for a second?

9. Make sure you are continually asking the child about his prayer time for others. Praying for others is key to our own healing (Jas. 5:16).

10. Besides the fact that Jesus loves us enough to take the horror of our sin upon himself, why would he do battle for us? 'To make plain to everyone the administration of this mystery, which for ages past was kept hidden in God, who created all things. His intent was that now, through the church, the manifold wisdom of God should be made known to the rulers and authorities in the heavenly realms' (Eph. 3:9–10). Jesus does battle for us so that we can walk strong in him. When we walk according to his will, the angels and demons observe and bow before the Lord in honour. We can bring honour or disgrace to Jesus.

11. The prayer should be from the depths of the heart. Do not be afraid to yell, plead and cry in your prayer. 'During the days of Jesus' life on earth, he offered up prayers and petitions with loud cries and tears to the one who could save him from death, and he was heard because of his reverent submission' (Heb. 5:7).

12. Teach the child how to put on the spiritual armour of God each day.

13. You, the discipler, should pray for total repentance and healing for the child. Pray the word back to Jesus. 'Your Father in heaven is not willing that any of these little ones should be lost' (i.e., their lives be ruined) (Matt. 18:14). 'Let the little children come to me, and do not hinder them, for the kingdom of God belongs to such as these' (Mark 10:14).

Case study

Esther is the regional co-ordinator of a ministry that trains disciplers to disciple children. Esther was visiting one particular church on a regular basis to work with the team at that church. In modelling discipling for the team, she had worked with all the children but one. Matthew kept avoiding her.

Finally, one day, she was able to sit down with him to work on his homework. She soon discovered that though he was in the sixth grade, he was unable to read. He was obviously embarrassed.

Later that week she spoke with her national director and asked for suggestions about what to do with Matthew. 'How do we help children like this?' The national director laid out the above steps.

The next week at the centre, Matthew was sitting with his discipler. Esther went to them and said, 'Mary, would you be willing to pray for Matthew every day? Would you pray that Jesus would help him learn to read?' Mary said she would love to do that.

Then, turning to Matthew, Esther said, 'And Matthew, would you be willing to pray for Mary?' Matthew was a little surprised and replied, 'I'll try.'

Two weeks later, Esther was helping another child when she heard someone reading out loud. She looked up. At the other end of the table, Matthew was reading a book out loud to Mary.

Mary explained to Esther that the week she began praying for Matthew, his schoolteacher decided to put him in an accelerated phonics programme. In two weeks, he was able to read. For six years, no teacher had taken any special interest in Matthew. The week that intensive prayer began for him, a teacher suddenly cared.

For a child to learn to function and be comfortable in the body of Christ, it is important that she be 'folded' into a local church at the earliest age possible (Deut. 6:6–9). In recipes, the term 'fold in' is used to describe the gentle blending of flour into a mixture of butter, sugar and spices (as opposed to whipping or mixing). Children need to be gently brought into the body of Christ. They must know that they are special, that they are wanted. A child's first experiences in the body of Christ set the stage for how he will view the body of Christ for the remainder of his life. This view of the church can also strongly influence the attitude he has towards Christ.

Each Sunday, ten-year-old Thomas was at church early to meet with the elders for their time of prayer. He was included in the circle as the men stood holding hands. They would ask him to pray. He felt included. He felt as though he was a viable part of the body of Christ. Thomas had to get himself up in the morning; there was no parent to encourage him.

To disciple children who demand the intensity that 'children at risk' require, it is important that you have your own support team. Never go it alone (Mark 6:7). Have individuals to whom you are accountable (Mark 6:30).

Mark was ready to give up. He was the only single staff member living in the slum. There was no one else with whom he could relate his struggles or his joys. Often his cry to the Lord was 'Why, Lord? Why have you put me here?'

Then a believer from a middle-class church reached out to Mark. They began to meet regularly. The weight of the kids with whom he was ministering was lifted as another believer 'held up' Mark's arms. Without this support Mark would have left the slums, he would have left his kids to again fend for themselves. Expect to be drained, physically, emotionally and spiritually (Mark 5:30). Thus you must go away by yourself and be refreshed (Mark 6:31).

– Questions to consider –

1 Describe how we can involve children in the church. Why do you think that so often their place in the church is not honoured?

2 If you were to begin a discipling relationship with a child, what things would you need to consider? How would your life, schedule or habits need to change? What things would you be able and willing to give up? What support structures would you put in place?

CHAPTER 25

Rediscovering Children at the Heart of Mission

Keith White

A little child will lead them. (Isa. 11:6)

Introduction

THERE is a misconception of serious proportions among Christians that the Bible says very little about children. After a brief survey of biblical material, this chapter will suggest the beginnings of a theological framework for our role in God's mission among 'children at risk'.

Let us not underestimate the significance of our task today. What if we have misheard or neglected God's revealed teaching about children and childhood? How does mishearing or neglecting God's word on these issues affect the history and current life and shape of the church? What if by default we have not been salt and light in God's world? What if our vision of the kingdom of heaven is a pale reflection of what Jesus revealed? The stakes are very high, and today marks the start of a process of what could in time have a significant impact on the development of theology and mission and the shape of the church.

What is offered here is a tentative outline. It has been written while the responsibilities of caring for 'children at risk' have taken priority over writing. It comes from the heart as well as the head, and from one who has spent much of the last 12 years working on a new version of the Bible, designed for children of every culture who are encountering the Scriptures for the first time.

Children in the Bible

An Old Testament cast of children

- **Ishmael** (Gen. 16) means 'God hears'. His pregnant mother, Hagar, had all but given up hope, but God was infinitely concerned about this single mother and her future son.
- **Isaac** (Gen. 22) prefigured Jesus' sacrifice in the story of the testing of Abraham.
- **Joseph** (Gen. 37), the seventeen-year-old dreamer, was the one through whom his father and the children of Israel were saved.
- **Benjamin** (Gen. 44, 45) was the boy through whom reconciliation came between Joseph and his brothers.
- **Moses** (Exod. 1) was saved by the vigilance of his sister **Miriam**.
- The story of the exodus begins with the murder of 'Jewish baby boys', foreshadowing the birth of Christ. The final plague involved the death of 'firstborn sons'.
- The climax of the book of Ruth is the birth of a baby, **Obed**, one of the ancestors of Jesus.

- **Samuel** (1 Sam. 3) was the child through whom God was able to reveal his will when adults failed. He is a model for human spirituality and obedience.
- **David** (1 Sam. 17) was the person through whom it was revealed that God was not dependent on adult power or training. Through a boy, the Philistines were routed.
- Elijah and Elisha each brought a **widow's son** to life (1 Kgs. 17; 2 Kgs. 4).
- God used a **young servant girl** in the healing of Naaman, the army commander (2 Kgs. 5).
- **Josiah**, who reformed politics and religion, was a boy-king (2 Kgs. 22). He was a boy when he began his dramatic reforms (2 Chr. 34).
- **Esther**, the future queen who would save the Jewish people, was an orphan girl (Esth. 2:7)
- **Jeremiah** was chosen by God, though he was 'only a child' (Jer. 1).

It is not just that these people happened to be children. But God performed some of his most significant acts and revelations through these children. Their faith and actions are critically important in the unfolding and outworking of God's purposes.

Childhood in the Old Testament

The Old Testament is much more than a record of the significance of individual children. Children and childhood are of great significance in the social life of Israel and in the way the Old Testament is presented as a whole.

Worship was visual and dramatic – equally accessible to children and adults. The instructions for the Passover assume that children will ask what it means (Exod. 12:26–28). So, too, the 12 stones set up after being taken from the bed of the river Jordan stand as a sign for instructing future generations (Josh. 4:6–7). God's people serve and worship him through the rituals and practices described in Exodus and Leviticus. There is little, if any, separation of children from adults. In Ezra 10, when the law is read out, children are mentioned as part of the crowd, recalling the occasion of the renewal of the covenant in Joshua 8:35.

Children are seen as a sign of God's blessing throughout the Old Testament, and yet they are the first to suffer when sin, deceit, war and famine affect a tribe or city. Achan's children die as a result of his sin (Josh. 7). There are desperately sad and vivid depictions of the suffering of children throughout the Old Testament (Ps. 106; Jer. 31; Lam. 1, 2, 4; Joel 3; Amos 2; Zeph. 1).

One of the primary concerns of any responsible adult is the well-being and care of children. In most situations families will provide for them, but when this is not possible because of disease, death, famine or war, then the care of the fatherless is dear to God's heart (Pss. 10; 146; Isa. 1; Zeph. 1:8).

God's relationship with his people is portrayed in different ways in the Old Testament, but one of these portrayals (subsequently developed in the New Testament) is as a Father. In Deuteronomy 8, God disciplines those whom he has chosen. Psalm 27:10 says that a child may be abandoned by father and mother, but not by God, the heavenly Father. God's compassion is like that of a father to a child (Ps. 103). The Wisdom literature is written largely as from a father to a son (Ps. 34; Prov. 1–7). The Jewish people are often called 'children of Israel' or 'daughters of Zion'.

The mother/child relationship is significantly used to describe the bond between God and us, his children. There is a beautiful description of the weaned child in Psalm 131 representing the stilled and quietened soul. A mother may forget the child at her breast, but God will never do so (Isa. 49:15–16). Isaiah closes with a tender description of childbirth that concludes, 'As a mother comforts her child, so will I comfort you' (Isa. 66:13). Hosea movingly relates the early days of the Israelites thus: 'When Israel was a child, I loved him, and out of Egypt I called my son' (Hos. 11:1).

You will find much food for thought in Ecclesiastes 11 and 12: 'Remember your Creator in the days of your youth'; Song of Songs 8 and the younger sister; Ezekiel and the 'son of man' (2:1ff.), and the Old Testament closes with a renewed relationship across the generations between children and fathers (Mal. 4:6). And that's only a skim through!

Old Testament themes

There are three deeply significant themes that we have not yet touched upon, and before we leave the Old Testament we must deal with them.

First, in Psalm 8, there is a truth that is easily overlooked alongside the immensity of the night sky. Jesus specifically draws attention to it, so that should be reason enough for us to stop and take note: 'From the lips of children and infants you have ordained praise because of your enemies, to silence the foe and the avenger' (8:2). Children are ordained and designed to praise God and his glory. They are not consumers or future adults, but worshippers of the Creator God. Their ears, eyes, feet, hands and voices have been created to praise God. This is their true nature and purpose. But, more than this, they have a special role in silencing the enemies of God. When all else fails, it is children (like Samuel and David, for example) who will be the means of moral and spiritual virtue and power. Is this not remarkable? The child is being portrayed, morally and spiritually, as the 'father of the man'.

This leads to the second great insight, found in Isaiah 11. This passage vividly portrays the messianic kingdom: 'The wolf will live with the lamb, the leopard will lie down with the goat, the calf and the lion and the yearling together; and a little child will lead them.' What is the place of the child? Leading! And it will be a safe environment in which children can play – unlike the urban, war-torn, consumer market-dominated jungle of today (see also Isa. 65). The kingdom of heaven has children at its heart. We must never lose sight of this if we want to understand the teaching of Jesus, our relationship to God and our joint mission on earth.

There is one crowning role for the child in the Old Testament. Isaiah talks of God's righteous anger against the sin and hypocrisy of humankind. This situation seems unimaginably bleak and hopeless, and yet God gives a sign: 'The virgin will be with child and will give birth to a son, and will call him Immanuel' (Isa. 7:14). The culmination of God's saving action is a light to those living in the shadowlands: 'to us a child is born, to us a son is given, and the government will be on his shoulders. . .' (Isa. 9:6).

The focus is not a warrior king, a wise rabbi or a high priest, but a child. The natural and normal place to look for salvation is everywhere else and to everyone else . . . but the government will rest on this child's shoulders. And so the scene is set, the stage is ready, for us to venture into the New Testament.

The New Testament and children

It is in the Gospels that we encounter the working out and development of each of these themes from the Old Testament.

Jesus encounters many different children throughout his life, for example: the daughter of the Canaanite woman (Matt. 15; Mark 7); the boy with a demon (Matt. 17; Mark 9; Luke 9); the official's son at Capernaum (John 4); Jairus' daughter (Matt. 9; Mark 5; Luke 8); the son of the widow at Nain (Luke 7); and the boy who offered Jesus the five loaves and two fish (John 6). Jesus has a heart for children, and they are drawn to him. His preferred method of teaching by story and sign is, like the Old Testament worship and ritual, equally accessible to children and adults.

There are four aspects of the gospel narratives that call for our particular respect and attention. The first is the birth of Jesus, *the incarnation*. The Gospels of Matthew and Luke devote their opening chapters to this. Matthew quotes the passage from Isaiah about the virgin and child (Isa. 7:14). The wise men come in search of the child. When they find him, they worship him by kneeling and presenting gifts. The exodus narrative is recreated and revisited as Herod realizes he has been tricked. Once again, young boys are killed. In Luke there are extensive accounts of the births of John the Baptist and Jesus. Luke tells of a sign for the shepherds that replicates the prophecy of Isaiah, 'You will find a baby wrapped in cloths and lying in a manger' (Luke 2:12). Simeon tells of the significance of the child, 'This child is destined to cause the falling and rising of many in Israel, and to be a sign . . .' (2:34). And when those who looked forward to the redemption of Jerusalem came to the prophetess Anna, she spoke about 'the child' (2:38).

The word 'child' is repeated again and again in both Gospels at this point in the story. The significance of all of this is that God has chosen to enter the world, to reveal himself as a baby and as a child. Perhaps we are so accustomed to Christmas that we do not realize how radical this is. The theologian Nestorius was so upset about the implications of this that he wrote, 'I deny that God is two or three months old!' Karl Barth, describing the helpless baby, wrote, 'This is your God!' The fullness of the creator God is a tiny child? Is it possible? If so, what does it mean?

The hymn writers have pondered the paradox and come up with 'Lo within a manger lies, He who built the starry skies . . .', and other ways of expressing total amazement. If it is difficult to see how the fullness of the Godhead could dwell in a human being, how much greater is the challenge to see almighty God contracted to the span of a baby! From God's point of view there is no problem, but it shakes our preconceptions. A baby is small, weak, dependent and vulnerable, lacks education and training and language . . . and God says that we must learn to move from the palaces and encounters with the learned and the powerful to the manger and the child.

The second strand in the Gospels concerns *children and childhood*. To see this requires some work on your part as we seek to understand the mind of Jesus. You will need to turn to Matthew 17 and be ready to look through to chapter 21. The story here spans the period from the transfiguration to Jesus' entry into the temple at Jerusalem. (It is also told in Mark 9–11 and Luke 9–19 with many of the same elements.) These chapters contain some of Jesus' clearest teaching about the nature of the kingdom. The first action of Jesus after the transfiguration is to heal the boy with a demon. Then he teaches about taxation, payment and sonship. Chapter 18 contains the famous statement 'unless you change and become like little children, you will never enter the kingdom of heaven', as well as a curse on those who cause harm to children and the story of the lost sheep applied to children.

Next comes teaching on forgiveness and divorce prompted by adult questions and concern, and once again Jesus places children in the centre of the kingdom (19:13–15). A rich young ruler is then told to sell everything in order to enter the kingdom (i.e., to become like a child). The parable about workers in a vineyard demonstrates the upside-down nature of the kingdom and is followed by more teaching about Jesus' death. The mother of James and John wants to claim prestigious places in the kingdom for her boys, completely misunderstanding the nature of the kingdom and what childhood teaches us about it. The two blind men (20:29–34) do a lot better! Then Jesus enters Jerusalem and crowds welcome him. In the temple, things carry on as if the Christ had not arrived and the kingdom of heaven did not exist. Only children continue to praise Jesus. They are rebuked. But Jesus confirms that these children are doing exactly what they are designed for: to praise and worship God (Ps. 8:2).

What have we discovered? A thread from transfiguration to the temple, from one mountain top to Mount Zion, links the teaching about the death of Jesus and the kingdom of heaven. All of the major commentaries miss the fact that children are the linking strand, and some translators do not help by translating '*nepioi*' (little children) as 'the simple' (Matt. 11:25; Luke 10:21).

The third strand to note in the Gospels is about the *kingdom of heaven*. What is Jesus teaching about the kingdom of heaven?

- Greatness in his kingdom has nothing to do with status, power, strength, influence, wealth, or any of the things normally associated with human greatness.
- You need to change (to repent) to enter the kingdom.
- You need to become like a little child if you are to enter the kingdom of heaven.
- In welcoming little children, we welcome the Lord of the kingdom!
- The kingdom belongs to the childlike.

The kingdom is in fact not like an earthly kingdom at all – it's the opposite in every way. The best way of describing it is not as a place or territory, but as 'God's way of doing things'. When we understand that, all the stories of the kingdom fall into place.

Another great paradox of the kingdom concerns when it will be fully realized, or when it started. It is both inaugurated (i.e., it has begun) but not yet (i.e., it has not been fully realized). In this children help us: for children are both fully human (now) and not fully developed (not yet). Childhood and the kingdom illuminate each other. No wonder Jesus is seething with anger at the thought of anyone harming a child, made in God's image and a sign of his kingdom!

The fourth and final strand is a powerful and common description of entering the kingdom that we have allowed to become detached from children and childhood. That is the teaching of Jesus to Nicodemus (John 3): 'You must be born again'. What is Jesus teaching? Exactly the same truth: you've got to repent, to let go of all your adult, culturally-laden preconceptions and become a little baby. You have to start all over again . . . in Christ. It is not a separate metaphor or teaching. Like Matthew, Mark and Luke, John is recording the need for an adult to become like a child – otherwise, he or she cannot see the kingdom of God.

This truth is embedded in John's Gospel in the relationship between Jesus and his Father. This is a model for us. So when we pray we are to say not 'Almighty God', 'Creator' or 'Lord God', but . . . *Our Father*. This relationship is the realization of the hope of the Old Testament. The Gospel of John begins by talking about 'children of God', and Jesus' life shows most tenderly and plainly what this means.

In the Gospels and in the kingdom, children are at the centre – like the boy offering his five loaves and two fish to adult disciples who felt it right to point out to Jesus that they weren't enough!

And what of the rest of the New Testament? Romans and Galatians flesh out the whole nature of our relationship with God in Christ. We are adopted into God's family and enabled to know God as 'Abba', or father. We are to enter into every aspect of the life of Christ and to live as children of the light. One of the favourite descriptions of the followers of Jesus is 'dear children'. The epistles describe a new way of living, in Christ, in which there is neither male nor female, Jew nor Gentile, bond nor free!

As we have seen, the Bible has much to say about children. What are the implications of all this?

Preparing the ground

Let's look first at some of the errors from past experience to avoid before we begin to outline a theological framework for the future.

1. We have made fundamental mistakes about the *kingdom* of God and about mission. We separate it from our own culture. Kingdom, empires and colonialism were all about power, territory and conquest. We thought mission was what we did; that God's kingdom depended on our activity.

2. We have gone about *theology* in the wrong way. It has been an adult-orientated pursuit placing tremendous emphasis on philosophy, doctrine, systematic theology and hermeneutics. Very little attention has been paid to the stories, paradoxes and signs of the kingdom.

3. We have made mistakes in the *church*. We have got our priorities mixed up. Sometimes we did not distinguish between kingdom and church. Often we underestimated the place and contribution of children. We honestly did not think that we had anything to learn from them!

4. We have contributed to *societies* in which adults, power, wealth and possessions seem to count for almost everything and in which Jesus' teaching to sell everything becomes, for many, impossible to contemplate. Childlikeness is marred, or squeezed into adulthood, by our commercialism and adult programmes of education. Children are second-rate concerns of the political system. They suffer hugely, and the wrath of God does not seem to have stirred us into appropriate action.

With this in mind by way of preparation, let's consider a theological framework for our future mission alongside and among children.

I draw from that wonderful work *Transforming Mission* by David J. Bosch, the South African theologian who was killed in a car crash in 1992, and from the Lausanne Covenant and subsequent Manila statements. They make the life of Jesus a central organizing principle. It is, in shape and emphasis, a christological framework.

We are, along with every follower of Jesus Christ, called to present our bodies as living sacrifices in his service; to allow the world-view and mind of Christ to permeate our every thought and attitude; to serve Jesus as Lord; to live in new relationships and a new community in such unity and love that people know we are his disciples; to continue his priorities and mission. This is our common calling. But what is the particular calling for those of us committed to work with children and young people at risk?

A Christ-centred framework for our mission

Let's take six of the major events of Jesus' life as our framework and see how they clarify our mandate and tasks.

The incarnation (the model of our mission)

Evangelical Protestant theology has tended to be comparatively weak at this point, rather stressing the cross and redemption. We must seek out the implications and demands of the astounding event of the incarnation. God entered the world in time and space, and Jesus in his life and teaching brought forgiveness and healing to people irrespective of role, gender or class.

Parenting, families, communities, work and play all matter to Jesus so much that he brought restoration to people and relationships. The New Testament sees such relationships as central to our calling as followers of Jesus. Jesus calls us to follow him, and as we ask 'what would Jesus do?' we find his ministry to be a vivid and simple guide.

Christians are seeking to continue Jesus' work in every family, city and street, along each track, mountain, river and well, in every wound and disease. The transcendence and divinity of Jesus are revealed distinctively in John's Gospel through his humanity. Through his daily life, with dust on his feet and thirst in his mouth, he revealed God's grace and glory.

The social and political dimension of the gospel is implicit in the agony, sweat and blood of Jesus – not only on the cross, but also in his life and ministry. The wrestling and struggle at the heart of the Lausanne Covenant represents a struggle at the heart of the gospel. Evil is not only in the human heart but also in our social structures, and there is no gospel without solidarity (incarnation).

In all this and more we recognize the implications of the incarnation for our life and calling in Christ. But our life alongside 'children at risk' leads us to shed light on hidden aspects of the incarnation. Traditionally, Western theological creeds have stressed that Jesus became man ('*homo factus est*'). The gospel narratives, in contrast, stress the *child* Jesus. Drawing on Isaiah, the sign in Luke's Gospel that this was indeed God's chosen One, the Messiah, was the fact that 'a baby was lying in a manger'.

The implications of the incarnation involving a baby and a child have not been fully worked into Western theology. Do the creeds need reformulation? *'Puer factus est'*: he became a boy-child? This tendency to overlook the significance of the child Jesus finds its way into the commentaries on his ministry and teaching. The centrality of childhood for understanding and entering his kingdom has been generally overlooked or marginalized. We have not seen children as signs of the kingdom. A Christian is one who has been born again, who has become like a child. This process is deeply interwoven with the incarnation: the child Christ in us, and we in him.

The cross (the cost of our mission)

The life and death of Jesus cannot be separated. They are indissolubly linked. Philippians 2 sums up his life and death: 'being found in appearance as a man, he humbled himself and became obedient to death – even death on a cross!' 'When Christ calls a man he bids him come and die', Bonhoeffer wrote not long before his execution. The cross is the symbol of our salvation, through Christ's sacrificial death. The cross is also the reminder that 'suffering is the divine mode of activity in history . . .' (Schutz, 1930, p. 245) There is no following Jesus without scars.

As followers of Jesus, we live under the shadow of the cross. It is a constant reminder and emblem of the reality and savage cruelty of human sin, rebellion and suffering. We delude ourselves if we ever minimize the extent of human suffering and degradation. The cross reminds us of the constant necessity for repentance and reformation as individuals and as a community of believers. There is no mission without tears.

The cross is God's reminder that we cannot save ourselves by human means: our plight is too serious. We are not just lost, but dead in our sins. The cross also points to the sacrifice of Jesus, the sinless one, so that we might be right with God. There is no healing or forgiveness without shedding innocent blood. The cross constantly challenges our own motives and commitments: it calls us to love irrespective of reward or return.

The cross is also a symbol of reconciliation, uniting people irrespective of creed, gender or class. It is the place where we meet as equals.

Through all of this we recognize the implications of the cross for our life in Christ. But as those called to live among and alongside children, we are constrained to cry out on behalf of the silent suffering of children worldwide in every culture and economy. Children are suffering like silent lambs on the altars of our gods.

As adults we have become so obsessed with our own ambitions, fears and agendas that we have allowed generations of children to suffer. Our institutions and structures reflect this. The cross calls us to identify most of all with those who are oppressed and suffer chronically. The innocent children who suffer in our world find, in Jesus on the cross, one who understands more than others will ever know.

The resurrection (the mandate for our mission)

We are an Easter people and 'Hallelujah' is our song! Through the resurrection of Jesus the forces of the future – joy, hope and victory – stream into the present.

Christians are not bitter, angry and consumed by a desire to destroy and exact revenge, because the cross has replaced that desire with love, and because the empty tomb opens up whole new horizons.

We believe there is no situation that cannot be transformed by the power of the risen Lord. And having glimpsed the transforming reality of God's reign we identify and stand against the forces of death, exploitation and destruction. We are not afraid to unmask idols and false gods.

We are prepared to become seeds that die in order that God's life might be revealed in all its glory. We value each person on earth and each relationship in the light of God's love . . . and yet we see beyond human life, beyond the graves and killing fields.

In all of this we identify with our brothers and sisters in Christ worldwide, but as those alongside and living among 'children at risk' we find ourselves moved to consider the ways in which children speak to us of resurrection.

We see, in the ability and resilience of children in the face of appalling loss, suffering and humiliation, the desire to work for a better world – resurrection in action. Children in our world are Easter signs, like green shoots after the grip of winter.

The ascension (the incentive for our mission)

The significance of the ascension of Jesus for our life and God's mission has also often been overlooked. The ascension is the sign that Jesus Christ is King and that the kingly reign has begun. We are called to live as the Messiah people, in a world that does not as yet acknowledge Jesus as Lord. We are to resist being squeezed into worldly moulds and ecclesiastical and institutional patterns that distort the values and priorities of Christ.

There is a rich biblical vision of this new kingdom all through the Scriptures, and we are called to realize it in our lives, our families, our countries, our culture and in the wider world.

In the history of mission other visions have unconsciously shaped the living out and proclamation of God's reign. In particular territory, power and status have been valued more than gift-love and servanthood. This kingdom demands that we invert the status quo. Children are central in this vision; this is a revolutionary contrast to contemporary political kingdoms that have lost touch with the childlike spirit in their preoccupation with adult concerns and solutions.

Children and childhood present us with insights into the nature and dynamics of God's kingdom, especially the 'now' and 'not yet'. This is a creative tension. We see a child and a sacrificed lamb at the heart of that vision. It is an everlasting kingdom where every aspect of creation lives in harmony and without fear or pain.

Pentecost (the power for our mission)

God's Spirit is powerful in the life and witness of God's people. The love and fellowship of God's people are part of the message that the church proclaims.

This community is distinctive in that it exists for others, to be servants of the wider community by revealing righteousness and justice in action. The church community is a picture of God's kingdom (on earth), but not the kingdom itself.

It is a fellowship of followers of Jesus, on the move and responsive to God's agenda, call and timing. No Christian individual or organization exists independent of the Spirit's enabling and *koinonia*. We are accountable to Christ through his people.

As those alongside children and living with them we are aware that the church has all too often replicated the assumptions and institutions of the culture in which it has been set, at the expense of Christ's example. Children have not been at the heart of our life and our worship together. Too often, like the infant Jesus, they have been relegated to the stable-like margins. We have agonized over matters like infant baptism, participation in the Lord's Supper and whether they are saved and at what age. All the while we have been unaware of the ways in which, like the disciples of Jesus, we have come between children and the love of Jesus. We have tended to see work with children as outside the mainstream of church life and worship. We need to recognize the biblical call to refocus our corporate agenda.

The second coming (the urgency of our mission)

All our work, our initiatives and structures, like our celebration of the Lord's Supper, are interim. We occupy the period between his first and second comings. We see in part; the kingdom is realized in part. But then we shall see him face to face, and the kingdom will be fully revealed.

We are alert; we listen; we work in the knowledge that he may come at any time. We operate in every part of the world, for that is his command. He has no preferred people or cultures: all are objects of his mercy and love, and all peoples will be equally joyful as they participate in the new kingdom. We acknowledge that, should Jesus come again today, the suffering of millions of children will provoke his burning anger and judgement upon those peoples and institutions that oppress them and cause them harm.

As those living alongside and among children we must acknowledge the special place and role that they have in his kingdom. They will lead the worship because this is what they are ordained to do. They will be at the centre, as centuries of marginalization, victimization and abuse will be replaced by an experience of perfect freedom and harmony.

Some of the implications
of the rediscovery of children in mission

This approach and outline has radical, potentially world-shattering implications. Let us list some of the most obvious and begin the task of working out others.

Theology

There have been major challenges to the Western tradition of theology in recent decades from women and from non-European peoples and cultures. The old colonial-type edifice is crumbling. We cannot read the Old Testament, see Jesus, or understand the New Testament and the Gospels in the same way. How could we have missed the great transcendent truths and been squeezed by the constraints of our narrow, parochial approach and assumptions? We have begun to understand our Lord and Saviour in fresh and living ways: the Jesus we never knew!

Children have been all but invisible in theology, in its formal sense. The starting point of theology should be Jesus' teaching: doing, not just hearing, being born again and becoming like children. There would be much that we would 'need to unlearn – all the adult structure and the cumbering years' (Arnold, 1997, pp. 29–30).

Church

Alongside the shifts in theological understanding and process have come fresh insights into the nature of 'church'. For centuries, the European consensus across denominations has been of institutions usually worshipping in a building with a male leadership. In Europe, this model has reached a crisis point: there is widespread and chronic decline, especially among children and young people.

Are there new ways of being church? In their recent study, Anne Wilkinson-Hayes and Stuart Murray (2000) look at examples from different parts of the world. And one of their discoveries was that, in several cases, 'children are very central to the way of being church'. I recall the excitement and sense of discovery at the last Cutting Edge Conference when Stuart Christine told of his discovery of the dramatic change in his understanding of church when he saw children at the heart of ministry, life and worship.

We need to redefine the core and margins of the church . . . always reforming. And the core is clearly identified in the Scriptures: widows, orphans, strangers and the 'little ones'.

We have radical work to do if we are to be God's avant-garde.

Society

Ours is a calling to change the world in line with the contours of God's kingdom. Christians cannot accept the status quo and should be salt and light at every level: living in a new way, challenging evil, power and traditions. Graham Kendrick's prophetic hymn, 'Who Can Sound the Depths of Sorrow in the Father Heart of God?' may become like an anthem for those of us involved with 'children at risk'.

Christians working with 'children at risk' must challenge adult assumptions and preferences and the market forces that corrupt children and childhood. Patterns and understandings of families and parenting need to be rethought. Christians should be involved personally and corporately in action and policy, with individuals and institutions, with ideologies and structures.

Obedience

We did not choose Jesus; he chose us. He loved us and gave himself for us. He fills us with his spirit and leads us into his mission. In leading us to be alongside children, Jesus entrusts us with the heart of his mission and kingdom. He warns us of the costs and dangers and also promises that, as we open our hearts to one child, we welcome Christ himself.

At the dawn of a new millennium we have an awesome calling to be alongside 'children at risk', and to reshape the processes, nature and structures of church, mission and society. If we fail, it is not just children who continue to suffer but civilization as God sees it. Not only will children fail to have their rightful place, but Jesus himself will be misunderstood and unrecognized. He will have knocked at the door of our souls and fellowships in vain. But when we welcome a child in his name, we have opened our hearts afresh to him.

– Questions to Consider –

1 So often in our work with children, children can become problems and issues rather than people. Reflect on the challenges presented in this chapter and discuss how you would respond to them.

2 Create a forum with your colleagues or fellow students and discuss how to place children at the heart of mission. Write up your discussion as a proposal for your organization.

3 Write a theology of mission, integrating the biblical material and insights contained in this chapter.

– CHAPTER 26 –

What the Bible Says about Why Children Suffer

Glenn Miles with Coleen Houlihan

Author and lecturer Leo Buscaglia once talked about a contest he was asked to judge. The purpose of the test was to find the most caring child. The winner was a four-year-old child whose next door neighbour was an elderly gentleman who had recently lost his wife. Upon seeing the man cry, the little boy went into the old gentleman's yard, climbed onto his lap, and just sat there. When his mother asked him what he had said to the neighbour, the little boy said, "Nothing, I just helped him cry."

The biblical view of suffering

ALL of us working with 'children at risk' come into contact with suffering every day and have probably thought, prayed and used Scripture to make sense of what we have thought and seen. 'Children at risk' in some ways is an inaccurate description, because many children are no longer simply at risk; they are actually suffering.

Recently my wife, who is working with families affected by HIV/AIDS, told me of a family who was being helped. The husband had died and left his wife with four children. Even though the wife knew that the children could now be helped, she had sold them. The staff in the centre could not understand why, because she received very little money and the centre had agreed to help her. When questioned further, she asked why her children should have a better life than the terrible life she had suffered. The staff were numbed. What suffering leads a woman to sell her children even when relative safety was at hand? What suffering are those children now to be exposed to in the form of sexual slavery and organized crime?

How did Jesus respond to the suffering he saw among children? Jesus healed the boy with the evil spirit (Luke 9:37–45) and, while the disciples were still marvelling, he told them what was about to happen to him, of his own suffering in being 'betrayed into the hands of men'. It seems strange that he would bring this up at this particular moment in time unless it was for a purpose. What is that purpose? Was it to somehow relate his own suffering to the suffering of children?

Faith

It is interesting that the disciples ask why they could not heal the boy, and Jesus chooses this moment to rebuke them for their lack of faith. He concludes 'If you have faith . . . Nothing will be impossible for you' (Matt. 17:20).

Sometimes when I have been involved in evaluating programmes working with children in very difficult situations, I am amazed at the faith that people have had to push through against all odds, believing that it was possible when everyone said it was not. The fruits of their faith are evident in the work. I believe that people are responding to the challenge of Jesus in Matthew 17:21.

In a world where there is so much hopelessness it is important that Christians believe that change is possible. This is especially important among many cultures in which there is a strong element of fatalism. We need to be like the friends of the paralysed man who had enough faith to bring him to Jesus; when Jesus saw this, he healed him (Luke 5:20).

Obedience

The argument among the disciples about who will be greatest occurs soon after the healing of the boy with the evil spirit. It seems ironic that they should be arguing over who should be the most powerful after they had just demonstrated that they were unable to heal the boy. But is this not typical of human nature? Jesus took a child and stood him among them and said, 'Whoever welcomes this little child in my name welcomes me; and whoever welcomes me welcomes the one who sent me' (Luke 9:48). So when we reach out to a child at risk we are, in effect, reaching out to Jesus.

But Jesus doesn't finish there. 'For he who is least among you all – he is the greatest' (Luke 9:48). Those involved in ministry among 'children at risk' are reminded that in God's kingdom the power differential between adults and children is nullified. We should not exercise our power over children or colleagues in a way that humiliates them. How much pain and suffering do adults cause children? Are we any better if we exert power and authority over the children we seek to serve or over the staff who work under us or over us? We must be obedient to God and servants to one another if we want to see his kingdom.

Compassion

Perhaps the reason we ask why children suffer is because we see their vulnerability and feel that they are too innocent to deserve to suffer. As a paediatric nurse who has worked in Asia for many years, I have seen children dying in hospital, sometimes slowly and painfully. I have seen children with disabilities in huge wards of abandoned children with little physical contact. I have seen girls who have been raped into submission and then kept as sexual slaves. I have seen child soldiers who have lost their limbs and part of their hearts to a war they do not understand. I have seen babies dying of HIV/AIDS. And the chances are, if you are reading this, that you have also seen these things, or worse. Jesus instructs us to reach out to the most vulnerable and unlovely with compassion. When we do so, we are touching the very heart of the gospel (Luke 9:48).

Even in the midst of crisis, Jesus was a model of compassion and thoughtfulness in the way that he healed children and included the family. He asked Jairus to get his daughter some food after she was raised from the dead (Luke 8:55). He gave the widow's son back to his mother after he was healed (Luke 7:15) and the boy with an evil spirit back to his father (Luke 9:42). We also must seek God's help to respond compassionately.

Forgiveness

The healing and redeeming power of the cross is a unique resource to the Christian child-care worker. We need to respond to those who cause others to suffer in an attitude of forgiveness. If we do not, then things cannot change. Forgiving others will enable us to be forgiven ourselves. 'Forgive us', we pray, 'as we forgive others who sin against us.' Children who have themselves caused suffering and feel responsible, such as the child soldier, will need a special touch of God's forgiveness as they come to the cross. Forgiveness is a legal act, releasing the offender and the offended from the bond of the wound, enabling both parties to let go of the burden. But before we can forgive, we need firstly to acknowledge the wound and the pain, to feel the anger and hurt, to have our reactions heard and honoured by ourselves and others. Then, and only then, can we truly forgive. Forgiveness is *not* saying that it did not matter, nor is it forgetting the wrong and trusting the offender without first expecting some demonstration that they have changed and become worthy of trust anew. It is releasing ourselves from the past to live and grow for Christ. The debt has been paid, and we have the choice of life.

Wounded healer

Perhaps the suffering also reminds us of our own vulnerability. Many people working with 'children at risk' (including some of the contributors to this book) have suffered through prejudice, through persecution, through misunderstandings and/or through personal tragedy. I believe that this is because God uses the weakest to make his kingdom.

> God chose the foolish things of the world to shame the wise; God chose the weak things of the world to shame the strong. He chose the lowly things of this

world and the despised things – and the things that are not – to nullify the things that are, so that no one may boast before him. (1 Cor. 1:27–29)

Ironically, it is through our own understanding of suffering that we are able to help others. As Paul said, 'For just as the sufferings of Christ flow into our lives, so also through Christ our comfort overflows' (2 Cor. 1:5). And, because Jesus himself suffered when he was tempted, 'he is able to help those who are being tempted' (Heb. 2:18).

We are reminded that nothing can separate us from the love of Christ: 'neither death nor life, neither angels nor demons, neither the present nor the future, nor any powers, neither height nor depth, nor anything else in all creation, will be able to separate us from the love of God that is in Christ Jesus our Lord' (Rom. 8:38–39).

Children who have suffered can also contribute to the healing of others, in spite of their own suffering. A young slave girl who had been captured from Israel told her mistress about Elisha, and Naaman was subsequently healed (2 Kgs. 5). What a wonderful example of graciousness towards her slave master. At the same time, we need to encourage children to be like the young men Shadrach, Meshach and Abednego and say that the God we serve can save us and rescue us from the blazing furnace, 'But even if he does not . . . we will not serve (other) Gods' (Dan. 3:18). This is where there is real sacrifice, because children (and we) need to learn to say that if things do not work out the way we want them to, we will still trust God.

No more suffering

It is comforting for those of us exposed to so much suffering in children that one day he will 'wipe every tear from their eyes. There will be no more death or mourning or crying or pain, for the old order of things has passed away' (Rev. 21:4). Isaiah 11 gives us a picture of a time when the needy will be judged with righteousness, decisions for the poor will be made with justice and the wicked will be slain. The wolf will live with the lamb, the leopard will lie down with the goat and the calf and lion will be together. Perhaps most extraordinary of all is that 'a little child will *lead* them'. Once again, children are put in our midst as a symbol of power being turned upside down.

In their own words

Children can experience profound suffering even when, in the world's eyes, there is no obvious disaster present. The following poems and thoughts by children and young people speak volumes about their suffering.

Cardboard City
by Coleen Houlihan (aged 16)

I get shivers when I sit alone,
Don't wanna go back don't wanna go
   home.
Ice cold hearts in a cardboard street,
All day staring, people's passing feet.
Insomnia, joint pain and a headache,

All thrown in together with a stomach
   ache.
Just lying here listless on a cardboard
   street,
All day staring at people's passing feet.
My life is a balancing act, real life truth or
   dare,
My cardboard cupboard is empty now
   discarded and left bare.

All this happens under your feet,
Unnoticed in your concrete street.
Just lying here listless on a cardboard
        street,
All day staring at people's passing feet.

Silence

by Coleen Houlihan

In the loudness all around,
I will never make a sound.
They take for granted their own sweet
        voice,
And I am left silent but not of choice.
Their voices loud and smoothly clear,
I am contented just to hear.
In my silence I see new things,
The little children playing on swings.

So they take for granted what they think
        they own,
And I am left so silent and alone.

Divorces

by Coleen Houlihan

In the darkness of the night,
I can feel a deadly fight.

And as all the hearts are broken,
I have finally spoken.

This fight lives on,
And no-one has won.

Winter Dreams

by Coleen Houlihan

Listen to the words leave me,
Watch the glistening snow.
All that's gone and now I'm sadder,
No dark places to ever go.

Nothing noticed nothing cared.
Lightness crept in on my life,
But darkness belongs in there.
Feel the emptinesses control,
Let the black take on my soul.

Sitting here all by myself,
Like something unused on the shelf.
Happy here I am alone,
Never caring, just alone.

Watch the world it passes by,
Like I'm sitting way up high.
Winter comes I am at peace,
Happy as a dead world sleeps.

Now you're gone I'm left in light,
No one listens to my plight.
No one noticed, no one cared,
Now I watch them as they stare.

Listen to the winter dreams,
No more spaces left for me.
Standing out here in the cold,
Watching as my life grows old.

Little sounds they leave my head,
As I die here in my bed.
Go unnoticed go uncared,
Now I leave the Earth's bright glare.

All alone in winter dreams,
Nothing quite is how it seems.
I have gone where I believe,
Never worry, you'll soon see.

The First Blossom

by Tiffany

Dear Daddy
This rose tree
was bought for you.
This is the first blossom.

I hope you like
this drawing it took
a long time.

I will always
love you.

p.s. I hope you are having a good
time with the Angels.[1]

Dear God
Nobody wants
to be your
Buddy when your
fat.

Martha[2]

I wish Jesus would come back and stop the
fighting because I think they've all had
enough by now. (Alan, aged 7)

I have been praying to God for over a year
now to stop the fighting and wars but he
hasn't done anything about it – yet. (Zarab,
aged 7)

I feel very sad for children left alone in war and
I would like to love them but they never put
their names in the paper. (Liz, aged 7)

Sometimes when there's lots of wars they
ration love. (Tessa, aged 8)

I wish they could declare love instead of war. (Deirdre, aged 11)[3]

'When your mum dies, you have to decide whether to grow-up as she would have wanted or to follow your heart and grow up to be yourself.' (Elizabeth, aged 14)

'My dad did not worry about dying; he just worried bout leaving us all. Now he'll never see me grow-up – or give me away when I marry . . . But I do worry about dying, it's weird to think that one day I won't be walking on this earth.' (Emma, aged 13)

'They're dead but not buried cos they might come alive again.' (Adam, aged 6)[4]

Notes

1. From P. Milner and B. Carolin (eds.), *Time to Listen to Children* (London: Routledge, 1999).
2. *Children's Letters to God* (compiled by E. Marshall and S. Hample; Glasgow: Collins, 1976).
3. N. Newman, *God Bless Love* (Glasgow: Collins, 1972).
4. Milner and Carolin, *Time to Listen to Children*.

– Questions to Consider –

1 What kind of things have you experienced yourself that help you appreciate the suffering of others?

2 How can children use their own suffering to help other children and even adults (thinking about the powerful poetry and quotations above, for example)? What evidence have you seen of the way children are empathetic and compassionate to others? How can you encourage this in the children with whom you work?

3 Having had a glimpse into how children experience and work with suffering, we realize that children need a response from us that mirrors what the Bible says they feel and need. In your work with children, how can you encourage them to explore what the Bible says about suffering and apply it in their own lives?

– PART FIVE –

Working with Children: Practical Issues

Introduction THE *previous chapters of this book have sought to provide a frame-work for working effectively with children in a wide variety of circumstances. Here in Part Five, we explore the practical issues that are pertinent to someone working in this field, thus enabling workers to develop hands-on skills for being with children and working with them.*

Tom Riley and Josephine-Joy Wright, writing with the experience of Novi Most International in Chapter 27, provide ways of assessing the qualities and skills needed by an effective worker in this field. In Chapter 28, Andrew Tomkins discusses how to respond to the medical needs of 'children at risk'. Chapter 29 examines specific practical skills necessary for working with children: discipline and behavioural management (Steve Bartel), supporting parenting (Josephine-Joy Wright) and sharing your faith (Cheryl Barnes). Heather MacLeod provides a critique of key child protection issues in practice, and then in Chapter 31 Rushika Amarasekera discusses selection criteria, monitoring and training of staff. Finally, in Chapter 32, Sally Clarke and Emily McDonald continue this theme by exploring data protection and the effective storage and management of information. **Josephine-Joy Wright**

– CHAPTER 27 –

Identifying and Assessing the Skills and Qualities of Those Who Work with Children

Tom Riley and Josephine-Joy Wright and the experience of

Novi Most International

WHEN one is reviewing the holistic needs of children which may be considered in childcare and therapeutic work, one is struck by the wide range of needs which need to be, or could be, addressed by any given project. When leaders of Christian organizations working with 'children at risk' reviewed the approaches and foci of their work at a recent international conference, the emphasis of most people's organizations was on spiritual care, evangelical outreach, education and recreation. A few were taking on the challenge of holistic work (i.e., physical, moral, spiritual, cognitive, emotional, social and recreational).

We tend to put ourselves and the children whom we serve into boxes, often for very pragmatic reasons. But, in reality, children's lives do not fit neatly into categories. Workers need to be aware of this before leaving for the field. One aspect of my work is supporting returning missionaries, and I have noticed how often their pain and their trauma comes from being unprepared for what they would find, especially emotionally and spiritually. As one aid worker said:

> I went out as a nurse. Our task was to feed 50,000 children. I suppose we thought we could do it. I hadn't expected them to die in the numbers in which they did. I thought our project would be different. I hadn't expected them to cry so much, the silent stares of children without a mother. I could not find God for a while. He hadn't left; I know that now that I've been able to share. He was silent because he was weeping.

Thankfully, this lady's organization encouraged her to get help and she was able to allow herself to do so. Too often we meet workers in the field of children's work who are not able get such help – either for practical reasons or because of cultural and familial beliefs that internally command them to keep things private. In this chapter we will consider how we can assess the needs and practical skills of children, their families and the workers who walk with them. We will also look at how we can apply such knowledge in practice. A friend, Elizabeth Ewers, aged eleven, has written a poem about how we often make knowledge too complicated, too unwieldy. When we come to the final knowledge, it's all about Jesus and his creative, transforming extravagant power and love, encapsulated so beautifully, so simply in the gift of an apple, which we marred in its role in our fall.

The Apple of Knowledge
by Elizabeth Ewers

The apple falls,
The idea is sown,
And out of it a huge tree has grown,
Branches into different streams,
A spectrum of colours and light of
dreams.

From the fallen apple on the ground,
A rocket has high heavens found,
The laws of science,
And measurements too,
Hold the weight of expectations of what
science can do.

The core of science,
In the Millennium,
Is still held by the apple that fell on
Newton.

We need to communicate to children that their feelings, their thoughts, their very selves as they are, are precious – and that we want to hear them. In our desire to develop learned systems, we too often create complex, impenetrable forests. Simplicity and openness to God, as well as a spirit of permission-giving to oneself and to children, are the keys.

The principles of assessment

Gosling and Edwards (1995), in their superb analysis of assessment, monitoring and evaluation in the field, present a clear outline for project analysis which can be easily translated into the needs of the individual worker, project and community. They discuss how the usual programme cycle should more accurately (and, incidentally, biblically) be seen as a spiral.

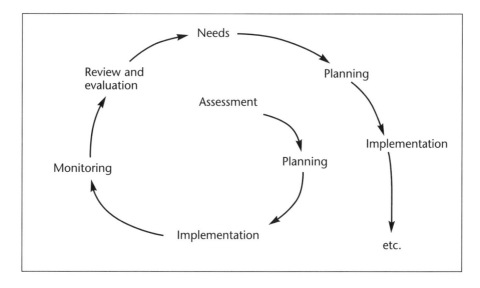

Figure 1: Project analysis

Christ requires that we are honest with him about our needs, willing to change and to grow, to be vigilant and self-controlled, testing new happenings against the yardstick of his wisdom and willing to be transformed (Rom. 12:2). These steps are mirrored in the programme or person spiral illustrated in Figure 1.

So how can we begin to assess the practical skills that workers need to have? Any assessment needs to be underpinned by certain key principles, whose roots can be found in the Bible:

1. *Be systematic.* Any assessment needs to have a focus and a vision, or it will be in danger of being seen as a critical appraisal to be resisted, sabotaged and feared. Assessments need to be in line with the aims and objectives of the organization.

2. *Involve the relevant people.* Participatory assessment involving the key stakeholders gives people a voice, a sense of being heard and honoured, and thus enhances their support for any initiative stemming from the assessment.

3. *Be non-discriminatory.* Often workers who are less skilled in terms of paper qualifications will need encouragement to see assessment as positive and to feel fully part of the process. Christ does not call us all to be the same, but he does call us to live in unity with one another. We need to develop ways of assessing, monitoring and evaluating that allow for differences in people's ways of working.

4. *Be aware.* When developing effective assessments one needs to be aware of what is possible, of where people are psychologically and spiritually at that moment in time, and of how to help people to move to new beginnings. As with children, we have to work with people, not on them.

5. *Be effective agents of change.* Usually the motivation behind any assessment is to identify what needs to change in the current situation in order to see how we can develop.

From the world of management, two useful frameworks for assessing the factors that will facilitate change include:

1. Force field analysis

In this analysis, based on 'field theory' (Lewin, 1951), one identifies which factors would make the change more/less likely to occur/be possible, and which factors instigate 'pushing'/'restraining' forces against the achievement of clear targeted change. The outcome indicates the forces that would enable change to be possible.

2. SWOT analysis

This form of analysis was developed by Ansoff (1987) and enables one to assess the strengths and weaknesses of a given change and the opportunities and threats which will arise from any given change taking place. The results of the SWOT analysis give people a clear cost-benefit analysis of any change taking place.

Novi Most International

A powerful example of how such an analysis has often apparently been performed by God before we even arrive there is seen in Novi Most International, a charity whose vision and purpose is to work long-term to transform the lives of young people following the war in Bosnia-Herzegovina. A few months ago, Paul Brooks, Director, Tom Riley, Deputy Director, and the other managerial, office and field staff became aware that God was halting them in their tracks. The finances were a permanent toil, the workers were tired and questioning. God was saying 'stop'. In the weeks of prayer and fasting that followed, as prayer networks were activated, they felt God lay upon their hearts the challenge: 'How dare we?'.

- How dare we think we can give anything to children if we are not willing to open ourselves to being transformed?

- How dare we contain and constrain God? As the song says, 'I have made you too small in my eyes, O Lord, forgive me; and I have believed in a lie that you were unable to help me, but now, O Lord, I see my wrong: heal my heart and show yourself strong, and in my eyes and with my song, O Lord, be magnified, O Lord, be magnified. Be magnified, O Lord, you are highly exalted; and there is nothing you can't do, O Lord, my eyes are on you. Be magnified, O Lord, be magnified.'[1]

- How dare we not dare and step out of our comfort zones and go and care and be with God's hurting people, either supporting others to go or going ourselves?

The staff at Novi Most began to think into the worlds of the children and, rather than thinking of how the children needed to change and grow, they began to ask themselves what the children needed from them. What were the qualities and skills which they needed to have in order to serve the children more effectively? Table 1 is the result of their prayerful brainstorming and analysis:

Table 1: Novi Most brainstorming

Corporate characteristics needed in team members	Characteristics needed in child's key worker
Respect	*All the characteristics listed opposite, plus...*
Love (unconditional)	
Safe/secure	Reliability
Integrity	Friendship (regular, frequent contact)
Trustworthiness	Closeness
Humility	Visionary
Fruits of the Spirit	Able to assess needs
Saying sorry	Informed (of services available, etc.)
Firm/fair/justice	Able to monitor progress
Impartiality	Able to take appropriate responsibility for self and others
Forgiveness	
Living in the light	Committed to children, fellow workers and the project
Grace	
Understanding of weaknesses	Able to listen to children and other workers and to be self-aware
Mercy	
Availability (as appropriate)	Recognizing uniqueness and responding appropriately
Shrewdness	
Modelling consistency	Having realistic expectations
Inspiring	Organized
Clear boundaries	Proactive and reactive
Prayerfulness	Able to challenge behaviour/attitudes/ lifestyle/beliefs
Affirming	
Encouraging	Accountability
Supporting	Receiving attitude
Advocating	Culturally sensitive
Believing	
Motivating	
Consistent	
Providing growth opportunities	
Providing responsibilities	
Confidential (keeping confidences except when inappropriate)	

They realized that there were certain characteristics and practical skills necessary for all members of a team at field and office level, and that additional characteristics and skills were necessary for the workers specifically involved in face-to-face work with children and their families.

As we explored this area together, we became powerfully aware of the need to gather these thoughts into a systematic framework of continuous assessment, monitoring and evaluation pertinent to the specific tasks of Novi Most International. As we did so, we became aware of how many of the needs of Novi

Most were in fact similar to those of other Christian organizations. The resultant pathway clarified our thinking. Now we have to walk the gentle, sensitive, wise steps to hear everyone's ideas on the proposal and to walk forward together in unity as we try to put them into practice (Fig. 2).

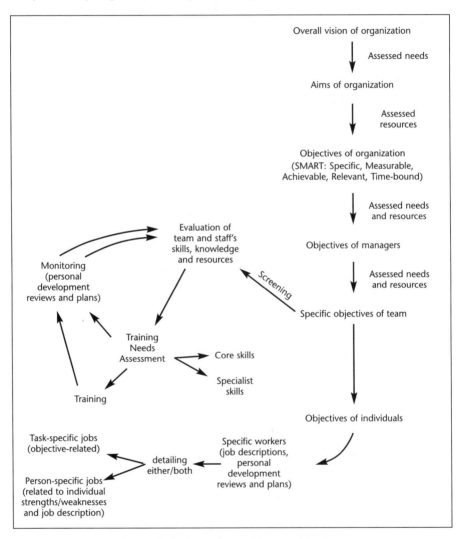

Figure 2: Pathway from vision to objectives

The cycle of monitoring and evaluating is a dynamic one, regularly reassessing (every six months, at least) with the workers their objectives, tasks and action points for both themselves and their managers against both their own and their managers' objectives and progress. This enables workers to feel that they are an intrinsic and vital part of an organization as they can clearly see their role, their purpose and their value. As we discussed in Chapter 8, both adults and children have the same core needs for security, significance, boundaries, community and creativity (White, 1999).

Too often in Christian organizations, there is only a brief induction training and no ongoing training. Or skills are simply learned ad hoc, with no frameworks within which the workers can: process or understand their knowledge; identify gaps without feeling ashamed or a failure; or feel a sense of purpose in their achievements (see Chapter 8, Frank Lake's Dynamic Cycle, 1986). We need to enable the workers, the children and the families whom we serve to be part of the assessment and needs evaluation process. Lester (1985) discusses how, in the pastoral care of children in crisis, we have to remember that children are an equal part of the community of the church. We have to look for ways of involving them in the assessment of what skills children need from the workers. In my experience, adults can too often get distracted and focused on the process, whereas children's wisdom often takes them arrow-like to the heart of the matter.

However, we also need to be clear in our focus, our aims and our objectives in order to show how we are being effective; to be able to assess ways of enhancing our effectiveness; and to be able to see change. Even though we know that works do not increase God's love for us (Eph. 2:8, 9), we are called by God to be effective and to use his resources and talents wisely (Luke 19:11–26).

Over the past few years in the UK, many large organizations have applied for 'Investors in People' awards. And, although the awards have been the subject of many wry comments among the staff, the principle is sound: every staff member has a Personal Development Review (PDR), in which objectives based on their job descriptions are set, and from which time-based, achievable tasks are enumerated. The key concepts are accountability and the development of a sense of organizational commitment and purpose so that the personnel operate as one body, their own objectives coming both from their own aspirations and from those that their manager has to achieve.

A Personal Development Plan (PDP), or training plan, is devised from the PDR, highlighting the additional skills, insights and experience needed in order to achieve objectives. Items in the PDP may involve study time, reflective learning, mentoring, working alongside another colleague, time to observe children in different activities and time to process ideas and feelings, as well as to attend specific training courses and conferences. This model of ongoing assessment, appraisal and support seems eminently applicable to the Christian world where, as part of a family, we are called to be interdependent even as we are all individuals and have value.

How do we use such assessment pathways to analyse our specific needs? As we have said, it is crucial at all points to involve workers and children and their families. Whether we are working in a statutory or in a voluntary context, participative development is vital so that we really ascertain what is necessary to children's well-being. If not, we are in danger of being like the grown-ups in Antoine de Saint-Exupery's *The Little Prince*:

> If I have told you these details about the asteroid, and made a note of its number for you, it is on account of the grown-ups and their ways. Grown-ups love figures. When you tell them that you have made a new friend, they never ask you any questions about essential matters. They never say to you, "What does his voice sound like? What games does he love best? Does he collect butterflies?" Instead, they demand: "How old is he? How many brothers has he? How much does he weigh? How much money does his father make?" Only

from these figures do they think they have learned anything about him.

If you were to say to the grown-ups: "I saw a beautiful house made of rosy brick, with geraniums in the windows and doves on the roof", they would not be able to get any idea of that house at all. You would have to say to them: "I saw a house that cost £4,000." Then they would exclaim: "Oh, what a pretty house that is!"

Just so, you might say to them: "The proof that the little prince existed is that he was charming, that he laughed, and that he was looking for a sheep. If anybody wants a sheep, that is a proof that he exists." And what good would it do to tell them that? They would shrug their shoulders, and treat you like a child. But if you said to them: "The planet he came from is Asteroid B-612," then they would be convinced and leave you in peace from their questions.

They are like that. One must not hold it against them. Children should always show great forbearance toward grown-up people.

But certainly, for us who understand life, figures are a matter of indifference. I would have liked to begin this story in the fashion of the fairy-tales. I should have liked to say: "Once upon a time there was a little prince who lived on a planet that was scarcely any bigger than himself, and who had need of a friend . . ."

To those who understand life, that would have given a much greater air of truth to my story.

Hopefully we can rise to the challenge of finding a bridge between these two worlds as we explore together the practical skills needed by the effective worker in this field.

Qualities and practical skills

Christian organizations are increasingly aware that passion and love are not always enough – we need good tools and good materials if we are to be most effective with our scarce resources. But training should not simply be seen as skills development. It is fundamentally a pathway of personal transformation before God. When children respond to workers, they are responding not so much to their skills but to who they are before Christ. The two are intertwined and interdependent, but the qualities are the fundamental key since children have the wisdom and insight of hawks. A child will quickly assess if a person is not true, genuine or enjoying him as a person. Richard Cole of Lifeline International has experienced this truth time and time again in his work with child soldiers in Sierra Leone (as instruments of healing as well as recipients of care), to rehabilitate them back into their communities. For him, truth, steadfast love and acceptance are the keys to freedom. If we have problems with intimacy, with appropriate boundaries, with dealing with conflict, with creating healthy relationships, we will not be able to be the powerful vessels of healing that Christ desires us to be. We will be more effective if we are willing to let God in to heal us. It is sometimes easier for us to hide behind a position of superiority, afraid of our own darkness yet asking others to confront theirs. But God can, and will, use our darkness, our suffering and our sin, to help others. When we have walked through our dark places and looked to Christ to be healed of their fear, we can walk with children in humility into their darkness, with Christ, and walk with them gently into the light.

Recently I (Wright) was with Mike McGill from Asha Ministries, exploring frameworks that could be developed for working globally with sexually exploited children and specifically with the children of Sri Lanka in children's homes, street dwellings and communities. Although the worlds of Novi Most, Lifeline and Asha are, in human terms, very different, as we exchanged ideas, visions and models I saw how, at a practical and spiritual level, they are very similar.

When looking for frameworks for assessment of the practical qualities and skills needed by workers, we are aware that the main principle used in management, and particularly in personnel management, is that of 'profiling'. That is, the assessor measures the strengths and vulnerabilities of a worker against the skills and qualities profile of the task and makes a judgement. In the Christian world, however, we are confronted by the dilemma of God's way of working and fitting people to jobs. We have probably all encountered situations in which personnel are not able to do their tasks without a great deal of training and transformation. We have probably all been touched by the fear and insecurity of others in manipulative, destructive, controlling activities and power games (Stewart and Joines, 1987). But the reality is that God often does use ordinary people to accomplish extraordinary tasks and uses apparent job mismatches to achieve great changes. There does not seem to be an easy answer. We cannot contain God. We need to use our wisdom and knowledge to promote best practice 'thinking complex yet talking simple' (Carr, 1999) as we walk with people on their journeys of healing. But we always need to be willing to be amazed and surprised by God (Rom. 11:33–36).

To a large extent, the skills needed will depend on the worker's role in the team. These key roles, shown in Table 2, were initially developed by Belbin in 1981 (p. 78). He revised the roles in 1993 (p. 23, revisions shown in italics).

Table 2: Belbin's team roles

Team leader	Chairman/co-ordinator
Resource investigator	Specialist
Completer finisher	Shaper
Practice innovator	Plant (planting ideas, etc.)
Monitor evaluator	Team worker
Company worker/implementator	

The following model is an assessment of the key roles and facilities which a team or project leader would require in order to achieve an effective team and meet the needs of both workers and children or young people (Fig. 3).

A model of ways of assessing and addressing workers' needs, using the framework of White's key theological and childcare practice-based basic needs of children (and adults).

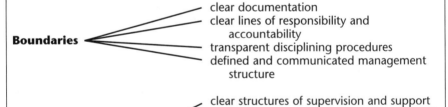

Community
- encourage integration with the local community
- encouragement for workers to link with communities at home and abroad
- encourage workers to look beyond their worlds

Creativity
- opportunities for training and personal development
- provide ways in which workers' personal gifts can be heard, valued and exercised
- stimulate workers' own personal development, spiritually and practically
- flexibility and adaptability

Significance
- ways for workers' voices to be heard and their ideas honoured
- affirmation at all levels, especially by the leaders
- team work
- person-centred, not solely process-driven
- valuing people as they are

Boundaries
- clear documentation
- clear lines of responsibility and accountability
- transparent disciplining procedures
- defined and communicated management structure

Security
- clear structures of supervision and support
- comprehensive systematic assessment at all levels
- clear job description
- clear task definition
- clear contract
- specified financial budgeting and legitimate expenses
- basic physical needs met related to work and personal needs

Figure 3: Needs assessment model

Key worker – child's pathway of interaction and the practical skills necessary to enable the key workers to fulfil their roles. The development of the skills should be seen as a step by step cumulative process as one passes down the pathway, each step a building block supporting the next.

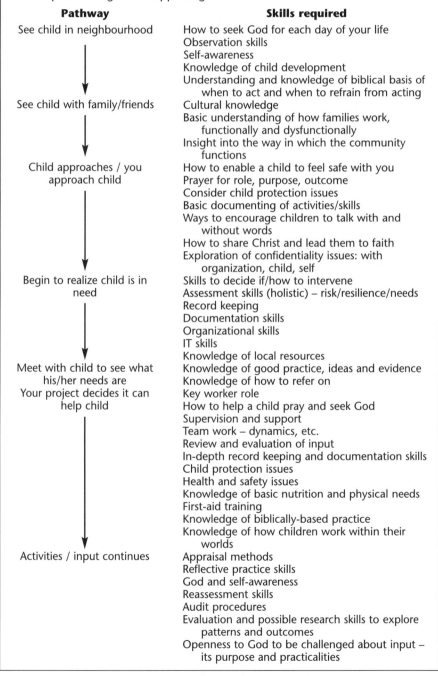

Pathway	Skills required
See child in neighbourhood	How to seek God for each day of your life
	Observation skills
	Self-awareness
	Knowledge of child development
	Understanding and knowledge of biblical basis of when to act and when to refrain from acting
See child with family/friends	Cultural knowledge
	Basic understanding of how families work, functionally and dysfunctionally
	Insight into the way in which the community functions
Child approaches / you approach child	How to enable a child to feel safe with you
	Prayer for role, purpose, outcome
	Consider child protection issues
	Basic documenting of activities/skills
	Ways to encourage children to talk with and without words
	How to share Christ and lead them to faith
	Exploration of confidentiality issues: with organization, child, self
Begin to realize child is in need	Skills to decide if/how to intervene
	Assessment skills (holistic) – risk/resilience/needs
	Record keeping
	Documentation skills
	Organizational skills
	IT skills
	Knowledge of local resources
Meet with child to see what his/her needs are	Knowledge of good practice, ideas and evidence
Your project decides it can help child	Knowledge of how to refer on
	Key worker role
	How to help a child pray and seek God
	Supervision and support
	Team work – dynamics, etc.
	Review and evaluation of input
	In-depth record keeping and documentation skills
	Child protection issues
	Health and safety issues
	Knowledge of basic nutrition and physical needs
	First-aid training
	Knowledge of biblically-based practice
	Knowledge of how children work within their worlds
Activities / input continues	Appraisal methods
	Reflective practice skills
	God and self-awareness
	Reassessment skills
	Audit procedures
	Evaluation and possible research skills to explore patterns and outcomes
	Openness to God to be challenged about input – its purpose and practicalities

Figure 4: Pathway of interaction

Looking within the team at the key workers' roles, a role which may also be taken on by the team leader, the following diagram summarizes the interaction which one might have with a child and the relevant skills required (Fig. 4).

Our discussions with various organizations, however, have highlighted that regardless of how good the process is, regardless of how effective the procedures, the strategic plan and the operational pathways are, the most crucial skills and knowledge people need are an understanding of God and an understanding of themselves and others before him. Workers also need to develop skills for living, such as good boundaries (Cloud and Townsend, 1998).

The diagram on the next page illustrates some of these organizations' observations of the key practical qualities necessary for effective work in this field (Fig. 5), drawing mostly on the work of White (1999) for a framework of key needs which need to be met.

So often in the Christian world we meet burned out, desperately busy Marthas (Luke 10:38–42). The challenge of our work is to be in but not of the world, not to be seduced into fitting the world's moulds, but to find our worth and our identity in God. Barry Adams summarizes this powerfully in the following extract, which is called 'My Child':

You may not know me, but I know everything about you . . . Psalm 139:1

I know when you sit down and when you rise up . . . Psalm 139:2

I am familiar with all your ways . . . Psalm 139:3

Even the very hairs on your head are numbered . . . Matthew 10:29–31

For you were made in my image . . . Genesis 1:27

In Me you live and move and have your being . . . Acts 17:28

For you are my offspring . . . Acts 17:28

I knew you even before you were conceived . . . Jeremiah 1:4–5

I chose you when I planned creation . . . Ephesians 1:11–12

You were not a mistake, for all your days are written in my book . . . Psalm 139:15–16

I determined the exact time of your birth and where you would live . . . Acts 17:26

You are fearfully and wonderfully made . . . Psalm 139:14

I knit you together in your mother's womb . . . Psalm 139:13

And brought you forth on the day you were born . . . Psalm 71:6

I have been misrepresented by those who do not know me . . . John 8:41–44

I am not distant and angry, but am the complete expression of love . . . 1 John 4:16

And it is my desire to lavish my love on you . . . 1 John 3:1

Simply because you are My child and I am your father . . . 1 John 3:1

I offer you more than your earthly father ever could . . . Matthew 7:11

For I am the perfect Father . . . Matthew 5:48

Every good gift that you receive comes from my hand . . . James 1:17

For I am your provider and I meet all your needs . . . Matthew 6:31–33

My plan for your future has always been filled with hope . . . Jeremiah 29:11

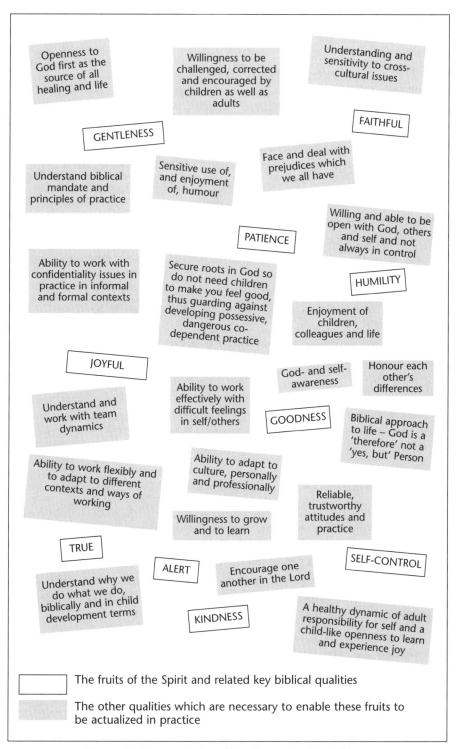

Figure 5: Key practical qualities for work with children

Because I love you with an everlasting love . . . Jeremiah 31:3

My thoughts toward you are countless as the sand on the seashore . . . Psalm 139:17–18

And I rejoice over you with singing . . . Zephaniah 3:17

I will never stop doing good to you . . . Jeremiah 32:40

For you are My treasured possession . . . Exodus 19:5

I desire to establish you with all My heart and all My soul . . . Jeremiah 32:41

And I want to show you great and marvellous things . . . Jeremiah 33:3

If you seek Me with all your heart, you will find Me . . . Deuteronomy 4:29

Delight in Me and I will give you the desires of your heart . . . Psalm 37:4

For it is I who gave you those desires . . . Philippians 2:13

I am able to do more for you than you could possibly imagine . . . Ephesians 3:20

For I am your greatest encourager . . . 2 Thessalonians 2:16–17

I am also the Father who comforts you in all your troubles . . . 2 Corinthians 1:3–4

When you are brokenhearted, I am close to you . . . Psalm 34:18

As a shepherd carries a lamb, I have carried you close to My heart . . . Isaiah 40:11

One day I will wipe away every tear from your eyes . . . Revelation 21:3–4

And I'll take away all the pain you have suffered on this earth . . . Revelation 21:3–4

I am your Father, and I love you even as I love my son, Jesus . . . John 17:23

For in Jesus, my love for you is revealed . . . John 17:26

He is the exact representation of my being . . . Hebrews 1:3

He came to demonstrate that I am for you, not against you . . . Romans 8:31

And to tell you that I am not counting your sins . . . 2 Corinthians 5:18–19

Jesus died so that you and I could be reconciled . . . 2 Corinthians 5:18–19

His death was the ultimate expression of My love for you . . . 1 John 4:10

I gave up everything I loved that I might gain your love . . . Romans 8:31–32

If you receive the gift of My son Jesus, you receive Me . . . 1 John 2:23

And nothing will ever separate you from My love again . . . Romans 8:38–39

Come home and I'll throw the biggest party heaven has ever seen . . . Luke 15:7

I have always been Father, and will always be Father . . . Ephesians 3:14–15

My question is . . . Will you be My child? . . . John 1:12–13

I am waiting for You . . . Luke 15:11–32.

Love, Your Dad, Almighty God (Barry Adams, 1999)

While in the process of revising this chapter, I was reading 'Word for Today', a daily devotional by United Christian Broadcasts. I was struck by the relevance of its content for this chapter about the choices we make concerning the fruits we exercise in our lives – fruits that are essential to our effective work with children:

'Choose you this day . . .' (Joshua 24:15). 'If you want your life to glorify God and bless others today, here are seven choices you must make:

Choose joy: Since God's directing your steps, resist the temptation to be negative or fearful (Ps. 37:23).

Choose patience: Instead of cursing the one who takes your place, invite him to do so. Instead of complaining that the wait is too long, be grateful for a moment to pray (Rom. 5:3–4).

Choose kindness: Be kind to the poor, for often they're alone. Be kind to the rich, for often they're afraid. Be kind to the unkind, then you'll understand how God treats you (Col. 3:12).

Choose goodness: be quicker to confess than to accuse, to be overlooked than to boast, to go without than to accept anything dishonest (Isa. 3:10).

Choose faithfulness: Keep your promises so that your creditors will never regret their trust, your friends question your word or your family doubt your love (1 Cor. 4:2).

Choose gentleness: Nothing is won by force. If you raise your voice, let it be in praise. If you clench your fist, let it be in prayer. If you make a demand, let it first be on yourself (Jas. 3:17).

And if you succeed in living by these principles today, put your head on your pillow tonight and have a good night's sleep; you deserve it!' ('The Word for Today', 31 May 2001)

So often we are influenced by the sense of achievement, power and pride that comes from our positions, our posts, our potential, our perceived power, the ability to change a child's life, the ability to open a child up emotionally, the ability to lead an organization, to feed five thousand. But such gifts become clanging symbols. Worse, they become vessels for Satan to change what God meant for good and twist it to be an evil charade of its God-given and God-purposed commission. We need to be willing to take up the challenge to let go to God's will, as this text explains:

To 'Let go' does not mean to stop caring, it means I can't do it for someone else.

To 'Let go' is not to cut myself off, it's the realization I can't control another.

To 'Let go' is not to enable, but to allow learning from a natural consequence.

To 'Let go' is to admit powerlessness, which means the outcome is not in my hands.

To 'Let go' is not to try to change or blame another, it's to make the most of myself.

To 'Let go' is not to care for, but to care about.

To 'Let go' is not to fix but to be supportive.

To 'Let go' is not to judge, but to allow another to be a human being.

To 'Let go' is not to be in the middle arranging all outcomes but to allow others to affect their own destinies.

To 'Let go' is not to be protective, it's to permit another to face reality.

To 'Let go' is not to deny but to accept.

To 'Let go' is not to scold, nag or argue, but instead to search out my own shortcomings and correct them.

To 'Let go' is not to adjust everything to my own desires but to take each day as it comes and cherish myself in it.

To 'Let go' is not to criticize and regulate anybody but to try to become what I dream I can be, and what God knows that I can be.

To 'Let go' is not to regret the past but to grow and live for the future.

To 'Let go' is to fear less and to love more. (Anonymous)

'My people have committed two sins: They have forsaken me, the spring of living water, and have dug their own cisterns, broken cisterns that cannot hold water'(Jer. 2:13). This verse gives us our challenge powerfully and clearly. We are so often tempted to create our own cisterns to hold children's pain and lead them into healing. Such potential cisterns include our knowledge and their knowledge, understanding, skills or experience, or even their relationship with us (and we need to take care that cisterns such as this book do not become another such vessel).

We have to seek God daily on these issues, taking our wisdom ultimately from him. He will transform our gifts into his miracles. As Jeremiah 2:13 shows us, we need to seek him with all our hearts (Jer. 29:13), committing our ways to him, knowing that he will act (Ps. 37:1–7), waiting patiently for him (Isa. 64:4) and seeking to use our time of waiting wisely. Children respond to us, children are willing to be vulnerable with us to the extent to which we are mirrors of him – of his love, his joy, his compassion, his genuineness, his power, his truth, his stillness and his peace. So, 'Ask and it will be given to you; seek and you will find; knock and the door will be opened to you' (Matt. 7:7).

God does not require us to be anything but ourselves. We are of value as we are. He purposed us to be as we are (Eph. 1:4) and each of us only has to be what God meant us to be for him to weave the carpet of our lives together and create an incredible picture (see 'Jigsaws and God', p. 439). The greatest gift that we can give to children is Christ – the transforming reality of what he has done for us. Our task is always to bring children to the only true source of real healing rather than holding them by the broken clay pots of the past, which we sometimes refuse to release for God to give us new ones filled to overflowing with his Holy Spirit. We need to use our qualities and our skills to enable our work to be carried out most effectively and holistically for children, their families and ourselves. But ultimately these qualities and skills are only of use if they are the hands of God. Only then will they really be instruments of healing (Cloud, 1995).

So come aside awhile and stay with him. He will nurture and refresh you. He will challenge and amaze you. He will turn your life upside-down and around and set you free to be all that he wants for you to be. Trust him, stay with him. It's wonderful. It's free. For his sake, for our sake, for the children.

The Deaf Child

by Josephine-Joy Wright (aged 15 years)

You cannot touch me, you out there amidst your babble.
I am soft, floating in this world of mine.
You screw your eyes and gallop in the madness,
You wave your arms and point at bread and wine.
Mouths quiver, flash like birds slurred out of focus,
Moist fruits of tongues, you tell me that I should.
I move my mouth like yours and squash my voice out,
My voice? It must have come – you smile and nod.

When the sun has gone I lie there in the darkness,
To sleep? But why; the silence already come.
You sit and watch my eyes, willing dream last –
The sun in my mind lingers on,
Bursting golden, dying amber blue across the waves,
Turning clouds to newborn pink skin rose.
My Lord press out to touch at what you're calling,
What you're doing to your face above the clothes.
I cannot really tell you that I love you.
These words I write are in my world alone.
Take my eyes and fill them with your laughter.
Fill me with a time for your tomorrows.
Do to my lips things you say is speaking –
I push against that wall through to you,
I'll sleep now, or pretend, so you'll go creeping,
In the night I am awake but I'm alone.

This person that I feel; someone's with me,
I find him when we go to hills and streams,
I find him in the old crumpled ruins, running
Silver hopes through all my dreams.
I think you call him God; he is my true lips.
To blossom flowers of verdant grass walk on.
He lets me feel you mother and to love you.
One day I'll hear you, and we'll talk in tongues.

Note

1. 'I have made you too small in my eyes (Be Magnified)' by Lynn De Shazo. © Copyright 1992 Integrity's Hosanna! Music / Sovereign Music UK. P.O. Box 356, Leighton Buzzard, LU7 3WP UK. Reproduced by permission.

– Questions to Consider –

1 How would you begin to determine the practical skills required by a worker in your organization? What are the factors that you would need to consider when making such an assessment?

2 Using the frameworks provided in this chapter, appraise your own qualities and skills and develop your own Personal Development Plan. How would you begin to address in practice the development needs that you have identified?

3 What would you do if you had an applicant for a post within your organization who apparently lacked the necessary qualities and/or skills for the post but who felt that God was calling him or her to it? Would you differentiate between skills and qualities – if so, how? Why?

CHAPTER 28

Caring for the Medical Needs of 'Children at Risk'

Andrew Tomkins

Caring for children at risk of malnutrition

Types of malnutrition

THE term 'malnutrition' is used to describe a number of nutritional disorders that result from interaction between these three factors:

1. Deficient food intake

2. Infection

3. Poor childcare.

Nutritional disorders resulting from malnutrition include the following:

- *Low birth weight* (less than 2.5 kg.). Caused by premature delivery or by lack of proper growth in the womb.

- *Poor growth in infancy and childhood.* This includes being underweight, stunted or thin (expressed as weight/age, height/age and weight-for-height, respectively, by comparison with international standards).

- *Thinness.* Assessed by measurement of mid-upper-arm circumference.

- *Severe malnutrition.* Including the life-threatening conditions of marasmus (being severely underweight) and kwashiorkor (underweight children who retain fluid).

- *Anaemia.* This results most commonly from iron deficiency caused by a poor diet, poor absorption because of intestinal disease or blood loss from intestinal parasites.

- *Iodine deficiency.* Causing decreased production of thyroid hormone, which is essential for good foetal brain development. Swelling of the thyroid gland in the neck ('goitre') is a sign of this condition.

- *Vitamin A deficiency.* A lack of vitamin A can cause eye changes (xerophthalmia), which may lead to blindness, as well as immune deficiency, which increases the risk of mortality from infection.

- *Zinc deficiency.* Causes immune deficiency, impaired growth and slow recovery from infection.

- *Obesity.* Increasingly common, this is primarily a result of carrying too much weight over a long period, which leads to increased risk of degenerative disease in later life.

- *Short-term food shortage.* Such as missing breakfast, leads to poor concentration span in school and decreased learning capacity and school achievement.

- *Toxicity.* Pollution is increasing globally, with more children being damaged intellectually by lead and immunologically by arsenic (found in some tube well waters). Malnourished children are less able to withstand the toxic effects of these and other pollutants.

Several types of malnutrition can occur at the same time. Children are especially vulnerable because their brains, immune systems, muscles and skeletons are developing rapidly. They need much more food per body weight than adults do if they are to grow and develop to their potential. It is now well recognized that populations of children all across the world can grow to a similar height and weight if they receive enough food, are free from infection and are cared for properly. Thus child development programme managers worldwide can use the World Health Organization (WHO) international reference standards (available from WHO Geneva) for monitoring the nutritional state of the children in their programmes.

Children may also suffer from 'micronutrient malnutrition' (micronutrients are very small amounts of dietary components such as iron, vitamin A, iodine and zinc), which can cause a slow down in growth and, in severe cases, stunting, as well as anaemia and decreased resistance to infection. The section on infection, below, describes different infections contributing to malnutrition. The ability of a mother/carer to look after a child is influenced by many external factors (including time, poverty, inadequate household resources such as water supply and sanitation, permission from her husband and other family members), as well as her own education, experience and intuition.

Malnutrition can also lead to several further problems:

- *Increased risk of getting infected.* This is especially true for diarrhoea and pneumonia. A malnourished child is more susceptible to getting diarrhoea and pneumonia, and cases of these illnesses in malnourished children are more likely to be severe.
- *Greater tendency to have a prolonged illness.* With long convalescence, leaving the child vulnerable to the next illness.
- *More likely to die.* Over 12 million children under five years of age die every year (most of them in poor countries). Underlying malnutrition is a major factor in over 50 per cent of child deaths globally.
- *Learning ability* (cognition) and school achievement are impaired.
- *Shortened attention span.* There is some evidence in malnourished children of a decreased ability to cope with mental stress.
- *Shorter stature.* Leading to increased risk of producing small babies (who have increased risk of morbidity, mortality and impaired intellectual development) and fewer opportunities for employment (both because employment often takes the form of physical labour and because of prejudices against those who are shorter).

Reasons why children become malnourished

Causes of malnutrition need to be assessed in the local situation in order to plan interventions appropriately. It is helpful to use the 'life cycle' approach, in which the interaction of nutrition and human development and function is seen at different stages of life.

Unborn children

Infants in the womb are especially vulnerable, because many metabolic processes are 'set' during this time. Certain adult diseases, such as diabetes, hypertension and heart attacks, are more common among adults who were born small. Low birth weight affects the immune status and leads to an increased risk of infection and mortality, especially in the first few years of life and particularly in poor communities if the child is not breastfed. Low birth weight affects not only babies who are born prematurely (mostly due to maternal infection), but also infants who are 'small for gestational age', or who are born on time but are malnourished in the womb. There are many reasons for this, including maternal factors such as shortness of stature, illness, malnutrition, poor energy (protein, iron and iodine intake are important), exposure to toxic substances such as are found in certain dietary items (e.g., coffee and alcohol) and possible mental stress.

Infants during the first year of life

Breast milk provides immune factors that prevent infection and promote brain development. Breastfeeding also reduces the risk of certain allergic diseases such as eczema. While many women start off by breastfeeding, the proportion of mothers who continue to breastfeed exclusively is dangerously low. The early introduction of complementary foods ('solids') increases the risk of several infections.

Children receiving complementary solid foods

Most cereals (such as rice, maize and millet) have high levels of phytate ('dietary fibre') that makes it difficult to absorb iron and zinc, so children face the risk of micronutrient deficiency. They tend to grow more slowly and become anaemic. In malarious areas, the extra burden of parasitic infection worsens their anaemia and many infections, such as diarrhoea, pneumonia and intestinal infection, decrease the appetite and reduce the absorption of food. A child who contracts malaria is more prone to diarrhoea, pneumonia and intestinal infection – and also less able to fight these infections once they get them.

School-age children

School-age children often receive less than they need in terms of energy and protein and are therefore underweight, short and thin. They also find it difficult to obtain enough micronutrients from a predominantly cereal diet, especially if they do not eat foods (such as green vegetables) containing minerals and vitamins. In addition, they frequently have high levels of intestinal parasitic infections, which cause poor appetite, blood loss and malabsorption. Many schoolchildren are anaemic, which limits their ability to benefit from school. Many children go to school without breakfast, which further disadvantages their scholastic ability and learning performance. Stunted ('short') children do less well at school.

Nutrition as part of a child programme

There are many different ways of improving nutritional intake in a programme for 'children at risk', including:

- *Community development.* There are many opportunities for improving household security and the availability of food. Issues of household security include making homes safe from burglars and abusers as well as making homes safer places emotionally, where parents stay together and care for their children. Social development activities within communities including pregnancy advice, parenting training, 'keep safe' programmes with children, nutrition programmes and building physically safer housing would address these problems.

- *Introduce a life cycle approach.* It is important to improve the nutrition of this generation of children directly (by feeding them, giving them better food) and indirectly (by teaching their parents to understand nutrition and to be healthier themselves). By doing so, we improve the nutrition of the next generation of parents, infants and children.

- *Provide better nutrition for children.* This may mean providing food supplements (including breakfast, lunch or snacks) or micronutrient supplements (such as iron or vitamin A).

- *Tackle infection at all ages.* If a child has better overall health, she will be better able to respond to the benefits of a good diet.

- *Include nutrition in the curriculum.* Use Child to Child approaches. Children are keen to learn about nutrition in practical ways – for example, in school gardens, making choices about their diets and food preparation.

Caring for children at risk of infection

Many children in child-care programmes come from disadvantaged families who live in poor environments where infections and toxic exposures are common. Unless interventions are introduced to prevent and treat infection, the educational performance of these children will be damaged. Infection can interfere with intellectual development in several ways:

1. Through direct damage to the brain (e.g., from malaria or meningitis).
2. Malnutrition affects the actual function and development of the brain, and therefore one's ability to concentrate and think, which in turn affects one's ability to learn and the level of scholastic achievement.
3. Inflammation of the brain (and other areas of the body) causes the release of chemicals that disturb the function of the brain.
4. By decreasing the appetite and jeopardizing food absorption.

Problems of infection during the life cycle

Infections of various sorts can seriously impair growth and development in different ways and to varying degrees at each stage of the life cycle.

Unborn children

Alcohol, cigarettes and drugs taken by the mother during pregnancy have a toxic effect on child development. The mother can also transmit to the infant infections that damage the brain, immune system and specific organs. These include syphilis, hepatitis B and HIV/AIDS. Unfortunately breast milk can transmit HIV, and therefore HIV-positive mothers are advised to use breast milk substitutes in industrialized countries. However, poor hygiene and sanitation and the lack of resources to afford adequate supplies make it dangerous to use infant formula in poor communities. Fortunately, recent evidence suggests that mothers who exclusively breastfeed their infants are less likely to transmit HIV than if they introduce mixed feeding with infant formula early. Pending further research, HIV-positive mothers are advised to breastfeed exclusively for as long as possible and then make an early transition to solid foods.

Infants and young children

Infants are susceptible to a range of infections that affect their development. Severe malaria and meningitis can lead to brain damage and deafness. Children living in high-density housing are particularly susceptible to meningococcal meningitis in certain key geographical areas (especially dry sub-Saharan Africa). Dengue and haemorrhagic fevers are increasingly common (especially in Asia), leading to forms of encephalitis and brain damage. Respiratory infections such as pertussis ('whooping cough') may lead to chronic lung damage, making it difficult for the child to be healthy and energetic. Respiratory infections may also cause chronic ear diseases leading to deafness. Measles can cause blindness. Poliomyelitis can cause weakness of the limbs.

Diarrhoea and intestinal parasites cause chronic ill health leading to malabsorption and nutrient loss from the intestine. Intestinal parasites such as trichuris and hookworm set up inflammatory responses which decrease the ability to concentrate and learn at school. These infections are often more pronounced if the child is HIV-positive.

School-age children

Children at school are vulnerable to intestinal infections, malaria, schistosomiasis (a parasitic infection of the bladder and sometimes intestine and liver which is transmitted by snails in water in which children paddle or swim) and skin infections (such as scabies and leg ulcers). Although a large number of HIV-positive children die before they reach school age, with increasing awareness and antibiotic treatment more children are surviving, and they are susceptible to frequent infections. It must be emphasized that HIV-positive children are not likely to pass the virus to other children. Teachers, parents and governors of schools need to know this and ensure that the confidentiality and right to education of HIV-positive children are respected. This is a complex, increasingly common issue that has been examined in AIDS-related educational literature and research publications.

Adolescent children

Adolescents are liable to become infected by the same diseases that affect younger children, as well as being vulnerable to the risks of sexual activity (pregnancy, sexually-transmitted disease, violence and abortion). All of these take a heavy toll on child health and impair a child's social and intellectual development. In some countries, up to a quarter of pregnancies occur in children (younger than eighteen years old), and this almost always excludes them from further educational opportunities.

In addition, adolescents are susceptible to pressures to abuse cigarettes, alcohol, marijuana, heroin and solvents. They are also often caught up in exploitative occupations, such as hard labour. They may be coerced into violent behaviour, even murder, which damages them psychologically and emotionally. Nightmares, fears and (vivid and terror-filled) dreams may be common in this age group. The danger here is that their fears are not contained or they do not know how to deal with them because of poor emotional literacy (their parents never taught them to make sense of their worlds).

Children of all ages

Occupations involving substances such as lead and cadmium may damage children's brains and lungs. Industrial effluents and 'cottage industries', such as recycling batteries and making matches, can be highly toxic.

Children of all ages are susceptible to parasitic infections causing chronic disability such as filariasis (causing 'elephantiasis' in severe forms) and onchocerciasis (leading to 'river blindness') and leishmaniasis (causing severe skin damage and even invading the liver and spleen). These infections are transmitted by insects and are therefore more likely to affect poor children who live in environments that favour the breeding of insects. These chronic infections impair their learning ability.

Disability can be present from birth or acquired as a result of a disastrous event during childhood. Learning difficulties, problems with speech and language, deafness, blindness and impaired gait all contribute to a delay in learning unless special arrangements are made to accommodate disabled children within 'mainstream' schools or, if this does not work, to provide special facilities.

Child-care programmes and infection

The damaging impact of infection on child development is often so serious that all child-care programme managers need to make specific plans, including:

- *Prevention.* Make sure that all children are completely immunized; clean up the environment to prevent insect-transmitted infections (use insecticide treated bed nets, for example); improve hygiene and sanitation to prevent diarrhoea and intestinal parasites and ensure that children have soap and water for their own personal hygiene.

- *Preventive treatment.* In those areas where intestinal parasites and schistosomiasis are common (often suspected by a high prevalence of children passing blood in their urine), deworming medication should be given regularly.

- *Treatment of infection.* It is important to take illness seriously, recognizing symptoms at an early stage and ensuring that children see a health professional.

- *Encourage children to learn about infection.* Include health issues in the curriculum, teaching about disease prevention, symptom recognition and treatment. Child to Child methods should be used in all child-care programmes.

– Questions to Consider –

1 What have you learned that can help you to improve the nutritional status of children in your care?

2 Identify the key factors that need to be borne in mind when establishing a nutrition programme. How would you meet the challenge of a field-based, or headquarters' office-based, situation where evidence suggests that the demands are often greater than the supply? Consider the strategic, practical and emotional issues that may arise and how you would manage them.

3 List some specific ways in which you can help to improve the health of the children in your care?

– CHAPTER 29 –

Key Practical Skills: Discipline, Supporting Parents and Sharing Your Faith

Appropriate discipline with children (and colleagues)

Steve Bartel

ONE of the greatest challenges that people who work face-to-face with children encounter is the fear that they will not be able to control the children's behaviour. Imagined scenes of children screaming in classrooms, throwing things, swearing and making obscene gestures and disobeying each and every order, plea or request coming from an adult can totally dissuade potential candidates for a staff position in a children's ministry. Interestingly, many directors of children's ministries often state that their staff are actually more of a challenge to discipline than the children!

Experienced parents, teachers, child-care workers and others who work with children are often asked about their techniques for disciplining both staff and children. Indeed, the techniques that are effective with some children and adults are disastrous with others. There are no magic formulae for 'discipline', but there are some underlying principles that will help us channel behaviour correctly.

First of all, the terms 'authority', 'discipline', 'consequences' and 'punishment', since they are often confused, should be properly understood. Authority implies the permission that someone grants another to influence him. Discipline is a positive concept that refers to the overall ordering of one's life. Consequences can be either positive or negative – they are the results that one would expect from his actions. Punishment is a negative term that implies negative consequences meted out as a result of negative behaviour.

Authority is often misunderstood as stemming from one's position, area of responsibility or even title. But true authority comes through establishing trust. Jesus taught as 'one having authority' – not because he had been recognized by the religious leaders, but because the multitudes trusted that his teachings were true. When we are influencing an adult's or a child's behaviour, we will be able to do so if she trusts us, our principles and our motives. Authority is based on relationship.

Discipline is always necessary. 'Self-discipline' or 'team discipline' help the functions of the individual or the ministry to be more 'ordered'. When we say that we will 'discipline the child' for his behaviour, we must view the action as a positive opportunity to teach the child how to better order his life. (This is based on taking the child's best interests into account, not on feeling obligated to provide a reaction to his behaviour.) The same is true for adult colleagues.

Consequences should be understood by staff members and children alike as the natural or imposed results of their actions. When guidelines on behaviour are clear, the consequences should also be clear. Positive consequences (e.g., 'when I finish my homework, I can go out and play') tend to govern behaviour better than negative ones (e.g., 'if I don't finish my homework, I have to sit in the corner'). When we must discipline a child by allowing him to experience the consequences of his actions, our motive should be to expose the child to learning valuable lessons for his future. When the child trusts us to have his best interests in mind, he will accept the consequences – whether positive or negative – more readily. Many 'children at risk' will blame others for their plight and actions, even when it's clear to the adult caregivers that the children themselves are responsible for them. Consequences that are correctly administered will help the child take responsibility for her actions.

Punishment is often a reaction by the person in control to make the child pay for his negative behaviour. Often punishment will reinforce the child's notion that the person punishing him really doesn't like him, does not have his best interests at heart, is struggling with maintaining control or even wants to take vengeance upon him. The result is that punishment is likely to divide, or at least distance, a relationship. Punishment is the least effective way to modify behaviour.

The best way to provide discipline is to model it! Colleagues and children will follow the patterns of self-discipline that they consistently see in those they respect. Yet situations in which a colleague or child will require corrective discipline are inevitable. The following are effective principles that help leaders handle staff and children in these situations:

- *Consistently pray for the staff member or child that needs discipline.* This will allow you to see her through God's eyes, make you aware of the underlying needs that might be influencing her behaviour and help you to build a personal compassion for her. (Note: Praying over children as they sleep dramatically improves their behaviour the next morning. Try it!).

- *Don't act alone.* Seek other mature and trustworthy Christians to help you pray for the individual and advise you on how you can approach him with understanding. Does the staff member or child trust you, and does he know that you have his best interests in mind?

- *Use the Bible.* Biblical phrases and principles cut through many barriers and get to the heart of the situation. The word of God brings awareness, repentance and hope for change when it is read out loud to the individual needing discipline. Don't use it unfairly to bring condemnation or to back up what might be strictly your opinion instead of a true godly principle.

- *Be positive.* The discipline situation is an opportunity to teach. Pray with the individual. Allow him to sense your commitment through your prayer. Evaluate once again your motivation while you pray. (For example, if you are angry at the person rather than at their infraction, ask God to change your attitude towards the person to one of love, or postpone the intervention until a later time.)

- *Be clear.* Don't beat about the bush. Allow the other person to express his reasons and feelings. Accept what is reasonable; gently point out fallacies or excuses. Be willing to change your own preconceived opinions.

- *Consider consequences.* Will the consequences punish, or will they rather positively reinforce the discipline that's desired?

- *Act.* Don't leave the situation hanging. The younger or more immature the child, the sooner the discipline intervention is necessary. Procrastinating in discipline is counter-productive.

- *Follow through.* After the intervention, check to see how the person's behaviour has changed and whether he needs encouragement or additional correction.

When we discipline a child we must explain the infraction clearly. Show the child through the Bible the sadness that God feels about his actions, but emphasize that God still accepts him as a person. Allow the child to express repentance, if he chooses to. (Never coerce or manipulate his repentance, or force an apology that does not come from his heart.) Pray with the child. After discipline, show acceptance and love for the child. Hug her if she allows you. Spend time with her to strengthen the relationship.

Discipline must take into account that every child is an individual who will respond to correction in different ways. Discipline done in a godly manner and motivated by love can be one of the most positive influences upon a child's or a colleague's life. It's actually a great gift that you, as his leader, can give him.

Supporting parents who care for children who are difficult to care for

Josephine-Joy Wright

I often hear the pleas of workers and parents around the world: how do we manage our children, how do we parent them effectively? Many of us breathed a sigh of relief when studies were first published on 'good enough' parenting and its effectiveness in mitigating adverse influences on children and their families. Rutter's (1981; 'Continuities', 1987) studies on the importance of a child's resilience greatly assisted our understanding of what enables children not just to survive childhood but also to be moulded (and not defined) by childhood experiences. As his research and the research of others (e.g., Dwivedi, 1997) has shown, the greatest protective factor in helping a child to overcome and work with risk factors positively is the presence of a securely attached, reliable, safe adult (Cassidy and Shaver, 1989). Many of the children and young people with whom we work have never had that experience – or they have had it and it has been taken from them.

The principles of supporting and promoting not just 'good enough', but Christ-centred good parenting, are as follows:

1. To establish/re-establish stable, secure attachments and to encourage children and parents to dare to attach and get close (Bowlby, 1979; 1982).

2. To build/rebuild relationships between children and adults which focus on gently overcoming fear, mistrust and abuse with honour and respect.

3. To build/rebuild relationships between children and their parents/ caregivers.

4. To enable parents/carers to understand the children's developmental world (Vasta, Haith and Millar, 1999) and how their experiences can damage their holistic growth.

5. To enable parents/carers to hear children's voices, and especially to learn how children show or tell that their world is not OK (Herbert and Harper-Dorton, 2001).

6. To enable parents/carers to recognize, understand and address, with God and others, their own personal needs. This process must include opportunities for healing the pain from their own childhoods. They must also be enabled to understand and honour the needs, fears and wants of their child within – in the past and now. Such unresolved pain may impact their own children and their relationships with them – for example, competing with their children, expecting their children to parent them, developing co-dependent relationships with their children.

7. To enable parents/carers to learn how to interact with children in ways with which they and their children feel comfortable and which are culturally appropriate. It is important for parents to feel free to explore their own ways of doing this. Both they and their children have many 'voices' (e.g., play, games, creative activities, being still; Richmond, 1993).

8. To develop strategies (praise, rewards, consequences, etc.) to enable

parents/carers to consistently manage their children's normal, defiant and more difficult behaviour, as well as their emotional needs. Such consistency provides the children with security, safety and clear, reliable boundaries. This consistency also assures them that they are significant, special, precious and freely loved with no strings attached (Herbert, 1994).

9. To enable parents/carers and children and young people to enjoy one another as they grow.

10. To enable good parenting to be a mirror of God's love for us and thus to enable children to release, recognize and act upon their hunger for God and come to know him and have their own committed, personal relationship with him.

The following guidelines, when used in conjunction with references on biblically based parenting such as Dobson (1982) and 'Care for the Family' publications,[1] and others, can enable us as workers to achieve these principles in our practice more effectively. We can thus help children and parents/carers to move towards rebirth in their own identities and relationships as we give them knowledge and support to change. This renewal breaks the cycles of sin and sets parents and children free to be themselves before God and to grow up in him.

It is fundamental to our work and lives as Christians that we support other parents, and also parent effectively ourselves, always underpinning our practice with biblical principles (Matt. 18:6). Furthermore, consistent, loving, biblical parenting is an incredible witness, glorifying God, to the world around us.

Guidelines for parents who are finding it difficult to control their children

These guidelines are to help parents who have children who can sometimes be difficult to control. Children need to learn that their world is consistent, predictable and yet appropriately flexible. This enables them to develop a sense of continuity and equips them to utilize their healthy frames of references and cognitive ability to make sense of their experiences. To be in control is a big responsibility, and if your child is usually the one in control he will be relieved if you take this responsibility from him. You should only use the following plan if you feel comfortable and happy with it and are willing to try it for a minimum of three months. It will help to guide children to do what you want them to do and stop them doing things you do not want them to do. It is important that you follow all the steps in the correct order, that you don't leave anything out and that you follow the guidelines regularly. In the first instance you will have to work hard to prove to your child that things are going to be different and that you are in charge – not your child. It will be very tiring, but you must not give up as this will confuse your child. The guidelines are particularly helpful for young children, but the principles also apply to older children and teenagers with very little adaptation. (It is important to remember that children still need to have times when they can safely and appropriately be in charge so that they can develop a sense of mastery and learn to make good choices.)

Children need to feel important and special

The most important rule to keep in mind is that all children need love, affection, praise and encouragement. Whenever a child does something well or pleases you, you need to show them that you have noticed. You can do this by giving them a smile, a cuddle, talking to them or, on very special occasions, giving them treats or presents. Children and young people love getting lots of positive attention, especially when they are used to hearing that they are naughty. Once they are used to hearing good things about themselves and feeling loved and special, it will matter more to them when you are cross or unhappy with them.

Here are some questions to help you think about how to show your children that you care:

- How often do you tell them that you are pleased, proud or happy?
- In what ways do you show them that you are pleased with them?
- How much special time do you have with your children to play with or talk to them?
- How much interest do you show in their school work, hobbies and friends?
- What regular fun or pleasurable activities do you do with your child?

Guidelines for disciplining children who will not do as they are told

Carry out the following instructions step by step. Make sure beforehand that your child does not have a genuine physical problem that is causing her to behave badly. If she is hungry, sick or has been hurt and needs medical attention, these rules may not work.

- *Step 1.* When you see your child misbehaving, call him by name and make sure that you have eye contact with him. Explain clearly what it is that you want him to do or stop doing. Be gentle and firm. If the child will not look at you, gently touch her arm or leg and say, for example, 'Sally, I want you to put that book away now please.'
- *Step 2.* If the child does not obey, make eye contact again. Repeat her name and what you said in step 1, but this time say it a little louder.
- *Step 3.* If the child continues to be disobedient repeat step 1 again, speaking a little louder than in step 2, and this time add a warning about what you will do if the child does not follow your instructions. You might say, for example, 'Sally, I want you to put that book away please. If you do not do as I say then you will have to go to your room.' Remember, never use a warning that you cannot carry through.
- *Step 4.* If the child continues to be disobedient, then carry out your warning with the minimum of fuss and attention. You might ask the child to stand in the hall or sit on a particular chair – or, if you are outside the home, remove him from the situation in which he is misbehaving. Do not shout or hurt the child in any way.
- *Step 5.* Always explain to the child that they can come back when they say that they are sorry and will change their behaviour. If the child does not want to apologize, then you should tell them how long you expect them to be banished. This should not last longer than ten minutes; for smaller children five minutes may be enough. When that time is up, go to the child and say that she can come back. Warn her that if she is disobedient the same thing will happen again. Do not ask her to apologize but, if she does, always give her a cuddle and a 'well done'.

- *Step 6.* If the child apologizes and then refuses to do as he is told again, simply return to step 1. Go through all three steps before carrying out the warning; never jump straight to step 4. Repeat steps 1–5 as many times as necessary; never give in; never leave out a step; and always remain calm and in control.

Important things to remember

You do not have to explain to young children why you have rules. You must show them that you are the adult in charge, rather than justifying your actions. As children get older and develop more complex emotional and cognitive reasoning, they will require reasonable explanations for why certain rules and decisions are made. This does not, however, mean that parents are no longer in charge.

It is important that you are always calm. Never shout or scream, never hit, push or hurt children: this would simply show them that you have lost control and that they can dictate how you behave.

Always begin at step 1 as soon as the child becomes defiant. This will help the child learn that there is no point pushing things to steps 2, 3 or 4. In the end this will help them change their behaviour and be in control of themselves. They will feel proud of themselves and you will be working less hard and achieving more.

These guidelines can be very hard to carry out, and you may need lots of help and practice. If they do not work, it is likely that one or more of the following is occurring:

- One of the adults in your family does not agree with the rules and is giving a different message to the child and confusing him.
- You are not using all of the rules all of the time. This may be because you are tired or because you think you can relax a bit when the child is behaving better.
- You are jumping steps or are not always starting from step 1.
- You want to give up the rules because the child does not appear worried about being banished to her bedroom or another room.
- You are finding it hard to remain calm and you are losing control of yourself.
- You are forgetting to allow the child to say 'sorry' or are banishing him for more than ten minutes at a time.
- You have forgotten to praise the child when she is behaving well or you are pleased with her.
- You have given up and stopped using the guidelines before the three months are over.
- Someone who is important to the child (perhaps you yourself) is ill or unhappy, causing her to worry.

Learning to build a relationship with your child through play

- Follow your child's lead and pace.
- Be an attentive and appreciative audience. Talk about what your child is doing but be careful not to ask too many questions.

- Do not expect too much – give your child time and be aware of his level of ability so that he experiences success instead of constant failure and learns the skills to overcome difficulties firstly with you and, gradually, independently.
- Do not compete with your child or criticize.
- Praise and encourage your child's ideas and creativity.
- Engage in role-play and make-believe with your child.
- Curb your desire to give too much help. Your child needs to 'have a go' herself, and the end result does not need to be perfect.
- If your child is playing quietly, try to sit and watch and remain interested rather than walking away.
- Encourage your child's problem solving.
- Laugh and have fun.

Children need praise

- A child's behaviour improves if good behaviour is praised and attended to (positive reinforcement). Children will behave in such a way as to get attention – even negative attention – but they respond even more to attention coupled with praise.
- Do not worry about spoiling your children with praise.
- Give labelled and specific praise, clearly linked to the child's action.
- Praise can take the form of smiles, eye contact, hugs, other forms of affection and enthusiasm – rewards do not have to be material.
- Give heartfelt, genuine praise – not teasing or sarcasm (passive aggression).
- Praise immediately.
- Use praise consistently and reliably so that your child is able to build up a sense of the patterns of the world.
- Praise your child both when you are alone together and when you are with other people.
- Praise your child's attempts and approximations, not just her perfect end results.
- Children who are not used to praise may find it difficult to receive. Gently enable them to do so by moderating your words and responses to their emotional needs. Ask the child to tell you how he feels about what he has done and then gently shape his reactions by responding more positively.
- Take care not to discount your child's interpretations of her world – they need to be honoured even if they differ from your own.
- Children need praise even when you are finding them difficult – in fact, they need praise even more at these times.

Children need clear boundaries established by setting clear limits

- Give one command at a time – be specific and clear.
- Be realistic in your expectations and use age-appropriate commands.
- Use commands that communicate clearly what is required of your child.

- Use 'do' commands rather than 'stop' commands.
- Make commands positive and polite.
- Give children ample warnings and helpful reminders – they do not always deliberately forget. They often get distracted by learning about new aspects of their worlds and do not always share or understand your priorities.
- Give children options wherever possible.
- Make commands short, to the point and useful. Do not issue commands just for the sake of issuing commands.
- Gradually give over age-appropriate control for children to make decisions themselves in a supportive environment.
- Encourage your child to do problem solving with you, and to gain independence as appropriate to the child's age and emotional maturity.
- Be consistent – talk to your partner or fellow carer to ensure that you agree on what to praise and what consequences to use for non-compliance.

Children need clear, specific, consistent consequences for their actions with opportunities for learning and changing

- Consequences need to be age-appropriate. One minute is a long time for a two-year-old, and 'tomorrow' is meaningless for a child under five years of age.
- Never threaten what you will not or cannot carry through.
- Consequences need to be immediate and clearly related to the child's actions.
- Agree the consequences with the child in advance, giving them choices where appropriate so that they are involved in planning their discipline. This promotes self-discipline in the future.
- Involve your child wherever possible in deciding the behavioural management programme.
- Make consequences natural and non-punitive.
- Use consequences that are short and to the point.
- Enable your child to experience opportunities to learn and to be successful.
- Enable your child to see consequences as helpful, and not punitive, by being positive, conciliatory and warm rather than frightening and punishing in your manner.

Children need to be rewarded for changes in behaviour and attitudes – rewards increase the desired behaviour

- Try to make rewards relational.
- Define appropriate child behaviour clearly.
- Do not make programmes too complex – choose one or two behaviours to start with, and choose behaviours where the child is likely to be able to succeed in making the desired change fairly easily so that she builds up her confidence and hope with frequent positive feedback.
- Make the steps small.
- Gradually increase the challenge.

- The focus needs to be on increasing positive behaviours rather than just eliminating undesirable behaviours.
- Involve your child in choosing the rewards (within appropriate and defined limits), making them relational where possible and certainly inexpensive.
- Reward everyday achievements, as well as significant changes.
- Be clear, specific and consistent about what rewards are for.
- Show your child that you expect success and do not confuse rewards and negative consequences.
- Make the system of monitoring appropriate to the child with respect to her age, interests and temperament (e.g., a 'star chart' in the kitchen for a younger, extrovert visual child; a diary [chart or prose] for an older, less outgoing child).

Guidelines for withdrawing attention

Another possible method of discipline that can be effective, but that should be used sparingly and for short periods of time only, is ignoring. Ignoring involves looking or moving away and not giving the child eye contact (which is very rewarding) so that they are not getting your attention. Ignoring is particularly useful in stopping the parent or carer from getting into a vicious cycle of negative reinforcement. Because children respond to attention, withdrawing attention in a clear, non-punitive way often decreases undesirable behaviours.

- Physically move away from the child, but stay in the room if possible.
- Be subtle in the way you ignore and be careful not to snub or taunt the child non-verbally.
- Do not have a long discussion about the consequences of a behaviour – this again is very rewarding.
- Be consistent.
- Return your attention as soon as the misbehaviour stops so the child does not feel unloved.
- Choose a few specific child behaviours to ignore and make sure they are ones you *can* ignore.
- Give attention to the child's positive behaviours to enhance them.
- Be prepared for the child to test you to see if you can hold him to the boundary you have set.
- Use ignoring/withdrawing attention within a range of management techniques. Especially with a younger child, distraction or diversion can be just as effective.
- Arrange with a friend or fellow carer to give one another emotional support – withdrawing attention from younger children can bring up a range of conflicting emotions within you, especially if this technique was used as a punishment when you were younger

A specific type of withdrawing attention is called 'time out'. The child is placed in a room or space away from anybody for a set period (no more than 5 minutes). This technique should only be used as a last resort in response to one or two specific behaviours. Generally speaking, withdrawing rewards (attention is a reward) as a result of undesired behaviour is more effective than punishment. Time out needs to be clearly explained to the child and seen as part of a planned management strategy – not as an impulsive last option by an exasperated, angry carer. Make sure the place chosen for the time out is safe and not wildly interesting or associated with bad memories or key activities in a child's life. As with any consequences, positive or negative, time out needs to be used within a considered, consistent and planned management strategy developed by the child and parent or carer together.

One of the fringe benefits of time out is that it also gives both the parent or carer and the child a break from the emotional dynamics and projections of their interaction and enables both parties to calm down, reconsider their actions and assumptions and move towards an alternative resolution. This enables healing rather than damage and abuse. It is part of our effective protection of our children to take this space, even if not an actual time out – children and young people are ours to nurture and love, not to batter with our pain.

Children need help to develop self-discipline and skills in problem solving

If a parent or carer is inconsistent, illogical and punitive, a child learns that the world is a frightening, unpredictable place. He becomes watchful, submissive and withdrawn or rebellious as a way of keeping himself safe – becoming either a permanent peacemaker or tyrant. Neither role enables a child to develop skills in safe self-management and the confidence and self-esteem to dare to take appropriate risks and to develop her own identity within her culture and society. Parenting skills which enable children to develop appropriately in this way include:

- Not reacting just to what you see or what you assume when you encounter a problem (e.g., one child saying that the other has hit him).
- Gathering information from all parties concerned about what happened.
- Not interrogating the child.
- Be sure the child realizes that you want to understand his feelings and appreciate that his feelings may differ from yours. Be honest with children if you cannot make sense of where they are coming from and ask them to help you.
- Help the child to look at the other child's feelings as well as her own.
- Ask the child to help develop a solution for what has happened.
- Give praise and attention for the positive ways the child has at least attempted to solve the problem.
- After the child has suggested a solution, help him to think about the consequences of the action and other possible options.
- If the consequences are not positive, ask the child to suggest another solution and to think this through in the same way.

In this way we are enabling children to learn to understand their worlds and to understand themselves within those worlds. Good parents are cycle breakers, equipping children with the skills for living to enable them to feel secure, safe and accepted as they are and to feel challenged, encouraged and guided to become all that God intended them to be.

Organizations

Mental Health Foundation

www.mentalhealth.org.uk/index/html

The website for the Mental Health Foundation is comprehensive and includes a site for children and young people. It contains a summary of the 'Big Picture' report promoting children and young people's mental health. Publications can be ordered on-line.

Association of Infant Mental Health

Child and Family Department
Tavistock Centre
120 Belsize Lane
London NW3 5BA
UK
Tel. +44 20 7447 3810

Infant Mental Health Journal www.wiley.com.

For professionals concerned about the mental health of infants and parents.

Resources for fathering

Joseph Rowntree Foundation
The Homestead
40 Water End
York, YO3 6LP
UK
Tel. +44 1904 629241
Fax +44 1904 620072
www.jrf.org.uk

This foundation is an independent, non-political body that supports research and innovative projects with funding. Their excellent website includes research summaries that are available to download.

Websites – Parenting for parents and professionals

Fact sheets for parents

www.bbc.co.uk/parenting

Information on this site is reliable and provided through the health education authority.

Parenthood.com

www.abcparenting.com

This American site is very comprehensive and provides good resources for fathers. It also addresses the needs of parents of premature babies with information for professionals provided separately.

Parentline Plus

www.parentlineplus.org.uk

Helpline: +44 808 8002222

Office: +44 20 7284 5500

Provides leaflets, publications and information on parenting courses such as Family Caring Trust, Webster-Stratton and Positive Parenting (from whose excellent briefs information was drawn for these guidelines).

Sure Start

Caxton House
Tothill Street
London SW1H 9NA
UK

www.surestart.gov.uk

Sure Start's website provides up-to-date information about the programme and on-line editions of Sure Start publications. Sure Start is an initiative to help mothers and young children who live in areas of extreme deprivation so that the children get a good start in life.

Sharing your faith with a child

Cheryl Barnes

Sharing the gospel with children is a subject that has been written about extensively, and there is much advice on 'how' to lead a child to Christ. Many of us experience a sinking feeling when we hear the word 'evangelize' and remember difficult times trying to witness to our friends. We need to be encouraged to share our faith with children and to realize how fruitful it is.

Child evangelism is a simple and natural process. Children, especially young children, readily believe the truth and willingly make a commitment to Jesus. Sharing our faith follows naturally from spending time with children, as part of our relationship with them. We need to live our lives as examples to them, present the gospel and answer their questions simply. Our faith is based on a relationship with our Lord, and it seems right that to share our faith with a child is to introduce her to the one who loves her, really knows her innermost needs, and died for her to become a child of God.

Children from all nations and situations respond to the message and hope of the gospel – from street children to those traumatized by war. While they may not grasp the deeper concepts and doctrines, their hearts believe and joyfully turn to Christ. Childlike faith is simple, sincere, genuine and characterized by wholehearted commitment – yet we as adults keep looking for them to demonstrate their faith in a way that is measurable, evident or adult. In doing this we do not accept children's faith for what it is. As adults we are reluctant, hesitant in the face of circumstances, and at times we lack discernment over the spiritual battle for the child's life. The Bible simply says, 'if you confess with your mouth, "Jesus is Lord," and believe in your heart that God raised him from the dead, you will be saved' (Rom. 10:9). We enter the kingdom like little children; later we go on to learn about 'what' we believe.

Sometimes adults are reluctant to share their faith with children because they feel that there are things children should know before they give their lives to Christ. We feel that they should fully understand the seriousness of what they are doing and the lifestyle changes making a commitment to Jesus requires. We also question our own ability to present the gospel in a relevant way, and we worry that the child may only be coming to Christ to please us.

It is a spiritual battle for the child's life. What if the reluctance on our part is fuelled by an enemy who definitely does not want a child saved? There may never be another chance to pray with that child; you may never see the child again. Often well-meaning Christians put stumbling blocks in front of children to make it as difficult as possible for them to come to faith, so that they will know the child really wants to become a Christian. Only when they are sure that this is the case will they pray with the child.

In Africa it is quite common to find evangelistic crusades setting up tent meetings. Children flock to these meetings. It is probably quite a spectacle for them – the sound system, the tent, the musicians and wonderful songs, the great man who stands and speaks passionately and finally calls for a response to his message. Children flow up to the front – constituting, on average, 50 per cent of those who respond. The children are often shepherded aside, sometimes prayed for with a blessing of sorts and sent back to their seats. The salvation call is explained to the adults, and they are led in the sinners' prayer. Occasionally the children are given the opportunity to pray, but everyone knows that they will respond over and over again, so generally they aren't taken seriously.

Particularly tragic is a belief that is widespread in southern and central Africa, that a child cannot truly come to know Jesus as Saviour until about thirteen years of age – a type of 'age of accountability' concept. Consequently, no one takes the younger ones seriously at all. There is no follow-up or discipleship with them, and the local church does nothing more than keep them entertained or make them sit quietly during the preaching and adult worship service. People sometimes say that 'children are the church of tomorrow'. On the contrary, children are the church of today. There is no 'junior' Holy Spirit. They are soldiers in God's army the moment they believe. Our ignorance of this fact will be fully exploited by Satan, who 'prowls around like a roaring lion looking for someone to devour' (1 Pet. 5:8). Statistics show that the majority of Christians become believers before they reach the age of fourteen (see Chapter 23). This fact proves that the child's simple response to Jesus, not fully knowing what it's about, can be effective and lasting. There are many of us who could testify to this truth.

'Children at risk' have no other hope to turn to, and they know that the gospel is truth and will change them and the life they lead. We cannot approach these children in a complex way – they want a simple, genuine message of hope and truth. A child prostitute, for example, may not be able to be rescued from her 'prison', yet a true faith will sustain her during the trauma and bring healing and comfort where no other is found. The Holy Spirit is our comforter and teacher, a 'very present help in time of need'. He will never leave or forsake his children.

We need to pray against the paralysis among adults with regard to evangelizing children. No one would think twice about giving a thirsty child water, or helping him out of a deep pit, yet people are reluctant to speak openly about Jesus. Wonderful projects provide food, shelter, medicine and care, while sharing the gospel through good relationships and spending time with the children receive less emphasis. If we are only meeting physical needs we are no different from other 'secular' organizations and projects. Jesus said to the woman at the well, 'the water I give him will become in him a spring of water welling up to eternal life' (John 4:14).

Fears of offending other authorities or breaking the law also constrain us. Where is the boldness of Peter and John? In Acts 4, particularly verses 17 to 20, they were severely warned 'to speak no longer to anyone in [Jesus'] name'. Peter's answer was, 'Judge for yourselves whether it is right in God's sight to obey you rather than God'.

It is faith that pleases God, and we need to approach children with the faith that our prayers make a difference, and that as co-workers with Christ we are rescuing these beautiful little children from eternity in hell. If we only have one moment with a child, let us put aside our reluctance and make it count eternally.

Note
1. Care for the Family, 53 Romney Street, London SW1P 3RF.

– Questions to Consider –

1 Christians are often accused of over-disciplining or under-disciplining their children. How would you answer such assertions? What does God require of us? Use biblical references, national and international policy documents to support your answer.

2 Parenting is said to be the hardest job in the world and yet, ironically, it is perhaps the only one for which we have no previous training. Identify the key qualities, skills and approaches of a good parent and discuss how parents can most effectively respond to children's difficult behaviours.

3 Consider a child whom you know well and discuss how you might explore sharing your faith with him. What might be some of the stumbling blocks to this? How would you overcome them?

CHAPTER 30

Child Protection

Heather MacLeod

Introduction

CHILD-FOCUSED projects aim to provide safe and friendly environments where children can develop and grow in a healthy way. There are many challenges to creating such environments. These may involve cultural, social, economic, religious and political realities. Abuse of children prevents their healthy development, and therefore any organization working with children needs to consider the extent of abuse in the community. Child abuse generally falls into three main categories: physical, emotional and sexual abuse.

This chapter focuses on the protection of children from within your own organization. In particular, we will focus on the development of policies that will reduce the risk of children being abused within your organization. While the notion that abuse can come from within a child-focused organization is difficult to contemplate, the reality is that working with 'children at risk' is attractive to those who may want to harm children. Increased media attention in the last decade has highlighted this fact, identifying cases of physical, emotional and sexual abuse of children by staff and volunteers. Christian organizations and church groups have been included in this attention.

The following concerns and recommendations are in line with the CRC, which specifically mentions the protection of children from child abuse and neglect and also looks at providing appropriate measures to ensure the physical and psychological recovery and social reintegration of children.

Before discussing the development of policies, we need to understand more about child abuse.

Definitions of abuse

Child abuse, or maltreatment, occurs in all cultural, ethnic, occupational and socio-economic groups. Some people think only parents are to blame or, in the case of sexual abuse, that strangers are to blame. In reality, children can become victims of abuse by parents, relatives, neighbours, family friends, acquaintances and strangers. Those people trusted to care for children such as teachers, child-care providers, church workers or foster parents may also abuse children. Abusers may be male or female and they may be adults, adolescents or children. There is no single profile of someone who abuses. Adults abuse children for many different reasons.

The World Health Organization defines abuse as follows:

> Child abuse and maltreatment constitute all forms of physical and/or emotional ill treatment, sexual abuse, neglect or negligent treatment or commercial or other exploitation, resulting in actual or potential harm to the child's health, survival, development or dignity in the context of a relationship of responsibility, trust or power.

Many communities will acknowledge that physical and emotional abuse does occur, but sexual abuse is often not discussed due to taboos surrounding the subject. Christina Sands (1999) explains the silence in this way:

> Ignorance is bliss . . . but it is "killing" society's most precious resource – its children. Satan uses our ignorance for his gain as he chokes the innocence out of millions of children wounded by abuse. Fear, the root of our ignorance, is Satan's weapon to silence us and make us believe that if we don't talk about the evil it will go away.

Because of this silence, we need to look at sexual abuse in more detail. There are many definitions of sexual abuse. The National Committee to Prevent Child Abuse in the US defines child sexual abuse as 'sexual contact between a child and an adult or older child for the sexual gratification of the offender'. The Action for the Rights of Children (ARC) Resource Manual uses this definition:

> Sexual Abuse should be understood not only as violent sexual assault but also other sexual activities, including inappropriate touching, where the child does not fully comprehend, is unable to give informed consent, or for which the child is not developmentally prepared.

Paedophilia

Finkelhor (1986) is a leading expert in this issue. He explains that the terms 'sexual abuse and child molesting refer to the actual behaviours, whereas paedophilia is essentially a state in which a person is predisposed to use children for his or her sexual gratification'. He continues,

> We define paedophilia as occurring when an adult has a constant sexual interest in prepubertal children. We infer that sexual interest from one of two behaviours: 1) The adult had some sexual contact with the child (meaning that he or she touched the child or had the child touch him or her with the purpose of becoming sexually aroused) or 2) The adult has masturbated to have sexual fantasies involving children.

He then discusses the multi-factor explanations of why adults become sexual abusers. His book is an excellent reference for detailed information about profiles of abusers. As we develop child protection policies, it is important to keep in mind the following points about child sexual abusers:

- There is no reliable 'profile' of a sexual abuser. You can't tell by looking at a person.

- They come from all walks of life. The majority of child sex offenders are male. However, women can also offend.

- Sex with children is much more about power and control than sex.

- The paedophile/sexual abuser may appear to be a caring, skilful person. He may appear to be an excellent applicant with impressive experience.

- They can be seen as invaluable workers who apparently relate well with children.

- They actively pursue contact with children both during work time and on a private basis after hours.

- They may have poor social skills and relate better to children than to adults.

- Very few paedophiles have criminal records. It is estimated that only 2–3 per cent are ever convicted, and the recidivism (likelihood of repeating an offence) rate is high.

- They often have an age and gender preference.
- They often select children who are vulnerable – exactly the kinds of children with whom many NGOs work.
- There is no 'test' to detect a paedophile, so we need to be alert to patterns of behaviour.
- Pictures of children and child pornography play a key role. It is important to note that the huge photo libraries on the Internet, the availability of photos and pornographic videos in circulation mean that children can suffer over and over again.
- It is important to remember that it is not a crime to be a paedophile – it is the action that is the crime. However, we do not want to put people in situations where they are tempted.

Developing a child protection policy

Child protection policies are aimed at reducing the risk of anyone who is associated with the organization abusing children. Such policies also give strong messages to the community that you take your commitment to protecting children seriously, and they encourage others to do likewise. A policy is much more effective if it is wide-ranging. One single action or emphasis is inadequate to meet your goal. The following are the key components of a child protection policy.

Statement of commitment

This statement summarizes why you have a policy and places it in a broader context. It normally includes:

- An explanation of why your organization is particularly concerned with this issue.
- Definitions of abuse, the definition of a child (UNICEF and the majority of organizations use 'under the age of 18 years') and other terms.
- An analysis of the major child right violations and, in particular, child protection issues in your country and local context.
- An analysis of the legal and cultural framework related to children in which you work.

Communicating the issue

This section of the policy usually includes:

- Your commitment to speaking out on the issues of child abuse and breaking the silence. The method with which you choose to 'speak out' may depend on the political, social and cultural environment, but the intention is always to increase awareness.
- An explanation of specific awareness-raising activities and specific training for staff and volunteers.
- A statement that ensures that the policy is to be included in your organization's staff/volunteer/board manual.

Behaviour protocols

This component of the policy clearly spells out the expectations with regards to interaction with children. It is recommended that this section be formulated in such a way that it can be easily extracted from the larger policy and reproduced as a reader-friendly document. These protocols are for all those who work with your organization and for those who are associated with the work (e.g., employees, volunteers, visitors, consultants, interns and board members). Visitors include staff from other offices, donors/sponsors and visitors from other organizations. There are additional protocols for sponsorship projects due to the special nature and the responsibility associated with that relationship.

Behaviour protocols are given to visitors to ensure that they understand and agree to abide by the organization's commitment to protect children. Staff, volunteers and others working under the umbrella of your organization have additional responsibilities. The universal behaviour protocols include:

- Introductory statements about treating children with dignity, respecting them and valuing them as precious in the eyes of God.

- A description of appropriate interaction with children in your culture. Consider this in terms of different ages of girls and boys (young children, middle childhood and adolescents) and the differences between male and female visitors. In most cases, children will feel more comfortable in the presence of another child, and this may be part of your description.

- A statement that your organization will take any accusation of abuse seriously and will take appropriate action.

- 'Two adult rule': This rule states that an adult should not be alone with a child. Even if an adult is having an individual conversation with a child, another adult must be within visual contact. This protects both the adult from false accusation and the child from abuse. In cases where individual counselling is deemed appropriate, the counsellor must inform another adult/supervisor in advance that this will happen, and where.

- A statement about the adult's responsibility in the case of a child behaving in a 'seductive' way.

- A statement that visitors and non-project staff will always be accompanied by project staff

Additional behaviour protocols for close associates of the organization (e.g., staff, volunteers, interns, consultants and board members) usually include:

- Provisions to inform communities and children of the protocols, and an assurance that project support will not stop if they report a suspicion.

- Clearly stated procedures related to appropriate discipline where direct care of children is involved.

- A statement that no hiring of children (under 18 years) as household help is tolerated. The high level of abuse of domestic child workers is well documented. In the definition of child domestic workers we do not include occasional babysitters/help during school holidays or out of school time, provided it is not exploitative in nature.

- Having the person concerned sign a statement that he/she has read the complete policy, understands it and will adhere to it also provides additional protection in the event that an allegation is made.

- Clear notice that if anyone is found to break these protocols, including inappropriate behaviour with children, this will be grounds for discipline including dismissal.

Project partners

This component of the child protection policy identifies the role of our project partners in protecting children. Partners need to know about and share our commitment to child protection. This section therefore includes statements that expect:

- Written agreements with partners which reflect and include child protection policy commitments.
- Partners to create their own child protection policies.

Recruitment and screening

This component of the policy makes statements about the importance of careful screening of all potential candidates and recruiting procedures. It identifies procedures that reduce the risk of hiring someone who may abuse children. As you write this component of your policy, pay very close attention to local law regarding recruitment and what you are and are not permitted to ask or learn. Local lawyers need to be consulted. It includes statements that cover the following areas:

- The protection of children and child protection policies, which will be stated clearly from the beginning of the recruitment process and then reviewed during orientation.
- A signed statement by the applicant, stating that he/she has no criminal convictions for abuses against children.
- An agreement by the applicant that he/she will abide by the policy.
- Detailed reference checks.
- A signed agreement for a background check will be obtained during the recruitment process. Where legally possible, a criminal record check of related abuses against children is strongly recommended for applicants who will be associated with the organization.

Response to allegations

This component of the policy details specific actions related to any allegations of abuse by staff/visitors and others associated with the organization. It includes statements that:

- Create a culture in which suspicious behaviour is reported.
- Indicate that both the victim and the alleged perpetrator are treated with respect and dignity while an investigation takes place.
- A child is believed until proved otherwise.
- Outline reporting procedures.
- Emphasize a team approach (e.g., child protection worker, legal, personnel, management).

- Reflect high levels of confidentiality.
- Written documentation of facts related to the investigation and outcome will be kept and stored in a confidential file.
- Local laws will be followed as required and extraterritorial issues recognized if a foreigner is involved.
- Someone competent will be designated to deal with the media.
- In the event of an employee being dismissed for suspected abuse, then the organization may disclose such information, if requested, by a prospective employer.
- Ongoing support will be given to the child and the accused.

Advocacy

This component of the policy indicates a commitment to working with other groups interested in child protection and includes statements about:

- Learning from other groups that have experience in this area.
- Being involved in community, national and regional activities to lobby government, police and others for better child protection laws, procedures, and so on.
- Encouraging and supporting training initiatives.
- Networking with others.

This section can also include statements about praying for wisdom and strength as you address this difficult issue of child abuse.

Confidentiality

This component relates to information dissemination between people and written information about children and child abuse situations. This specifies:

- The sharing of information about an incident and who is informed. Generally a child abuse allegation is shared with the designated child protection team, which decides who else needs to know.
- That care needs to be taken with prayer requests related to a child abuse situation, as this sometimes gives more information than required.
- Procedures for ensuring the security of information – for example, the locking of files with child information and limited access.
- That correspondence from donors to children should be screened to check that they are not developing inappropriate relationships with children.
- That information on the Internet is especially vulnerable, due to its global nature and the ease of access, therefore procedures related to website development and Internet access are necessary.

Conclusion

Writing a comprehensive child protection policy may seem an overwhelming task. Although it does require time and commitment, it can be done with team effort. It is best to begin with a detailed implementation plan. Identify the person/people responsible for each component and set realistic time frames.

Begin with an analysis of child abuse in your country and local environment. This helps frame your policy. Raising awareness about the issues within the organization is crucial to the shared commitment to this issue. Remember that your goal is to create safer environments for children and to protect children from those who may harm them. The implementation of effective child protection policies within your organization is one significant contribution towards this goal.

– Questions to Consider –

1 Critically appraise the key issues relating to child protection policy development within an organization. How would you develop such a policy within a project? How would you transfer such a policy to a field project-based situation?

2 You come into work one day and a colleague meets you with the news that a child in the care of your organization has disclosed that he has been touched inappropriately by another member of staff. What would you do? Discuss each step of your approach, detailing your rationale for each aspect of your response.

3 How would you respond to a colleague's comment that, 'We don't need those sorts of [child protection] policies here. We are *called* to this work by God. No missionary would ever hurt a child. Those policies are just for secular organizations.'

– CHAPTER 31 –

Selection Criteria, Monitoring and Training of Staff

Rushika Amarasekera

Lift up your hands towards him for the lives of your children, who faint from hunger at the head of every street. (Lam. 2:19)

WE are often moved with compassion when we hear of 'children at risk in diverse situations' in various parts of the world. Many programmes have resulted from compassionate, committed people responding to their needs. Although when we reach out to hurting children we feel a sense of fulfilment and are able to help the children, such work also brings us face to face with a difficult reality.

A time for preparation and training

Because working with hurting children brings us into worlds and situations that are so painful, complex and different from our own, it is essential that all workers have appropriate training. We must be adequately prepared for the sake of the children as much as for ourselves. This concept of preparation is a biblical principle. Moses, for instance, was grieved at the plight of his people. He received a calling from God, but it took training in Pharaoh's court and 40 years in the desert before God considered his people ready to enter the promised land. Through these times of training, Moses and his people were challenged, nurtured, disciplined and guided by God into a state of greater maturity before they were ready to do what God required of them. Likewise, we must not just rush off to help children. We need to be trained and matured by God and by human mentors in order to work effectively and safely with children. In the same way King David was chosen by God and anointed when he was just a shepherd boy, but he had to come a long way before he finally became king. The same could be said of Joseph, who in the time between his calling or vision and its fulfilment was prepared spiritually, physically and in terms of skill and knowledge.

Jesus commanded his disciples not to depart from Jerusalem until they were baptized with the Holy Spirit, 'you will receive power when the Holy Spirit comes on you; and you will be my witnesses . . . to the ends of the earth' (Acts 1:4–8). Jesus taught them, led by example, empowered them with the Holy Spirit and only then commanded them to go forth.

Similarly, working with 'children at risk' requires training and preparation. The worker may be dealing with children who have experienced physical, sexual or emotional abuse, or with children who have been traumatized by war. The resulting emotional and behavioural problems and the ways in which children have adapted to the situations they face may be difficult to understand or cope with. An untrained worker who struggles with a child's aggressive or sexual behaviour after trying the usual means of discipline may label the child as 'impossible' or 'bad'. On the other hand, if a worker understands the background and intervenes appropriately, the outcome will be rewarding for the worker and constructive for the child.

Another reality is that the children and families we are trying to help often have values and expectations different from our own. A child who has adapted to the lifestyle of the streets may initially prefer to earn money rather than go to school. His parents may also resist our intervention. This can be a frustrating situation for both the child and the worker unless the worker has the skills to handle it. It is no wonder, then, that the fields related to social services, although the work can be rewarding and fulfilling, have some of the highest rates of staff turnover and burn-out.

Good practice

Lack of appropriate training and support can lead to further abuse of children and emotional fatigue and burn-out for the worker. Basic good practice is essential to ensure that the work we set out to do is effective. It is important that organizations involve professionals for specialized roles and when drawing up procedures, so that they are able to follow best practice guidelines – for example, with up-to-date child protection procedures and child-care and therapy practices. Some points to consider when working out a code of good practice for a project with 'children at risk' include:

- *Competence.* Each worker should be aware of the children's context and understand the psychological and social impact of difficult circumstances on the children, as well as being aware of possible interventions.
- *Training.* This needs to be provided for workers at all levels (including volunteers and part-time workers), in keeping with their various roles.
- *Confidentiality.* Personal information about the children and their families should be respected. Often, trust is undermined and untold damage is unwittingly done when the 'cases' of children are discussed or published.
- *Clarity.* It is important to clearly define roles, duties and procedures.
- *Consistent strategy.* A project should have an agreed plan of action for all situations that can be anticipated.
- *Team work.* Working together as an effective team ensures prayer support, emotional support, opportunities for problem solving and discussion, and consistent good practice

Protecting the child and the worker

There is a tendency to think that the problem of sexual abuse of children does not exist in Christian organizations. The fact is that it can, and does, happen. Children are at risk of sexual abuse in any setting, and especially when they are in residential care. We need to acknowledge this possibility and build in safeguards to protect children from abuse. The following points focus on protecting the child as well as providing clear boundaries to protect the worker from allegations of inappropriate conduct.

Suggested procedures

- Talking to, playing with and working with a child needs to be done in full view of another responsible adult. That adult also needs to be aware that you are looking to them to externally regulate and assist in monitoring your practice.
- No one touches another person without permission.
- In a residential setting, no children are allowed to get into bed with each other or with a staff member.
- No one should touch the area covered by the swimsuit or underwear (except a doctor during a medical examination or if a young child needs assistance bathing).
- When doing home visits, take another worker along.
- Never go anywhere alone with only one child.
- Do not permit strangers on the property. Make sure that all visitors are accompanied by a member of staff at all times. (Goodwin, 1993)

Monitoring

Once guidelines and procedures have been drawn up and established, it will be possible to compare good practice with current practice. An objective standard will be available so that an individual worker, or the project as a whole, can be monitored. For instance, if confidentiality is breached, if a worker does not follow appropriate good practice guidelines, does not engage in training and supervision, or if she works alone with one child when others are not present, reference can be made to the code of good practice.

It is necessary for all workers to read and understand the procedures and guidelines and make a commitment to follow them. It will be necessary for the team leader to uphold good practice, since it is likely that the staff will include both those who accept the practice and others who do not see the need for it. Identifying one person to whom each worker is directly accountable will ensure that the worker is monitored and supported. Regular meetings need to be held to set goals, to monitor progress and to discuss and deal with issues that arise daily.

Selection criteria

Since it is not always easy to find workers, most projects would welcome all those who volunteer their time. When working with 'children at risk', however, we are constantly reminded of the fact that our every action can have a significant impact on another person's life and, therefore, special care has to be given to the selection of staff. It is also worth noting that many people want to do something to help but are not sure what to do. A clear idea of what the work entails and the skills and aptitude required is essential to avoid future frustration and disillusionment. When screening potential workers:

- Ask for references and make personal contact with the referees.
- Discuss their Christian commitment and experiences.
- Take time to speak to the person and get as much background information as possible.
- Has the applicant carefully considered her decision to come forward to work with 'children at risk'?
- What is this person's reason for wanting to work with children?
- What is his reason for wanting to be involved in this particular project?
- What experience does the person have of working with children?
- What did she learn from this experience?
- What does the person think his skills and aptitudes are?

We also need to be aware of the applicant's attitudes:

- to children.
- to abused children or children facing the particular set of difficult circumstances the project is handling.
- to working with communities that have values different from the worker's own.
- to working with people from different religious backgrounds.
- towards any past experiences of abuse suffered (consider whether the job will place further stress on the person).
- to counselling.
- to training.

- to procedure, guidelines, monitoring processes and good practice.

Keep in mind that abusers are good at winning trust and using spiritual arguments to get their own way. They seek out jobs that have little supervision and that allow them to get close to children. They also show an unwillingness to work under authority. Good practice and monitoring act as a deterrent to those who want to take advantage of the vulnerability of children. Even with the best screening processes, there are no guarantees. It is essential, therefore, to maintain procedures and guidelines to ensure good practice.

– Questions to Consider –

1 What training and support do you think you need to enhance your skills as a worker with 'children at risk'? How and where can you get this training?

2 What, if any, procedures and guidelines does your project have to maintain good practice? How can you improve existing guidelines, to make sure that you cover as many angles as possible? If you do not have any such guidelines, how can you realistically draw them up for your project to protect both children and workers?

3 In the light of Amarasekera's discussion, think about either your own organization or a project with which you are familiar. How you would create a climate of awareness and establish the procedures to enable child protection issues to be addressed?

CHAPTER 32

Information Systems: Data Collection, Protection, Storage and Usage

Emily McDonald and Sally Clarke

By wisdom a house is built, and through understanding it is established; through knowledge its rooms are filled with rare and beautiful treasures. (Prov. 24:3–4)

ONE seasoned project leader echoed this proverb when he likened the research and preparation phase of his organization to building strong foundations for a building: the deeper the foundations, the taller the building can be. Too many initiatives are launched with inadequate knowledge of the environment in which they are setting out – a fact that contributes to the high closure rate of 'children at risk' projects. This chapter explains why research is important and how to collect and store useful data. Alastair Ager provides a slightly more academic approach to research methods in Chapter 33.

Careful research can save you months and years of wasted time. Your projects are more likely to succeed if you set out to understand:

- The real needs of the children you propose to work with so that you can more clearly define the goals and nature of your response.

- What resources are available to you within the church and community at large.

- Who is already working in your target area and how your work may complement the initiatives that already exist.

- The legal and practical implications of your proposed work with children.

Most people and organizations have limited resources in terms of time, money and people. Jesus exhorts us to count the cost before beginning a project in Luke 14:28–33. Research helps us avoid starting things we cannot complete. Ultimately, undertaking careful research honours the children and the Lord as we strive for excellence in our work with the world's most precious treasures.

General guidelines

- *Involve potential co-workers.* Bear in mind that those involved at this stage will gain a stronger sense of ownership of the project than those who are simply presented with your results.

- *Avoid re-inventing the wheel.* Find out what research has already been done before embarking on original studies yourself.

- *Make use of networks and directories.* In many places around the world, groups working with 'children at risk' are forming networks in order to get to know each other and share information. Try contacting your local network as you start your research, or try Viva Network's regional or international offices.

- *Share what you learn.* Do not simply approach networks or organizations for what you can get from them, but also be prepared to share any additional

information you collect.
- *Be culturally aware.* Learn about local cultural issues relating to children. These may affect the way you can work, as well as the ways in which you can involve local people in your project.
- *Personal contact is most effective.* Table 1 shows the effectiveness of communication methods in getting information back and may help you plan your research methods.
- *Share your findings with those you involve.* Do not be like the many researchers who treat project workers poorly by taking up their time but fail to share copies of the completed research. Find out who is interested in getting copies and follow through.

Table 1: The effectiveness of various methods for gathering information (results of a study by the *Harvard Business Review*)

Most effective

⬆

| Personal contact, one-on-one |
| Small group discussion |
| Large group discussion |
| Telephone call |
| Handwritten personal letter |
| Typed personal letter |
| Non-personal circular |

⬇ | Handouts |

Least effective

Researching the situations and needs of children

Make use of existing research

The following groups may have produced research documents on the situation in the area in which you intend to work, so check with them before you begin:
- Government departments of health, education and family welfare. The attention generated by the CRC has provoked recent new research.
- The local/national UNICEF office. Many of these offices have carried out situation analyses on women and children and on 'children in especially difficult circumstances'.
- The World Health Organization
- NGOs
- Networks of NGOs
- Professional organizations and special interest groups
- Indigenous organizations

The place of children in the 'system'

Find out how the national legal system relates to children. Think about which areas of law are relevant to the children for whom you are concerned. Possible areas of interest include: laws on family life, such as those relating to adoption, registration of births and deaths, social security and welfare systems; laws on employment, such as minimum ages for employment of different kinds and rules for street vending; and laws affecting particular groups of children such as refugees and immigrants.

Carrying out first-hand research

Once you have an overview of existing research, you will have identified gaps in the information you need. Carefully consider the information you lack, and focus your research on that. Avoid long, complicated studies and focus instead on the concerns and interests of children and on designing appropriate action on their behalf. Make yourself aware of research methodology and analysis, especially the research methods most appropriate to your field of work.

The children will be able to tell you more about their real needs than almost anyone else will. Make every effort to find out about their daily lives, their joys and burdens, their hopes and fears for the future. You could organize children and families into discussion groups to serve as vehicles for them to express themselves (see below). At this piloting stage take a listening role, and do not promise too much.

Many social research projects rely on surveys and questionnaires, but these are not the only useful research methods and can give misleading results if designed with inadequate background understanding. In some contexts, for example on the street, children may well have been approached with questionnaires before, and they sometimes 'act up' and exaggerate their answers to create a more dramatic impression. Other methods of research can usefully precede the use of a questionnaire (Ennew, 1994) such as observation and focus group discussions.

Place yourself in situations where you can observe the lives of children and their context. This can be done in a relatively unstructured way, by simply being in the company of the children and recording occurrences and impressions in a diary immediately following each period of observation. You can either keep a low profile or involve yourself in some way with the children, playing games or offering a simple service. In time you may wish to structure your observations further to answer specific questions about one or more aspects of the children's activity, for example their daily or weekly routines. Observation methods are time-consuming, but they help you hone further research more precisely.

Discussions can be helpful, especially if you ensure a small group of people from a similar background (e.g., age or situation) and keep the discussion topics focused. These discussions can shed light on the views of local people and the vocabulary they use in relation to 'children at risk' situations. Children may find it easier to talk freely about sensitive issues when in a group of peers than when talking one-on-one with an adult. You should aim to create a comfortable informal environment free from distractions and to generate understanding and agreement within the group about the purpose of the discussion. Establish some ground rules for the discussion so that everyone feels the right to be heard. (See also Part Two on guidelines for listening to children and involving them in programme design.)

Sources of information

1. National newspapers: journalists often summarize key points and use statistics to back up their arguments.

2. Journals (see 'Key journals' in 'Further Reading'). Set aside a 'research hour' each week.

3. Internet (see 'Key websites' in 'Further Reading').

4. Publishers' catalogues: get your name on relevant mailing lists.

5. Leaflets and newsletters produced by local projects.

Finding out what kind of work can be done

Find your peers

Having listened to the children, their families and the local people, the next step in working out what kind of programme will be most effective is to contact those who have experience in working in the field. Getting to know your peers is invaluable. Ongoing positive communication and co-operation with other groups need never cease to be a major source of ideas, encouragement and guidance. Your peers will fall into two groups:

1. Local peers, or those already working in the same *place* that you propose to work.

2. Topical peers, or those in the same *field of ministry*, or with the same *type of programme* that you propose.

Consider yourself and these peers as part of a single team fighting to improve the lives of 'children at risk'. Avoid the temptation to have a competitive or jealous attitude. This temptation can be surprisingly strong, since disunity is one of the devil's number-one tactics to reduce the impact of Christians on the situations of 'children at risk' around the world.

The following groups of people may be able to point you to those already working with the children. Where possible, ask for as many types of contact information as possible (i.e., postal and e-mail addresses, telephone and fax numbers – if one piece of this information is out of date, another may prove fruitful).

- Project leaders you know already
- Church leaders in the area
- The local Evangelical Alliance or pastor's confederation
- Government-related social welfare and children's committees and institutions
- Intergovernmental organizations such as UNICEF
- The children themselves
- Local schools
- Media (Internet, newspaper, television, radio)
- Local police

Approach your peers for advice and help

Actually visiting the site where your peers work is by far the best way to find out what is being done, and it can be worth a long and costly journey. Speaking on the telephone can also be helpful for less accessible projects, and e-mail forums on different 'children at risk' subjects do exist. Writing to project leaders is another option, but bear in mind that such people are usually very busy (see Table 1). The following are some guidelines for approaching your peers:

- Have a teachable attitude and communicate with humility.
- Do not turn up unannounced, or expect to hold a long telephone conversation out of the blue, but make an appointment for a convenient time.
- Record your impressions as soon as possible after your visit/conversation.
- Decide what kind of questions you want to ask beforehand, but avoid turning up with a typed list since this may seem intimidating.
- Explain to your peers that you want to learn from them to improve what you do.
- Be sensitive and alert to areas in which you may be able to work together and pool resources.
- Do not set out to point out flaws in their work, but do record any impressions of weaknesses after your visit and seek to learn from them.

Information your peers may be able to give you

The following questions are examples of the kinds of things you may wish to ask your peers.

Spiritual principles

What do you feel God says about ministry to 'children at risk'?

How did you draw from God's strength and guidance when starting out?

What spiritual truths are helpful for you in encouraging and sustaining your ministry?

Motivation for ministry

What do you feel are healthy motivational factors for a person starting out?

What are unhelpful factors?

The working model

What are the objectives of your programme?

How do you work out these objectives in practice?

What are the different activities of your organization?

How do you select the children with whom you work?

How do you monitor the progress of the children?

Initial steps

What were the most important lessons you learned during the establishment of your ministry?

What were the main hurdles? And how did you overcome them?

Staff training

What training do your staff have?

Which resources (e.g., books and reports) and training opportunities have you found helpful?

Administration

How is your organization structured?

How do the different components relate to one another?

How is the project administrated?

What management principles can you recommend?

What methods of fund-raising have you found fruitful?

Can you offer basic advice for handling finances and bookkeeping?

Personal advice

What advice would you offer someone starting out in ministry with regards to family life, personal walk with God, rest, time off, continued motivation, energy and so on?

Legal matters

> Therefore, it is necessary to submit to the authorities, not only because of possible punishment but also because of conscience. (Rom. 13:5)

You may have a strong sense of God's call and authority over your work, but you should also seek to respect the earthly authorities over you. Although it will probably seem a long and tedious task, it will save you time, money and potentially serious disruption to your work in the long run if you make sure you have understood and complied with legal requirements. Communicate with the following regulatory bodies:

- The health department, about sanitation permits.
- The zoning or city planning department, to find out whether you can establish your project in certain areas.
- The fire department, regarding safety regulations in the facilities.
- The labour and tax collection departments, to discover how financial records must be kept and to learn about tax responsibilities and required reports.

You can learn from the experience of other leaders, who may be able to help you save time finding out which legal requirements will apply to your work and how to best set about working towards meeting those requirements. Christian lawyers are often willing to offer advice. Obtain copies of the specific regulations that apply to your type of ministry. Be sure you understand them and put them into practice. Be prepared to spend money for qualified advice.

Data protection

Ensure that organizations (e.g., Viva Network International and other networking organizations, government bodies and large child-care agencies as well as smaller projects) are aware that you are storing data about them, and that they understand why. Obtain permission from these organizations if you intend to distribute the information to other projects in the form of a directory or on a website. Be particularly aware of the use of information about projects working in restricted or sensitive countries. It is advisable to ask organizations about the level of security they require.

The UK Data Protection Act (1998) provides useful guidelines. It states that data must be:

- fairly and lawfully processed
- processed for limited purposes
- adequate, relevant and not excessive
- accurate
- not kept longer than necessary
- secure
- processed in accordance with the data subject's rights
- not transferred to countries without adequate protection.

For further details about the Data Protection Act and its application, see the website of the Office of the Information Commissioner, http://www.data protection.gov.uk/. If you are outside the UK, it is important to find out what data protection regulations apply to your organization. If no such regulations exist, consider investigating and campaigning for similar data protection regulations. Sadly, paedophiles and others will make use of any loopholes in our data protection systems.

Storing information

As your collection of information develops, you will find a classification system useful. The following is an example of a broad classification system for resources about 'children at risk'. The breadth of your own system will depend on your own needs and interests. This example can be adapted to suit your own situation, and new categories can be added.

A	**News and information about 'children at risk'**	**B**	**Working with 'children at risk'**
A1	Street children	B1	Working with street children
A2	Orphans	B2	Working with orphans
A3	Children affected by AIDS	B3	Working with children affected by AIDS
A4	Abused children		
A5	Children affected by war	B4	Working with abused children
A6	Children suffering from chemical/drug addiction	B5	Working with children using drugs, etc., for all categories as above
A7	Disabled children		
A8	Orphans	B6	Counselling children
A9	Sexually exploited children	B7	Child protection
A10	Children in exploitative/slave labour	B8	Advocacy
		B9	Evangelism and discipleship materials
A11	Refugees and children in emergency situations	B10	Literacy and educational materials
A12	Malnourished children		

C	Planning and running a project	D	Working with 'children at risk' locally
C1	Planning your project	D1	Reports from local ministries
C2	Evaluating your project	D2	Reports about 'children at
C3	Management of project and staff		risk' in the local area
		D3	etc., (other categories specific
C4	Finances and fund-raising		to your context)
C5	Spiritual preparation for ministry		

Books, reports and magazines can then be kept in order according to category, so it is easy to identify what information you have on a particular topic. In general it is more useful to keep resources sorted by category rather than by type of resource.

Resource library

Share the materials you have with others so that they can benefit. You will need to establish guidelines for outside organizations borrowing from the library and keep track of who has borrowed which books. Loans can be recorded on your database or, for a smaller library, a paper record of loans can be kept.

One organization in Cambodia asks people to give US$5 to borrow a book and then gives them US$4 when it is returned. This encourages people not to hold onto books too long, to value them, and it also provides a small fund from which to purchase new materials (or at least to pay the phone bill when they remind borrowers to return them!).

Setting up a database

A database is useful for recording details of the information you have and allows you to search easily for information on a particular topic. The following is an example of a simple database for resources that can be created using any database software. The fields and information can be tailored to fit the needs and resources of your organization.

Resources database

In creating a database of your organization's resources, you may find the following fields helpful:
- Title
- Author
- ISBN
- Cost
- Type (e.g., book, video, report, newsletter)
- Description (A summary of what the resource is about. You can also indicate how many pages it has and for whom it would be useful.)
- Geographic focus (The country or region the resource focuses on, if applicable.)

- Category (The category the resource falls into, from the category system suggested above or your own category system [e.g., C2, D1, etc.])
- Library (A tick box to indicate whether this resource is in your library collection.)
- Contact (Address of publisher or organization producing the resource.)

You may include the address of the organization in the contact field or, if you are also setting up a contacts database, your software should give you the option of assigning a unique contact identification number for the publisher. You can then link these contacts in each table. You should also be able to assign a unique reference identification number to each record in the database (some software packages call this 'autonumber'). When you have tailored the table to your needs and saved it, you will be able to record the details of all of your resources using this format.

Contacts database

You can also set up a table within the same database to record details of local projects and contacts. You might also want to include contact details for organizations who supply resources. Such a table might include the following fields:

- Organization
- Leader
- Contact name (contact other than the leader)
- Phone number(s)
- Fax number(s)
- E-mail address(es)
- Address lines (usually 2 lines)
- City
- Country
- Postcode

As in the resource database above, you can specify that your software automatically give a unique reference number to each record which can then be linked with other records (e.g., you could search your resource database using a given organization's reference number).

To extend the usefulness of your database you could also add the following fields:

- *Field of work:* Record the type of work the project does. Create your own list of the types of work carried out locally (e.g., drop-in centre, rehabilitation) and select from this list for each project.
- *Target group:* Create a list of the type of children different projects work with (e.g., street children, AIDS orphans, etc.) and select from this list for each project. It will then be possible to use a query or filter to produce a list of projects working with a particular group of children.
- *Involvements:* Use this field to record the involvement of the other organization with your work. You may also wish to record correspondence and their attendance at any training courses you run.
- *Newsletter subscription:* Use this to indicate whether the organization subscribes to your newsletter or other publications. It would then be

possible, for example, to produce mailing labels from this list.

Recording loans

Another possible use of your database is to record items loaned from your resource library. The following fields may be helpful in maintaining such a record:

- Resource identification number (again, linked to other areas of your database, see above)
- Contact identification number (see above)
- Date borrowed
- Date due back
- Reminder sent (Tick box to indicate whether a reminder has been sent if the loan is overdue.)
- Date returned
- Notes (Record any extra information, e.g., the name of borrower if you have more than one contact in an organization.)

It is also possible to create drop-down lists of all the resources, organizations and contacts in your database, to make it easy to record loans. You will, of course, want to tailor your database to your organization's individual needs (e.g., you may loan items mainly to individuals, rather than organizations, or you may want to maintain a similar record of people to whom you give handouts, newsletters, etc.).

Once you have set up the various areas of your database and entered your data you will be able to add to it and update as necessary, perform searches for resources and information according to different categories, generate reports, produce mailing labels, and so on.

– Questions to Consider –

1 What are some practical and administrative issues that need to be considered when establishing an information system for an organization or project?

2 Reflect on the constraints and benefits of setting up such a system in a remote, isolated situation and in a city-based project. Compare the difference, problems and potentials of these two situations.

3 Someone within your organization presents you with a question that you feel is a potential research issue. How would you go about turning it from a query into a research hypothesis? What are some of the issues that may arise in this process?

4 You have been appointed as a research officer within your organization and you feel honoured by this appointment but ill-equipped to meet the challenge. What are some of the training and practice needs which may arise for you? How would you meet them within the constraints of your current post?

– PART SIX –

Development, Evaluation and Monitoring of Programmes

Introduction MANY *programmes working with children are acutely aware of the need to evaluate what they are doing – not just for the sake of the donors, but also because they appreciate that the only way to improve the programme is to measure its progress with some kind of tool.*

In the first chapter in this section Alastair Ager and Josephine-Joy Wright describe the aims and objectives and means of implementing different research methods. Sue Birchmore draws on her experience in evaluation with World Vision in Chapter 34, where she explores the principles of evaluative practice for different programmes. She demonstrates how to identify and evaluate a programme's strengths and effectiveness as well as its weaknesses and vulnerabilities. In Chapter 35, Glenn Miles and Paul Stephenson explain Tearfund's principles of good practice in programmes working with children and introduce a tool for applying these principles. Gustavo Crocker's chapter describes key aspects of organizational assessment in order to evaluate organizational strengths and weaknesses. Finally, in Chapter 37, Andrew Tomkins takes the issue of risk reduction and resilience enhancement one step further in his appraisal of the importance and power of prevention and rehabilitation.

Glenn Miles

– CHAPTER 33 –

Research Methods

Alastair Ager and Josephine-Joy Wright

ALTHOUGH formal research methodology and terminology may not be familiar to many child-care workers, it is important to learn correct research methods so that our projects can be properly evaluated. Publishing and disseminating the results of our research will result in improved child-care practice and an expanded body of knowledge on which child-care workers can base future work. It will also enable others in the field to learn about our work and learn from it, giving appropriate glory to God for the work God is doing through us.

It is important in the context of researching prior to setting up an intervention programme to be able:

1. To articulate clear aims and objectives.

2. To identify appropriate means of achieving such aims and objectives with respect to a rigorous analysis of the prevailing context.

In other words, what are we appropriately seeking to achieve? And what is the best way of going about this?

The key questions below express the core principles of research methodology. These questions are particularly geared to programme evaluation, but the approach and the principles which they reflect are equally valid for any stage in project planning.

A checklist for programme evaluation

Aims and objectives

Any researcher must first of all identify what she is trying to achieve and how that achievement can be measured. All objectives must be measurable (e.g., 'more children now go to school compared with six months ago, before the project started, and nothing else has changed'). The key questions to ask at this stage, then, are:

1. What are the explicit aims and objectives of the project? (Objectives and outcomes must be able to be demonstrated or measured.)

2. What are the targeted outcome variables (i.e., what is the goal of the project or intervention, what is its purpose and what is the proposed outcome)?

3. What is the targeted population (i.e., who are the intended beneficiaries)?

Measurement

It is essential to determine how we can measure changes in the factors or indicators that we have selected. For example, how is it possible to measure changes in children's health or emotional well-being? The methods of measurement must be both reliable and valid.

1. What are the most appropriate measures for operationalizing targeted outcome variables (i.e., how can we measure the change; what are the best indicators of change)?

2. What evidence exists – or could be gathered – to support the reliability of these measures (e.g., 'How can I reliably measure good parenting, discipline or feeding?')?

3. What evidence exists – or could be gathered – to support the validity of these measures?

4. To what extent are chosen measures likely to be *sensitive* to the degree of change targeted by the project? (E.g., a child's weight would be a sensitive measure in evaluating the effect of a feeding programme. A child's attendance at school would be a related measure, since well-fed children tend to go to school better, but it is not a directly sensitive measure to a child being well fed.)

5. What can be done to minimize (social, cultural or other) *bias* in the chosen measures?

6. To what extent are the outcome variables considered *grounded* in the

experience of those who may benefit from the intervention and *relevant* to the people who are taking part in the project?

Interpretation

1. What means can be adopted for selection of participants in the evaluation to maximize the *trustworthiness* of findings with respect to the full targeted population?

2. What comparisons are available to allow outcomes to be meaningfully related to programme activity (e.g., pre- to post-scores, outcomes for non-programme participants, etc.)?

3. What bases are there for linking up the findings of this particular research project with other sources of data?

4. Does the analysis provide a *comprehensive* account of the experience of participants in the programme?

5. To what extent are participants *representative* of other groups/situations of potential interest (e.g., are the children like other street children or a special group within this broad category)?

6. Otherwise, is theoretical analysis potentially *transferable* to other settings (i.e., can you undertake a similar study in another setting to compare the two results)? (Ager, 1999)

Information gathering

Once objectives have been defined and measures chosen to reflect them, information can be gathered. A key consideration is how it is to be interpreted. Careful selection of participants or respondents in research activities will support the trustworthiness of findings. This might involve a statistical approach requiring random selection of a specified sample. With other approaches there may be other methods used to ensure that what is found can be trusted to be a 'genuine' finding, rather than the experience of an unrepresentative sub-group.

Gaining information from multiple sources and comparing them (triangulation) can be a powerful means of supporting confident interpretation. To interpret information appropriately, a researcher needs to have confidence that measures are providing a suitably comprehensive account of relevant beneficiary experience. In quantitative studies this may mean ensuring that questionnaires address a suitably broad range of issues. In qualitative work it may mean ensuring that selection of material from transcripts, or the reporting on discussions from focus groups, does not 'leave out' too much of the story told. Focus groups are groups of people brought together to discuss the particular (or 'focus') topic which needs to be addressed. For example, you can have focus groups to discuss anything from a birth control programme to a road-widening project, a parent-support programme, or a child protection strategy for a church or an organization.

It should be clear that the vast majority of issues surrounding project implementation are best addressed early. However, this ideal is frequently not met, and project managers and evaluators frequently have to work knowing that if some previous decisions had been made differently, their current task would be a lot easier. Nevertheless, the principles outlined above at least provide a 'reference point' with respect to which decisions can be made towards achieving the 'best possible' project structure or evaluation attainable in a given, maybe constrained and difficult, situation. The fact that it is generally impossible to keep operating theatres completely free of bacteria does not detract from the importance of seeking the most sterile environment attainable in a given circumstance for the benefit of patients. By analogy, we should not apologize if our research lacks the robust, empirical rigour of an experimental study if we are genuinely seeking the most rigorous methodology available to us within the constraints of an applied setting. With commitment, imagination and foresight many of the principles outlined here can be addressed even in the most complex of circumstances.

Examples

1. A project decided to try a new way of teaching children about Jesus. They had two methods – Method A and the new Method B. They wanted to see which was the more effective. They split the children of similar ages into two groups. One group was taught by Method A, and the other by Method B. The teachers for both groups were similar in terms of their experience, style and ability to engage with the children. Before and after the teaching period, they gave the children a simple questionnaire asking them about Jesus. An independent person interviewed the children about what they had learned and how that had affected their faith. The results of the two groups were compared and used to modify the project's teaching programme in the future.

2. A project was helping families in a poor area of town. There was so much to do, the project did not know where to focus its resources. They decided to ask the families themselves what they needed, and so they held focus groups (although they didn't use this terminology) in the local community hall to discuss ideas and priorities. This helped the families to feel involved and to prioritize their needs appropriately. Those involved with the project also discussed with the families how they could evaluate the impact of the intervention. (They could also have given the parents a questionnaire to elicit their views, instead of using focus groups.) The parents said that their priorities were discipline and how to enjoy their children. The project organizers had been focusing on giving them good vegetables and playtimes! As a result of these findings, the project organizers enlisted the help of a child-care worker who ran parenting groups. They ran these parenting groups for the parents, assessing by interviews the attitudes of the parents to parenting both before and after the programme. They also started an ongoing parenting support group so that parents had a safe place to take their queries and concerns. This helped the project to maximize the effects of the parenting programme and to identify future training needs.

– Questions to Consider –

1 In the light of this chapter, identify some of the key issues in your organization that would lend themselves to being researched.

2 Select one area or variable and write a proposal describing how you would design a research project to study the effect of a given intervention on that variable.

3 How would you help other members of your project to undertake such research?

– CHAPTER 34 –

The Principles of Evaluative Practice

Sue Birchmore

THE prospect of a project evaluation is often worrying for project workers, especially if it is to be carried out by a team of external evaluators representing the project donors. This is unfortunate, as it turns what could be a positive experience – affirming achievements and taking corrective action where needed to achieve even more in the future – into an ordeal to be endured and forgotten as quickly as possible. An evaluation should not be an audit or a fault-finding exercise. The aims of a project evaluation should be:

1. To learn lessons that can be used in future work – what worked well and can be applied in other programmes, what was less successful and needs to be changed.

2. To provide accountability – to the beneficiaries, to the donors and possibly to other interested parties, such as the local government.

An evaluation can take different forms. It can be:

- Externally led, with the advantage of fresh insights from an outside viewpoint.

- A self-review by project staff and/or beneficiaries, with the advantage of inside knowledge.

- Conducted with a combination of external facilitation and participation by project staff and beneficiaries.

An evaluation might require as much as several weeks of fieldwork by ten or more people, or as little as a few days of work by three or four people. The size and complexity of the project will determine what is appropriate.

The project cycle

The project cycle (see Figure 1, below) is a fundamental concept in project planning. In the ideal model, initial assessment and planning is followed by implementation and monitoring, and finally by evaluation. The results of the evaluation are fed back into the planning process for the next phase of the programme in order to create a 'virtuous circle' of never-ending learning and improvement.

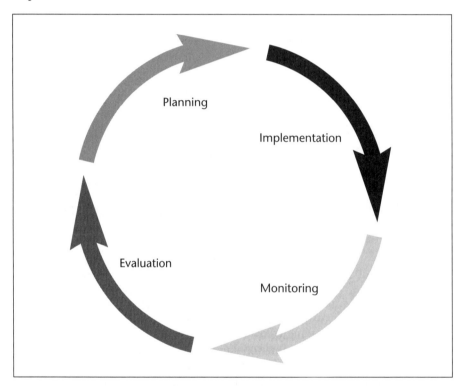

Planning

Implementation

Evaluation

Monitoring

Figure 1: The project cycle

There is sometimes some confusion about the difference between monitoring and evaluation. As I shall use the terms, monitoring looks at progress towards goals. Evaluation looks at what impact our goals have made on people's lives. Monitoring continues regularly throughout the life of a project. Evaluation may only take place at the end. For longer projects, it may also be appropriate to carry out one or more interim evaluations.

Planning an evaluation

Figure 2 maps the process for planning an evaluation. Ideally, planning for evaluation should start at the very beginning of the project life, when project plans and budgets are still being drawn up. This is important because:

1. Impact evaluation is about assessing change. To do this successfully, data is needed on the nature of the situation at the start of the project. A 'baseline survey' needs to be done right at the beginning, to gather information on the things it is hoped the project will change. For example, if the project aims to improve children's health in a community, the baseline survey will need to collect information on the most common health problems, the percentage of children sick at any one time, and other data such as rates of immunization or mothers' awareness of good health practices.

2. Evaluations cost money, and this needs to be included in the project budget. The flow chart in Figure 2 assumes that an external evaluator will be leading the process, but similar principles would apply for self-evaluation.

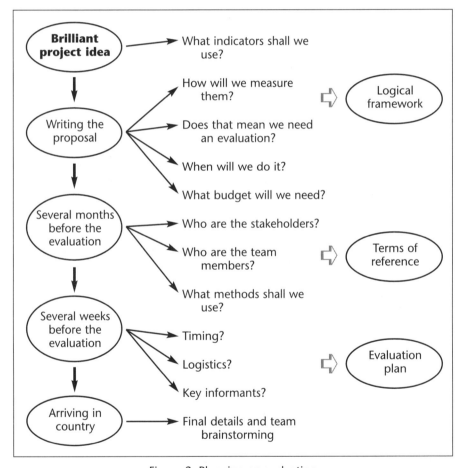

Figure 2: Planning an evaluation

Indicators

At the project planning stage, impact indicators need to be identified. Indicators are the specific pieces of information that will tell us whether the project is having the desired effect. For example, in a child health project an indicator of success might be: 'By the end of the five-year project life, the percentage of children who have had an episode of diarrhoea within the two weeks before the survey is reduced from 15 per cent to five per cent.'

Notice that this indicator is SMART:

- *Specific.* It identifies a particular health problem which has been assessed as part of the baseline survey.

- *Measurable.* We know how we will assess it (with a survey asking a number of families about their children's health in the last two weeks).

- *Achievable.* People sometimes ask why we set targets at less than the ideal state. However, it is unlikely that the project will succeed in completely eliminating diarrhoea.

- *Relevant.* The project objective is improved child health, and diarrhoea is among the most potentially dangerous childhood diseases.

- *Time-bound.* The project aims to achieve this result in five years.

In this example, the indicator is quantitative – it sets a numerical target. Qualitative indicators, looking at things that cannot be expressed in numbers, are also useful.

The set of indicators should encompass a range of both qualitative and quantitative indicators, and where possible a quality and quantity component should be included in each indicator statement, along with the relevant time factor. Whether qualitative or quantitative, however, indicators should be objectively verifiable in that two independent observers would be able to come to the same conclusion regarding the status of achievement. Indicators may be:

- *Direct indicators.* The percentage of children suffering from diarrhoea is a direct indicator of their health status.

- *Indirect indicators and / or proxy indicators.* These measure things which represent (or approximate) changes in areas which cannot be measured directly. For example, improvement in mothers' attitudes to health education is difficult to measure directly, but the number of mothers who participate in sessions would be a proxy indicator.

- *Process indicators.* These show whether planned activities were carried out effectively and include volume, efficiency and quality of work.

- *Impact indicators.* These assess the changes resulting from activities/processes.

It is important, however, not to get too carried away by setting indicators. In some projects, the staff time, energy and cost needed to collect, analyse and use information to monitor indicators have exceeded the resources available for the actual project implementation!

Terms of reference

Several months before the evaluation, terms of reference need to be drawn up. This document is sometimes also referred to as the 'scope of work'. It describes what the evaluation aims to achieve and outlines the methods for carrying it out.

Drawing up terms of reference should be a collaborative exercise. All the major *stakeholders* (people with an interest in the project) need to be involved. These may include field staff, headquarters staff, donors and beneficiaries. By the end of the process, they should all be on board and heading in the same direction. The terms of reference should specify:

- The objectives of the evaluation
- The key questions to be answered
- What methods will be used
- How the evaluation will be organized.

The evaluation plan

A few weeks before the evaluation, a more detailed plan needs to be drawn up. The plan should build on the terms of reference, specifying who will carry out various activities and when. It will normally include:

- People to be interviewed
- Sites to be visited
- Documents to be reviewed
- Team meetings to review findings
- Presentation of findings and feedback
- Report writing.

The lead evaluator needs to:

1. Discuss the purpose and methods of the evaluation with the team, identify suitable techniques, allocate tasks and ensure that all those involved have an adequate understanding of what they are to do.
2. Prepare a work plan, listing dates, locations, evaluation techniques to be used and team members to carry them out.
3. Carry out the planned exercises, monitoring the other team members to ensure that they are using the techniques correctly.
4. Review results with the team regularly as the evaluation progresses, changing the work plan if necessary in the light of experience.

Choosing sites and interviewees

To make sure that the sites visited, people interviewed, and so on are as representative as possible of the whole project, the following steps need to be followed:

1. Identify key characteristics which are different for different places/people involved in the project – for example: gender, income, ethnic group (people); urban/rural, highland/lowland (places).
2. Divide lists or maps into groups or areas according to the characteristics identified.
3. Select a sample from each group/area using a method that will ensure random selection – for example, picking every tenth name from an alphabetical list. The size of the sample will be limited by the time and team members available for the evaluation.

Table 1 shows a typical sampling plan for a child-based project. There is a representative number of boys and girls across the age range from pre-school to secondary school. In this case, the register of children in the project area has been divided into six groups. One hundred and fifty of the total 1,500 children were interviewed (10 per cent is usually taken as a statistically reliable sample size).

	Total number	Sample size		Total number	Sample size
Pre-school girls	246	25	Pre-school boys	267	27
Primary-age girls	234	23	Primary-age boys	263	26
Secondary-age girls	230	23	Secondary-age boys	260	26

Table 1: Sampling plan

Evaluation tools

Most evaluations will need to use a range of complementary techniques – quantitative and qualitative, office-based and field-based. Some of the most common techniques used in evaluations are:

1. *Review of project documents to examine the history of the project and the logic of its design.* If the design did not include a logical framework, it can be a useful exercise to construct one on the basis of the documentation; this helps to test and understand the project logic.

2. *Statistical surveys of beneficiaries using structured questionnaires.* A team of surveyors is trained to carry out interviews in a predetermined format. The questions will usually be yes/no or multiple choice. For example: 'When your child has diarrhoea, do you (a) Take her to the clinic, (b) Treat her with medicines from the shop, (c) Treat her with herbal remedies, or (d) Other'.

3. *Semi-structured interviews with beneficiaries and other stakeholders.* In this type of interview the interviewer has a prepared checklist of questions, but it is less formal than a survey questionnaire, and the questions are open-ended to encourage discussion. For example: 'When your child has diarrhoea, what do you do?' It is useful to work in pairs, with one person asking the questions and the other taking notes.

4. *Collection and analysis of data from other sources such as local government health statistics, residents' association minutes, or school attendance records.* In a recent evaluation of a World Vision project, the most significant impact indicator from a school feeding programme was that school attendance records were up by 25 per cent, demonstrating that it was meeting a felt need and improving the children's educational prospects.

5. *Observation.* For example: Do children play energetically, or are they listless? Are there any visible signs of malnutrition? Do they show a healthy curiosity in the evaluation team, or are they fearful or withdrawn?

More on specific evaluation techniques can be found in Feuerstein (1986) and Gosling and Edwards (1995).

Participatory Evaluation Process

Various participatory assessment techniques have been developed, including Participatory Learning and Action (PLA) and Appreciative Inquiry (AI). One such technique, the Participatory Evaluation Process (PEP), was developed by the WVI evaluation department in 1983–86. It is being used in a number of World

Vision community development project communities.

The process may be more accurately described as a participatory planning process that includes monitoring. If participatory principles have been incorporated in a community development project, the results can then be included when an external evaluation takes place and community members can be encouraged to participate in the planning and implementation of the external evaluation.

If participatory techniques have not been used during the project life, then the level of participation that can be achieved during the evaluation will be limited. However, the three principles on which the participatory process is based should still be applied so far as possible. Frank Cookingham (1995) writes:

> First, no matter how poor they may be, people have great creative capacities. These capacities can be exercised when they are respected, loved and listened to.
>
> Second, change is most likely to occur when a person is engaged in an experience with all the senses, emotions and personal experiences of his or her background.
>
> Third, change is most likely to occur when people use resources they already have to learn more about their situation.

Development workers are required to facilitate rather than direct the process.

Writing the report

If possible, a draft report should be completed and presented to local stakeholders before the evaluation team departs. If time pressure does not allow this, then the main conclusions need to be written up and an invitation for feedback extended.

When writing the report, verifiable evidence on which conclusions are based needs to be stated. It is often helpful to begin each section with a factual description of what the evaluation team saw, heard, measured or otherwise found out, followed by a discussion of the achievements and constraints of the project with respect to the particular aspect being reported.

When writing recommendations, it should always be kept in mind that the objective is to prompt useful action. Recommendations need to be very clearly expressed and well supported by evidence. In some cases, where the subject is sensitive, recommendations should be made privately to the individual or group concerned rather than being included in a report.

The following section headings are suggested as an outline for an evaluation report; others may be included if it is helpful.

1. Contents
2. Summary and recommendations
3. Introduction
4. Evaluation methodology
5. Background
6. Project design: this should examine the method by which the project was designed and choice of interventions and methods of analysis, including the

rationale for all these aspects of the design.

7. Project implementation: this should look at the degree to which the planned objectives were met in the planned timescale.

8. Project impact: this is the key section, which examines the changes achieved through the project interventions and assesses their sustainability.

9. Monitoring and reporting

10. Appendices

Using the results of evaluation

Evaluation without effective feedback is useless . . . Only if this is done systematically and continuously can we even begin to convince ourselves that we are near to making the maximum impact with the limited resources we have. – J.K. Wright, Under Secretary, Economic Service, ODA – Proceedings of 1983 ODA Conference at IDS, University of Sussex

The ultimate aim of all appraisal, monitoring and evaluation is to make informed decisions that will improve the effectiveness of our work. If no action is taken as a result of gathering information, it would be better not to have used scarce resources in gathering it. The information generated by appraisal, monitoring and evaluation should be used to:

• Inform planning of future projects to make them as effective as possible.

• Identify concerns at an early stage and suggest possible actions.

• Satisfy donors that their contributions are being used effectively, thereby retaining existing donors and attracting new ones.

• Be part of a continuous learning and improvement process.

In practice, it is at this stage that the cycle most commonly breaks down. Particularly where the evaluation has been seen primarily as satisfying donor requirements, evaluation reports disappear into filing cabinets and the lessons they contain vanish with them. The more all stakeholders have been actively involved throughout the evaluation process, the more likely they will be to 'own' and put into practice the findings. Actions that can be taken after an evaluation to increase active use of the findings include:

• Presentations to other staff by evaluation team members. These can be used both to share findings and to exchange experience of evaluation techniques.

• Periodic meta-evaluations – studies of collected reports from a number of different evaluations to draw out any common findings or trends.

• Inclusion of some members from previous evaluations in later evaluations of the same programme to allow continuity and historical perspective.

• Use of technology such as computer databases to make information more accessible.

The principles of evaluative practice outlined in this chapter are key to every aspect of our work with children – our mandate is to give our best – to the children and to God. Evaluative practice enables us to be able to assess and implement our best work.

<hr>

– Questions to Consider –

1 When Christians get together, they often speak of the amazing work that God is doing within their project – and yet such work is often never evaluated so that others can learn from it. How would you go about correcting this, both at the level of a given project and generally from a world-view perspective?

2 What do you feel are some of the practical and philosophical obstacles that discourage staff from evaluating their practice? How can such obstacles be overcome?

3 Draw up a sample evaluation plan, keeping in mind all of the above considerations and techniques, for a project you have worked on or for a project you would like to undertake in the future.

<hr>

– CHAPTER 35 –

The Principles of Good Practice in Programmes Working with Children

Glenn Miles and Paul Stephenson

The Tearfund 'Child Development Framework for Good Practice'

THE Tearfund 'Child Development Framework for Good Practice' can be used to analyse good practice when looking at any programme working with children. The framework is based on the following principles of good practice:

1. *Building relationships*

   Priority is given to building relationships with the child, family, community, organization or institution and between agencies.

2. *Parental responsibilities*

   Parental responsibilities towards children are encouraged, as is the development of a caring, child-friendly community.

3. *Working at different levels*

   There is awareness of what levels the programme is addressing:

   • Individual

- Peer
- Family
- Community
- Organizational/institutional
- National
- Policy/political
- Spiritual

4. *Identifying needs and priorities*

- Children's (and parents') needs are identified. This includes listening to and involving both children and parents.
- Staff are experienced and trained in communicating with children and their families and in helping facilitate children's participation.
- There is awareness of the spiritual, physical, mental, emotional and social aspects of the child's development (including educational and vocational aspects).

5. *Children's participation*

Children's abilities and needs are taken into consideration as adults co-operate with them individually and collectively. The following should remain a focus:

- Ability rather than disability or inability
- Resilience to change and trauma as well as vulnerability
- No prejudice based on gender, age, parentage, ethnicity, social class or caste, religious background or disability.

6. *Children in context*

- Children are considered in the social, political and historical context of their community.
- Parents, caregivers and families are involved and affected.
- The child's community is involved and affected.
- Links (networks) are developed with other local, national and international organizations, including organizations from other sectors.
- The cultural and religious context of the child, family and community is taken into consideration.

7. *Advocacy*

- Lobbying and interceding with, or on behalf of, children and their families take place at local, national or international levels.
- The programme staff are aware of the importance of the CRC and other relevant human rights conventions.
- The challenges and risks involved in advocacy work should be analysed so that they can be understood and addressed.
- There is dialogue with parents and caregivers so that they can make informed decisions and advocate for their families.
- There is dialogue with children so that, depending on their ages and

abilities, they can make informed decisions and advocate for themselves and their peers.

- There is awareness of the biblical basis of advocacy on behalf of children and the importance of prayer.

8. *Child-sensitive indicators*[1]

- The impact of work on the children and their families is measured both qualitatively and quantitatively.
- Indicators show how the programme has an impact on the lives and environments of the children (by age and gender) and their families.
- Parents, caregivers and children (according to age and ability) are involved in the evaluation of the child and the care given.
- The programme reflects on and uses the results of the evaluation.

The Reflective Question Tool

The Tearfund 'Child Development Reflective Question Tool' enables individuals and groups to reflect on the principles listed above. These questions can be used in an evaluation process (both self-evaluation and external evaluation).

1. *Building relationships.* How is priority given to building relationships with the child, family, community, organization or institution and between organizations?

2. *Parental responsibilities.* How does the programme encourage the development of parental responsibilities towards children and a caring, child-friendly community?

3. *Working at different levels.* At what level(s) does the programme work and how does it consider other levels?

- Individual
- Peer
- Family
- Community
- Organizational/institutional
- National
- Policy/political
- Spiritual

4. *Identifying needs and priorities.*

- How are children's (and parents') needs identified? How have children and parents been listened to and involved?
- What experience and training do the staff have in communicating with children and their families and in facilitating children's participation?
- How does the programme try to meet the spiritual, physical, mental, emotional and social aspects of the child's development (including educational and vocational aspects)?

5. *Children's participation.*

- How does the programme take into account children's abilities? And what are its attitudes to prejudice?

- How do the adults listen to and co-operate with children, according to their ages and abilities?

6. *Children in context.*

- To what extent is the child considered in the historical, political and social context of his community?
- How are parents, caregivers and families of the children involved and affected?
- How is the child's community involved and positively affected?
- In what ways are links developed (networking) with other local, national and international organizations (including organizations from other sectors)?
- How is the cultural and religious context of the child, family and community taken into consideration?

7. *Advocacy.*

- In what ways does the programme lobby with, or on behalf of, children and their families at local, national or international levels?
- Are the programme staff aware of the importance of the CRC and other human rights issues and conventions?
- What are the barriers to advocacy work? How can these be overcome?
- Is there dialogue with parents and caregivers so that they can make informed decisions and advocate for their families?
- Is there dialogue with children so that, based on their ages and abilities, they can make informed decisions and advocate for themselves and their peers?
- To what extent are the programme staff aware of the biblical basis of advocacy for children and the importance of prayer?

8. *Child-sensitive indicators.*

- How does the programme measure the impact of its work on children and their families? Do the indicators measure quantitative as well as a qualitative impact?
- Do these indicators show how the programme has an impact on the lives and environment of the children and their families? Is the data broken down into age and gender groups?
- How are parents, caregivers and children (according to age and ability) involved in the evaluation of the child and the care given?
- How does the programme reflect on and use the results of evaluation?

The full framework, together with its biblical basis, is available in the Tearfund 'Child Development Study Pack', which also contains case studies applying the principles in practice. The principles have also been expanded into a number of themes in the Tearfund 'Children at Risk Guidelines'.[2]

Notes

1. See also Chapter 34.
2. The full text of the 'Child Development Study Pack' is available from Tearfund, 100 Church Road, Teddington, Middlesex, TW11 8QE, UK. E-mail: enquiries@tearfund.org. This is available in English, French, Spanish, Portuguese and Cambodian. A series of 'Children at Risk Guidelines' are also available, based on the same eight principles and covering areas such as residential care and alternatives, child health, children and disability, children and family breakdown, children and armed conflict and children and sexual abuse/exploitation. They are available in English, French, Spanish and Portuguese.

– Questions to Consider –

1 Using the Tearfund 'Child Development Framework for Good Practice' principles listed above, evaluate the overall practice of your organization or a project with which you are familiar.

2 Having identified one area of relative weakness from the above analysis, use the 'Reflective Question Tool' to identify and suggest methods for strengthening this area in your organization.

3 Using the full Tearfund 'Child Development Study Pack' and / or the information contained in this chapter, undertake a full review of your organization's practice, ensuring that everyone you work with is involved in the evaluation.

CHAPTER 36

Organizational Assessment and Evaluation of Strengths and Weaknesses

Gustavo Crocker

THE number of international Christian ministries for children has grown in response to the need to tackle social, economic and environmental issues from a value-based perspective. Hundreds of new organizations have sprung up with the purpose of responding to the ever-increasing needs of developing nations. The growth of this sector since World War II has led to increasing competition to secure resources in a highly restricted environment (Christian Reformed World Relief Committee, 1997). Along with the competition, the growth in the size and influence of these ministries has resulted in increased visibility and scrutiny by diverse constituencies including governments, overseeing agencies, private donors and foundations, clients, the media and the public at large (Kearns, Krasman and Meyer, 1994).

While this scrutiny has threatened the survival of many organizations, it has also brought several excellent and worthwhile initiatives into the public eye. Although these considerations of excellence are good for the few organizations that are managing to succeed and survive, there is little information for struggling organizations about what makes a Christian children's ministry excellent and, consequently, worthy of public support.

One of the frustrations for leaders and practitioners involved in Christian ministry for children is the public opinion that 'a large number of non-profit organizations are full of do-gooders and bleeding-hearts who, unfortunately, do not know how to manage and operate with effectiveness' (Knauft, Berger and Gray, 1991). The poor reputation of the sector as a whole has resulted in limited access to public and private donations, as well as government funding. This lack of resources has threatened the survival of numerous ministries that have not been able to achieve the levels of organizational development needed to succeed in accomplishing their mission to serve the needy.

The survival of Christian ministries

Christian ministries are like children. They follow the normal cycle of conception, birth, christening, childhood, adolescence, adulthood and even death. A ministry normally begins as the vision of one or two individuals, who 'birth' it. As they develop an identity, ministries are often 'absorbed' or 'endorsed' by the local church (the christening phase). It is at this point that most ministries face the first threat to their survival. Institutionalization often demands a new ethos in the life of the ministry. It demands more accountability and structure. It demands planning and marketing. It demands good nutrition and monitoring. At this point, the early childhood organization requires good development practices to secure survival and life beyond survival.

Cultural, social and political environments

Van Til (1994) points out that non-profit organizations exist as the direct result of the cultural, societal and political forces that interact in their society. This is especially true for Christian ministries. The main cultural forces that shape the life of Christian ministries are the family, the church and the school (Van Til, 1994). Each of these influences the scope and scale of the ministry. A significant number of Christian ministries are organized to respond to the needs of these three major cultural elements in society. Changes in the family structure, the educational systems and the religious culture determine the direction of those ministries.

Van Til (1994), Firstenberg (1996) and Drucker (1990, *Managing*) contend that social problems are the largest market generators for non-governmental organizations. Van Til cites poverty, racism and alienation as the major social forces that determine the need for those types of ministries to exist. Furthermore, Christian ministries provide the avenue for Christians to channel their desires to improve their society through Christian witness, altruism and civic responsibility (p. 11). Drucker's (1990, *Managing*) argument is that these types of organizations create a sphere of meaningful citizenship by responding to the societal needs through human change (p. 3). The changes in the social fabric of a group would, therefore, change the environment in which Christian ministries operate.

The political dimension is perhaps the most evident influence on Christian ministries for the poor. As Carroll, Delacroix and Goodstein (1990) point out, political systems often determine the boundaries of operation of a given organizational population (p. 69). This is especially true for Christian social ministries. The forces of political power create conditions that shape communities and influence public policy in such a way that they develop a complex set of problems that threaten the survival of weaker ministries (Herman and Heimovics, 1991, p. 33). Van Til (1990) argues that government and politics influence voluntary organizations both directly and indirectly. Directly, the government decides which organizations it will recognize as legitimate civil societies for providing services. Indirectly, government and political systems affect Christian ministries by selecting the types of services they can provide and by creating a market niche for specific organizations in the whole sector (Van Til, 1990, p. 52).

Market competition among Christian ministries

'Competition, the pursuit of the same objective by two or more firms, creates rivalry among non-profit organizations for capital, labor, customers, and revenues' (Tuckman, 1998, p. 175). Herman and Heimovics (1991) point out that the competitive factors in the marketplace cause non-governmental organizations (and, consequently, Christian ministries) to strive for survival (p. 18). Tuckman's (1998) study on competition, commercialization and the evolution of charities explores competition both in settings where charities compete among themselves and where they compete with the business community. His main contention is that, as a result of the competition in the marketplace, organizations engaged in social services are pressured toward commercialization, which may in turn affect the unique charitable nature that motivated their creation (Tuckman, 1998). Thus, Christian ministries, in order to secure a place in the marketplace, end up creating 'income generating' mechanisms that include service fees for help that otherwise would be provided free of charge.

Resource dependency

A vast majority of writers in the charitable sector focus on financial resources as the main factor that determines the life of a social service organization (Firstenberg, 1996; Herman and Heimovics, 1991; Herman, 1994; Drucker, 1990, *Managing*; and Weisbrod, 1998). Recent studies suggest that Christian ministries are especially threatened as they are highly resource-dependent (Firstenberg, 1996, p. 67). Furthermore, access to financial resources is one of the main leadership challenges for Christian ministries in a pluralistic society. Christian ministries are highly dependent upon external resources for financial support (Firstenberg, 1996, p. 28). Financial support for Christian ministries usually comes from the following sources:

- donations from international organizations and partner organizations
- governmental funding through contracts and grants
- sales of services and goods in the marketplace
- donations from individuals, local donors and corporations.

The dependency on resources and the need to secure them on a daily basis is perhaps the biggest challenge for Christian ministries to remain true to their original purpose. Leaders of Christian social ministries need to make sure that they do not focus solely on fund-raising so that the focus remains where it should be, on caring for the needy. When organizations are less dependent on funds, they are more likely to work in terms of their mission than in terms of finding resources for themselves. Whether their goals are lofty or modest, Christian ministries depend heavily on appropriate financial support to accomplish their goals. The key question, then, is how Christian ministries balance time and effort between fund-raising and mission work, and how they discern which sources of funding are appropriate and will not cause them to compromise their mission.

Age and organizational survival

Organizational scholars consider that youth is a liability for an organization (Bielefield, 1994). Consequently, the expectation is that older ministries live longer than those organizations facing their institutional infancy. In their studies on the strategic implications of size and age in organizational survival, Bielefield (1994) and Aldrich and Auster (1990) contend that, although organizations cannot improve their age as a strategy for survival, they must understand the liabilities associated with their youth. As a result, younger organizations must develop contingency plans to secure their survival.

Inertial pressures

High-quality management, an uncommon feature of most Christian organizations, is nevertheless a factor in their survival. Hiding behind altruism and service, many ministries fall into the trap of mediocrity. Consequently, they cannot compete with other local social service organizations for securing resources and accessing the national mechanisms of social transformation. As recent studies in organizational excellence of Christian relief and development organizations show (Crocker, 2001), administrative excellence, programmatic excellence and excellence in donor relations are key factors in securing survival and success.

Successful ministries are those which have moved beyond their point of survival. They have reached such a point of organizational balance that they are less vulnerable to the changes in the environment because they have properly balanced their values, strategy, structure, systems, style, skills and staff (Peters and Waterman, 1982). Therefore, a successful Christian ministry is identified by the public and by the experts by its ability to: a) achieve its purpose, b) set an example of quality among Christian ministries, c) gain a good reputation among Christians and the larger constituencies of donors, and d) survive the various changes in the financial, political and social environments.

Organizational excellence as a strategy for ministry survival

In his landmark piece for non-profit management, Peter Drucker (1990, *Managing*) suggests that, if non-profit organizations are to survive their environment, they must focus on achieving high degrees of excellence. Kearns, Krasman and Meyer (1994) contend that 'in an era of growing public scrutiny and calls for greater accountability in the non-profit sector, Total Quality Management offers one approach for non-profit organizations to enhance their responsiveness to various customers and constituencies' (p. 458). Although these authors are aware that Total Quality Management may be another organizational fad, they also contend that 'the fundamental principles of customer satisfaction, problem prevention, employee empowerment, and quality measurement are, and always have been, the bedrock of effective management and organizational success. The systematic application of these principles in nonprofit organizations should be a component of a long-term strategy for survival and growth' (Kearns, Krasman and Meyer, 1994, p. 459).

In their book *Profiles of Excellence: Achieving Success in the Nonprofit Sector*, Knauft, Berger and Gray (1991) suggest that excellence is the key component that makes the difference between outstanding success and just mediocrity (and even survival) of the nearly three million non-profit organizations that operate across America. Their contention is that it takes more than just good programmes to differentiate a truly great non-profit organization from the merely good and struggling ones, and excellence is the 'something extra' that makes the difference (Knauft, Berger and Gray, 1991; Firstenberg, 1996).

Measuring organizational excellence in Christian ministries

Knauft, Berger and Gray (1991) summarize the theoretical dilemma of measuring organizational excellence in the non-profit sector:

> At the outset, constructing a definition of "excellence" seemed straightforward, but, in fact, the task turned out to be quite challenging. Scores of books have been written on organizational excellence – including many specifically for the nonprofit world – but the findings offer no clear consensus. If measuring excellence is an inexact science, the challenge to do so is compounded by the very nature of the nonprofit sector. What, after all, do you measure? Should a nonprofit be judged by its capacity to survive over time, to skillfully adapt to

changes and challenges over its life cycle? Or perhaps the best measure is current performance. If so, do we consider the organization's financial condition or the number of people it serves, the size of its membership, the quality of its programmes and staff, the extent of volunteer engagement? And what about the spirit of the organization and how it is perceived in its community? (Knauft, Berger and Gray, 1991, p. xviii)

As a result of the various approaches to measure organizational effectiveness, contemporary authors suggest the use of integrating approaches to the issue. Their perspective is to incorporate the natural systems model, the goal model and the decision process model into one comprehensive model that answers the major questions of organizational excellence. This model includes four main components:

- constituent satisfaction
- resource acquisition effectiveness
- internal process effectiveness
- goal attainment.

These components impact the overall excellence of the organization in a particular sequence (Kushner and Poole, 1996). The overall causal logic of Kushner and Poole's model is as follows:

> Constituent satisfaction can be treated as both first cause and first result of organizational effectiveness. Constituent satisfaction is based on utility received in exchange for resources offered. When resources are scarce, organizations have to both identify needed resources and supply acceptable returns to factor owners (constituents). This is resource acquisition effectiveness. Organizations require internal process effectiveness; that is, technical efficiency and internal social and technological systems matched to each other so that they can use acquired resources. The final component, given resources and transformation process, is goal attainment, or how the organization reaches stated objectives. Ultimately, constituents evaluate utilities in terms of how organizational goal attainment meets their conditions for contributing resources, and the sequence repeats. (Kushner and Poole, 1996, p. 122)

Other models suggest that the four components of excellence in non-profit organizations are:

- a clearly articulated sense of mission
- an individual who truly leads the organization
- an involved and committed volunteer board
- an ongoing capacity to attract sufficient financial and human resources.

Let's look at each of these components in more detail. According to this model, the mission is an organization's reason for existence. 'Broad but clear mission statements are written into bylaws, highlighted in brochures, and promoted in fund-raising overtures. The mission is on the tongue of board members and staff – and most important, is reflected in their actions. In other words, effective nonprofit organizations convey a single-mindedness of purpose' (Knauft, Berger and Gray, 1991, p. 3). In reference to the mission of the organization, Collins and Porras (1994) contend that mission is the evidence of a core ideology that the organization uses as a source of guidance. These ideological statements, they argue, are more than words on paper. The mission of the organization guides the organization to bring consistency between good ideals and actions.

The second criterion of excellence in the model of Knauft, Berger and Gray is effective leadership. According to them, 'the best leaders embody their organizational mission. They can clearly articulate the mission and transmit it to others with a sense of excitement, even if the mission was originally developed by a board or a founder long since departed' (Knauft, Berger and Gray, 1991, p. 8). Several writers in non-profit effectiveness support this argument. In addition to inspiring their followers to fulfil the mission of the organization, non-profit leaders must also manage the organization efficiently (Nygren, et al., 1994; Drucker, 1990, *Managing*). Leadership excellence in the non-profit sector is also connected with the initiation and maintenance of organizational structure, the integration between individual needs and the organizational goals, and the creation of a vision for the desired future state of the organization (Kay, 1994).

The third component of excellence in this model is the presence of an involved board of directors that relates to the executive director and the organization's top leadership. According to scholars who adhere to this model, the best non-profits enjoy the governance of a group of committed volunteers who are legally responsible for the organization and for its strategic directions. As the best-managed non-profit organizations demonstrate, both the board and the executive director are essential for the proper functioning of a non-profit entity (Drucker, 1990, 'Lessons'; Fletcher, 1992; Boeker and Goodstein, 1991; Provan, 1980).

Finally, Knauft, Berger and Gray contend that the last hallmark of an excellent non-profit organization is the capacity to attract and sustain sufficient financial resources. Although respondents in their study suggest that 'the ability to attract resources' is one of the most crucial factors determining the success of a non-profit, Knauft, Berger and Gray equally emphasize the importance of sustaining the sources of funding. In this regard, donor integrity and accountability are as important as resource acquisition (Fry, 1995; Balda, 1994; File, Prince and Cermak, 1994).

Both integrated models (Kushner and Poole, 1996; Knauft, Berger and Gray, 1991) have been tested in the non-profit sector. However, both models miss the importance of programmatic and administrative excellence in the success and survival of Christian social ministries. Although the factors that both models suggest are worth evaluating, a more comprehensive model needs to include programmatic and administrative excellence as variables of organizational excellence in non-profit organizations (in addition to leadership, mission and quality of resource development). Furthermore, such a comprehensive model needs to be tested in light of the realities of the Christian ministries working with children.

The comprehensive model suggested above was tested in a recent study of Christian relief and development organizations in America. This study suggests that excellence in ministry is achieved as organizations balance the concerns of the various constituencies through operational, financial, customer-related and marketplace performance (Dalrymple, et al., 2000). The following five components of excellence reflect this balance:

1. *Mission excellence and clarity.* The organization must have clear statements of

vision, values and ideology with the intent to use such statements as sources of guidance (Collins and Porras, 1994). For the purpose of this study, mission excellence and clarity are measured in terms of specificity, ownership, realism, practicality and congruence with the Great Commission.

2. *Programmatic excellence.* Refers to the practical expression of mission and is measured in terms of practicability and congruence between the organization's mission and its programmatic intervention (including planning and implementation).

3. *Excellence in resource development.* Refers to the organization's capacity to secure, maintain and grow the support base. In considering excellence in donor relations, this study evaluates each organization's ability to identify a donor base, develop a systematic donor strategy, mobilize volunteers, explore new donor opportunities and provide clear avenues for industry and donor accountability and scrutiny (Knauft, Berger and Gray, 1991).

4. *Administrative excellence.* Refers to the quality of management and personnel relationships. 'Organizations require technical efficiency and internal social and technological systems matched to each other so that they can use acquired resources' (Kushner and Poole, 1996, p. 122). For the purpose of this study, administrative excellence is the evidence that the organizations have a history of conscious attention to quality management disciplines, which include management development, staff development and training, personnel relations, sound planning and budgeting practices and efficient information and auditing systems (Collins and Porras, 1994).

5. *Leadership excellence.* This is the evidence that the organization has been led by 'top executive(s) who have displayed high levels of persistence, overcome significant obstacles, attracted dedicated people, influenced groups of people towards the achievement of goals, and played key roles in guiding their organizations through crucial episodes in their history' (Collins and Porras, 1994, p. 280). In considering leadership excellence, this study evaluates leadership in terms of mission orientation, servanthood, empowerment, vision, achievement motivation, administrative skills, approachability and the overall urgency for leadership succession.

Application of the model to Christian ministries

Using the excellence in Christian ministry questionnaire (see below), a recent study on the excellence of Christian relief and development organizations in America revealed that there are several factors that help Christian organizations move beyond the point of survival to be recognized as successful ministries.[1] The most significant qualitative differences evidenced by the most reputable Christian ministries can be broken down into ten main strategic features. The very different ways in which successful and struggling ministries approach each of these factors appear to determine their level of success. The majority of successful ministries, therefore, show strong evidence of intentionally focusing attention on most, or all, of the following ten areas:

1. Reason for establishing the organization

2. Nature and application of the mission statement

3. Process of mission articulation

4. Organizational structure
5. Emphasis of administrative systems
6. Resource dependency
7. Programme evolution
8. Evaluation systems
9. Leadership visibility
10. Leadership succession.

Reason for establishing the organization

A review of the history of Christian ministries shows that successful ministries clearly articulate the reason for their establishment to respond to the overwhelming needs of the poor. Many successful ministries were founded at a time in which wars, famine and disasters had exposed Christians to worldwide suffering and poverty. These ministries had very humble beginnings and started mainly as 'one man dreams'. At the time of their founding, philanthropy was not well known and the founders had to rely on the support of churches personally known to them.

Ministries that struggled and experienced less success were established primarily in response to the overwhelming giving of Christians to ministries of disaster relief (Weber and Cook, 1989). Unlike the successful ministries, struggling organizations were established with an organizational start-up in mind. At the time of their foundation, these ministries had a funding base that supported them, qualified staff who understood relief and development and a professional approach to marketing and donor development. The subtle philosophical differences in the creation of the organizations are reflected more strongly in the way in which each organization instrumentalizes its mission statement.

Nature and application of the mission statement

Collins and Porras (1994) suggest that visionary organizations are those for which the core ideology is more than just a philosophical statement. For successful ministries, the mission statement and the core ideology are more than just words. Recent studies show that these organizations have invested time and resources in developing a clearly articulated core ideology, which includes an organizational purpose, a mission statement, a corporate vision, a set of corporate beliefs and a set of organizational principles. Most of the senior and junior executives, as well as a vast majority of staff members, have the ability to refer to the mission of the organization as the framework of reference for answering most organizational and programmatic questions. The value that those organizations place on their core ideology is essential for maintaining their organizational quality (Collins and Porras, 1994).

Conversely, struggling ministries have more general mission statements and very few foundational principles. The study on organizational excellence in Christian relief and development organizations (Crocker, 2001) revealed that struggling organizations have not reviewed their mission statement since the founding of the organization. Furthermore, none of these organizations has documentation (internal or public) that reflects the operational definitions of the mission statement, and leaders have difficulty articulating the mission of their organization, or at least expressing its uniqueness. One of the reasons for such difficulty seems to be the way in which the core ideology was developed.

Process of mission articulation

A key distinctive of successful ministries is their 'completeness of the people orientation'. Such completeness is evident not only in the role which people play when implementing the organizational mission and vision, but also in the way in which such core ideology is 'claimed' or 'owned' by the entire organization (Bennis and Nanus, 1997, p. 101). Successful ministries normally employ participatory methods and consultation to shape and share the organizational mission, vision and values. Although they do not abdicate their responsibility to inspire and elaborate the vision of their respective organizations, leaders in successful ministries recognize the important role that the different layers of the organization (and even external constituencies) play in articulating and contextualizing the organizational core.

Struggling ministries, on the other hand, develop their mission statement only with the participation of the organizational apex (if at all). In a struggling ministry, middle-level (and even upper-level) employees are unable to clearly remember or articulate the mission of the organization.

Organizational structure

Organizations move beyond mere success when they set their basic mission and when they create the organism capable of fulfilling it. The study of successful ministries revealed that their organizational structures are conducive to responding to changes in the environment. Successful organizations display structures that focus on the function. Roles and flows of services are more important than titles and hierarchy, and positions are not assigned based on deserving individuals. In many cases, ministries have changed their structure several times in order to respond to their programmatic evolution, the globalization of the donor base and the changing demands both in the field and in the donor culture.

The organizational structures of struggling ministries are more nominal than functional. Looking at the organizational charts, it is clear that the organizational architecture focuses primarily on the form at the expense of the function. Such focus is evident in the emphasis that mediocre organizations put on titles rather than on the actual delivery of services.

Emphasis on administrative systems

By their nature (and by the fact that they are subject to external laws and regulations), most ministries have basic administrative systems in place (employee relations, communication systems, filing and reporting systems, etc.). However, the administrative systems in a successful social ministry focus on consistent strategic planning, budgeting and evaluation, while the mediocre organization emphasizes administrative systems with the purpose of accountability and compliance. From a distance, both groups of organizations seem to have good systems in place. However, when it comes to the purpose of the systems, it is clear that the top organizations highlight the strategic nature of the administrative systems (without abdicating their commitment to accountability and integrity).

Resource dependency

This is perhaps the most evident threat to the survival of organizations. One of the features that successful ministries display is a constant mechanism for generating revenue. Whether it is through monthly sponsorships or service fees, successful ministries have secured a solid resource base for their operations. Although these funding sources require maintenance, they at least secure the self-sustainability of the ministry without depending on third parties for their support.

Conversely, struggling ministries are heavily dependent on external factors to secure their funding. If a ministry is developed under the auspices of external funding, and if this ministry doesn't develop a local support base, the life of such a ministry will depend on either the life or the choices of the external funding source.

Programme evolution

A symbol of organizational maturity is the evidence of purposeful evolution (Collins and Porras, 1994; Peter and Waterman, 1982) – or, in other words, a history of consciously embracing the concept of moving towards progress by making significant strategic shifts to stimulate progress and respond to the demands of the environment (Collins and Porras, 1994).

The programmes of most successful ministries have progressed so that they can respond to the needs of the communities they serve and to the constituencies that support them. Some ministries, for example, have evolved from focusing on child assistance to working with communities on social transformation and justice. In the case of health-care programmes, programmes in successful ministries have evolved from supplying pharmaceutical shipments to community-based programmes addressing total health.

Programmes of most less successful ministries have also evolved over time. However, the patterns of evolution are more erratic than those of the ministries that have succeeded beyond survival. The programmes of many organizations have not evolved since their inception. For other ministries, resource availability and opportunities have mainly dictated programmatic evolution. These struggling ministries have shown very creative instances of programme implementation. However, we have often been more creative in developing methods of fund-raising than in developing services to meet the needs of people we are trying to help.

Evaluation systems

One of the major flaws of non-profit organizations is their inability to engage in self-evaluation to review their performance in fulfilling their mission and responsibilities to the public as trustees of the charitable funds they receive (Knauft, Berger and Gray, 1991). Focusing on one constituency only (e.g., industry watchdogs or the field) results in either mediocre programmatic impact or lack of public trust. Reputable organizations are known for being accountable both to their mission and to the public. They have built-in mechanisms to secure financial accountability and programmatic impact.

Leadership visibility

This is perhaps one of the major areas of contrast between successful ministries and those who have not moved beyond survival. A study of the history of successful ministries reveals that these organizations have been known because of their mission and not necessarily because of their leaders. This finding is congruent with current writings that suggest that 'a high-profile, charismatic style is absolutely not required to successfully shape a visionary organization'. Interviews, surveys and documentary analysis of successful ministries reveal that the public and the staff know about the organizations and their mission, but not necessarily the names of their past or present leaders. In fact, some of the most significant presidents and chief executive officers in successful ministries did not have the archetypal charismatic traits that people would expect of them.

Most of the young, struggling ministries on the verge of survival, on the other hand, are better known by their founders/CEOs than by their mission or programmatic quality.

Leadership succession

One of the difficulties of high-leadership profile is the problem of engaging in effective leadership succession. Successful ministries with low-profile, high-quality leaders have been able to develop and promote highly competent leaders from inside the organization. Furthermore, these competent leaders have achieved 'great continuity of excellence at the top through many generations' (Collins and Porras, 1994, p. 34). In general, successful social ministries display various levels of success in leadership succession. Most of those ministries have succeeded at growing leadership from within 'in spite of their growing pains' (Erickson, 1997).

The picture is different in the ministries that have not reached the point beyond survival. Some ministries are still struggling to recruit a replacement for their founders. Such vacancies have left the organizations without leadership for longer periods of time, and the perspectives of leadership selection are still not clear. Other ministries have experienced several attempts to bring leaders from the outside to lead the organization, but such attempts have been unsuccessful. Moreover, in many cases, the life and sustainability of the ministry after the retirement of its leader remain in question.

Conclusions: Ten principles for ministry beyond survival

1. Successful ministries respond to the needs around them – they are not opportunity-driven.
2. In order for a ministry to succeed, it has to be driven by a mission that is owned by more than just the leaders.
3. The mission must be articulated and shaped by beneficiaries, volunteers and workers.
4. The structure of a social ministry must be functional.
5. Successful ministries break the cycle of mediocrity by emphasizing administrative quality.
6. Ministries that move beyond survival are able to secure a sustainable support base.

7. Ministries remain relevant to the needs of their communities when they evolve with its needs, and not only with the opportunities.

8. Successful ministries constantly evaluate their programmes, themselves and their impact on those they minister to.

9. Successful ministries are known for their mission, and not necessarily for their founders/leaders.

10. Successful social ministries evidence maturity when they are able to promote new leadership from within.

Excellence in Christian ministry questionnaire

Please note that the following questionnaire is a tool to help you identify some of the issues that such an investigation needs to consider. As we have seen in other chapters on research methodology (e.g., Chapter 32), it will be important to vary the way questions are framed so, for example, the 'correct' answer is not always at the same end of the scale.

Name of the organization: ....

You are:

☐ An executive of the organization

☐ A non-executive staff member of the organization

☐ A former employee of the organization

☐ A non-employee who knows the organization

Score:

1 — No, the statement doesn't reflect the organization at all.

2 — There are some indications that this happens in the organization. However, the organization does not explicitly claim to do this.

3 — Some of it happens in the organization. However, much improvement is needed.

4 — It happens most of the time.

5 — This statement absolutely reflects the organization.

1. Mission of the organization

a) The organization has a clear mission statement that is used as a source of guidance for ministry.

| **1** | **2** | **3** | **4** | **5** |

b) The mission of the organization is consistent with the Great Commission and shaped by Christian principles.

| **1** | **2** | **3** | **4** | **5** |

c) As a member of the organization, you are satisfied with the mission statement.

| **1** | **2** | **3** | **4** | **5** |

d) The organization's mission has been properly reviewed to make it relevant to the needs of the poor and societal demands.

1   **2**   **3**   **4**   **5**

e) If you asked an executive or a board member of the organization, they would be able to articulate the mission statement.

1   **2**   **3**   **4**   **5**

f) Employees at all levels of the organization identify themselves with the mission.

1   **2**   **3**   **4**   **5**

g) The mission of the organization is visible in its strategies, actions and programmes.

1   **2**   **3**   **4**   **5**

h) The mission is clear and operational in that it states the expected outcome of actions and not just good intentions.

1   **2**   **3**   **4**   **5**

i) The mission is understandable to the general public.

1   **2**   **3**   **4**   **5**

2. Organizational arrangements

a) The structure of the organization is conducive to the implementation of its mission.

1   **2**   **3**   **4**   **5**

b) The organization has policy and procedures manuals that are updated regularly.

1   **2**   **3**   **4**   **5**

c) Every staff member has access to the organization's policies, procedures and foundational documents.

1   **2**   **3**   **4**   **5**

d) The organization practices sound budgeting, up-to-date bookkeeping, complete/timely reporting and regular audits.

1   **2**   **3**   **4**   **5**

e) The management information system of the organization is used regularly and effectively to enhance organizational effectiveness.

1   **2**   **3**   **4**   **5**

f) People in the organization have the opportunity to be trained and learn on the job.

1   **2**   **3**   **4**   **5**

g) People in the organization have access to staff development opportunities.

1   **2**   **3**   **4**   **5**

h) The organization has employee orientation and training materials which are updated regularly.

1   **2**   **3**   **4**   **5**

i) The employee rewards and incentives are clearly articulated and understood by the employees and their managers.

1   **2**   **3**   **4**   **5**

j) Team building is promoted at all levels.

1   **2**   **3**   **4**   **5**

k) Planning, implementation and evaluation is promoted and practised at all levels.

1   **2**   **3**   **4**   **5**

l) Every staff member has a clear work plan for meeting the organization's mission and strategies.

1   **2**   **3**   **4**   **5**

m) There is no nepotism in the organization.

1   **2**   **3**   **4**   **5**

3. Resource development

a) The organization has systematically identified those constituencies or groups of individuals that would be willing to give support.

1   **2**   **3**   **4**   **5**

b) The organization has clearly articulated the reasons it deserves to be supported (which distinguish it from other groups).

1   **2**   **3**   **4**   **5**

c) The organization involves key volunteers who are willing to make personal contributions (time, talent, finances) and are willing to engage in personal solicitation of funds on behalf of the organization.

1   **2**   **3**   **4**   **5**

d) The organization has successfully engaged in direct mail solicitation.

1   **2**   **3**   **4**   **5**

e) The organization has successfully engaged in media-based solicitation.

1   **2**   **3**   **4**   **5**

f) The organization's reliance on government grants is minimal compared to the other sources of sustained income.

1   **2**   **3**   **4**   **5**

g) The organization has a plan to recruit and select volunteers.

1   **2**   **3**   **4**   **5**

h) There is a match between the fund-raising message and the realities of the programmes the organization implements.

1   **2**   **3**   **4**   **5**

i) The organization has systems in place that allow donors to verify the use of their donations.

1   **2**   **3**   **4**   **5**

j) Board members are engaged in resource development.

1   **2**   **3**   **4**   **5**

k) A key role of the organization's CEO is to secure funding for the organization.

1   **2**   **3**   **4**   **5**

4. Programmatic focus

a) Programmes of the organization are relevant to the needs of the people and are effective.

1   **2**   **3**   **4**   **5**

b) Programmes reflect the mission, vision and goals of the organization.

1   **2**   **3**   **4**   **5**

c) The organization shows a steady improvement in the cost-effectiveness of programmes over time.

1   **2**   **3**   **4**   **5**

d) Programmes support and enhance the redemptive work of the church where they are implemented.

1   **2**   **3**   **4**   **5**

e) Programmes are evaluated by both the organization and the implementing partners (communities).

1   **2**   **3**   **4**   **5**

f) The organization has shown innovation by adapting its programmes to the evolving needs of the communities they serve.

1   **2**   **3**   **4**   **5**

5. Leadership

a) Key leaders in the organization have ownership and the ability to clarify, apply and exemplify the core values, which are understood, accepted and practised by members of the organization.

1   **2**   **3**   **4**   **5**

b) Leaders are available, open and vulnerable enough to support opportunities for staff members to be guided, mentored and trained to maximize their gifts and potential for service.

1   **2**   **3**   **4**   **5**

c) Leaders are characterized by humility, perseverance, discipline and a simple lifestyle.

1   **2**   **3**   **4**   **5**

d) Leaders are committed to the vision.

1   2   3   4   5

e) Leadership is based on justice, love and righteousness.

1   2   3   4   5

f) Leaders have the ability to attract dedicated people to the organization.

1   2   3   4   5

g) Leaders have been heavily involved in securing integrity in the organization's financial, programmatic and promotional activities.

1   2   3   4   5

h) The organization has successfully survived the transition between its founders and new leadership.

1   2   3   4   5

i) During the history of the organization, the executive leaders (CEO) have had the capacity to significantly influence its direction.

1   2   3   4   5

j) The organization is identified by the public because of its ministry and not necessarily because of its CEO.

1   2   3   4   5

k) The organization has grown its top leadership from within.

1   2   3   4   5

l) The organization has intentionally taken leadership succession into consideration as a priority.

1   2   3   4   5

m) The organization has developed clear selection processes and criteria for its leadership.

1   2   3   4   5

Note

1. The study focused on the 40 member organizations of the Association of Evangelical Relief and Development Organizations (AERDO). AERDO is a professional network of non-profit Christian agencies and individuals engaged in relief and development work. This network represents a wide variety of organizations that differ in terms of their type of ministry, longevity, size and resource base. Each of the organizations has its own board of directors, strategic plans, reporting systems and organizational structures. Some of the AERDO members are covered by larger umbrella organizations that support them both legally and financially. Other organizations are completely independent entities. Very few of these organizations are connected to a denomination, local church or church group.

The central purpose of this research was to identify the characteristics of excellence in the top three organizations in the sector as compared to three others. The key issue, then, was the objective selection of the 'top three' organizations and the comparison organizations among all the AERDO members. The first step in the selection process was to rank the organizations based on their success as perceived by experts and leaders of the Christian relief and development sector. Using a phone/postal interview, respondents were asked to rate the AERDO member organizations in terms of their success. In rating the organization, respondents were asked to consider which organizations have been more successful in: a) achieving their purpose, b) setting an example of quality in the Christian relief and development sector, c) gaining a reputation among Christians and the larger constituencies of donors, and d) surviving the various changes in the financial, political and social environments they have faced. A scale graded each organization from a score of minimal success (1) to outstanding success (5). Respondents included: a) the current and past members of AERDO's executive committee (9 top executives), and b) scholars who have been identified with Christian relief and development (5 individuals).

Results of the survey were tabulated to determine the ranking of all AERDO member organizations. The initial research identified the most reputable organizations among leaders in the sector. The 'measure of success' scores were then compared with the organizations' indicators of survival (as outlined above). The main comparison factors were: a) size, expressed in annual income, b) longevity, expressed in years operating, c) financial performance, expressed as the percentage of income that the organization spends on charitable purposes, and d) level of resource diversification, expressed as the percentage of funds received from governmental and other non-traditional sources.

Using a multiple regression analysis, the scores generated by the survey were used to determine the weight that each of these factors has in the success of the organizations. The formula: A (size) + B (age) + C (financial performance) + D (resource diversification) = success helped find the weight (A, B, C, D values) of each factor. These values were then applied to each organization's data. The top three organizations were those with the highest weighted score. The comparison organizations were selected based on similar age and type of ministry, but with scores in the middle of the rank.

– Questions to Consider –

1 Analyse the key issues in organizational assessment and the implications of such issues for practice.

2 Taking an organization (Christian or non-Christian), develop a profile of its strengths and weaknesses. Critically appraise the impact of such organizational attributes on the organization's vision and development.

3 How would you counter the following statement from a project worker: 'I don't need to know all the information about my organization – I just get on and do my job. There's no point anyway – they don't want to know, as long as you don't make a mess.'

CHAPTER 37

Prevention and Rehabilitation Working Together[1]

Andrew Tomkins

Children: Their potential

CHILDREN have enormous potential but, if they are to develop fully, families and the caring organizations which help them need to understand their make-up and needs very clearly. Together with the children themselves, they can ensure that the children are properly nurtured. As we saw in Chapter 22, child development can be likened to the 'tender shoot' described in Isaiah chapter 53. The care and nurture necessary for the development of a young plant is a superb image of how God provides for the development of children so that they may grow up to a life 'full of meaning and purpose' as in John chapter 10. The next five years will see a massive increase in the numbers of 'children at risk', for one reason or another, on nearly every continent. The challenge for programme managers and the children, families and communities is how to provide a nurturing environment, using limited resources cost-effectively.

This chapter explores how families, civil societies and NGOs can respond to the needs of 'children at risk', with a special focus on those situations where parents are poor, or one or both are ill or even dead. While there are many millions of 'children at risk', the scale is greatest in sub-Saharan Africa, where 15 million children have already lost their mothers or both parents.

There are no simple prescriptions for child development programmes which are suitable for all families and programmes globally. The make-up of children varies from culture to culture and from one social environment to another. A child in a wealthy community may grow well physically, remain healthy, attend a good school with supportive teachers and become smart, but he may be 'stunted' socially if he lacks social and/or family support. Another child may do well at school and function well socially at home and eventually in the workplace but may be starved of any spiritual values or experience, thus growing up spiritually stunted. Another child may be malnourished to the point of increased risk of severe illness or even premature death but may have greater social and spiritual stature than the previous two children. Around the world, there are many millions of children who are stunted in some way – becoming much less of a person than God intended. This chapter addresses some of the generic issues that are suitable for discussion, reflection and action within specific contexts. For this reason, we will first examine the common elements of the make-up of a child. What are children made of? Then we will discuss specific, possible activities and interventions. What could be done to support children more effectively? We will review the need to listen to children and see them more as players rather than passive recipients. What do they think and wish for? In this way we can explore a range of specific activities that churches and other organizations can introduce to promote child development.

Child development workers need to 'prevent scars' as well as 'bind up the hurts of the wounded'. Children often have scars. Sometimes they are easily visible, such as those on the knee where skin damage lasts for many years after a child has fallen down and cut the tissues deeply. Sometimes they are less visible, such as the scar of bad emotional experiences; children may have a lifelong, deep-seated fear of adults because of abuse in early life. Children may have scars in their brains from being malnourished at critical periods of brain development; this results in impaired learning and problem solving which may never develop fully. Sometimes children respond abnormally to stress as a result of 'programming' during early life; children may behave violently, seeking to resolve conflict by violence rather than 'sorting things out' in a reasoned way. Children who are brought up in violent homes are often violent themselves, and children who have been abused are more likely to abuse their children when they are parents themselves. Children may have different disabilities that make life much harder. Blindness, deafness, learning difficulties, communication disorders, cerebral palsy and lameness can all occur as a result of illness in the womb or early childhood. They are especially likely to develop in communities where disease is prevalent and medical treatment is unavailable or unaffordable.

The problem with scars is that they are very difficult, if not impossible, to heal. However caring, safe, healthy and wholesome the social and physical environments in which the child is reared and nurtured subsequently are, there is often lifelong evidence of scarring. 'Children at risk' programmes can provide wonderful support for the physical, emotional, social, cognitive, physical and spiritual development of children, but 'scars are scars' – and they prevent children from reaching their full potential, however intensively and compassionately the support for a scarred child is provided. It is all a question of achieving a balance between providing for the urgent problems of the child 'here and now', and seeking to prevent those problems occurring in the first place.

Health workers face this challenge daily in their work among sick children. While 'saving lives' is more dramatic and results in great job satisfaction, if all the resources were put into 'saving lives' there would not be enough time to 'prevent illness in the first place'. Many health workers are familiar with the 'Lifesaver Story'. It also has major relevance for those in child development.

> There was once a lifesaver who sat at the bottom of a large waterfall and tried to save the lives of people as they fell down and drowned in the strong currents. He saved many people's lives, but one day he had an idea. He decided it would be better if he climbed up to the top of the waterfall and put up notices and rails to warn people of the danger of swimming at the top of a waterfall. He enlisted the help of the local community, including the leaders and school children. Everybody became aware of the importance of preventing people from swimming in this very dangerous place. The lifesaver was amazed at how few people fell over the waterfall once the preventive programme had been set up.

This story provides the basis for this chapter. It describes the ways that child development workers can prevent problems and promote effective child development through preventive programmes. There will always be a need to 'treat' children with arrested development and to provide support for the urgent 'here and now' problems facing 'children at risk', but the challenge is to ensure that 'prevention' and 'cure' go hand in hand. This is important for all aspects of child development. Both the Scriptures and professional groups encourage us to look at the development of children through a 'life cycle' approach in which the health, nutrition and welfare of the mother and her child are enhanced. Healthy mothers are more likely to produce healthy babies. There is now strong evidence that the physical, emotional and immunological health of children is influenced by prenatal factors. There are further important influences during infancy and early childhood. Many programmes focus on pre-school or school-age children. It may be too late by these stages, however, to overcome the adverse effects suffered prenatally and during early childhood. For this reason, more and more child development groups are moving into community-based projects that seek to limit the damage so that poor children will have the best possible chance of growing up as God intended. Such children are more likely to be able to grow out of the poverty trap into which they were born. There are many examples of child development programmes producing children who are smarter, more skilled and better able to improve their status. The provision of 'preventive' and 'curative' programmes is a key element in reducing poverty.

Key components of child development

There are many aspects of a child's life. All of these areas require attention.

* Growth and nutrition
* Health and immunity
* Cognition and educational achievement
* Social and relational attitudes and behaviour
* Self-esteem
* Life skills
* Spirituality

Children may falter in one or more of the above domains. There are specific factors that can influence how a child feels, thinks, learns, solves problems and lives with her family and peers. These include diet, illness, psychomotor stimulation, social environment, Christian teaching and care and the influence of a relationship with Jesus Christ. The importance of many of these influences has been largely established through careful observational studies. Most of these have focused on individual factors such as malnutrition, infections and social stress rather than on combinations of factors. Furthermore, most studies have examined the effects of those factors which are present at the time of the study. Thus the difficulty that children face in learning anything if they are hungry or sick is well known. Many child development programmes recognize this and provide food and health care for poor children. There is now clear evidence that the health and nutrition of the mother during pregnancy also affects child development.

Intergenerational effects

In addition to the effect of maternal health on child development there is now increasing evidence of intergenerational effects, whereby stressors for child development are passed down from grandparents to mother to child and so on. This has important implications for setting priorities for intervention. Should we focus on the immediate, or should we take a longer-term view on the development of children in the next generation?

For example, the following are some physical intergenerational effects:

- Low birthweight leads to poor growth and physical stunting, resulting in less healthy and less intelligent children. Such children may grow up to be shorter, more malnourished mothers, who in turn are more likely to produce low birth-weight babies.

- Iodine deficiency in pregnancy leads to poor physical and mental development in the womb, resulting in less intelligent children. Unless iodized salt is introduced, the result will be generation after generation of brain-damaged children.

- HIV infection is acquired in the womb, during delivery and through breast milk (although the chances are considerably less if the child breastfeeds exclusively). While many children with HIV die in infancy, there are increasing numbers of children with HIV who survive to school age. Their health problems, developmental delay and psychological problems related to HIV in themselves or their parents may be considerable. Not all children with HIV/AIDS die, and it is possible for a sexually active adolescent who acquired the infection from her mother to transmit it to her infant.

- Infection (especially malaria) is transmitted in the womb, leading to babies with lower birthweights who are also more anaemic, especially during the first few years of life. This may lead to intellectual delay that may not be reversible

- Toxins such as alcohol, lead, arsenic and cadmium can be transferred from mother to infant and, unless there are effective interventions, these deficiencies or toxins may be transmitted to the next generation.

In the psychomotor domain, an environment that lacks psychosocial stimulation is detrimental and often associated with a lack of parental awareness of the benefits of education. These attitudes may be passed down from parent to child. Such issues are often regarded as 'cultural', and therefore not something which should be 'interfered with', but is it right that a child should be 'stuck' in a vicious cycle of psychomotor deprivation because grandparents and parents feel that their way is the best way?

In the social domain, environments that include physical and psychological violence and abuse tend to persist such that parents exposed to violence tend to be violent parents themselves. There are now many areas of the world, including industrialized countries, where generation after generation of children grow up with little hope of employment or harmonious family relationships. Unless ministries include programmes to break out of the unemployment cycle, children who are capable of more will continue to be less able and less visionary.

Developing a vision for child development programmes

Before deciding on what key elements from the menu of possible interventions should be included in a programme for children, it is important to examine the different stages of building a programme:

- Producing a vision of what can be achieved
- Reviewing the necessary resources and training

- Assessing the levels and type of needs
- Monitoring the effectiveness, especially cost-effectiveness, of activities
- Identifying and promoting examples of good practice
- Becoming 'advocates' as well as 'carers' for 'children at risk'
- Becoming informed and involved with the provision of children's rights
- Interacting with and learning from other agencies who have had good programme experience
- Promoting discussion and planning of activities with children themselves
- Avoiding the stigma of children in programmes, especially related to HIV.

Many programmes focus on the development of individual children. They support disadvantaged children in rather structured programmes. Many NGOs ensure that such children are well fed, attend a good school and are cared for by motivated, skilled and compassionate staff. Many of these programmes are run in association with lively churches that support the children physically and emotionally and also provide Christian programmes that are popular with the children. Many child sponsorship programmes use this model, citing examples of ways in which extremely able adults have developed as a result of careful nurture during their childhood years. Their lives before entry into the programme seemed rather hopeless, with severe poverty and family discord being compounded by lack of education. The crucial support that these programmes provide is a fine example of what can be achieved by dedicated people and finance from caring, praying, Christian donors.

Other programmes focus on whole communities, recognizing that children are a key part of society but preferring to seek to achieve a reduction in poverty in the poorest families. They aim to improve the chances of better child development if families are more able to support their children. Such NGOs tend to emphasize the importance of listening to children in making plans for future activities within their communities. These more participatory approaches aim to enlist ownership of the programme by the community. They have the advantage of moving at speeds that are determined more by communities themselves than by the NGOs. They are much less dependent on external resources than the sponsorship model. When the community is very poor, however, it is difficult to be certain whether there is much change in child development or any other aspect of a child's life as a result of these more 'social development' approaches. In particular, it is difficult to know how much effect such programmes have when children are hungry, sick and unable to afford to go to school and their parents are ill, dead, absent or dysfunctional.

In addition to these two somewhat 'polar' and contrasting programmatic approaches, there are many other examples of programmes that seek to improve the experience and outcome of childhood by providing a 'treatment' and 'preventive' approach together.

In all programmes, the speed at which ideas, information and vision can be developed, modified and disseminated is now extremely fast. Similarly, the needs of children and the pressures that they are under are changing rapidly. The term 'globalization' is perhaps overused, but there are now many situations where children feel more at home with children of the same age in another culture than with their parents or even older siblings. The international influence of television, radio and the press means that children, even those in some of the most deprived areas, have become more aware of the behaviours and values of people in other countries and cultures. Children' s attitudes towards clothes, music, sport, social customs, sexual behaviour and values are now much more similar across the world than in previous decades. This has considerable influence on the sort of programme that children wish for, although fundamental issues of love, compassion and nurture remain the basis of what children need to develop fully. All of this means that there are several possible interventions within a child development programme.

Child-focused programmes

- *Nutrition* – promotion of breastfeeding and improved intake of iron, zinc and vitamin A in late infancy and early childhood, improved diet for growing children, breakfast, school lunch, improved iron and multiple micronutrients for schoolchildren (diet, fortification, supplements).

- *Health* – immunization, deworming, treatment of mild illness (scabies), detection and management of disability.

- *Psychomotor stimulation* – especially important from six months to three years through toys, play and safe risk-taking.

- *Education* – provided by government, churches or community schools, encouraging regular attendance with teachers who are present, committed and competent, and providing learning materials.

- *Social* – parenting, mentoring, befriending, enhancing self-worth by creating an environment where children are valued as individuals rather than just as a labour force or an investment for the future; listening to children and supporting them in times of stress.

- *Life skills* – for negotiating in relation to sexual pressures, employment, health damaging practices involving solvents, drugs and alcohol; creating an environment that promotes resilience in the face of violence, conflict, criticism, loneliness, emotional and physical pain.

- *Spiritual* – making the gospel understandable, enabling personal belief and a deep experience of God, relevant for children in their own context, emphasizing the limitless and powerful love of Jesus for children in all life situations.

Community-focused programmes

- The *physical environment* can be improved by providing infection control. Transmission of malaria and gut parasites can be prevented by using bed nets treated with insecticide, potable water, latrines and simple drugs. These could include anti-malarials during pregnancy and anti-helminths at the beginning of each school term.

- *Nutrition* can be improved by stronger promotion of a better maternal diet, particularly during the second and third trimesters of pregnancy when the foetal brain is developing. This will lead to improved birthweights and better micronutrient levels for the mothers (especially iron and iodine). Taller, better nourished women produce healthier, more intelligent babies.

- The *mental environment* can be improved by creating skills in development workers in psychomotor stimulation, early childhood education, schools and community groups.

- The *social environment* may be improved through creating greater awareness of promotive parenting, supporting dysfunctional families and using children's groups to enhance self-esteem and confidence, with a particular emphasis on life skills in relation to sexual behaviour.

- As the epidemic of HIV/AIDS orphans gathers pace, there will be an increasing number of families in which the primary caregiver for children will be the grandparent. It will be necessary to provide support for elderly carers as they care for children. In most societies, men play a minor role in childcare. There are many cultural reasons for this, and men have been excluded by programmes such as 'maternal and child health' programmes that reinforce the role of women. With the devastating effects of HIV/AIDS on child development, there is a new role for men – not only in nurturing their own children, but also in supporting the welfare of the elderly as they care for the many orphaned children.

- The life cycle approach – this holistic view of child development takes a look at what parental, family and societal pressures influence the child –in the present, past and future. It shows specific vulnerable periods at which child development may be affected and identifies specific interventions that focus on eliminating these problems:
  - 0–3 years – breastfeeding, infection control, psycho-motor stimulation
  - 4–5 years – micronutrient nutrition, infection control, psychomotor stimulation, social stimulation
  - 6–12 years – infection control, educational provision, nutrition (especially micronutrients)
  - 12–18 years – nutrition, life skills, educational provision for girls
  - 18–40 years – women's health, nutrition, birth spacing, decision-making in relation to pregnancy and prevention of low birthweight
  - 40+ years – care for elderly as they care for orphans and vulnerable children.

Family- and community-level interventions

Some examples of these programmes include:

- Helping HIV-positive parents to fulfil their roles for as long as possible and enabling children to express their fears about their illness and death. Death is often not discussed with children, and the unknown may cause far more stress than the undiscussed.

- Encouraging children and parents to plan for the future – by making wills, photograph albums, deciding on who will look after children when the parents are dead.

- Exploring traditional cultures for methods of grieving that can be helpful to children, and exploring other possibilities to alleviate stress (e.g., allowing children to attend funerals may be culturally taboo, but it may allow children to grieve more effectively).

- Financially and emotionally supporting families with orphans and vulnerable children.

- Facilitating the community to make its own plans for the future, recognizing the scale of problems that orphanhood will produce over the next 10–20 years.

- Avoid stigmatizing those with AIDS or poverty – with the best intentions in the world, some programmes have 'marked out' children for special care.

- Involving older children and adolescents in planning the programme.

- Supporting school attendance and even developing new programmes – where traditional government schools are so understaffed or under-resourced or just too expensive, it may be necessary to establish community schools.

- Protecting the property and inheritance rights of widows and orphans.

- Monitoring and evaluating the process of community support, indicating the percentage of families with orphans, the percentage of children attending school and the numbers of support groups formed, together with some indication of impact on growth, health and social development.

Many child development programmes are 'free-standing', being run with very little interaction with government groups. While this decision is often made after consideration of all the options, it is difficult for governments and associated agencies to learn of the good experiences if they are not shared. Furthermore, it is crucial to look at the 'big picture'. For example, how can a programme that works be scaled up into a national or regional programme? A major challenge here, then, is for Christian agencies to establish programmes that can be taken on by others.

District / regional- and national-level interventions

In these situations, churches and NGOs have a key role in being advocates and ensuring that government plans take account of the needs of children. These could include:

- Exchange of information

- Setting up collaborating organizations

- Review of existing policies, considering manpower, resources and politics

- Identifying and/or developing new policies and being advocates to ensure their adoption and implementation

- Ensuring that protective laws for children are developed, especially avoiding exploitative labour

- Providing protection and support for street children

- Supporting regulation for foster parents and guardians, including sustainable financial support

In all of these activities there are many opportunities for monitoring and supporting the evaluations by district and regional task forces.

International-level interventions

With the increasing numbers of children who are orphaned and the decreasing numbers who are attending school in many sub-Saharan African countries, there will be many opportunities for enhancing school attendance through the provision of school fees, books and regular salaries for teachers. NGOs can therefore be active in the following:

- Exchanging information about what works (large international donors really need to have some good examples of what they can invest in).
- Networking so that the impact of a small number of NGOs can be shared and key strategies developed for international funding organizations.
- Developing new policies for use by donors and advocating their adoption.

Interface between churches, NGOs and international agencies

Many Christians are nervous about working with secular organizations. There are indeed many problems, and there is a real need to have high standards and a solid Christian base of prayer, commitment, compassion and spiritual growth among the staff. Yet high-quality care is not something that should be kept within Christian organizations. There are many 'kingdom values' which can be translated and need to be at least acknowledged in the practice of as many organizations as possible, both Christian and secular. There are many NGOs who wish to support communities as they enhance child development activities. The benefits of working with existing groups are now well recognized, and all programmes need to emphasize the interaction between NGOs and communities and families, religious groups and local and national governments. Increasingly, there will be opportunities for international funds for support of children. Children themselves require information and support as they work out their own response.

Many church leaders feel that their role is to preach the gospel and care for those who are disadvantaged. There is strong scriptural mandate for that. However, we live in a world that is increasingly interconnected. What happens in one country may profoundly influence another country, however far away, for good or bad. Furthermore, there are some countries and groups of countries in the West that have enormous financial resources. With the great burden of debt that many countries are now under as a result of paying interest rates on loans, there is considerable resistance to take on any more debt. However, there are such serious situations with regards to orphanhood in some countries that, unless international aid is given, there will be a generation of children in which only the minority attend school. Thus careful planning, in which risks of dependency are discussed and resolved, is possible and financial support is available for child development.

The churches have a key role to play in being advocates for children and ensuring that, whatever loan or aid is given, it will reach those most in need and will not damage local initiatives or resources.

Managing child development programmes in today's world

We live in a world that is vastly more complex than ever before. The interaction between the geographical and economic climates is close, and fine balances can be disturbed or destroyed very rapidly. The management of programmes that aim to promote child development is therefore complex and has to take account of many competing demands. Traditional ways of planning and managing, in which rigid approaches are used, are unlikely to be efficient. New styles of leadership and management with imagination and a preparedness to innovate, change and initiate, while at the same time being responsible and accountable, are needed. In this situation the Christian manager needs to be inspired and empowered by Jesus Christ, who led a team of ordinary people to do extraordinary things. Some of his activities were extremely radical. Jesus saw that slavish adherence to tradition did not help the poor and needy; in fact, it excluded them. Those with leprosy and other illnesses were excluded from the temple. One of the major effects of Jesus' miraculous healings was that people were made well enough to access the spiritual, social and physical benefits of worship. Children need to be made as physically well as possible so that their minds and bodies can be 'temples of the Holy Spirit'.

There are several exciting challenges for programme managers over the next ten years. They will need to be visionary and incisive in their analysis of the problems facing children and their families, not relying on others' analyses uncritically. They will need to have skills in formulating plans in a participatory manner that will unlock existing resources. They will also need to be humble enough to realize that, try as they will, communicate as they will and liaise as they will, it will be difficult to please everybody.

The environment that Christian organizations working for child development need to develop, therefore, will be rather like the 'road to Emmaus'. It will be puzzling at times, but managers need to be assured that Jesus is there to guide with his presence, power and plans. It will be more important than ever for managers to connect, communicate, advise, encourage and inspire one another as they share experiences of what is happening globally.

Note

1. I have been very privileged to work with staff at Compassion International, Tearfund, Viva Network and other organizations in a number of ways over the last few decades, and I am extremely grateful for their interaction, experience and insights. I have also been fortunate in having some extremely talented research colleagues with a wealth of experience in child development at the Centre for International Child Health, Institute of Child Health in London. This chapter, however, does not necessarily reflect their views. Any errors and misconceptions are mine.

– Questions to Consider –

1 Look at a child-care programme with which you are familiar and consider whether there is a balance between prevention and rehabilitation. If that balance is not present, how could the programme develop to ensure that there is a balance?

2 What is the interface between the church and the child-care programme with which you are familiar? How could it be further enhanced?

Putting What You Have Learned Into Practice: Development, Evaluation and Monitoring of Programmes

Profiles of Children and Projects

HAVING considered the various aspects of development, evaluation and monitoring of programmes in Part Six, the reader will find it helpful to use the case studies in Part Eight to see and evaluate projects in action. These profiles of children, and of projects working with them, come from around the world. These different projects give a broadly based understanding of how different programmes address different needs in different contexts. They also give the reader an idea of the potential of different interventions, the resources required, possible problems and likely outcomes. Some of the organizations described are high-level, experienced, government-supported programmes. Others are newer and much more basic, but they are all in their own way serving Christ by serving children.

When reading the case studies or visiting projects it will also be useful to consider the programme(s) with which you are familiar and consider:

- What are the similarities and differences between the programmes? How can you explain these?
- How does the programme impact and involve the family and the community?
- How is the programme involving the local church?
- How is evaluation being carried out, or how might this be done?
- What can you learn from this for your own context?

– PART SEVEN –

Development of Self and Staff

Introduction THROUGHOUT *this book we have emphasized that working with children is a dynamic, relational process which, if it is effective, enhances the mutual growth of both child and adult. We are not working* on *children from a position of power, but rather* with *them as we learn from one another, each with our differing strengths and vulnerabilities.*

Sadly, a high ratio of field workers and base staff 'burn-out' and leave their work suddenly, in a very vulnerable state. This has significant effects both on them and on the children who have come to know them. Here in Part Seven, therefore, we will examine the key issues of self-awareness and self-care.

Kelly O'Donnell profiles these needs in detail and also explains how both individuals and organizations need to be able to assess them. Josephine-Joy Wright and Eileen Taylor discuss practical guidelines for the Christian caregiver in Chapter 39. Steve Bartel (Chapter 40) and Josephine-Joy Wright (Chapter 41) provide a biblical foundation for self-care as well as some practical considerations to guard against damaging stress and burn-out. Self-care is not selfish or self-centred, but a means of enhancing our effectiveness to care for others. In Chapter 42, Sharon Prior, Colin Bennett and Steve Bartel address crucial issues for preventing and resolving conflicts – factors which often contribute to stress levels and to the inability of workers to perform their tasks effectively. Finally, Cressida Pryor considers team dynamics and how to work effectively in groups.

The chapters that follow provide a mandate for effective practice: we cannot care for others, and especially not for children, unless we care for ourselves and, more importantly, unless we make space for God to care for us all.

Josephine-Joy Wright

– CHAPTER 38 –

Staff Strengths, Vulnerabilities and Needs[1]

Kelly O'Donnell

Whoever welcomes a little child like this in my name welcomes me. But if anyone causes one of these little ones who believe in me to sin, it would be better for him to have a large millstone hung around his neck and to be drowned in the depths of the sea. (Matt. 18:5–6)

CHILDREN deserve to be treated with dignity and respect. Christ encourages us to receive children in his love, and he gives a stern warning to those who do not. Woe especially to those who, through their behaviour, attitudes and teaching, might cause children to stumble in their belief in God.

Our work with children is not restricted to the programmes that we provide. Of utmost importance is what we offer of *ourselves*. Who we are and how we do things is very important. Proverbs teaches us to 'train a child in the way he should go, and when he is old he will not turn from it' (Prov. 22:6). Training takes place in each interaction that children have with us. Children are watching how we respond to pressure, to one another and particularly to them.

It is important for caregivers to monitor their own and their colleagues' spiritual and emotional health. Organizations and leaders are responsible for encouraging the health of their members, and they should provide opportunities for personal growth through training and pastoral care.

The following material is a series of tools to help individuals, teams and organizations look at their strengths and weaknesses. There are two short reflections on personal vulnerability (giants) and sin (flies), along with discussion questions and application sections. I conclude with three worksheets to give examples of selection guidelines, personal growth plans and job feedback forms. Let me encourage you to use these materials, and others like them, regularly. Share them with colleagues as part of your commitment to self-care and care for others. They will help you remain a healthy and significant source of Christ's love in the lives of children.

Fighting giants, facing vulnerabilities

There are some tall troublemakers lurking out there, waiting to take advantage of our vulnerabilities. How do we prepare our workers to handle these troublemakers and their own vulnerabilities? And how does the Lord use these things to train 'my hands for war, my fingers for battle' (Ps. 144:1)? We can find some strategies in King David's last battlefield experience.

Once again there was war with Philistia (2 Sam. 21:15). David and the men of Israel made the familiar trek down to fight at Gob, the border area between the two nations. David was probably an older man, without the robust strength of his youth, and a Philistine giant called Ishbi-Benob was out to get him. The battle commenced. In the midst of the fighting, David became exhausted. It would seem that the giant had been waiting for such a moment – when David was the most vulnerable – to make his move. Interestingly, the text points out that Ishbi-Benob was wearing something 'new' on his waist, perhaps a belt or a sword. The interpretation of this is not entirely clear, but its inclusion in the account is significant. Perhaps he was wearing a belt of honour, suggesting that he was a champion among the Philistines. Another possibility is that he wore a new sword, which may have been forged or dedicated for a specific task like killing David.

Abishai comes to David's aid, surely at the risk of his own life, smites the giant and kills him. David's valiant men gather around him and make him swear that he will never go into battle again, not just for David's own safety, but 'so that the lamp of Israel will not be extinguished'. David, as king, was like a lamp that reflected the character and purposes of God to Israel and the surrounding peoples. To extinguish this witness would be an assault on God's redemptive purposes for the nations.

Christian workers, likewise, are lamps to the particular people groups and ministries in which they work. We are the light of the world, the Lord tells us (Matt. 5:14). As David experienced, the forces of darkness seek to prey upon our vulnerabilities in order to diminish the intensity of our light. It's an age-old tactic, the response to which should be to fight the giants and face our vulnerabilities with the strength of the Lord and with the help of close friends.

Suggestions for personal growth

Let's look at 2 Samuel 21:15–17 and do some self-exploration. Read through the eight items below and discuss your responses with a colleague or as a team.

1. Like David, we all have vulnerabilities. These become even more visible for those who are in leadership positions. Sometimes we may not be aware of them until a crisis brings them to light. What are a few areas of vulnerability for you?

2. What might the 'giants' represent in your life? Are they metaphors for spiritual forces, or vulnerabilities?

3. It was said that Ishbi-Benob had a premeditated plan to kill David. Have you sensed a similar spiritual strategy to hinder God's work through you?

4. David, as the leader of Israel, was a lamp reflecting the character and purposes of God. Which aspects of God's character and purposes do you, or would you like to, reflect in your life?

5. Let's look at mutual support between workers. What does this passage imply about teamwork, our need for each other and our willingness to let others speak into our lives?

6. David's battlefield experiences started with a giant (Goliath) and ended with a giant (Ishbi-Benob). Verses 18–22 of chapter 21 go on to talk about other encounters with giants. How does God equip us to subdue the various giants in our lives? Are giants ever finally vanquished?

7. These giants did not just show up one day on the battlefield in order to be promptly slain by a God-appointed warrior. The giants must have inflicted many casualties on the Jewish army. Are casualties among workers inevitable? Which personal wounds are you aware of that have resulted from your battles with giants? Take time to bring these areas before the Lord in prayer.

8. Can you make any other applications of this passage for yourself, family or team?

Suggestions for training

Training is an ongoing process – its purpose is not only to develop additional ministry skills, but it also provides opportunities to reassess one's strengths and weaknesses. Like David and his men, we must rise to the challenge and venture down again into the border areas within our hearts, to take a closer look at our own giants and vulnerabilities. Our giants, or vulnerabilities, can meet us there, ready to assault us. Each person's vulnerabilities are unique and uniquely painful. They can include eating struggles, a need to control others, self-hatred, depression, painful memories, marital problems, sexual identity issues related to childhood sexual abuse, addiction to pornography. Some of these problems require professional help and can be identified through proper screening and selection procedures. Eating disorders, addictions, obsessional behaviours, and so on are coping strategies that people adopt to help them manage very difficult feelings. But then the strategy that they developed initially as a way of getting back in control begins to control them, and they become stuck and trapped in a cycle.

Sharing about any sort of personal struggle is risky, of course, and it is best done in training settings where there are caring people with big hearts and good helping skills, where confidentiality is honoured, and where weaknesses are seen as opportunities for growth.

In light of this, the following are important considerations for Christian training programmes for children's ministries:

• Relevant personal growth opportunities (times to look at oneself and share with supportive people)

• Applicants/trainees should know in advance about this emphasis on both personal and skill development

• Trainers and staff should model both vulnerability and strength

• Staff should demonstrate the overall organizational ethos (group culture) that allows for weakness and offers mutual care opportunities.

These components not only help to prevent problems later down the road, but they also reflect an important part of the body life described in the New Testament (e.g., 'carry each other's burdens [giants!], and in this way you will fulfil the law of Christ', Gal. 6:1ff.).

Proverbs 4:23 instructs us to watch over our hearts with all diligence, for from them flow the streams of life. Self-awareness and accountability are essential for both personal growth and ministry effectiveness. The initial training phase for ministry is a critical time to encourage and model this process for our future workers. One practical way of doing this is through small group Bible studies on this passage about David and other passages with similar themes.

Folly from flies: Facing personal sin

In many places, summer brings with it the nuisance of flies. It's not unusual to find a fly in one's glass of water, as I did one hot and humid day in Thailand. Maybe it was just going for a swim, I told myself. Or maybe this is someone else's glass. Yet there I was, sitting in a conference room with 40 expatriate leaders, discussing work strategies and praying, and because I was included in this gathering I was feeling, well, rather special. And everything was fine, except for that wee pest in my glass.

Contamination by flies

Quickly I flashed back to my morning devotions, pondering the verse I had meditated upon that would help me make sense out of my unsolicited visitor: 'Dead flies cause the ointment of the perfumer to putrefy and send forth a vile odor; so does a little folly (in him who is valued for wisdom) outweigh wisdom and honor' (Eccl.10:1; Amplified). The application started to become clear to me.

Was I fancying myself to be just a bit too special by virtue of my inclusion now as a 'leader'? This attitude was folly and would contaminate the fragrance of Christ in my life and work (2 Cor. 2:15), just as dead flies putrefy precious perfume. This special envoy had done its job by getting my attention!

Characteristics of flies

No one deliberately adds flies, be they dead or alive, to valuable perfume. The two are incongruous. Likewise, few of us deliberately try to pollute our own lives. Yet like flies in perfume, our folly can alight in our souls and wreak havoc on our wisdom, honour and work.

Some types of folly are more damaging than others. A few household flies are just a nuisance. Think of these, analogously, as things like unwanted habits in our life and minor character weaknesses of which we are trying to rid ourselves. But lots of flies, especially those that can bite, sting and carry diseases, could really hurt us. Think of these as serious folly: unconfessed sin, unrecognized arrogance, compulsive addictions and personality patterns that are unhealthy and unholy. Have you ever noticed how just one public, or even private, manifestation of these wrong behaviours and attitudes can neutralize our work effectiveness, compromise our integrity, destabilize our emotional life and hurt others? 'Wisdom is better than weapons of war, but one sinner destroys much good' (Eccl. 9:18).

Sometimes our folly takes the form of a one-off event – we recognize the problem and learn our lesson quickly. We can brush away such flies fairly easily. Folly can also take the form of intermittent events that can be hard to predict and that seemingly just creep up on us. Folly can also manifest itself in ongoing events in our lives, marked by a serious lack of self-control. In these situations we can feel like there is a host of flies swarming around us.

The bottom line is that folly, whatever form it takes, leads to disgrace. It only takes a little bit to damage our reputation (and God's), no matter how virtuous our life is otherwise or how noteworthy our accomplishments. Disgrace results not only from the actual content of the folly (e.g., rash words, questionable financial dealings, physical and emotional affairs). Disgrace can also come in the aftermath of our inappropriate actions when we do not avail ourselves of God's grace either by denying or minimizing our sin or by not believing in God's desire to forgive and help us in our time of need (Heb. 4:16).

Spotting flies

It often takes an outside source, such as a close friend, the word of God or the Holy Spirit, to help us recognize the flies in our life. One of the biggest sources of folly is not to be in regular contact with these three 'fly spotting' sources. Let's look at some of the more common flies:

1. *Addictions.* These compulsions distort our judgement and our relationships and take time away from other things. After awhile you can smell their stench, even though they may be covered up at first. Excessive behaviours involving over- or under-eating, exercise, preoccupation with one's appearance, withdrawing from other people, shopping, watching television, Internet use and so on are all part of this. We sedate and stimulate ourselves in many ways in order to avoid seeing ourselves clearly and having to deal directly with problems. Other addictions, such as pornography, gambling

and drug dependence, can be even more crippling.

2. *Bitterness.* Henri Nouwen has observed that, in this life, 'love and wounds are never separated'. We hurt those we love, and vice versa. Although working through such hurts and practising forgiveness is challenging, it is certainly more desirable than the alternative: harbouring the hurt and developing a pervasive, entrenched bitterness that can defile our own souls and damage others as well (Heb. 12:15). Forgiveness, an act of mercy that pardons others for specific offences, is the only sure antidote for such bitterness. It is important to emphasize that we need to be given space and permission to acknowledge and work through the hurts before we can move on to a place of forgiveness. If we are pushed to forgive too soon, the act is simply a ritual and not a release, and is therefore a mockery of what Christ has done as a legal spiritual act, releasing us from the power of darkness and our pasts. Forgiveness enables us to move from a place where we are chained by our pasts to a place where our pasts, although they may have moulded us, do not need to define us. Forgiveness does not mean that we will never be hurt again, but it is a decision to be free, to reinvest our energy from past pain into the future and to live again. The timing in the process of grieving is crucial but the effect, at the right time, is profound.

3. *Improprietous comments.* Our mouths are sources of both honour and embarrassment. Surely no one can tame the tongue (Jas. 3:8). Some of our greatest verbal faux pas include making hasty, inappropriate promises, especially to God (Prov. 20:25, Eccl. 5:1–7); spewing out 'brain sludge' – nonsensical things, questionable stories or jokes, or coarse jesting that does not edify (Eph. 5:4); gossip, which involves repeating a matter that unfairly or unnecessarily damages another person; and insensitive (poorly timed and overly harsh) criticism.

4. *Arrogance.* Some of us like to be at the top. How easy it is to be seduced by our positions of influence and by our desires to be important. Inflated pride and self-aggrandizement are two of life's greatest dangers. People can start to believe that they are more special than they really are, and that their success has come more through their own efforts than through God's favour and anointing (Deut. 8:17).

5. *Personal flies.* The list of flies that can plague us is almost endless. Can you identify any flies, dead or alive, floating in the waters of your soul?

Swatting flies

How do we rid ourselves of such menaces? It can be tricky, and it is a process. We hit some and we miss some. The first line of defence is to proactively attend to our personal growth: staying close to the Lord, in touch with ourselves and aware of the influence of our surroundings.

When flies do come around, they are best dealt with through honestly admitting their existence and impact (confession), choosing to make serious changes and amends in order to limit their influence (repentance and restitution), and getting ongoing supportive input from others to help us deal with them (accountability). Guidance from the Holy Spirit, trusted friends, Scripture meditation, counselling and a good support group (e.g., a 12-step programme) are all important sources of help, especially to deal with some of the more lethal varieties of flies.

Confession, repentance and restitution, and accountability are like strands of the three-fold cord that is not easily broken (Eccl. 4:12). We can use this cord to knit a protective fabric, which like a mosquito net can keep the folly out, and like a safety net can catch us if we fall.

Let's pull these thoughts together by considering Christ's words to Peter right before Gethsemane. 'Simon, Simon, behold, Satan has demanded permission to sift you [plural] like wheat; but I have prayed for you [singular], that your faith may not fail; and you, when once you have turned again, strengthen your brothers' (Luke 22:31–32, NASB). Note that this is a prediction primarily of Peter's faithfulness, not his failure. As we struggle through areas of folly, vulnerability and sin, God sees the potential in us. In spite of our weaknesses, he still entrusts us, as he did Peter, to feed his sheep and to be his faithful and refreshing fragrance among the nations (John 21).

Suggestions for organizations

How do we help those who struggle with more serious types of flies, like character disorders and addictions? Here are some suggestions for organizations as they discuss the issues:

1. *Identification of problems.* Which problem areas significantly affect us and our workers? Begin by briefly describing a few cases (e.g., financial mismanagement, child fondling, pornography addiction, abusive leadership from someone who is self-centred and mean, and the person whose sense of self is so fragile that she frequently becomes emotionally volatile under stress). How common are these and other serious problems?

2. *Protocols for problems.* Develop a protocol for dealing with people who have 'significant' problems. Are there any approaches to study from other organizations? Be careful not to scapegoat those who are simply 'different' or to inappropriately blame others. Consider these three 'S's' to guide your approach – screening, support, separation:

   * *Screening.* How do we recognize and help people with significant struggles? How effective is our selection process? Candidates these days have some very different characteristics from their predecessors, often resulting from 'bruised' backgrounds (family dysfunction, abuse, neglect). These characteristics vary by culture and nation. How can we screen for these problems, disciple further when we can, and refer people for more help?

   * *Support.* How do we help those who are part of the organization and who want to keep working? Accountability, a support group and counselling are usually needed. What types of resources are available to provide more help in the nations where we work and live? Should we try to run a support group in a field location? Most professionals would say that people with significant struggles do not belong on the front lines as they deplete others' energy and time and thus distract them from their primary objectives. Is this always true? Is it better to redeploy them in the home office? What is the place of agape love and Christian community in light of such problems?

   * *Separation.* What are the conditions under which we will ask a person to leave the work or organization for the purposes of restoration? Do you

know of cases where this has worked? What can we learn from such cases? How can we prevent just 'kicking people out', or their moving on to another organization or location?

3. *Leadership and problems.* The leaders in each organization have a responsibility to develop guidelines for the selection, support and separation of its staff. It is also important to put into place an organizational review process to monitor how the organization is doing in these areas. How are we helping people in our organizations, our colleagues on the field and ourselves, when personal problems such as addictive behaviour or character problems significantly disrupt our lives? Further, what are we doing to help develop our workers and to prevent the occurrence of significant struggles?

Leaders must also be willing to look beyond the problems and assess the whole area of organizational health and dysfunction. What are our strengths and weaknesses as a ministry and institution? Remember that wounded people form wounded organizations; and wounded organizations wound people, too.

Selection criteria

Following are 11 important factors that should be assessed prior to someone becoming part of an organization or a team. This list can be used for screening potential workers or for newly formed teams, as a point of departure to discuss who they are, their backgrounds and their motivations and expectations for the team. It can also be useful for teams going through a major transition period, such as a change in goals or the addition of new members.

1. *Calling* to your job or profession, to a country, a people, the organization, the team
2. *Character* – emotional stability, resilience, strong and weak points
3. *Competence* – your gifts and skills, training, preparation and experience
4. *Commitment* to your 'calling', job, cross-cultural work, organization, team, people
5. *Christian experience* – spirituality, previous related work
6. *Cross-cultural experience* – living and relating with people from different cultures
7. *Compatibility* with team goals, organizational ethos and doctrine, cultural, relational, spoken and unspoken expectations
8. *Confirmation* from family, friends, organization, church; inner peace
9. *Corporal health* – overall physical wellness
10. *Cash* – financial assets and overall support network
11. *Care network* – friends and senders to encourage and support you

Personal growth plan

This exercise is based on a self-assessment tool put together by the personnel department of the US Center for World Missions. The purpose is to plan for, stimulate and monitor your own growth in your character, skills and spirituality. Complete this worksheet (or something like it) once a year and talk about it with a friend or leader.

Part one: Personal profile

1. List your current interests – things you do which give you personal satisfaction and pleasure (like reading, sports, music).
2. List your current dislikes – things you do which you do not enjoy (teaching, poor habits, exercise).
3. Describe a few of your strengths.
4. Describe some of your limitations and growth areas.
5. List your current work responsibilities. Summarize your job clearly in one sentence.
6. List any other responsibilities you have (personal, professional, social, family).
7. How do your current responsibilities compare with your stated interests and strengths as well as with your limitations and dislikes?
8. What would you like to be doing in the next five years? Write a brief statement about your future roles and responsibilities – both personal and work-related.
9. What are you doing to further your spiritual life? What are your specific struggles?
10. What helps you maintain emotional stability and keeps you emotionally healthy?
11. In what ways do you continue to learn and build upon your strengths and skills?
12. Describe your relationship with your family. Are there areas to improve?
13. Describe your relationship with your team, department or work community. Are there areas to improve?
14. Describe your relationship with the local community or nationals. Are there areas to improve?

Part two: Personal and professional development plan

Based on your answers to the questions above, identify five specific objectives that you want to accomplish this year. Choose objectives that are reasonably obtainable and that can be measured. Set dates for when you want to have them completed. For example, lose five kilograms by 1 September, read two books on cross-cultural relief work within the next three months, or raise my support level by 50 per cent by the end of the year. Outline the steps you will take to accomplish each objective. Describe how you will evaluate your progress. Focus on changes that you can make – not on changes that you think others need to make. For example:

Objective: Send newsletters to 50 friends, three times a year.

Date: Mail newsletters in late April, August and December.

Strategy: Address envelopes in advance, keep the newsletter to two pages, revise it twice, include a one-page insert of interest.

Evaluative assessment: Show each newsletter to my team leader and ask for feedback from a few supporters on the content and style of the newsletter.

Job feedback form

This form will help you look at how your overall team or department is doing. It is intended to stimulate mutual feedback between you and your supervisor or leader, and between group members when it is done as a joint exercise. It is also meant to complement, but not replace, the use of performance appraisals or personal development reviews. Your assessment should ideally lead to constructive changes for you and your work. Use the five-point scale below to rate the 15 different areas. Feel free to make additional comments regarding any of the items.

Job feedback form

1 —————————2 —————————3 —————————4 —————————5
Strongly disagree   **Basically agree**   **Strongly agree**

1. The objectives of my team/department are clear to me.
   Rating: _____   Comments:

2. The objectives were formed with ample discussion.
   Rating: _____   Comments:

3. I am involved in the decision-making process.
   Rating: _____   Comments:

4. We meet often enough as a group.
   Rating: _____   Comments:

5. There is a good sense of team spirit in our work.
   Rating: _____   Comments:

6. The communication process is adequate in our group.
   Rating: _____   Comments:

7. I understand what is expected of me.
   Rating: _____   Comments:

8. I receive timely and sufficient feedback on my work.
   Rating: _____   Comments:

9. I feel respected and encouraged by my leader or supervisor.
   Rating: _____   Comments:

10. I feel encouraged and respected by my colleagues.
    Rating: _____   Comments:

11. I regularly try to encourage and support my colleagues.
    Rating: _____   Comments:

12. Communication with my leader or supervisor is good.
    Rating: _____ Comments:

13. I have sufficient time to fulfil my responsibilities.
    Rating: _____ Comments:

14. I am growing as a person from my work involvement.
    Rating: _____ Comments:

15. Overall I am satisfied with, and enjoy, my work.
    Rating: _____ Comments:

Now find your overall rating (total divided by 15), and then the composite score for your group (total scores divided by 15 then divided by the number of people in the group). Please make any additional comments on the following areas: ways to work better as a team; personal areas of struggles that affect my work; any additional concerns or suggestions.

Note
1. Special thanks to Diane Gohl for her editorial help with this material. Parts of this chapter have been adapted from 'Folly from Flies' and 'Fighting Giants, Facing Vulnerabilities' (*Reaching Children at Risk* 3.2, pp. 26–29; 2.3, pp. 11–14) and have been used with permission.

– Questions to Consider –

1 Using O'Donnell's framework, identify those flies that are contaminating the fragrance of Christ in your life and work. How are they affecting your emotional well-being, spiritual development and practical performance? What steps can you take to get rid of them? What support systems will you need to help you in this process?

2 How would you meet a colleague's assertion that: 'We don't need to get into that psycho-stuff – just pray and it will all be fine. Christians are too "namby-pamby" and "fluffy" nowadays. They need to toughen up and get on with what God has called them to or his work just won't get done. We are not here to just gaze at our navels.'

3 Think about your 'giants' or vulnerabilities. How do these affect you in your work and how can you work with God to turn your weaknesses into his opportunities?

CHAPTER 39

Practical Guidelines for Christians Working with Children

Josephine-Joy Wright and Eileen Taylor

VARIOUS chapters in this book have explored many of the key issues that arise when working with children – from ethics to politics, from safe practice guidelines to ways of understanding the different worlds of children. Here we will consider, in partnership with the other contributors to Part Seven, the specific needs of those who work with children and young people – whether abroad or in their home countries. The purpose of this chapter is to address the practical issues that arise for people working in this area and to give practical guidelines that can ensure their safe and healthy practice. Over the past few years, practitioners have become more aware of issues such as 'burn-out' and the large numbers who leave their work with children due to work-related, as well as personal, stressors. Just as we have examined the basic needs of children and young people and how we can meet them (in particular how we can enhance their resilience, see especially Part Three), we need to understand how to meet our own needs as well as the needs of those with whom we work and those we manage. In Chapter 27, Riley and Wright look at the practical skills workers need, drawing on the work of Keith White (1999) and the five core needs (security, significance, boundaries, community and creativity) which must be met for all of us if we are to develop effectively. These core needs have to be met to ensure effective healthy development in any child. They underpin the model developed by Josephine-Joy Wright which describes the necessary conditions for the journey of healing from difficult experiences to take place for adults and children: 1) firstly they need to be *held* (spiritually, emotionally, physically and practically – thus providing boundaries and security); 2) they need to be *heard* (and thereby given self-worth and significance); and this enables them then to 3) be able to access *healing* (both within ourselves and within our communities). This is a creative journey, and it is heartbreaking to witness the stunted creativity of many Christians working in this field in positions that do not allow them to release and nurture their strengths and gifts. Even worse, their gifts are sometimes seen as threatening by others within the organization and thus are destroyed or denied. Jealousy and pride are indeed at the root of so many problems in organizations, teams and families. Each one of us needs to be equipped with skills to recognize and change these hurtful patterns and experience forgiveness and healing.

The following practical guidelines are designed to help mitigate such difficulties. Safe practice and child protection guidelines require that we keep ourselves safe, and that we keep children safe. We need to be safe from children emotionally, physically and also spiritually, since many of the children with whom we work will have been involved with occult practices or abused by individuals or organizations giving windows of opportunity to satanic forces. We also need to be safe from one another and ourselves. We are often working with colleagues who, as a result of their own difficult childhoods, work with their worlds in damaging or dysfunctional ways practically, spiritually and emotionally, dumping their baggage on one another in order to deal with their pain and internal conflicts.

We need to learn ways of working effectively with our pasts so that they do not define our futures and so that we do not repeat cycles of abuse, neglect and loss. The practical guidelines we will be looking at here can be grouped under three main headings. They all describe points of good practice and resilience building, using Grotberg's (1995) model:

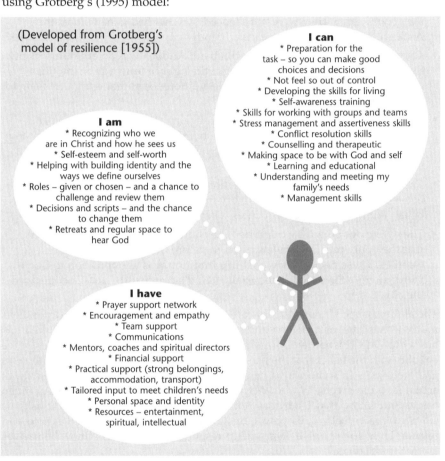

(Developed from Grotberg's model of resilience [1955])

I am
* Recognizing who we are in Christ and how he sees us
* Self-esteem and self-worth
* Helping with building identity and the ways we define ourselves
* Roles – given or chosen – and a chance to challenge and review them
* Decisions and scripts – and the chance to change them
* Retreats and regular space to hear God

I can
* Preparation for the task – so you can make good choices and decisions
* Not feel so out of control
* Developing the skills for living
* Self-awareness training
* Skills for working with groups and teams
* Stress management and assertiveness skills
* Conflict resolution skills
* Counselling and therapeutic
* Making space to be with God and self
* Learning and educational
* Understanding and meeting my family's needs
* Management skills

I have
* Prayer support network
* Encouragement and empathy
* Team support
* Communications
* Mentors, coaches and spiritual directors
* Financial support
* Practical support (strong belongings, accommodation, transport)
* Tailored input to meet children's needs
* Personal space and identity
* Resources – entertainment, spiritual, intellectual

Figure 1: Enhancing the resilience of Christians working with children and young people

'I am' guidelines

Those who are secure in Christ and in their identity in him are better able to withstand the pressures of this work as they seek to transform horror into peace. Society often regards Christian child-care workers as heroes, angels or fools – as committed, dedicated, patient and without needs of their own. Sometimes we even think of ourselves in this way and have a strong tendency to put one another on pedestals. But the Bible clearly describes how God in fact uses not heroes or people of high status, but ordinary people who are faithful.

Acts 11:19–21 is an encouragement to all of us as it records how God powerfully used Christians whose names are not even recorded – they were ordinary church members. The Antioch church was the first fellowship to fulfil Christ's command to go to the rest of the world. Ross Paterson (2000), in his book *The Antioch Factor*, identifies the qualities that made them so successful.

- They were undaunted by persecution. These men and women walked into Antioch while they were under much pressure, fleeing from persecution. They had only the clothes on their backs and whatever personal possessions they could carry. They were not silenced by what had gone before, or by Antioch, which was by no means a friendly city.

- They were unsullied by their environment. Antioch was a very immoral city. But these unknown Christians brought the light of Jesus Christ into that darkness. These ordinary people made a difference in that world, refusing to allow its darkness to cover them.

- They were not compromised by other religions. These ordinary men and women proclaimed Jesus uniquely and faithfully. (How else would so many have known to turn to Christ?) They proclaimed boldly and clearly that all religions are not equal.

- They were uninhibited by their position. They were lay people. They believed that God could use ordinary men and women. They acted on their belief, with powerful consequences. They were real and honest.

- They were not bound by tradition. The church had a tradition (Acts 11:19) that they only preached to Jews, and therefore they did not preach to Gentiles. These people knew that this tradition was in opposition to God's word, so they discarded it and exalted God's command – and God changed the city.

The ability of the Christian child-care worker to take up a position depends as much on her level of *confidence* and *self-esteem* as it does on the specific skills she has. Often in Christian work (more so than in non-Christian environments) we collude with the belief that the person who is busy and overwhelmed with tasks and feelings is in some way a better worker – or at least a better Christian. In actual fact, the reverse is true. We need to accept the reality of sin in our fallen world and know that God does not call us to change the world. He asks us simply to be vessels of his power, healing and peace. Vessels receive, hold and release. They do not strive. Instruments respond to the players – they themselves are not the players.

We need *space* and *time* to read the Bible and to be able to hear God. Resources such as reference books and meditations can help us to hear what God is saying and interpret his word correctly. Our response to problems, conflicts and fears should be to take them to God *first*. We need to wait with him long enough to hear his response, to feed on him, to be affirmed again for who we are in him. Only then should we walk out into the situation (and only if he tells us to), protected with his armour and equipped with his truth about ourselves and our situation, with his wisdom, knowledge and peace. Retreats (whether for an hour, a day, or more) and Sabbaths need to be part of the rhythm of our lives. God has given us a model in his creation and in Ecclesiastes – the tide ebbs and flows, the moon waxes and wanes, the seasons change, death is part of life, rest is part of activity. Rest is not something to feel guilty about or to reserve for a special treat. It is part of the guiding rhythm of safe practice – rest, play, laughter, listening, being, doing.

'Observe the Sabbath, because it is holy to you.' (Exod. 31:14)

If we do not care for ourselves, we become clanging symbols, useless to God and perhaps even damaging to the children with whom we work. If we are hungry, angry, lonely or tired, we need to HALT. This acronym, used by Alcoholics Anonymous, reminds us that without God we cannot achieve anything. We need to live in the present, pace ourselves and work with today (as children do), dependent on God and honest about our needs and vulnerabilities. In order to live effectively we need to set a pace and rhythm for each day and each week. God's final act in the process of creation was to bless the seventh day and rest in it (Gen. 2:2–3). This idea of rest was revolutionary to the Romans, who saw Christians as lazy because Roman law allowed for no concept of a Sabbath rest. Although we have taken up the concept of 'holy days' in our term 'holidays', the Sabbath is more than a holiday. God ordained that the Sabbath was not just a day of rest and leisure, but a holy day – a day set apart from our ordinary work for drawing close to God, a day for honouring and enjoying one another as children of God in our families and communities.

Dwight Pryor, in his Haverim School teaching tapes, says that the Sabbath rest is also entering into God's presence and holiness and being refreshed by it. There we receive the ultimate blessing – our spiritual adoption as God's children. We are adopted by his grace not as a reward for our frenetic activity and work, but because he loves us. Pryor also speaks of how the Pilgrim fathers of America said that 'Good Sabbaths make good Pilgrims'. Pryor says that 'observance of the Sabbath gives us back our humanity'. 'We are not just human doings, we are human beings.' God is a jealous God. He wants time with us – not as a taskmaster, but as a father who delights simply in being with his children. The Sabbath is a gift from God (Ezek. 20:12), not a set of laws and commandments as it was made into by the Pharisees (Luke 6:1–11) and which Jesus confronted, reclaiming its true identity – and ours.

When we spend time with God we can see beyond our fears and dreams to God's reality and certainty for our lives. We are able to let go of our pasts instead of clinging to the pain and lies in the fantasy that in so doing we can replace or restore the past. We can release ourselves to God's true restoration (Isa. 43:18–19; Joel 2:18–27) and live out that pathway of transformation for the children that we care for.

When we work with children it is very easy to buy the lie that more is better. It is tempting to believe the social and subconscious myth that we can single-handedly save the world. Many Christian and non-Christian organizations perpetuate this lie. It is often harder to repudiate this false and damaging martyrdom within Christian organizations. It is good biblical practice, as well as incredibly enjoyable, to observe the Sabbath on whatever day it is practical to keep it. If we do not feel able to observe a regular Sabbath rest, we need to ask ourselves what false beliefs or messages in our heads or hearts are preventing this from happening (e.g., 'I have to be busy to be a good Christian'). We need to create organizations in which Sabbath observance is part of the normal rhythm and culture of the organization. This will enable people to feel that it is more than 'okay' to take one day off each week – to be with God, to come into a holy rest in whatever way they rest most effectively, to be with their families and friends – it is fundamentally good practice and to be welcomed. Not only will such observance make us more effective, safer practitioners and biblically-grounded in our work and lives, but it will also model such good practice for children and young people and break the cycle of lies and abuse that has stemmed from this false work ethic. We owe this rest to ourselves, to our God, to our children, to our Father who delights in his children and wants to love and bless them. It is part of God's creative love for us in his world.

> "Are you tired? Worn out? Burned out on religion? Come to me. Get away with me and you'll recover your life. I'll show you how to take a real rest. Walk with me and work with me – watch how I do it. Learn the unforced rhythms of grace. I won't lay anything heavy or ill-fitting on you. Keep company with me and you'll learn to live freely and lightly." (Matt. 11, *The Message*)

'I can' guidelines

'I can' factors enable Christian workers to cope with their situations, and to manage themselves in these situations, more effectively. These guidelines include the following:

Preparation for the task

Brad Lincoln, of International Nepal Fellowship (INF), writes:

> At INF we are re-evaluating the way in which we handle the issue of recruiting missionaries. In particular, instead of advertising vacancies, we want to provide more of a service to Christians who feel that God may be calling them to mission work, but are not sure. Because of our network of supporters, and our involvement in mission work for over 50 years, we may have something to offer to those who are seeking to understand if God is calling them to mission work. We plan to offer to link these potential missionaries up with some of our supporting prayer groups who would be prepared to pray with and for these people, in helping them to understand the calling on their lives. The other support we can give is some basic practical advice on becoming a missionary, in partnership with other missionary organisations. The objective here is not to convince people to serve in Nepal, but to help people understand if they are called to work overseas.

Preparation involves being able to explore whether the path that is appearing is the right one to take, as well as exploring how to walk on that path if it is the right one. Each of us has different needs in terms of what we personally need to be able to prepare. Preparation is not just an issue for those who work abroad as missionaries. Those of us who work primarily in our own countries, in Christian or non-Christian organizations, equally need to prepare as we undertake each step on our journey. What does that preparation require?

Skills for living

Very often, people are attracted to working with children (consciously or unconsciously) because of difficulties or traumas in their own childhoods. As a result of these experiences, potential workers may have difficulties in the following areas: attachment (emotional security, intimacy); boundaries; saying no and yes effectively; self-care; working in groups; peer relationships; working with authority; and conflict resolution. These issues may arise from the traumas themselves. Often they arise because the person has not been allowed or given the opportunity to develop these skills for living. Those who have experienced difficulties in childhood may be driven by scripts, or childhood messages and decisions that control their adult lives. These scripts might include, for example, 'Be strong', 'Hurry up', 'Be nice to and please everyone', 'Try hard', 'Be perfect', 'Don't be a child', 'Don't be you', 'Don't be a girl/boy', 'Tears are bad/dangerous', 'No one cares about you'. Workers need practical guidance from a variety of others who are willing to help them to develop these skills. We need safe people to 'reparent' us and also to help us learn as equal adult peers. Cloud and Townsend's (1995, 1998) books provide an excellent pathway of healing, equipping Christians to work with these issues. Such materials should be offered to all workers as part of equipping them for their journey in this field. Other chapters (e.g., Chapters 27 and 38) seek to equip workers with some of these key skills, including establishing good boundaries and clear roles.

Counselling and therapeutic help

Far from being shameful or an admission of weakness, it is a manifestation of strength to ask for help when we need it.

> There is now a recognition that those who work full-time in the service of the Church sometimes need help. Hopefully a culture is emerging where it is recognised that to seek help when it is necessary is not a confession of weakness but a manifestation of strength and integrity and that the best [missionaries] are those wounded healers who have experienced both pain and renewal. To take the risk of seeking help may be an act of personal courage and also the beginning of personal and professional renewal. (Lyall, 1995, p. 133)

Educational skills and learning input

When working either at home or abroad, one can get so bound up with the practical issues of the job that the result is both intellectual and spiritual starvation. We need mental stimulation for our growth as professionals, as people and as Christians. Ask friends, colleagues or senders back home to recommend books that they have found interesting. One idea is to keep four books on hand to read, maybe a chapter at a time – enabling you to persevere in reading necessary, but heavy, books as well as disciplining you to pace your reading of more interesting and readable novels. While others may prefer to immerse themselves totally in one book at a time, the important issue is to be aware of one's own needs in this area and to address them. Do you need books, music, computer-based learning, educational activities, tapes? It is important to be aware of your learning styles and those of your colleagues in order to promote a stimulating environment that renews mind (intellect), body and soul.

'I have' guidelines

'I have' guidelines concern ways in which friends, family, church, community and others can support the person or team, both at home and abroad.

Prayer support

It is both sad and interesting that often, when one thinks of doing any specific mission or Christian charity-based work, the first plea is for finance rather than prayer. Yet we can have all the financial support we need, but unless we have God (daily and hourly) at the root and centre of what we are doing it is all a dangerous charade, a clanging symbol.

Praying together is an essential part of being in a team. Those who have sent us are also part of the team, closely involved with us. Indeed, it would be impossible to fulfil the vision God has given us without this help (Rom. 10:14, 15). Ross Paterson (2000) quotes Neal Pirolo, who heard that 'in secular war, for every one person on the battle front, there are nine others backing him up in what is called the "line of communication".' Since he learned this, Pirolo has 'encouraged, exhorted – even implored – anyone going into cross-cultural outreach ministry not to leave home without a strong, committed support team – a group that accepts the ministry of serving as senders'. Such supporters join in the spiritual warfare that rages around our work and pray for us at all times, especially during long silences when we are too busy or too tired to communicate. Such 'senders' hear from God and share with you what they have heard. They also encourage through letters, parcels, birthday and Christmas cards. The following story beautifully sums up all the aspects of this sort of prayer support. May it be a lovely encouragement to those of us who, faced with need and pain in so many lives, in moments of depression ask, 'can God really?'

> One night I worked hard to help a mother in the labour ward. In spite of all we could do, she died leaving a tiny premature baby and a crying two-year-old daughter. We would have difficulty keeping the baby alive, as, although we lived on the equator, nights were often cold and we had no incubator or even a hot-water bottle.
>
> As I did most days, I went to have prayers with some of the orphanage children. I told them about the tiny baby and the two-year-old sister, crying because her mother had died. During the prayer time, one ten-year-old girl, Ruth, prayed: "Please God send us a water bottle. It'll be no good tomorrow, God, as the baby will be dead, so please send it this afternoon." While I gasped inwardly at the audacity of the prayer, she added, "And while You are about it, would You please send a dolly for the little girl so she'll know You really love her?"
>
> I was put on the spot. Could I honestly say, "Amen"? The only way God could answer this prayer would be by sending me a parcel from home. I had been in Africa for almost four years at that time, and I had never received a parcel. Anyway, if someone did send me a parcel, who would send a hot-water bottle to the equator!
>
> Halfway through the afternoon, I found a large parcel on my veranda. I felt tears pricking my eyes. I could not open the parcel alone, so I sent for the children. Some thirty or forty pairs of eyes were focused on the large cardboard box. I lifted out brightly coloured jerseys, knitted bandages, a box of mixed raisins and sultanas. Then, as I put my hand in again, I felt something else . . . could it really be? I grasped it and pulled it out. Yes, a brand-new, rubber hot-water bottle. I cried. I had not asked God to send it; I had not truly believed that He could.
>
> Ruth was in the front row of the children. She rushed forward, crying out, "If

God has sent the bottle, He must have sent the dolly too!" Rummaging down to the bottom of the box, she pulled out the small, beautifully dressed dolly. Her eyes shone! She had never doubted. Looking up at me, she asked: "Can I go over with you and give this dolly to that little girl, so she'll know that Jesus really loves her?"

That parcel had been on the way for five whole months. Packed up by my former Sunday school class, whose leader had heard and obeyed God's prompting to send a hot-water bottle. And one of the girls had put in a dolly for an African child in answer to the believing prayer of a ten-year-old to bring it "that afternoon". (Carey, 2002)

Such stories are beautiful testimonies to the fact that God is here. He does care, and we need to stay still and silent. We need to believe radically. We need to be as children and learn from them as God speaks in his power, love and wisdom.

Encouragement and empathy – and thank yous

Working with children and young people can be both incredibly rewarding and incredibly deskilling as the young people and our colleagues challenge our assumptions, our cultural norms and values, our family's rules and myths. In the face of the enormity of our task, it is very easy to lose confidence in ourselves. The work environment and, for some, even a living situation, can bring incredible challenges. Eileen cites an example from her own experience:

Sharing a home with others always requires sensitive adjustment. When sharing is in a multi-cultural, multi-lingual setting, misunderstandings and conflict abound. There is certainly a need for conflict resolution! As a new missionary, I spent my first year being accident-prone. I put it down to culture shock. I felt very inadequate and wondered if it was only me until my senior missionary felt safe enough with me to share how, years before in her home country, she had experienced great difficulty with an Irish work colleague. She was empathizing with me and realizing that we both had a need to know that we were normal and were not alone – that it was OK to share our vulnerability.

Empathy is an important ingredient in conflict resolution. Jesus taught us about empathy in a startling way (Matt. 7:12).

[Jesus] did not condemn our needs as selfish. Instead, he used them as a starting point for learning how to love. In other words, he was saying, "You know how terrible you feel sometimes? That's also how others feel. You know how being loved and understood by another person helps you deal with those feelings? That's also what helps others. Give them what you're also needing". If we're all taking our needs to safe people and those safe people are taking their needs to us, love is created – and the Law and the Prophets are fulfilled. (Cloud, 1995)

We need to look for safe people in our lives – people who can be trusted, who do not play games with our emotions, who are consistent, who are interested in discovering and providing what we need to grow up in Christ, people who encourage, challenge and enjoy us. This enables us to grow up and to be safe people for others. One of our great sadnesses from our experiences of working within the so-called 'mission world' and other areas (although all the work Christians do is mission work for God) is the lack of encouragement and 'thank yous'. When working in disasters or major incidents, the impact of employers saying 'thank you' and showing their appreciation of the extraordinary work done by their staff is great. Such appreciation is a powerful protective factor in mitigating against staff developing long-term post-traumatic stress symptoms. Staff who feel valued, heard, appreciated, held and significant (White, 2000) are much less likely to develop burn-out and depression, even with very high workloads. We need to develop a culture of thanksgiving among one another as a witness to the world and as a resilience protective factor for ourselves.

Visitors

Encouragement can also come from visitors – those who are sensitive to our situation and who listen prayerfully to our joy and pain. Henri Nouwen expresses it well:

> Simply being with someone is difficult because it asks of us that we share in the other's vulnerability, enter with him or her into the experience of weakness and powerlessness, become part of uncertainty, and give up control and self-determination. And still, whenever this happens, new strength and new hope is being born. (Quoted in Huggett, 1988, p. 94)

It also needs to be recognized that it can be difficult, when visitors are with you, to juggle their needs and your desire to see them with the demands of your job. Equally it can be a painful grief when they leave, and colleagues need to be aware of this grief in their practical and emotional interactions with one another after a visit.

Financial support

The work that we do requires money, and this can be a source of stress when we are faced with such need around us. Our team, both at home and in the country where we work, can together covenant to pray the money in. Hudson Taylor, the founder of the China Inland Mission, was often heard to say that God's work done in God's way will never lack God's supply (Huggett, 1988, p. 94).

It is important to be aware of the financial needs of people who work part-time for Christian organizations. It is also essential that guidelines on funding within these organizations be responsive to the roles of these personnel. Our experiences as both full-time and part-time workers have demonstrated that people often make assumptions about the financial stability of salaried workers. Our full-time missionary colleagues have often been better supported financially than our part-time colleagues, as the former attract more goodwill donations and regular giving by individuals and churches. The matter needs to be addressed within organizations and churches in order to encourage more professionals and experienced lay personnel to give of their time and expertise to this work, thus enhancing the practice of full-time staff (through training) and broadening the scope of this work.

Practical support

Whether one is in full-time or part-time work, there are many practical needs which arise for workers in the field, including:

- *Medication.* Self-care includes knowing how to access medical support, expert opinion and medication when needed.
- *Finances.* Help is needed with tax forms at home and in the host country.

There are also questions of insurance and provision for pensions.

- *Storage.* Those working abroad need places to store belongings and family memorabilia.
- *Food.* People abroad often get incredibly focused about particular foodstuffs that they miss (e.g., peanut butter, Bird's custard powder or Cadbury's chocolate!). For those at home, such desires can seem at variance with the task these workers are doing – but providing for such details symbolizes care and empathy, a recognition of sacrifices being made and an awareness of the person as a human being.
- *Music.* As well as the provision for other creative activities.
- *Communications.* Letters, faxes, e-mails, telephone calls, parcels – all are crucial to maintaining morale and a sense that one is cared for and significant in someone else's world. They are not luxuries, but as essential as basic food or shelter.

Needs of families and children

There is a greater awareness of the needs of the children of missionaries, and a network of care is now in place in many cross-cultural organizations. For example, holiday camps have been organized for children returning to live in their country of origin. These children need a place to connect with others who have similar experiences and deal with similar issues.

It is essential that the needs of these children are properly and regularly recognized and responded to, in consultation with the children and young people themselves, to ascertain what they feel that they need, working as they do with their home culture(s), their overseas culture(s) and their own 'third hybrid culture'. It is not just politically expedient. It is good practice and a sure foundation for any of our work. We cannot expect to care for other people's children effectively and to be supported for so doing if we do not firstly care for our own. Equally we cannot, as parents and fellow workers, care effectively for other children while we worry about our own children's unmet needs. We need to be creative and responsive in our solutions so that the experience of being a missionary's child does not turn the young person away from Christ, but rather is a witness in their world. Children are part of the mission team. We can learn from one another to enhance our mutual practice and growth. Organizations need to explore practical guidelines to enable this to happen as part of a routine of good practice.

Mentoring and coaching

We need a safe person, or persons, who will give us pastoral support, challenge us on occasions and guide us with wisdom. This relationship does not necessarily need to be face-to-face; it can even be by e-mail. There are many good books being published about the importance of coaching (e.g., Collins, 2001). Confidentiality is essential; personal details are not to be spread around the team 'for prayer'. A mentor's role is to reflect with us on our personal development and on how God is speaking into our lives. The mentor may take on the role of spiritual directorship as well. When working in the field we were horrified and saddened by the great number of missionaries and people working with children and young people who do not have mentors. Jesus mentored and coached his disciples. This enabled them to grow, to work with their mistakes as opportunities for learning not failures, to learn to take risks appropriately and to grow 'in wisdom and stature, and in favour with God and men' (Luke 2:52) as Jesus did, tutored and mentored by the wise elders in the temple and his Father, God.

Mentors can also act as 'safety nets', enabling workers to talk through difficult dynamics and relationships in a safe environment and to explore options for resolution and develop new perspectives and skills. They need to be a key focus of good personnel practice in the preparation and renewing of all staff at all levels.

Conclusion

Through this overview of key practical needs and guidelines for addressing them, we have seen that workers are part of a wider system. We operate as part of our families, our friendship circles, our organizations, our cultures. It is the interplay of these factors that enhances the richness of our world – spiritually, emotionally and practically. This interplay, however, also highlights our vulnerability. It is essential that organizations do not get so focused on 'the mission' that they become vessels of pain or even abuse. We have a mandate to be lights to the world. We cannot do that if our very organizations are rife with jealousy, self-righteous defensiveness, non-communication, inappropriate use of authority and lack of good management, staff support and development.

Hypocrisy in any of these areas will not fool the children – they are the first to see through it. Our first witness needs to be to one another, allowing God's cleansing into our own worlds to confront, nurture and heal with grace and truth. Practical guidelines of good practice build upon the resilience of workers and enable them to become more like Christ to one another and to the children.

– Questions to Consider –

1 Assess yourself in terms of the qualities of the Christian caregiver listed above. Which quality would you identify as your particular area of strength? How could you effectively develop that area to be an even greater asset to the children with whom you work? Which quality comes least naturally to you? What is one thing you could do to develop that area?

2 Think through the list of goals and objectives of the Christian caregiver. How do you prioritize these in your everyday work? What might you add to this list in your own practice?

3 Using the material in this chapter, as well as what you have learned and read throughout this book, write a 'vision statement' for your own work with children. How would you describe your calling, your passion and your goals in a paragraph or two?

CHAPTER 40

Motivation, Spiritual Refreshment, Encouragement and Rest

Steve Bartel

I hardly recognized the voice on the other end of the phone. It was a young lady who had been on our team, but she sounded broken-hearted. 'I just can't take it anymore! I don't know what's happening . . . but I just can't stay,' she sobbed. 'I'm sorry . . . I've got six boys . . . street kids . . . living in my apartment. And I hate to put them back out on the streets.' Her cries became almost a wail. 'They've been with me for nine months . . . they're like my own sons. Please, please, can't you take them? I've got to leave the country next week . . .' I'd had similar conversations several times before. We'd all seen it coming. But she just wouldn't listen.

I remember when she first came to Colombia. In the comfort of her home country, she'd heard about the plight of street kids and had a tremendous 'burden' for them. She'd also heard about our work and wanted to be part of it. So she joined us, full of enthusiasm. Her 'I'm going to save the world' attitude was just wonderful. But, two weeks later, she was frustrated at how 'slow' we worked. We prayed too much. We weren't going out to the streets enough. The decision-making process involved in bringing a child into our homes was too cumbersome. So she decided to strike out on her own. Nothing could dissuade her.

After the first week, she called me. She was so excited. She'd 'gotten in' with a small gang of street kids in an area I instantly recognized as a tough part of downtown. One ten-year-old street boy and two of his friends had agreed to go and live with her in her fifth-floor apartment. I was happy for her, but already the red flags were waving in front of my eyes. She was headed for trouble.

A couple of months went by and I called her, just to say that we were thinking of her and praying for her. But her excitement was gone. 'Why are the kids so ungrateful?' she said. 'Here I am doing everything for them, and they can't even help out any. And they want to do their own thing, and they're starting to disobey me.' Eventually there were six boys living with her. She didn't have time to go out on the streets anymore. She didn't have time for grocery shopping. She couldn't trust them alone in the apartment. She had to take them everywhere she went. She locked herself up in her room at night. She 'didn't have a life'. Did I hear a tinge of resentment in her voice?

We tried to help, but our advice went unheeded. Less than a year after her arrival she went back home – sad, defeated, resentful and wishing she'd never come. When she left, she also deeply wounded six street boys who felt betrayed by a string of broken promises and expectations. Why did she come? Why did she go? The reasons are deep-seated and go back to long before she ever came to Colombia. The main issue was her motivation for ministering.

Over the years, we've seen several types of motivations that encourage or compel people to work with 'children at risk'. They are centred either on the person himself; on the child who is suffering; or on God's honour. While some motivations are not negative themselves, they are not strong enough to sustain the person working with children. In order to have the strength to persevere in this challenging work, the staff member must have a combination of motivations based upon a desire to honour God in all that he does.

Motivations centred on the person who is helping the children

It is absolutely essential that each person working with children examine himself and his motives for doing so. As numerous tragedies in Christian circles have served to underline, there are many people working with children who have unhealthy secondary, or even hidden, motivations. The following motivations for working with children are not appropriate or valid, since they focus entirely on the worker himself.

The saviour

'If no one else can do it, I will. I can be the answer to these children's needs. I won't let them down. I won't leave them; they can count on me.'

A need to be needed or appreciated

'These children need me. It gives me such a great feeling to know that I saved a life today. They'll be thankful for what I do for them.'

Emotional needs that only children can fill

Some applicants have lost or have never had children, and they need children in their lives to fill emotional voids. Others have insecurities around adults, or cannot relate to them, but feel accepted and wanted by children.

'By helping others who suffer, maybe I can heal my own sufferings'

Many of the enquiries we receive for staff openings are from adults who suffered as children – through poverty, abuse, abandonment or rejection. Some applicants have gone through recent failures in their jobs, marriages or relationships and believe that they can alleviate their own hurts by helping others who hurt.

A need to make restitution

A few applicants are former drug addicts or pushers, pimps, assassins, gang members or alcoholics. Many have lost their families, manipulated or destroyed others, or otherwise affected people negatively. 'I've hurt so many people in the past, I need to make up for it. I can't undo the past, but I can affect the future.'

Paedophiles

Some applicants may be adults who get abnormal sexual gratification by finding access to vulnerable children. As many countries are developing registers of child abusers and requiring extensive background checks for people working directly with children, paedophiles are increasingly going to countries and organizations that do not look into their pasts. (Christian organizations, due to their trusting natures and desperation for staff, are especially vulnerable.)

When individuals are motivated to help children solely because of their own needs, hurt and disillusionment are inevitable. The following are some typical responses:

- When we do not feel good (either emotionally or physically), we often lose interest in the children or the ministry.
- When a child does not show gratefulness, we tend to withdraw our commitment.
- When the child becomes an obstacle to our realizing our own desires, we become resentful.
- Pressure and stress, so common in children's ministries, tend to totally overwhelm us.
- We may revert to child abuse when a child acts contrary to the way we think he should be acting.

Human institutions such as governments and businesses can gain influence and respect by helping 'children at risk'. When these are the sole motivations behind a project, the focus tends to be on the programme, the influence or the publicity instead of on the children themselves. Once there is no longer anything to gain by helping the children, those so motivated retract the help to the children.

Motivations centred on the child who is suffering

It is quite common and natural for people to respond to the suffering of children by wanting to help in some way. Following are some of the motivations that spring from a focus on the needs of the child.

Pity

The child's obvious needs horrify us. 'Those poor children are suffering so! They're hungry. They're cold. My God, look at those infections! This is where they live? It's a rubbish dump! She's a prostitute? She's so young! They're actually cooking that garbage in a paint can? Somebody has to do something!'

Correcting injustice

'What the world needs is equality. The rich become richer, and the poor become poorer. That's not fair. With the food surpluses in so many nations, no one should have to go hungry.'

Compassion

Compassion is deeper, longer lasting and more thoughtful than pity, and it touches our spirit. Jesus himself had compassion for the multitudes. It was partly out of compassion that he gave them bread and fish, healed their sicknesses and raised their dead. But, by itself, compassion is still centred on the needs of the child: 'This child has no future. Let's get him into school . . . any school that will take him. This family is constantly sick. Let's bring them a doctor. Let's replace their cardboard shack with something decent. Children shouldn't be hungry all of the time . . . let's give them something to eat now. Maybe we should run a feeding programme downtown, a soup kitchen.'

The problems with individuals being motivated to help solely because of the child's needs are that:

- Our response tends to be superficial, often addressing the child's most obvious needs.
- Our response tends to be immediate, often without thinking through the long-term implications.
- Our personal involvement may be short-term.
- The magnitude of the needs that surround us can easily discourage us because we cannot meet all of the needs.
- When one of the children is disrespectful or unappreciative, we feel that he no longer needs or deserves our help.

Individuals who are motivated by the children's needs can be valuable to a ministry to children, as long as they are also motivated by God-centred motives (see below).

Motivations centred on God:
His love, his will, his honour and his name

When God is the centre of our focus and attention, our desire to reach out to the children that he loves flows naturally out of our desire to please and glorify him.

Unconditional love

Out of our love for God, we can love even the most unlovable. 1 Corinthians 13:3 states that ' . . . if I give all I possess to the poor and surrender my body to the flames, but have not love, I gain nothing.' Verse 7 goes on to say that love 'always protects, always trusts, always hopes, always perseveres'.

Obedience to God's commands

Christians who have clearly heard that God wants them to work with 'children at risk' often obey God, and at great personal sacrifice. The key to the obedience, however, is to ask God for unconditional love for him and the children. (Obedience without love will soon result in relationships that are shallow and impatient.)

Honouring God's holy name

Ezekiel 36 has an interesting comment on God's restoration of a people. Verses 22–32 list several problems that 'children at risk' face – either personally or in their families and communities. After describing these problems, God solves them. For example, God cleans them, changes their hearts of stone, encourages them to follow his decrees, puts a new spirit within them, provides a home, food, belonging to a community, and even the chance of repentance.

The key to this passage is found at the beginning and the end. God says: 'It is not for your sake . . . that I am going to do these things, but for the sake of my holy name . . .' (verses 22, 32). In the context of restoring the badly hurt, God clearly says that his name is to be honoured above the needs of the people.

Emphasizing God in all of our activities is the highest of all motivations. Protecting and restoring 'children at risk' honours God's name and gladdens his heart. God's honour is the noblest of reasons for a person to dedicate her life to children. When circumstances around us are difficult, when ungratefulness could discourage, when the children themselves do not show the progress we would expect – even when they fall back into the streets – if we are convinced that we have obeyed God, and thus honoured his holy name, we can keep going.

Spiritual refreshment, encouragement and rest

Regardless of our solid motivations, we will be simply unable to cope with the inevitable stresses and strains of working with 'children at risk' if we do not take care of ourselves. God holds us up and gives us the strength to bear our burdens and, to a certain extent, those of others – and he never gives us more than we can endure. But God does require us to support our ministries and ourselves on the three-legged stool of spiritual refreshment, encouragement and rest. We will be well-equipped for every good work if we allow God to minister to us through his word.

Spiritual refreshment

Every Christian understands the theory that we need to spend time with God in order to maintain, strengthen and deepen our relationship with him. Just as human relationships cannot mature without an investment of ourselves and our time, so it is in our relationship with God. Why, then, does it seem so much easier to fill our lives with doing things (often good things, many of them 'for God') without actually spending time reading the Bible? The Bible is God's word to us to challenge us to grow in faith, to encourage and strengthen us for the battles we face daily. How can we speak *for* God when we rarely, or inadequately, speak *with* him in prayer? Can our lives really be showing forth the joy of the Christian life when we are not regularly praising God? Why do we burden ourselves with trying to point out and correct the sins of those around us when we have not confessed our own? In all of this, those who work with children in need must realize that we cannot give what we have not received.

Encouragement

The gift of encouragement is perhaps of as much benefit when it is given away as when it is received. Each human being, created in God's image, needs to be affirmed and feel worthy. Those who work with 'children at risk' see these children blossom when they are carefully nurtured with regular doses of thoughtful encouragement. It is sometimes easy to forget, when giving so much away, that such nurture is not one-way. Likewise, it is important to understand the nature of encouragement and what it is not. While it is wonderful to receive the praise of others for things that we do, such affirmation can often be like a sugar high, giving us a temporary jolt of energy before we crash, looking for the next 'fix' to buoy us up again. 'I love your new dress.' 'You did a great job on that report.' 'I don't know what this office would do without you.' These are all statements of praise that make us feel affirmed, loved and wanted. Encouragement, though, is based primarily on who we are. While encouragement may initially take the form of a compliment for an action, it does not end there but speaks fundamentally of motivation and character. Encouragement is an offer, not a full-stop statement. 'You have persevered through some hard times, and I'd like to know how I can help you.' 'Thank you for saying what you did in that meeting. I know it was hard for you, but I want you to know I'm with you and support you.' The ultimate encouragement, of course, is knowing how God has worked in the past and trusting that he will be faithful to his promises to work through us and for us again. Encouragement instils hope and confidence in the context of an ongoing, supportive relationship.

All of us need to be in relationships of mutual encouragement in Christ. Again, we must realize that we cannot give what we have not received.

Rest

To be a Christian means that we depend on God for everything. The drive to work 24/7 is not a biblical one. When our ultimate trust is in God through Christ, who is our Sabbath rest (Matt. 11:28; Heb. 4:9–11), we are freed to rest one day in seven. This is a principle that we can apply in our lives on a very practical level. Rest includes proper physical self-care, a good diet and exercise, as well as achieving a balance in our lives, taking time out for God, for family, for solitude and for friends. Rest also means finding hobbies that we find relaxing and stimulating, taking 'retreats' away from daily demands. While it should go without saying that human beings need to take time to rest, it does not go without saying – because so many of us completely ignore this creation ordinance. God created the world in six days and rested on the seventh. Note that God is not resting to recover, but to enjoy the results of creation. Likewise, our rest is not simply to get over one week of work and prepare for the next. Our rest, modelled on God's own pattern, is to enjoy our Creator and his creation as we look forward to our heavenly rest.

– Questions to Consider –

1 Our motivations lie at the heart of who we are. If we do something 'good' out of a selfish motivation, God is not honoured. Think of something you did recently and analyse your motivations. If they were not purely God-centred, how do you think this affected your action and its consequences?

2 Using Bartel's breakdown of motivational assessment (self, other, God), how would you help those considering work with 'children at risk' examine and unravel their motivations?

3 Do you make time for spiritual disciplines? Are you in one or more relationships of mutual encouragement? Do you take adequate time for rest? Based on your answers to these questions, identify areas for improvement and write down some specific steps for achieving a more biblical balance in your life.

CHAPTER 41

Emotional Awareness and Meeting Our Own Needs

Josephine-Joy Wright

The dangers of emotional blindness: Power games, abuse and mistrust

OVER the past few years there has been a growing consciousness of emotional awareness and emotional literacy in both our working and personal lives. This has been particularly evident in the business world. Assessment centres, which evaluate candidates in terms of their suitability for a given post, often assess not just skills, but also look at areas such as a person's ability to work effectively in a team and how he or she responds to conflict and stress. One aspect of such an assessment is to ascertain safety. Staff who are poor at reflecting with constructive, honest criticism on their own practice and that of others and who are unable to accept constructive feedback on their emotional or skill-based responses are potentially a greater risk to the organization in terms of safety – their own as well as that of other staff and those whom they serve.

This area of safety is particularly crucial when those whom they serve are young children or vulnerable young people. The caring professions have a built-in potential power imbalance – I am offering or providing care; you are in need. However we attempt to minimize this imbalance by our personal behaviour and organizational policies, the issues remain. Wherever power exists within a relationship, there is the potential for abuse – the misuse of power and trust within a relationship. This potential for abuse is therefore very real for employees and volunteers as well as for those receiving the service. All of those who have worked in the caring professions have probably witnessed that abuse in some form, and perhaps have been its victims as well. It is important, and very sad, to note that this abuse occurs within Christian as well as non-Christian organizations.

People come into the caring professions, and particularly into the mission field, for many reasons. Many are consciously or unconsciously motivated by their own childhood needs (see Ch. 40). They may have needs for power and autonomy that were not appropriately met as they grew up. They may personally identify with children in difficult circumstances. They may want to 'be there' and fight for children in a way that no one was or did for them as children. If the wounds of the past have been healed and the person is open to the transforming power of being loved by Christ and others, then some aspects of this motivation can be wonderfully used by God. Other issues, such as a person's need for power and autonomy, will need to be transformed into appropriate assertiveness, healthy interdependence and servant-inspired leadership. Workers who are thus transformed will not be afraid of the emotional and spiritual darkness of raw pain and thus will be able to stay and journey with children, young people and adults through it. In the Warner Child Protection personal staff interviews, recently developed in response to revelations of abuse in children's homes in the 1990s in the UK, interviewers examine the candidates' attitudes to power, autonomy and control; accountability; ethical issues and beliefs and value systems; motivations for doing the work; and emotional awareness and team work. An effective and 'safe' worker in the caring professions must be able to be a good reflective practitioner and be honest and open to working on their personal and professional issues. Sadly, no such standard interview procedures occur within most Christian organizations. Moreover, the potential for the abuse of power is even greater in Christian organizations, since people who are placed in management positions are often not gifted or properly trained in this area. Visionaries who conceive organizations are rarely gifted with the skills to properly run them once they grow to a certain size. Neither do these people always have the insight and humility to relinquish their 'babies' to the care of better equipped staff and able managers who will nurture the staff's emotional, intellectual and professional needs. Often organizations stumble on, with staff being badly hurt in the process by ill-defined or non-existent job descriptions, staff development (mentoring, training, supervision), safe practice guidelines, personal and professional boundaries and good practice guidelines. All of this results in a poorer service and even harm to those whom God has sent us to serve, as well as damage to the staff involved. Valuable staff members often leave missionary organizations and child-care agencies because of these issues. These problems can also result in staff who are poorly motivated, deskilled, less effective and fearful. Sadly, they can even feel trapped by their own sense of God's calling on their lives – they do not want to let God down, so they remain in what they know is an unhealthy situation in order to do God's work. In situations of emotional abuse people often find themselves in a 'fog' (blinded by fear, obligation and guilt). They are often thus unable to cope with their own personal needs and dilemmas and are frustrated by the lack of union support and autonomy to challenge the power games of their organization. They feel trapped, powerless to release themselves from or successfully confront the cycles of abuse. Managers and staff within Christian organizations too often play the 'spiritual card', negating their staff with comments falsely attributed to God or ostensibly stemming from their sense of spiritual oversight and care of the person when, in fact, they are simply abusing God in their power games.

The way forward: Emotional awareness

What is the way forward? This book has begun to address many of these issues and offer some solutions in terms of better organizational and personal practice. However well-equipped we are in terms of our skills and knowledge, if we do not have an awareness of our emotional world and the impact of that world on our own development, on the development of others and on our interactions and relationship dynamics, we are but clanging cymbals (1 Cor. 13:1).

So what is emotional awareness? Emotional awareness requires that we understand the dynamics of our emotional world, how emotions work, what our emotional needs are and how to manage our stress (Baker, 1995). We need to be able to see what factors lead us to react to our current events with responses learned from our pasts (what Transactional Analysis calls 'script behaviour', since it is as if we are reacting to internal scripts of decisions we made as children to keep safe). We also need to be aware of what events we are able to react to in a congruent, real way based simply on the present. Frank Lake, in his book *Clinical Theology* (1986), describes us as living within a dynamic cycle of acceptance, which leads to sustenance, which leads to significance, which leads to achievement. Emotional awareness is a dynamic progressive process of growth as we journey as people, and especially as Christians, towards accepting ourselves and others with our differences and similarities – rather than expecting or needing others to merge with us in order to feel safe. Emotional awareness requires us to recognize the impact of stress on our lives and how we can work with it effectively, thus providing ourselves with sustenance, status, strength and vitality. We need not to be handicapped by our pasts or paralysed by stresses in our present situations but free to achieve and confront our fears and develop our gifts.

The Bible speaks of our goal as Christians to experience the freedom of knowing that we are adopted as God's heirs (Rom. 8:15–17). When we give our lives to Christ, he gives us back our lives in true fullness. Eric Berne, in his exposition on Transactional Analysis (1964), speaks of the goal of therapy as being 'autonomy', which he defines as being a combination of awareness, spontaneity and intimacy. If a person is emotionally free (from his past life), then he can be more aware of his world (as a child is) and can respond in a real and spontaneous way (as a child can) – free from constraints imposed by others. Such a person is also able to freely express thoughts, feelings and behaviours with another person. Berne speaks about how many of us are closed off from our feelings, desires and reactions to our world because we are caged by scripts and fears. If we are unaware of our problems, we will be unable to identify the roots of them in the chains of our past experiences or to find solutions for them to enable us to be free of them. Even if we become aware that we have a problem, we may be too fearful to go into the pit of our pain to discover the truth and learn the skills and insight to walk towards freedom. Berne's ideas throw some light on what Christ meant when he said that we need to become as little children in order to enter the kingdom of God. For humanistic therapists, the goal is for the client to achieve enough security with the therapist so that she can enter the pit of her pain. The therapeutic relationship is the anchor and the vessel for reworking old damaging relationships, releasing pain, enhancing awareness and developing new skills to equip us to work effectively with others.

So how do we as Christians, working with colleagues, children, young people and their families who are often holding incredible bundles of pain which prevent them from becoming the people God wanted them to be, achieve emotional awareness? Most people in the world would not be able to access psychotherapies, even it were the norm in their culture for them to talk about difficulties or to see themselves as individuals separate from their family or group. Most of us find it difficult to acknowledge our emotional needs and provide ourselves with the rest and rhythm in our lives that Christ modelled so powerfully (Luke 5:16) – never mind accepting that we need counselling or therapy. As a result, we are caught in dysfunctional games of interacting, playing out parent-child dynamics of victim, rescuer and persecutor (Stewart and Joines, 1987) and condemning ourselves for having needs. However, as well as calling us to be self-controlled, alert and wise (1 Pet. 5:8), Christ also calls us to be honest with him and with one another about our needs (Isa. 58:11; Phil. 4:19) and calls us to be in relationship with one another and with him. Poverty of relationship is often the most damaging influence in a person's life. As Henri Nouwen (1990) explores so powerfully, we are called to be in relationship. Larry Crabb takes this up in his book on connecting (1997), in which he challenges the humanistic views that emotional awareness, motivation and insight alone are the keys to a person's journey of change. As Keith White (2001) has discussed (see Chapter 16), human beings have five core needs: security, significance, boundaries, community and creativity. Community is one of our basic needs. Community and unity bring a sense of peace and release our creativity. As Brother Roger from the Taize Community (2002) states:

> . . . peace in found in creativity. How can we begin to trust in all simplicity? Peace is perhaps created step by step, discreetly in the relationships between individuals, tiny bridges of friendship across the map of Europe and the world, bringing reconciliation and hope, seeds of true understanding among nations, of course with obvious limits but also holding out a new hope in the history of mankind.

Such relationships – bridges built out of humility, awareness and love – are not built by 'magic'. As Crabb explains, they are built by us becoming more like Christ himself.

1. They provide us with a taste of Christ delighting in us – the essence of connecting is accepting who we are and envisioning who we could be.

2. Christ diligently searches for the good he has put in us (an affirming exposure) – remaining calm as our badness and past is made visible, keeping confidence that good lies underneath.

3. He gently exposes what is bad and painful (a disruptive exposure) – claiming opportunities to reveal the grace that the difficult contents of our hearts need.

As we grow in our awareness of ourselves and others, we grow towards true maturity, wisdom and true freedom as children of God. We build relationships based on honesty, grace and truth that strengthen us as individuals and as a family in Christ. All of this stems from growth not only in psychological awareness, but also in spiritual awareness. As we realize what damage has been done in our pasts and how we are at risk of repeating that damage in our present and future, true freedom comes from realizing that Christ does not bring us out of our wilderness to take us back again. He takes us out to take us on to the promised land. He takes us to a place where we can be emotionally free, learning to understand the seasons of our lives and the need for 'successful wintering so we can develop depth, hardiness and the ability to grow to full potential when the spring thaws set in' (Munday, 2002). Many of us feel that we need to permanently be in the driving seat. We are afraid even to sleep, lest the world perish without us being in control. Life is difficult, pilgrimage is difficult. But God spreads a table for us in the presence of our enemies (Ps. 23). He makes us a place of springs in Baca (Ps. 84:6). Yet, as we come to be more aware of God and of ourselves in relationship to others, we realize that it is often in the places of difficulty, of risk and setback that joy, rest and peace are found. Jesus promises us that he has overcome the world (John 16:33). God promises that he will restore the years that have been taken from us (Joel 2:25). But he also requires that we do not rob others, and especially children, of their heritage by being dishonest about who and what we are. God requires us to embrace discipline – to walk with him each day in humility and trust. We need to seek out safe people (Cloud and Townsend, 1995) who can mentor us and teach us the new skills that we need to learn, who can challenge us about the health and wisdom of our current relationships (Cloud, 1995) and who can help us to learn to make safe attachments and have good boundaries. In so doing we will be witnesses of Christ's transforming power in our lives and a light to his world. Without God, we who are called 'wise' so often cannot extract ourselves from the problems that we have created.

> Our greatest challenge today in the midst of all the confusion, conflict and struggle in our lives, and in the lives of those around us is the task of bringing hope to our world. Your task when you leave this cathedral tonight is to go out and to be bearers of the Gospel to people you meet, in word, in deed, sometimes in the sharing of pain or anguish or anger but above all in love. (Murphy-O'Connor, 2002)

> So don't deny the tangle and the talents – the varied web of what has made you who you are. Every step is part of the journey. On this journey even the false starts are part of the journey, experience that moves you on towards truth. "You are my especial patrons," said Helena, "and patrons of all latecomers, of all who have a tedious journey to make to the truth. Pray for me and for my poor overloaded son." It won't do to think of Christianity as a faith that demands of you an embarrassed pretence of a simplicity that has no connection with reality. Isn't this what often leads people not to take Christianity seriously? Evelyn Waugh, in his book *Helena* (1950), like so many writers knew what it was for imagination to twist around on itself like a snake. He knew about the gaps that open between work and life, how a work, finished and beautiful in its own terms, emerges out of a human background of failure and confusion. His Helena is praying for her literary creator. The writing is a prayer for absolution. The Wise Men stand at the cradle with a clear job to do for us and Helena addresses them unforgettably: "For his sake who did not reject your curious gift, pray always for all the learned, the oblique, the delicate, let them not be quite forgotten at the throne of God when the simple come into their kingdom." (Williams, 2002)

Thanks to God's grace and love, we will not be forgotten. We simply need to continue to trust him each day in humility and truth as we seek to be instruments of his transforming power, bringing light to his world.

– Questions to Consider–

1 Honestly assess yourself in terms of your ability to reflect critically on your own practice and accept feedback from others. What is one thing you could do to gain strength in this area?

2 Reflect on the 'safety' of your organization, identify the potential power imbalances and assess the general levels of emotional awareness. What steps could you take to improve these factors?

3 Try to see yourself through Christ's loving and pure eyes. What would he affirm in you? What is he calling you to give up or change in order to grow more like him?

CHAPTER 42

Conflict Resolution
with Colleagues and Children

Sharon Prior and Colin Bennett with Steve Bartel

Introduction

FOR most people, conflict is something to be avoided at all costs. It is seen at the very least to be an irritation and at the very worst to be destructive and dangerous. Many Christians consider conflict to be unbiblical and therefore not something with which they should be involved.

However, this does not have to be the case. Usually negative experiences with conflict are a result of the conflict not being understood and resolved. Conflict in itself can be a very positive experience. It can help to develop ideas, to encourage creativity and to develop healthy debate. It can help young people to establish boundaries in their lives, as they learn to take responsibility for themselves and to respect the boundaries of others. Cloud and Townsend develop this thinking in their book *Boundaries* (Cloud and Townsend, 1992). So it is important when working with colleagues and young people that conflict is not always seen as negative.

Whenever two or more parties (individuals, groups or nations) are in contact with one another, there is potential for conflict. This potential becomes even greater when the two people are from different backgrounds or generations or have different belief systems, when one person is being supervised by another, and when the two have differing goals. Conflict is a natural part of life and should not be avoided or covered up. It does not necessarily have to be a problem, if it is understood and resolved properly.

The Bible teaches us about conflict and different ways of handling it. From Genesis to Revelation we can see how God's people were involved in conflict situations. There will also, inevitably, be conflict among Christians working to help 'children at risk'. But the Bible offers us some practical principles for solving conflicts in a godly way.

Preventing destructive conflict

Understanding how conflict might escalate in certain situations may help to prevent it from getting to the stage where parties are completely at loggerheads. There are many theories of conflict resolution.[1] In this chapter we will look at the theory put forward by David Cormack in his book *Peacing Together*, because it sets out the conflict escalation and resolution in easy to follow stages. This model gives a clear view of the way in which intervention can happen at each stage.

Cormack describes the three main phases of conflict escalation (Cormack, 1989, p. 36). The first phase is 'separation', where people begin to recognize their differences. Open, honest communication at this stage will help to prevent conflict from going any further. If that communication does not occur, however, one of the parties will start to see the other as the opposition and will distance herself from the other. If both parties follow the biblical advice of Matthew 18:15–20 at this stage, then it may be possible to stop the conflict before it proceeds to the next phase.

If the conflict is not resolved at the first stage of separation it proceeds to the second stage, which Cormack calls the divergence stage. The interaction between the two parties begins to get more heated at this stage and people's differences become much more pronounced. The conflict starts to get nasty, as one or both parties look for opportunities to undermine the other. At this stage it may be necessary to bring in someone who can negotiate between the two parties to bring some semblance of order. By the time the conflict has escalated to this second stage, the hostilities need to be addressed and calmed before healthy communication can begin.

If this calming down period is not forthcoming, then the conflict develops into Cormack's third stage, which is the 'destructive' stage. At this stage the parties see each other as enemies and try to inflict as much damage on the other party as possible. This stage can continue for some time and may only stop if the parties move away from each other or if the conflict exhausts them. However, the fact that the heat of the conflict cools does not mean that the conflict has been resolved. All the hurt feelings, anger and bitterness can still be there.

Sadly, people working overseas often tend to leave conflict that has reached the destructive stage unresolved. There are many reasons for this. Sometimes it is just easier to come home and try to forget about it. In other cases, people take such conflict as the excuse they are looking for to return without losing face, because they are finding their work difficult. Missionary organizations say that one of the main reasons for people returning from the field is the breakdown of relationships with other missionaries. Leaving the field may be the only way that someone can get out of the situation, but such action leaves conflict unresolved and people go into other jobs carrying their baggage with them.

So how can people prevent conflict from reaching the destructive phase? There are various things that can be done to prevent such escalation of conflict situations. The following list gives some ideas, although it is not exhaustive:

- *Build healthy relationships* with those with whom you are working. This will help open channels of communication so that issues can be discussed before they get to the divergence phase. There is no substitute in building healthy relationships for spending time and having fun together. Whether you are building relationships with colleagues or the children with whom you are working, spending this time will create a good foundation for discussing differences of opinion, expectations and ways of working. Good communication is the key to preventing conflict situations arising. Some very powerful emotions can surface when conflict arises, and it is important to deal with these emotions in an appropriate way. Fear and anger are the two most common emotions, and these need to be acknowledged and talked about before people can move on. Failure to do this properly will almost certainly result in the conflict escalating.

- *Prayer* can help bind people together and help us to see other people's ways of doing things. It can also help in changing the negative attitudes that one person might have against another. The Bible tells us, 'as far as it depends on you, live at peace with everyone' (Rom. 12:18). This does not mean that we should sweep our differences under the carpet, but rather that we should get them into the open and resolve them together. We are to be 'peacemakers' rather than 'peacekeepers' (Matt. 5:9).

Exodus 34:6–7 sets out the Christian's example: 'The LORD, the LORD, the compassionate and gracious God, slow to anger, abounding in love and faithfulness, maintaining love to thousands, and forgiving wickedness, rebellion and sin . . .' It is difficult to harbour negative thoughts about someone when we love that person as God loves us.

- *Being clear about goals and expectations* is another way that we can prevent potential conflict situations. If people know where they are heading and what is expected of them, it is less likely that misunderstanding and resentment will build up.

- *Using positive discipline* when working with young people also helps to prevent confrontation and conflict. We are often quick to discipline children when they have done something wrong, and this gives them the impression that they only get attention when they are naughty. Giving rewards for good behaviour reverses this trend and shows them that good behaviour will receive attention as well. If the purpose of the bad behaviour is to get attention, then positive discipline will mean that you are less likely to get into a situation where you have to confront a young person, thus avoiding a conflict situation.

- *Being aware of the attacks of the devil* is another way that we can prevent conflicts from arising. Although Satan does not cause all conflicts, his influence to bring division through lies and unfair judgements cannot be underestimated. Christians need to daily 'put on the armour of God' in the area of defending their relationships (Eph. 6:11).

- *Learn to live with each other's differences.* The fact that different people on a team have different views can be very healthy, as long as the tensions are well managed. We should not expect everyone to agree with everything that is discussed. The world would be a very boring place if we all thought the same things!

Resolving conflict

Sometimes conflict escalates to such a degree that people find themselves in a full-blown argument before they realize what has happened. Once the conflict has reached the destructive phase, serious remedial action needs to be taken.

Cormack sets out three phases for trying to resolve conflict when it has reached the destructive phase (Cormack, 1989, p. 108). The first phase is that of 'disengagement'. The people involved must admit that there is a problem and that they want to do something about it. Sometimes it takes a third party to enable the people involved in the conflict to do this. There needs to be a ceasing of hostilities and a desire to sort out the problem. Both parties also have to want to find a solution and recognize that each side may need to take some of the blame for what has happened. Once this has been done they can move to the next phase, which is 'convergence'.

In this phase, the facts and feelings of the issue need to be aired in a safe environment and the people involved need to look to the future and what they would like to see happen. In order to move forward, it is essential that there is open communication at this stage. People need to express their feelings and frustrations so that there will not be ongoing and lingering bitterness and resentment. It is important that people are in an environment where they feel listened to in a non-judgemental way. It is important that we are working towards peace (*'shalom'*) rather than a cessation of violence. Resolution has to be active and not passive.

Once this has been accomplished, the parties reach the third and final phase of conflict resolution, 'integration'. In this phase both sides need to confess their part in allowing the conflict to escalate, repent of it and ask for forgiveness. This is normally the most difficult of the three stages. In order to reach complete reconciliation, it is important to work through all three stages. Too often, Christians try and jump to the third stage without working through the facts and feelings that caused the problem. This short-circuiting results in papering over the cracks rather than achieving real reconciliation. The problem will almost certainly raise its ugly head again in the future if the parties take such short cuts.

Resolving conflict: A real-life situation

The three phases outlined above can be seen very clearly in the following case study.

John and Jeff, two thirteen-year-old boys, did not feel that church was for them. However, both sets of parents were committed church members and made John and Jeff attend every Sunday. The young people stayed for the first ten minutes of the service and then went out to their Sunday school classes, where John and Jeff were disruptive, argued a lot and created stress for their long-suffering youth leader. One Sunday this became intolerable for the youth leader and so he marched the two boys back into the church to sit with their parents. This humiliated the boys, embarrassed the parents and felt like a relief to the youth leader.

After a cooling-off period and at the instigation of an elder in the church, the two boys, their parents and the youth leader sat down and discussed the problem (the disengagement phase). The boys were angry with the youth leader for humiliating them in front of the whole church and for the fact that their parents had grounded them for a week. Larsen and Brendtro, in their book *Reclaiming Our Prodigal Sons and Daughters*, says,

> Young people who act in cruel and mean ways are seething with anger, possessing what Louis Ramsey termed "free-floating anger." This anger is accompanied with feelings of frustration and helplessness which make them perpetually irritable like a person who wakes up on the wrong side of the bed day after day.

The parents were angry with the youth leader for not being able to control their sons and for interrupting their worship time. They were also angry with the boys for embarrassing them in front of the whole church. The youth leader was angry with the parents because he perceived that they did not want to take responsibility for the boys. He was also angry with the boys for making his job as youth leader so difficult. He was, after all, volunteering to work with these young people.

Things were quite tense at first, but eventually, with the elder's help, they began to discuss their anger and frustration openly. Once their feelings were out in the open, they were able to work through a vision for the future (the convergence phase). The youth leader wanted to suspend the boys for at least two weeks, as punishment for what they had done, and he also wanted them to sign a behavioural agreement when they returned to the group after the two weeks. The parents were not very receptive to this, but after some discussion they decided to support it. The parents wanted the youth leader to deal with disciplinary issues differently in the future and not repeat the incident of returning the boys to them during the service. The youth leader agreed to this. The boys wanted to make the Sunday school more interesting by introducing other methods of communication and they suggested topics that they could discuss in the future. They also wanted their parents to understand that they did not always want to attend church. Sometimes they wanted to play with their local football team on a Sunday morning. The youth leader agreed to work with the boys on the programme for the term. The parents were not very happy about the boys missing church to play football, but they did eventually agree to this.

All three groups apologized to each other and made a decision to try and work together to meet all their needs, even though they did not necessarily agree with some of them (the integration phase).

Interestingly, the rest of the Sunday school students were also fed up with the behaviour of the two boys. They drew up a code of Christian behaviour for the group. When the two boys returned to Sunday school, the rest of the group expected them to sign this code of conduct, which they did.

Conflict was not always avoided subsequently, but things did settle down. It was a turning point in the relationship between the church and the boys. Because the boys now felt that they had some choices in their lives, the relationships between the boys and their parents also improved. The youth leader started to enjoy his work with the Sunday school class because they were interested in what he was trying to teach them, since it was relevant to them. The youth leader and parents also made a conscious decision to communicate more together for the sake of the boys. They finally realized that they were actually on the same side, wanting the best for the boys. Things were not perfect, but conflict resolution did bring about reconciliation.

When working with children and adolescents in the whole area of conflict it is important that adults recognize the developmental characteristics of the child's age group. It is essential that we do not try and move a young person too quickly through the process of resolving conflict. While we must treat them with respect and encourage them, we should not try to force them to talk through their feelings and forgive the other party.

Children who have been mistreated, abused, abandoned or malnourished, or children who are fiercely independent (such as street children), will have a 'life view' that is vastly different from that of most Christians, and the parties in conflict will view the disagreements in very different ways. Both the causes and the solutions (and even the procedures for resolution) will be perceived differently. This may also be true for adults who were 'at risk' as children. It is up to the more mature of the parties, or the neutral mediator, to make sure that resolution can be conducted in a way that is both sensitive to the differences and that will result in a process that all involved can clearly understand.

Role conflicts

It would be wrong in a chapter such as this if the whole area of role conflict was not mentioned. This can be a major area of conflict when working with children and young people.

A role conflict is a conflict that arises 'when the demands of one role are incompatible with the demands of another role' (Johnson and Johnson, 1997, p. 569). An example of this is when a very depressed young person asks a professionally trained counsellor for help. There might appear to be no problem in this situation. However, if the counsellor is also the mother of the young person, then there is a serious conflict in her role. Is she the mother or a professional counsellor in this situation? Is it possible to separate the two roles?

Another example can be found in the movie *Star Wars*. Darth Vader and Luke Skywalker were sworn enemies, but when Darth told Luke that they were actually father and son a role conflict arose. How could Luke now kill his own father? Darth tries to seduce Luke into joining his side (the dark side) in order to overcome the role conflict, but Luke puts his role as a champion for good before his relationship with his father.

Role conflict could be a problem for the children's worker in various realms of ministry (e.g., professional standards, spiritual development, pastoral care versus therapeutic care, etc.).

Of all the conflicts we may encounter, the notion of role conflict in children's work is immensely significant. How can a worker handle such conflicts and maintain ethical standards without being overcome by the issue?

The following examples illustrate real-life role conflicts and the tensions surrounding them.

> As a freelance management trainer, my role demanded me to travel extensively and work long hours away from home. My Christian 'role' (responsibility) as a father of three young children and a husband seemed to challenge and clash with this work role. The conflict between these two roles had to be dissipated. I chose to be a responsible Christian and changed job.

This example, however, is not only about family and work. There is also a conflict here concerning spiritual roles. What would God think if I chose money over family? Or even status from this prestigious post over family? In this one example, the role conflicts cross the boundaries of family, employment, money, power, spirituality and even gender (in that the choice, and the career, belonged to a male). In reality this may not be a difficult choice, but for many these role conflicts present regular tensions and dilemmas. For example, how does the woman careerist feel about leaving a sick child at home? How does a husband feel staying at home to be a house-husband and giving up a career? What about a youth and children's minister who works with a pastor who feels that adult preaching is the true ministry of the church and therefore commands a higher salary?

In all of these examples, the complex mix of money, sex, power, family and spirituality causes tensions as roles conflict. Because it is difficult to escape these tensions in daily life, it is vital to consider and analyze them as an aspect of both professional Christian ministry and other vocations as well.

Conclusion

We have seen from this chapter that conflict is not always negative; it can also be creative and positive. However, it is necessary for the worker to understand his attitude to conflict before he can effectively resolve conflict situations with other parties. Resolving conflict is not always easy. Conflict resolution can take time, and the worker needs to realize this and not go for a quick solution, which only papers over the cracks. Although it is difficult and time-consuming, it is something that is worth working at in all areas of life.

The professional worker also needs to understand the different role conflicts she may face when working with children so that she does not become confused about the role she is assuming at any one time.

Note
1. See, e.g., Jones (1995), pp. 65ff., or Chalke (1995), pp. 103ff.

– Questions to Consider –

1 What is your attitude to conflict? Do you try to ignore it and hope it will go away or do you face it and deal with it head-on? What are the advantages and disadvantages of these different approaches?

2 Think of a conflict situation you have been in and try to identify how you might have been able to break the cycle of separation, divergence and destruction.

3 What are some of the role conflicts that you encounter in your daily life? How do you handle the tensions surrounding them?

– CHAPTER 43 –

Group Processes, Socio-Cultural Variables and Team Dynamics

Cressida Pryor

AN old rabbi once asked to be shown the difference between heaven and hell. He was taken to a room with a big table. In the centre of the table was a bowl of delicious food and around it sat a group of starving people. Each one held a spoon. They could reach the food because their spoons were very long, but they could not turn them around and put the food into their mouths. They were in hell. Then the rabbi was taken to another room. Here again there was a table with a bowl of wonderful food and around it a group of people holding long-handled spoons. But these people looked cheerful and well fed. They were in heaven. What was the difference? The second group had learned to feed each other, and no one was hungry.

Dr S.H. Foulkes, the founder of group analysis in Britain after World War II, maintained that the so-called 'individual' is, for practical purposes, an abstraction. We can therefore only make sense of people in terms of the groups they belong to or were part of in the past. The most influential group for each of us is the earliest: our family. Foulkes further maintained that only through new and beneficial group experience could any damaging effects of the earlier group experiences be corrected.

Foulkes (through his observations of what happens in therapy groups) saw the group as something that all of its members help to create, with two types of contribution. The first is what each member brings in terms of his or her 'relating' difficulties or strengths. This becomes more apparent as the group meets over a period of time (e.g., verbal domination of the group, persistent lateness, always feeling marginalized). The other type of contribution that people bring to groups is that each member has an inherent urge towards group understanding and communication, which ultimately breaks down the isolation and individualistic destructive behaviour which perhaps led them to such a group in the first place (Foulkes and Anthony, 1984). This perhaps rather optimistic and idealistic view of human nature has been challenged more recently with Nitsun's description of the destructive forces in the group, the anti-group. Acknowledging and harnessing this aggression can help to contain and limit the destructive potential of the group, transforming it into a more therapeutic entity (Nitsun, 1996). For most of us, working in different groups, either as a leader or as a participant, is a fact of life. Being part of a group can be very rewarding, and at times it can also be frustrating. With some of these basic theories from Foulkes and Nitsun in mind, let's turn to consider how research into group dynamics can assist us in facilitating different groups and avoiding some common pitfalls.

The following are important points to be aware of when leading groups:

1. There should be clarity regarding the venue, time and 'housekeeping' issues.
2. The group's aims, objectives and boundaries should be clear to everyone.
3. Provide ground rules (these can be negotiated with the group).
4. In training groups, agree upon a learning contract negotiated between students and trainers.
5. Be aware of your own competencies and limitations.
6. Be aware of potential difficulties and how to deal with them.
7. Encourage people to commit to attending the group.
8. Be aware of your own power and the risk of abusing it.
9. Know where to go for support and supervision.

What to look for in groups

Part of the art of leading effective groups is cultivating an awareness of what is happening within the group on different levels in terms of participation and influence.

Participation

One indication of involvement is verbal participation. Look for differences in the degree of participation among members.

1. Who are the high participators?
2. Who are the low participators?
3. Do you see any shift in participation? Do you see any possible reason for this in the group's interaction?

4. How are the silent people treated? How is their silence interpreted (e.g., as consent, disinterest or fear)?

5. Who talks to whom? What are your ideas or assumptions about why this happens?

Influence

Influence and participation are not the same thing. Some people may speak very little yet capture the attention of the whole group. Others may talk a lot but are generally not listened to by other members.

1. Which members are high in influence? (That is, when they talk others seem to listen.)

2. Which members are low in influence? (Others do not listen to or follow them.) Is there a shifting of influence?

3. Do you see any rivalry in the group? Is there a struggle for leadership? If so, what effect does it have on other group members?

Styles of influence

Influence can take many forms. It can be positive or negative; it can enlist the support of others or alienate them. How a person attempts to influence another may be the crucial factor in determining how open or closed the other will be towards being influenced. The following are four styles that frequently emerge in groups.

1. *Autocratic.* Does anyone attempt to impose his will or values on other group members or try to push them to support him? Does anyone evaluate or pass judgement on other group members? Do any members block action when the group is not moving in the direction they desire? Who pushes to get the group organized?

2. *Peacemaker.* Who eagerly supports other group members' decisions? Does anyone consistently try to avoid conflict or unpleasant feelings by pouring oil on the troubled waters? Is any member typically deferential toward other group members? Do any members appear to avoid giving negative feedback?

3. *Laissez faire.* Are any group members getting attention by their apparent lack of involvement in the group? Does any group member go along with group decisions without seeming to commit herself one way or the other? Who seems to be withdrawn and uninvolved? Who does not initiate activity, participates mechanically and only in response to another member's question?

4. *Democratic.* Does anyone try to include everyone in a group decision or discussion? Who expresses his feelings and opinions openly and directly without evaluating or judging others? Who appears to be open to feedback and criticisms from others? When feelings run high and tension mounts, which members attempt to deal with the conflict in a problem-solving way?

Team dynamics

It is no surprise to learn that most of the problems that groups experience also apply to work teams. Therapy groups and work teams are differentiated mainly by the amount of time people spend with each other and a certain expectation of workplace etiquette that may preclude the more direct expression of feeling often fostered in the therapy setting.

To minimize the potential problems in a work team and maximize its performance, it may be useful to use the analogy of a football team manager wanting to get players into their best possible positions. You would need to find out quickly what skills each team member had and where each could play best. You could then assign certain players to defensive roles and others to attacking, or offensive, roles. When the actual game begins you would get your players, with their individual skills and preferences, to play together as a team. They should pass the ball rather than try to do all the work themselves. They should help and encourage each other – particularly when one member is under pressure.

Margerison and McCann (1985) have formulated a model, the 'team management wheel', which puts together the major work functions and relates them to people's major skills. Major work functions are divided into the following areas:

- Advising
- Innovating
- Promoting
- Developing
- Organizing
- Producing
- Inspecting
- Maintaining

While people may adopt several functions in a group, they usually have one preferred role or function that they adopt, or try to adopt, in different groups (e.g., social situations, work meetings, etc.). These functions in turn fall into five main categories, or roles: explorers, organizers, controllers and advisors, united by the crucial function of linkers (who may also take on other functions but who may also be primarily linkers). All teams need people who can co-ordinate and integrate others, regardless of their role preferences. On most occasions this person should be the manager.

The 'team management wheel' is based on the view that there are two major elements in any team:

1. Required behaviour
2. Role preferences

Required behaviour consists of:

- Exploring behaviours associated with searching, creativity, opportunity, contacting, selling and other externally orientated activities
- Controlling behaviours associated with concern for detail, precision, standards, systems, rules, regulations and ordered ways of doing things according to a plan.

Role preferences generally fall into:

- Advisory roles which provide the invaluable support services of information, planning, research, training and design
- Organizational roles which concentrate more on the 'front' end and delivering the product or service.

Some people will prefer to work in an exploring role while others may prefer to work with a more controlling approach. Sometimes people choose their role based on their preference for advising or organizing.

Conclusion

Research into which factors encourage healthy, happy and fully functional families has identified four main points that also apply to good group work and efficient team working (Skinner, 1995):

1. Being able to have fun together with laughter and humour.
2. Negotiating time apart and time together that is mutually satisfying and agreeable.
3. Upholding clear and consistent boundaries both inside and outside the group.
4. Being able to communicate openly and clearly with each other.

We need to promote these good practice factors so that the teams we work with become vessels of growth and development that are honouring and fruitful for all participants.

– Questions to Consider –

1 Missionaries returning from the field and people working in office headquarters often speak of the way in which the dynamics of the team can have a greater, or as great, an impact upon them as the work with the children themselves. Discuss how a greater understanding of group dynamics, and the processes underpinning them, can improve our ability to work more effectively in groups in the future.

2 Use your understanding of team roles, dynamics and processes to analyse your current work situation or a previous situation in a team setting. What are the pitfalls and benefits of your team's group processes? How could you improve both your own practice and the way in which the team works together as a whole in order to enable everyone to become more effective in their different roles?

3 God's command is 'to love our neighbour as ourselves'. Describe an example of 'tough love' from your own experiences (either towards yourself or another). What prevents us from consistently behaving in a way which witnesses to that love both in and for one another? How can you use what you have learned in this book to change and enable you to be a 'light in the darkness and a signpost on the way' to and with others and the children?

– PART EIGHT –

Case Studies from around the World: Children and Projects

Introduction PART Eight contains a wide range of different case studies, each of which gives a profile of children who are at risk or who have already become victims in a particular area. These profiles are intended to be a representative cross-section, describing the different ways in which children are 'at risk' around the world and explaining the various types of assistance that can be offered to them. The names and identification indicators of those children profiled below who are not entirely fictional have been altered to ensure their protection.

We have avoided using the categories that some agencies typically employ (e.g., 'children in prison'), because many children who fall outside these categories are excluded from care. A 'child at risk' will often need assistance according to the definitions of several categories. Helping a family, or better still a community, to be more resilient through spiritual and physical transformation will therefore have far more impact than assistance focused on a single issue. When categorizing 'children at risk' it is best to avoid attaching labels to groups of children that are unhelpful and even damaging (for example, 'former child prostitutes' or 'handicapped children').

Each case study in the four chapters that follow consists of a profile of a child, followed by a profile of a project seeking to address some of the issues presented in the child profile. The purpose behind profiling different projects is to give a broadly based understanding of how different programmes address different needs in different contexts and to give the reader an idea of the potential of different interventions, the resources required, possible problems and likely outcomes. Some of the organizations described in the following case studies are high-level, experienced, government-supported programmes. Others are newer and much more basic, but they are all in their own way serving Christ by serving children.

There are profiles below from Europe, the Americas, Africa, Asia and Australasia. This diversity enables the reader to see how individual children experience life very differently in a wide range of environments. It also highlights the fact that projects need to be appropriate to the context. While it is right that some projects address the root causes of a problem through prevention and education, other projects will focus on rehabilitation.

It will be helpful for you, as you work with different children, to put together a portfolio of child profiles and case studies after listening to children tell their own stories and visiting and observing the work of other secular and Christian NGOs in your area. When you are writing such case studies yourself, however, it is absolutely crucial to understand the confidential nature of these documents. All case notes with identifying details for children in your own programme should be carefully and securely filed. Names should be changed and identifying details removed (as we've done with the case studies below) for any materials not filed in this way.

Glenn Miles and Josephine-Joy Wright

– Questions to Consider –

You will not have enough information to answer all of the questions below for each organization, but the vulnerability of the organizations to be critiqued in this exercise might encourage you to constructively look at your own organization.

When looking at each case study you primarily want to ask, on the one hand, how the child is vulnerable and at risk and, on the other hand, how she is resilient and what resources she has access to. Secondly, you will want to ask what the strengths of the organization are as well as how it could be improved. You will also want to continuously be assessing how you can use what you are learning in your own context.

The following questions will help to guide you through a more in-depth analysis of any of these profiles.

Child level

1 Do you think the child would describe his own situation in the same way he has been described, or differently? (See Glenn Miles, Chapter 2.) What can we learn from this analysis?

2 Using Susan Greener's approach, look at the child in terms of a 'dynamic systems perspective'. What environmental conditions exist that influence the child's development? What qualities does the child bring to her physical and social worlds? How do cultural beliefs influence the child and her treatment by others? What resources are available to the child? (See Susan Greener, Chapter 5.)

3 Look at the child's environment and assess what key risk factors are operating at a local level. (See Josephine-Joy Wright and Keith White, Chapter 16.)

4 What are the risks to the child on a broader national, regional and global level? (See Glenn Miles, Chapter 15 and Bryant Myers, Chapter 14.)

5 To what extent is the child considered in the cultural, religious, historical, political and social context of their community?

Programme level

6 How does the programme give priority to building relationships – with the child, family, community, organization or institution and between organizations?

7 How does the programme work with, and consider, other levels – peer, family, community, national, international, spiritual? In what way does it balance preventative strategies with rehabilitation?

8 How does the programme try to meet the holistic – spiritual, physical, mental, emotional and social – aspects of the child's development (including educational and vocational aspects)?

9 How are strategies for promoting children's resilience integrated into the programme? What type of interventions or training are being used or would be appropriate for parents, caregivers and children-at-risk workers? (See Susan Greener, Chapter 18.)

10 How do the adults actively listen to and co-operate with children, according to their ages and abilities, in things that affect them? How are children actively involved in planning and programme development?

11 How does the programme encourage the development of parental responsibilities towards children? How has the organization listened to and involved parents or caregivers?

12 In what ways does the programme advocate with, or on behalf of, children and their families at local, national or international levels?

13 How does the programme use the CRC, or how could they use it? How are Christian principles embedded in the work, or how could they be? How can either be used to inspire, rather than place boundaries around, practice? (See Paul Stephenson, Chapter 7.)

14 What is distinctly Christian about the programme that would make it stand apart from secular organizations working in the same sector?

15 How does the programme measure the impact of its work on children and their families? How effective is the programme in improving the lives and environments of the children and their families?

CHAPTER 44

Children at Risk of Not Receiving the Basic Needs of Food, Health, Education and Shelter

Children at risk because of malnutrition (East Africa)

Andrew Tomkins

Profile of a child

Fatima was born in a poor household in rural East Africa. Her mother's labour was long and hard, and neither she nor the traditional birth attendant had much knowledge of childbirth. So when the baby took a long time to breathe, they were really worried. Fatima's mother was only seventeen years old. She found it difficult to establish breastfeeding, but eventually baby Fatima attached and suckled. When she was a few days old, Fatima was taken to the health centre for a BCG immunization. The nurses there were concerned when they saw that she weighed less than 2.5 kilograms, because such a low weight is associated with decreased immunity, health and development.

Initially Fatima grew, but her grandmother persuaded her mother to give Fatima some fruit juice and diluted porridge from around the age of six weeks. Not surprisingly Fatima developed diarrhoea, became dehydrated and was not strong enough to breastfeed successfully. Fortunately the diarrhoea was treated with oral rehydration solution, but Fatima lost weight. When she was taken to the clinic, the nurses emphasized the importance of maintaining breastfeeding throughout illness and she regained her growth. She did well for the next few months of life and the nurses recorded satisfactory weight gain on the 'Road to Health' card each time she visited for another immunization. Unfortunately, the clinic had run out of the vitamin A capsules that they were supposed to give to increase the baby's immunity.

At around four months of age Fatima developed chronic diarrhoea, would not eat and even refused breast milk. Her eyes became glazed as she developed vitamin A-deficiency. The clinic prescribed a large dose vitamin A capsule, thereby averting the danger of blinding malnutrition. She started suckling again

and took porridge regularly, but there were few vegetables available in this season and the family could not afford meat or fish (other important sources of vitamin A). By the end of the first year she weighed only six kilograms (compared with the 10 kg. which would be expected in a healthy, well-nourished baby). By now Fatima's mother was back at work in a stall at the market for many long hours, returning in the early evening. Fatima was left in her grandmother's care. Fatima's mother had asked the grandmother to feed her pulses, some oil and even a few dried fish, but the grandmother fed Fatima diluted porridge because she did not think it important – or perhaps because she did not have the time or the money to go to the market.

One evening the family noticed that Fatima's breathing was fast and laboured. The local transport service had stopped and nobody had any money for the expensive taxi, so Fatima remained breathless all night and was very ill in the morning. Fortunately Fatima's mother managed to get somebody to look after the stall while she took Fatima to the clinic for an antibiotic. The nurses were worried about the late presentation of the illness and her very low weight. They explained that if Fatima had been better nourished she would not have had such a severe episode of pneumonia. Fatima's mother did not say anything, but resentment burned inside her at being insulted in front of the other mothers.

Early in Fatima's second year of life she developed several episodes of malaria and some more diarrhoea. It was difficult to take Fatima to the clinic and the local traditional birth attendant advised the mother, with great confidence, to stop breastfeeding because her milk was obviously poisoned. Fatima's mother was really worried. She noticed that Fatima had pale eyes and tongue, especially after an episode of malaria, and that she was very weak and not moving properly.

By now Fatima's mother was pregnant again. There were several community nutrition groups in the village where mothers supported each other in the feeding of nutritious foods to infants and young children, but she was too busy to go, and the grandmother was unimpressed by all the advice. Food was in short supply because it was now the pre-harvest period when all the stores from last season were used up. People were more worried about this year's harvest because of the lack of rain than about a baby that did not seem to be growing very well.

Fatima remained a quiet child, apparently happy to sit without exploring or playing. She never got into mischief but had a rather sad countenance. Her hair grew ginger and her lips became paler as the combination of anaemia and malnutrition started to take a further toll on her development and on her resistance to infection. Fortunately one of the neighbours in the nutrition group noticed how badly she was doing and agreed to get support from the community. By now Fatima was big enough to be taken to the group by other mothers, even though Fatima's mother had to keep working. Fatima's father visited the child a few times after she was born but was never around after that.

Fatima survived the rigours of life in a poor home, but the impact of severe malnutrition and anaemia left scars and she never grew up to be as healthy or as intelligent as she could have been. Projects like the one described below are vital for the health and development of babies like Fatima.

Profile of a project

Many children in the village of Elala are short or thin or both, many are anaemic and about 10 per cent of them die, especially in the first month of life. The staff in the local government health centres had received training in nutrition, and they emphasized the importance of growth monitoring. The nurses set up cooking demonstrations, used flip charts and gave lots of talks. However, this community was poor; their diet consisted mainly of plantains with occasional groundnuts (or cassava when the rains were bad). In recent years they had been eating more cassava than plantains. Not surprisingly, much of the information from the nurses went over the heads of the mothers. They smiled politely as the nutritionists described foods that they could not afford and food preparation techniques that

they did not have time to do. The church leaders did not see what nutrition had to do with their preaching, and the community leaders felt that most of the nutritional problems were due to 'lazy' farmers and 'ignorant' mothers. There was not much sympathy for the malnourished children.

As part of an agreement that had been set up in the capital town of the district, without any consultation with people in the village, an NGO with funding from overseas arrived in the village. After a few meetings, they said they were going to provide food that should be targeted towards the most malnourished children. The people were excited about this, especially as they said they had enough food to support around one-third of the children. But, when the food was distributed, there were a lot of quarrels over which family should receive the food, and there was a lot of bitterness towards those who made the decisions. Again, the recipients had to listen to more lectures on the types of foods that they should have been giving to their children. Three years later the NGO ran out of money, the food stopped and the children were just as malnourished as they had been before the programme. Most mothers knew that nutrition was important for the health and well-being of their children but were not clear what they could do about it.

Several years later a new NGO arrived in the village, with considerable experience of working with communities and the government, but this time they brought no food, no supplies and did not have a four-wheel drive vehicle. Rather, they said they wanted to hold meetings with a wide range of people in the village to find out what some of the root causes of malnutrition were and how people could tackle the problems themselves. Initially people were very cynical and suspicious. However, people were getting desperate. Some harvests recently had been very poor.

After preliminary visits, the NGO sent two workers to live in the village for several weeks. During this visit they established friendships and set up meetings with different social groups. This time the leaders of the churches became much more interested. They were challenged to accept that their preaching and teaching could include issues of support and respect for women and better health and nutritional care for children. The pastors found that the people listened to their sermons better if they included real-life issues such as diet, disease and development. People were surprised when the NGO introduced participatory drama in the main village square on special festival days. The people noted that the NGO staff often asked the community and religious leaders to open with a speech or a prayer. The leaders felt important, the people were happy about the play and everybody enjoyed themselves – but the children were still malnourished.

The community did not at first realize that these were plays with a difference. The actors stopped after each act and developed a dialogue with the audience about issues related to nutrition. People were amazed at how wide-ranging the plays were; the plots covered relevant issues to do with water, pregnancy, the health of animals, child-spacing, HIV and alcoholism. As a result of the community meetings and the plays, the village and religious leaders agreed that they really ought to take nutrition more seriously. But they did not know whether they had a problem in their community or not.

The NGO agreed to do a survey in the village to identify what proportion of children were malnourished. They measured the weight and height of 300 children under five years of age and involved the children in working out and displaying the results. People were particularly interested to see how their results compared with the results of some villages in the next district. Charts were prepared and the results of the survey were fed back to the elders, religious leaders and community women's groups. People were really surprised to see the high level of stunting and thinness.

The NGO staff were specially trained in how to promote discussion of the results, leading always to analysis and plans. Initially people blamed the climate, the government and neighbours. Then they recognized that they themselves had many resources with which they could improve things. Not everybody joined in. There were some 'problem' families who many people in the community were rather annoyed about. They always made a mess, became involved in fights and quarrels, their children were ill behaved and dirty. But the church community leaders explained that these families needed to be considered, involved and supported.

The churches took a key role in including nutrition within their own groups, particularly in the groups for young mothers and youth. The parent-teachers' association started a school-feeding programme, collecting money from parents to provide a nutritious meal at

midday. Women attending the immunization clinics started their own growth monitoring activities in which the 'road to health' cards were examined every month – not just by the health workers who had previously shouted at them for using the wrong food, but also by the mothers themselves. They came to understand what it meant to have a line on a chart explaining the satisfactory, or otherwise, growth and development of their child.

A new Child to Child programme was started, based in the school, with the support of the teachers. These children started a vitamin A capsule distribution programme. Using a simple plastic strip, they monitored the thinness of all children under five years of age in the village. They reported back to the clinics, and their information was a key means of monitoring change in the programme. It may not have been rigorous enough to satisfy an epidemiologist, but it certainly gave evidence of trends and identified particularly thin children who needed early attention if they were not to be severely malnourished.

Several of the groups asked for some information in relation to childcare and family planning, and slowly the appearance of the village changed. There were more families using latrines, there were protected water supplies and the women's group started some new market gardens. These provided important vegetables for provision of vitamins within the diet and also increased the amount of money that the women had so that they could purchase more nutritious food items. The growth cards were filled in properly, the children were fed better and seemed cleaner and there was a general reduction in the attendance of children at the clinic with severe illness.

Life remained hard. There were still seasonal food shortages, major problems with malaria and diarrhoea and severe underlying poverty. But the local social safety nets that had been prepared by the community seemed to protect some of the more vulnerable children. There was a greater awareness of 'togetherness'. The church and community leaders promoted this, and people noted that the atmosphere in the community became much better. There were certainly fewer children with severe malnutrition.

Soon after their arrival, the NGO staff had explained that they would only be able to keep making visits for a three-year period. They would then need to move on to other communities and work to help them improve their quality of life with a particular focus on nutrition. They emphasized the importance of setting up links with government and development officers. The local community groups sometimes paid for the petrol of the government officers to leave the capital city and come out to them in the rural area with advice or supplies, or both. The community knew that they were entitled to a lot of advice and supplies, but they also knew that being remote cut them off from government provision. The community was surprised to see that the government officers quite liked coming out to visit them.

The village set up a nutrition committee. It had some key people on it, including the political leader, the headmaster and several pastors of the local churches. They played a key role in keeping the activities going, encouraging people to recognize that many of the resources for improving nutrition were available within the village.

Eventually the NGO moved away, as promised, to start up a programme in another community. However, the staff came back from time to time just to check how things were going. They were really pleased to see the way that the vision, skills, participation and activities were continuing. As a result of the positive initiatives that they had developed through their work with the NGO, the villagers noted that they could do a lot of things themselves and that the overall nutritional state of their children was getting better. It felt good.

Children at risk because of poor health (Cambodia)

Peter Sidebotham

Profile of a child

Dara, a three-year-old, was brought by his mother to the local district hospital near where they lived in Cambodia. His mother's main concern was that Dara could not walk.

Dara had been born at full term but had a low birthweight. He was reported to have problems with recurrent diarrhoea and chest infections. Dara had received his first two immunizations in infancy but had never completed the full course. Examination by a doctor showed that Dara was stunted and malnourished. He was pale and showed little interest in his surroundings, although he did respond to his mother. He had areas of infected, broken skin. The tone and power was reduced in all his muscles and he was unable to support his weight on his legs.

Health workers entered Dara in the community nutrition programme, through which he received food supplements, and his mother received training and support in budgeting, nutrition and health care, along with birth-spacing advice. He was treated for intestinal worms and given vitamins and iron supplements for anaemia. His immunizations were brought up to date. Over the following six months Dara gradually gained weight and muscle bulk. With the input of a therapist working with his mother, Dara started to take weight on his legs and eventually learned to walk. Over the same time period, Dara gradually became less withdrawn and began to show more interest in his environment.

Dara's case illustrates a number of issues related to poor health. He presented with one problem – his inability to walk. Assessment (through a history and examination) revealed other, underlying health issues. The most important of these was his poor nutrition. The mother's report illustrated the dangerous cycle of poor nutrition leading to increased susceptibility to infections, including diarrhoea, which in turn lead to worsening nutrition. The main target of health intervention was to tackle Dara's poor nutrition, without which any improvement would be marginal. Health workers also treated him for worms, anaemia and skin infections. Questions about his background revealed several factors contributing to his poor health, including his low birthweight and lack of immunizations and other preventative health care. Home visits brought other issues to light, such as overcrowding in the home, lack of access to sanitation or a reliable water source and the meagre and unstable family income. These visits also gave opportunities to work with the mother, family and wider community to tackle the root causes of Dara's health problems.

Servants to Asia's Urban Poor

As part of a wider urban community development programme in Phnom Penh, Cambodia, Servants to Asia's Urban Poor (Servants) is involved in a community health programme for 'children at risk'. The programme is primarily preventive in nature and operates at several levels in the family and community. What follows is a brief overview of the different aspects of the programme and a discussion of how the various aspects fit into a health strategy.

Primary prevention: Community immunization programme

A study in the local district in 1993 and a review of official health statistics showed that immunization levels in the district were low. Further research in the community revealed that, although levels improved over the following four years, there were large pockets with low coverage – particularly among the Vietnamese minority. Servants worked alongside the government health staff and the community women's association to improve immunization uptake. They established outreach teams to visit different slum areas on a weekly basis. These teams offer immunization and limited consultative health care for minor problems. Over the past few years Servants have supported the local workers in taking part in National Polio Immunization days. An impressively high uptake resulted from offering immunizations in a large number of community sites. This success has highlighted how much can be achieved even in very deprived communities.

'Child to Child' health education

Small teams of local workers visit schools in their area on a regular basis. In each class the team presents a health education lesson on a particular topic following the 'Child to Child' material (Hawes, Bailey and Bonati, 1994). Each session is interactive, involving the children in songs, quizzes and other activities, and the class is left with material to work on following the session. The programme has led to practical action in many of the schools – for example, teams of children clearing up rubbish in the school or neighbourhood; provision of wells for safe water; building toilet blocks with access for able and less physically agile children; and deworming children in schools.

Secondary prevention: Community nutrition programme

During the course of the overall programme, a number of malnourished children have been identified. Workers see these children for an initial medical assessment and deal with their immediate health needs. They then provide a home-based nutritional support programme for the families. This has included encouragement of breastfeeding, nutritional supplements where necessary, weekly home visits with training in budgeting, food preparation and other aspects of health and hygiene. Where staff workers identify other issues, such as domestic violence, birth-spacing needs or lack of income, they take steps to help the family or community identify resources and tackle the problem. Workers have found that many children in this programme are suffering from TB, and are therefore in need of both in-patient and out-patient treatment. Other children have been affected by HIV – either in themselves or their families.

Hospital-based health services

One of the major emphases of the health programme in its early stages was the training and empowerment of local hospital staff. The community made poor use of the hospital facilities, and local perceptions of the hospital services were generally negative. Early on, workers set about improving the hospital environment and tackling issues such as waste and sharps disposal. Both of these had presented significant risks to children who could often be seen playing with disposed needles in and outside the hospital grounds. Workers provided drugs and organizational support for the pharmacy in conjunction with the government strategy. They also offered the staff a programme of clinical training as well as management support.

Tertiary prevention: 'Little Conquerors' childhood disability programme

The 'Little Conquerors' programme offers support and rehabilitation to children with disabilities and their families. Community health workers, hospital clinics and others in the Servants' programme identify the children in need. A trained therapist undertakes an initial assessment, together with a doctor. Through this assessment they identify specific health issues, attempt to establish a diagnosis and clarify the child's and family's strengths and needs. The child attends a weekly therapy/play session at a community centre, although therapeutic work is primarily carried out by the family and reinforced by regular home visits. One important aspect of the programme is the ongoing support to the families. Caring for a disabled child can be extremely demanding and does not end with a short course of treatment.

Key issues

The programme as a whole focuses on a number of key aspects. Although not all programme activities have been successful, these aspects have contributed to the relevance and effectiveness of the programme.

A holistic approach

In aiming to promote child health and protect those children at risk from poor health, Servants have tried to view health in a holistic way. The programme therefore tackles different levels of health care and prevention. At a primary preventive level, two key components for good health are immunization, through the national expanded programme of immunization, and health education. Health education was targeted at children through the 'Child to Child' approach and at mothers through the nutrition programme and women's health and immunization outreach.

Secondary prevention, the early recognition and appropriate treatment of disease, involves the promotion of good nutrition and emphasizing training and supporting hospital staff. Ideally this should follow the 'Integrated Management of Childhood Diseases' protocols (www.who.int/chd/publications/imci/index.htm). Very often, aspects of secondary prevention will also incorporate primary prevention through teaching the family.

Tertiary prevention involves the ongoing support of children with ill health or disability, to minimize the effects of such disability and to promote children's participation in their society. Other aspects of tertiary prevention would include care for children with chronic illness, such as epilepsy or HIV/AIDS, and care for children with HIV-infected parents.

A targeted approach

Because it is unrealistic to try to meet all health needs at every level, three key strategies have been used. The first is to identify and prioritize the needs in the community – through an initial health survey and knowledge of national health priorities and policies, and through liaison and integration with other programmes, both governmental and non-governmental. The second strategy is to identify and build on the strengths of the team. For example, those team members who had particular skills in communication were used in the 'Child to Child' health education programme, while those with specific medical training were directed to more clinical activities. Team members continuously sought ongoing training opportunities. The third strategy is one of evaluation, or audit. This can involve formal evaluations using an external evaluator, regular reports to the ministry of health and funding bodies, or less formal evaluation through team discussions.

A participatory approach

In health care, as in any other work with communities, a participatory approach is essential for good outcomes. Rather than imposing 'solutions' on a family or community, team members have tried to work with family or community members at all stages. In the Servants' programme, community leaders and community health workers were consulted regularly and worked with the team to identify children in need and to determine the best approaches to help those children. The recruitment and training of community volunteers encourage further participation at a community level.

One of the distinctive elements of the Servants' programme is that all of the team members are actually living in the community where they are working. This is not without its costs, but it has proved to be one of the greatest strengths of the programme. By living in the community, team members have been able to gain an unusual degree of understanding of the needs of the community, its resources and the cultural values affecting health.

Children at risk because of little or no education (India)
Pamela MacKenzie

Profile of a child

In central India, along the banks of the Godavari in an area that crosses four state borders, live the people of the ancient tribal kingdom of Bastar. Several tribal groups make up this kingdom, among them the Koya. Kalyani is a nine-year-old Koya tribal girl. She is looking after the goats for the day. She has come home for a few weeks now that it's the hot season and the schools are closed. She is thinking of how different her life is, now that she goes to school.

Over a year ago she had heard her parents talking about whether or not she could attend the new school. She desperately wanted to. She wanted to learn to read and write, to learn more about the world outside and to be less dependent on others than her parents were. She wanted to be more confident than so many of the women around her, to be able to understand money and handle the market traders and bus conductors. But how could they afford the uniform and books? No, it was too far for her to go anyway. Four kilometres was a long way for a young girl. She might get hurt, or molested – then who would want to marry her? Besides, if she was away for so long every day she wouldn't be able to work in the fields, or look after the children while her parents worked there. Who would fetch the water and the firewood and help in the house? And what was the point of educating a girl? She would soon be married and stay at home. Educating a girl is like 'watering another man's garden', the Telugu say. All that investment ending up in her husband's household? Better to send her younger brother when he was old enough!

The teachers came and talked to her parents. They said it was important to educate girls, they said that the whole family would benefit. Kalyani could live at the school so she wouldn't have to walk. The uniforms and books would be free. And, what was more, they would help her family during the holidays when they would have another mouth to feed.

Her family agreed and Kalyani went to school, where the pastor's family and the teachers looked after her. She loved it there. She made new friends, learned about other people and places and also learned to read and to do sums. It took her some time to learn the new

language. She had never spoken Telugu much before. She had only known her own tribal language, but that did not have a script and Telugu did. They always used their own language, though, while they were playing.

Now she had come home and was helping her parents. She was up at five o'clock every morning to sweep the floor and yard of the little mud house. Then she would fetch water from the nearby bore well. Later she would walk with her mother into the forest to cut the wood and carry it home for cooking on the open fire. Now she is tending the goats. Yes, she liked being back home, but she loved being at school too. And maybe if she did well at this school she could go to the secondary school. Then she wouldn't have to get married so early, or have quite so many children – and those children she did have could go to school too!

Profile of an intervention

The Koya used to live as hunter-gatherers, using the fruits, animals and fish of the forest for their own needs and for selling in local markets. Much of the forest has now been destroyed, and many of the tribal people find work as farm labourers for about six months of the year. The rest of the time they still gather the fruits of the forest, hunt and fish, from dwindling resources. In the rainy season the river often floods, destroying homes and fields. During the hot season when rivers and even the wells dry up, water is scarce. Forest fires at this time are also a hazard, and sometimes villages burn down.

The tribal people are subject to exploitation in every area of their lives – at market, on buses, at work and when dealing with government officials. Most tribal people use thumbprints as their signatures and have to rely on the honesty of others. In the past some have even lost lands. A lack of sufficient knowledge of the state language (Telugu), weights, measures and money, lack of confidence, and a prejudice against tribal people are some causes of these injustices.

Although the situation is improving slowly, there are few educational opportunities in this region and schools are not accessible from every village. Even where there are schools, teachers may not be available. Where teachers are employed, the teaching itself may be sporadic and of indifferent quality.

Some parents understand the value of their children learning to read and write, but the struggle to survive influences their decisions to use their children for labour instead. Other parents may try hard to prevent their children from going to school so that they can work and earn money instead. Some children are required to work in the fields or look after their siblings while parents are working. Boys mainly cut wood, plough the land or carry heavy things. Girls plant and harvest. Any child may have to care for their own or another family's cattle, sheep and goats. They take the animals to the nearby fields or forest by eight o'clock in the morning – sometimes alone, sometimes with other children. They return by evening, but even in the day there are dangers from snakes and wild animals. Some children become bonded labourers for rich farms and houses. Girls are often abused sexually, or given to the flesh trade if they are beautiful.

Ninety per cent of girls in rural India marry before they are sixteen, while those with secondary education usually marry later. Boys will be married before they are eighteen. There is probably enough provision for secondary or higher education, but the opportunity to attend, particularly for girls, is limited.

One church in this region has set up 12 primary schools, several hostels giving access to government schools, a Telugu Medium secondary school, an English Medium school and a junior college, a vocational training centre and an engineering college. The reason for this growing educational programme is to provide the most marginalized with access to education. Children are taught to read and write, to understand both their rights and responsibilities, and they are given the opportunity to enjoy their childhood. Their horizons are widened through the ability to read books and newspapers. At the very least they will be able to sign their names and know what they are signing for.

Education is a protection for the present and the future. Children are gaining a better understanding about themselves, their lives and the world around them. They are learning to make choices and to know their own worth and value so that greater respect is given to them. With sufficient education come greater opportunities for employment. Vocational education provides more possibilities, whether through local business or by generating self-employment. Although boys currently dominate the job market, parity for girls will develop as discriminatory practices diminish.

The results of the education programme provided by the church are slowly beginning to be seen. Girls are marrying later and having smaller families, and more attention is being paid to the healthy growth of children. Their understanding about society and the world is much wider, and they are learning to respect themselves as they gain self-confidence. Even eight- to ten-year-old girls and boys are growing in self-confidence, and girls and boys are interrelating without regard to traditional gender feelings and differences. Non-tribal people are beginning to show more respect for the tribal people.

Educational provision in this region has a long way to go to reach the number of children in need and, as UNICEF points out, government commitment to it is essential. To ensure that 'the right of all children to learning' is achieved, parents, civil society organizations, communities, educationalists and government must realize that it is a shared responsibility and work together. A rigorous training programme is required so that the curriculum and teaching methods strengthen initiative, creativity and individuality. While this programme does attract some criticism for using hostels, not teaching in the mother tongue and imposing new cultural practices on a traditional community, it is providing children with the ability to make their own choices to transform their own and their communities' futures.

Many now agree that one of the most critical factors for a child's well-being and for a country's economic and social development is a strong education system. Education creates opportunities that children would not otherwise have had. It helps to build self-esteem; it can provide the skills, information and self-confidence needed to be a better parent and an active participant in civil affairs. It can help individuals to become better decision-makers – personally, politically and economically – and to respond positively to changing and challenging situations. It can help to develop a proper respect for individuals and communities, reducing misunderstanding and intolerance. It can help eradicate poverty and increase family income by producing a more productive and better-equipped work force. Women in particular, if educated beyond primary school age, have an improved quality of life. They tend to be healthier, marry later, better protect themselves against such things as HIV/AIDS, raise healthier children and invest in their own children's education.

And yet, out of the 625 million children of primary school age in the world, 130 million never enrol. A further 150 million drop out before completing primary school. This means that 280 million children do not have the kind of education they need to give them the opportunity to improve their own lives and develop their fullest potential. Sixty per cent of these are girls. Some of the reasons for this are:

- *Poverty.* Children are sent to work, often in exploitative and hazardous labour markets. Children are often kept home from school to look after siblings while parents are working.

- *Cultural practices and traditions.* This is a particular cause of discrimination against girls. Many parents feel that education for girls is a waste of money as there are no

employment opportunities and society does not allow them to pursue a career.

- *Schools are often too far from home.* Girls are more affected by this than boys.

- *Gender discrimination, sexual harassment and insecurity.*

- *Facilities and the curriculum are often inappropriate.* The quality of education and the relevance of what is being taught are often questioned.

- *Armed conflicts, political instability, migration.*

Ensuring access and improving the quality of education, particularly for girls, is a major priority. The treaty on the CRC, in which there is a clear commitment to education as a universal and unconditional obligation, has now been ratified by 191 governments. How each country will meet this obligation remains a serious question.

Children at risk because of little or no shelter (Thailand)

Don Strongman

Profile of a child

Timothy is ten years old and lives with both parents, next to relatives, in a slum community on the outskirts of Bangkok, Thailand. The house is a wood and tin shack built against a larger house. The family built the house in a single day with the help of relatives, and it provides minimal protection against the elements. When it rains, it leaks. Timothy sleeps on the floor with his parents, who alternate shifts for work. While one parent sleeps, the other works. There is no privacy.

Lack of self-esteem is a problem for Timothy. There is little that would give him a sense of pride or self-worth. In a crowded shelter it is difficult for Timothy to have personal space to think, play and reflect on his world.

Timothy suffers from neglect. His parents are caring, yet they have little time to give him. One or the other of his parents is gone all the time, leaving Timothy with little supervision. Cramped quarters, inadequate protection from the weather and lack of the basic necessities force the ten-year-old outside to seek belonging and care elsewhere where he is exposed, among other things, to the temptation of drugs available in the community. Timothy is a good student and attends school. Yet going to school and learning necessitate foun-

dations that only adequate shelter can provide, such as a place to study, to learn and to be safe.

Timothy is vulnerable because of poverty, but his future is at greater risk. Inadequate shelter limits possibility and choice. For a child, building a house is a tangible sign of increased hope. A simple, decent home provides a margin of safety; a welcome place to feel esteemed and grounded.

In the house, on a simple wooden shelf, is a trophy. Timothy won the trophy at the local elementary school in a running contest. Bright and shiny, it is a source of pride and esteem to the family. Like the trophy, a simple, decent shelter testifies to hope and esteem. It is a step on the way to breaking the cycle of poverty and points to a safe future of greater choice.

Habitat for Humanity International

Habitat for Humanity International is an ecumenical Christian organization working alongside communities to address housing problems. Beneficiary families invest hundreds of hours of their own labour – sweat equity – in building their own house and the houses of others. When the houses are complete, the families move in and pay a no-interest mortgage on affordable repayment terms. The monthly mortgage payments go into a revolving fund that is used to build more homes in the area. Habitat for Humanity International is rooted in developing communities and enabling people to solve their own problems.

There are 498 families, or 1,557 people, in the slum community outside Bangkok. Before 15 February 2001, the people were illegally encroaching on land owned by a hospital foundation. Through negotiations they have managed to sign 21-year land lease contracts, and through their own housing co-operative they became legal tenants of the land. Hoping to access financial assistance, the people, with the help of NGos, have begun working to form revolving savings groups. Currently there are 148 families with nearly 300,000 baht in a revolving fund. This is the foundation for the future of housing in the community.

Roughly half of the people in the community labour as general or daily workers. The other half are food service vendors or work in scrap collection, sales, as civil servants or in transportation. Parents working in shifts are forced to neglect family time and child supervision. In a small shack with one of the parents sleeping at any given time the children are forced to be outside, where they are vulnerable to the problems and temptations in the community.

Efforts began in 1996 to organize the community. Various NGOs have contributed to assist the community in accessing internal resources. A Danish NGO provided money to establish a child development centre; another group stepped in to organize rotating savings groups and a women's organization came forward to organize a women's savings group. These efforts build foundations that continue growth in the community. Habitat for Humanity International has tied into this foundational work and is beginning to organize the people into a local affiliate.

The problems that impact the whole community affect the children most acutely. Water and electricity are expensive and difficult to acquire. Money spent for these necessities subtracts from the funds available for food, clothing, savings and school supplies. Prior to the land tenancy negotiations families lived with housing insecurity, which meant that there was no stable environment for safety and learning. While this is changing, there continue to be questions and uncertainty. Chief among the concerns of parents for the well-being of their children is a growing drug problem. Already the effects are being felt in the community. Without adequate housing, children lose the safety of home life. Boredom and lack of security create an environment in which drug abuse proliferates among young people.

Providing a source of adequate housing is only the beginning. Building community strength is a significant result of providing housing. Families sense greater choice and children have secure homes in which to thrive, to be safe and to grow.

CHAPTER 45

Children at Risk Because of Prejudice and Inequity

Children at risk because of gender (India)

Raymond Samuel

Status of a girl child

Mrs Arunathayee is twenty-two years old and a resident of Ayyan Kovil Patti village in Usilampatti District, South Tamil Nadu, India. She comes from a peasant family with marginal land holdings. There is only one crop harvest each year because there is no proper irrigation facility. The village is located in an interior rural area with no scope for earning any other steady income beyond seasonal manual labour in fields belonging to other farmers. Mrs Arunathayee also belongs to the Kallar community, which is predominantly known for its practice of female infanticide. She already had a daughter when she became pregnant again. Her husband and in-laws were determined to kill the second child if it was a girl. Members of the Kallar community incur huge expenses for various ceremonies related to gender (from birth through different stages in the child's life). Because the bride's family suffers a poor social status, they are compelled to finance all special events and festival celebrations for at least the first two or three years of the marriage. The father of the child receives all of the special 'bridegroom' treatment even after the child is born, and the members of the mother's family do all they can to please him. So Mrs Arunathayee began to worry about these matters even before the child was born. Some of the expenses for a family with a female child include:

1. Dowry at the time of marriage (a minimum of 5–10 sovereigns, even for the poorest families – 1 gold sovereign is presently equivalent to Rs. 3400). The average daily wage (when work is available) for a woman is 45–60 Rs., and 80–100 Rs. for a man. Usually the dowry is paid from years of family savings or from mortgaging land and selling animals.

2. Household articles to start a family when the bride goes to the groom's home.

3. New clothes for each family member for at least the three main festivals – Pongal, Diwali and Adi.

4. Cradle ceremony expenses for the new-born child (including delivery care expenses).

5. Circumcision expenses for the birth of a grandson (although this practice is now on the decline, the mother's family would invite all of the relatives of both families to a celebration at which financial gifts were given).

6. Ear-piercing ceremony for girl child when it comes of age (again, this ceremony is traditionally financed by members of the mother's family).

7. Funeral expenses in case of death in the family (the parents of a daughter are expected to meet these expenses, too).

The expenses for all of these rituals, ceremonies, festivals and events are compulsory in the tradition of the Kallar community and are mostly paid for by the girl's family. With all of these financial concerns in mind, Mrs Arunathayee's family moved to another village before her baby was born so that they could commit the crime there if a female child was born.

The Women's Development Association in the village formed by SISU (meaning 'infant', the acronym for the 'Society for Integrated Social Upliftment', a voluntary organization set up in 1991 to address the female infanticide problem in South India) kept a watchful eye on the expectant mother. They were able to track the whereabouts of the family and, on the birth of the child that did turn out to be a female, they immediately informed the SISU project office.

The members of the project team immediately visited the home and the mother was taken by surprise, since she thought no one would know where they were. In spite of repeated counselling and support from the field staff, the mother was determined to do away with her newborn daughter. Hence she refused to feed the baby, saying that the child was ill and not taking any feeds.

Later the SISU community health nurse checked the baby's condition and found it to be normal. The team then had to deal firmly with the mother and her family, making them aware of the severe legal consequences that would follow if they continued with their plan to kill the child. The government of Tamil Nadu has also taken precautionary steps to curb the killing of female children. Such an act is now legally considered to be first-degree murder – a crime which carries a sentence of life imprisonment.

The team also helped the mother to realize how sinful and cruel it would be to think of murdering her own daughter. The mother then began to nurse the baby. After regular follow-up and counselling, as well as medical assistance for both mother and child, the baby's life was saved. Because the Women's Development Association respected the mother's co-operation and recognized her financial difficulties, they gave her the opportunity to participate in a loan scheme to buy a goat with a subsidy to generate additional income for her family. Through this, Mrs Arunathayee gained the confidence to participate in the Women's Development Association's 'Micro Credit Scheme for Economic Development'.

Society for Integrated Social Upliftment

The Kallar community became notorious when its practice of female infanticide was exposed in 1985. It is understood that they were a happy peasant community until a dam was built which increased poverty by depleting water in their countryside. The Kallars accepted female infanticide as the only solution to escape from the evils of the dowry practice that was prevalent among most of the caste communities.

SISU began its work after an extensive community survey among this people group. They started a community-based project with a health programme for expectant women and lactating mothers in ten rural villages within a 15-kilometre radius. This became the entry point to work in this tough community.

The village communities were organized into action groups to engage in specific initiatives to enhance their own community's economic and social status. A need-based development plan was conceived with the following strategies:

- Health awareness and teaching for expectant and lactating mothers
- Health training for volunteers
- Training in agricultural and animal husbandry practice
- Income-generating models and feasible micro-credit schemes
- Village action groups to serve as monitoring cells to save female babies from being killed
- Christian adult literacy programmes to benefit elders (mostly women)
- Vocational training programmes (sewing) for young girls

The following significant achievements have been made:

- The Women's Development Association has been activated in 20 villages in a 35-kilometre radius.
- The action groups have, with the project team's guidance, saved about 195 female babies at risk (i.e., second or third babies in a family subject to a killing threat).
- A federation of all the associations has emerged for joint community action for advancement.
- About 95 adult women have become literate.
- A church, with more than 100 members, has been established.
- The project has become a model for social transformation in the surrounding Kallar community villages.
- The government has recognized their good work and supported SISU with a substantial grant for a food processing training centre.
- Female infanticide is no longer seen as a problem to fear, but rather as an issue for the community to face with confidence.
- The local government court of law for the first time sentenced a Kallar woman in the adjacent region to life imprisonment for the infanticide offence last year.
- The economic upliftment scheme for women has been able to achieve better social status for women in the Kallar community.

SISU seeks to empower the target group economically as well as to activate the social transformation process among the Kallars. Their holistic approach encourages the target group's participation at all levels. Timely social intervention, along with a commitment to the integrated development of the Kallars, have saved innocent female babies at risk in the Kallar community in spite of much opposition.

SISU is a Christian NGO that stands as a testimony to declare God's mighty ways of working in the lives of people and to pronounce his liberating power to those in need.

Children at risk because of ethnicity, displacement and refugee status (Bosnia-Herzegovina and Mozambique)

Alastair Ager

Profiles of children

Nedim, age eight, fled with his family from his home in Bosnia-Herzegovina. Ethnically Muslim, he was accommodated in a makeshift refugee camp just across the border in Macedonia for several weeks while his mother sought to make arrangements to stay with relatives further south. Asked to recall life in his home town, he draws a picture of his family sharing a meal while he plays with neighbouring children. Later Nedim will draw an uncle hanging by a rope from a tree, with camouflage-clad soldiers mocking beneath. But such pictures do not come for some time. For now the pictures are of happy times, with intact houses, flowers and sunshine. Making sense of all that has happened in the last few months is difficult. 'I know that the Serbs did bad things, and that our people are good . . . but if I was a Serb, maybe I'd think that Serbs were good . . .'

Luciano, an eleven-year-old Mozambican boy, sleeps on the floor of the mud-and-thatch hut of his best friend, Jiva. Since the theft of the family's remaining blankets, Luciano's mother has slept under a plastic sheet in their home with his sister, while he and his older brother Francisco have stayed with friends. They have been in temporary homes in Biriwiri, Malawi, since they fled across the border two years ago. Luciano hopes to get into the local school, where they have begun classes with the Portuguese textbooks he used to use back in Mozambique. His widowed mother hopes for that too, but she is not sure if she can pay the school fees (and get uniforms) for both Luciano and Francisco, who has been in school for the last year. Luciano is worried about his mother's health, as she has to travel further and further from home to collect firewood and struggles to make the food ration last the two weeks for which it is allocated. He seldom talks of his father, shot dead by the 'bandits' when he refused to leave their home, but he remembers the silence after the shot as he fled into the bush with his mother.

Profiles of projects

There remains considerable debate concerning the key attributes of effective programmes addressing the psychosocial needs of children impacted by displacement, refuge and war. Despite the substantial increase in the number of programmes addressing the broader experience of children caught within complex emergencies, there has been little consensus within the humanitarian world regarding appropriate programme design. Rigorous evaluations of the impact of differing forms of approach have been scarce.

There have, however, been a number of initiatives seeking to define some 'ground rules' in evaluating psychosocial project response to non-material needs within complex emergencies. These have included the establishment of the Impact Assessment Committee through Save the Children Federation (USA), the 1999 ICRC/Colombia University consultation on Humanitarian Response in the Context of Complex Emergencies and the establishment of the Psychosocial Working Group by the Andrew Mellon Foundation, bringing together practitioners and academics active in the field. The following four key design principles are suggested for psychosocial interventions with children impacted by displacement, refuge and conflict:

1. Programmes should use knowledge of *both* local culture *and* relevant technical understandings of child adjustment. There has been much debate between those proposing programme design based upon facilitating the re-establishment of pre-existing local coping strategies and those urging education and training in the detection and treatment of traumatic stress reactions, and other conditions not currently 'recognized' in many cultures. Good programmes pay more than 'lip-service' to the value of local cultural practices. They try to work with these practices and also aim to be sensitive to the emo-

tional as well as practical needs of children and their families, especially regarding the impact of traumas on such families. These two sources of knowledge need, therefore, to be kept in balance.

2. Programmes need to address *both* the personal *and* the mediated experiences of children. The individual experiences of children are important, but the experiences of children mediated by such structures as the family, the church or mosque and the school have substantial influence on their understanding and adjustment. Many programmes necessarily emphasize intervention through the structures of society that support children in their growth and socialization. Such programmes are seen by many to be preferable to those which risk importing an overly westernized, individualistic approach to understanding the lives of children. Such sensitivity should not blind workers to the importance of the personal experience of children, and their potential need to tell their own story, shaped as it is by their social context.

3. Programmes should acknowledge that displacement and refuge generally expose children to *both* specific traumatic events *and* more chronic ongoing stresses and adjustments. Many programmes 'foreground' the former experiences in their appraisal of children's needs. However, chronic stressors such as housing problems, racism in school, language and communication difficulties can play a huge part in the adjustment of children and their families to life in refuge, and they need to be addressed.

4. Programmes need to be informed by an understanding of both child development *and* child rights. The growth of awareness of child rights issues (particularly participation rights, in addition to rights regarding safety and protection) is to be welcomed. Issues of child rights are now significantly shaping the approach of many NGOs in their work with children impacted by complex emergencies. However, such an emphasis should not be at the expense of an awareness of the circumstances which support child development, reinstatement of which is commonly a key programming goal.

The displacement of populations resulting from conflict in the former Yugoslavia in the early 1990s brought the human dimensions of uprooting and flight to the attention of many.

Scores of psychosocially-oriented programmes were developed across Croatia, Serbia, Bosnia-Herzegovina and Macedonia. Many of these programmes failed to meet the criteria of 'good practice' suggested above. In particular, many (see the review by Adjukovic and Adjukovic, 1998) threatened inappropriate importation of approaches and understandings of trauma, and a devaluation of insights and capacity of local personnel, including social workers and mental health professionals. The reorientation of the expertise of local professionals in the face of the unprecedented challenges set by the prevailing conflict and population upheaval constituted a key component of the ongoing and effective work with impacted children.

One example of such work is the programme organized by the Macedonian psychologist Lena Kostaravo-Unkovska. This work built upon the early assessment of the impacts of war reported in such publications as 'Children Hurt by War' (1993, General Children's Consulate of the Republic of Macedonia). A long-term programme of activities supported children such as Nedim at one of the displaced person's camps in Macedonia. These activities were rooted in analysis of child development processes, shaped also by an understanding of the impact of the broader climate of fear and uncertainty on the social, cognitive and emotional development of children. Activities were paced over several months, acknowledging the time it took children to establish some sense of security in this uncertain environment. Through creative use of games, structured artwork and discussions, children were given the opportunity to express some of their fears and uncertainties and – once more secure – to address some of the challenges and complexities of growing up in what had become part of the 'former Yugoslavia'. There was no fixed agenda here to get children to 'work through' their experience (as some programmes expect). The programme was at the outset structured as ongoing support for displaced children growing up in a complex and uncertain setting.

The programme thus met many of the suggested 'quality standards'. It combined sensitive insight into the social and cultural dimensions of those displaced with an acute awareness of processes facilitating and constraining children's social, emotional and cognitive development. It worked primarily with the children themselves, but it also provided resources to the families and communities to enable them to foster the children's development. Counsellors did not deny the traumas of some children's experiences, but they allowed the children the freedom to identify and explore issues of concern to them, such as the present challenges of life as a refugee child and the future as a citizen of the country, as well as dark memories of the past. In particular, the programme modelled the value of children participating in their own activities, as both a human right and as a means of supporting the development of confidence and co-operation.

These same principles can be seen to be at work in 'Consolacao Psychosocial Support' in Malawi. This programme grew out of initial child tracing and family reunification work with Mozambican refugees in the early 1990s. Children like Luciano who had been displaced by the conflict in Mozambique were targeted for support by a programme whose name (meaning 'consolation') gives a clue to its defining principle – providing activities which can support children through the difficult circumstances of flight and refuge.

The programme was based upon a psychological appraisal of children's developmental needs, which involved, in the early stages, the deployment of doctoral interns from a US programme in clinical psychology. The set-up costs were thus high, and were the subject of some criticism. However, such investment may – several years later – be seen to have supported significant local capacity development (enabling, for example, the subsequent development of related initiatives with AIDS/HIV orphans). The programme became the site of an internship for psychology students from the University of Malawi, who were able to integrate psychological understandings with a strong appreciation of local cultural resources. Programme assistants

recruited from the Mozambican refugee community strengthened the programme in this latter area, with a heavy emphasis on the use of traditional song and dancing with the children.

Again work with key 'mediators' in the community was a key feature, with school teachers and community leaders involved in programme planning and development. The programme targeted children between the ages of six and around twelve years of age. While screening tools were adopted, these were to guide work with particular children rather than to select those who met specified criteria (e.g., with regard to specific symptomology) for inclusion within the programme. The programme sought to reflect children's current concerns as well as past experiences. It aimed to develop a sense of confidence and competence through work that gave them exposure to appropriate adult Mozambican role models of both sexes (with many of the children drawn from single-headed households and a significant minority being unaccompanied minors). While participation was a key theme in the programme, through the 1990s subsequent SCF programmes have perhaps come to reflect more the emphasis on other aspects of children's rights. The 'guide to good practice' being produced by the SCF's impact assessment committee documents a number of case studies showing this trend, though many of the key features of the Consolacao programme remain in evidence.

Although these examples depict hugely differing situations, the four issues highlighted serve as a useful basis for identifying – and seeking to enhance – good practice in psychosocial services for displaced and refugee children.

Children at risk because of disability (Thailand)
Wasan and Chariya Saenwian

Profile of a child

Dum was born with cerebral palsy to a poor family in the rural north-east of Thailand. His father and mother were rice farmers working for landlords, and they had no land of their own. They lived with Dum's mother's parents. Dum had a sister who was about five years older. His mother kept him at home for the first three years of his life, but it was difficult because she was unable to work and they

were very poor. Dum's muscles were very weak, and she had to do everything for him.

Dum's parents decided that they could not continue to look after Dum, so they went to the social worker. It was decided that Dum should go to the government home in Bangkok. The parents did not want to abandon him, but they could not see how they could support him.

When he arrived in Bangkok he was placed in

a 'ward' for sick and handicapped children with 45 other children. The 'ward' was part of a large complex of nine different wards for 500 disabled children. The one psychiatrist, one physiotherapist and two teachers were only able to concentrate on a few children. Dum received little, if any, care. In the dry season his father came to visit him regularly (every 3 months), but otherwise there was no one to give him one-to-one attention.

Christian Care Foundation for Children with Disabilities (CCD) noticed Dum in the ward and asked the social worker's permission to care for him and nine others. Dum's father was informed that CCD would provide individual care for Dum free of charge, and cooperation with the government home would continue. So Dum came to 'Rainbow House', where he received medical care and the staff ensured that he received physiotherapy to learn to walk properly as well as speech therapy to learn to speak.

Meanwhile, Dum's father continued to visit his son every three months (transport money was provided), and eventually he was invited to take Dum back home. The CCD staff took Dum to visit his family on a number of occasions, and after two years he returned home. By this stage the family were more resilient. They had their own home and a more secure source of income – a small hand-pump petrol station and a small grocery shop.

At first the local school refused to accept him, but the social worker from CCD went to visit the teacher. The teacher had thought that Dum's jerking movements were disrespectful, but the social worker explained that this was due to his cerebral palsy and was not intentional. Now he is happy at school and even cycles there! CCD maintains regular contact with the family, and when they have concerns they telephone and ask for advice.

Christian Care Foundation

This study demonstrates the following principles:

- The cultural and religious contexts of the child, family and community need to be taken into consideration.

- Lobbying and interceding with or on behalf of children and their families take place at local and national levels.

- Those working with children need to communicate with parents and caregivers so that they can make informed decisions and advocate for their families.

Christian Care Foundation for Children with Disabilities (CCD) was set up in 1997 as a government-approved Thai foundation. It took over the work originally set up by Christian Outreach (CORD) in 1986, working in the government home for babies, which was actually for children from birth up to seven years old.

Children with disabilities in Thailand (especially children with learning difficulties and those with severe physical disabilities) generally experience severe discrimination in all areas of life. People believe in superstition and ancient traditions that say that disability is the result of past sins in this or a previous life.

Many children with disabilities are unwanted by their parents and are therefore abandoned. Some of them end up in hospitals, and many die prematurely. The Thai government established three children's homes in a suburb of Bangkok, with admission depending on age and disability. Of those children who are able to stay with their families, some are left at home by themselves for much of the day, while others are physically maltreated.

CCD are responsible for two day centres at the government homes and a small residential unit called 'Rainbow House' that also has daycare facilities for children with disabilities from the local community. CCD have also been developing a Community-Based Rehabilitation (CBR) programme in Kamphaeng Saen, Nakhonpathom Province (60 kilometres west of Bangkok). They recognize that such programmes, which aim to provide support to rehabilitate children within their own communities, reach a greater number of children and are also often more effective in the long term than those projects that take children into residential placements.

A comparative survey into the needs of children with disabilities, conducted by CCD with Handicap International in a rural and an urban area, found that families in the rural area were more likely to be optimistic about the child's future, whereas urban families felt that putting the child in a home was the solution for a child with disabilities. CCD felt that this was due to the breakdown of traditional values in the urban setting.

Usually relationships between parents and children with disabilities stop as soon as they are transferred to the government home, but CCD are trying to change this. CCD try to trace families, especially families of those children with minor disabilities. Often they are able to trace parents by talking with local church pastors in the district in which there was last contact with the parents. A programme worker then approaches parents and, after careful explanation and showing photographs and describing the progress of the child, many parents are willing to be reunited. CCD then spend time preparing both children and parents so that they can live together again. In cases where parents cannot be found, adoption into a new family is sometimes possible. Where neither tracing nor adoption is possible, the programme is committed to caring for children until they are old enough to care for themselves. Some of the earliest admissions to the centre are now teenagers, so preparations are being made for a group home where teenagers can learn to integrate into society and do things for themselves instead of being institutionalized.

The CBR programme is well aware of the spiritual needs of the family, and it sees children and their families in a holistic way. A parents' support group has been formed in which they can help each other and receive training and encouragement. Praying with families is an integral part of the work. On an individual level, the emphasis of the relationship approach to parents means that the needs of the whole family are taken into consideration.

The CBR programme works in close co-operation with the local Disabled Persons Organisation to advocate on behalf of children and other people with disabilities in the community. CCD is a member of the Federation of Health Voluntary Organisations. The CBR programme is seeking to impact and receive help from district health and education authorities. Relationships are being developed with the local church.

CCD are considering how they can:

- develop the CBR programme to involve children who are less able in decision making.

- increase the awareness of the local church and the general public about disability, fostering and adoption, and involve church members in volunteering.

- become more sustainable with less need for outside financial support.

Children at risk because of inappropriate cultural practices (Nigeria)

Ojoma Edeh

Profile of a child

In a paper presented at the World Congress on Future Special Education in Scotland (1978), Mba noted that the education of children with disabilities in Nigeria 'has hitherto been left in the hands of voluntary organizations, owing to a general negative attitude toward disability in communities characterized by mass illiteracy'. Several myths abound with regard to the causes of disability, which give rise to superstitions and fear of such afflictions. This has resulted in discrimination, even in educational institutions, against the handicapped children.

Nigeria (which has about 250 tribes) is rich in varied cultures and different cultural practices. One of the many such practices is 'Ebo-eta'. Ebo is a god, and Ebo-eta means that this god is out searching. While it is important for men to see Ebo, women must run into their houses and hide because they are not allowed to see him. Most of the time, Ebo comes out when there is a child born with disabilities. Ebo takes the child and the curse is lifted from the family.

The following is a true story about a boy called Alex. Though this is Alex's story, it is not unique to him; it is true for all children born with disabilities in this culture. Like most newly married Nigerian women, Alex's mother was a teenager when she became the second wife of a man much older than she was. Shortly afterwards, she became pregnant and hoped to have a baby boy. When Alex was born there was great joy – but only for a moment.

It was not long before it was discovered that Alex looked different. His head was smaller than normal, he did not open his eyes and his 'neck could not hold his head'. The elderly women who delivered Alex recognized the 'signs' right away, but they thought that he could be cured if appropriate sacrifices were made to the gods. Alex's father was willing to do anything to save his only son from these evil spirits. Six months later Alex did not 'get better', but instead was 'getting worse'. At eight months, Alex was taken to a hospital and seen by a medical doctor. The doctor told

Alex's parents that he was healthy and would live to be about forty years old.

That afternoon, a bell rang and music began. The eldest woman in town gave a high-pitched yell and every woman ran inside and hid. Moments later, pleasant music signalled that the women could come out. They did not hear what went on during Ebo's search because the music was loud and the men were dancing. When they came out, baby Alex was no more and there was no body to bury. Ebo had taken Alex! Alex's mother, her family and friends were left crying. The older women knew the true identity of Ebo, but they never told the younger girls. What actually happened to Alex? And what was the true identity of Ebo?

Ebo is one of the gods that this culture trusts to come out and take away their 'problems' and remove the curse from the targeted family. Alex was killed by the older townsmen and buried where the grave could not be found. It is not important to reveal where Ebo ends and men take over or to discuss whether or not Ebo is real. What is important is that many children like Alex are killed daily due to cultural practices such as this one, and it must be stopped. 'Children at risk' of this type of practice include those born with cleft palettes, severe disabilities, no clear sexual organ, both sexual organs, and so on. Most of these children could grow up to be productive members of society if only they could be provided with minimal medical interventions to break the cycle of their deprivation.

The MOM Programme

MOM is a non-profit Christian organization that focused initially on rescuing children with disabilities like Alex. How can this be done? What can one organization do to minimize or stop children from being killed through this and similar cultural practices? Where does one start? The founders of MOM were faced with these and many more questions. These sorts of cultural practices are very difficult to change, and so MOM started by helping four older boys who were not born with disabilities, but who became physically disabled due to polio or medical errors during childhood.

Having made this 'public connection' with children with physical disabilities, MOM spoke with people from different villages and churches and told them that the programme would also take newborn children with disabilities. With this information, mothers of children born with physical disabilities started

to bring their children to the programme – usually at night. At first, it was difficult to establish guidelines for admission but, through trial and error, the admission guidelines were established.

The general guidelines for admission include, but are not limited to, the following requirements: 1. The parent(s) bringing the child to the program provides a detailed history of the family's health and a history of the pregnancy and birth of the child; 2. Parents give legal permission for MOM to educate their child with disabilities (in front of the local chief and the village representatives); 3. Parents agree to bury their child at the family compound in the event of death; 4. Parents agree to come and visit their child regularly. When the parents fulfil these four requirements, the child is admitted into the programme.

Providing a 'dumping ground' for these children was not MOM's intention. The type of cultural practice described above must be stopped, and the beliefs that view disabilities as diseases or curses must be changed. With this goal, MOM put 'a reversed form of inclusion' programme in place. This educational programme, which consists of an attractive curriculum, was designed for children with disabilities. The teachers receive the same training as public-school teachers, in addition to training enabling them to appropriately and respectfully teach children with disabilities. The programme is called 'a reversed form of inclusion' because the goal is to attract children without disabilities through this innovative educational programme.

It was three years into the programme, during which public-school teachers were constantly on strike, that MOM made the first connection with 'normal' children. Teachers at the MOM school taught consistently without going on strike, and the society started to notice. One educated man asked to have his two children schooled at the MOM school. He said, 'MOM have a good programme and the teachers do not go on strikes.' MOM accepted his children on the condition that he pay tuition of about one US dollar per month for each child – and his children would eat and play with MOM's children.

All the necessary papers were signed and his children began schooling at MOM. A year later, his children did not 'become disabled', and no misfortune befell the family. At this point, the public became curious and parents started asking for their children to be educated at MOM as well. Having 'proved' that disabilities are not 'contagious diseases' and that children with disabilities are not 'possessed by evil spirits', MOM started to educate the public about what disabilities are and some of their possible causes.

MOM continue doing this sort of education by regularly accepting children with disabilities into the programme and by supporting parents to keep their children with disabilities while MOM provide educational and medical

support. It became evident that no amount of preaching could change cultural beliefs, but getting people actively involved can change their ways of thinking. Are children like Alex still being killed today due to cultural practices? The answer is yes, but fewer numbers are being killed today compared to the past. The society is learning more about the true nature of disability and is more accepting of children with disabilities.

Children at risk of unwanted pregnancy and babies at risk of abortion (Nigeria)
Ojoma Edeh

Profile of a child

According to the *Women's International Network News* ('Nigeria', 2000), ten per cent of the 585,000 women who die annually worldwide from pregnancy and childbirth-related complications are Nigerian. Many of the pregnancy-related deaths in Nigeria occur among teenage girls, who account for some one million births in the country annually. Among the unmarried girls under the age of nineteen, 72 per cent of all deaths result from abortion complications. Most of the unmarried teenage girls who were pregnant had been sexually abused. In their study of childhood sexuality and child sexual abuse in south-west Nigeria (1999), Obisesan and Adeyemo found that as many as one in every 20 men and women had sexual intercourse between the ages of six and ten years.

Oloko and Omoboye (1993) found that more girls than boys were sexually involved during childhood. This is in sharp contrast to the findings of Ogbuagu and Charles (1993), who reported much higher figures for boys. There is no doubt as to why there are contradictions in findings among studies in Nigeria regarding sexuality among children. Discussion on sexual matters still remains taboo in Nigerian culture (Obisesan and Adeyemo, 1999). Interviewing children about sexual issues is often difficult and rarely permissible. More interestingly, most of the studies referred to 'children who had sexual intercourse' instead of 'children who were sexually abused' (Obisesan and Adeyemo, 1999).

Jane is one of those 'children who has had sexual intercourse' between the ages of six and ten years. She is the oldest of 15 children. Jane and her family live in a very populated

village. Her father and his three wives 'became Christian' after her father had already married his third wife. The family were then known as 'churchgoers'. At the age of seven Jane had her first experience of sexual intercourse with her father's best friend (known to the family as the 'second father'). He told Jane never to tell anyone, and that he was having sex with her because he loved her more than the rest of the family members.

So Jane felt very special, even though she was in pain. At about ten and half years of age, she found out through the second father (contrary to tradition) that the plan had begun for her arranged marriage. Not long afterwards, Jane became pregnant with the second father's baby. He arranged for her to have an abortion by a local native medicine man, telling him that Jane was a rebel. About six months after the first abortion Jane had a second abortion during which she almost lost her life.

When Jane was about twelve years old, her future husband's family planned to visit Jane's family. But the local native medicine man where Jane had received the two abortions had spread the news in the village about Jane's rebel sexual behaviour. Jane's family found out about her 'filthy rebel' nature when the future husband's family did not turn up. Jane turned to the one person she knew loved her and who could explain this whole misunderstanding, but the second father turned against her and denied the truth. Instead, the second father told Jane's family that he paid for the abortions when he learned of the pregnancies in order to prevent the family's shame. He said that his only regret was that he had not informed Jane's family when he learned of her abominable behaviour.

According to SIECUS (1996–2001), Nigeria's youth are sexually active. Among unmarried adolescents, unwanted pregnancies are a common problem. The medical risks associated with early pregnancy include, but are not limited to, anaemia, bleeding, toxaemia and prolonged and difficult labour complications. Early pregnancy poses special health risks not only for the mother, but also for the child. The infants of teenagers suffer higher mortality than those of older mothers. The babies are also more likely to be born prematurely and have low birth weight. These conditions frequently contribute to long-term mental and physical handicaps. In addition, many babies are killed daily by teenage girls aborting their unwanted pregnancies.

The MOM Project

In a culture where discussion of sexual matters still remains a taboo and sexual abuse of children is not reported, it is difficult to know which children are being abused and need help. MOM opened the door to 'children at risk' in August 1992, aiming to spread the gospel through actions among neglected members of society. At first, MOM focused on rescuing children with disabilities. Within three months after MOM began, Jane (now fourteen and half years old) came to MOM in the middle of the night with her little boy, John. He was born with mental retardation and Jane could not bear to see him killed as cultural tradition demanded. MOM set out on a mission to rescue children like Jane.

MOM receives such children through a variety of channels. The children may turn up at MOM having fled from unbearable home lives or because they have had enough of living on the streets. Sometimes 'good Samaritans' feel sorry for these girls and bring them to MOM for help. MOM staff also go out into the streets to invite needy children to the project.

MOM offered Jane help, but she needed to agree to specified processes of admission and support. MOM fed and clothed Jane and her son and took them back to her father's compound. Jane's father had died and the second father was taking care of the family. MOM talked with Jane's mother, who believed the second father's version of the story. This is the kind of pattern that dialogue with families tends to follow:

MOM: Your daughter ran away from home and we brought her back to you.
Mother: The girl is not my blood. She is a parasite who came out of me.
MOM: What are you going to do with her now?
Mother: I don't want her at home to pollute the rest of the children.
MOM: Where are you going to send her? Do you have extended family who could care for her? We can provide some education and vocational training.
Mother: She can go back to the street where she belongs.
MOM: What would you do if harm befalls her out there?
(Jane's mother did not want to answer that question, but it was evident that she was fighting back tears.)
MOM: Do you need help in taking care of her?
Mother: If you are not ashamed of her, go ahead, she is yours.
(At this point MOM always uses the opportunity to share the gospel with the family.)
MOM: We need your approval in front of a local chief and village representatives that you are giving us permission to help educate your daughter and that you will welcome her home when she comes to visit regularly.

When this process is completed, the girls are brought to the MOM compound for Christian counselling. They must agree to be active members of the new family. This includes attending devotions, Bible studies, Sunday schools and worship services. MOM staff get to know the girls' interests, and if the girls are of school age, they enrol in MOM's school. Later they go to good Christian boarding schools that teach biblical values. MOM pays all expenses in order for the girls to complete their education. If the girls are too old for school, they learn vocational skills such as tie-dying and sewing. MOM also provides care and treatment for medical needs.

MOM's non-judgemental approach means that the girls soon begin to find new purposes for living. They learn to respect their bodies, to strive to please God and not humans and (perhaps the most difficult thing of all) to accept themselves the way God accepts them.

The first visit to their families, villages and old friends is a traumatic experience for every girl; however, the visits are one of the requirements of the programme. MOM sends one staff member with each girl for the first three visits. One purpose of these visits is to show that changes are taking place in the girls' lives. The girls also have an opportunity to apologize to anyone they have wronged, especially family members. The villagers begin to learn that God loves everyone and is able to help anyone who comes to him. The visits are also set up in order to communicate the truth about the girls' past behaviour to the parents. Knowing and accepting the truth helps the family to accept their daughters again, and to believe other girls with similar stories.

For Jane, being able to communicate her childhood true stories about the second father was only possible during her fifth visit home. She had accepted Christ as her Saviour about six months earlier, which she shared with her family on visit number four. By the time of visit number five, Jane had just completed her training to become a seamstress and MOM had bought her a sewing machine. A Christian man had been courting her for two months. Armed with her new accomplishments, Jane was ready to tell all. A staff member and her prospective husband accompanied her. Jane talked first with her mother, then with her brothers and unmarried sisters. Surprisingly, everyone believed her version of events and professed to have been aware of the truth all along. Jane doesn't know why none of them supported her during her traumatic experience or why she was blamed for it. Why was she excluded from her family when it was not her fault?

Her questions may not be answered, but the truth remains – many girls like Jane go through this type of sexual abuse daily in Nigeria. These girls are known at best as youth who are sexually active or at worst as rebellious girls who deserve to be expelled from their families. MOM is educating parents to talk with their daughters about sexuality. MOM also encourages them to believe their daughters when they have stories to tell regarding sexual contact with adults. Jane has continued to reach out to girls in situations similar to her own. She has connected with them and believed them.

CHAPTER 46

Children at Risk Because of Abuse and Exploitation

Children at risk because of exploitive labour (Bolivia)

Carmen Rivera and Paul Stephenson

Profile of a child

Maria is eleven years old. She is an ordinary girl. Her interests and hopes are similar to those of her peers, including those peers who live behind the high walls of their houses in the middle-class suburbs nearby. She lives with her parents and three sisters in a one-room house on the outskirts of Cochobamba. They own a television. Maria's father works as a labourer and earns £56 a month. Her mother washes clothes. The money that Maria's mother earns, combined with that of her husband, is barely enough for them to survive on, so the girls go out to work. Maria works alongside her sister Pamela, who is seven years old. They sell bags and earn about £1.70 a day. The 'bolseras' (bag-sellers) watch out for each other and the market sellers also protect them from potential threats. Girls have been robbed and preyed upon by older men. On weekdays, Maria and Pamela go to school in the afternoon. Maria has good friends at school. Mosoj Yan (see below) supports Maria and Pamela through school and also works with them in the market place. Here is how Maria describes her life:

I wake up at 7:30 am. Wash my hands and face then drink some tea. At 8:30 am I dress and make my bed. At 9am, me and my sister take the bus to the market. It takes 30 minutes to get there from my house. My neighbourhood has both good and bad people living there. Some drink and others are thieves. They are poor and come from all over Bolivia. I am not ashamed of my room. My mum is called Maria and the baby, Yan Carla. When we get to the market, we buy plastic bags and sell them to shoppers. We call ourselves 'bolseras' (bag sellers). A pretty lady helped to teach us about how to look after ourselves. I like the market. I have fun with my friends, we help each other and we also earn money. I work until 12 o'clock. Then we take a bus to another market for lunch. I like it better

there because the women are nicer and we can play. On Saturdays we work all day until 7 pm in the market and stay here for lunch. At 1 o'clock we go to school. It's good to study. My teacher is good to us. In the market [the girls learn in the market on a stall that is set apart for informal classes, facilitated by a promoter from Mosoj Yan] we learn about our rights, health, changes that happen to our bodies.

We get back home at 7 pm and eat. We help to clean and wash up, then watch some TV until 9 o'clock. We do some homework for half an hour then go to bed. I like to go to school, but I also like working. I want to continue to do both. In the future I dream of becoming a teacher and owning a house in the city. I hope that my mother is healthy and that all my family is happy, and that my friends who are also 'bolseras' can study too.

Mosoj Yan

'Mosoj Yan', meaning 'New Life' in Quechua, is a ministry that started in Cochobamba, Bolivia in 1991. It focuses on helping girls and adolescents who live in or work on the street. The programme's vision is a society in which human beings have equal opportunities to live with dignity in accordance with the values of the kingdom of God: love, justice, solidarity, peace, goodness, honesty, respecting the identity of people and responsibly administrating natural resources. The mission is to accompany both girls and adolescents in the transformation of their lives and their community, meeting their needs and reaching for the goal of fullness of life.

Bolivia, South America's poorest country, has a population of around 8,327,700. According to UNICEF, five per cent of the population live well, 15 per cent are on the poverty line, 20 per cent are poor but not destitute, 40 per cent are destitute and 20 per cent live in extreme poverty.

Cochobamba, the city where Mosoj Yan works, has a total population of 1,445,990 and is known for its agricultural and petroleum production. Its pleasant climate and location attract many immigrants. Many of these immigrants live at the edge of the city, where there are no basic amenities. The resulting social problems are complex and difficult. Children become involved in exploitative work on the streets that deprives them of time to play, relax and go to school. It is calculated that in Bolivia there are around 569,000 child and adolescent workers (both in urban and rural areas). They work long and exhausting hours without legal protection. These children constitute 22.4 per cent of the country's workforce.

There are also children and adolescents who leave dysfunctional families for the relative freedom of the street. They flee from alcoholism and violence. Society considers them to be its 'negative face' due to their survival activities, including the use of glue and petty crime. The situation of these impoverished children becomes even more tragic and critical when one considers their exposure to delinquency, sexual abuse, teenage pregnancy, prostitution, HIV/AIDS and other dangers.

Mosoj Yan runs three independent projects that facilitate the process of change and transformation in the lives of the children they serve. Two of these projects focus on rehabilitation and the other on prevention.

Their Centre for Motivation is a rehabilitation centre that aims to orientate adolescents towards reintegration with society. The centre also works to raise awareness of the problems in local communities.

The second rehabilitation centre is called the House of Restoration and provides a home for up to ten children and adolescents who have decided to leave the street or who are leaving their homes for the street. Here the children can gain stability, enter full-time education and prepare for the future.

The Centre for Working Girls and Adolescents assists working girls to maintain high educational standards. The centre also helps families to improve relationships and trains adolescents to find good job opportunities and to know their rights and responsibilities. In addition, the centre runs four workshops for technical training in card making, baking, making recycled paper and computing. Some of the adolescents who have graduated from these workshops are now studying for technical careers or are at university.

The three centres provide services such as canteens, showers, washing facilities and savings accounts. They also offer psychological support for individuals, groups and families; handicraft training for occupational therapy; career advice; legal defence and health checks.

The children are involved in the decision-making of the organization and the evaluation of each project. They hold monthly assemblies to discuss various aspects of the work within the projects and give suggestions for improvement. Last year, a local committee was formed to advise and direct the programme. Members included one parents' representative, one children's and adolescents' representative from each centre, two representatives of institutions that work for 'children at risk' in Cochabamba, three representatives of Mosoj Yan and one member of the board. This committee approves the programme plans and budgets.

Working and reflecting with these children has taught Mosoj Yan a great deal. For example, we are convinced that to work with women is vital for the future of society; that the power of God can and does transform lives; and that these girls have great potential but a lack of opportunity to study and progress. As Alejandro Cussianovich said, 'To be a boy and to be poor is a double tragedy. To be a girl and to be poor is a triple tragedy.' Monthly prayer bulletins foster support from brothers and sisters around the world. Each team holds daily devotionals and one day of prayer and fasting a month is dedicated to the Lord. All the staff of Mosoj Yan trust that this is God's work and that it is a privilege to be like him and reflect his love.

Raising funds for these ministries is very difficult. Mosoj Yan actively looks for donors or individuals to support the work while also trusting in God's provision. A key factor in the success of the programme is the support of the local church. Mosoj Yan now counts on five churches that support its work through donations and prayer.

Future objectives include:

- Establishing a union for working girls and adolescents

- Documenting and evaluating different areas of the work

- Involving local church members as volunteers

- Raising awareness of the rights of child workers in the street.

Children at risk because of sexual abuse (Sri Lanka)

Subhadra Tidball

Profile of a child

Rani lives in a slum community of displaced people between the train tracks and the beach outside Colombo, the capital city of Sri Lanka. She is a part of the 'gypsy' community that speaks the minority language, Tamil, and is known for selling incense and telling fortunes. Many of the men are alcoholics and abuse the women who, in turn, are abusive to anyone beneath them in the community hierarchy. Their small huts are constructed out of scraps of wood and cardboard. When the monsoons come these houses fall apart, and sometimes the ocean becomes so rough that it floods them. During the dry seasons, which are unbearably hot, everyone crowds under whatever shade they can find.

Rani lives with her mother, stepfather, stepsister and occasionally her older brother. Her hut is hardly big enough for the single mat, small table and chair that it contains. At night they all sleep on the ground, fitting themselves in like pieces of a jigsaw puzzle.

At eight years old, Rani was an expressionless, quiet child. The physical abuse she endured was no secret. She had been responsible to take care of her three-year-old stepsister from the day she was born, and she was expected to carry her everywhere. Rani's stepfather favoured his own daughter and treated Rani as if she were a personal servant. On one occasion, when she had set the child down to fill a pot with water, he slapped her across the face and yelled obscenities at her. Her mother's loyalty lay with her husband, to whom she felt indebted for taking her in after her first husband left her. She would take her frustration out on Rani – even if it had nothing to do with her.

The stepfather's drunken nights were the worst. Rani tried to stay out of sight during the day to avoid his abuse but, when everyone else was asleep, her stepfather would turn to her and sexually do as he pleased. He threatened to kill her if she even resisted and told her he would leave her mother if Rani told. She remained silent. Rani was withdrawn and, because she had to take care of her stepsister, she did not interact with other children. As her stepsister grew older and needed less care, Rani had more time of her own. She did not

know how to play, however, so she often just watched the other children. A social worker noticed Rani and, after many visits and investigations, her situation came to light. Social workers were able to work with Rani and her family. Rani learned to play with other children and gradually became energetic and excited, much like other children her age.

Save Lanka Kids

The aim of this programme is to develop relationships with children in 'at risk' areas, using sports as a vehicle to teach and explain simple rules about how to stay safe from sexual abuse. The programme is designed to fit a three- to six-month time period, during which volunteers visit the chosen area for weekly hour-long sessions.

Training, which occurs a month before the work begins, involves cultivating a basic awareness of sexual abuse, becoming familiar with profiles of perpetrators, and having an understanding of children's views of and reactions to abuse. Volunteers are also taught skills to help them understand and be a good friend to a child. They are encouraged to develop leadership skills and the ability to work in a team.

Volunteers are recruited from churches near the areas in which we work, to encourage those churches to adopt the neighbourhoods and sustain relationships established during the programme. The majority of our volunteers are young people (they have to play sports and keep up with the children), and it is best to have an even combination of male and female volunteers (as children relate best to same-sex volunteers).

During the week prior to the programme, volunteers visit the area and go from house to house, explaining the programme to the parents and obtaining permission for the children to attend. The community's support is vital. Typically we find parents and other community members to be appreciative of the time spent with their children as they are poor and otherwise neglected by society.

Approximately 30 to 50 children participate in a programme. During a typical meeting, volunteers coach the children in playing sports and, for the last fifteen minutes, the children gather together for the day's lesson (a five-

minute talk followed by ten minutes for discussion). Issues covered include self-esteem,
body safety, 'No, Run, Tell' rules, the difference between good and bad secrets, and
standing up for the kids around you. It is
important to note that these programmes
were designed to promote prevention of
abuse. It is expected that there will be children
who have already suffered abuse and that,
during the course of the programme, they will
often share this with a trusted volunteer.
When this happens, volunteers refer the case
to a trained professional.

The programme has seen many successes. The

communities have been encouraging, and
building relationships has been easy. The kids
are always ready to play, and they grow fond
of the volunteers who are good role models.
The lessons are short and to the point, so the
kids pick them up well and remember them
when quizzed over the following weeks. There
are, however, many difficulties. The incentive
to work hard and remain committed to the
project and the team depends on the maturity
and self-motivation of each individual to do
so. It is usually best to train twice as many volunteers as needed, with the expectation that
at least half of them will remain dedicated for
the required amount of time.

Children at risk because of sexual exploitation (Thailand)

Patricia Green

Profile of a child

Saouw grew up in a small village in the north-
east of Thailand. She completed her primary
schooling at twelve years of age because there
was no money for the further education of
girls. Her family was poor, but there was
always enough to eat and friends to enjoy.
Although Saouw had to work hard to help her
family in the house, caring for the younger
children and sometimes working in the rice
fields, her childhood was a happy one. Often
she would have to take the buffalo to the
fields to eat and wallow in the mud. There she
would meet her friends with their buffaloes
and they would talk and dream of the day
when they would go to the city to find work.

One day, when Saouw was fifteen, a woman
from a neighbouring village came and offered
her and her friends work as waitresses in a
restaurant in Pattaya, a city in the south. The
girls were excited, and it was not difficult to
persuade them to go. The youngest of the five
girls was fourteen.

They arrived in Pattaya with their meagre possessions, and Khun Sarang took them to a tiny
room where they would sleep. She showed
them a bar where they were to sell drinks 'for
two days', after which she would come and
take them to the restaurant. That night, the
outreach team from Rahab Ministries visited
the bar and talked to Saouw and her friends.
They told the girls what would probably happen. 'Oh no', they said, 'that won't happen to
us, Khun Sarang promised to come for us.'
But Khun Sarang never returned, and the bar

owner ordered the girls to talk to the customers and said that if a foreigner asked for
them they must go with him and sleep with
him.

Saouw and her friends had been trafficked
into the sex industry. She was one of the ten
million children working in the sex industry
worldwide, one of the one million children
who are trafficked into the sex industry every
year, one of the one million children in Asia
'expected' to sell her body for sex to support
her family, one of the 300,000 child prostitutes in Thailand.

As the days went by, Saouw was terrified. She
tried to hide behind the bar and not speak
with the customers. The bar owner became
very forceful and said that Saouw must go
with the next customer who asked for her.
The next night, as Saouw slowly walked to the
bar, she saw the team from Rahab Ministries
again. She ran to them and pleaded, 'Will you
help me? What you said is true. Will you take
me away?'. With the help of a local pastor,
Saouw and one of her friends were rescued.
She came to Rahab House in Bangkok.

A few days later Saouw accepted Jesus Christ
as her Saviour and enrolled in evening high
school. During the day she worked at Rahab,
making greeting cards to earn money for her
family.

Today Saouw is eighteen. She has nearly fin-
ished her third year of high school and plans
to go on to technical school. Saouw loves
Jesus and has been baptized. She still lives in

the girls' house and helps with the younger girls in the prostitution prevention programme. Saouw is on the staff of Rahab Ministries and was recently appointed a manager of the greeting card project. Saouw says, 'God rescued me and gave me a new life.'

Rahab Ministries

Rahab Ministries began in 1989 as an evangelistic and social outreach to women and girls working in prostitution in the sex tourist area of Patpong Road, Bangkok. The initial objective was to share friendship and the love of Christ with the women and girls. The ministry has developed to include evangelism, discipling, self-development through skills training and sponsorship for education and vocational training. Rahab Ministries is also involved in advocacy, networking with other organizations and raising awareness to combat child prostitution and international sex trafficking of women and children. Rahab Ministries' programme is registered with the Evangelical Fellowship of Thailand.

It is estimated that there are more than two and a half million women and girls in prostitution in Thailand. Annually, thousands of children and young women are tricked, lured and bought from the northern and tribal areas and forced to work in exploitative and often slave-like conditions in brothels and bars. Increasingly, they are also being trafficked into Thailand from the surrounding Mekong countries. In Patpong Road in downtown Bangkok it is estimated that 4,000 women, some as young as fourteen years old, work in the bars every night. The majority of these women, along with the 20,000 who work in the bars and on the beaches in the city of Pattaya, come from poor families and villages in the north-east of Thailand and work to make money to support their families. Most have minimal education and no job skills and so have few alternatives for earning a viable wage. Thailand is the epicentre for HIV/AIDS in Southeast Asia. Although boys are also sexually exploited in Thailand, Rahab Ministries focuses on helping girls. There is a need for Christians to work to help boys as well.

Rahab began making contact with these women by visiting them in their places of work, the bars, and making friends with them. Relationships were built and a weekly Bible study and support group developed out of this. The women were invited to a simple meal, could share their hearts and hear a simple Bible story. The group wanted its 'own place', so Rahab opened a centre, a small beauty shop, to meet the immediate needs for hairdressing and make-up. The centre, located in the middle of the bar area, offers friendship, counselling, prayer, skills training and education on safe sex, general health, HIV/AIDS and other relevant topics. The beauty shop provides a non-threatening environment where women can relax and feel free to share their stories and problems with the hairdressers, who are also trained in basic counselling and social work skills.

Involvement in the centre's activities – such as daily worship, helping with tasks, learning basic life skills, hairdressing and make-up – develops the women's confidence and contributes to increased self-esteem, self-worth and personal dignity. A greetings card programme employs several women, offering an alternative means of making an income. Rahab also has a house that currently accommodates nine girls who have left prostitution and are sponsored for vocational training or furthering their education.

Visiting women and girls in the bars is still the focal part of the ministry, and this has extended to other areas of Bangkok and to Pattaya, a coastal resort. Several of the women who previously worked in the bars and have benefited from the Rahab Ministries programme are now staff members.

Future plans for Rahab include:

- Working with other national groups in Thailand and throughout the region to support, encourage and assist them in setting up similar ministries amongst their own people

- Continuing to network with international organizations and NGOs to combat international sex tourism and trafficking.

Children at risk because of organized crime (Cambodia)

Valeria Peres

Profile of a child

Phat comes from a very poor family in Cambodia. Her father is a farmer. She has six brothers and sisters. Her father and mother used to drink and gamble, and the family did not have enough to eat. Then her mother got very sick and died. Everyone was very sad, and Phat missed her mother. Her father had 'too many children' so Phat, who was about eight years old, along with her younger sister, went to live with her aunt. The aunt was cruel and punished her for small mistakes. Her aunt and uncle had many problems and quarrelled quite often. They also used to gamble and had many debts.

One day, Phat's aunt took her and her little sister to a house and said that she should stay there because they would give her food and nice clothes to wear. The house had shining lights and the girls there wore lots of make-up, and there were a lot of men coming in and out of the house. Phat and her little sister had been sold to a brothel. Sexual slavery is big business in Cambodia. It is well known that officials work together with mafia at every level. Children like Phat are also bought and sold across borders into begging rings.

Phat and her sister were not used as prostitutes, but they were being groomed for the sex industry. They saw everything from sexual relations to pornographic movies.

Figure 1: Phat's family

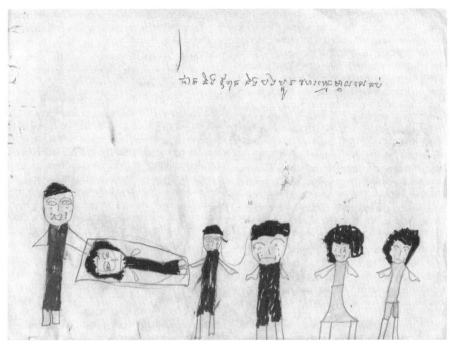

Figure 2: Her mother's funeral

Cambodia is slowly emerging from decades of war and devastation and is now on the road to recovery. While this progress is encouraging, its benefits are uneven and are often felt only in society's upper income levels. The vast majority of Cambodians, especially children, continue in poverty and difficult living conditions.

Significant numbers of Cambodia's children are homeless, abused, neglected and exposed to the lawless conditions of Cambodia. Most disturbing is the increase in children being sold or kidnapped into various networks that feed off the region's sex, petty theft and trafficking networks. These 'children at risk' are becoming expendable elements of society, supporting the ravenous desires of the rich and powerful.

The YWAM Hagar Programme

In response to the needs of Cambodia's children, the Hagar Project places 'children at risk' in group homes where they can receive long-term care. Hagar's Foster Home Programme (FHP) currently provides shelter and care for almost 40 children in five different homes. All of the children help with various household chores according to their ages and abilities. Older children learn skills such as sewing and

dancing and are responsible for teaching the younger children. Each of these activities contributes to their development and increases their confidence.

The ongoing objectives of the FHP are:

• To provide care, protection and rehabilitation in a family unit for children in difficult circumstances

• To provide a wholesome supportive environment for children to develop holistically – that is physically, spiritually, emotionally, intellectually, socially and professionally – in order to function in society as responsible productive adults

• To build the capacity of house parents to lovingly care for children with difficult backgrounds.

Over the next few years the number of orphans is expected to increase to 350,000 (in a population of 11 million). These children need families. God is 'A father to the fatherless . . . God sets the lonely in families' (Ps. 68:5, 6). Group homes care for children in a family setting rather than in an institutional one. These homes also care for the individual, and not just for the group.

The task of fostering a child is almost impossible for most Cambodian families. Many parents have little knowledge of how to parent effectively because they did not know their own parents or were separated from them during the war. Many parents are not even able to deal with their own children, let alone traumatized foster children. The present reality is that, in Cambodia, there are not enough families available to provide good care for children. Therefore the Hagar Project cannot keep to the ideal of one foster child per family, but instead seeks out good families and places more than one child with them. The Hagar Project trains, encourages and works together with house parents to care for a small group of children, who will have a sense of belonging and all they need for holistic development. Large families are an integral part of Cambodian culture. These group homes, therefore, provide support and a natural family model for the children.

The children benefit from being loved, cared for and nurtured in Christian values. They can also be part of the house parents' church, benefiting from the support of that church and community. While Cambodia experiences high levels of corruption, the hope is that this will not be a problem in a Christian home.

The recruiting process has been developed over a period of time. The Hagar Project looks for house parents with no more than three children themselves. This means that they have experience with children, but that their family is not so large that they cannot take in more children. The parents should not be too young or too old and should have some education in order to be able to give some input into the children's education. The project looks for families with good reputations in their neighbourhoods and who are prepared to make a long-term commitment to these children.

The project asks questions about the house parents' personal life, education and work experience. The staff talk with them about their childhood and give them a case study to see how they would solve potential problems. The programme staff and the house parents discuss the idea with the house parents' children. If the children and their parents are well-prepared for the experience, these families can be a real asset to the group home.

Our series of training programmes includes discussion about:

- Reasons for fostering
- The kinds of environments the children come from

- Some of the problems the children may struggle with, including low self-esteem, trauma and addiction
- Some of the children's needs, such as learning how to deal with anger and how to express love.

Many parents in Cambodia believe that raising children is an easy job because they focus on practical, physical needs and do not recognize the underlying emotional needs. As parents began to care for these traumatized and abused children, it became clear that specialized training was necessary to equip the parents to care effectively for them. Through this training they have developed a better understanding and are more gracious with the children who come from difficult backgrounds.

Prospective house parents spend a week in an established home. This time of observation is mutually beneficial as we get to know each other better. It also allows the staff to observe their attitudes before they officially start working with them. Their children are allowed to come as well, so that the staff can observe how they behave and interact with the other children.

One or two children move into the new group home initially and additional children arrive later. This helps in the process of attachment and bonding and also gives the house parents some time to adapt. The project selects the children based on the assessments of both the family and the child. By this stage, based on previous assessment, staff are usually 90 per cent sure that parents will work well with the children selected. They want to avoid placing children in families that they may later have to leave.

There are regular meetings for Bible study, worship, prayer, fasting and group discussion about child-related issues. Since the house parents have begun to meet like this, they have been able to share their problems with one another. This has encouraged teamwork and group support. The group shares the task of finding solutions to problems and everyone learns from the different situations encountered. Mrs Chantom is a housemother. She says, 'in the beginning I did as is Khmer custom and did not think about the children. After we studied different lessons about children's issues, I am much more aware of their feelings'. During the time for prayer, house parents can share their burdens. Many of them have experienced God changing situations and lifting their burdens.

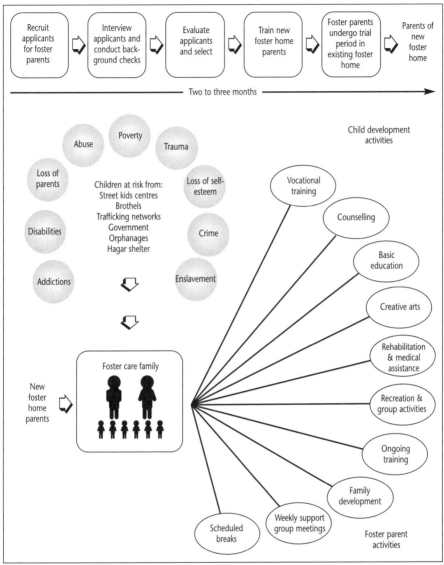

Figure 3: Hagar Foster Home programme overview

Children at risk because of substance abuse (Kazakhstan)

Belinda Johnson

Profile of a child

Dima came to Teen Challenge Kaz (TCK) from a local narcology rehabilitation hospital one month after his fifteenth birthday. He had been an intravenous opium user for five years. He has now been drug-free for 19 months, has completed the TCK rehabilitation programme and is currently training as a programme worker.

Dima lived with his mother and stepfather, both drug users and dealers. They used and sold drugs in their home, which is a common practice in Kazakhstan. Many people use drugs in the presence of other, non-using, family members such as children or parents. Because of this practice, it is also common for more than one family member to become a drug addict.

When Dima was thirteen years old, his parents went to prison for selling narcotics and he was left alone with his oldest brother, who was sixteen. In order to support themselves and their habits, they began stealing. The police eventually caught them, and Dima's brother went to prison. Dima was considered too young to be held responsible.

With no adequate social care system, Dima was left alone and spent his time with adult drug addicts. Later he began to go from city to city, stealing from people's pockets to buy drugs and to live. In 1998, the police in Almaty stopped him and took him to a narcotic rehabilitation hospital connected with the prison system. It was here that Dima learned about the TCK programme. The director of the hospital consented to have an interview with the TCK director, who agreed to take Dima into the programme.

One of the greatest contributors to generational drug addiction appears to be the high incidence of co-dependency evident in this culture. Other contributing factors include a strong sense of hopelessness brought about by the collapse of an ineffective social system, little or no prospects of work and the fact that it is a society without faith. Dima was brought up in this environment, not knowing that it was possible to change the circumstances that governed his life.

Prior to coming into the programme, Dima had not attended school regularly for over six years. He is currently working towards finishing his schooling. Because of his involvement in the programme he is now bilingual (speaking both Russian and English), and he is planning to become a pastor.

Dima's mother is now out of prison, but he has chosen to stay within the strict disciplined life of TCK as he continues his studies and training.

Teen Challenge Kazakhstan

Teen Challenge began in New York in 1959, when a man named David Wilkerson began to work with troubled young people who were addicted to drugs and involved with criminal gangs. Today there are more than 150 Teen Challenge centres in 53 countries. Each Teen Challenge centre operates as a national organization in its own country, self-governing and financing, but all share the unique Teen Challenge philosophy, which states that drug addiction is a crime, not a sickness. It is a crime against God, self, family and society. In order to change this, a person must accept responsibility for his or her drug addiction and then take positive steps to bring about change. Lasting change occurs progressively as people are taught and trained how to deal with life's problems in a responsible manner.

Teen Challenge Kazakhstan operates under the auspices of TCI. TCK's programme focuses on preventing drug abuse and on curing and rehabilitating drug addicted children in Almaty, Kazakhstan. It began its work as an adult drug and alcohol rehabilitation centre in 1995. It has developed a children's drug rehabilitation programme and a women and children's refuge in response to the overwhelming needs in the local community. An initial staff of seven workers and 10 students has grown to over 400 workers, students and children living, working and studying together in the residential and non-residential programmes of the TCK ministries. The residential programmes include detoxification and rehabilitation for both men and women and rehabilitation and refuge for teenage girls and juvenile boys. TCK runs the longest programme of any TCI centre (all students entering TCK commit to staying for 18 months), because life-controlling problems are endemic in this culture. Alcoholism, opium addiction and co-dependency are prevalent. The non-residential programmes of TCK include a school, providing the full Kazakhstan curriculum, a sports club focusing on drug prevention and a family recovery programme.

The first child addict came into the programme in 1998. He was fifteen years old and had been injecting opium for five years. Since then, the programme has taken in five other boys who had been addicted to a variety of drugs. TCK has also taken in two girls, ages twelve and fourteen, who were working as prostitutes to help feed themselves and their families, as well as a dozen other children who were living on the streets and thus at risk of drug or other forms of abuse.

Kazakhstan is a member of the Commonwealth of Independent States in Central Asia and was formerly part of the USSR. It became independent after the collapse of the Communist system and has had to readjust to this new political environment. It has a population of approximately 18 million, of which 44 per cent are ethnic Kazakh, 35 per cent ethnic Russian and the remainder a mix of many Central Asian and Slavic people groups. Over 60 per cent of the world's opium trade passes through Kazakhstan, including what is grown here.

Kazakhstan has many societal problems. Many marriages are very unstable and most adults are not living with their original spouses. The incidence of sexually transmitted diseases is very high. The legacy of three-quarters of a century of atheistic totalitarianism, combined with economic difficulties and very cheap, available drugs have all led to a very high rate of drug abuse. The social welfare system is seriously inadequate. Prior to the collapse of Communism there was a system that was able to house and feed these people, at least to a subsistence level. Now, many of the local institutions for children are overcrowded and underfunded, so often the children are left to themselves.

There are an estimated 80,000 homeless children in Kazakhstan. Their parents are either dead, in prison or drug addicts, or marriages have broken down and the new step-parents do not accept the children. The children survive by stealing or prostitution and become used to a life of hopelessness at a very early age. Drug addiction is a common result. Many children will try drugs for the first time in their own homes because their parents or older siblings are addicted. Others will begin through peer pressure while they are living or playing on the streets. Some will even begin in their schools.

The typical TCK programme has four stages, which each student passes through. When the children enter the programme, they must go through physical withdrawal from the drug(s) they have been using. During withdrawal they are never left alone and are offered comfort and companionship to help them stick it out. While physical withdrawal lasts no longer than one week (usually 2–3 days), the students remain in this first stage for one month. Physical rehabilitation continues as they begin to eat regularly and properly (many are malnourished and undersized for their ages). Gradually they recover from any illnesses they had and their physical growth improves. The following three stages involve the children completing a number of individual and group studies which

help them learn to understand and deal with their problems. These studies cover issues such as anger management, families and understanding sin. The students only progress to the next stage once the studies for their current stage have been completed. They also take on more responsibility as they move through the stages. For example, the boys have dairy cows which must be milked twice a day and cared for, without exception. The boys are given duties relating to the cows as they grow and show that they are ready to take on more responsibility.

TCK has a very strict discipline system that requires the child or young person to accept responsibility for all of his actions. The punishments usually involve work that takes time out from their free time. They may have extra duties to perform or lessons or Scriptures to write. Every discipline is given for the purpose of teaching the child why her action is wrong and how to behave correctly. Over time it is expected that behavioural patterns will change permanently through this teaching.

TCK started a school in October 1999 to accommodate child addicts who were unable to attend normal schools. The school follows the complete curriculum of Kazakhstan schools but is flexible in order to cope with children who have not attended school for a number of years, if at all. All of the teachers are qualified nationals, and the children are prepared for all required national examinations by the completion of their studies. The children study until they graduate from school and then decide what they want to do. Because Kazakhstan has a high rate of unemployment, many of the children see their future linked to TCK and church service, and some see university as an option. All of the children participate in sport, usually football or basketball, and they also have free time to read, relax, watch television or just play.

Each child has daily 'housekeeping' duties in addition to a few other work duties as required. During their school holidays, these duties will include such things as tree trimming and other gardening, building walls, making bunk beds and painting. As a child progresses through the programme and matures, he is given greater responsibility, including some responsibility for younger children.

The children have regular contact with people outside the programme. Many of the children do not have family members, but those who do can begin fellowship with them after they have completed the first month of the pro-gramme. This contact is limited to every second weekend, since this time puts a lot of emotional pressure on all concerned. Emotional rehabilitation is an incredibly important part of the process, since these children have had little emotional support throughout their lives. Opiates also stunt emotional development. The children receive counselling and a lot of hugs and 'parental' support. The programme is designed to be as little like an institution as possible so that the children can mature normally and will be able to enter into healthy relationships in the future.

The children's day begins and ends with private devotional times, and they attend a short chapel service before school begins each morning. They are encouraged to develop a personal relationship with God from the time they enter TCK.

TCK is currently working on a family recovery programme for family members who are co-dependent. Co-dependency can be defined as

> . . . a compulsion to control and rescue people by fixing their problems. It occurs when a person's God-given needs for love and security have been blocked in a relationship with a dysfunctional person, resulting in a lack of objectivity, a warped sense of responsibility, being controlled and controlling others (three primary characteristics); and in hurt and anger, guilt and loneliness (three corollary characteristics).
> (Springle, 1990)

Co-dependency is the major cause of an addict returning to addiction. The family recovery programme will teach family members about their own problems and how to change their behaviour towards their addicted partner or child.

Children at risk because of violent abuse and neglect (UK)

George Hosking

Profile of a child

David was fourth in a family of eight children. His father was a gardener and his mother a cook and cleaner. Until he reached the age of seven, David's grandmother was the dominant figure in the family. She used to hit him frequently. Once, David's little brother fell into the water at the docks. He would have drowned, but David dived in and saved him. His grandmother gave him a good thrashing because they should not have been there.

David saw little of his parents. His father spent the evenings as a singer and comedian and his mother played bingo or visited friends. After his grandmother died, David was left in the care of his older brothers and sisters. He started wandering around at night. Soon he started stealing sweets, smoking and playing truant. He found other boys living nearby who were also free to wander. They started challenging each other to do things for a dare. 'How far can you go without being caught?'

He was caught shoplifting when he was thirteen years old and his father disowned him. His parents sent him to a remand home. After he was released, still with no parents around at home, he went out and continued to steal.

David was sent to another remand home. As an anti-bedwetting measure, children were wakened every hour and taken to the toilet, even though David never wet the bed. One staff member shook his penis 'to get the last drop out'. Soon after, David became a victim of sexual abuse by the supervisor of the remand home. Children were abused, both individually and in groups. He ran away twice but did not dare tell anyone, as the children were warned they would never see their parents again if they 'told stories'.

David was not protected – from physical abuse and neglect when at home, or from sexual abuse when put into the care of authorities. David developed a very violent personality out of his early experiences as a recipient of violence, and anger at his neglect. Being the victim of sexual abuse as a child resulted in him later sexually abusing children. David spent much of his life in prison.

Happily, in his forties, David successfully took part in WAVE's 'An End to Violence' programme, let go of his violent ways and sexually abusing behaviour, found a job and began a peaceful life. In the UK, the British government spends 300 times more on dealing with the adult Davids of this world, long after the consequences have taken effect, than they spend on prevention by protecting the Davids while they are young. WAVE's goal is to prevent children like David from suffering physical abuse, sexual abuse and neglect, and so to avoid there being many more victims like David, his brothers and sisters, and the children whom David abused.

WAVE

The bulk of violence in modern societies occurs within the family. Most sexual abuse is perpetrated by family members. Despite decades of dedicated work by charities, levels of child abuse are as high, or higher, than they were 50 years ago. Numerous studies have demonstrated the cycle of violence. Forty-two per cent of children who suffer abuse or neglect go on, as parents, to abuse or neglect their own children.

In Dunedin, New Zealand, every child born in 1972 has been followed since birth, with extensive tests at two-year intervals, and careful tracking of educational, employment and criminal records. At age three, nurses observed the children at play for 90 minutes and identified an 'at risk' group of children. Eighteen years later, two and a half times as many males in the 'at risk' group had two or more criminal convictions. Fifty-five per cent of their offences were violent (versus 18 per cent of the offences perpetrated by those not part of the 'at risk' group). Further, offences by the 'at risk' group were much more serious, including robbery, rape and homicide. Forty-seven per cent abused their partners (versus 9.5 per cent for others). Although fewer females became violent, 30 per cent of females in the 'at risk' group had teenage pregnancies (there were no teenage pregnancies among those outside the 'at risk' group), and 43 per cent were in abusive relationships. The next generation of 'at risk' children was already being created.

What is happening to children to turn them violent by the age of three? Harsh parenting styles, neglect and a failure by parents to 'attune' with their babies' emotions and needs during the first 12 months of life are primary causes. Recent research has traced a pathway from poor parent-baby interactions at 10 to 12 months of age through aggression and temper tantrums at 18 months, non-compliance and hitting at age two, problems with other children at age three, coercive behaviour at age four, to fighting and stealing at age six.

It does not have to be this way. There are cost-effective programmes which reduce child abuse in 'at risk' families. A New York state early infancy project, involving home visits by nurses to low-income, teenage, pregnant mothers, until children were two years old, significantly reduced child abuse, neglect, injuries, poisonings and subsequent pregnancies. The long-running Hawaii Healthy Start Programme of home visits from birth to five years old also demonstrates reduced child abuse. There is evidence that child abuse and neglect can be prevented by appropriate proactive intervention; and that the earlier intervention takes place, the better.

In April 1996, a group of people who had been discussing on the Internet the unacceptable levels of cruelty to children throughout the world decided to form WAVE (Worldwide Alternatives to ViolencE). Meeting on-line, this group observed that almost all charity and government initiatives tackling child abuse: 1. addressed the symptoms of the problem, and 2. were not reducing child abuse. They therefore decided that an effective approach must tackle root causes, not symptoms. They decided that understanding the root causes of violent behaviour would be the focus of their early work.

In October 1996, the 46 members of WAVE created a vision, 'to create a world without violence, where everyone acts with respect for all others'. Their mission statement was 'to build an international network dedicated to understanding the root causes of violence, to finding and promoting effective practical solutions and to direct action to create a world of peace'. Membership spread over four continents and included psychologists, therapists, teachers, doctors, business people, mothers, computer specialists and two very eminent former prison psychiatrists. They set up an international panel of world-renowned expert advisers and created a strong organizational structure. WAVE became first a limited company and then an international charity. The goals and long-term strategy of WAVE include identifying the root causes of child abuse and violence; finding the most effective methods known, worldwide, to address these; promoting adoption of these proven methods in pilot studies; managing, evaluating and supporting successful implementation of the pilot studies; and educating political leaders on the application of the lessons learned from successful pilot studies.

CHAPTER 47

Children at Risk Because of Their Unsafe Environment

Children at risk because of armed conflict (Croatia and Bosnia)

Ela Balog

Profile of a child

The following is a true story about how war changed the life of one girl in Croatia. Jovana was a nine-year-old girl. She had lived with her parents in a village near Vukovar. Her mother Marija was Croat, and her father Vojo was Serb. Before the war, that was not important. Many couples were mixed and lived normal lives without having to think about who was who.

The family had a little house, a big yard, a garden and a cornfield. There were many domestic animals in their yard. They were a hard-working family and they had everything that was important for a good life. Jovana liked learning, singing and playing with her school friends.

During spring and summer her father taught her how to catch fish in the river Danube. Very often they swam together, and in the autumn they spent time in the woods learning how to tell good mushrooms from bad ones. Jovana and her father were very close; he was the most important person in her life.

The spring of 1990 saw the first democratic election in Croatia. Many parties were established, including nationalistic ones. Jovana's father enrolled in the Serbian nationalistic party and her mother sympathized with the Croatian nationalistic party. There was no peace in their home anymore. Vojo was very active in his party and, because of that, his wife was very frustrated. They started to have conflicts. Jovana was shocked by how her parents lost their good relationship. In the beginning they shouted and it was very noisy in their house. Later, they stopped talking. Jovana could feel that they hated each other.

One night in July 1991 her father disappeared without explanation. Marija was disappointed and angry. She told Jovana that he was now to be regarded as their enemy. One morning

there was an attack on the village. Marija told Jovana that her father was the leader of terrorists and rebels. It was very dangerous for Croats, so they decided to escape from the village. Many of them took only a few things in plastic bags and ran away through cornfields. On the main road, Croatian soldiers picked them up and put them on the bus to Zagreb. When they arrived, all displaced people were accommodated in big gymnasiums. Jovana and her mother had to sleep on mattresses on the floor with 80 other people. Most of these people were children, women and elderly people.

The children reacted badly to Jovana because they recognized her name as Serbian. Some of her villagers said things about her father and called her names and started beating her. They wanted to send her away because, according to them, her place was with her father on the other side with the enemies. She was shocked, speechless and felt that she was alone in the world. Her mother did not protect her. She didn't even pay attention to her. She did not think about Jovana's feelings. Marija was tired of the situation. Jovana could not sleep, eat or react normally. She became very aggressive and refused to do anything.

She had a nightmare about her father. In the beginning they were together swimming in the river, smiling and laughing, but then her father changed his mood; his face became angry and he wanted to do something bad to her. How could her good father become so evil? Did he love her any more? She screamed during the nights and wet the bed.

Her mother tried to convince her that it would be best for her to change her name to the Croatian Ivana. Jovana did not know what to say, because she got her name from her grandpa. Why should she change it? Would her new name give her protection and safety?

But they decided to change her name, and her mother thought that it solved the problems.

They were housed in a room in one of Zagreb's hotels, and Ivana went to school. But she was very sleepy and disinterested and used to sit and look at the floor. She did not like to talk about her past life, and she did not play with others. When her classmates asked about her father, she told them that she had no father. Other children were very proud of their fathers, because they were in the Croatian army and were heroes.

In the meantime, her mother found a new man and they moved to a village near Osijek. They worked in the garden and life was very hard. Her stepfather was very cold to Ivana and humiliated her at every opportunity. He spoke very badly about her father and how she would be the same in the future. Ivana was afraid that he would hit her and, when she tried to abuse her, she told her mother.

Marija was angry with her daughter and assumed that Ivana hated her stepfather and wanted to blame him. He had given them a home and they had enough food and could live a normal life. But Ivana became more and more afraid of him. She decided to run away from them. The first night, Ivana slept in the woods and cried a lot because she had nobody to take care of her and give her protection . . . she was ready to kill herself.

After the intervention of the centre for social care, Ivana was placed in a Christian family. Her mother agreed with this decision because she felt she would be free of her daughter the troublemaker. The family were Christians, they invited Ivana to church and Sunday school. In the summer she visited children's camp and she heard the message about God who sent his own Son to save the whole world – Croats, Serbs and Muslims. It was a surprise for her. Everybody had rejected her because she belonged to the 'enemy' nation, and yet she found that Jesus loves her and doesn't differentiate. Ivana felt comfortable among her Christian peers. The Christians were very friendly and kind to her.

Ivana thinks about her father often. She knows that he was killed and buried on the 'other side', but she has a special place in her heart for him. He showed her his love and care, and she knows that he did not go away because he stopped loving her.

Agape

During the war in Croatia and Bosnia, a humanitarian organization called Agape ran children's camp projects. The following story illustrates the kind of work that Agape was able to do.

A family that lived in a big house in Sarajevo had two children. Twelve-year-old Ana was the best pupil in her class, played the piano very well and had a sense of humour that made her popular among her classmates. Miro was ten years old and a very lively boy. His family was especially proud of him because he was a gifted football player and there were often articles about him in the local newspaper. Their father, Ivo, was an economics expert in the chemical industry and their mother, Eva, worked as a secretary in the city hall. The family had everything. They often spent weekends on picnics with relatives and friends in the mountains and during vacations they travelled to the Adriatic coast.

When the war started, they decided to stay in their house in Sarajevo. They didn't leave, because somebody else would probably move in and steal their possessions. Moreover, they had a sizeable basement in which they could find shelter. During the air alarm they could stay there for days. Some of their friends and neighbours came to stay during dangerous days. In the beginning it was not so bad, but it got harder. There was not enough food and no gas, water or electricity. They ate macaroni and rice and stayed in bed to keep warm. They started to dream about sunshine and carefree days spent with friends. The children were upset and could hardly wait to be with friends in the playground.

At last there was a quiet period and people cautiously resumed normal life. They moved back to the upper part of the house and Eva visited the market to buy food. She saw some of Miro's friends in the playground, and they asked if he could come out to play. Ivo and Eva were afraid, but Miro begged them to let him go out, and in the end they gave him permission.

Miro spent the next two afternoons with his friends, playing football and enjoying the fresh air. On the third day, he did not come home. Ana and her mother heard on the radio that there was a sniper in their neighbourhood. They went out and found Miro and his friend lying dead in the grass near the playground.

That moment changed their life. They could not believe it at first. How could anybody shoot and kill their Miro? They began to ask themselves why they had not fled the country as others had. Blaming themselves, they spent many days without sleeping, eating, washing or talking to each other. There was no future. Ivo decided to go to the front as he had promised his son during the funeral. He wanted revenge.

Ana was very sad and suffered a lot. She thought that she did not deserve to be alive. She stopped having contact with her peers; she could not sleep, eat or concentrate on anything. Their world was falling apart. The Chetnik's brutality was breaking their dreams. One day her mother heard about the counselling centre in Sarajevo. She recognized that they needed help. They found out that there were many people who lost members of their families. The children drew pictures and spoke about happiness and unhappiness, about their wishes, the worst and the best days in their lives. Ana watched and listened and drew pictures, but she did not talk.

The therapists respected Ana's reactions and wanted to find the best technique to help her begin to overcome her problems. There was another silent girl. She had green eyes and was called Sonja. She had lost her mother during the bombing of Sarajevo. She and Ana became close. They were very good at drawing, and they started to share thoughts about their pictures. Sonja became Ana's great support. She was a 'shoulder to cry on' and they started to visit each other.

Ana was encouraged to write a diary. In it she could express her feelings without having to speak in front of others. It was a special moment when she visited her brother's grave with her parents. She left a letter there, a confidential conversation between her and her brother. She wrote to him about her love and how she would never forget him.

Ana's father's story is one of real victory. He was a Bosnian army sniper, and on one occasion he had a child of his son's age in his sights. He remembered how he had promised to retaliate for Miro. His hand shook, seeing the image of his son shivering in front of him. And then his finger slipped down. No, he was not able to do that. His son would not like his father to be a murderer.

During visits to the counselling centre, the family rebuilt their relationships and started life again. Ana went on to study at Sarajevo's university and her mother gave birth to a baby girl.

Some of the techniques used by the counselling centre with children in Ana's age group included:

- *An ideal day.* Children sit in a circle and are encouraged to make a plan for an imaginary day, from the moment they get up in the morning until they go to bed. This enables children to make their wishes and needs come true. Their parents agree to provide such a day, and it is discussed at the next meeting.

- *The saddest day.* Children talk about the saddest day for them during the war. The leaders help them to tell their painful stories.

- *My favourite gift.* Children sit in a circle and the leader asks each child to think of the best present she has ever received, who it was from and on what occasion. This facilitates understanding of wishes and needs, oneself and others.

- *A mirror.* Each child is asked to write his name at the top of a piece of paper and then draw a mirror. In the mirror they draw a symbol or picture which characterizes them. Then the pieces of paper are passed around for each member of the group to draw or write a message in each mirror. When each child gets her own paper back, they discuss how they feel about what is drawn or written there.

Children at risk on the streets (Colombia)

Steve Bartel

Profiles of children

Libardo was fifteen years old when our team members, who find and befriend children on the streets, first met him. He'd been on the streets for at least six years. He was easy to

recognize because his eyes were bluish green and his hair was a dirty blond. He was softspoken and serious, even when we tried to have fun with him and his gang.

One of the few times we saw him smile was at

a Christmas picnic we held. Among the activities were competitions testing skills that were useful on the streets. Libardo won the rubber band shooting contest!

One day Libardo asked me if he could come up to our farm for the day. He knew he couldn't stay overnight because only children under thirteen 'lived in', but he'd heard he could glean potatoes from our field. I worked alongside him, hoeing, and we had a great time. I never realized it would be the last time we'd really talk.

A couple of weeks later, some of his gang came to our drop-in centre and asked for prayer for Libardo. He had 'problems'. Two days after that, one of our staff members recognized him as the coroner turned his body over before loading it onto the van for the morgue. The story came out: an off-duty policeman had harassed and beaten his friends, and Libardo had punched him, knocking him to the ground. The policeman had vowed revenge. Three nights later, at midnight, the policeman returned with another man and took Libardo away for 'questioning'. When he didn't return, the gang got anxious, but it was too late. They found Libardo six blocks away, next to a freeway overpass, with six shots in his head.

When we talked to the gang about justice, all of them said they recognized the policeman because they had given him a nickname months before. They were even willing to testify, but all of them backed out for fear that they, too, would be killed. Officials we were friendly with warned us that it was too dangerous to keep digging, and so we dropped it. Our only consolation is that Libardo knew how to pray . . . and he probably did . . . in the short walk to his death. I believe we will see him in heaven.

Margarita was six years old when her mother was murdered. Her father, Juan, turned to drugs and alcohol. He became a wanderer on the streets of the capital city of Colombia, Bogotá. He took his daughter with him.

Her father loved and protected Margarita when he was sober, but most often he used her to support his habits. When she was seven, she and a nine-year-old street friend pickpocketed a businessman. They were running off with his money when the man turned and shot her friend. Her friend fell. She kept running, turned the corner, and looked back in time to see him pump two more shots into her friend's head.

When Margarita was ten years old, she was invited to 'The Other Way', a Christian drop-in centre in Bogotá. Margarita enjoyed the relatively peaceful atmosphere, the games and the Bible stories. The staff befriended her. Soon Margarita came consistently and participated in all of the activities, proving her desire to leave the streets and make a life for herself. She was moved to the 'Oasis', a transition home, where her thankfulness and sincerity of worship to the Lord were immediately noticed. She became very motivated, helpful, responsible and conscious that her future would be better with an education. Within a year she was studying at an alternative school for street children, 'Light and Life', and a few months later was living with a Christian family.

Today Margarita is an adult. She has been on evangelism outreaches where God has used her to bring others, even hardened criminals, to him. She helps care for the smaller children in the home where she lives. She is finishing high school and has a deep desire to help the poorest children in India. She believes that she can best serve God as a medical doctor.

Street Children's Ministry

Street Children's Ministry traces its beginnings to three separate but interconnected events. In 1973, a couple received God's call to work with street children. In 1981, a Youth With A Mission (YWAM) base expressed a deep desire to work with street children. Then, in 1982, eight Christian women dedicated themselves to prayer and fasting for the children according to Lamentations 2:19.

The common denominators for all three groups were prayer and intercession – the essential conditions for the birthing of the ministry. But there were other factors as well. An initial investigation was begun into who the street children really were; what programmes were already working with them and how; and what God's strategy might be for the children's permanent rehabilitation. New team members dedicated to God and to these children were found. A ministry philosophy was developed. And, finally, face-to-face work with the children was initiated in 1983 with Saturday 'picnics' for the kids at a large city park in the centre of Bogotá.

The early investigation had shown that many of the street kids were children and grandchildren of street people, some of whom had already been rehabilitated. But since the parents had never experienced a correct model of parenting, they raised their children as they had been raised: to go to the streets! This confirmed, first of all, that the rehabilitation process needed to be carried out within a family setting. Also, the generational cycle needed to be broken, the commitment to the children needed to be long-term, and the children needed to be reached early enough to provide them with a 're-parenting' stage with Christian principles that they could later model with their own children.

Parameters were set: the ministry would work with boys and girls both 'of' and 'on' the streets, as well as with those at high risk of going to the streets. The initial age range would be from birth to twelve years. Once at the residential phase, children could stay until they were integrated into a Christian family (either their restored biological family, an adoptive family or a substitute family) or they could remain at the centre until they became independent adults.

The ministry evolved as the team prayed, learned by experience and adjusted. The experience with the first child brought directly from the streets to a ministry family was a difficult situation which led to the development of a step by step process for preparing the children to live in the ministry's centre and finally to be integrated into a Christian family.

Today, our general strategy for restoring a street child in a comprehensive way consists of the following sequential stages. However, since each child has individual needs, some of the sequence may be modified, often with a child functioning in two stages at a time, depending on how he can best be served.

- *Friendship evangelism.* Spending time with the children where they live, providing for some of their immediate basic needs, gaining their trust and sharing God's love.

- *The Other Way.* This is a drop-in centre where the children can shower, eat, play, learn basic reading and numeracy skills and participate in a Bible club. The Other Way is also a short-term emergency shelter for children in emotional or physical crisis.

- *Light and Life School.* This school is specially designed for the street child who has behavioural problems or learning disabilities. Its purpose is to prepare the child to function in a community school or vocational training programme. Once a child has 'graduated', she still returns to Light and Life for individual tutoring and spiritual discipleship.

- *The Oasis.* Children just off the streets live

in this transition home full-time. Here they are prepared to live with a family, study, go to church and participate in positive group activities.

- *The Restored Heritage.* The child lives in a semi-rural location in a family environment until a permanent family (either his restored biological family or an adoptive family) can be found for him. Christian values, work and mutual respect are modelled for the child. Local Christian families can also help raise children in their own homes, under supervision by the ministry team. Local Christian families can also be recruited to re-parent children in their own homes. These are similar to foster families, having been approved by the local government child protection agency, yet, in the case of Street Children's Ministry, they do not receive payment from the government to raise the children.

- *Re-integration.* The child is returned to the biological family or placed in an adoptive or foster family. His siblings are placed in the same home if possible – if not, they are placed in homes in the same locality. When a child cannot be placed in his biological, adoptive or long-term foster family, he is allowed to stay with the family who has been re-parenting him within the programme until he is ready to leave. At that time several options are available to him to ease him through the transition from dependence to independence as an educated, self-supporting adult.

- *Follow-through.* The ministry team makes frequent visits to the home where the child has been placed in order to monitor the family's progress and provide help and advice if necessary. As the family's local church becomes more responsible for the family and as the family's stability is recognized, the visits by the ministry team become less frequent.

Street Children's Ministry is concerned for the orientation, training and ongoing spiritual development of its staff members. Weekly staff meetings emphasize intercession, spiritual principles and decision making as a group. New staff receive initial and ongoing orientations. Formal training for staff is offered each year, in courses ranging from weekend seminars to three-month 'live-in' schools. Street Children's Ministry trains its own staff and also opens courses to other ministries for staff training.

At any given time, the ministry works directly

with over one hundred children on a consistent (at least four contacts per week) basis. Since its inception, several hundred children have passed through at least two stages of the programme, and at least 60 children have left the streets permanently.

Children at risk because of sudden disaster (UK)

Josephine-Joy Wright

Profile of a child

'I didn't know where they were. I didn't know whether they were alive or dead. I ran everywhere looking. There were masses of people, people looking angry, frightened, scared like me – but none of them was my mother or my little brother. No one would tell me. No one could tell me. I was cold, wet. I hadn't brought a coat – I just ran when I heard the news. My mind was going crazy. I'd left my little sister and middle brother at home. They were only five and eight years old – too young to be left I'm sure you'd say now, but I didn't know what to do. I still don't know what to do. Nothing has been the same since my mum died. We lost our home, my aunt took us in but then she's in hospital now so we're on our own really. I'm the mum and at thirteen it all feels too much somedays. I want to die – but I can't leave them. I get nightmares, can't eat some days and feel all shaky. My mate's dad and his two friends died in that football match and he feels the same, but at least he still has his home – somewhere to feel safe. I don't feel safe anywhere and no one really wants to know, not now. It's old news. But I'm still running. I've been running for three years now just my dream isn't a dream, it's my life – I started running that moment they said "King's Cross Station, fire in the Underground." If only she had never gone shopping that day. It wasn't really necessary. Lots of life isn't really necessary I see now. Did anyone help, did anything help? That lady near the station who gave me a cup of tea and her coat 'cos I was shivering, still got the coat, means the world to me, means kindness. And the policeman who took mum and Tim's details, he really listened, really wanted to know and he had a team with him, normal folks it looked like but they were calm and working together. It gave you hope. And they found Tim.'

Response: An NHS and voluntary organizations partnership

Esther was thirteen years old when we spoke.

She encapsulates the fears and needs of children, young people and adults whose lives have been turned upside down by a sudden disaster – whether by an earthquake in East Timor, by severe flooding in the UK as in 2000, by the terrorist attacks in the United States on 11 September 2001 or by a train fire, aeroplane crash. I have worked both within statutory (NHS and social services) and voluntary services (pastoral and Christian counselling, victim support and CRUSE bereavement counselling) in major incidents and disasters such as these since my first personal experience with the M1 aircrash as a newly qualified psychologist. Through these experiences, I have been able to identify key elements that encapsulate the experiences of people working with a major disaster in their own lives and in the lives of their families and communities. We have begun to learn the keys to effective project work and service response to such disasters. With the King's Cross fire, the M1 aircrash, the Hillsborough football stadium crush, the Piper Alpha aeroplane bombing (all UK-based disasters in the late 1980s and early 1990s), those of us who were there to help were running with the survivors to plan, detail the logistics and implement major psychological and community response programmes within 24 hours. Inevitably, there were unnecessary casualties in terms of staff, volunteers and survivors. The Cutting Edge 2000 and the Nairobi Children of War in Africa Conference (2000) stimulated thinking about what different organizations, including World Vision, Medair, YWAM and Red Cross, are doing. How are we all responding in war-torn countries to the short- and long-term needs of survivors and of helpers? How should we respond? Some points for good practice have resulted from this reflection. Combining these points with those raised by survivors such as Esther, we can see that in sudden disaster situations we need to:

- Work together at all levels with statutory and voluntary organizations, combining their gifts.

- Pre-plan – both in terms of logistics and in identifying the gifts and resources of different organizations and individuals, but also in terms of building relationships. In the midst of disasters, people can become fearful and defensive. Those in charge of such work need to know that the teams involved are pre-trained, trusted, emotionally aware workers who have been identified in advance to do the work.

- Prioritize – neither individuals nor organizations can achieve everything at once and, without clear priorities, those involved end up working against one another.

- Train all workers to recognize the normal symptoms of post-traumatic stress (expressed and repressed) which they and others (children, young people and adults) will probably demonstrate in response to being involved in such work. It is important that workers are able to identify these symptoms in themselves and in their co-workers as well as in those they are trying to help. Workers also need to know how to respond to such symptoms (normalize them, help the person to tell their story in whatever way is appropriate and help them to feel heard and safe). Workers need to know how they can reduce their stress through leave, time out and so on, as well as how to identify who needs specialist help and where to obtain it.

- Train all workers in the resilience building, preventative strategies which can be used to mitigate against the development of severe physical, spiritual and psychological reactions (e.g., meeting basic needs such as food and shelter; being honest about why disasters happen and God's role in suffering; not pretending to have all the answers; allowing people to be real with

their feelings even if they are difficult; having regular, clearly communicated team briefings and times to talk; being together; showing people that they are appreciated and valued; having clear guidelines on how to protect oneself emotionally regarding levels of involvement).

- Be able to rapidly establish clear communication centres that give the best accurate information – and thus valid hope.

- Remember that staff and volunteers responding to the disasters, as well as those personally involved in the disaster, are all survivors and therefore all have needs. Routine debriefing and follow-up for everyone involved are essential for being a safe missionary organization, relief agency or statutory organization. Support for those on home leave is also essential.

- Educate those offering ongoing general services in the country about what the long-term needs of survivors will be after the crisis relief organizations go home, and train these people to offer effective follow-up services.

These are just a few of the findings of this partnership group, gleaned from working in this field since 1989. The greatest key is focusing on Christ's example – his example of humility, of compassion, of valuing people, of being real with his own needs and of working as part of a team of differently gifted individuals. Three cords are better than one – nowhere is this seen more clearly as we struggle together through the chaos and fear of a major sudden disaster (on a nationwide or personal level) to try to restore order and hope. Nowhere is there a greater need for the reality of his love to restore and renew, to provide a turning point and a future.

Children at risk because of HIV/AIDS (Zimbabwe)

Gill Grant and Heather Mkandawire

Profile of a child

Gertie is now sixteen. She was only twelve when her parents died. Her father was living and working in the small mining town of Zvishavane, while the rest of the family lived in their rural home and worked the fields, for economic reasons. After being sick for some

time with HIV, Gertie's father died of AIDS. Six weeks later, her mother died. Their bodies were buried just outside the family's kitchen hut in the rural homestead. For Gertie, every day there is a constant reminder of her loss, as she has to pass the graves of her beloved ones.

Gertie has one brother, Nigel, who is twelve. Her little sister Isabel is six. Both of them are

HIV-positive. This fact just adds to the strain on Gertie as she has to give them extra care and attention through their times of illness. At times when one or both are sick, she gets very little sleep as she has to sit with them and comfort them. She realizes that, one day, she will lose them too. Nigel, in particular, gets sick with TB and other infections in addition to his asthma. His growth is stunted because he was malnourished when he was younger. Medical fees are a problem, as they have no income. Although Bethany Project successfully advocated for free treatment at the district hospital, the drugs are often out of stock, so they have to be paid for at the pharmacy.

Gertie and Nigel are able to go to school, since Bethany has paid their fees. The children take Isabel to a Bethany volunteer (Vatete) in the neighbourhood, and collect her afterwards. Sometimes Gertie misses school because she doesn't like leaving either child when they are sick. 'I am afraid,' she says, 'because both my parents passed away while I was at school.' She works very hard, getting up early, doing the household chores and cooking the children's breakfast before school. After school she fetches water and firewood, cooks the evening meal, washes the dishes, washes the children, makes the beds, helps with their homework and cleans the house. She is then supposed to do her homework and study for exams, but she says she is often too tired.

The Vatete visits the children often and Gertie says, 'you will never know what Vatete's visits mean to us'. In their local culture, when someone dies of HIV people believe the family have been cursed, and they won't associate with them. In spite of all of Gertie's problems, she still thanks God that she's going to school and has Bethany's support. Bethany arranged for her to go to a Christian camp that organized activities, bereavement counselling and classes in teenage parenting skills. Gertie's outlook has certainly changed. Previously she would cry whenever we visited her, but now she is a delightful, confident girl who knows she is loved.

The project's 'Vatetes' receive little or no recompense for their work, but they are dedicated to serving God by looking after orphans. They say their motivation is 'to see the children smiling again', and 'to help nurture the future of Zimbabwe'.

The Bethany Project

The Bethany Project is a Christian NGO based in the mining town of Zvishavane, Zimbabwe. The town has a population of 129,000, and the district has one of the highest rates of HIV infection in the country. The project's main activities are training and mobilizing local communities to provide loving care and support for the orphaned children in their area. It also helps establish children's and youth clubs covering HIV prevention teaching and psychosocial support. Bethany Project has a fulltime team of four and works with 650 community volunteers.

The project was set up after local research in September 1995, and it was registered as a Private Voluntary Organisation in February 1998. Its mission statement is as follows:

- To help meet the mental, physical and spiritual needs of the most vulnerable orphan children in the Zvishavane District, and of other children living in especially difficult social circumstances

- To help mobilize local communities and churches to care for such children

- To raise awareness of the rights of children.

Since 1995, there have been 22 Community Based Orphan Care (CBOC) programmes established. Currently, 8,200 of the neediest orphans and vulnerable children are registered under the CBOC programmes, receiving varying degrees of support.

Three-day training workshops are held in the target community, using participatory approaches. The team asks questions to help the community members identify orphans' needs. The team then suggests activities that they themselves can do, without financial input, which will increase the children's quality of life.

The group elects a committee and volunteers who will visit families on a regular basis to befriend and help them (known as Vatetes). This group is then taught how to carry out an enumeration survey and to compile a register of the neediest orphans and vulnerable children. Their activities include:

- Practical help such as fetching firewood and water, ploughing fields, washing clothes and the children, re-roofing huts, taking sick children to the clinic

- Emotional support such as showing them love and care, listening to the children, playing with them, encouraging and nurturing them and being a friend

- Spiritual support such as praying with the children, reading the Bible to them, taking them to church, teaching spiritual values and demonstrating God's love

- Material support such as sharing food and clothing
- Other help such as teaching cultural traditions, values and basic skills such as sewing and hut repairs
- Advocacy (i.e., in school, for free medical treatment, for social welfare intervention in cases of neglect or abuse, for assistance with acquiring birth certificates, etc.).

The Bethany Project itself, although not a relief agency, also assists with a small amount of material help such as second-hand clothing, basic foodstuffs and school fees for as many of the children as possible.

Bethany is also involved in teaching youth groups. For the first few groups, teaching focused exclusively on the biblically-based syllabus on HIV awareness, with a variety of age-appropriate participatory methodologies. Topics covered include:

- Why I am special
- Respect for each other
- Respect for our bodies
- Choices
- Differences between the two sexes
- Signs of puberty

- Consequences of good and bad decisions
- Good and bad touches (related to sexual abuse)
- What is HIV/AIDS?
- How HIV/AIDS can and cannot be spread
- Caring for someone with HIV
- Peer education.

Current programmes, in addition to covering the above topics, include income-generation projects, psychosocial support and leisure activities. The groups mix orphan children and those with both parents in order to discourage stigmatization.

The project aims to decrease dependency and to promote sustainability within communities. Bethany is developing further income-generating projects by training community groups, youth groups and individual households. They are working in partnership with other NGOs who have the appropriate experience and skills to impart, such as small business management and identifying a market.

Community Based Orphan Care is far more effective than institutional care because it allows thousands more children to be reached and is far more economical. It is also more appropriate for children to grow up in their own environment and culture.

Children at risk because of family breakdown (UK)

Keith White

Profile of a child

Steven was abandoned at birth. His mother left him in the hospital. He was suffering from breathing difficulties and was often in hospital during his first year. When he finally came home, his mother and father's relationship had deteriorated to such a point that the family dwelling had become a battleground. He was locked in his room because his mother judged him to be out of control.

When it came to schooling, he stood no chance. He probably inherited a form of dyslexia, but the bigger problem was his inability to relate to people. He found the classroom situation impossible. He was excluded from school after school. He was placed in one foster family after another. Eventually he was sent to a special residential

school for those with behavioural difficulties and was referred to a Christian residential community called Mill Grove.

Steven has come to see Mill Grove as his (second) home. He still has behavioural problems and finds it difficult to sleep because he worries about the dark and being alone in his room. He finds eye contact and meeting new people very threatening. He needs to be active and finds it hard to talk about his feelings. He has, however, developed a sense of identity, responsibility and self-worth. He has begun college courses and is keen to relate with understanding to his mother and siblings. What has accounted for this change? It is difficult to make specific links of cause and effect, but the important elements in his progress include the following:

- *Unconditional acceptance.* He has been welcomed into our home and our hearts and knows that this acceptance does not depend on good behaviour. We are there for him as long as we live.
- *Being 'held'.* It soon became clear that Steven's anger had never been 'contained'. He never felt safe, because he had never experienced the strong and loving arms of a parent. It was at Mill Grove that he first experienced this security.
- *Being affirmed.* Steven is an intelligent and very sensitive boy. He has very high standards and usually fails to achieve them. We needed to encourage and praise him consistently – in time he came to believe in certain of his abilities and feelings. He did not have a concept of personhood and would whimsically say 'hello' to people in a room with him in order to gain confirmation that he still existed for them. The process of affirmation of his existence took several years.
- *A basis for confidence.* In the light of his 'failure' at school and at home he desperately needed to achieve something, to find something he could do, in order to build his confidence. His gifts emerged slowly: he was superb with Lego and engines. We entrusted him with responsibility for our lawn mowers. He also showed great aptitude for rock climbing, and after a lot of practice together he found he had become more proficient than I had. A special time came when he helped me up a rock face! He also sailed and gained his first certificate ever in power boating. He treasures this and carries it around with him almost everywhere.

Our faith in Jesus motivated us, and we sought to live it out alongside Steven. He listened to the Bible stories and worshipped with us. The place in which he feels most comfortable, apart from Mill Grove, is a Christian Outdoor Centre – there he finds others living out the gospel. He has a good relationship with some of the team and finds a consistency of life and example.

He still has difficulty sleeping, is shy and finds writing very problematical. Yet the disorganized and ambivalent attachments of his earliest years have been replaced by dependable ones. He has found a place where he belongs. A foster or adoptive family would not have worked – they would have been too demanding from his point of view. He is beginning to realize that people like him to be around. He

has a wonderful sense of humour, and his enthusiasm is infectious. In some ways, the lost has been found . . . in the name of Jesus and in the power of his spirit.

Mill Grove

Mill Grove is the home of a unique family and residential community in South Woodford on the outskirts of London. It began as an informal foster family in 1899 and is still a place of love and care for children and young people who cannot live with their own families. It is a lively place where Christians are seeking to respond to the needs of children and young people by sharing their lives with them in a homely setting and atmosphere.

The story of 'the family' is one of a simple faith expressed in daily living. Through the twentieth century the community has adapted to many changes and pressures while seeking to remain true to the aims of its founders. Since 1899, over 1,000 children have lived at Mill Grove for all or part of their childhood and many of these, spread all over the world, regard Mill Grove as their home.

In 1899, Herbert White asked Rosa Hutchin to provide a home for a destitute girl, Rosie. It was a spontaneous expression of their Christian commitment and love. Herbert was himself an orphan and knew from experience something of the pain of separation. They also saw clearly the appalling poverty and deprivation of children on the outskirts of London. In time, the property being used was given to Herbert White. Herbert had no desire to own anything himself, so he established the 'Children's Home and Mission' under a trust deed. Mill Grove is a registered charity, independent of any denomination or organization.

The aims of Mill Grove are:

1. To care for children in need: every child needs the unconditional love and commitment of at least one adult. Where this is lacking, Mill Grove seeks to provide it. Our approach has adapted to the changing social context and patterns of life. We make no distinction on grounds of race, gender, creed or ability, and we seek to respond to each child and family with sensitivity.

2. To encourage the spiritual development of children. The adults who live as part of the Mill Grove family believe that God is concerned for and loves every child and family. We believe that we can know God as our heavenly father in and through Jesus Christ and with the help of the Holy Spirit. We believe that the love of God is the source of

individual human growth, development and personal relationships. We take his commands to be the basis for the well-being of communities and society.

3. To rely on God alone to meet all the needs of Mill Grove. Herbert White's intention was that the home would be a venture of faith, testifying to the love and power of God. For this reason, there is no fund-raising or advertising. Needs are shared only in private prayer and we offer care irrespective of anyone's ability to pay. Most of our income comes from gifts of Christian individuals, families and churches. Many churches send us their harvest produce. We receive no formal government or local authority funding.

Children usually come because there have been major problems in their own families such as death, separation, illness, homelessness or physical and emotional traumas. As a consequence of the severity of the problems in their situations, there is little or no prospect of them living with relatives – even if support and financial help are given. Parents, families, churches and local authorities who turn to Mill Grove asking for help with children and young people see it, perhaps above all, as a stable and caring environment where children can thrive, maintain links with family and friends (where that is desirable) and where they can stay until they are ready to move on. Sometimes we are also asked to care for siblings who would otherwise have been separated.

In more recent years we have also received whole families that have been homeless or needed support. Children and families come from a wide variety of backgrounds and cultures and have a great diversity of gifts as well as needs. We seek to understand a child's strengths and potential before focusing on any problems or needs. We believe that shared-living based on God-given rhythms and patterns can provide a therapeutic context in which the deepest personal and social wounds can be healed, and in which creative growth and expression can be encouraged.

People of all ages live in Mill Grove. Typically some are at home, some at school, some at college, some at work, some retired. From Monday to Friday, there is education at local schools and a work routine. Evenings are spent together or with friends. Weekends are times of relaxation and include practical tasks and shopping. Sundays are special, with time for worship. Friends often come to share with us, as do members of the wider family. Sometimes the children have been tragically let down in their natural families. We seek to create a setting in which they can put down new roots, live through and come to terms with unhappy previous experiences and begin to develop self-esteem, a sense of trust and identity and a willingness to accept choices and responsibilities. Mill Grove family members include adults who keep abreast of childcare knowledge and have access to a nationwide network of resources, which we use to assist in the understanding and development of a child. Such resources (educational, psychiatric, therapeutic) will always be appropriate within the context of ordinary family and community life.

Some children stay at Mill Grove for a comparatively short time, but many stay until they are ready to set up their own home, go to college, move in connection with work or settle down and marry in the same way as their contemporaries. As part of a transition to independent living we do have some self-contained accommodation at Mill Grove, and we encourage those at work or college to accept some responsibility for their own household chores.

We are an accepted part of the community. Neighbours often come in, and Mill Grove helped to set up a lively local community association, pre-school playgroup and a parents and toddlers group. Many other local activities and events take place in the Mill Grove hall. Premises have been adapted to provide facilities for the local community without encroaching on our daily life.

Children at risk because of domestic violence (UK)

Amanda Jones and Trudie Rossouw

Profile of a child

John is a three-year-old boy who was referred to me because of his violent behaviour towards his mother and the other children at his nursery. He was an only child, and his mother was a single parent. When I met them, his mother explained to me how hyperactive he was. He would wake her early in the morning and scream his demands at her all day, treating her like a brainless slave, showing no regard for her feelings. In the first session his mother looked at me with dark, tired rings under her eyes, while John bounced around like a little angel.

I asked her to describe to me the worst episode of the day before. She told me that John didn't want to eat his dinner and was just playing with it. She told him that if he didn't eat it she was going to take it away, which of course was what happened. John was furious and went into the sitting room and started to throw the sofa cushions on to the floor. His mother went to tidy up, but this made him even more furious and he started to throw things at the TV. He was beginning to lose control, running and screaming with his mother hot on his heels, screaming and threatening. In this way the two of them got lost in a cycle in which both were getting increasingly loud and frightened. Violent eruption was becoming more and more inevitable.

Then the bubble burst for John's mother. She grabbed him forcefully and carried him under her arm to his bedroom. She put him down on his bed with great force and covered him with his blankets to 'straitjacket' him. Inside, she felt she could kill him. I think he was aware of this. Both of them were, at this stage, utterly terrified of the feelings inside him. After telling him to stay in his bed, she left his room. He, possibly in a frozen state, stayed in his room and didn't make a sound. She phoned her mother. She cried on the phone and said that she had almost killed her son.

While listening to the story I felt a sense of empathy for both John and his mother. It seemed that something so small tipped them so easily into an escalating pattern of violence and fear. I was also very aware of her tremendous sense of guilt about the way she felt. I commented that it seemed that when John was upset about the food, it was difficult for her to just let him be. She behaved as if she wanted to stop him from being cross, and the more she became involved with him at that stage, the worse the situation became. I wondered what it was in his behaviour that frightened her. She replied that she was afraid that his scream would get worse and he would hurt himself.

I didn't think he was endangering himself at the point when he screamed, so I wondered what was triggered for her unconsciously, which made her perceive his behaviour as more dangerous than it really was. I asked her what his scream reminded her of. Without a second's thought, she said, 'my sister'.

It emerged that her sister, who was born when she was four years old, was developmentally delayed and had many emotional and behavioural problems. Her sister was also often left in her care. She described in detail how her sister used to have terrible tantrums in which she would bash her own head repeatedly against the wall. Often on these occasions John's mother would be alone with her sister and be terrified that she was going to kill herself. She would be overwhelmed with a sense of helplessness and fear.

Understanding the loneliness and terror of a little girl who had the responsibility to care for such a disturbed young child made me understand John's mother's anxiety when her son displayed a 'normal' temper tantrum. If his experience of his angry feelings was that it evoked that overwhelming state of anxiety in his mother, he would be likely to conclude that his emotions, and he himself, were very destructive and bad. If he sees himself as bad, he is likely to start behaving in that way.

Once I understood the nature of the problem, we were able to separate John's mother's past from the present. We were then able to reframe John's behaviour in more realistic terms. Slowly, over time, she was able to see John more for who he was. She also became more able to feel a sense of strength within herself, which enabled her to be less frightened by him. Consequently, he was less frightened by himself.

Redbridge Infant Mental Health Service

Redbridge is a London borough consisting of a multicultural social environment with a high proportion of ethnic minority groups, refugees and single parent families. A new Infant Mental Health Service (IMHS) has just been established there. It works with families who have children of four years and younger where there are concerns about emotional or behavioural difficulties. These problems present in many different ways, including sleeping difficulties, feeding difficulties, attachment problems, hyperactivity, aggression and temper tantrums. The IMHS also intervenes where children are not yet showing signs of distress, but where they are at risk of developing emotional or behavioural difficulties later on – for example, in families where there is domestic violence, parental mental illness, cases of suspected abuse or neglect or children with chronic medical illnesses.

'Mental health difficulties' in such a young age group seem daunting, but early intervention focusing on the relationship between the infant and the caregivers can have powerful preventative functions. Research has indicated that early treatment of disturbed behaviour in the young, as well as enhancing mother-child bonding, could also prevent the development of criminal and violent behaviour later on. The project also provides treatment for those mothers with postnatal depression after the first line of intervention (either medication and/or involvement from a health visitor) has proved unsuccessful, or when the bonding does not improve after this first line of treatment.

The IMHS forms part of the local Child and Adolescent Mental Health Service and is housed in the same premises. The service has active links with community workers, GPs, health visitors, paediatricians, midwives, obstetricians, social services and adult psychiatric services. A consultant child and adolescent psychiatrist and a psychotherapist run the service. The two professionals were successful in raising funding and will continue to do so in order to be able to employ more professionals.

We receive referrals from health professionals and social services, as well as self-referrals from parents. We provide a rapid response, aiming to see cases within the first two weeks of referral. A family is then offered a six-session intervention focusing on the parent-child relationship. Many other aspects are interwoven into the rich texture of that relationship – such as the relationship of the parents with one another; the parents' past relationships with their parents; the parents' internal representation of the child; the child's temperament and health and social factors, to mention just a few. Our interventions therefore focus on an intergenerational and psychodynamic understanding of all these elements and their influences on the parent-child relationship. Psychodynamic understanding can often bring about a shift in the coherence of the narrative of the past, which makes integration and coherence of the present possible. This understanding can free a parent to see her child for who he is, and not through the veil of past 'ghosts and monsters'.

Children at risk in the church (World-wide Missionary Kids/UK)

David and Pauline Pearson

Profile of a child

Sasha Brown sat in her room – confused, upset and angry all at the same time. How could she have been so stupid? She was ten years old. She ought to know better. Her mum and dad were always saying how clever she was. But how was she supposed to know that the 'touching' thing would happen again? After all, Jenny was one of the leaders, a wonderful Christian. All the other kids loved her. How could she tell her mum and dad that Jenny had been touching her between her legs and had then got Sasha to touch her in the same

place? How could she talk about those pictures Jenny had shown her on the Internet?

Sasha decided she could not tell her mum. Jenny had warned her that her mother wouldn't do anything anyway, that her mother thought it was OK. But was it? She decided to talk to her dad once he came out of the meeting with the other mission workers. It was a long two hours, and she could not meet Jenny's eyes when she came out laughing and talking with the others.

Sasha grabbed her dad's hand when, finally, he emerged from the room. 'I need to talk to you, Dad,' she whispered. 'It's really important.' He looked at her and nodded, 'I can spare you two minutes, love . . .'

Half an hour later, Sasha's dad was looking and feeling devastated, but he gave her arm a brief squeeze and said, 'Thank you for telling me, Sasha. That must have been so hard. I need to do something about this – Jenny mustn't be allowed to do this again to you or anyone else. I'll let you know what I decide.'

Ed Brown knocked on the field director's door. He had spent the last hour walking blindly in the burning heat of midday, weeping, asking God for help and then shouting at God for not intervening. Now he was angry enough to do something he might regret later, so he figured he should let the boss know the situation.

The field director, to put it mildly, was shocked. Jenny had been a vibrant personality for the two and a half years she had been on the campus. She had a natural rapport with the children and young people she taught in the mission school and took camping in the hill country. She volunteered to run the kids' club and would be there, often on her own, until all hours.

'She'll have to go,' he said firmly, 'back to England. I can't have her putting children at risk here.'

'What about her fiancé?' queried Ed. 'They're getting married later this year and were planning to take over from the Frobishers up north. Are you going to tell him? And are we going to involve the police? After all, it's my child who's been abused. Is there going to be any help for her? How am I going to tell my wife? This is such a mess!'

When confronted, Jenny said it was a pack of lies and packed her bags to return to her teaching job in England.

The Churches' Child Protection Advisory Service

This case study raises a number of issues, such as how an allegation of a serious offence against a child should be investigated, what kind of help children like Sasha need, and how procedures can be improved to minimize the risk of such incidents occurring in the first place.

Involving the authorities should always be considered. Sexual abuse such as that experienced by Sasha would be recognized in the UK, Australasia, USA, Canada and in some other parts of the world as grounds for legal action and as a child protection issue, but not everywhere. In some cultures and countries the attitude that 'sexual abuse doesn't happen here' is ingrained. It is important to know what would be the expected action in child protection and abuse situations in the place where you are working.

Let's assume that the country's authorities could not deal with Sasha's situation. She needs to be protected from further abuse and may also need help to deal with the emotional turmoil that she is in. It will not be helpful for her to see Jenny wherever she goes and, in any case, Jenny should now be denied access to any children. Perhaps the field director will meet with Jenny, tell her about the allegations and invite her response.

A careful note of Sasha's allegations should have been taken, using her exact words and anything said to her by a parent or worker, and similar notes should also have been taken of Jenny's response when confronted. The field director would also need to record details of all action taken. In Britain, we would advise that the matter should only be discussed with those named in a Child Protection Policy and that the allegations should be reported directly to social services or the police without alerting Jenny.

Jenny should have no further access to the computer – the Internet pictures could be incriminating. We would advise the mission that Jenny should return to the sending country and that the matter should be investigated as independently as possible. The Churches' Child Protection Advisory Service (CCPAS) can offer step-by-step guidance to any agency placed in such a situation. If Jenny is returned to the UK, the agency should give social services full written information about the allegations and the action taken.

It could be that there have been previous concerns in Jenny's teaching career. She is going to need some specialist help to deal with this abusive behaviour. Her church leader needs to ensure that children in the congregation are protected from her. This leader may need to think about establishing a contract with Jenny, which will set out the boundaries of her church involvement while still offering her pastoral support.

Back on the campus, the field director would have to consider the needs of other children who may have been abused. (Sasha is unlikely to be the only victim.) What will he tell the other workers about Jenny's sudden departure? What will her fiancé and other friends think? Sasha's parents will need pastoral support and counselling from the organization. In all circumstances the reporting chain should be kept to a minimum, with people being informed on a 'need to know' basis so as not to jeopardize any enquiry and to preserve confidentiality.

In the short-term, Sasha will need reassurance that she was right to tell and that she has not been naughty. Someone with whom she feels comfortable and who is in authority will need to make an age-appropriate explanation to her about what is happening. All children should routinely be helped to develop personal safety skills in order to prevent abuse in the first place or bring matters to light quickly when devious adults break through those defences. This will be especially important for children who have been abused, as so often they are vulnerable to further abuse. In the longer term, a child may need specialist counselling help. However, in circumstances where there are going to be formal proceedings, counsellors will need to be aware of the various issues regarding therapeutic help for child witnesses prior to a criminal trial.

To prevent abusive incidents from occurring, it is important to ensure that workers work as a team, responsible to and for each other. There should be practice guidelines on touch, sleep-ing arrangements and transport. This is not just for the protection of the children, but also in order to protect workers from possible false allegations.

CCPAS is the leading Christian child protection agency in Britain, working uniquely across denominations and children's organizations. The work is strongly supported by the department of health and the association of chief police officers and church leaders. CCPAS provide some one hundred training events in Britain every year. In addition, they have developed video training materials used by churches and organizations both at home and abroad and have a range of other child protection resources. A team of Christian social workers and counsellors with extensive experience in child protection staffs the CCPAS helpline. Services are available to leaders, workers, individual families, children and young people.

All the practice issues outlined above are covered in more detail in 'Guidance to Churches', published by CCPAS. This is a comprehensive child protection manual for leaders and workers relating to churches, children's groups, camps, counselling centres and overseas missions.

Children at risk of abuse on the Internet

Nigel Williams

What happened to one family

In February 2000, a stranger entered the Smith's home without their knowledge or consent. The intruder was not a normal housebreaker and his intentions were far more sinister than merely stealing replaceable possessions. From a cowardly and anonymous vantage point, many miles away, he had logged onto a teenage chat room via the Internet and was waiting for his intended prey – a young girl who had also logged on, with the intention of corresponding with her peers. She became instead the unwitting subject of a relentless campaign to rob her of her childhood and innocence.

In the same way in which a spider weaves a web to trap his victim, this perpetrator spun many 'expressions of love' and managed to appear as a friend. Once obtaining her e-mail address, he bombarded her with messages, with the goal of getting to meet her alone. All of this took place over a period of weeks, within the confines of the family house, and went undetected by her parents.

Caught in an unequal, abusive relationship, the young girl was unable to rebuff this man's endeavours to arrange a rendezvous. She finally gave way and agreed to a meeting in a public place. Her 33-year-old assailant arrived by car and, after identifying himself to her, removed her to his flat many miles away, and so began a series of indecent assaults.

The young girl finally broke down and shared the event with her parents, who were stunned and completely numb. Immediately they informed the police, who arrested the perpetrator and confiscated a number of items pending analysis, including his home computer, which was found to contain indecent pictures of children stored on the hard drive. He was released on police bail pending further investigation and results of the laboratory analysis.

Within days, he had used the computer at his place of work to contact another young underage girl and, using similar tactics, drove hundreds of miles across the country to commit a similar assault. Thankfully, his work colleagues discovered some disturbing e-mails and tipped off the police who mounted a surveillance operation and re-arrested him, just as the next young victim was getting into his car.

The Internet is fast becoming as important to our lives as good roads. However, unlike a public highway on which children are taught how to cross and keep safe, the Internet, and chat rooms in particular, can be dangerous places for children. This one tragedy, whilst being the first case in the UK to be tried in court, is by no means isolated. In this case the victim's father worked in the computer industry and was very familiar with the Internet. However, he did not realize what could happen in chat.

The victim in this incident, along with the wider family, have gone through acute pain and heartache. However, they have managed to show enormous courage in seeking to publicize this incident in the hope of alerting others to the risks.[1]

How a child is at risk

The Internet has increased the opportunities for people to be in touch with one another. The medium offers e-mail, bulletin boards, news groups and, for communication in real time, instant messaging and chat. Chat rooms are places online where people can meet other people, perhaps with a similar interest, and have conversations in real time, essentially like an on-line 'living room' in which people from all over the world can chat to each other.

In a chat room a person can pretend to be whoever she wants to be. Although this may be one of the great attractions of chat rooms for children, ironically this is also the source of a new kind of danger.

Although Internet chat rooms can be used in creative ways to connect children together, the unsupervised use of chat rooms can be very dangerous for children – especially when adults use them to seek to strike up sexual relationships with young teenagers or children. Paedophiles have recognized the opportunity the Internet affords them to contact children at a safe distance, building up a rela-

tionship with them for the sole purpose of persuading them into sexual activity.

The techniques which sex offenders use to entice children into sexual activity are known as 'grooming', and this follows a recognized sequence. The adult makes initial contact with the child in a chat room. Once this contact has been established, the adult invites the child into a private area of the chat room to get to know them better.[2] Next in the grooming sequence comes private chat via an instant messaging service, and then e-mail contact, telephone conversations (often on mobile phones) and finally a face-to-face meeting. The grooming process can go on for weeks and months, as it may take this long for the child to feel truly comfortable. The patience of the predator may also be explained partly by the fact that it is not uncommon for them to be grooming several children at the same time. Therefore, even if a child begins to feel uncomfortable and breaks off the relationship, there are others lined up.

It is in this context that the Internet has been called the 'school yard of the twenty-first century'. Chat rooms can afford the predator invisible access to children from a safe distance, enabling contact even while the child is using the Internet in the secure surroundings of her own home – even her own bedroom.

The Internet thus gives the paedophile the possibility of daily contact with a child – a degree of contact that would be impossible unless the paedophile was a family member or a care worker. The paedophile is thus able to manipulate the emotions of a young child over a long period of time to the point that the child feels safe enough to have a face-to-face, off-line, meeting – and thus to the point that the child is sexually abused.

There have been numerous cases of such abuse in the USA. This crime is also occurring increasingly in the UK, and there are cases in other countries all over the world. It seems clear that this new type of crime is not going to go away – at least not on its own.

How Childnet addresses the problem

In a Europe-wide research study,[3] Childnet International identified and grouped the dangers facing children on the Internet under three broad headings: content, contact and commercialism. 'Content' is defined as accessing inappropriate content including pornography, child pornography, racist/hate and violent sites. 'Contact' refers to being contacted through chat rooms and e-mail by those who would seek to harm or lure them. 'Commercial' danger is found in the blurry distinction between much content and advertising, direct marketing to children and collecting information that violates privacy. Of these three, 'contact' is the danger about which parents are the most concerned.

Childnet International set up the website www.chatdanger.com to inform children and parents about the potential dangers in chat rooms and to advise them how to keep safe while chatting. This website contains a contact form, and since the website has been live they have received thousands of e-mails from concerned children and parents giving Childnet staff details of their experiences using chat rooms. Many of these were seeking advice or even assistance.

Childnet are also active in trying to raise awareness among children, parents and teachers about such potential dangers and also in offering advice on how to stay safe online. The Childnet International website gives details of some of their awareness-raising work, which has spanned the globe. Recently they were involved in a Kidsmart programme aimed at getting key safety messages to children in schools (see www.kidsmart.org.uk).

Childnet has also been very active in the public policy response to this situation, particularly in the UK. We are members of the Home Office Task Force on Internet Safety for Children, and are helping to formulate legislation that would offer children a degree of protection from online predators that they are not afforded at present. We are also calling for a review of law enforcement techniques in this area.

Childnet have also been active in lobbying the chat service providers to take steps to make the chat rooms more child-safe. Measures here include, for example, displaying clear and visible safety messages in the chat room and offering moderated chat services.

Childnet have been active in trying to assure a policy response around the world, and they have raised this issue at international platforms such as the Yokohama Congress 2001 and other international conferences. They have also been in consultation with several national governments with regard to this issue and to more general Internet safety strategies.

Childnet are especially concerned about the links between the use of the Internet to contact children and the use of mobile phones to extend or even initiate such contact. This is an area that Childnet will be researching further.

Notes

1. This story is taken from www.chatdanger.com and used with permission.
2. Although there is no blueprint for the language of grooming, there are some characteristics of the communication that may give clues as to the true nature of a new online 'friendship'. Such warning signals include the 'friend' constantly asking the child for information before revealing anything about himself; sending numerous messages; asking for personal contact details; asking private questions; and asking for photographs. These more clear-cut characteristics of grooming would be accompanied by more subtle signals, such as showing an excessive interest in the child or flattering the child. Given that all this could be contained in communications stretching over a period of months, and that the initiator is conscious of the need for subtlety in this delicate and intricate manipulation, these warning signals would not necessarily be obvious.
3. See www.netaware.org.

– Appendix –

Celebrating Children Course Syllabus

– Part 1 –

Understanding the Child in Context

1 'What is a child?' as a physical, moral, spiritual, cognitive, emotional and social being.
2 Who are children? How do they describe themselves?
3 What does the Bible say about children?
4 How do children develop in their families and communities?
5 What are the factors that optimize a child's development in his or her particular context?
6 What are the key theoretical frameworks and their applications (physiological, cognitive-developmental, learning theories, ethological, anthropological and socio-ecological)?
7 What are the 'rights' of the child (CRC) and how should the Christian respond?

– Part 2 –

Key Issues in Listening to Children

8 How can we listen to children and enable their involvement?
9 How can we involve children in assessment and therapy?
10 What 'rights' does a child have to speak and be heard? What are the implications of silence?
11 How can we listen to children and involve them in programme and policy planning that affects them?
12 What is the purpose of advocacy for and with children?
13 What are the ethical issues involved in listening, or not listening, to children?

– Part 3 –

Risk and Resilience

14 What are the strategic trends affecting children at risk?
15 How can you examine how and why children are 'at risk'?
16 What are the various theoretical frameworks defining risk and resilience?
17 How can needs be evaluated using an integrated biblical and theoretical typology of children's needs?
18 What happens when a child's needs are not met, and what are the affects on the child, her family and community?
19 How can you explore and release children's strengths, gifts and potential?
   (Explore individual profiles of 'children at risk', see Part Eight.)

– Part 4 –

Holistic Mission to Children

20 What is the churches' ministry to children and their families – globally, nationally and locally?
21 What are the practical and spiritual implications, lessons and responsibilities for the current practice of the church's ministry to children (including the ministries of Christian organizations and missions)?
22 What is the basis for the design of child development programmes?
23 What are the implications of 'the 4/14 Window'?

24 What is the child's place in the church?

25 Why are children at the heart of mission?

26 What does the Bible say about suffering? Why do children suffer?

– Part 5 –

Working with Children: Practical Issues

27 What kinds of skills and qualities does a worker need to effectively meet the holistic (i.e., physical/medical, moral, spiritual, cognitive/educational, emotional, social, recreational) needs of children (and their families) in practice?

28 What are the basic medical needs and symptoms of children at risk of malnutrition and infection?

29 What additional practical skills will workers need to be effective in their various contexts (e.g., discipline, supporting parents caring for 'difficult' children and sharing your faith with a child)?

30 What is child protection, and how can you develop a child protection policy?

31 What are the key issues involve in selecting, monitoring and training staff?

32 Why, how and where can you store, access and use key information?

– Part 6 –

Development, Evaluation and Monitoring of Programmes

33 What are some effective methods for doing research, documentation and data collection?

34 What are the principles of evaluative practice?

35 What are the principles of good practice in programmes working with children?

36 What are some methods for assessment and evaluating organizational strengths and weaknesses?

37 How can prevention and rehabilitation be used together in working with children? (Consider different projects working with 'children at risk', see Part Eight.)

– Part 7 –

Development of Self and Staff

38 How can you address your own personal strengths and vulnerabilities and those of others working with children?

39 What are some practical guidelines for Christians working with children?

40 Why are motivation, spiritual refreshment, encouragement and rest both biblical and essential for good practice?

41 How can you develop emotional awareness and meet your own needs and those of others working with children?

42 What are some appropriate techniques for conflict resolution with children and colleagues?

43 How can you work effectively with group processes, socio-cultural variables and team dynamics?

– Part 8 –

Case Studies from around the World

Bibliography

Ager, A., *Refugees: Perspectives on the Experience of Forced Migration* (London: Cassell, 1999).

Ainsworth, M.D.S., 'The Development of Mother-Infant Interaction among the Ganda', in *Determinants of Infant Behaviour*, II (ed. B.M. Foss; New York: Wiley, 1963), 67–112.

Alderson, P., *Listening to Children: Children, Ethics and Research* (Ilford: Barnardos, 1995).

Aldrich, H., and E. Auster, 'Even Dwarfs Started Small: Liabilities of Age and Size and Their Strategic Implications', in *The Evolution and Adaptation of Organizations* (ed. L. Cummings and B. Staw; Greenwich, CT: JAI Press, 1990), 33–66.

Anastasi, A., *Psychological Testing* (New York: Macmillan, 6th edn, 1988).

Anderson, W.T., *Reality Ain't What It Used To Be* (New York: HarperCollins, 1990).

Ansoff, H.I., *Corporate Strategy* (London: Penguin, 1987).

Ariès, P., *Centuries of Childhood* (London: Penguin, 1962).

Arnold, J.C., *A Little Child Shall Lead Them* (Farmington, PA: Plough Publishing, 1997).

Backett-Milburn, K., and L. McKie, 'A Critical Appraisal of the Draw and Write Technique', *Health Education, Research Theory and Practice* 14.3 (1999), 387–98.

Baker, R., *Understanding Panic Attacks and Overcoming Fear* (Oxford: Lion Books, 1995).

Balda, J.B., 'The Liability of Nonprofits to Donors', *Nonprofit Management and Leadership* 5 (1994), 67–83.

Barclay, W., *Daily Study Bible: Romans* (Edinburgh: St Andrew's Press, 1962).

Barker, P., *Basic Child Psychiatry* (Oxford: Blackwell, 1995).

Barkley, R.A., *Taking Charge of ADHD: The Complete, Authoritative Guide for Parents* (New York: Guilford Press, 1995).

Barnard, P., I. Morland and J. Nagy, *Children, Bereavement and Trauma: Nurturing Resilience* (London: Jessica Kingsley, 1999).

Barrett, D., and T. Johnson, *AD2000 Global Monitor* (Jan. 1990).

——, *AD2000 Global Monitor* (April 1991).

Barton, S.C., *Towards a Theology of the Family* (Crucible: Board for Social Responsibility, 1993).

Bayley, A., *One New Humanity: The Challenge of AIDS* (International Study Guide 33; London: SPCK, 1996).

Beacham, M., 'He Loves Me, He Loves Me Not: God, Spiritual Development and Recovery from Childhood Trauma', *Introduction to Transpersonal Psychology*, www.tmn.com (1994).

Beardshaw, T., G. Hordern and C. Tufnell, *Single Parents in Focus* (Cardiff: Care for the Family, 2000).

Belbin, R.M., *Original Management Teams: Why They Succeed and Fail* (London: Butterworth Heinemann, 1981).

——, *Team Roles at Work* (London: Butterworth Heinemann, 1993).

Benke, W., and M. Bryan, 'The World's Most Fruitful Field', *Evangelizing Today's Child* (Nov./Dec. 1977), 4–8, 44–45.

Bennis, W., and B. Nanus, *Leaders: Strategies for Taking Charge* (New York: HarperCollins, 2nd edn, 1997).

Berg, D.V., and S. Van Brockern, 'Building Resilience through Humor', *Journal of Emotional and Behavioral Problems* 4.3 (1995), 26–29.

Berk, L., *Infants, Children, and Adolescents* (Boston: Allyn and Bacon, 1999).

Benard, B., 'Fostering Resilience in Children', *ERIC Digest* database EDO-PS-95-9 (1995).

Berne, E., *Games People Play* (New York: Grove Press, 1964).

Bielefield, W., 'What Affects Nonprofit Survival?', *Nonprofit Management and Leadership* 5 (1994), 19–36.

Bindé, J., 'Going Backwards into the Future', *The Star (South Africa)* (UNESCO Analysis and Forecasting Office, 31 Aug. 1998).

Blackburn, C., 'Resilient Children and Families', www.ecdgroup.com/cn/claudia.html (2000).

'Black Hole: The Shadow Economy', *The Economist* (28 Aug. 1999).

Blake, W., *Songs of Innocence* (Oxford: Oxford University Press, 1970).

Blankenhorn, D., *Fatherless America: Confronting Our Most Urgent Social Problem* (New York: Basic Books, 1995).

Boeker, W., and J. Goodstein, 'Organizational Performance and Adaptation: Effects of Environment and Performance on Changes in Board Composition', *Academy of Management Journal* 34 (1991), 805–26.

Bosch, D.J., *Transforming Mission: Paradigm Shifts in Theology of Mission* (Maryknoll, NY: Orbis Books, 1991).

Bowlby, J., 'The Growth of the Independent Child', *Royal Society of Health Journal* 76 (1956), 587–91.

——, *The Making and Breaking of Affectional Bonds* (London: Tavistock, 1979).

——, *Attachment and Loss*, I: *Attachment* (New York: Basic Books, 1982).

Boyden, J., 'Childhood and the Policy Makers: A Comparative Perspective on the Globalisation of Childhood', in *Constructing and Reconstructing Childhood* (ed. A. James and A. Prout; London: Falmer Press, 2nd edn, 1997).

——, and S. Gibbs, *Children of War: Responses to Psycho-Social Distress in Cambodia* (Geneva: United Nations Research Institute for Social Development, 1997).

Bronfenbrenner, U., *The Ecology of Human Development* (Cambridge, MA: Harvard University Press, 1979).

——, 'The Ecology of Cognitive Development: Research Models and Fugitive Findings', in *Development in Context* (ed. R.H. Wozniak and K.W. Fischer; Hillsdale, NJ: Erlbaum, 1993), 3–44.

Brown, L., C. Flavin and H. French, *State of the World 2000* (New York: Norton, 2000).

——, M. Renner and B. Halweil, *Vital Signs 1999* (Washington, DC: Worldwatch Institute, 1999).

——, and E. Politt, 'Malnutrition, Poverty and Intellectual Development', *Scientific American* 274.2 (1996), 38–43.

Browning, D., 'Practical Theology and the American Family Debate: An Overview', *International Journal of Practical Theology* 1.1 (1997), 136–60.

Bruce, J., C.B. Lloyd and A. Leonard, *Families in Focus: New Perspectives on Mothers, Fathers and Children* (New York: The Population Council, 1995).

Buchannan, A., and A. Katz, *Factors Associated with High and Low Self-Esteem in Boys and Girls* (London: Mental Health Foundation, 1999).

Butler, S., J. Gross and H. Hayne, 'The Effect of Drawing on Memory Performance in Young Children', *Developmental Psychology* 31 (1995), 597–608.

Cameron, C., *Resolving Childhood Trauma: A Long-Term Study of Abuse Survivors* (London: Sage Publications, 2000).

Capaldi, D., and G. Patterson, 'Relation of Parental Transitions to Boys' Adjustment Problems: I. A Linear Hypothesis. II. Mothers at Risk for Transitions and Unskilled Parenting', *Developmental Psychology* 27 (1991), 489–504.

Carey, C., 'A Hot Water Bottle and a Dolly', *Connect* (Viva Network) 14 (Sept. 2002), 7.

Carnoy, M., M. Castells, S. Cohen and F. Cardosa, *The New Global Economy in the Information Age* (University Park: Pennsylvania State University Press, 1993).

Carr, A., *Child and Adolescent Clinical Psychology* (London: Routledge, 1999).

Carroll, G., J. Delacroix and J. Goodstein, 'The Political Environment of Organizations: An Ecological View', in *The Evolution and Adaptation of Organizations* (ed. B.M. Staw and L.L. Cummings; Greenwich, CT: JAI Press, 1990), 67–100.

Cassidy, J., and P.R. Shaver (eds.), *Handbook of Attachment: Theory, Research and Clinical Applications* (London: Guilford Press, 1999).

Castells, M., *The Power of Identity* (Oxford: Blackwell, 1997).

Castro, H., 'Venezuela, the Church and Child Rights' (e-mail forum, August 2000).

Cattanach, A., *Children's Stories in Play Therapy* (London: Jessica Kingsley Press, 1997).

Cavolletti, S., *The Religious Potential of the Child* (Chicago: Catechism of the Good Shepherd Publications, 1992).

Cetron, M., and O. Davies, *Crystal Globe: The Haves and Have Nots of the New World Order* (New York: St Martin's Press, 1991).

Chalke, S., *Making a Team Work* (Eastbourne: Kingsway, 1995).

Chen, L., 'World Summit Goals: Achievements and Shortfalls' (address at the First UN Prepcom for the 2001 World Summit for Children, Prepcom Summaries; New York: UNICEF, 2001).

'Children at Risk', *Footsteps* (Tear Fund) 28 (1996), 1–16.

Christian, J., S. Commins, K. Currie and L. van Straaten, *Development and Children: An Integrated Paradigm for Transformation* (Monrovia, CA: World Vision International, 2001).

Christian Reformed World Relief Committee, *Partnering to Build and Measure Organizational Capacity* (Grand Rapids: The Christian Reformed World Relief Committee, 1997).

Church, A.T., M. Katigbak and G. Velazco, 'Psychometric Intelligence and Adaptive Competence in Rural Philippine Children', *Intelligence* 9 (1989), 317–40.

Clapp, R., *Families at the Crossroads: Beyond Traditional Roles and Modern Options* (Downers Grove, IL: InterVarsity Press, 1993).

Clarke, N., S. McGregor and C. Powell, 'Nutrition and Health Predictors of School Failure in Jamaican Children', *Ecology of Food and Nutrition* 21 (1990), 1–11.

Cloud, H., *Changes that Heal: How to Understand Your Past to Ensure a Healthier Future* (Grand Rapids: Zondervan, 1995).

——, and J. Townsend, *Safe People* (Grand Rapids: Zondervan, 1995).

——, and J. Townsend, *Boundaries* (Grand Rapids: Zondervan, 1992).

——, and J. Townsend, *Boundaries with Kids: When to Say Yes, When to Say No to Help Your Children Gain Control of Their Lives* (Grand Rapids: Zondervan, 1998).

Collier, P., and A. Hoeffler, 'Greed and Grievance in Civil War' (draft of a World Bank paper, 26 April 2000).

Collins, G.R., *Christian Coaching: Helping Others Turn Potential into Reality* (Colorado Springs: NavPress, 2001).

——, *Christian Counselling* (Waco, TX: Word Books, 1985).

——, *How to Be a People Helper* (London: Tyndale, 1995).

Collins, J., and J. Porras, *Built to Last: Successful Habits of Visionary Companies* (New York: HarperCollins, 1994).

Collins, M., J. McWhirter and N. Wetton, 'Researching Nursery Children's Awareness of the Need for Sun Protection: Towards a New Methodology', *Health Education* 4 (1998), 125–34.

Cookingham, F., *Directing Community Development Evaluation Work: Principles and Guidelines* (Monrovia, CA: World Vision International, 1995).

Corey, G., *Theory and Practice of Counselling and Psychotherapy* (London: Brooks/Cole, 6th edn, 2001).

Cormack, D., *Peacing Together* (Monrovia, CA: MARC Monarch Publications, 1989).

Cox, M., *Children's Drawings* (Harmondsworth: Penguin, 1992).

Crabb, L., *Connecting* (Nashville, TN: Word Books, 1997).

Cranfield, C.E.B., *A Critical and Exegetical Commentary on the Epistle to the Romans* (The International Critical Commentaries; Edinburgh: T. & T. Clark, 1975).

Crocker, G., 'Total Quality of Charitable Service: Profiles of Excellence in Christian Relief and Development Organizations' (PhD Diss., Regent University, Virginia Beach, 2001).

Crompton, M., *Children, Spirituality, Religion and Social Work* (Aldershot: Arena, 1998).

Dalrymple, J., R. Edgeman, M. Finster, J. Guerrero-Cusumano, D. Hensler and W. Parr, 'A White Paper: Quality at the Crossroads of Organizational Excellence and the Academy' (www.geocities.com/WallStreet/District/1798/whitepaper.html, 2000).

De Berry, J., and P. Stephenson, 'Entering the New Millennium: Children's Rights and Religion at a Crossroads' (conference report, Tearfund in-house paper, 1999).

De Saint-Exupery, A., *The Little Prince* (London: Mammoth Press, 1991).

Dixon, P., *Out of the Ghetto and into the City* (Milton Keynes: Word, 1995).

Dobson, J., *Preparing for Adolescence* (Eastbourne: Kingsway, 1982).

Doherty, W.J., and R.H. Needle, 'Psychological Adjustment and Substance Use Among Adolescents before and after Parental Divorce', *Child Development* 62 (1991), 328–37.

Donaldson, M., *Children's Minds* (Fontana Press: William Collins, 1988).

——, *Understanding Children* (Glasgow: Fontana, 1978).

Drucker, P.F., 'Lessons for Successful Nonprofit Governance', *Nonprofit Management and Leadership* 1 (1990), 7–14.

——, *Managing the Nonprofit Organization: Principles and Practices* (New York: HarperCollins, 1990).

Drucker, P.M., C. Greco-Vigorito, M. Moore-Russell, J. Avaltroni and E. Ryan, 'Drawing Facilitates Recall of Traumatic Past Events in Young Children of Substance Abusers' (paper presented at the Biennial Meeting of the Society for Research in Child Development, Washington, DC, 1997).

Dwivedi, K.N., *Enhancing Parenting Skills: A Guide for Professionals Working With Parents* (London: Wiley, 1997).

Edwards, M., 'New Approaches to Children and Development: Introduction and Overview', *Journal of International Development* 8.6 (1996), 813–27.

Egan, G., *The Skilled Helper* (Pacific Grove, CA: Brooks Cole, 6th edn, 1998).

Ellsberg, R., *Gandhi on Christianity* (Maryknoll, NY: Orbis Books, 1991).

Ennew, J., 'The History of Children's Rights: Whose Story?', *Cultural Survival Quarterly* 24.2 (www.culturalsurvival.org/quarterly, 1999).

———, *Street and Working Children: A Guide to Planning* (Save the Children Development Manual 4; London: Save the Children, 1994).

Epstein, P.R., 'Is Global Warming Harmful to Health?', *Scientific American* (Aug. 2000).

Erdich, L., *The Blue Jay's Dance* (London: HarperCollins, 1995).

Erikson, E.H., *Identity: Youth and Crisis* (New York: Norton, 1968).

Erickson, W., 'Transition in Leadership', in *Leaders on Leadership* (ed. G. Barna; Ventura, CA: Regal Books, 1997), 297–316.

Evans, D., *HIV/AIDS Briefing Manual: An Evangelical Christian Response to a Global Relational Issue* (Teddington: Tear Fund, 1996).

Evans, J.L., 'Children as Zones of Peace', in *Working with Young Children Affected by Armed Violence* (The Consultative Group on Early Childhood Care and Development, www.ecdgroup.com, 2000).

Evans, T., *The Battle Is the Lord's* (Chicago: Moody Press, 1998).

Feuerstein, M.-T., *Partners in Evaluation: Evaluating Development and Community Programmes with Participants* (London: Macmillan, 1986).

File, K.M., R.A. Prince and D.S. Cermak, 'Creating Trust with Major Donors: The Service Encounter Model', *Nonprofit Management and Leadership* 4 (1994), 269–83.

Fine, G.A., and K.L. Sandstrom, *Knowing Children: Participant Observation with Minors* (Qualitative Research Methods 15; Sage University; London: Sage Publications, 1988).

Finkelhor, D., et al., *A Sourcebook on Child Sexual Abuse* (Beverly Hills: Sage Publications, 1986).

Firstenberg, P.B., *The Twenty-First Century Nonprofit: Remaking the Organization in the Post-Government Era* (New York: The Foundation Center, 1996).

Fischer, K.W., and T.R. Bidell, 'Dynamic Development of Psychological Structures in Action and Thought', in *Handbook of Child Psychology*, I: *Theoretical Models of Human Development* (ed. R.M. Lerner; New York: Wiley, 5th edn, 1998), 467–562.

Fletcher, K.B., 'Effective Boards: How Executive Directors Define and Develop Them', *Nonprofit Management and Leadership* 2 (1992), 283–93.

Foulkes, S.H., and E.J. Anthony, *Group Psychotherapy: The Psychoanalytic Approach* (London: Maresfield, 2nd edn, 1984).

Frangoulis, S., N. Jordan and R. Lansdown, 'Children's Concept of an Afterlife', *British Journal of Religious Education* 18 (1995), 114–23.

Freeman, M., 'The Sociology of Childhood and Children's Rights', *The International Journal of Children's Rights* 6 (1998), 433–44.

Freud, S., *Introductory Lectures on Psychoanalysis* (trans. J. Strachey and A. Richards; Harmondsworth: Penguin, 1976).

Fry, R.E., 'Accountability in Organizational Life: Problem or Opportunity for Nonprofits?', *Nonprofit Management and Leadership* 6 (1995), 181–95.

Fuller, C., *When Children Pray* (Portland, OR: Multnomah, 1998).

Garcia, F.N., 'Reactivity', *Transactional Analysis Journal* 12.2 (1982), 123–26.

GCOWE, *The AD 2000 and Beyond Movement Participants' Book* (Seoul, Korea: May 1995).

Geldard, K., and D. Geldard, *Counselling Adolescents* (London: Sage Publications, 1999).

———, *Counselling Children* (London: Sage Publications, 1997).

General Synod Board of Education, *Children in the Way* (The National Society of the Church of England for Promoting Religious Education, 1988).

Ginsburg, H., *Entering the Child's Mind: The Clinical Interview in Psychological Research and Practice* (Cambridge: Cambridge University Press, 1997).

Gleick, P., *The World's Water: 1998–1999* (Washington, DC: Island Press, 1998).

Goodall, J., 'A Social Score for *Kwashiorkor*: Explaining the Look in the Child's Eyes', *Dev Med Child Neurol* 21.3 (1979), 374–84.

Goodwin, D.C., *Child Abuse in the Church* (Hastings: Camp David Ministries, 1993).

Goodwin, J., 'Use of Drawings in Evaluating Children Who May Be Incest Victims', *Children and Youth Services Review* 4 (1982), 269–78.

Gorkin, M., 'The Four Stages of Burnout' (*The 'Stress Doc'*, http://www.shpm.com/articles/wf/burnout.html).

Gosling, L., and M. Edwards, *Toolkits for Appraisal, Monitoring and Evaluation of Development Projects* (London: Save the Children, 1995).

Gourley, S., *Child Labour and Salt Production in Kompot Province, Cambodia* (Phnom Penh: International Labour Organisation International Programme for the Elimination of Child Labour, 2000).

——, et al., *Look Before You Leap: Strategic Approaches to Urban Child Labour* (Phnom Penh: World Vision Cambodia, 2000).

Gross, J., and H. Hayne, 'Drawing Facilitates Children's Verbal Reports of Emotionally Laden Events', *Journal of Experimental Psychology: Applied* 4.2 (1998), 163–79.

Grotberg, E., *A Guide to Promoting Resilience in Children: Strengthening the Human Spirit* (Early Childhood Development: Practice and Reflections 8; The Hague: Bernard van Leer Foundation, 1995).

Hanbury, C., *Working with Children in Refugee Camps* (St Albans: Child to Child Trust, 1994).

Handy, C., *The Empty Raincoat: Making Sense of the Future* (London: Arrow Business Books, 1995).

Hansen, W., 'Young People in Young Nations – Strategic Objective', *EMQ* II (Summer 1966), 218–27.

Hart, A.D., *Stress and Your Child* (Dallas: Word Books, 1992).

Hartnup, T., 'Divorce and Marital Strife and Their Effects on Children', *Archives of Disease in Childhood* 75 (1996), 1–3.

Hawes, H., and C. Scotchmer (eds.), *Children for Health* (London: Child to Child Trust/UNICEF, 1993).

——, D. Bailey and G. Bonati, *Child-to-Child: A Resource Book* (London: Child to Child Trust, 1994).

Hay, D., and R. Nye, *The Spirit of the Child* (London: Fount, 1998).

Hendrick, H., *Child Welfare: England 1872–1989* (London: Routledge, 1994).

Hendriksen, W., *New Testament Commentary: Romans 1–8* (London: Banner of Truth Trust, 1980).

Herbert, M., *The ABC of Behavioural Management* (Parent and Child Training Series [PACTS]; Leicester: British Psychological Society, 1994).

——, and K. Harper-Dorton, *Working with Children, Adolescents and Their Families* (Leicester: British Psychological Society, 2001).

Herman, R., 'Preparing for the Future of Nonprofit Management', in *The Jossey-Bass Handbook of Nonprofit Leadership and Management* (ed. R. Herman, et al.; San Francisco: Jossey-Bass Publishers, 1994), 616–26.

——, and R. Heimovics, *Executive Leadership in Nonprofit Organizations: New Strategies for Shaping Executive-Board Dynamics* (San Francisco: Jossey-Bass Publishers, 1991).

Herrera, E., A. Mora, L. Palma and L. Cesari, 'The Church and Child Rights' (e-mail forum, 2000).

Hetherington, E.M., 'The Role of Individual Differences and Family Relationships in Children's Coping with Divorce and Remarriage', in *Family Transitions* (ed. P.A. Cowan and E.M. Hetherington; Hillsdale, NJ: Erlbaum, 1991), 65–194.

Hetherington, P., 'The Changing American Family and the Well-Being of Children' (Master lecture presented at the biennial meeting of the Society for Research in Child Development, Indianapolis, 1995).

Hoghughi, M., et al. (eds.), *Working with Sexually Abusive Adolescents* (London: Sage Publications, 1997).

Huggett, J., *Listening to Others* (Sevenoaks, Kent: Hodder & Stoughton, 1988).

Hunter, S., and J. Williamson, *Children on the Brink* (Washington, DC: USAID, 2000).

Hurding, R., *Roots and Shoots* (London: Hodder & Stoughton, 1985).

——, *Understanding Adolescence* (London: Hodder & Stoughton, 1989).

James, A., C. Jenks and A. Prout, *Theorizing Childhood* (Cambridge: Polity Press, 1998).

Jayakumar, C., S. Commins, K. Currie and L. van Straaten, *Development and Children: An Integrated Paradigm for Transformation* (World Vision International, Jan. 2001).

Jenks, C., J. Qvortrup, I. Rizzini and B. Thorne, 'The UN Convention on the Rights of the Child as a Touchstone for Research on Childhoods', *Childhood* 6.4 (London: Sage Publications, 1999), editorial.

Jennings, S., *Play Therapy with Children: A Practitioner's Guide* (Oxford: Blackwell Scientific Publications, 1993).

Johnson, D., 'Averting a Water Crisis', *The Futurist* 32.2 (1998), 7.

Johnson, D., and F. Johnson, *Joining Together* (Needham Heights, MA: Allyn and Bacon, 1997).

Johnstone, P., and J. Mandryk, *Operation World* (Carlisle: Paternoster, 2001).

Jones, G., and R. Jones, *Teamwork* (Scripture Union, 1995).

Kay, R., 'The Artistry of Leadership: An Exploration of the Leadership Process in Voluntary Not-for-Profit Organizations', *Nonprofit Management and Leadership* 4 (1994), 285–300.

Kearns, K.P., R.J. Krasman and W.J. Meyer, 'Why Nonprofits are Ripe for Total Quality Management', *Nonprofit Management and Leadership* 4 (1994), 447–60.

Kennedy, P., *Preparing for the Twenty-First Century* (New York: Vintage Books, 1993).

Kilbourn, P. (ed.), *Healing the Children of War* (Monrovia, CA: MARC Publications, 1995).

——, *Children in Crisis: A New Commitment* (Monrovia, CA: MARC Publications, 1996).

Kimball, C., *These Things I Wish for You: Reflections from a Father's Heart* (Portland, OR: Multnomah, 2000).

King, M., and C. Elliott, 'Averting a World Food Shortage: Tighten Your Belts for CAIRO II', *British Medical Journal* 313 (1996), 995–97.

Knauft, E.B., R.A. Berger and S.T. Gray, *Profiles of Excellence: Achieving Success in the Nonprofit Sector* (San Francisco: Jossey-Bass Publishers, 1991).

Konrad, K., and J. Bronson, 'Handling Difficult Times and Learning Resiliency', in *Deeply Rooted, Branching Out* (Annual Association for Experiential Education International Conference Proceedings from 25th Meeting in Asheville, NC, 1997).

Kramer, R., L. Allen and P.J. Gergen, 'Health and Social Characteristics and Children's Cognitive Functioning: Results from a National Cohort', *American Journal of Public Health* 85 (1995), 312–18.

Kushner, R.J., and P.P. Poole, 'Exploring Structure-Effectiveness Relationships in Nonprofit Arts Organizations', *Nonprofit Management and Leadership* 7 (1996), 119–36.

Lahad, M., 'Story-Making in Assessment Method for Coping with Stress: Six-Piece Story Making and BASIC-Ph', in *Drama Therapy, Theory and Practice*, II (ed. S. Jennings; London: Routledge, 1992).

Lake, F., *Clinical Theology* (London: Darton, Longman & Todd, 1986).

Landers, P., 'Arthritic Nation', *Far Eastern Economic Review* (16 July 1998), 11.

Larsen, S., and L. Brendtro, *Reclaiming Our Prodigal Sons and Daughters* (Bloomington, IN: National Educational Service, 2000).

Latourette, K.S., *A History of Christianity*, II: *Reformation to the Present (A.D. 1500–A.D. 1975)* (San Francisco: HarperCollins, 1975).

Lazarus, R.S., 'Hope: An Emotion and a Vital Coping Mechanism Against Despair', *Social Research* 6.2 (1999), 653–78.

Lederer, E.M., 'UNICEF: Children Still Suffer' (AP press release, Jan. 2001).

Lester, A.D., *Pastoral Care with Children in Crisis* (Philadelphia: Westminster Press, 1985).

Levin, P., *Cycles of Power* (Florida: Book Print Publication, 1980).

Lewin, K., *Field Theory in Social Science* (London: HarperCollins, 1951).

Lindström, B., and N. Spencer, *Social Paediatrics* (Oxford: Oxford University Press, 1995).

Litvin, D., 'Development and the Environment', *The Economist* (21 March 1998).

Locke, J.S., *Some Thoughts Concerning Education* (Oxford: Clarendon Press, 1989).

Luthar, S.S., 'Annotation: Methodological and Conceptual Issues in Research on Childhood Resilience', *Journal of Child Psychology and Psychiatry* 34 (1993), 441–53.

Lyall, D., *Counselling in the Pastoral and Spiritual Context* (Buckingham: Open University Press, 1995).

Machover, K., *Personality Projection in the Drawing of the Human Figure* (Springfield, IL: C.C. Thomas, 1949).

Mailbach, E., and D. Murphy, 'Self-Efficacy in Health Promotion Research and Practice: Conceptualization and Measurement', *Health Education Research* 10 (1995), 37–50.

Margerison, C.J., and D. McCann, *How to Lead a Winning Team* (Bradford: MCB University Press, 1985).

Maslach, C., 'Job Burnout', *Annual Review of Psychology* (http://www.findarticles.com, 2001).

Maslow, A.H., 'A Theory of Metamotivation: The Biological Rooting of the Value of Life', *Journal of Humanistic Psychology* 7 (1967), 93–127.

Mba, P.O., 'Issues of Social Adjustment and Society Attitudes: A Comparative Perspective' (paper presented at the World Congress on Future Special Education, Scotland, 25 June–1 July 1978).

McClung, F., *The Father Heart of God* (Eastbourne: Kingsway, 1985).

McDonald, P., and E. Garrow, *Reaching Children in Need: What's Being Done, What You Can Do* (Eastbourne: Kingsway, 2000).

McDowell, J., *His Image, My Image: Biblical Principles for Improving Your Self-Image* (San Bernadino, CA: Here's Life Publishers, 1984).

McLanahan, S., and G. Sandefur, *Growing Up with a Single Parent: What Hurts, What Helps* (Cambridge, MA: Harvard University Press, 1994).

Menconi, P., et al., *Keeping It Together When It Falls Apart* (Colorado Springs: NavPress, 1988).

Mercer, N., *The Guided Construction of Knowledge* (Clevedon: Multilingual Matters, 1995).

Miles, G.M., 'Children Do Not Do Sex with Adults for Pleasure: Sri Lankan Children's Views on Sex and Sexual Exploitation', *International Journal of Child Abuse and Neglect* 24.7 (2000), 995–1003.

——, 'Drawing Together Hope: "Listening" to Militarised Children', *Journal of Child Health Care* 4.4 (2000), 137–42.

——, 'Prevalence, Acceptability and Accessibility of Tobacco, Alcohol and Illegal Drugs among School Children in a Rural Market Town in Isaan, Thailand', *Journal of Population and Social Studies* 7.1 (1998), 85–94.

——, P. Sidebotham and M. Young, 'Mean Chey District Health Survey – Part 1: Urban Child Health 3rd Quarter 1994', *Cambodia Disease Bulletin* (1994).

——, and P. Stephenson, 'Child Development Study Pack' (London: Tearfund, 2000).

Miller, D.K., 'Implications of United Nations Policy on Canadian Domestic Law' (paper presented at a training seminar, New York, 2000).

Milner, P., and B. Carolin (eds.), *Time to Listen to Children* (London: Routledge, 1999).

Minirth, F., D. Hawkins, P. Meier and R. Flournoy, *How to Beat Burnout* (Chicago: Moody Press, 1986).

Morgan, E., and C. Kuykendall, *What Every Child Needs* (Grand Rapids: Zondervan, 1997).

Morrow, V., and M. Richards, 'The Ethics of Social Research with Children: An Overview', *Children and Society* 10 (1996), 90–105.

Munday, D., 'Editorial', in *Christians in Caring Professions* (PO Box 2828, Reading, RG30 2GE, UK, Sept. 2002).

Murphy-O'Connor, C., '"We Must Never Give Up Hope"', Edited highlights of the address by the Archbishop of Westminster, given at the Christmas Eve Midnight Mass at Westminster Cathedral', *The Times*, 26 Dec. 2002.

Murray, S., and A. Wilkinson-Hayes, *Hope from the Margins: New Ways of Being Church* (Cambridge: Grove Books, 2000).

Myers, B.L., *Walking with the Poor* (Mary Knoll, NY: Orbis Books, 1999).

Myers, N., *Environmental Exodus: An Emergent Crisis in the Global Arena* (Washington, DC: Climate Institute, 1995).

Myers, R., *The Twelve Who Survive: Strengthening Programmes of Early Childhood Development in the Third World* (London: Routledge, 1992).

Nader, K., N. Dubrow and S. Hudnall Stamm, *Honoring Differences: Cultural Issues in the Treatment of Trauma and Loss* (Ann Arbor, MI: Edwards Brothers, 1999).

Neill, S., *A History of Christian Missions* (Harmondsworth: Penguin, 1964).

Newman, N., *God Bless Love* (London: Collins, 1972).

'Nigeria: High Maternal Mortality Due to Teen Pregnancy', *Women's International Network News* 26.4 (Autumn 2000), 24.

Nitsun, M., *The Anti-Group: Destructive Forces in the Group and Their Creative Potential* (London: Routledge, 1996).

Nouwen, H., *Reaching Out* (London: Fount, 1990).

——, *Gracias! A Latin American Journal* (Maryknoll, NY: Orbis Books, 1993).

Nygren, D.J., M.D. Ukeritis, D.C. McClelland and J.L. Hickman, 'Outstanding Leadership in Nonprofit Organizations: Leadership Competencies in Roman Catholic Religious Orders', *Nonprofit Management and Leadership* 4 (1994), 375–91.

Obisesan, K.A., and A.A. Adeyemo, 'Childhood Sexuality and Child Sexual Abuse in Southwest Nigeria', *Journal of Obstetrics and Gynaecology* 19 (1999), 624.

Ogbuagu, S.C., and J.O. Charles, 'Survey of Sexual Networking in Calabar', *Health Transition Review* 3 (1993), 105–19.

Oloko, B.A., and A.O. Omoboye, 'Sexual Networking Among Some Lagos State Adolescent Yoruba Students', *Health Transition Review* 3 (1993), 151–57.

O'Toole, B., and R. McConkey (eds.), *Innovations in Developing Countries for People with Disabilities* (Chorley, Lancashire: Lisieux Hall Publications, 1995).

Parker, R., and J. Gagnon, *Conceiving Sexuality: Approaches to Sex Research in a Postmodern World* (New York: Routledge, 1995).

Paterson, R., *The Antioch Factor* (Tonbridge: Sovereign World, 2000).

Perry, B.D., 'Bonding and Attachment in Maltreated Children', *Child Trauma Academy* 1.4 (www.childtrauma.org, 1999).

——, 'Memories of Fear: How the Brain Stores and Retrieves Physiologic States, Feelings, Behaviors and Thoughts from Traumatic Events', in *Splintered Reflections: Images of the Body in Trauma* (ed. J. Goodwin and R. Attias; New York: Basic Books, 1999).

——, 'Neurobiological Sequelae of Childhood Trauma: Post-Traumatic Stress Disorders in Children', in *Catecholamine Function in Posttraumatic Stress Disorder: Emerging Concepts* (ed. M. Murburg; Washington, DC: American Psychiatric Press, 1994), 253–76.

——, and I. Azad, 'Post-Traumatic Stress Disorders in Children and Adolescents', *Current Opinions in Pediatrics* 11.4 (1999), 310–16.

——, and J.E. Marcellus, 'The Impact of Abuse and Neglect on the Developing Brain', *Colleagues for Children* (Missouri Chapter of the National Committee to Prevent Child Abuse) 7 (1997), 1–4.

——, and R. Pollard, 'Homeostasis, Stress, Trauma and Adaptation: A Neurodevelopmental View of Childhood Trauma', *Child and Adolescent Psychiatric Clinics of North America* 7.1 (1998), 33–51.

Peters, T.J., and R.H. Waterman, Jr., *In Search of Excellence: Lessons from America's Best-Run Companies* (New York: Harper & Row, 1982).

Piaget, J., *The Child's Conception of the World* (trans. J. Tomlinson and A. Tomlinson; Totowa, NJ: Littlefield, Adams, 1976).

Pinstrup-Andersen, P., R. Pandya-Lorch and M. Rosegrant, *The World Food Situation: Recent Developments, Emerging Issues and Long-Term Prospects* (Washington, DC: International Food Policy and Research Institute, 1997).

Pope, S., *The Evolution of Altruism and the Ordering of Love* (Washington, DC: Georgetown University Press, 1994).

Pridmore, P., 'Visualising Health: Exploring Perceptions of Children Using the Draw-and-Write Method', *Promotion and Education* 3.4 (1996), 11–15.

——, and G. Bendelow, 'Images of Health: Exploring Beliefs of Children Using the "Draw-and-Write" Technique', *Health Education Journal* 54 (1995), 473–88.

Pritchett, L., 'Divergence Big Time', *Journal of Economic Perspectives* 11.3 (1997), 3–17.

Provan, K.G., 'Board Power and Organizational Effectiveness among Human Service Agencies', *Academy of Management Journal* 2 (1980), 221–36.

Pryor, D., 'Haverim School Teaching Tapes' (Eastbourne: Christian Friends of Israel, info@cfi.org.uk).

Pullan, B., *Orphans and Foundlings in Early Modern Europe* (Reading: University of Reading, 1988).

Rae, W.A., 'Analysing Drawings of Children who are Physically Ill and Hospitalised Using the Ipsative Method', *Children's Health Care* 20 (1991), 198–207.

Reapsome, J., 'Editor's Analysis: Where Do Kids Fit in Mission Priorities?' *EMQ* 22.3 (July 1985), 320–21.

'Red Cross Says Three Diseases Kill More Than Disasters', *The New York Times* (29 June 2000).

'Refugees: Exporting Misery', *The Economist* (17 April 1999).

Richman, N., *Communicating with Children: Helping Children in Distress* (London: Save the Children, 1993).

Roberts, H., and D. Sachdev, *Young People's Social Attitudes: Having Their Say: The Views of 12–19 Year Olds* (Ilford: Barnados, 1996).

Roger, B., 'Keeping Peace' (letter from Taize, available from 71250 Taize Communauté, France, Oct.–Nov. 2002).

Rogers, C., *A Way of Being* (Boston: Houghton Mifflin, 1980).

Rosenau, J., *Turbulence in World Politics: Theory of Change and Continuity* (Princeton: Princeton University Press, 1990).

Rutter, M., 'Continuities and Discontinuities from Infancy', in *Handbook of Infant Development* (ed. J.D. Osofsky; New York: Wiley, 2nd edn, 1987).

——, 'Protective Factors to Children's Responses to Stress and Disadvantage', in *Primary Prevention of Psychopathology*, III: *Social Competence in Children* (ed. M.W. Kent and J. Rolf; Hanover, NH: University Press of New England, 1979).

——, 'Psychosocial Resilience and Protective Mechanisms', *American Journal of Orthopsychiatry* 57 (1987), 316–31.

——, 'Stress, Coping and Development: Some Issues and Some Questions', *Journal of Child Psychology and Psychiatry* 22 (1981), 323–56.

——, H. Giller and A. Hagell, *Antisocial Behaviour in Young People* (Cambridge: Cambridge University Press, 1998).

Sachs, A., 'Men, Sex and Parenthood', *Worldwatch* 7.2 (1994), 13.

Sameroff, A.J., R. Seifer, A. Baldwin and C. Baldwin, 'Stability of Intelligence from Preschool to Adolescence: The Influence of Family and Social Risk Factors', *Child Development* 64 (1993), 80–97.

Sands, C., *Learning to Trust Again* (Grand Rapids: Discovery House Publishers, 1999).

Scanlon, T., M. Lynch and A. Tomkins, *A Database for Workers among Streetchildren in South America* (available from Andrew Tomkins at CICH, Institute of Child Health, University of London, 1998).

Schutz, P., *Zwischen Nil und Kaukasus* (Munich: Chr. Kaiser Verlag, 1930).

Scwartz, P., *The Art of the Long View* (New York: Doubleday, 1991).

Serageldin, I., *Toward Sustainable Management of Water Resources* (The World Bank Directions in Development Series; Washington, DC: World Bank, 1995).

Sharp, S., and H. Cowie, *Counselling and Supporting Children in Distress* (London: Sage Publications, 1998).

Sieber, J., 'The Ethics and Politics of Sensitive Research', in *Researching Sensitive Topics* (ed. C. Renzetti and R.M. Lee; London: Sage Publications, 1993).

Silverman, W., 'The Line between Knowing and Doing', *Archives of Disease in Childhood* 71 (1994), 261–65.

Skinner, R., *Family Matters: A Guide to Healthier and Happier Relationships* (London: Methuen, 1995).

Smith, D., 'Health Risks', 'National Income' and 'Population', in *The State of the World Atlas* (London: Penguin Books, 1999).

Snarey, J., *How Fathers Care for the Next Generation: A Four-Decade Study* (Cambridge, MA: Harvard University Press, 1993).

Springle, P., *Rapha's 12-Step Program for Overcoming Codependency* (Houston: Rapha Publishing, 1990).

Spurgeon, C., *C.H. Spurgeon's Sermons on Revival* (ed. C.T. Cook; London: Marshall, Morgan & Scott, 1958).

Stephenson, P., 'Child Rights: Has Anyone Got It Right?' (Plenary talk, Cutting Edge Conference, Amsterdam, March 2001).

Stewart, I., and V. Joines, *TA Today: A New Introduction to Transactional Analysis* (Nottingham: Lifespace Publishing, 1987).

Stibbe, M., *From Orphans to Heirs* (Oxford: Bible Reading Fellowship, 1999).

Strange, W.A., *Children in the Early Church* (Carlisle: Paternoster, 1996).

Stress Fact (McKinley Health Center, Student Affairs, University of Illinois at Urbana Champaign, http://www.mckinly.uiuc.edu/health-info/stress/vul-stres.html, 2002).

Stroop, D., *Understanding Your Child's Personality* (Chicago: Tyndale, 1998).

Theis, J., *Child-Focused Development: An Introduction* (Asia regional office: Save the Children, 1996).

Thelen, E., and L.B. Smith, 'Dynamic Systems Theories', in *Handbook of Child Psychology*, I: *Theoretical Models of Human Development* (ed. R.M. Lerner; New York: Wiley, 5th edn, 1998), 563–634.

Thomas, A., and S. Chess, *Temperament and Development* (New York: Brunner/Mazel, 1977).

Thomas, G.V., and A.M.J. Silk, *An Introduction to the Psychology of Children's Drawings* (Hertford: Harvester Wheatsheaf, 1990).

Tolfree, D., *Restoring Playfulness: Different Approaches to Assisting Children who are Psychologically Affected by War or Displacement* (Stockholm: Radda Barnen/Swedish Save the Children, 1996).

Tomkins, A., 'Population Challenges for the Two-Thirds World: With Specific Reference to Mother and Child Health', *Transformation* 13 (1996), 10–14.

——, 'Malnutrition, Morbidity and Mortality in Children and Their Mothers', *Proc Nutr Soc* 59.1 (2000), 135–46.

——, and F. Watson, 'Malnutrition and Infection' (ACC/SCN State of the Art Series, Nutrition Policy Discussion Paper No. 5; Geneva: World Health Organization, 1989).

Trawick-Smith, J., *Early Childhood Development: A Multicultural Perspective* (Upper Saddle River, NJ: Merrill, 1997).

Tuckey, C., 'Sexism and the Church', in *Archbishop Tutu: Prophetic Witness in South Africa* (ed. L. Hulley, L. Kretzschmar and L. Pato; Cape Town: Human and Rousseau, 1996).

Tuckman, H.P., 'Competition, Commercialization, and the Evolution of Nonprofit Organizational Structures', *Journal of Policy Analysis and Management* 17 (1998), 175–94.

Tymchuk, A.J., 'Assent Processes', in *Social Research on Children and Adolescents: Ethical Issues* (ed. B. Stanley and J.E. Sieber; London: Sage Publications, 1992).

UK NGO AIDS Consortium, *Vulnerability of the Girl Child to HIV/AIDS* (London, 2000).

UNDP, *Human Development Report 1998* (Oxford: Oxford University Press, 1998).

UN High Commissioner for Refugees, *The State of the World's Refugees: The Challenge of Protection* (New York: Penguin, 1993).

UNICEF, *A New Global Agenda for Children* (New York: UNICEF, 2000).

——, *Emerging Issues for Children in the 21st Century* (New York: UNICEF, 2000).

——, *The Child in South Asia: Development as if Children Mattered* (New Delhi: UNICEF, 1998).

——, *The State of the World's Children* (Oxford: Oxford University Press, 1995).

——, *The State of the World's Children 2000* (New York: UNICEF, 2000).

United Nations, *UN Convention on the Rights of the Child* (New York: UNICEF, 1989). (The text of the CRC can be obtained on the website for the UN Commission for Human Rights at http://www.unhchr.ch.)

US Committee on Refugees, *World Refugee Survey 2000* (Washington, DC, 2000).

Van Til, J., 'Nonprofit Organizations and Social Institutions', in *The Jossey-Bass Handbook of Nonprofit Leadership and Management* (ed. R. Herman, et al.; San Francisco: Jossey-Bass Publishers, 1994), 44–64.

Varghese, R.A. (ed.), *The Intellectuals Speak Out About God: A Handbook for the Christian Student in a Secular Society* (Chicago: Regnery Gateway, 1984).

Vasta, R., M.M. Haith and S.A. Millar, *Child Psychology* (London: Wiley, 1999).

Veerman, P., and C. Sand, 'Religion and Children's Rights', *International Journal of Children's Rights* 7 (1999), 385–93.

Velazco, G., 'Development of an Instrument for the Assessment of Adaptive Competencies of Rural Filipino Children as an Alternative to Traditional Intelligence Measurement', *Philippine Journal of Educational Measurement* (1985), 65–69.

——, 'JC, a Bully No More: A Case of Behaviour Modification Plus' (in conference reader for Cutting Edge 2000, compiled by Viva Network, 2000).

——, *Manual of Operations of the Therapy Centre for Children Victims of Abuse and Exploitation* (Manila: Programs and Special Projects Bureau, Department of Social Welfare and Development, 1999).

Viva Network, *The Oxford Statement* (from the consultation at the Oxford Centre for Missions Studies, Oxford: Viva Network, 1997).

Vygotsky, L., 'Thinking and Speech', in *The Collected Works of L.S. Vygotsky*, I: *Problems of General Psychology* (ed. R.W. Rieber and A.S. Carton; trans. N. Minick; New York: Plenum Press, 1934/1987), 37–285.

Wallerstein, J., 'Children of Divorce: The Psychological Tasks of the Child', *American Journal of Orthopsychiatry* 53 (1983), 230–43.

Walvin, J., *A Child's World: A Social History of English Childhood 1800–1914* (Middlesex: Penguin Books, 1982).

Watt, G., 'All Together Now: Why Social Deprivation Matters to Everyone', *British Medical Journal* 312 (1996), 1026–29.

Weber, S., and F. Cook, *The Crisis* (Kansas City, MO: Nazarene Publishing House, 1989).

Weisbrod, B.A., 'The Nonprofit Mission and Its Financing', *Journal of Policy Analysis and Management* 17 (1998), 165–74.

Weiss, L.H., and J.C. Schwarz, 'The Relationship Between Parenting Types and Older Adolescents' Personality, Academic Achievement, Adjustment and Substance Use', *Child Development* 67.5 (1996), 2101–114.

Werner, D., and B. Bower, *Helping Health Workers to Learn* (Palo Alto, CA: Hesperian Foundation; St Albans: TALC UK, 1988).

Werner, E., and R. Smith, *Overcoming the Odds: High Risk Children from Birth to Adulthood* (Ithaca, NY: Cornell University Press, 1992).

Westerhoff, J.H., III, *Bringing Up Children in the Christian Faith* (Minneapolis: Winston Press, 1980).

White, K., 'Foundations for Ministry: "A little child will lead them" Rediscovering Children at the Heart of Mission' (Paper presented at the Cutting Edge Conference, Amsterdam, March 2001).

——, 'A Theology of Childhood: Understanding Children's Needs from a Theological and Child Development Perspective' (Paper presented at the Cutting Edge Conference, Brighton, UK, 1999).

'WHO and Private Sector Set Up Foundation for Fighting Malaria', *Financial Times* (29 Nov. 1999).

Wilkins, R.G., 'International Law, the International Criminal Court and National Sovereignty' (unpublished paper, 1999).

Williams, R., 'Unwise World Created by the Wise Men, the Edited Christmas Message', *The Times*, 26 Dec. 2002.

Winnicott, D.W., *The Maturational Processes and the Facilitative Environment* (London: Hogarth Press, 1960).

Woodhead, M., *'Children's Perspectives on their Working Lives': A Participatory Study in Bangladesh, Ethiopia, the Philippines, Guatemala, El Salvador and Nicaragua* (Stockholm: Radda Barnen, 1998).

——, and D. Faulkner, 'Subjects, Objects or Participants? Dilemmas of Psychological Research with Children', in *Conducting Research with Children* (ed. A. James and P. Christensen; London: Falmer Press, 1999).

World Bank, *Entering the 20th Century: World Development Report 1999/2000* (Oxford: Oxford University Press, 2000).

World Health Organization, *World Health Report 1999* (Geneva: WHO, 1999).

Wright, C.J.H., *God's People in God's Land* (Carlisle: Paternoster Press, 1997).

——, *Walking in the Ways of the Lord: The Ethical Authority of the Old Testament* (Leicester: Apollos, 1995).

——, *Human Rights* (Bible Study Booklet 3; London: Tearfund, 1980).

Yates, M., 'Eglantyne Jebb and Save the Children' (www.leader-values.com, 1998).

Zurheide, K.J., and J.R. Zurheide, *In Their Own Way: Accepting Your Child as They Are* (Minneapolis: Augsburg Fortress, 2000).

Zwi, A.B., and S. Rifkin, 'Violence Involving Children', *British Medical Journal* 311 (1995), 1384.

Suggested Further Reading

Texts

The following are recommended supplementary texts in different subject areas covered in various parts of the book.

Ager, A., 'Psychosocial Programs: Principles and Practice for Research and Evaluation', in *Psychosocial Wellness of Refugees* (ed. F. Ahearn; New York: Berghahn, 2000).

African Network for Prevention and Protection Against Child Abuse and Neglect, *Child Abuse: We are All Guilty: A Media Analysis on Child Abuse 1986 – 1996* (Uganda Chapter, June 1998).

Anderson, B., *When Child Abuse Comes to the Church* (Minneapolis: Bethany House Publishers, 1992).

Barton, S.C. (ed.), *The Family in Theological Perspective* (Edinburgh: T. & T. Clark, 1996).

Beasley, N.M., A. Hall, A.M. Tomkins, et al., 'The Health of Enrolled and Non-Enrolled Children of School-Age in Tanga, Tanzania', *Acta Trop* 76 (2000), 223–29.

Benard, B., *Fostering Resilience in Children* (ERIC Clearinghouse on Elementary and Early Childhood Education, Urbana, IL; http://resilnet.uiuc.edu, 1995).

Blanchet, T., *Lost Innocence, Stolen Childhoods* (Radda Barnen: University Press Limited, 1996).

Bowers, J. (ed.), *Raising Resilient MKs: Resources for Caregives, Parents and Teachers* (Colorado Springs: ACSI, 1998).

Bowlby, J., *A Secure Base: Parent-Child Attachment and Healthy Human Development* (New York: Basic Books, 1988).

Bruner, J., *Child's Talk: Learning to Use Language* (New York: Norton, 1983).

Buchanan, A., *Cycles of Child Maltreatment: Facts, Fallacies and Interventions* (New York: John Wiley & Sons, 1996).

Bundy, D.A., and N.R. de Silva, 'Can We Deworm this Wormy World?', *British Medical Bulletin* 54 (1998), 421–32.

Callouste Gulbekian Foundation, 'Children and Violence' (Report of the Commission on Children and Violence, convened by the Gulbekian Foundation, 1995).

Cavalletti, S., *The Religious Potential of the Child* (Mt. Ranier, MD: Catechesis of the Good Shepherd Publications, 1992).

Child Abuse Prevention and Treatment Act (CAPTA), Public Law 104–235, section 111; 42 U.S.C. 5106g (Oct. 1996).

Cockett, M., and J. Tripp, 'The Exeter Family Study: Family Breakdown and Its Impact on Children' (Exeter: Family Policy Study Centre, 1994).

Conway, H.L., *Domestic Violence and the Church* (Carlisle: Paternoster Press, 1998).

Costello, A., 'Integrated Management of Childhood Illness', *Lancet* 350 (1997), 1266.

Crabb, L., *Inside Out* (Colorado Springs: NavPress, 1992).

Davies, C.A., *Reflexive Ethnography: A Guide to Researching Selves and Others* (London and New York: Routledge, 1999).

Delange, F., 'The Role of Iodine in Brain Development', *Proc Nutr Soc* 59 (2000) 75–9.

Dennison, J., *Team Ministry: A Blueprint for Christian Ministry* (London: Hodder & Stoughton, 1997).

Dubois, S., C. Coulombe, P. Pencharz, O. Pinsonneault and M.P. Duquette, 'Ability of the Higgins Nutrition Intervention Program to Improve Adolescent Pregnancy Outcome', *J Am Diet Assoc* 97 (1997), 871–78.

Dujardin, B., R. Van Cutsem and T. Lambrechts, 'The Value of Maternal Height as a Risk Factor of Dystocia: A Meta-Analysis', *Trop Med Int Health* 1 (1996), 510–21.

Elliot, M., 'Protecting Children: Training Pack for Front-Line Carers' (London: KIDSCAPE, 1992).

ECPAT Australia and MacKillop Family Services, *Choose with Care: A Recruitment Guide for Organisations Working with Children* (www.ecpat@ecpat.org; PO Box 1725, Collingwood, VIC 3066, Australia).

Erikson, E., *Childhood and Society* (New York: Norton, 1950).

Fernald, L.C., and S.M. Grantham-McGregor, 'Stress Response in School-Age Children Who Have Been Growth Retarded Since Early Childhood', *Am J Clin Nutr* 68 (1998), 691–98.

Ford, L., *Transforming Leadership: Jesus' Way of Creating Vision, Shaping Values and Empowering Change* (Downers Grove, IL: InterVarsity Press, 1991).

Freeman, H.E., P.H. Rossi and S.R. Wright, *Evaluating Social Projects in Developing Countries* (Paris: Development Centre, Organisation for Economic Cooperation and Development, 1979).

Freud, S., *The Standard Edition of the Complete Psychological Works of Sigmund Freud* (London: W.W. Norton, 1989).

Friere, P., *Pedagogy of the Oppressed* (trans. M. Bergman Ramos; Harmondsworth: Penguin, 1972).

Fuchs, V., and D. Reklis, 'America's Children: Economic Perspectives and Policy Options', *Science* 255 (1992), 41–46.

Golding, A., 'Violence and Public Health', *Journal of the Royal Society of Medicine* 89 (1996), 501–05.

Goodhall, J., *Children and Grieving* (London: Scripture Union, 1995).

Gorman, K., and E. Politt, 'Does Schooling Buffer the Effects of Early Risk?', *Child Development* 67 (1996), 314–26.

Grantham-McGregor, S.M., and L.C. Fernald, 'The Effects of Health and Nutrition on Cognitive and Behavioural Development in the First Three Years of Life', Parts 1 and 2, *Food and Nutrition Bulletin* 20 (1999), 53–99.

Grieve, R., and M. Hughes (eds.), *Understanding Children* (Oxford: Blackwell, 1994).

Gross, J., and H. Hayne, 'The Development of Children's Drawings: Implications for Clinical and Legal Interviews' (paper presented at the Biennial Meeting of the Society for Research in Child Development, Washington, DC, 1997).

Harris, P.L., *Children and Emotion* (Oxford: Blackwell, 1989).

Hart, A., *Healing Life's Hidden Addictions: Overcoming Inner Compulsions that Waste Your Time and Control Your Life* (Eastbourne: Crossway, 1991).

Hart, R., 'Children's Participation: From Tokenism to Citizenship' (*Innocenti Essays* 4; New York: UNICEF, 1992).

Hill, C., and R. Curtis, 'Family Matters: Report to the Home Secretary, the Rt. Hon Jack Straw MP' (Bedford: The Centre for Contemporary Ministry, 1998).

Hunter, R.J., *Dictionary of Pastoral Care and Counseling* (Nashville: Abingdon, 1990).

Iwaniec, D., *The Emotionally Abused and Neglected Child* (New York: John Wiley & Sons, 1998).

James, A., 'Forward', in *Children and Social Competence: Arenas of Action* (ed. I. Hutchby and J. Moran-Ellis; London: Falmer Press, 1998).

Johnson, V., J. Hill and E. Ivan-Smith, *Listening to Smaller Voices* (Somerset: Action Aid, 1995).

——, E. Ivan-Smith, G. Gordon, P. Pridmore and P. Scott, *Stepping Forward: Children and Young People's Participation in the Development Process* (London: Intermediate Technology Publications, 1998).

Jung, C.G., *Psychological Types* (London: Routledge & Kegan Paul, 1944).

Kagitcibasi, C., *Family Human Development across Cultures: A View from the Other Side* (Mahwah, NJ: Lawrence Erlbaum Associates, 1996).

Kane, C., and N. Thomas, 'Effective Communication with Children in Research and Practice' (unpublished paper; University of Wales, Swansea; 1997).

Keepers, T.D., and D.E. Babcock, *Raising Kids O.K.* (California: Menalto Press, 1986).

Kirk, J., and M.L. Miller, *Reliability and Validity in Qualitative Research* (Qualitative Research Methods Series, I; Newbury Park, CA: Sage Publications, 1986).

Knell, M., *Families on the Move: Growing Up Overseas and Loving It* (London: Monarch Books, 2001).

Kurtz, Z., 'Do Children's and Young People's Rights to Health Care in the UK Ensure Their Best Interests?', in *Adolescent Health* (ed. A. Macfarlane; London: Royal College of Physicians, 1996), 141–67.

Lahad, M., *Creative Supervision: The Use of Expressive Arts Methods in Supervision and Self-Supervision* (London: Jessica Kingsley, 2000).

Larkin, S., 'Introducing Evaluation' and 'Steps in Organising an Assessment' (Guidelines on Assessment Series; Tearfund, enquiries@ tearfund.org, 2001).

Lawrence, P., and J. Lorsch, *Organization and Environment* (Cambridge, MA: Harvard University Press, 1967).

Leberg, E., *Understanding Child Molesters: Taking Charge* (Thousand Oaks, CA: Sage Publications, 1997).

Linney, B., *Pictures, People and Power: People-Centred Visual Aids for Development* (London: Macmillan Education, 1995).

Lorenz, K.Z., *The Foundations of Ethology* (New York: Springer-Verlag, 1981).

Mahler, H., 'The Safe Motherhood Initiative: A Call to Action', *Lancet* 1 (1987), 668–70.

Mahon, A., and C. Glendinning, 'Researching Children: Methods and Ethics', *Children and Society* 10 (1996), 145–54.

Maldonado, J., *Even in the Best Families* (Geneva: WCC Publications, 1994).

Mayall, B. (ed.), *Children's Childhoods: Observed and Experienced* (London: Falmer Press, 1994).

McAuley, C., 'Child Participatory Research: Ethical and Methodological Considerations', in *Making Research Work: Promoting Child Care Policy and Practice* (ed. D. Iwaniec and J. Pinkerton; New York: John Wiley & Sons, 1998).

McFayden, A., 'The Abuse of the Family', in *The Christian Family: A Concept in Crisis* (ed. H.S. Pyper; Norwich: The Canterbury Press, 1996).

McGregor, A.S.T., C.E. Currie and N. Wetton, 'Eliciting the Views of Children about Health in Schools through the Use of the Draw and Write Technique', *Health Promotion International* 13.4 (1998), 307–18.

Meeks-Gardner, J.M., S.M. Grantham-McGregor, J.H. Himes and S. Chang, 'Behaviour and Development of Stunted and Non-Stunted Jamaican Children', *Journal of Child Psychology* 40 (1999), 819–27.

Miles, G.M., 'Violence and its Effects on Our Children', *Child* (British Paediatric Association, 1997).

Miles, M.B., and A.M. Huberman, *Qualitative Data Analysis* (Newbury Park, CA: Sage Publications, 2nd edn, 1984).

Morrow, V., *Understanding Families: Children's Perspectives* (London: National Children's Bureau, 1998).

Mott, S.C., *Biblical Ethics and Social Change* (New York: Oxford University Press, 1982).

Myers, B., *Walking with the Poor: Principles and Practices of Transformational Development* (Maryknoll, NY: Orbis Books, 1999).

Nanchalos, S., 'How To Do (or not to do) . . . The Logical Framework', *Health Policy and Planning* 13.2 (1998), 189–93.

Neustatter, A., 'A Market in Innocence', *Children First* 32 (UNICEF, 1996), 14–15.

Oates, J. (ed.), *The Foundations of Child Development* (Oxford: Blackwell, 1994).

O'Donnell, K. (ed.), *Missionary Care: Counting the Cost for World Evangelization* (Pasadena, CA: William Carey Library, 1992).

——, and H. O'Donnell (eds.), *Helping Missionaries Grow: Readings in Mental Health and Missions* (Pasadena, CA: William Carey Library, 1988).

O'Hagan, K., *Emotional and Psychological Abuse of Children* (Buckingham: Open University Press, 1993).

Olmsted, P.P., and D.P. Weikart (eds.), *How Nations Serve Young Children: Profiles of Childcare and Education in 14 Countries* (Michigan: Highscope/Educational Research Foundation, 1989).

Parton, N., and C. Wattam (eds.), *Child Sexual Abuse: Responding to the Experiences of Children* (New York: John Wiley & Sons, 1999).

Pavlov, I.P., *Conditioned Reflexes* (Oxford: Oxford University Press, 1927).

Pelletier, D.L., E.A.J. Frongillo, D.G. Schroeder and J.P. Habicht, 'The Effects of Malnutrition on Child Mortality in Developing Countries', *WHO Bulletin* 73 (1995), 443–48.

Petty, C., and P.J. Braken, *Rethinking the Trauma of War* (London: SCF Publications, 1998).

Piaget, J., *The Origins of Intelligence in Children* (New York: International University Press, 1952).

——, *The Psychology of Intelligence* (New York: Harcourt Brace, 1950).

——, *The Construction of Reality in the Child* (New York: Basic Books, 1954).

Porras, J., *Stream Analysis: A Powerful Way to Diagnose and Manage Organizational Change* (Reading, MA: Addison-Wesley, 1987).

Riddell, R., 'Judging Success: Evaluating NGO Approaches to Alleviating Poverty in Developing Countries' (Working Paper 37; London: Overseas Development Institute, Regent's College, May 1990).

Rose, J., *For the Sake of the Children: Inside Barnardos 120 Years of Caring for Children* (London: Futura, 1987).

Rossetti, S.J., *A Tragic Grace: The Catholic Church and Child Sexual Abuse* (Collegeville, MN: Liturgical Press, 1996).

Rubin, F., *A Basic Guide to Evaluation for Development Workers* (Oxfam, 1995).

Rugh, J., *Self-Evaluation: Ideas for Participatory Evaluation of Rural Community Development Projects* (Oklahoma City: World Neighbors, 1986).

Salter, A.C., *Transforming Trauma: A Guide to Understanding and Treating Adult Survivors of Child Sexual Abuse* (Thousand Oaks, CA: Sage Publications, 1995).

Sande, K., *The Peacemaker: A Biblical Guide to Resolving Personal Conflict* (Grand Rapids: Baker Book House, 1997).

Sanders, J.O., *Spiritual Leadership* (Chicago: Moody Press, 3rd edn, 1994).

Sands, C., and J. Ellis (eds.), *Learning to Trust Again: A Young Woman's Journey of Healing from Sexual Abuse* (Grand Rapids: Discovery House, 1999).

Sarino, E.M., *Youth Participation: UNICEF's Experience with Working for and with Young People* (New York: UNICEF, 1998).

Scanlon, T.J., A. Tomkins, M.A. Lynch and F. Scanlon, 'Street Children in Latin America', *British Medical Journal* 316 (23 May 1998), 1596–1600.

Scrimshaw, N. (ed.), *Community Based Longitudinal Nutrition and Health Studies: Classical Examples from Guatemala, Haiti and Mexico* (International Nutrition Foundation for Developing Countries, 1995).

Seabrook, J., *No Hiding Place: Child Sex Tourism and the Role of Extraterritorial Legislation* (London: Zed Books & ECPAT, 2000).

Skinner, B.F., *Science and Human Behaviour* (New York: Macmillan, 1953).

Smith, P.K., and H. Cowie, *Understanding Children's Development* (Oxford: Blackwell, 1994).

Stonehouse, C., *Joining Children on the Spiritual Journey: Nurturing a Life of Faith* (Grand Rapids: Baker Books, 1998).

Svedin, C.G., and K. Back, *Children Who Don't Speak Out About Children Being Used in Child Pornography* (Radda Barnen: Swedish Save the Children, 1996).

Taylor, G., *Managing Conflict* (London: The Directory of Social Change, 1999).

Tomkins, A.M., 'Protein-energy Malnutrition and Risk of Infection', *Proc Nutr Soc* 45 (1986), 289–304.

——, 'Improvingj Nutrition in Developing Countries: Can Primary Health Care Help?' *Trop Med Parasitol* 38.3 (1987), 226–32.

——, and F.E. Watson, *Malnutrition and Infection: A Review* (Geneva: WHO, 1999).

Tutu, D., *The Rainbow People of God: The Making of a Peaceful Revolution* (ed. J. Allen; New York: Doubleday, 1994).

UNESCO, *Sexual Abuse of Children, Child Pornography and Paedophilia on the Internet: An International Challenge. Final Report, Declaration and Action Plan* (Paris: Jan. 1999).

UNICEF, *A Picture of Health? A Review and Annotated Bibliography of the Health of Young People in Developing Countries* (New York and Geneva: WHO, 1995).

——, *Action for the Rights of Children Resource Pack. Critical Issues: Abuse and Exploitation* (2001).

University of Virginia, Center for Survey Research, *What Do Christians Expect from Christian Relief and Development* (A report of the National Survey of Evangelicals on Christian Relief and Development, 1992).

Van Der Weele, T., *From Shame to Peace: Counselling and Caring for the Sexually Abused* (Monrovia, CA: MARC Monarch Publications, 1996).

Watt, G., 'All Together Now: Why Social Deprivation Matters to Everyone', *British Medical Journal* 312 (1996), 1026–29.

Webster-Stratton, C., *The Incredible Years* (New York: Umbrella Press Publishing, 1992).

Weitzman, L.J., *The Divorce Revolution: The Unexpected Social and Economic Consequences for Women and Children in America* (New York: The Free Press, 1985).

Werner, E.E., *Childcare: Kith, Kin and Hired Hands* (Baltimore, MD: University Press, 1984).

Whitaker, D., L. Archer and L. Hocks, *Working in Children's Homes* (New York: John Wiley & Sons, 1998).

WHO, *Action for Adolescent Health: Towards a Common Agenda* (Geneva: WHO, 1997).

WHO/UNICEF, *The Role of IMCI in Improving Family and Community Practices to Support Child Health and Development* (Geneva: IMCI Information, 1–5, 1999).

Williams, G., and T. Nassali, 'Strategies for Hope' Series (St. Albans, UK: TALC).

World Vision International, *The Commercial Sexual Exploitation of Children: A Bibliography* (Prepared on behalf of the NGO Group for the CRC for the World Congress Against the Commercial Sexual Exploitation of Children, Aug. 1996; c/o Defense for Children International, PO Box 88, 1211 Geneva, Switzerland).

Yamamori, T., 'Furthering the Kingdom through Relief and Development: Where and How Is it Happening?' (AERDO Occasional Paper; www.aerdo.org, 1996).

Zuck, R.B., *Precious in His Sight* (Grand Rapids: Baker Books, 1996).

Key journals

Child Abuse and Neglect: The International Journal (ISPCAN: International Society for Prevention of Child Abuse and Neglect; Denver, CO, http://www.ispcan.org).

Childhood: A Global Journal of Child Research (London: Sage Publications, http://www.sagepub.co.uk).

Footsteps (Teddington: Tearfund, enquiry@tearfund.org).

Hope for Children in Crisis (Rainbows of Hope, Fort Mill, SC, http://www.wec-int.org/rainbows/books.htm).

My Name is Today (New Delhi, India, bflies@sdalt.ernet.in).

Reaching Children at Risk (Oxford: Viva Network, http://www.viva.org).

The Best of Caring (Swanley, Kent, http://www.pcca.co.uk).

Key websites

American Bible Society
http://www.americanbible.org

American Tract Society
http://www.gospelcom.net

Amnesty International
http://www.amnesty.org

Anti-Slavery International
http://www.antislavery.org

Barnardos
http://www.barnardos.org

Bernard van Leer Foundations
http://www.bernardvanleer.org

Bible Society
http://www.biblesociety.org

Bible Visuals International
http://www.biblevisuals.org

Brigada Today
http://www.brigada.org

British Agencies for Adoption and Fostering
http://www.baaf.org.uk

Child Evangelism Fellowship
http://www.gospelcom.net/cef

Child Rights Information Network (CRIN)
http://www.crin.org

Child Workers in Asia
http://www.cwa.tnet.co.th

Childhope UK
http://www.childhopeuk.org

Children and Armed Conflict Unit
http://www2.essex.ac.uk

Children of the Andes
http://www.children-of-the-andes.org

Children's Aid Direct
http://www.cad.org.uk

Children's Missions Resource Centre
http://www.uscwm.org

Childrens Society
http://www.the-childrens-society.org.uk

Childwatch
http://www.childwatch.uio.no

Christian Outreach
http://www.cord.org.uk

Christian Vocations
http://www.christianvocations.org

Compassion International
http://www.ci.org

Council of Europe Presse
http://www.book.coe.fr

CPAS
http://www.cpas.org.uk

Directory of Social Change
http://www.dsc.org.uk

Disability Awareness in Action
http://www.daa.org.uk

ECPAT
http://www.ecpat.net

Evangel Publishing House
http://www.evangelpublishing.com

Focus on the Family
http://www.family.org

Friends Puppet Company
http://www.friendspuppets.org

Good News Family Care
http://www.gnfc.org.uk

High Scope Press
http://www.highscope.org

Human Rights Watch
http://www.hrw.org

INTERDEV
http://www.ad2000.org/adoption/Coop/
Partner/PidMenu.htm

International Child Development Centre
http://www.unicef-icdc.it

International Justice Mission
http://www.ijm.org

International Labour Office
http://www.ilo.org

Interserve
http://www.interserve.org

KIDSCAPE
http://www.kidscape.org.uk

Marc Publications
http://www.marcpublications.com

Mission Frontiers
http://www.missionfrontiers.orgset.htm

Multi-Language Media
http://www.multilanguage.com/feature.htm

National Children's Bureau
http://www.ncb.org.uk

No Frontiers
http://www.nofrontiers.com

One Way Street
http://www.onewaystreet.com

OSCAR Mission Resources
http://www.oscar.org.uk

Oxfam Publishing
http://www.oxfam.org.uk

Pangaea
http://pangaea.org/street_children/kids.htm

Paternoster Publishing
http://www.paternoster-publishing.com

PCCA
http://www.pcca.co.uk

Puppet Productions
http://www.puppetproductions.com

Sage Publications
http://www.sagepub.co.uk

Save the Children
http://www.savethechildren.org.uk

Scripture Gift Mission Africa
http://www.sgm.org.za

Scripture Union
http://www.scripture.org.uk

Teaching Aids at Low Cost
http://www.talcuk.org

Tearfund
http://www.tearfund.org

Toybox Charity,
http://www.toybox.org

UFM Worldwide
http://www.ufm.org.uk

UNAIDS
http://www.unaids.org

UNESCO
http://www.education.unesco.org

UNICEF
http://www.unicef.org

Viva Network
http://www.viva.org

Viva Network Research Index
http://www.viva.org/tellme/research

VSO Books
http://www.vso.org.uk

WEC International
http://www.wec-int.org

WEF Publications
http://www.wefbookstore.org

World Health Organisation
http://www.who.int

World Vision
http://www.wvi.org

Index

– Epilogue –

Butterflies or Boxes?

The young boy sat in the corner of the playroom, carefully picking the pink pen from the box of crayons and marking the paper in a concentrated, constrained circle of colour. He looked up at me, fear flickering in uncertainty behind the soft hazel of his three-year-old eyes. He picked up the pink pen again and drew another line, his eyes casting shadows in the cage of his feelings. He looked over at the box of crayons, an overwhelming myriad of colours, exciting, frightening, forbidden. His gaze shot again to mine and I smiled gently and nodded. He watched the pink pen in his hand for a moment, caught between the worlds of his experience where cultures and faiths meet and war, castrating creativity and freedom in a charade of life.

Slowly I poured out the crayons onto the table, tumbling childhood before his eyes. He looked up half-light, for a second restoring his birth. He picked a purple-pink pen as I nodded, a tiny step as he marked the paper with daring delight. As I coaxed him with my eyes, his hands, his heart, his being found the colours and first, like a fleeing deer, next a darting nut-collecting squirrel and finally as a bird laughing in the rainbows of rain splashed sunlight, the pens sparkled and swirled, dancing with him across the page as we laughed into freedom, cocooned in a world within the chaos of the playroom, where, in the silence of belonging, hope and life were being reborn. I watched and laughed with him as we hugged our joy.

But it was not to be. A solemn hand came down, logically ordering the crayons, fitting them back into their neat packages of convention, disapproval holding her body hard in its brown box of socially acceptable goodness. The little boy's eyes again met mine, a wistful smile touching the freedom we had shared for a moment in that corner of a hospital cavern – forbidden fruits, or childhood rights to promises of reality? The message was clear. A sad smile acknowledged our grief. We dutifully pushed the crayons into the cold reality of the prisons man had created.

Later that day as I sat musing into bowls of hot chocolate, my heart took my eyes back to that gentle fair-haired child and I thought of another babe whom we too put in a box – Christ Jesus. A box of Fear, a box of Love, a box of unattainable Joy in suits of the world's approval, deceit carved in their backs.

Which box do you put him in?

Which box do you put yourself or others in?

We have created boxes to constrain, to control, to order, to contain – but in the process we have created coffins. As we read in Isaiah 43:16–21 we are encouraged, nay commanded, to forget the former things, not to dwell in the past, for he is doing a new thing. He is making a way in the desert and streams in the wasteland. Maybe it is too simple. Maybe freedom is too beautiful, too dangerous. It requires that we become as that child, willing to dare to be, willing to dare to fly, to find ourselves in the wisdom of wonder. Instead we build our cages and our rockets, weaving the lies of our past into cloaks of chains, trapping ourselves and one another in our first beginnings. But Christ gives us rebirth, a chance to redo the years of our lives when our identities and stories were formed, to have a new song. No boxes, just butterflies. Butterflies?

Trinia Paulus writes of a story about a caterpillar whose name was Yellow. She used to dream of becoming a butterfly but doubted that this liberating thing could ever happen to her: 'How can I believe there's a butterfly inside me when all I see is a fuzzy worm?' One day, Yellow met a fellow caterpillar who encouraged her to believe that she could be transformed. She decided to take the risk: to lose the life she knew, the caterpillar state, and to weave around herself the cocoon from which she would emerge as a butterfly. Her friends waited. Their patience was rewarded.

Rising before their eyes was a brilliant, yellow-winged creature. It was the same Yellow they had always known yet so very different. She looked awesome as she soared into the sky, circled around and gloried in the air she had now inherited. Her freedom was enchanting.

To be free, Yellow had to release herself to

being transformed – within the cocoon, every part of her former being was remoulded, used in the creation of something so beautiful, so free. That is what Christ does for us and with us. He takes every part of our pasts, every part of our being and uses them to create and recreate us in his likeness. Nothing is wasted, nothing is a mistake. God does not make mistakes.

When you look at me, you may see a little lady in a body that looks like it was whipped in a funfair top of alternatives. I may argue with it at times. I may get cross with it, sad, or jealous when I see beautiful straight women dancing or skiing in the mountains.

But it was not a mistake. God has used it and me in it, to challenge, to bear witness, to invite you to look again, to look behind the mask to see what he has done and will do with you if you will let him. Nothing is wasted.

Years ago, I laboured over a PhD, unable to say 'no' to the pressure to fulfil the academic accolade, fighting for freedom to be able to breathe, to paint, to sing, to play with the children he had called me to walk with. A recent trip to China showed me how he needed and used that prison to release others. As a Christian lady with a wiggly body and a strange profession, I was a reject within the Chinese culture; but as Dr Jo, I was to be honoured, respected, listened to, neither of us losing face, and able to teach and be heard and bear witness to how, as one Chinese lady said, 'I have a whole body but I am so broken inside and fear I can never be whole. Your body is broken yet you radiate with joy and are so whole. How? Why? Could it ever happen to me?' It was so beautiful that, before the end of the trip, she too became a butterfly for Christ.

So often in my life I have seen how as Christians we play the game of freedom. We put ourselves and others into boxes of acceptability. We judge, we gossip, we condemn. We label ourselves and others by our pasts. Yet why, when the Bible so clearly, so powerfully shows that Christ did the exact opposite? If this beautiful land of former Yugoslavia is to be released, to be healed, to be transformed, we need to be willing to dare to read and put into action what Christ really commanded us to do, to forget the former things for both ourselves and others and allow him to create through us rivers of joy and real new life, not the charades of

religiosity which we seem to almost worship and let control us. We need to be willing to be taken slowly and carefully apart and remade, as happens with the cocoon. We need to be willing to look for his miracles in unexpected places.

My mind goes back again to the playroom where we began our story. In another corner, two boys in turn are carefully building tissue boxes, painted to look like bricks, into castle walls around them. One works with all the red ones, putting them carefully on edge while the other places the blue and green ones the other way around. Both are building their own castles. They exchange the odd word but no more, just as we adults do as we build our own castles of our lives with drawbridges of conditional love.

A small boy watches them from afar, a quizzical expression fluttering across his face, half joyful, half bemused at their quest. Suddenly the joy wins and he runs and flings wide his arms as gates of freedom through the castle walls. The two lads look surprised, threat looming for a second, then laughter as they tumble in the ruins and rise and run. The small boy suddenly stoops, clutching a brick that has just flown free. He holds it to his ear. It rattles. He opens the box and releases the tiny, exquisite figure of a doll. 'I have been looking for that for ages', exclaims the Play Master with delight, 'I thought it was lost forever!'

This is the same delight with which the Father welcomed the prodigal son and with which Christ welcomes us. But we have to be willing to stop long enough to hear the rattle, to climb outside the false comfort zones of our lives, to give all we have to look for the pearls and treasures.

He wishes to transform – and we too need to encourage them to dare to be transformed; to dare for ourselves to be transformed. In so doing we may not just entertain angels, we may see and fly with the angels. We need to allow caterpillars to become butterflies, to expect caterpillars to become butterflies. It won't make sense through the looking glass of our adult eyes, but with the wise eyes of a child his plan will be wonderfully plain. Our pasts may, and are needed to, mould us, but they do not need to define us (John 8:7) – and neither must we let them.

Butterflies, not boxes. We can be, we shall be truly, joyfully, gloriously free.

Can we? Will you?

Come butterfly seeking and I promise you your life will never be the same again. The cages, the fear will be replaced by space to run and breathe and a solid, unbudgeable, illogical peace. It is scary yet so secure and wonderful. My name used to be Much Afraid, with Sorrow and Suffering as my companions (H. Hurnard, *Hind's Feet on High Places*). Now it is Joy. There is still pain at times. There are still times when the world does not make sense but the lies of my past are replaced with the Reality and Truth of my future. So come fly with me. He will set us free.

But do we?

This book will hopefully have enhanced your knowledge, stimulated your thinking and challenged your emotions to enable you to better understand your own child within and be able to work more effectively with the children without. Our prayer is that it leads you not to box and categorize children and their problems or yourselves but to work with them to release one another to grow – to be butterflies for God, all equally valuable to him.

Josephine-Joy Wright

(written in Mostar, Bosnia, 5 December 2000)

Jigsaws and God

My daughters, ages seven and nine, are having a craze on jigsaws at the moment and I'm really pleased. I've always enjoyed them myself, but they are so *slow*. It amazes me the mistakes the girls make, like not realizing a corner piece is a corner piece and putting it in the middle of the puzzle. They often recognize that two pieces should join up but don't know how to rotate them until they fit. Still, watching them struggle to try to make a complete picture out of individual pieces made me wonder if this is part of what God is trying to do with us.

Just imagine a jigsaw where each piece has a will of its own and all you are allowed to do is guide each piece, not force it, into place; the pieces themselves being involved in the work of completing the jigsaw. Say you have a picture of a boat sailing on the sea. The pieces which make up the boat consider themselves to be the most important as they are the most easily recognized and usually the first ones to be put together.

The sky pieces are all so like one another that a few of them wander off, saying that there are plenty of other sky pieces and surely they are not *really* needed. There are groups of pieces that have tried joining together and did it incorrectly so that they are convinced that they do not belong to the jigsaw at all, while other pieces are desperately searching for where they belong and are confused because their section of the puzzle is not complete enough for them to fit anywhere.

There are red pieces, blue pieces, large pieces, small pieces. Most pieces have holes to be filled and bits to fill other holes. No piece is expected to be anything but itself, but each piece needs to find its right place and needs every other piece to find its place as well in order to complete the picture . . . what a task!

. . . And my daughters can tell you how sad it is if one piece is missing when the puzzle is done – even if it is a piece of sky!

Sarah Ewers